See what students love about LearningCurve.

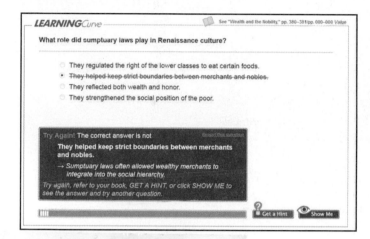

"With LearningCurve, students engage with the content and retain it better."

— Melissa Walker, *Converse College*

Students using LaunchPad receive access to LearningCurve for *Understanding Western Society.*

Each chapter-based LearningCurve activity gives students **multiple chances to understand key concepts**, return to the narrative textbook if they need to reread, and answer questions correctly.

Over 90% of students report satisfaction with LearningCurve's **fun and accessible game-like interface**.

Assigning LearningCurve in place of reading quizzes is easy for instructors, and the **reporting features help instructors track overall class trends** and spot topics that are giving students trouble so that they can adjust lectures and class activities.

To learn more about LearningCurve, visit **learningcurveworks.com**.

LearningCurve: Everyone's got a learning curve — what's yours?

Understanding
Western Society

A HISTORY

VOLUME 1

CONTEMPORARY EUROPE

ATLANTIC OCEAN

North Sea

Baltic Sea

NORWAY
Bergen
Oslo

SWEDEN
Stockholm
Göteborg

SCOTLAND
Edinburgh
Glasgow

NORTHERN IRELAND
Belfast

IRELAND
Dublin
Cork

UNITED KINGDOM
Liverpool
Birmingham
WALES
ENGLAND
Thames R.
London

DENMARK
Aarhus
Copenhagen

RUSSIA
Kaliningrad
Gdańsk

Elbe R.
Berlin
Vistula R.
Warsaw

POLAND

NETHERLANDS
Amsterdam
Rotterdam

Antwerp
Brussels
BELGIUM
Luxembourg
LUXEMBOURG

GERMANY
Rhine R.
Frankfurt

Prague
CZECH REP.
Brno
Kraków

SLOVAKIA
Oder R.
Miskolc

English Channel

Seine R.
Paris

Loire R.

FRANCE

Rhône R.
Lyons

Vienna
Bratislava
AUSTRIA
Munich
Danube R.
Innsbruck
Graz
Budapest
HUNGARY

LIECHTENSTEIN
Zürich
Vaduz
Bern
SWITZERLAND
A L P S

SLOVENIA
Ljubljana
Zagreb
CROATIA

Milan
Po R.

San Marino
SAN MARINO

BOSNIA AND HERZEGOVINA
Sarajevo
Belgrade
SERBIA

Bay of Biscay

Oporto
PORTUGAL
Lisbon
Madrid
SPAIN
Seville
Ebro R.
PYRENEES
ANDORRA
Andorra la Vella
Barcelona

Marseilles
MONACO

A P E N N I N E S
Adriatic Sea
Split
Podgorica
MONTENEGRO
Tiranë
ALBANIA

Corsica

Rome
ITALY
Naples

Gibraltar (Gr. Br.)

Balearic Is.

Sardinia

Tyrrhenian Sea

Ionian Sea

Algiers

Tunis

Palermo
Sicily

MOROCCO
Rabat

TUNISIA

Valletta
MALTA

Mediterranean

ALGERIA

Tripoli

LIBYA

Elevation

Feet	Meters
Over 13,120	Over 4,001
6,561–13,120	2,001–4,000
1,641–6,560	501–2,000
661–1,640	201–500
0–660	0–200
Below sea level	Below sea level

⊛ National capital
• Major city

0   150   300 miles
0 150   300 kilometers

THE CONTEMPORARY WORLD

Greenland
(Den.)

ICELAND

UNITED
KINGDOM

IRELAND

FRANCE

SPAIN

PORTUGAL

Azores
(Port.)

MOROCCO

Canary Is.
(Sp.)

Western Sahara
(Mor.)

Alaska
(U.S.)

CANADA

UNITED STATES

ATLANTIC
OCEAN

Bermuda (U.K.)

BAHAMAS

DOMINICAN
REPUBLIC

HAITI

MEXICO

CUBA

JAMAICA

BELIZE

HONDURAS

GUATEMALA

EL SALVADOR

NICARAGUA

COSTA RICA

PANAMA

Puerto Rico (U.S.)

ST. KITTS AND NEVIS

ANTIGUA AND BARBUDA

Guadeloupe (Fr.)

DOMINICA

Martinique (Fr.)

ST. VINCENT AND THE GRENADINES

ST. LUCIA

BARBADOS

GRENADA

TRINIDAD AND TOBAGO

GUYANA

SURINAME

French Guiana (Fr.)

MAURITANIA

CAPE
VERDE

SENEGAL

MALI

GAMBIA

GUINEA-BISSAU

GUINEA

BURKINA FASO

SIERRA LEONE

LIBERIA

CÔTE D'IVOIRE

GHANA

Hawaii (U.S.)

VENEZUELA

COLOMBIA

Galápagos Is.
(Ec.)

ECUADOR

PERU

BRAZIL

PACIFIC OCEAN

Equator

BOLIVIA

PARAGUAY

CHILE

ARGENTINA

URUGUAY

ATLANTIC
OCEAN

SAMOA

TONGA

Easter I.
(Chile)

Falkland Is.
(U.K.)

N
W   E
S

0   1,500   3,000 miles
0   1,500   3,000 kilometers

80°N

60°N

40°N

20°N

0°

20°S

40°S

60°S

80°S

160°W   140°W   120°W   100°W   80°W   60°W   40°W   20°W

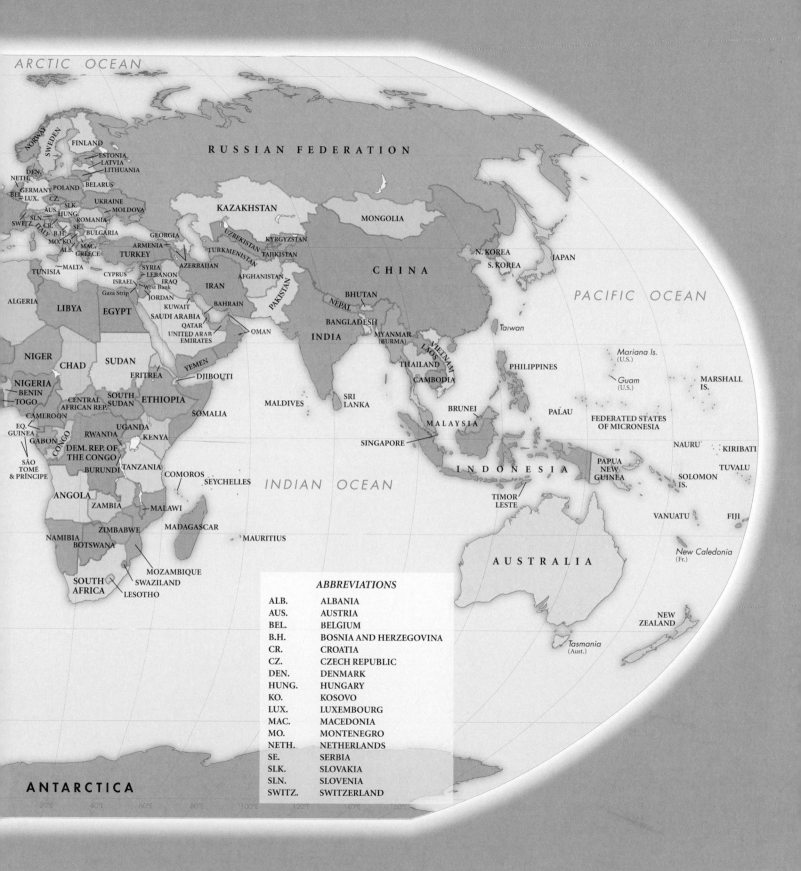

Understanding
Western Society

A HISTORY

SECOND EDITION

VOLUME 1 From Antiquity to the Enlightenment

John P. McKay
University of Illinois at Urbana-Champaign

Clare Haru Crowston
University of Illinois at Urbana-Champaign

Merry E. Wiesner-Hanks
University of Wisconsin–Milwaukee

Joe Perry
Georgia State University

Bedford / St. Martin's
Boston • New York

For Bedford / St. Martin's

Vice President, Editorial, Macmillan Higher Education Humanities: Edwin Hill
Publisher for History: Michael Rosenberg
Senior Executive Editor for History and Technology: William J. Lombardo
Director of Development for History: Jane Knetzger
Developmental Editor: Kathryn Abbott
Production Editor: Annette Pagliaro Sweeney
Senior Production Supervisor: Dennis Conroy
Executive Marketing Manager: Sandra McGuire
Project Manager: John Shannon, Jouve
Editorial Assistant: Emily DiPietro
Cartography: Mapping Specialists, Ltd.
Photo Researcher: Carole Frohlich and Elisa Gallagher, The Visual Connection Image Research, Inc.
Director of Rights and Permissions: Hilary Newman
Senior Art Director: Anna Palchik
Cover Design: William Boardman
Cover Art: Peasant Family at Meal time, c.1665 (oil on canvas), Steen, Jan Havicksz. (1625/26-79) /
    National Gallery, London, UK / Bridgeman Images.
Composition: Jouve
Printing and Binding: RR Donnelley and Sons

Manufactured in the United States of America.

9 8 7 6 5 4
f e d c b a

For information, write: Bedford/St. Martin's, 75 Arlington Street, Boston, MA 02116
(617-399-4000)

ISBN: 978-1-4576-8675-7 (Combined Edition)
ISBN: 978-1-4576-9490-5 (Volume I)
ISBN: 978-1-4576-9491-2 (Volume II)

Acknowledgments

Understanding
Western Society

A HISTORY

VOLUME 1

How to use this book to figure out what's really important

The **chapter title** tells you the subject of the chapter and identifies the time span that will be covered.

The **opening question** and **chapter introduction** identify the most important themes, events, and people that will be explored in the chapter.

15
ABSOLUTISM AND CONSTITUTIONALISM
CA. 1589–1725

> **What were the most important political trends in seventeenth-century Europe?** Chapter 15 examines seventeenth-century political developments. The seventeenth century was a period of crisis and transformation in Europe. Agricultural and manufacturing slumps led to food shortages and shrinking population rates. Religious and dynastic conflicts led to almost constant war, visiting violence and destruction on ordinary people and reshaping European states. While absolutism emerged as the solution to these challenges in many European states, a small minority, most notably England and the Dutch Republic, adopted a different path, placing sovereignty in the hands of privileged groups rather than the Crown.

✓ **LearningCurve**
After reading the chapter, use LearningCurve to retain what you've read.

Memorizing facts and dates for a history class won't get you very far. That's because history isn't just about "facts." This textbook is designed to help you focus on what's truly significant in the history of Western societies and to give you practice thinking like a historian.

> What made the seventeenth century an "age of crisis"?

> Why did France rise and Spain fall during this period?

> What explains the rise of absolutism in Prussia and Austria?

> What were the distinctive features of Russian and Ottoman absolutism?

> How and why did the constitutional state triumph in the Dutch Republic and England?

> What was the baroque style in art and music, and where was it popular?

The **chapter-opening questions** are also the questions that open each new section of the chapters and will be addressed in turn on the following pages. You should think about answers to these as you read.

Life at the French Royal Court. King Louis XIV receives foreign ambassadors to celebrate a peace treaty. (Erich Lessing/Art Resource, NY)

The Chapter Study Guide provides a process that will build your understanding and your historical skills.

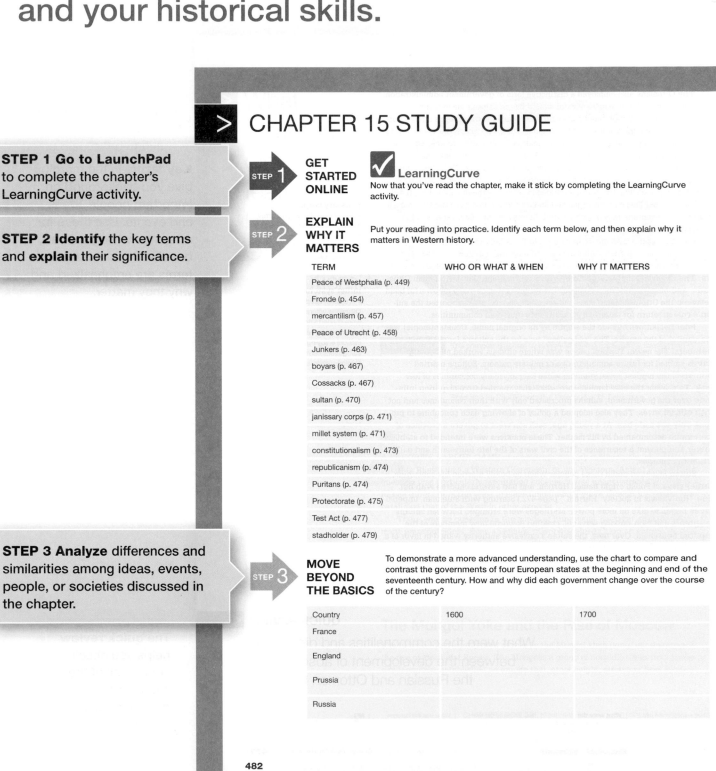

STEP 1 Go to LaunchPad to complete the chapter's LearningCurve activity.

STEP 2 Identify the key terms and **explain** their significance.

CHAPTER 15 STUDY GUIDE

STEP 1 GET STARTED ONLINE

✓ **LearningCurve**
Now that you've read the chapter, make it stick by completing the LearningCurve activity.

STEP 2 EXPLAIN WHY IT MATTERS
Put your reading into practice. Identify each term below, and then explain why it matters in Western history.

TERM	WHO OR WHAT & WHEN	WHY IT MATTERS
Peace of Westphalia (p. 449)		
Fronde (p. 454)		
mercantilism (p. 457)		
Peace of Utrecht (p. 458)		
Junkers (p. 463)		
boyars (p. 467)		
Cossacks (p. 467)		
sultan (p. 470)		
janissary corps (p. 471)		
millet system (p. 471)		
constitutionalism (p. 473)		
republicanism (p. 474)		
Puritans (p. 474)		
Protectorate (p. 475)		
Test Act (p. 477)		
stadholder (p. 479)		

STEP 3 Analyze differences and similarities among ideas, events, people, or societies discussed in the chapter.

STEP 3 MOVE BEYOND THE BASICS
To demonstrate a more advanced understanding, use the chart to compare and contrast the governments of four European states at the beginning and end of the seventeenth century. How and why did each government change over the course of the century?

Country	1600	1700
France		
England		
Prussia		
Russia		

482

STEP **4**

PUT IT ALL TOGETHER

Now, take a step back and try to explain the big picture. Remember to use specific examples from the chapter in your answers.

STEP 4 Answer the big-picture questions using specific examples or evidence from the chapter.

ABSOLUTISM

▶ What common challenges were faced by absolutist monarchs? How did the rulers of France, Austria, and Prussia respond to these challenges?

▶ What social and economic trends accompanied the rise of absolutism in eastern Europe?

CONSTITUTIONALISM

▶ Why did the efforts of English monarchs to build an absolutist state fail?

▶ In what ways was the Dutch Republic unique among seventeenth-century states?

RUSSIA AND THE OTTOMAN EMPIRE

▶ How did the Russian tsars gain control over Russia's landowning elite?

▶ How did the Ottoman absolutist state differ from its European counterparts?

MAKE CONNECTIONS

▶ How did the conflicts and tensions unleashed by the Reformation shape seventeenth-century political developments?

▶ What steps were taken during the seventeenth century toward the emergence of the modern nation-state?

> **IN YOUR OWN WORDS**

Imagine that you must give an oral report to the class answering the following question: **What were the most important political trends in seventeenth-century Europe?** What would be the most important points and why?

ACTIVE RECITATION Explain how you would answer the chapter-opening question in your own words to make sure you have a firm grasp of the most important themes and events of the chapter.

483

PREFACE: Why This Book This Way

U

Understanding Western Society grew out of many conversations we have had among ourselves and with other instructors about the teaching and learning of history. We knew that instructors wanted a Western Civilization text that introduced students to the broad sweep of history but that also re-created the lives of ordinary men and women in appealing human terms. We knew that instructors wanted a text that presented cutting-edge scholarship in new fields of historical inquiry. We also knew that many instructors wanted a text that would help students focus as they read, keep their interest in the material, and encourage them to learn historical thinking skills. It is our hope that *Understanding Western Society* addresses all of these concerns.

New Tools for Teaching and Measuring Outcomes

With requests for clear and transparent learning outcomes coming from all quarters and with students who bring increasingly diverse levels of skills to class, even veteran teachers can find preparing for today's courses a trying matter. The introduction of **LaunchPad** to the second edition offers a breakthrough for instructors. With LaunchPad we have reconceived the textbook as a suite of tools in multiple formats that allows each format do what it does best to capture students' interest and help instructors create meaningful lessons. But one of the best benefits is that instructors using LaunchPad will find they have a number of assessment tools that allow them to see what their students do and don't know and to measure student achievement all in one convenient space. For example, LaunchPad comes with **LearningCurve**—an adaptive learning tool that garners over a 90 percent student satisfaction rate and helps students master book content. When LearningCurve is assigned, the grade book results show instructors where the entire class or individual students may be struggling, which in turn allows instructors to adjust lectures and course activities accordingly—a benefit not only for traditional classes but invaluable for hybrid, online, and newer "flipped" classes as well. In addition, not only can instructors assign all of the questions that appear in the print book and view the responses in the grade book, they have the option to assign automatically graded multiple-choice questions for all of the book features. Plus many more pre-built **activities to foster critical reading and chronological reading skills** are available in LaunchPad, along with a **test building tool and additional primary sources** that all can be used for customized assignments than will report into the grade book for **simplified assessment**. With LaunchPad for *Understanding Western Society*, we make the tough job of teaching simpler by providing everything an instructor needs in one convenient space so instructors can set and achieve the learning outcomes they desire. To learn more about the benefits of LearningCurve and LaunchPad, see the "Versions and Supplements" section.

Understanding Western Society: Bringing the Past to Life for Students

At the point when the parent text, *A History of Western Society*, was first conceptualized, social history was dramatically changing the ways we understood the past, and the original authors decided to create a book that would re-create the lives of ordinary people in appealing human terms, while also giving major economic, political, cultural, and intellectual developments the attention they unquestionably deserve. We three new authors remain committed to advancing this vision for today's classroom, with a broader definition of social history that brings the original idea into the twenty-first century.

History as a discipline never stands still, and over the last several decades, cultural history has joined social history as a source of dynamism. The focus on cultural history has been heightened in the second edition in a way that highlights the interplay between men's and women's lived experiences and the ways men and women reflect on these experiences to create meaning. We know that engaging students' interest in the past is often a challenge, but we also know that the text's hallmark approach—the emphasis on daily life and individual experience in its social and cultural dimensions—connects with students and makes the past vivid and accessible.

Additional "Life" Chapters

Although social and cultural history can be found in every chapter, they are particularly emphasized in the acclaimed "Life" chapters that have always distinguished this book. In response to popular demand by reviewers of the previous edition, these have been increased to five in this edition and now include Chapter 4: Life in the Hellenistic World, 336–30 B.C.E. and Chapter 30: Life in an Age of Globalization, 1990 to the Present, which join Chapter 10: Life in Villages and Cities of the High Middle Ages, 1000–1300; Chapter 18: Life in the Era of Expansion, 1650–1800; and Chapter 22: Life in the Emerging Urban Society, 1840–1914.

An Inquiry-based Model Designed for Understanding

By employing innovative pedagogy, we believe that *Understanding Western Society* helps students not only understand the book's major developments but also begin to grasp the question-driven methodology that is at the heart of the historian's craft. Each chapter opens with a **NEW chapter-opening question** that drives students toward the overarching themes of the chapter, followed by a **brief chapter introduction** that identifies the most important events and people to be discussed. **Section-opening headings** expressed as questions and **section-ending**

quick review questions further model the kinds of questions historians ask and help students engage in inquiry-based reading and understanding.

Chapter Study Guides Designed for Active Learning

At the core of *Understanding Western Society's* unique pedagogical features are the revised **Chapter Study Guides** that provide a carefully structured four-step process to help students build deep understanding of the chapter material. In **Step 1**, students go to LaunchPad to complete the LearningCurve activity, to ensure that they have a grasp of the basic content and concepts of the chapter. In **Step 2**, students not only identify the chapter's key terms but also explain why each matters. In **Step 3**, they begin to apply their understanding of the chapter material through activities that ask them to consider comparison, change over time, or cause and effect. In **Step 4**, analytical and synthetic questions require students to engage in higher-order historical thinking. And, finally, in an active recitation exercise, students **answer the chapter-opening question** to realize their understanding of the chapter fully. In LaunchPad, instructors can assign the **NEW Guided Reading Exercise** for each chapter, which prompts students to read actively to collect information that answers a broad analytic question central to the chapter as a whole.

Primary Sources for Teaching Critical Thinking and Analysis

New assignable **Online Document Projects** in LaunchPad are tied closely to each chapter of *Understanding Western Society*. Each assignment, based on either the "Individuals in Society" feature described below or on key developments from the "Life" chapters (Chapters 4, 10, 18, 22, and 30), prompts students to explore a key question through analysis of multiple sources. Chapter 14, for example, asks students to analyze documents on the complexities of race, identity, and slavery in the early modern era to shed light on the conditions that made the story of Juan de Pareja, a mixed-race man who went from a life in slavery to a free artist, possible. The assignments feature a wealth of textual and visual sources as well as video and audio. Assignments based on the "Individuals and Society" feature include three to four documents in each assignment, while those based on the "Life" chapters include six to eight documents. These Online Document Projects provide instructors with a rich variety of assignment options that encourage students to draw their own conclusions, with the help of short-answer questions, multiple-choice questions that provide instant feedback, and a final essay assignment that asks students to use the sources in creative ways.

We have also revised our **primary source documents collection**, *Sources for Western Society*, to add more visual sources and to align the readings closely with the chapter topics and themes. Each chapter of the reader also includes a set of related documents called "Sources in Conversation." The documents are now available in a fully assignable and assessable electronic format within each LaunchPad unit, and the accompanying multiple-choice questions measure comprehension and hold students accountable for their reading.

Student Engagement with Biography

In addition to the primary source program, we are proud of the unique boxed essay feature in each chapter—**Individuals in Society**—that personalizes larger developments and makes them tangible. These popular biographical essays offer brief studies of individuals or groups, informing students about the societies in which they lived. We have found that readers empathize with these human beings as they themselves seek to define their own identities. The spotlighting of individuals, both famous and obscure, perpetuates the book's continued attention to cultural and intellectual developments, highlights human agency, and reflects changing interests within the historical profession as well as the development of "micro-history." **NEW** features include essays on Anna Jansz of Rotterdam, an Anabaptist martyr; Hürrem, a concubine who became a powerful figure in the Ottoman Empire during the sixteenth century; and Rebecca Protten, a former slave and leader in the Moravian missionary movement. As mentioned previously, the majority of these features are tied to **NEW Online Document Projects**, available in LaunchPad, that allow students to explore further the historical conditions in which these individuals lived.

Geographic and Visual Literacy

We recognize students' difficulties with geography and visual analysis, and the new edition retains our **Mapping the Past map activities** and **Picturing the Past visual activities**. Included in each chapter, these activities ask students to analyze the map or visual and make connections to the larger processes discussed in the narrative, giving them valuable practice in reading and interpreting maps and images. In LaunchPad, they are assignable, and students can submit their work. Throughout the textbook and online in LaunchPad, more than **75 full-size maps** illustrate major developments in the chapter. In addition, **50 spot maps** are embedded in the narrative to show specific areas under discussion.

Chronological Reasoning

To help students make comparisons, understand change over time, and see relationships among contemporaneous events, each chapter begins with a **chapter chronology** that reviews major developments discussed in the chapter. This chronology, available from every page in LaunchPad, allows students to compare developments over the centuries.

Better-Prepared Students

To help students fully understand their reading and come to class prepared, instructors who adopt LaunchPad for *Understanding Western Society* can assign the **LearningCurve** formative assessment activities. This online learning tool is popular with students because it helps them rehearse content at their own pace in a nonthreatening, game-like environment. LearningCurve is also popular with instructors because the reporting features allow them to track overall class trends and spot topics that are giving students trouble so they can adjust their lectures and class activities. When LearningCurve is assigned, students come to class better prepared and instructors can better evaluate and adjust their classes.

To further encourage students to read and assimilate the text fully as well as measure how well they do this, instructors can assign the **new multiple-choice summative quizzes** in LaunchPad, where they are automatically graded. These secure tests not only encourage students to study the book, they can be assigned at specific intervals as high-stakes testing and thus provide another means for analyzing class performance.

Updated Organization and Coverage

To meet the demands of the evolving course, we took a close and critical look at the book's structure and have made changes in the organization of chapters to reflect the way the course is taught today. Most notably, in addition to consolidating some coverage in the two new "Life" chapters described above, we have combined the three chapters on the High Middle Ages in the previous edition into two (Chapters 9 and 10), restructuring and in some cases shortening sections but retaining all key concepts and topics, resulting in one fewer chapter overall. Chapter 9 now focuses more tightly on political, legal, and institutional developments in church and state, and Chapter 10 on the life of both villagers and city folk.

This edition is also enhanced by the incorporation of a wealth of new scholarship and subject areas that immerse students in the dynamic and ongoing work of history. Chapters 1 through 6 have been revised intensively to incorporate the exciting cross-disciplinary scholarship that has emerged over the last several decades on the Paleolithic and Neolithic, river-valley civilizations, and the ancient Mediterranean. For example, archaeologists working at Göbekli Tepe in present-day Turkey have unearthed rings of massive, multi-ton, elaborately carved limestone pillars built around 9000 B.C.E. by groups of foragers, which has led to a rethinking of the links among culture, religion, and the initial development of agriculture. Similarly, new research on the peoples of Mesopotamia, based on cuneiform writing along with other sources, has led scholars to revise the view that they were fatalistic, and instead to emphasize that Mesopotamians generally anticipated being well treated by the gods if they behaved morally. Throughout these chapters, new material on cross-cultural connections, the impact of technologies, and changing social relationships has been added, particularly in Chapter 4, which has been recast as "Life in the Hellenistic World." Other additions include an expanded discussion of the historiography of the fall of the Roman Empire (Chapter 7); new material on the reconquista (Chapter 9); recent ideas on the impact of empire on the Scientific Revolution (Chapter 16); more on the experiences of African Americans, Native Americans, and women in the revolutionary era (Chapter 19); significant updates to the Industrial Revolution coverage, including increased attention to the global context (Chapter 20); revised treatment of ideologies and Romanticism (Chapter 21); new coverage of the popular appeal of nationalism (Chapter 23); new material on orientalism and European imperialism (Chapter 24); extensive updates on the Cold War (Chapter 28); up-to-date coverage of contemporary events in the final chapter, now called "Life in the Age of Globalization, 1990 to the Present," including the Euro crisis, issues surrounding immigration and Muslims in Europe, and the Arab Spring (Chapter 30).

Acknowledgments

It is a pleasure to thank the many instructors who critiqued the parent textbook, *A History of Western Society*, Eleventh Edition. Their feedback helped inform the shape this book has taken.

William M. Abbott, Fairfield University

Joseph Avitable, Quinnipiac University

Dudley Belcher, Tri-County Technical College

Amy Bix, Iowa State University

Nancy Bjorklund, Fullerton College

Robert Blackey, California State University, San Bernardino

Stephen Blumm, Montgomery County Community College

Robert Brennan, Cape Fear Community College

Daniel Bubb, Gonzaga University

Jeff Burson, Georgia Southern University

George Carson, Central Bible College

Michael Cavey, Northern Virginia Community College

Marie Therese Champagne, University of West Florida

Mark W. Chavalas, University of Wisconsin-LaCrosse

David Cherry, Montana State University, Bozeman

Benzion Chinn, Ohio State University

Thomas Colbert, Marshalltown Community College

Elizabeth Collins, Triton College

Amy Colon, Sullivan County Community College

Kristen Cornelis, Community Colleges of Spokane, Institute for Extended Learning

Michael H. Creswell, Florida State University

Andrea DeKoter, State University of New York at Cortland

Donna Donald, Liberty University

Kurt J. Eberly, Tidewater Community College

John Ebley, Anne Arundel Community College

Christopher Ferguson, Auburn University

Robert Figueira, Lander University

Paula Findlen, Stanford University

Jennifer Foray, Purdue University

Laura Gathagan, State University of New York at Cortland

Stephen Gibson, Allegany College of Maryland

Gregory Golden, Rhode Island College

Jack Goldstone, George Mason University

Chuck Goodwin, Illinois Valley Community College

Dolores Grapsas, New River Community College

Robert Grasso, Monmouth University

Robert H. Greene, University of Montana

Edward Gutierrez, University of Hartford

David Halahmy, Cypress College

Michael Harkins, Harper College

David M. Head, John Tyler Community College

Jeff Horn, Manhattan College

Barry Jordan, Cape Fear Community College

Cheryl L. Kajs, Pellissippi State Community College

Michael Kennedy, High Point University

Michele Kinney, Strayer University

Willem Klooster, Clark University

Pamela Koenig, Seminole State College

Roy G. Koepp, University of Nebraska at Kearney

James Krapfl, McGill University

Andrew E. Larsen, Marquette University

Kenneth Loiselle, Rice University

Susan Mattern, University of Georgia

Maureen A. McCormick, Florida State College at Jacksonville

James McIntyre, Moraine Valley Community College

Deena McKinney, East Georgia College

Linda A. McMillin, Susquehanna University

Jennifer McNabb, Western Illinois University

Michael Meng, Clemson University

Scott Merriman, Troy University

Ryan Messenger, Monroe Community College/Genesee Community College

Byron J. Nakamura, Southern Connecticut State University

Jeannine Olson, Rhode Island College

Lisa Ossian, Des Moines Area Community College

Jotham Parsons, Duquesne University

Margaret Peacock, The University of Alabama

Kathy L. Pearson, Old Dominion University

Amanda Podany, California State Polytechnic University, Pomona

Ann Pond, Bishop State Community College

Matthew Restall, Pennsylvania State University

Michael D. Richards, Northern Virginia Community College

Jason Ripper, Everett Community College

Russell J. Rockefeller, Anne Arundel Community College

Leonard N. Rosenband, Utah State University

Mark Edward Ruff, Saint Louis University

Ernest Rugenstein, Hudson Valley Community College

Anne Ruszkiewicz, Sullivan County Community College

Wendy A. Sarti, Oakton Community College

Linda Scherr, Mercer County Community College

Elise Shelton, Trident Technical College

Chris Shepard, Trident Technical College

Robert Shipley, Widener University

Sherri Singer, Alamance Community College

Daniel Snell, University of Oklahoma

Steven Soper, The University of Georgia

Susan Souza-Mort, Bristol Community College

James Taw, Valdosta State University

Alfred T. Terrell, Yuba College

Timothy Thibodeau, Nazareth College

Karl Valois, University of Connecticut, Torrington

Liana Vardi, University at Buffalo, The State University of New York

Joseph Villano, Indian River State College

Gregory Vitarbo, Meredith College

David Weiland, Collin County Community College

Scott White, Scottsdale Community College

Pamela Wolfe, Yeshiva of Greater Washington

James Wright, Triton College

Sergei Zhuk, Ball State University.

It is also a pleasure to thank the many people who have assisted us over the years, first at Houghton Mifflin and now at Bedford/St. Martin's and Macmillan Education. At Bedford/St. Martin's and Macmillan Education, these include developmental editors Kathryn Abbott and Annette Fantasia, associate editor Emily DiPietro, executive editor Traci Crowell, director of development Jane Knetzger, publisher for history Mary Dougherty, photo researcher Carole Frohlich, production editor Annette Pagliaro Sweeney, cover designer Billy Boardman, market development manager Katherine Bates, executive marketing manager Sandi McGuire, and marketing assistant Alex Kaufman. We would like to thank the staff at Jouve North America for composition and production services.

Many of our colleagues at the University of Illinois, the University of Wisconsin–Milwaukee, and Georgia State University continue to provide information and stimulation, often without even knowing it. We thank them for it. We also thank the many students over the years with whom we have used earlier editions of this book. Their reactions and opinions helped shape the revisions to this edition, and we hope it remains worthy of the ultimate praise that they bestowed on it, that it's "not boring like most textbooks." Merry Wiesner-Hanks would, as always, also like to thank her husband Neil, without whom work on this project would not be possible. Clare Haru Crowston thanks her husband Ali and her children Lili, Reza, and Kian, who are joyous reminders of the vitality of life that we try to showcase in this book. Joe Perry thanks his colleagues and students at Georgia State for their intellectual stimulation and is grateful to Joyce de Vries for her unstinting support and encouragement.

Each of us has benefited from the criticism of our coauthors, although each of us assumes responsibility for what he or she has written. Merry Wiesner-Hanks has intensively reworked and revised John Buckler's Chapters 1 through 6 and has revised Chapters 7 through 13; Clare Crowston has written and revised Chapters 14 through 19 and took responsibility for John McKay's Chapter 20;

and Joe Perry took responsibility for John McKay's Chapters 21 through 24 and has written and revised Chapters 25 through 30.

We'd especially like to thank the founding authors, John P. McKay, Bennett D. Hill, and John Buckler, for their enduring contributions and for their faith in each of us to carry on their legacy.

Clare Haru Crowston
Merry E. Wiesner-Hanks
Joe Perry

VERSIONS AND SUPPLEMENTS

Adopters of *Understanding Western Society* and their students have access to abundant print and digital resources and tools, including documents, assessment and presentation materials, the acclaimed Bedford Series in History and Culture volumes, and much more. And for the first time, the full-featured LaunchPad course space provides access to the narrative with all assignment and assessment opportunities at the ready. See below for more information, visit the book's catalog site at **bedfordstmartins.com/mckaywestunderstanding/catalog**, or contact your local Bedford/St. Martin's sales representative.

Get the Right Version for Your Class

To accommodate different course lengths and course budgets, *Understanding Western Society* is available in several different formats, including three-hole-punched, loose-leaf Budget Books versions and low-priced PDF e-books, which include the *Bedford e-Book to Go* from our Web site and other PDF e-books from other commercial sources. And for the best value of all, package a new print book with LaunchPad at no additional charge to get the best each format offers—a print version for easy portability and reading with a LaunchPad interactive e-book and course space with loads of additional assignment and assessment options.

- **Combined Volume** (Chapters 1–30): available in paperback, loose-leaf, and e-book formats and in LaunchPad
- **Volume 1, From Antiquity to the Enlightenment** (Chapters 1–16): available in paperback, loose-leaf, and e-book formats and in LaunchPad
- **Volume 2, From the Age of Exploration to the Present** (Chapters 14–30): available in paperback, loose-leaf, and e-book formats and in LaunchPad

As noted below, any of these volumes can be packaged with additional titles for a discount. To get ISBNs for discount packages, see the online catalog at **bedfordstmartins.com/mckaywestunderstanding/catalog** or contact your Bedford/St. Martin's representative.

NEW Assign LaunchPad — A Content-rich and Assessment-ready Interactive e-Book and Course Space

Available for discount purchase on its own or for packaging with new books at no additional charge, LaunchPad is a breakthrough solution for today's courses. Intuitive and easy to use for students and instructors alike, LaunchPad is ready to use as is, but it can be edited, customized with your own material, and assigned in seconds. *LaunchPad for Understanding Western Society* includes Bedford/St. Martin's high-quality content all in one place, including the full interactive e-book and the *Sources for Western Society* documents collection, plus LearningCurve formative quizzing, guided reading activities designed to help students read actively for key concepts, additional primary sources, images, videos, chapter summative quizzes, and more.

Through a wealth of formative and summative assessments, including short answer, essay questions, multiple-choice quizzing, and the adaptive learning program of LearningCurve (see the full description ahead), students gain confidence and get into their reading *before* class. Map and visual activities engage students with visual analysis and critical thinking as they work through each unit, while special boxed features become more meaningful through automatically graded multiple-choice exercises and short-answer questions that prompt students to analyze their reading.

LaunchPad integrates easily with course management systems, and with fast ways to build assignments; rearrange chapters; and add new pages, sections, and links, it lets teachers build the courses they want to teach and hold students accountable. For more information, visit **launchpadworks.com** or, to arrange a demo, contact us at **history@bedfordstmartins.com**.

✅ NEW Assign LearningCurve So Your Students Come to Class Prepared

Students using LaunchPad receive access to LearningCurve for *Understanding Western Society*. Assigning LearningCurve in place of reading quizzes is easy for instructors, and the reporting features help instructors track overall class trends and spot topics that are giving students trouble so they can adjust their lectures and class activities. This online learning tool is popular with students because it was designed to help them rehearse content at their own pace in a nonthreatening, game-like environment. The feedback for wrong answers provides instructional coaching and sends students back to the book for review. Students answer as many questions as necessary to reach a target score, with repeated chances to revisit material they haven't mastered. When LearningCurve is assigned, students come to class better prepared.

Take Advantage of Instructor Resources

Bedford/St. Martin's has developed a rich array of teaching resources for this book and for this course. They range from lecture and presentation materials and assessment tools to course management options. Most can be found in LaunchPad or can be downloaded or ordered at **bedfordstmartins.com/mckaywestunderstanding /catalog**.

▶ **Instructor's Resource Manual.** The instructor's resource manual offers both experienced and first-time instructors tools for preparing lectures and running discussions. It includes chapter content learning objectives, annotated chapter outlines, teaching strategies, and a guide to chapter-specific supplements available for the text, plus suggestions on how to get the most out of LearningCurve and a survival guide for first-time teaching assistants.

▶ **Guide to Changing Editions.** Designed to facilitate an instructor's transition from the previous edition of *Understanding Western Society* to the current edition, this guide presents an overview of major changes as well as of changes in each chapter.

▶ **Computerized Test Bank.** The test bank includes a mix of fresh, carefully crafted multiple-choice, short-answer, and essay questions for each chapter. It also contains volume-wide essay questions. All questions appear in Microsoft Word format and in easy-to-use test bank software that allows instructors to add, edit, re-sequence, and print questions and answers. Instructors can also export questions into a variety of formats, including Blackboard, Desire2Learn, and Moodle.

▶ *The Bedford Lecture Kit:* **PowerPoint Maps and Images.** Look good and save time with *The Bedford Lecture Kit*. These presentation materials are download-able individually from the Instructor Resources tab at **bedfordstmartins.com /mckaywestunderstanding/catalog**. They include all maps, figures, and select images from the textbook in JPEG and PowerPoint formats.

Package and Save Your Students Money

For information on free packages and discounts worth up to 50%, visit **bedfordstmartins.com/mckaywestunderstanding/catalog**, or contact your local Bedford/St. Martin's sales representative. The products that follow all qualify for discount packaging.

▶ *Sources for Western Society,* **Third Edition.** This primary-source collection— available in Volume 1 and Volume 2 versions—provides a revised and expanded selection of sources to accompany *Understanding Western Society*, Second Edition. Each chapter features five or six written and visual sources by well-known figures and ordinary individuals alike. With over fifty new selections—including a dozen new visual sources—and enhanced pedagogy throughout, students are given the tools to engage critically with canonical and lesser-known sources and prominent and ordinary voices. Each chapter includes a "Sources in Conversa-tion" feature that presents differing views on key topics. This companion reader is an exceptional value for students and offers plenty of assignment options for instructors. Available free when packaged with the print text and included in the LaunchPad e-book. Also available on its own as a downloadable PDF e-book.

▶ **The Bedford Series in History and Culture.** More than 100 titles in this highly praised series combine first-rate scholarship, historical narrative, and important primary documents for undergraduate courses. Each book is brief, inexpensive, and focused on a specific topic or period. For a complete list of titles, visit **bedfordstmartins.com/history/series**.

▶ *Rand McNally Atlas of Western Civilization.* This collection of over fifty full-color maps highlights social, political, and cross-cultural change and interaction from classical Greece and Rome to the postindustrial Western world. Each map is thoroughly indexed for fast reference.

▶ *The Bedford Glossary for European History.* This handy supplement for the survey course gives students historically contextualized definitions for hundreds of terms—from *Abbasids* to *Zionism*—that they will encounter in lectures, reading, and exams.

▶ **Trade Books.** Titles published by sister companies Hill and Wang; Farrar, Straus and Giroux; Henry Holt and Company; St. Martin's Press; Picador; and Palgrave Macmillan are available at a 50% discount when packaged with Bedford/St. Martin's textbooks. For more information, visit **bedfordstmartins.com/tradeup**.

▶ *A Pocket Guide to Writing in History.* This portable and affordable reference tool by Mary Lynn Rampolla provides reading, writing, and research advice useful to students in all history courses. Concise yet comprehensive advice on approaching typical history assignments, developing critical reading skills, writing effective history papers, conducting research, using and documenting sources, and avoiding plagiarism—enhanced with practical tips and examples throughout—have made this slim reference a bestseller.

▶ *A Student's Guide to History.* This complete guide to success in any history course provides the practical help students need to be successful. In addition to introducing students to the nature of the discipline, author Jules Benjamin teaches a wide range of skills, from preparing for exams to approaching common writing assignments, and explains the research and documentation process with plentiful examples.

▶ *The Social Dimension of Western Civilization.* Combining current scholarship with classic pieces, this reader's forty-eight secondary sources, compiled by Richard M. Golden, hook students with the fascinating and often surprising details of how everyday Western people worked, ate, played, celebrated, worshiped, married, procreated, fought, persecuted, and died.

BRIEF CONTENTS

CONTENTS

1

ORIGINS

TO 1200 B.C.E. *2*

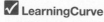

2

SMALL KINGDOMS AND MIGHTY EMPIRES IN THE NEAR EAST

1200–510 B.C.E. *32*

3

THE DEVELOPMENT OF GREEK SOCIETY AND CULTURE

CA. 3000–338 B.C.E. *58*

10

LIFE IN VILLAGES AND CITIES OF THE HIGH MIDDLE AGES

1000–1300 *274*

11

THE LATER MIDDLE AGES

1300–1450 *310*

12

EUROPEAN SOCIETY IN THE AGE OF THE RENAISSANCE

1350–1550 *342*

13

REFORMATIONS AND RELIGIOUS WARS

1500–1600 *376*

14

EUROPEAN EXPLORATION AND CONQUEST

1450–1650   *410*

15

ABSOLUTISM AND CONSTITUTIONALISM

CA. 1589–1725   *444*

16

TOWARD A NEW WORLDVIEW

1540–1789   *484*

MAPS, FIGURES, AND TABLES

Understanding
Western Society

A HISTORY

VOLUME 1

1
ORIGINS
TO 1200 B.C.E.

> **What similarities and differences were evident in the nature and development of the Mesopotamian and Egyptian civilizations?**

Chapter 1 examines early human history, tracing the evolution of human society from its origins to the emergence of cities, kingdoms, and empires. For most of their history, humans were foragers moving through the landscape, inventing ever more specialized tools. About 11,000 years ago, people in some places domesticated plants and animals. They began to live in permanent villages, some of which grew into cities. They created new technologies and social systems that facilitated further growth and development. The first places where these new technologies and systems were introduced were the Tigris and Euphrates River Valleys of southwest Asia and the Nile Valley of northeast Africa, areas whose history became linked through trade connections, military conquests, and migrations.

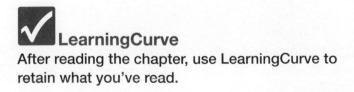

LearningCurve
After reading the chapter, use LearningCurve to retain what you've read.

Life in New Kingdom Egypt, ca. 1500–1300 B.C.E. In this wall painting from the tomb of an official, a man guides a wooden ox-drawn plow through the soil, while the woman walking behind throws seed in the furrow. (Deir el-Medina, Thebes, Egypt/The Bridgeman Art Library)

> What do we mean by "the West" and "Western civilization"?

> How did early human societies develop and create new technologies and cultural forms?

> What kind of civilization did the Sumerians develop in Mesopotamia?

> How did the Akkadian and Old Babylonian empires develop in Mesopotamia?

> How did the Egyptians create a prosperous and long-lasting society?

What do we mean by "the West" and "Western civilization"?

H HUMAN GROUPS HAVE LONG MADE DISTINCTIONS between themselves and others. Some of these distinctions are between small groups such as neighboring tribes, some between countries and civilizations, and some between vast parts of the world. Among the most enduring of the latter are the ideas of "the West" and "the East."

Describing the West

Ideas about the West and the distinction between West and East derived originally from the ancient Greeks. Greek civilization grew up in the shadow of earlier civilizations, especially Egypt and Mesopotamia. Greeks defined themselves in relation to these more advanced cultures, which they saw as "Eastern."

The Greeks passed this conceptualization on to the Romans, who saw themselves clearly as part of the West. To Romans, the East was more sophisticated and more advanced, but also decadent and somewhat immoral. Roman value judgments have continued to shape preconceptions, stereotypes, and views of differences between the West and the East to this day.

Greco-Roman ideas about the West were passed on to people who lived in western and northern Europe, who saw themselves as the inheritors of this classical tradition and thus as the West. When these Europeans established colonies outside Europe beginning in the late fifteenth century, they regarded what they were doing as taking Western culture with them. With colonization, *Western* came to mean those cultures that included significant numbers of people of European ancestry, no matter where on the globe they were located.

In the early twentieth century, educators and other leaders in the United States became worried that many people, especially young people, were becoming cut off from European intellectual and cultural traditions. They encouraged the establishment of college and university courses focusing on "Western civilization," the first of which was taught at Columbia University in 1919. In designing the course, the faculty included cultures that, as far back as the ancient Greeks, had been considered Eastern, such as Egypt and Mesopotamia.

After World War II, divisions between the West and the East changed again, with *Western* coming to imply a capitalist economy and *Eastern* the Communist

CHAPTER LOCATOR | What do we mean by "the West" and "Western civilization"?

4   CHAPTER 1
ORIGINS

ca. 250,000 B.C.E. – *Homo sapiens* evolve in Africa	**ca. 3000 B.C.E.** – Development of wheeled transport; beginning of bronze technology
250,000–9,000 B.C.E. – Paleolithic era	**ca. 2500 B.C.E.** – Bronze technology becomes common in many areas
9000 B.C.E. – Beginning of the Neolithic; crop raising; domestication of sheep and goats	**ca. 2300 B.C.E.** – Establishment of the Akkadian empire
ca. 7000 B.C.E. – Domestication of cattle; plow agriculture	**ca. 1800 B.C.E.** – Hyksos people begin to settle in the Nile Delta
ca. 5500 B.C.E. – Smelting of copper	**1792–1750 B.C.E.** – Hammurabi rules Babylon
ca. 3800 B.C.E. – Establishment of first Mesopotamian cities	**1258 B.C.E.** – Peace treaty between Egyptian pharaoh Ramesses II and Hittite king Hattusuli III
ca. 3200 B.C.E. – Development of cuneiform and hieroglyphic writing	**ca. 1200 B.C.E.** – "Bronze Age Collapse"; destruction and drought
ca. 3100 B.C.E – Unification of Upper and Lower Egypt	

A note on dates: This book generally uses the terms B.C.E. (Before the Common Era) and C.E. (Common Era) when giving dates, a system of chronology based on the Christian calendar and now used widely around the world.

Eastern bloc. Thus, Japan was considered Western, and some Greek-speaking areas of Europe became Eastern. The collapse of communism in the Soviet Union and eastern Europe in the 1980s brought yet another refiguring, with much of eastern Europe joining the European Union, originally a Western organization.

At the beginning of the twenty-first century, *Western* still suggests a capitalist economy, but it also has certain cultural connotations, such as individualism and competition. Islamist radicals often describe their aims as an end to Western cultural, economic, and political influence, though Islam itself is generally described, along with Judaism and Christianity, as a Western monotheistic religion. Thus, throughout its long history, the meaning of "the West" has shifted, but in every era it has meant more than a geographical location.

What Is Civilization?

Just as the meaning of the word *Western* is shaped by culture, so is the meaning of the word *civilization*. In the ancient world, residents of cities generally viewed themselves as more advanced and sophisticated than rural folk. They saw themselves as more "civilized," a word that comes from the Latin adjective *civilis*, which refers to a citizen, either of a town or of a larger political unit.

This depiction of people as either civilized or uncivilized was gradually extended to whole societies. Beginning in the eighteenth century, European scholars described any society in which political, economic, and social organizations operated on a large scale, not primarily through families and kin groups, as

How did early human societies develop and create new technologies and cultural forms? | What kind of civilization did the Sumerians develop in Mesopotamia? | How did the Akkadian and Old Babylonian empires develop in Mesopotamia? | How did the Egyptians create a prosperous and long-lasting society? | ✔ LearningCurve Check what you know.

5

civilization

▶ A large-scale system of human political, economic, and social organizations; civilizations have cities, laws, states, and often writing.

a **civilization**. Civilizations had cities; laws that governed human relationships; codes of manners and social conduct that regulated how people were to behave; and scientific, philosophical, and theological beliefs that explained the larger world. Civilizations also had some form of political organization through which one group was able to coerce resources out of others to engage in group endeavors, such as building large structures or carrying out warfare. Generally only societies that used writing were judged to be civilizations.

Until the middle of the twentieth century, historians often referred to the places where writing and cities developed as "cradles of civilization," proposing a model of development for all humanity patterned on that of an individual life span. However, the idea that all human societies developed (or should develop) on a uniform process from a "cradle" to a "mature" civilization has now been largely discredited, and some historians choose not to use the term *civilization* at all because it could imply that some societies are superior to others.

Just as the notion of "civilization" has been questioned, so has the notion of "Western civilization." Ever since the idea of "Western civilization" was first developed, people have debated what its geographical extent and core values are. Are there certain beliefs, customs, concepts, and institutions that set Western civilization apart from other civilizations and, if so, when and how did these originate? How were these values and practices transmitted over space and time, and how did they change? No civilization stands alone, and each is influenced by its neighbors. Whatever Western civilization was—and is—it has been shaped by interactions with other societies, cultures, and civilizations. Even so, the idea that there are basic distinctions between the West and the rest of the world in terms of cultural values has been very powerful for thousands of years, and it still shapes the way many people view the world.

> **QUICK REVIEW**

How have the meanings of the terms *Western* and *civilization* changed over time?

CHAPTER LOCATOR | What do we mean by "the West" and "Western civilization"?

How did early human societies develop and create new technologies and cultural forms?

Pillar at Göbekli Tepe

The huge limestone pillars arranged in rings at the Paleolithic site Göbekli Tepe are somewhat humanoid in shape, and the carvings are of dangerous animals, including lions, boars, foxes, snakes, vultures, and scorpions. (Vincent J. Musi/National Geographic Stock)

DURING THE NINETEENTH CENTURY, archaeologists coined labels for eras of the human past according to the primary material out of which surviving tools had been made. Thus the earliest human era became the Stone Age, the next era the Bronze Age, and the next the Iron Age. They further divided the Stone Age into the **Paleolithic era**, during which people used stone and other natural products to make tools and gained food largely by foraging. This was followed by the **Neolithic era**, which started around 9000 B.C.E. and saw the beginning of agricultural and animal domestication.

From the First Hominids to the Paleolithic Era

Sometime between 7 and 6 million years ago in southern and eastern Africa, groups of human ancestors (members of the biological "hominid" family) began to walk upright, which allowed them to carry things. About 3.4 million years ago, some hominids began to use naturally occurring objects as tools, and around 2.5 million years ago, one group in East Africa began to make simple tools, a feat that was accompanied by, and may have spurred, brain development. Groups migrated into much of Africa and then into Asia and Europe; by about 600,000 years ago, there were hominids throughout much of Afroeurasia.

About 200,000 years ago, again in East Africa, some of these early humans evolved into *Homo sapiens* ("thinking humans"), which had still larger and more complex brains that allowed for symbolic language and better social skills. *Homo sapiens* invented highly specialized tools made out of a variety of materials. They

Paleolithic era
▶ The period of human history up to about 9000 B.C.E., when tools were made from stone and bone and people gained their food through foraging.

Neolithic era
▶ The period after 9000 B.C.E., when people developed agriculture, domesticated animals, and used tools made of stone and wood.

| **How did early human societies develop and create new technologies and cultural forms?** | What kind of civilization did the Sumerians develop in Mesopotamia? | How did the Akkadian and Old Babylonian empires develop in Mesopotamia? | How did the Egyptians create a prosperous and long-lasting society? | ✔ LearningCurve Check what you know. |

7

made regular use of fire for heat, light, and cooking. They also migrated, first across Africa, and by 70,000 years ago, out of Africa into Eurasia. Eventually they traveled farther still, reaching Australia using rafts about 50,000 years ago and the Americas by about 15,000 years ago, or perhaps earlier. Gradually other types of hominids became extinct, leaving *homo sapiens* as the only survivors and the ancestors of all modern humans.

In the Paleolithic period, humans throughout the world lived in ways that were similar to one another. Archaeological evidence and studies of modern foragers suggest that people generally lived in small groups of related individuals and moved throughout the landscape in search of food. They ate mostly plants, and much of the animal protein in their diet came from foods gathered or scavenged rather than hunted directly. Paleolithic peoples did, however, hunt large game, often hunting in groups.

Paleolithic people were not differentiated by wealth. Most foraging societies that exist today, or did so until recently, have some type of division of labor by sex and also by age. Men are more often responsible for hunting and women for gathering plant and animal products. This may or may not have been the case in the Paleolithic era, or there may have been a diversity of patterns.

Beginning in the Paleolithic era, human beings have expressed themselves through what we would now term the arts or culture: painting and decorating walls and objects, making music, telling stories, dancing alone or in groups. Burials, paintings, and objects suggest that people may have developed ideas about supernatural forces that controlled some aspects of the natural world and the humans in it, what we now term spirituality or religion. Spiritually adept men and women communicated with that unseen world, and objects such as carvings or masks were probably thought to have special healing or protective powers. (See "Picturing the Past: Paleolithic Venus Figures," page 9.)

Planting Crops

Foraging remained the basic way of life for most of human history, and for groups living in extreme environments; it was the only possible way to survive. In a few especially fertile areas, however, the natural environment provided enough food that people could become more settled. About 15,000 years ago, the earth's climate entered a warming phase, and more parts of the world were able to support sedentary or semi-sedentary groups of foragers. In several of these places, foragers began planting seeds in the ground along with gathering wild grains, roots, and other foodstuffs. Intentional crop planting first developed around 9000 B.C.E., in the area archaeologists call the **Fertile Crescent**, which runs from present-day Lebanon, Israel, and Jordan north to Turkey and then south and east to the Iran-Iraq border. Over the next two millennia, intentional crop planting emerged, for the most part independently, in the Nile River Valley, western Africa, China, India, Papua New Guinea, and Mesoamerica.

Why, after living successfully as foragers for tens of thousands of years, did humans in so many parts of the world begin raising crops at about the same time? The answer to this question is not clear, but crop raising may have resulted from population pressures in those parts of the world where the warming climate provided more food through foraging. More food meant lower child mortality and longer life spans, which allowed populations to grow. People then had a choice: they could move to a new area or they could develop ways to increase the food supply.

Fertile Crescent
▶ An area of mild climate and abundant wild grain where agriculture first developed, in present-day Lebanon, Israel, Jordan, Turkey, and Iraq.

CHAPTER LOCATOR | What do we mean by "the West" and "Western civilization"?

8 CHAPTER 1 ORIGINS

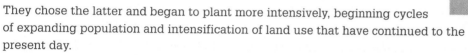

They chose the latter and began to plant more intensively, beginning cycles of expanding population and intensification of land use that have continued to the present day.

A very recent archaeological find at Göbekli Tepe in present-day Turkey suggests that cultural factors may have played a role in the development of agriculture. Here, around 9000 B.C.E., hundreds of people came together to build rings of massive, elaborately carved limestone pillars. The people who created this site lived some distance away, where archaeological remains indicate that at the time they first carved the pillars, they ate wild game and plants, not crops. We can only speculate about why so many people expended the effort they did to carve these pillars and raise them into place, but the project may have unintentionally spurred the development of new methods of food production that would allow the many workers to be fed efficiently. Indeed, it is very near here that evidence of the world's oldest domesticated wheat has been discovered. Archaeologists speculate that, at least in this case, the symbolic, cultural, or perhaps religious importance of the structure can help explain why the people building it changed from foraging to agriculture.

Implications of Agriculture

Whatever the reasons for the move from foraging to agriculture, within several centuries of initial crop planting, people in the Fertile Crescent, parts of China, and the Nile Valley were relying primarily on domesticated food products. They built permanent houses near one another in villages and planted fields around the villages.

A field of planted and weeded crops yields ten to one hundred times as much food—measured in calories—as the same area of naturally occurring plants. It also requires much more labor, however, which was provided both by the greater number of people in the community and by those people working longer hours. In

| How did early human societies develop and create new technologies and cultural forms? | What kind of civilization did the Sumerians develop in Mesopotamia? | How did the Akkadian and Old Babylonian empires develop in Mesopotamia? | How did the Egyptians create a prosperous and long-lasting society? | ✓ LearningCurve Check what you know. |

9

contrast to the twenty hours a week foragers spent on obtaining food, farming peoples were often in the fields from dawn to dusk. Early farmers were also less healthy than foragers were; their narrower range of foodstuffs made them more susceptible to disease and nutritional deficiencies. Still, farmers came to outnumber foragers, and slowly larger and larger parts of Europe, China, South and Southeast Asia, and Africa became home to farming villages.

At roughly the same time that they domesticated certain plants, people also domesticated animals. In about 9000 B.C.E., at the same time they began to raise crops, people in the Fertile Crescent domesticated wild goats and sheep. They began to breed the goats and sheep selectively for qualities that they wanted. Sheep and goats allow themselves to be herded, and people developed a new form of living, **pastoralism**, based on herding and raising livestock. Eventually other grazing animals, including cattle, camels, horses, yak, and reindeer, also became the basis of pastoral economies in Central and West Asia, many parts of Africa, and far northern Europe.

The domestication of certain large animals had a significant impact on human ways of life. Cattle, water buffalo, donkeys, and horses can be trained to carry people or burdens on their backs and pull against loads dragged behind them. Their use dramatically increased the power available to humans to carry out their tasks, which had both an immediate effect in the societies in which this happened and a long-term effect when these societies later encountered other societies in which human labor remained the only source of power.

Sometime in the seventh millennium B.C.E., people attached wooden sticks to frames that animals dragged through the soil, thus breaking it up and allowing seeds to sprout more easily. These simple scratch plows, pulled by cattle and water buffalo, allowed Neolithic people to produce a significant amount of surplus food, which meant that some people in the community could spend their days performing other tasks, thus increasing the division of labor. Some people specialized in making tools, houses, and other items needed in village life, or for producing specific types of food. Families and households became increasingly interdependent, trading food for other commodities or services.

The division of labor allowed by plow agriculture contributed to the creation of social hierarchies based on wealth and power. Although no written records were produced during this era, archaeological evidence provides some clues about how the hierarchies might have developed. Villagers needed more complex rules about how food was to be distributed and how different types of work were to be valued than did foragers. Certain individuals must have begun to specialize in the determination and enforcement of these rules, and informal structures of power gradually became more formalized. Religious specialists probably developed more elaborate rituals to celebrate life passages and to appeal to the gods for help in times of difficulty, such as illness.

Individuals who were the heads of large families or kin groups had control over the labor of others, and this power became more significant when that labor brought material goods that could be stored. Material goods—plows, sheep, cattle, sheds, pots, carts—gave one the ability to amass still more material goods, and the gap between those who had them and those who did not widened. Social hierarchies were reinforced over generations as children inherited goods and status from their parents.

Along with hierarchies based on wealth and power, the development of agriculture was intertwined with a hierarchy based on gender. In many places, plow

pastoralism
► An economic system based on herding flocks of goats, sheep, cattle, or other animals beneficial to humans.

CHAPTER LOCATOR | What do we mean by "the West" and "Western civilization"?

10 CHAPTER 1 ORIGINS

agriculture came to be a male task. Men's responsibility for plowing and other agricultural tasks took them outside the household more often than women's duties did, enlarging their opportunities for leadership. This role may have led to their being favored as inheritors of family land and the right to farm communally held land. Accordingly, over generations, women's independent access to resources decreased. The system in which men have more power and access to resources than women of the same social level, and in which some men are dominant over other men, is called **patriarchy** and is found in every society in the world with written records, although the level of inequality varies.

patriarchy
▶ A society in which most power is held by older adult men, especially those from the elite groups.

Trade and Cross-Cultural Connections

By 7000 B.C.E. or so, some agricultural villages in the Fertile Crescent may have had as many as ten thousand residents. One of the best known of these, Çatal Hüyük in what is now Turkey, shows evidence of trade as well as specialization of labor. Çatal Hüyük's residents made textiles, pots, figurines, baskets, carpets, copper and lead beads, and other goods, and decorated their houses with murals showing animal and human figures. They gathered, sharpened, and polished obsidian, a volcanic rock that could be used for knives, blades, and mirrors, and then traded it with neighboring towns, obtaining seashells and flint. From here the obsidian was exchanged still farther away, for Neolithic societies slowly developed local and then regional networks of exchange and communication.

Among the goods traded in some parts of the world was copper, which people hammered into shapes for jewelry and tools. By about 5500 B.C.E., people in the Balkans had learned that copper could be extracted from ore by heating it in a smelting process. Smelted copper was poured into molds and made into spear points, axes, chisels, beads, and other objects. Pure copper is soft, but through experimentation artisans learned that it would become harder if they mixed it with other metals during heating, creating an alloy called bronze.

Because it was stronger than copper, bronze had a far wider range of uses, so much so that later historians decided that its adoption marked a new period in human history: the **Bronze Age**. The Bronze Age began about 3000 B.C.E., and by about 2500 B.C.E., bronze technology was having an impact in many parts of the world. The end of the Bronze Age came with the adoption of iron technology, a development that began around 1200 B.C.E. (see Chapter 2).

Bronze Age
▶ The period in which the production and use of bronze implements became basic to society.

Objects were not the only things traded over increasingly long distances during the Neolithic period, for people also carried ideas as they traveled. Knowledge about the seasons and the weather was vitally important for those who depended on crop raising, and agricultural peoples in many parts of the world began to calculate recurring patterns in the world around them, slowly developing calendars.

The rhythms of the agricultural cycle and patterns of exchange also shaped religious beliefs and practices. In many places multiple gods came to be associated with patterns of birth, growth, death, and regeneration in a system known as **polytheism**. Like humans, the gods came to have a division of labor and a social hierarchy.

polytheism
▶ The worship of many gods and goddesses.

QUICK REVIEW

In what ways did the development and spread of settled agriculture constitute a revolution in human ways of life?

How did early human societies develop and create new technologies and cultural forms?

What kind of civilization did the Sumerians develop in Mesopotamia?

How did the Akkadian and Old Babylonian empires develop in Mesopotamia?

How did the Egyptians create a prosperous and long-lasting society?

☑ LearningCurve
Check what you know.

> What kind of civilization did the Sumerians develop in Mesopotamia?

Clay Letter Written in Cuneiform ca. 1850 B.C.E.

In this letter from a city in Anatolia, located on the northern edge of the Fertile Crescent in what is now Turkey, a Mesopotamian merchant complains to his brother at home, hundreds of miles away, that life is hard and comments on the trade in silver, gold, tin, and textiles. (© The Courtesy of the Trustees of the British Museum)

THE ORIGINS OF WESTERN CIVILIZATION are generally traced to Mesopotamia (mehs-oh-puh-TAY-mee-uh), the Greek name for the land between the Euphrates (yoo-FRAY-teez) and Tigris (TIGH-grihs) Rivers (**Map 1.1**). The earliest agricultural villages in Mesopotamia were in the northern, hilly parts of the river valleys, where there is abundant rainfall for crops. Farmers had brought techniques of crop raising southward by about 5000 B.C.E., to the southern part of Mesopotamia, called Sumer. In this arid climate farmers developed irrigation on a large scale, which demanded organized group effort but allowed the population to grow. By about 3800 B.C.E., one of the agricultural villages, Uruk (OO-rook), had expanded significantly, becoming what many historians view as the world's first city, with a population that eventually numbered more than fifty thousand. People living in Uruk built large temples to honor their chief god and goddess, and also invented the world's first system of writing. Over the next thousand years, other cities also grew in Sumer, trading with one another and adopting writing.

CHAPTER LOCATOR | What do we mean by "the West" and "Western civilization"?

MAP 1.1 ■ Spread of Cultures in the Ancient Near East, ca. 3000–1640 B.C.E.

This map illustrates the spread of the Mesopotamian and Egyptian cultures through the semicircular stretch of land often called the Fertile Crescent. From this area, the knowledge and use of agriculture spread throughout western Asia, North Africa, and Europe.

Environment and Mesopotamian Development

From the outset, geography had a profound effect on Mesopotamia because here agriculture is possible only with irrigation. Consequently, the Sumerians and later civilizations built their cities along the Tigris and Euphrates Rivers and their branches. They used the rivers to carry agricultural and trade goods, and also to provide water for vast networks of irrigation channels. In addition to water and transport, the rivers supplied fish, a major element of the Sumerian diet, and reeds, which were used for making baskets and writing implements. The rivers also provided clay, which was hardened to create bricks, the Sumerians' primary building material in a region with little stone. Clay was fired into pots, and inventive artisans developed the potter's wheel so that they could make pots that were stronger and more uniform than those made by earlier methods of coiling ropes of clay. The potter's wheel in turn appears to have led to the introduction of wheeled vehicles sometime in the fourth millennium B.C.E. Wheeled vehicles, pulled by domesticated donkeys, led to road building, which facilitated settlement, trade, and conquest, although travel and transport by water remained far easier.

Cities and villages in Sumer and farther up the Tigris and Euphrates traded with one another, and even before the development of writing or kings, it appears that colonists sometimes set out from one city to travel hundreds of miles to the north or west to found a new city or to set up a community in an existing center. These colonies might well have provided the Sumerian cities with goods, such as timber and metal ores, that were not available locally. The cities of the Sumerian

| How did early human societies develop and create new technologies and cultural forms? | **What kind of civilization did the Sumerians develop in Mesopotamia?** | How did the Akkadian and Old Babylonian empires develop in Mesopotamia? | How did the Egyptians create a prosperous and long-lasting society? | ✓ LearningCurve Check what you know. |

13

heartland continued to grow and to develop governments, and each one came to dominate the surrounding countryside, becoming city-states independent from one another, though not very far apart.

The city-states of Sumer continued to rely on irrigation systems that required cooperation and at least some level of social and political cohesion. The authority to run this system was, it seems, initially assumed by Sumerian priests. Encouraged and directed by their religious leaders, people built temples on tall platforms in the center of their cities. Temples grew into elaborate complexes of buildings with storage space for grain and other products and housing for animals. The Sumerians believed that humans had been created to serve the gods, who lived in the temples. To support the needs of the gods, including the temple constructions, and to support the religious leaders, temples owned large estates, including fields and orchards. Temple officials employed individuals to work the temple's land.

By 2500 B.C.E. there were more than a dozen city-states in Sumer. Each city developed religious, political, and military institutions, and judging by the fact that people began to construct walls around the cities and other fortifications, warfare between cities was quite common.

The Invention of Writing and the First Schools

The origins of writing probably go back to the ninth millennium B.C.E., when Near Eastern peoples used clay tokens as counters for record keeping. By the fourth millennium, people had realized that impressing the tokens on clay, or drawing pictures of the tokens on clay, was simpler than making tokens. This breakthrough in turn suggested that more information could be conveyed by adding pictures of still other objects. The result was a complex system of pictographs in which each sign pictured an object. These pictographs were the forerunners of the Sumerian form of writing known as **cuneiform** (kyou-NEE-uh-form) (**Figure 1.1**).

cuneiform

▶ Sumerian form of writing; the term describes the wedge-shaped marks made by a stylus.

Pictographs were initially limited in that they could not represent abstract ideas, but the development of ideograms—signs that represented ideas—made writing more versatile. Thus the sign for star could also be used to indicate

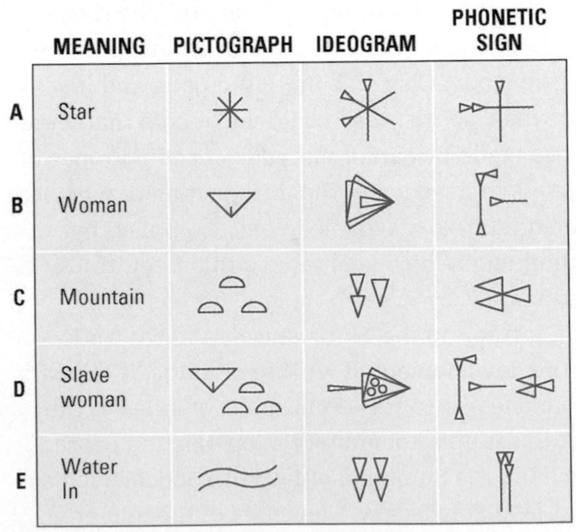

	MEANING	PICTOGRAPH	IDEOGRAM	PHONETIC SIGN
A	Star			
B	Woman			
C	Mountain			
D	Slave woman			
E	Water In			

FIGURE 1.1 ■ Sumerian Writing

(Source: S. N. Kramer, *The Sumerians: Their History, Culture and Character*. Copyright © 1963 by The University of Chicago Press. All rights reserved. Used by permission of the publisher.)

CHAPTER LOCATOR | What do we mean by "the West" and "Western civilization"?

heaven, sky, or even god. The real breakthrough came when scribes started using signs to represent sounds.

Over time, the Sumerian system of writing became so complicated that scribal schools were established; by 2500 B.C.E., these schools flourished throughout Sumer. Students at the schools were all male, and most came from families in the middle range of urban society. Scribal schools were primarily intended to produce individuals who could keep records of the property of temple officials, kings, and nobles. Thus writing first developed as a way to enhance the growing power of elites, not to record speech, although it later came to be used for that purpose.

Religion in Mesopotamia

To Sumerians, and to later peoples in Mesopotamia as well, the world was controlled by gods and goddesses, who represented cosmic forces such as the sun, moon, water, and storms. Each city generally had a chief god or goddess, or sometimes several, with a large temple built in his or her honor. The king of the gods was Enlil, who was believed to rule over the gods just as the king of a city-state ruled his population. Almost as powerful were the gods of the sun, of storms, and of freshwater.

People believed that humans had been created to serve the gods and generally anticipated being well treated by the gods if they served them well. The best way to honor the gods was to make the temple as grand and impressive as possible because the temple's size demonstrated the strength of the community and the power of its chief deity. Once it was built, the temple itself was often off-limits to ordinary people, who did not worship there as a spiritual community. Instead the temple was staffed by priests and priestesses who carried out rituals to honor the god or goddess. Kings and other political leaders might also visit the temple and carry out religious ceremonies from time to time, particularly when they thought the assistance of the gods was especially needed.

The peoples of Mesopotamia had many myths to account for the creation of the universe. According to one told by the Babylonians, in the beginning was the primeval sea, known as the goddess Tiamat, who gave birth to the gods. When Tiamat tried to destroy the gods, Marduk, the chief god of the Babylonians, proceeded to kill her and divide her body and thus created the sky and earth. These myths are the earliest known attempts to answer the question: How did it all begin?

In addition to stories about gods, the Sumerians also told stories about heroes and kings, many of which were eventually reworked into the world's first epic poem, the *Epic of Gilgamesh* (GIL-guh-mesh). It recounts the wanderings of Gilgamesh—the semihistorical king of Uruk—and his search for eternal life, and it grapples with enduring questions about life and death, friendship, humankind and deity, and immortality.

Sumerian Politics and Society

Exactly how kings emerged in Sumerian society is not clear. Scholars have suggested that during times of emergencies, a chief priest or perhaps a military leader assumed what was supposed to be temporary authority over a city.

How did early human societies develop and create new technologies and cultural forms?

What kind of civilization did the Sumerians develop in Mesopotamia?

How did the Akkadian and Old Babylonian empires develop in Mesopotamia?

How did the Egyptians create a prosperous and long-lasting society?

☑ LearningCurve
Check what you know.

15

Temporary power gradually became permanent kingship, and sometime before 2450 B.C.E. kings in some Sumerian city-states began transferring their kingship to their sons, establishing patriarchal hereditary dynasties in which power was handed down through the male line.

Kings made alliances with other powerful individuals, often through marriage. Royal family members were depended upon for many aspects of government. Kings worked closely with religious authorities and relied on ideas about the kings' connections with the gods, as well as the kings' military might, for their power. Acting together, priests, kings, and officials in Sumerian cities used force, persuasion, and taxation to maintain order, keep the irrigation systems working, and keep food and other goods flowing.

The king and his officials held extensive tracts of land, as did the temple; these lands were worked by the palace's or the temple's clients, free men and women who were dependent on the palace or the temple. They received crops and other goods in return for their labor. Some individuals and families owned land outright and paid their taxes in the form of agricultural products or items they made. At the bottom rung of society were slaves. Some Sumerian slaves were most likely prisoners of war and criminals who had lost their freedom as punishment for their crimes; others perhaps came into slavery to repay debts. Compared to many later societies, slaves were not widely used in Sumer, where most agricultural work was done by dependent clients. Slaves in Sumer also engaged in trade and made profits. They could borrow money, and many slaves were able to buy their freedom.

Sumerian society made distinctions based on gender. Most elite landowners were male, but women who held positions as priestesses or as queens ran their own estates, independently of their husbands and fathers. Some women owned businesses and took care of their own accounts. They could own property and distribute it to their offspring. Sons and daughters inherited from their parents, although a daughter received her inheritance in the form of a dowry, which technically remained hers but was managed by her husband or husband's family after marriage. The Sumerians established the basic social, economic, and intellectual patterns of Mesopotamia, and they influenced their neighbors to the north and east.

> **QUICK REVIEW**

What role did environmental factors play in shaping the development of Mesopotamian societies?

CHAPTER LOCATOR | What do we mean by "the West" and "Western civilization"?

How did the Akkadian and Old Babylonian empires develop in Mesopotamia?

THE WEALTH OF SUMERIAN CITIES also attracted non-Sumerian conquerors from the north, beginning with the Akkadians and then the Babylonians. Both of these peoples created large states in the valley of the Tigris and Euphrates, and Hammurabi, one ruler of Babylon, proclaimed an extensive law code. Merchants traveled throughout the Fertile Crescent and beyond, carrying products and facilitating cultural exchange.

The Akkadians and the Babylonians

In 2331 B.C.E., Sargon, the king of a city to the north of Sumer, conquered a number of Sumerian cities with what was probably the world's first permanent army and created a large state. The symbol of his triumph was a new capital, the city of Akkad (AH-kahd). Sargon also expanded the Akkadian empire westward to North Syria. He encouraged trading networks that brought in goods from as far away as the Indus River and what is now Turkey.

Sargon tore down the defensive walls of Sumerian cities and appointed his own sons as their rulers to help him cement his power. He also appointed his daughter, Enheduana (2285–2250 B.C.E.), as high priestess in the city of Ur. Here she wrote a number of hymns, especially those in praise of the goddess Inanna, becoming the world's first author to put her name to a literary composition.

Sargon's dynasty appears to have ruled Mesopotamia for about 150 years, during which time the Tigris and Euphrates Valleys attracted immigrants from

| How did early human societies develop and create new technologies and cultural forms? | What kind of civilization did the Sumerians develop in Mesopotamia? | **How did the Akkadian and Old Babylonian empires develop in Mesopotamia?** | How did the Egyptians create a prosperous and long-lasting society? | ☑ LearningCurve Check what you know. |

many places. Then his empire collapsed, in part because of a period of extended drought, and the various city-states became independent again.

One significant city-state that arose in the wake of the Akkadian empire was settled by the Amorites (AM-uh-rites), who migrated from the west. The Amorites were initially nomadic pastoralists, not agriculturalists, but they began to raise crops when they settled throughout Mesopotamia. One group of Amorites made their home in the city of Babylon along the middle Euphrates, where that river runs close to the Tigris. Like other Amorite kingdoms of the time, Babylon was more than a city-state. It included smaller kingdoms whose rulers recognized the king of Babylon as their overlord.

Life Under Hammurabi

Hammurabi of Babylon (r. 1792–1750 B.C.E.) was an extraordinarily successful military leader. Under his command, Hammurabi's forces moved from victory to victory, uniting most of Mesopotamia under his rule. The era from his reign to around 1595 B.C.E. is called the Old Babylonian period.

Hammurabi's most memorable accomplishment was the proclamation of an extensive law code, introduced about 1755 B.C.E. Like the codes of the earlier law-givers, **Hammurabi's law code** proclaimed that he issued his laws on divine authority "to establish law and justice in the language of the land, thereby promoting the welfare of the people." Hammurabi's code set a variety of punishments for breaking the law, including fines and physical punishment such as mutilation, whipping, and burning.

Hammurabi's code provides a wealth of information about daily life in Mesopotamia. Because of farming's fundamental importance, the code dealt extensively with agriculture. Tenants faced severe penalties for neglecting the land or not working it at all. Because irrigation was essential to grow crops, tenants had to keep the canals and ditches in good repair. Anyone whose neglect of the canals resulted in damaged crops had to bear all the expense of the lost crops. Those tenants who could not pay the costs were forced into slavery.

> ### > Hammurabi's Code

- Gave considerable attention to agriculture, marriage, and the family
- Established laws designed to protect consumers
- Demanded that the punishment fit the crime
- Individuals brought their own complaints to courts without prosecutors or district attorneys

Hammurabi gave careful attention to marriage and the family. As elsewhere in the Near East, marriage had aspects of a business agreement. The groom or his father offered the prospective bride's father a gift, and if this was acceptable, the bride's father provided his daughter with a dowry. As in Sumer, after marriage the dowry belonged to the woman and was a means of protecting her rights and status. No marriage was considered legal without a contract, and although either party could break off the marriage, the cost was a stiff penalty.

The penalty for adultery, defined as sex between a married woman and a man not her husband, was death. A husband had the power to spare his wife by

Hammurabi's law code

▶ A proclamation issued by Babylonian king Hammurabi to establish laws regulating many aspects of life.

CHAPTER LOCATOR | What do we mean by "the West" and "Western civilization"?

18 CHAPTER 1 ORIGINS

obtaining a pardon for her from the king. He could, however, accuse his wife of adultery even if he had not caught her in the act. In such a case she could try to clear herself, and if she was found innocent, she could take her dowry and leave her husband.

A father could not disinherit a son without just cause, and the code ordered the courts to forgive a son for his first offense. Men could adopt children into their families and include them in their wills, which artisans sometimes did to teach them the family trade, or wealthy landowners sometimes did to pass along land to able younger men, particularly if they had no children of their own.

The Code of Hammurabi demanded that the punishment fit the crime, calling for "an eye for an eye, and a tooth for a tooth," at least among equals. However, a higher-ranking man who physically hurt a commoner or slave, perhaps by breaking his arm or putting out his eye, could pay a fine to the victim instead of having his arm broken or losing his own eye. As long as criminal and victim shared the same social status, however, the victim could demand exact vengeance.

Hammurabi's code began with legal procedure. There were no public prosecutors or district attorneys, so individuals brought their own complaints before the court. Each side had to produce witnesses to support its case. In cases of murder, the accuser had to prove the defendant guilty; any accuser who failed to do so was to be put to death. Another procedural regulation declared that once a judge had rendered a verdict, he could not change it.

Consumer protection is not a modern idea; it goes back to Hammurabi's day. A boat builder who did sloppy work had to repair the boat at his own expense. House builders guaranteed their work with their lives. If inhabitants died when a house collapsed, the builder was put to death. A merchant who tried to increase the interest rate on a loan forfeited the entire amount.

Cultural Exchange in the Fertile Crescent

The Mesopotamians enjoyed a vibrant and creative culture that left its mark on the entire Fertile Crescent. Mesopotamian writing, mathematics, merchandise, and other aspects of the culture spread far beyond the Tigris and Euphrates Valleys. Overland trade connected Sumer, Akkad, and Babylon with the eastern Mediterranean coast. Cities here were mercantile centers rich not only in manufactured goods but also in agricultural produce, textiles, and metals. The cities flourished under local rulers. People in Syria and elsewhere in the Middle East used Akkadian cuneiform to communicate in writing with their more distant neighbors. Cultural exchange remained a mixture of adoption and adaptation.

Southern and central Anatolia presented a similar picture of extensive contact between cultures. Major Anatolian cities with large local populations were also home to colonies of traders from Mesopotamia. Thousands of cuneiform tablets testify to centuries of commercial and cultural exchanges with Mesopotamia, and eventually with Egypt, which rose to power in the Nile Valley.

QUICK REVIEW <

How did the advent of empires in Mesopotamia facilitate the dissemination and exchange of goods and ideas?

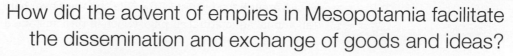

| How did early human societies develop and create new technologies and cultural forms? | What kind of civilization did the Sumerians develop in Mesopotamia? | **How did the Akkadian and Old Babylonian empires develop in Mesopotamia?** | How did the Egyptians create a prosperous and long-lasting society? | ✓ LearningCurve Check what you know. |

> How did the Egyptians create a prosperous and long-lasting society?

King Menkaure and Queen

In this sandstone sculpture made around 2500 B.C.E., the king and his wife look serenely toward the horizon. Stability and permanence were qualities prized by Egyptians in the Old Kingdom, and the sculptor captures them here. The figures are almost equal in size, suggesting the important role that queens sometimes played. (King Menkaura (Mycerinus) and queen. Egyptian, Old Kingdom, Dynasty 4, reign of Menkaura, 2490–2472 B.C. Findspot: Egypt, Giza, Menkaura Valley Tample. Greywacke. Overall: 142.2 x 57.1 x 55.2 cm, 676.8 kg (56 x 22½ x 21¾ in., 1492.1 lb.). Block (Wooden skirts and two top): 53.3 x 180 x 179.7 cm (21 x 70⅞ x 70¾ in.). Museum of Fine Arts, Boston. Harvard University-Boston Museum of Fine Arts Expedition. 11.1738. Photograph © 2013 Museum of Fine Arts, Boston.)

AT ABOUT THE SAME TIME that Sumerian city-states expanded and fought with one another in the Tigris and Euphrates Valleys, a more cohesive state under a single ruler grew in the valley of the Nile River in North Africa. This was Egypt, which for long stretches of history was prosperous and secure behind desert areas on both sides of the Nile Valley.

The Nile and the God-King

No other single geographical factor had such a fundamental and profound impact on the shaping of Egyptian life, society, and history as the Nile River. The Nile flooded once a year for a period of several months, bringing fertile soil and moisture for farming, and agricultural villages developed along its banks by at least 6000 B.C.E.

Through the fertility of the Nile and their own hard work, Egyptians produced an annual agricultural surplus, which in turn sustained a growing and prosperous

CHAPTER LOCATOR | What do we mean by "the West" and "Western civilization"?

population. The Nile also unified Egypt. The river was the region's principal highway, promoting communication and trade throughout the valley.

Egypt was fortunate in that it was nearly self-sufficient. Besides having fertile soil, Egypt possessed enormous quantities of stone, which served as the raw material of architecture and sculpture, and abundant clay for pottery. The raw materials that Egypt lacked were close at hand. The Egyptians could obtain copper from Sinai (SIGH-nigh) and timber from Lebanon, and they traded with peoples farther away to obtain other materials that they needed.

The political power structures that developed in Egypt came to be linked with the Nile. Somehow the idea developed that a single individual, a king, was responsible for the rise and fall of the Nile. The king came to be viewed as a descendant of the gods, and thus as a god himself.

Political unification most likely proceeded slowly, but stories told about early kings highlighted one who had united Upper Egypt—the upstream valley in the south—and Lower Egypt—the delta area of the Nile that empties into the Mediterranean Sea—into a single kingdom around 3100 B.C.E. Modern historians divide Egyptian history into periods (see "Periods of Egyptian History," page 21). The political unification of Egypt in the Archaic Period (3100–2660 B.C.E.) ushered in the period known as the Old Kingdom (2660–2180 B.C.E.), an era remarkable for prosperity and artistic flowering.

The focal point of religious and political life in the Old Kingdom was the king, who commanded wealth, resources, and people. The king's surroundings had to be worthy of a god, and only a magnificent palace was suitable for his home; in fact, the word **pharaoh**, which during the New Kingdom came to be used for the king, originally meant "great house." Just as the kings occupied a great house in life, so they reposed in great pyramids after death. Built during the Old Kingdom, these massive stone tombs contained all the things needed by the king in his afterlife. The pyramid also symbolized the king's power and his connection with the sun-god.

To ancient Egyptians, the king embodied the concept of **ma'at**, a cosmic harmony that embraced truth, justice, and moral integrity. Ma'at gave the king the right, authority, and duty to govern. To the people, the king personified justice and order—harmony among themselves, nature, and the divine.

Kings did not always live up to this ideal, of course. The two parts of Egypt were difficult to hold together, and several times in Egypt's long history, there were periods of disunity, civil war, and chaos. During the First Intermediate Period (2180–2080 B.C.E.), rulers of various provinces asserted their independence from the king, and Upper and Lower Egypt were ruled by rival dynasties. Warrior-kings reunited Egypt in the Middle Kingdom (2080–1640 B.C.E.) and expanded Egyptian power southward into Nubia.

PERIODS OF EGYPTIAN HISTORY

Dates	Period	Significant Events
3100–2660 B.C.E.	Archaic	Unification of Egypt
2660–2180 B.C.E.	Old Kingdom	Construction of the pyramids
2180–2080 B.C.E.	First Intermediate	Political disunity
2080–1640 B.C.E.	Middle Kingdom	Recovery and political stability
1640–1570 B.C.E.	Second Intermediate	Hyksos migrations; struggles for power
1570–1070 B.C.E.	New Kingdom	Creation of an Egyptian empire; growth in wealth
1070–712 B.C.E.	Third Intermediate	Political fragmentation and conquest by outsiders (see Chapter 2)

pharaoh
► The title given to the king of Egypt in the New Kingdom, from a word that meant "great house."

ma'at
► The Egyptian belief in a cosmic harmony that embraced truth, justice, and moral integrity; it gave the kings the right and duty to govern.

How did early human societies develop and create new technologies and cultural forms?

What kind of civilization did the Sumerians develop in Mesopotamia?

How did the Akkadian and Old Babylonian empires develop in Mesopotamia?

How did the Egyptians create a prosperous and long-lasting society?

✓ LearningCurve
Check what you know.

21

Egyptian Religion

Like the Mesopotamians, the Egyptians were polytheistic, worshipping many gods of all types, some mightier than others. They developed complex ideas of their gods that reflected the world around them, and these views changed over the many centuries of Egyptian history as gods took on new attributes and often merged with one another. During the Old Kingdom, Egyptians considered the sun-god Ra the creator of life. He commanded the sky, earth, and underworld.

Much later, during the New Kingdom (see page 21), the pharaohs of a new dynasty favored the worship of a different sun-god, Amon, whom they described as creating the entire cosmos by his thoughts. Amon brought life to the land and its people, they wrote, and he sustained both. Because he had helped them overthrow their enemies, Egyptians came to consider Amon the champion of fairness and justice, especially for the common people. As his cult grew, Amon came to be identified with Ra, and eventually the Egyptians combined them into one sun-god, Amon-Ra.

The Egyptians likewise developed views of an afterlife that reflected the world around them and that changed over time. During the later part of the Old Kingdom, the walls of kings' tombs were carved with religious texts that provided spells; these spells would bring the king back to life and help him ascend to Heaven, where he would join his divine father, Ra. Toward the end of the Old Kingdom, the tombs of powerful nobles also contained such inscriptions, an indication that more people expected to gain everlasting life. In the Middle Kingdom, new types of spells appeared on the coffins of even more people, a further expansion in admission to the afterlife.

During the New Kingdom, a time when Egypt came into greater contact with the cultures of the Fertile Crescent, Egyptians developed more complex ideas about the afterlife, recording these in funerary manuscripts that have come to be known as the *Book of the Dead*, written to help guide the dead through the difficulties of the underworld. These texts explained that the soul left the body to become part of the divine after death and told of the god Osiris (oh-SIGH-ruhs) who weighed dead humans' hearts to determine whether they had lived justly enough to deserve everlasting life. Egyptians also believed that proper funeral rituals, in which the physical body was mummified, were essential for life after death, so Osiris was assisted by Anubis, the jackal-headed god of mummification.

Book of the Dead

▶ Egyptian funerary manuscripts, written to help guide the dead through the difficulties they would encounter on the way to the afterlife.

Egyptian Society and Work

Egyptian society reflected the pyramids that it built. At the top stood the king, who relied on a sizable circle of nobles, officials, and priests to administer his kingdom. All of them were assisted by scribes, who used a writing system perhaps adapted from Mesopotamia and perhaps developed independently. Egyptian scribes actually created two writing systems: one called hieroglyphic, which was used for important religious or political texts and inscriptions, and a much simpler system called hieratic, which allowed scribes to write more quickly. Hieratic writing was used for the documents of daily life, such as letters, contracts, and accounts, and also for medical and literary works. In addition to scribes, the cities of the Nile Valley were home to artisans of all types, along with merchants and

CHAPTER LOCATOR | What do we mean by "the West" and "Western civilization"?

other tradespeople. A large group of farmers made up the broad base of the social pyramid.

For Egyptians, the Nile formed an essential part of daily life. During the season of its flooding, from June to October, farmers worked on the pharaoh's building programs and other tasks away from their fields. When the water began to recede, they diverted some of it into ponds for future irrigation and began planting wheat and barley for bread and beer, using plows pulled by oxen or people to part the soft mud. From October to February farmers planted and tended crops, and then from February until the next flood they harvested them.

As in Mesopotamia, common people paid their obligations to their superiors in products and in labor, and many faced penalties if they did not meet their quota. Peoples' labor obligations in the Old Kingdom may have included forced work on the pyramids and canals, although recent research suggests that most people who built the pyramids were paid for their work. Some young men were drafted into the pharaoh's army, which served as both a fighting force and a labor corps.

Egyptian Family Life

The lives of all Egyptians centered around the family. Marriage was a business arrangement, just as in Mesopotamia, arranged by the couples' parents, and seems to have taken place at a young age. Once couples were married, having children, especially sons, was a high priority, as indicated by surviving charms to promote fertility and prayers for successful childbirth. Boys continued the family line, and only they could perform the proper burial rites for their father.

Wealthy Egyptians lived in spacious homes with attractive gardens and walls for privacy. (See "Picturing the Past: Egyptian Home Life," page 24.) Poorer people lived in cramped quarters. Excavations at a city now called Tell el Amarna show that residents' houses were about 16½ feet wide by 33 feet long. The family had narrow rooms for living, including two small rooms for sleeping and cooking. These small houses suggest that most Egyptians lived in small family groups, not as large extended families. The very poor lived in hovels with their animals.

Life in Egypt began at dawn with a bath and clean clothes. The Egyptians bathed several times a day because of the heat and used soda ash for soap. Rich and poor alike used perfumes as deodorants. Egyptians generally wore linen clothes, made from fibers of the flax plant. Because of the heat, men often wore only a kilt and women a sheath.

Marriage was apparently not celebrated by any ritual or religious act; it seems to have been purely a legal contract in which a woman brought one-third of her family's property to the marriage. The property continued to belong to her, though her husband managed it. She could obtain a divorce simply because she wanted it. If she did, she took her marriage portion with her and could also claim a share of the profits made during her marriage. Most Egyptian men had only one wife, but among the wealthy, some had several wives or concubines. A husband could order his wife to her quarters and even beat her, but if a man treated his wife too violently, she could take him to court. If she won, her husband received one hundred lashes from a whip and surrendered his portion of their joint property to her. A man could dispense with his wife for any reason, just as she could leave him.

| How did early human societies develop and create new technologies and cultural forms? | What kind of civilization did the Sumerians develop in Mesopotamia? | How did the Akkadian and Old Babylonian empires develop in Mesopotamia? | **How did the Egyptians create a prosperous and long-lasting society?** | ✓ LearningCurve Check what you know. |

23

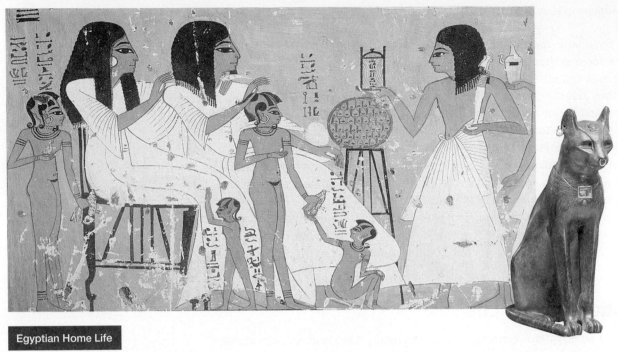

This grave painting depicts an intimate moment in the life of an aristocratic family, with the father and mother in the center and their children around them. Often found in Egyptian tombs are statuettes of cats (inset), family pets, and the symbol of the goddess Bastet.
(family: Gianni Dagli Orti/The Art Archive; cat: Courtesy of the Trustees of the British Museum)

> PICTURING THE PAST

ANALYZING THE IMAGE: What evidence do you find in the painting that Egyptian artists based the size of figures on people's status in the household?
CONNECTIONS: Based on your reading, how might an image of a poor family differ from this depiction?

Ordinary women were expected to obey their fathers, husbands, and other men, but they possessed considerable economic and legal rights. They could own land in their own names and operate businesses. They could testify in court and bring legal action against men. Information from literature and art depicts a world in which ordinary husbands and wives enjoyed each other's company alone, and together with family and friends.

The Hyksos and New Kingdom Revival

While Egyptian civilization flourished in the Nile Valley, various groups migrated throughout the Fertile Crescent and then accommodated themselves to local cultures (**Map 1.2**). Some settled in the Nile Delta, including a group the Egyptians called Hyksos, which means "rulers of the uplands." Although they were later portrayed as a conquering horde, the Hyksos were actually migrants looking for good land, and their entry into the delta, which began around 1800 B.C.E., was probably gradual and generally peaceful.

CHAPTER LOCATOR | What do we mean by "the West" and "Western civilization"?

24 CHAPTER 1 ORIGINS

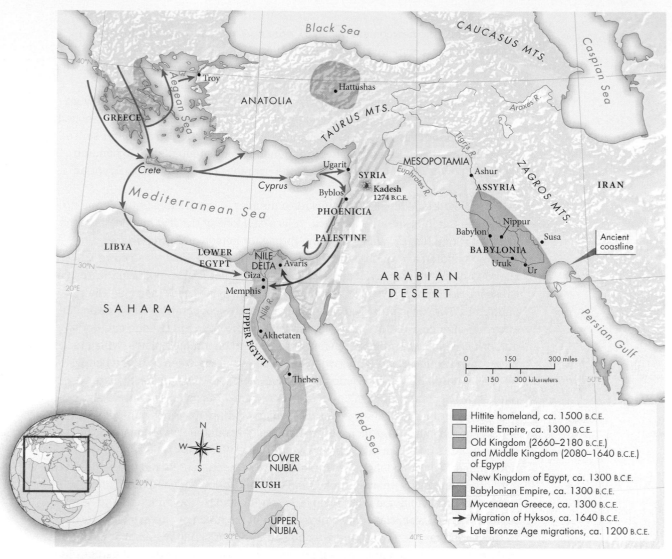

MAP 1.2 ■ Empires and Migrations in the Eastern Mediterranean

The rise and fall of empires in the eastern Mediterranean were shaped by internal developments, military conflicts, and the migration of peoples to new areas.

> MAPPING THE PAST

ANALYZING THE MAP: At what point was the Egyptian empire at its largest? The Hittite empire? What were the other major powers in the eastern Mediterranean at this point?
CONNECTIONS: What were the major effects of the migrations of the Hyksos? Of the late Bronze Age migrations? What clues does the map provide about why the late Bronze Age migrations had a more powerful impact than those of the Hyksos?

The Hyksos brought with them the methods of making bronze and casting it into tools and weapons that became standard in Egypt. The Hyksos also brought inventions that revolutionized Egyptian warfare, including bronze armor and weapons as well as horse-drawn chariots and the composite bow, made of laminated wood and horn, which was far more powerful than the simple wooden bow.

The migration of the Hyksos, combined with a series of famines and internal struggles for power, led Egypt to fragment politically in what later came to be known as the Second Intermediate Period (1640–1570 B.C.E.). During this time, the Egyptians adopted bronze technology and new forms of weaponry from the

| How did early human societies develop and create new technologies and cultural forms? | What kind of civilization did the Sumerians develop in Mesopotamia? | How did the Akkadian and Old Babylonian empires develop in Mesopotamia? | **How did the Egyptians create a prosperous and long-lasting society?** | ☑ LearningCurve Check what you know. |

25

Hyksos, while the newcomers began to worship Egyptian deities and modeled their political structure on that of the Egyptians.

In about 1570 B.C.E., a new dynasty of pharaohs arose, pushing the Hyksos out of the delta, subduing Nubia in the south, and conquering parts of Canaan in the northeast. In this way, these Egyptian warrior-pharaohs inaugurated what scholars refer to as the New Kingdom—a period in Egyptian history characterized by not only enormous wealth and conscious imperialism but also a greater sense of insecurity because of new contacts and military engagements. By expanding Egyptian power beyond the Nile Valley, the pharaohs created the first Egyptian empire.

The New Kingdom pharaohs include a number of remarkable figures. Among these was Hatshepsut (r. ca. 1479–ca. 1458 B.C.E.), one of the few female pharaohs in Egypt's long history, who seized the throne for herself and used her reign to promote building and trade. Amenhotep III (r. ca. 1388–ca.1350 B.C.E.) corresponded with other powerful kings in Babylonia and other kingdoms in the Fertile Crescent, sending envoys, exchanging gifts, and in some cases marrying their daughters. The kings promised friendship and active cooperation. They made alliances for offensive and defensive protection and swore to uphold one another's authority. Hence, the greatest powers of the period maintained peace, which facilitated the movement of gifts between kings and trade between ordinary people.

Amenhotep III was succeeded by his son, who took the name Akhenaten (ah-keh-NAH-tuhn) (r. 1351–1334 B.C.E.). He renamed himself as a mark of his changing religious ideas. Egyptians had long worshipped various sun-gods and aspects of the sun—Ra, Amon, Amon-Ra—but Akhenaten favored instead the worship of the god Aten (also spelled Aton), the visible disk of the sun. He was not a monotheist (someone who worships only one god), but he did order the erasure of the names of other sun-gods from the walls of buildings, the transfer of taxes from the traditional priesthood of Amon-Ra, and the building of huge new temples to Aten, especially at his new capital in the area now known as Amarna. In these temples Aten was to be worshipped in bright sunlight. Akhenaten also had artists portray him in more realistic ways than they had portrayed earlier pharaohs; he is depicted interacting with his children and especially with his wife Nefertiti (nehf-uhr-TEE-tee), who supported his new religious ideas. (See "Individuals in Society: Hatshepsut and Nefertiti," page 27.)

Akhenaten's new religion, imposed from above, failed to find a place among the people, however. After his death, traditional religious practices returned and the capital was moved back to Thebes. The priests of Amon-Ra led this restoration, but it was also supported by Akhenaten's son. This son was Tutankhamon (r. 1333–1323 B.C.E.), whose short reign was not particularly noteworthy and whose name would probably not be remembered except for the fact that his was the only tomb of an Egyptian king to be discovered nearly intact.

Tutankhamon's short reign was also marked by international problems, including warfare on several of the borders of the Egyptian empire. His grandfather and father had engaged in extensive diplomatic relations with rulers of states dependent on Egypt and with other powerful kings, but Tutankhamon was less successful at these diplomatic tasks. He also died childless. His successors were court officials, and in 1298 B.C.E. one of them established a new dynasty whose members would reassert Egypt's imperial power and respond to new challenges.

INDIVIDUALS IN SOCIETY
Hatshepsut and Nefertiti

Egyptians understood the pharaoh to be an avatar of the god Horus, the source of law and morality, and the mediator between gods and humans. The pharaoh's connection with the divine stretched to members of his family, so that his siblings and children were also viewed as divine in some ways. Because of this, a pharaoh often took his sister or half-sister as one of his wives. This concentrated divine blood set the pharaonic family apart from other Egyptians (who did not generally marry close relatives) and allowed the pharaohs to imitate the gods, who in Egyptian mythology often married their siblings. A pharaoh chose one of his wives, often a relative, to be the "Great Royal Wife," or principal queen.

The familial connection with the divine allowed a handful of women to rule in their own right in Egypt's long history. We know the names of four female pharaohs, of whom the most famous was Hatshepsut (r. 1479–1458 B.C.E.), the sister and wife of Thutmose II. After he died, she served as regent — adviser and co-ruler — for her young stepson Thutmose III. Hatshepsut sent trading expeditions and sponsored artists and architects, ushering in a period of artistic creativity and economic prosperity. She oversaw the building of one of the world's great buildings, an elaborate terraced temple at Deir el Bahri, which eventually served as her mortuary temple. Hatshepsut's status as a powerful female ruler was difficult for Egyptians to conceptualize, and she is often depicted in male dress or with a false beard, thus looking more like the male rulers who were the norm. After her death, Thutmose III tried to destroy all evidence that she had ever ruled, smashing statues and scratching her name off inscriptions, perhaps because of personal animosity and perhaps because he wanted to erase the fact that a woman had once been pharaoh. Only within recent decades have historians and archaeologists begun to (literally) piece together her story.

Though female pharaohs were very rare, many royal women had power through their position as "Great Royal Wives." The most famous was Nefertiti, the wife of Akhenaten. Her name means "the perfect (or beautiful) woman has come," and inscriptions also give her many other titles. Nefertiti used her position to spread the new religion of the sun-god Aten.

Together Nefertiti and Akhenaten built a new palace and capital city at Akhetaten, the present Amarna, away from the old centers of power. There they developed the cult of Aten to the exclusion of the traditional deities. Nearly the only literary survival of their religious belief is the "Hymn to Aten," which declares Aten to be the only god. It describes Nefertiti as "the great royal consort whom he, Akhenaten loves. The mistress of the Two Lands, Upper and Lower Egypt."

Nefertiti is often shown as being the same size as her husband, and in some inscriptions she is performing religious rituals that would normally have been carried out only by the pharaoh. The exact details of her power are hard to

Granite head of Hatshepsut. (Berlin/ Aegyptisches Museum, Staatliche Museen/ Margarete Buesing/Art Resource, NY)

Painted limestone bust of Nefertiti. (© Lebrecht Music and Arts Photo Library/Alamy)

determine, however. An older theory held that her husband removed her from power, though there is also speculation that after his death she may have ruled secretly in her own right under a different name. Her tomb has long since disappeared. In the last decade, individual archaeologists have claimed that several different mummies were Nefertiti, but most scholars dismiss these claims. Because her parentage is unknown, DNA testing such as that done on Tutankhamon's corpse would not reveal whether any specific mummy was Nefertiti.

QUESTIONS FOR ANALYSIS

1. Why might it have been difficult for Egyptians to accept a female ruler?
2. What opportunities do hereditary monarchies such as that of ancient Egypt provide for women? How does this fit with gender hierarchies in which men are understood as superior?

LaunchPad

ONLINE DOCUMENT PROJECT

Considering Egyptian views of gender roles, what complexities did Egyptian writers and artists face in depicting Hatshepsut? Keeping the question above in mind, analyze a range of written and visual representations of Hatshepsut, and then compose a short essay on your findings. *See inside the front cover to learn more.*

Conflict and Cooperation with the Hittites

One of the key challenges facing the pharaohs after Tutankhamon was the expansion of the kingdom of the Hittites. At about the same time that the Sumerians were establishing city-states, speakers of Indo-European languages migrated into Anatolia. Indo-European is a large family of languages that includes English, most of the languages of modern Europe, Persian, and Sanskrit. It also includes Hittite, the language of a people who seem to have migrated into this area about 2300 B.C.E.

Surviving records indicate that in the sixteenth century B.C.E. the Hittite king Hattusili I led his forces against neighboring kingdoms. Hattusili's grandson and successor, Mursili I, extended the Hittite conquests as far as Babylon. On his return home, the victorious Mursili was assassinated by members of his own family, which led to dynastic warfare. This pattern of expansion followed by internal conflict was repeated frequently, but when they were united behind a strong king, the Hittites were extremely powerful.

As the Hittites expanded southward, they came into conflict with the Egyptians, who were re-establishing their empire. The pharaoh Ramesses II engaged in numerous campaigns to retake Egyptian territory in Syria. He assembled a large well-equipped army with thousands of chariots and expected to defeat the Hittites easily, but he and his army were ambushed by them at the Battle of Kadesh in 1274 B.C.E. Returning to Egypt, Ramesses declared that he had won and had monuments carved commemorating his victory. In reality, neither side gained much by the battle, though both sides seem to have recognized the impossibility of defeating the other.

In 1258, Ramesses II and the Hittite king Hattusili III concluded a peace treaty, which was recorded in both Egyptian hieroglyphics and Hittite cuneiform. Returning to the language of cooperation established in earlier royal diplomacy, each side promised not to invade the other and to come to the other's aid if attacked. Each promised peace and brotherhood, and the treaty ended with a long oath to the gods, who would curse the one who broke the treaty and bless the one who kept it.

> **QUICK REVIEW**

How did the Nile River shape all aspects of Egyptian life?

CHAPTER LOCATOR | What do we mean by "the West" and "Western civilization"?

28 CHAPTER 1 ORIGINS

LOOKING BACK
LOOKING AHEAD

The political and military story of waves of migrations, battles, and the rise and fall of empires can mask striking continuities across the Neolithic and Bronze Ages. The social patterns set in early agricultural societies—with most of the population farming the land, and a small number of elite who lived off their labor—lasted for millennia. Disrupted peoples and newcomers shared practical concepts of agriculture and metallurgy with one another, and wheeled vehicles allowed merchants to transact business over long distances. Merchants, migrants, and conquerors carried their gods and goddesses with them, and religious beliefs and practices blended and changed. Cuneiform tablets, wall inscriptions, and paintings testify to commercial exchanges and cultural accommodation, adoption, and adaptation.

The treaty of Ramesses II and Hattusili III brought peace between the Egyptians and the Hittites for a time, which was further enhanced by Ramesses II's marriage to a Hittite princess. This stability was not to last, however. Within several decades of the treaty, new peoples were moving into the eastern Mediterranean, disrupting trade and in some cases looting and destroying cities. There is evidence of drought, and some scholars have suggested a major volcanic explosion in Iceland cooled the climate for several years, leading to a series of poor harvests. Both the Egyptian and Hittite Empires shrank dramatically. All of these developments are part of a general "Bronze Age Collapse" that historians see as a major turning point.

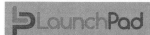

ONLINE DOCUMENT PROJECT

Hatshepsut

Considering Egyptian views of gender roles, what complexities did Egyptian writers and artists face in depicting Hatshepsut?

You encountered Hatshepsut on page 27. Keeping the question above in mind, analyze a range of written and visual representations of Hatshepsut. *See inside the front cover to learn more.*

| How did early human societies develop and create new technologies and cultural forms? | What kind of civilization did the Sumerians develop in Mesopotamia? | How did the Akkadian and Old Babylonian empires develop in Mesopotamia? | How did the Egyptians create a prosperous and long-lasting society? | ✓ LearningCurve Check what you know. |

CHAPTER 1 STUDY GUIDE

STEP 1

GET STARTED ONLINE

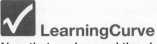 **LearningCurve**

Now that you've read the chapter, make it stick by completing the LearningCurve activity.

STEP 2

EXPLAIN WHY IT MATTERS

Put your reading into practice. Identify each term below, and then explain why it matters in Western history.

TERM	WHO OR WHAT & WHEN	WHY IT MATTERS
civilization (p. 6)		
Paleolithic era (p. 7)		
Neolithic era (p. 7)		
Fertile Crescent (p. 8)		
pastoralism (p. 10)		
patriarchy (p. 11)		
Bronze Age (p. 11)		
polytheism (p. 11)		
cuneiform (p. 14)		
Hammurabi's law code (p. 18)		
pharaoh (p. 21)		
ma'at (p. 21)		
Book of the Dead (p. 22)		

STEP 3

MOVE BEYOND THE BASICS

To demonstrate a more advanced understanding, compare and contrast key aspects of foraging and agricultural societies. How would you explain the similarities and differences you note?

	Foraging Society	Agricultural society
Social organization and labor specialization		
Gender divisions		
Religion and culture		

PUT IT ALL TOGETHER

Now, take a step back and try to explain the big picture. Remember to use specific examples from the chapter in your answers.

EARLY HUMAN HISTORY

▶ What were the advantages of settled agriculture over a foraging lifestyle? What were the disadvantages?

▶ What connections can you make between the development of social hierarchies and the advent of settled agriculture?

MESOPOTAMIA

▶ How did the Mesopotamians imagine their gods? How did they imagine their relationship to them?

▶ What does Hammurabi's Code tell us about the values and priorities of its authors?

EGYPT

▶ What role did the king or pharaoh play in Egyptian life?

▶ In what ways did the New Kingdom differ from the Old Kingdom?

MAKE CONNECTIONS

▶ What basic elements of Mesopotamian and Egyptian society can be traced back to the Neolithic period?

▶ What might explain the powerful influence of Mesopotamian and Egyptian culture on the societies that succeeded them in northern Africa and the eastern Mediterranean?

> IN YOUR OWN WORDS

Imagine that you must give an oral report to the class answering the following question: **What similarities and differences were evident in the nature and development of the Mesopotamian and Egyptian civilizations? What would be the most important points and why?**

2

SMALL KINGDOMS AND MIGHTY EMPIRES IN THE NEAR EAST

1200–510 B.C.E.

> **How did the Assyrians and the Persians win mighty empires, and how did they rule them once they had been won?** Chapter 2 examines the new political order that emerged in the wake of the so-called "Bronze Age Collapse" of the late thirteenth century B.C.E. In the absence of powerful empires, the Phoenicians, Kushites, Hebrews, and many other peoples carved out small independent kingdoms. In the tenth century B.C.E., this jumble of small states gave way to an empire that for the first time embraced the entire Near East: the empire of the Assyrians, which lasted for about three hundred years and then broke apart with the rise of a new empire centered in Babylon. Beginning in 550 B.C.E. the Persians conquered the Medes — nomadic peoples who had settled in Iran — and then the Babylonians and Assyrians, creating the largest empire yet seen, stretching from Anatolia in the west to the Indus Valley in the east.

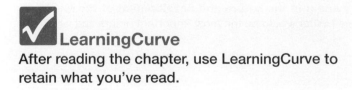

LearningCurve

After reading the chapter, use LearningCurve to retain what you've read.

> How did iron technology shape new states after 1200 B.C.E?

> How did the Hebrews create an enduring religious tradition?

> What explains the rise and fall of the Assyrians?

> How did the Persians consolidate their extensive empire?

Life in an Empire. In this colorful decorative frieze made of glazed brick, men wearing long Persian robes and laced ankle boots carry spears, bows, and quivers. (Erich Lessing/Art Resource, NY)

How did iron technology shape new states after 1200 B.C.E.?

This silver Phoenician coin shows an animal-headed ship containing soldiers with shields and helmets above the waves, and a hippocampus, a mythical beast, below. Phoenician gold and silver coins have been found throughout the Mediterranean, evidence of the Phoenicians' extensive trading network. (Erich Lessing/Art Resource, NY)

IF THE BRONZE AGE COLLAPSE was a time of massive political and economic disruption, it was also a period of the spread of new technologies, especially iron. Even though empires shrank, many small kingdoms survived, each with cultures that combined elements shared across a wide area with local traditions.

Iron Technology

Along with migration and drought, another significant development in the centuries around 1200 B.C.E. was the spread of iron tools and iron technology. Iron smelting was developed independently in several different places, including western Africa in what is now Nigeria, Anatolia (modern Turkey), and most likely India. In Anatolia, the earliest smelted weapon has been dated to about 2500 B.C.E., but there may have been some smelting earlier. Most of the iron produced was too brittle to be of much use until about 1100 B.C.E., however, when techniques improved and iron weapons gradually became stronger and cheaper than their bronze counterparts. Thus, in the schema of dividing history into periods according to the main material out of which tools are made (see Chapter 1),

ca. 1200 B.C.E.
- Bronze Age Collapse; end of the Hittite Empire

ca. 1100 B.C.E.
- Beginning of the Iron Age; Phoenicians begin to trade in the Mediterranean

ca. 1070–712 B.C.
- Third Intermediate Period in Egypt

ca. 965–925 B.C.E.
- Hebrew kingdom ruled by Solomon

911–609 B.C.E.
- Neo-Assyrian Empire

727 B.C.E.
- Kushite Dynasty established in Egypt

722 B.C.E.
- Kingdom of Israel destroyed by the Assyrians

626–539 b.c.e.
- Neo-Babylonian empire

ca. 600 B.C.E.
- Ideas of Zoroaster gain prominence in Persia

587 B.C.E.
- Kingdom of Judah destroyed by the Neo-Babylonians

587–538 B.C.E.
- Babylonian Captivity of the Hebrews

550 B.C.E.
- Cyrus the Great conquers the Medes and consolidates the Persian Empire

539 B.C.E.
- Persians defeat the Neo-Babylonians

525 B.C.E.
- Persians defeat the Egyptians and Nubians

the **Iron Age** began in about 1100 B.C.E. Iron weapons became important items of trade around the Mediterranean and throughout the Tigris and Euphrates Valleys, and the technology for making them traveled as well. From Anatolia, iron objects were traded west into Greece and central Europe, and north into western Asia. By 500 B.C.E., knowledge of smelting had traveled these routes as well.

Ironworkers continued to experiment and improve their products. Near Eastern ironworkers discovered that if the relatively brittle wrought iron objects were placed on a bed of burning charcoal and then cooled quickly, the outer layer would form into a layer of much harder material, steel. Goods made of cast or wrought iron were usually traded locally, but fine sword and knife blades of steel traveled long distances, and the knowledge of how to make them followed. Because it was fairly plentiful and relatively cheap when compared with bronze, iron has been called the "democratic metal." The transition from bronze to iron happened over many centuries, but iron (and even more so, steel) would be an important factor in history from this point on.

Iron Age
▶ Period beginning about 1100 B.C.E., when iron became the most important material for tools and weapons.

The Decline of Egypt and the Emergence of Kush

Although the treaty between the Egyptians and Hittites in 1258 B.C.E. seemed to indicate a future of peace and cooperation, this was not to be. Groups of seafaring peoples whom the Egyptians called Sea Peoples raided, migrated, and marauded in the eastern Mediterranean. Just who these people were and where they originated is much debated among scholars. They may have come from Greece, or islands in the Mediterranean such as Crete and Sardinia, or Anatolia (modern Turkey), or from all of these places. Wherever they came from, their raids, combined with the

| How did the Hebrews create an enduring religious tradition? | What explains the rise and fall of the Assyrians? | How did the Persians consolidate their extensive empire? | ✓ LearningCurve Check what you know. |

expansion of the Assyrians (see page 43), led to the collapse of the Hittite Empire.

In Egypt, the pharaoh Ramesses III (r. 1186–1155 B.C.E.) defeated the Sea Peoples in both a land and sea battle, but these were costly, as were other military engagements. Egypt entered into a long period of political fragmentation and conquest by outsiders that scholars of Egypt refer to as the Third Intermediate Period (ca. 1070–712 B.C.E.). The long wars against invaders weakened and impoverished Egypt, causing political upheaval and economic decline.

The decline of Egypt allowed new powers to emerge. South of Egypt was a region called Nubia, which, as early as 2000 B.C.E., served as a conduit of trade through which ivory, gold, ebony, and other products flowed north from sub-Saharan Africa. Small kingdoms arose in this area. As Egypt expanded during the New Kingdom (see Chapter 24), it took over northern Nubia, incorporating it into the growing Egyptian empire. The Nubians adopted many features of Egyptian culture, many Nubians became officials in the Egyptian bureaucracy and officers in the army, and there was significant intermarriage between the two groups.

With the contraction of the Egyptian empire in the Third Intermediate Period, an independent kingdom, **Kush**, rose in power in Nubia, with its capital at Napata in what is now Sudan. The Kushites conquered southern Egypt, and in 727 B.C.E., the Kushite king Piye (r. ca. 747–716 B.C.E.) swept through the Nile Valley to the delta in the north. United once again, Egypt enjoyed a brief period of peace during which the Egyptian culture continued to influence that of its conquerors. In the seventh century B.C.E., invading Assyrians (see page 43) pushed the Kushites out of Egypt, and the Kushite rulers moved their capital farther up the Nile to Meroë. Meroë became a center for the production of iron. Iron products from Meroë were the best in the world and were traded to much of Africa and across the Red Sea and the Indian Ocean to India.

The Rise of Phoenicia

While Kush expanded in the southern Nile Valley, another group rose to prominence along the Mediterranean coast of modern Lebanon, the northern part of the area called Canaan in ancient sources. These Canaanites established the prosperous commercial centers of Tyre, Sidon, and Byblos, and were master shipbuilders. Between about 1100 and 700 B.C.E., the residents of these cities became the seaborne merchants of the Mediterranean. Their most valued products were purple and blue textiles, from which originated their Greek name, **Phoenicians** (fih-NEE-shuhnz), meaning "Purple People."

The trading success of the Phoenicians brought them prosperity. In addition to textiles and purple dye, they began to manufacture goods for export, such as tools, weapons, and cookware. Phoenician ships often carried hundreds of jars of wine, and the Phoenicians introduced grape growing to new regions around the Mediterranean, dramatically increasing the wine available for consumption and trade. They imported rare goods and materials from Persia in the east and their neighbors to the south. They also expanded their trade to Egypt, where they mingled with other local traders.

Moving beyond Egypt, the Phoenicians struck out along the coast of North Africa to establish new markets in places where they encountered little competi-

The Kingdom of Kush, 1000 B.C.E.–300 C.E.

Kush
▶ Kingdom in Nubia that adopted hieroglyphics and pyramids, and later conquered Egypt.

Phoenicians
▶ Seafaring people from Canaan who traded and founded colonies throughout the Mediterranean and spread the phonetic alphabet.

CHAPTER LOCATOR | How did iron technology shape new states after 1200 B.C.E.?

tion. In the ninth century B.C.E., they founded, in modern Tunisia, the city of Carthage, which prospered to become the leading city in the western Mediterranean.

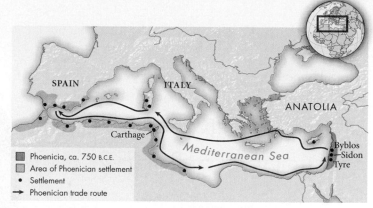

Phoenician Settlements in the Mediterranean

The Phoenicians planted trading posts and small farming communities along the coast, founding colonies in Spain and Sicily along with Carthage. Their trade routes eventually took them to the far western Mediterranean and beyond to the Atlantic coast of modern-day Portugal. The Phoenicians' voyages brought them into contact with the Greeks, to whom they introduced many aspects of the older and more urbanized cultures of Mesopotamia and Egypt.

The Phoenicians' overwhelming cultural achievement was the spread of a completely phonetic system of writing—that is, an alphabet. Writers of both cuneiform and hieroglyphics had developed signs that were used to represent sounds, but these were always used with a much larger number of ideograms. Sometime around 1800 B.C.E., workers in the Sinai Peninsula, which was under Egyptian control, began to write only with phonetic signs, with each sign designating one sound. This system vastly simplified writing and reading, and spread among common people as a practical way to record ideas and communicate. The Phoenicians adopted the simpler system for their own language and spread it around the Mediterranean. The system invented by ordinary people and spread by Phoenician merchants is the origin of most of the world's phonetic alphabets today.

QUICK REVIEW <

How did the Kushites and the Phoenicians take advantage of regional trade opportunities in the aftermath of the collapse of the Bronze Age empires?

How did the Hebrews create an enduring religious tradition?

What explains the rise and fall of the Assyrians?

How did the Persians consolidate their extensive empire?

☑ LearningCurve
Check what you know.

> How did the Hebrews create an enduring religious tradition?

Yahweh

▶ The sole god in Hebrew monotheism.

THE LEGACY OF ANOTHER PEOPLE who took advantage of Egypt's collapse to found an independent state may have been even more far-reaching than that of the Phoenicians. For a period of several centuries, a people known as the Hebrews controlled first one and then two small states on the western end of the Fertile Crescent, Israel and Judah. Politically unimportant when compared with the Egyptians or Babylonians, the Hebrews created a new form of religious belief, a monotheism based on the worship of an all-powerful god they called **Yahweh** (YAH-way). Beginning in the late 600s B.C.E., they began to write down their religious ideas, traditions, laws, advice literature, prayers, hymns, history, and prophecies in a series of books. These were gathered together centuries later to form the Hebrew Bible, which Christians later adopted and termed the "Old Testament." These writings later became the core of the Hebrews' religion, Judaism. Jews today revere these texts, as do many Christians, and Muslims respect them, all of which gives them particular importance.

CHAPTER LOCATOR | How did iron technology shape new states after 1200 B.C.E.?

The Hebrew State

The Hebrews were nomadic pastoralists who may have migrated into the Nile Delta from the east, seeking good land for their herds of sheep and goats. According to the Hebrew Bible, they were enslaved by the Egyptians but were led out of Egypt by a charismatic leader named Moses. The biblical account is very dramatic, and the events form a pivotal episode in the history of the Hebrews and the later religious practices of Judaism. Moses conveyed God's warning to the pharaoh that a series of plagues would strike Egypt, the last of which was the threat that all firstborn sons in Egypt would be killed. He instructed the Hebrews to prepare a hasty meal of a sacrificed lamb eaten with unleavened bread. The blood of the lamb was painted over the doors of Hebrew houses. At midnight Yahweh spread death over the land, but he passed over the Hebrew houses with the blood-painted doors. This event became known as the Passover and later became a central religious holiday in Judaism. The next day a terrified pharaoh ordered the Hebrews out of Egypt. Moses then led them in search of what they understood to be the Promised Land, an event known as the Exodus, which was followed by forty years of wandering.

According to scripture, the Hebrews settled in the area between the Mediterranean and the Jordan River known as Canaan. They were organized into tribes, each tribe consisting of numerous families who thought of themselves as all related to one another and having a common ancestor. In Canaan, the nomadic Hebrews encountered a variety of other peoples, whom they both learned from and fought. They slowly adopted agriculture and, not surprisingly, at times worshipped the agricultural gods of their neighbors, including Baal, an ancient fertility god.

The Bible reports that the greatest danger to the Hebrews came from a group known as the Philistines, who were most likely Greek-speaking people who had migrated to Canaan as part of the movement of the Sea

A Golden Calf

According to the Hebrew Bible, Moses descended from Mount Sinai, where he had received the Ten Commandments, to find the Hebrews worshipping a golden calf, which was against Yahweh's laws. In July 1990, an American archaeological team found this model of a gilded calf inside a pot. The figurine, which dates to about 1550 B.C.E., is strong evidence for the existence in Canaan of religious traditions that involved animals as divine symbols. (Courtesy of the Leon Levy Expedition to Ashkelon. Photo: Carl Andrews)

How did the Hebrews create an enduring religious tradition?

What explains the rise and fall of the Assyrians?

How did the Persians consolidate their extensive empire?

☑ LearningCurve
Check what you know.

Peoples and established a kingdom along the Mediterranean coast. The Philistines' superior technology and military organization at first made them invincible, but the Hebrews found a champion and a spirited leader in Saul. In the biblical account, Saul and his men battled the Philistines for control of the land, often without success. In the meantime, Saul established a monarchy over the Hebrew tribes, becoming their king, an event conventionally dated to about 1025 B.C.E.

The Bible includes detailed discussion of the growth of the Hebrew kingdom. It relates that Saul's work was carried on by David of Bethlehem (r. ca. 1005–965 B.C.E.), who pushed back the Philistines and waged war against his other neighbors. To give his kingdom a capital, he captured the city of Jerusalem, which he enlarged, fortified, and made the religious and political center of his realm. David's military successes enlarged the kingdom and won the Hebrews unprecedented security, and his forty-year reign was a period of vitality and political consolidation.

David's son Solomon (r. ca. 965–925 B.C.E.) launched a building program that the biblical narrative describes as including cities, palaces, fortresses, and roads. The most symbolic of these projects was the Temple of Jerusalem, which became the home of the Ark of the Covenant, the chest that contained the holiest of Hebrew religious articles. The temple in Jerusalem was intended to be the religious heart of the kingdom, a symbol of Hebrew unity and Yahweh's approval of the kingdom built by Saul, David, and Solomon. Along with discussing expansion and success, the Bible also notes problems. Solomon's efforts were hampered by strife. The financial demands of his building program drained the resources of his people, and his use of forced labor for building projects further fanned popular resentment.

A united Hebrew kingdom did not last long. At Solomon's death, his kingdom broke into political halves. The northern part became Israel, with its capital at Samaria, and the southern half became Judah, with Jerusalem remaining its center. War soon broke out between them, as recorded in the Bible, and the Assyrians wiped out the northern kingdom of Israel in 722 B.C.E. Judah survived numerous calamities until the Babylonians crushed it in 587 B.C.E. The survivors were forcibly relocated to Babylonia, a period commonly known as the Babylonian Captivity. In 538 B.C.E., the Persian king Cyrus the Great (see page 50) conquered the Babylonians and permitted some forty thousand exiles to return to Jerusalem. They rebuilt the temple, although politically the area was simply part of the Persian Empire.

The Jewish Religion

During and especially after the Babylonian Captivity, the most important legal and ethical Hebrew texts were edited and brought together in the **Torah**, the first five books of the Hebrew Bible. Here the exiles redefined their beliefs and practices, thereby establishing what they believed was the law of Yahweh. Fundamental to an understanding of the Jewish religion is the concept of the **Covenant**, an agreement that people believed to exist between themselves and Yahweh. According to the Bible, Yahweh appeared to the tribal leader Abraham, promising him that he would be blessed, as would his descendants, if they followed Yahweh. Yahweh next appeared to Moses during the time he was leading the Hebrews out of

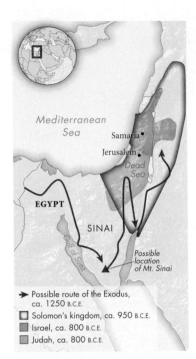

The Hebrew Exodus and State, ca. 1250–800 B.C.E.

➤ Possible route of the Exodus, ca. 1250 B.C.E.

☐ Solomon's kingdom, ca. 950 B.C.E.

◼ Israel, ca. 800 B.C.E.

◼ Judah, ca. 800 B.C.E.

Torah

▶ The first five books of the Hebrew Bible, containing the most important legal and ethical Hebrew texts; later became part of the Christian Old Testament.

Covenant

▶ An agreement that the Hebrews believed to exist between themselves and Yahweh, in which he would consider them his chosen people if they worshipped him as their only god.

Egypt, and Yahweh made a Covenant with the Hebrews: if they worshipped Yahweh as their only god, he would consider them his chosen people and protect them from their enemies. The Covenant was understood to be made with the whole people, not simply a king or an elite, and was renewed again several times in the accounts of the Hebrew people in the Bible. Individuals such as Abraham and Moses who acted as intermediaries between Yahweh and the Hebrew people were known as prophets; much of the Hebrew Bible consists of writings in their voices, understood as messages from Yahweh to which the Hebrews were to listen.

Worship was embodied in a series of rules of behavior, the Ten Commandments, which Yahweh gave to Moses. These required certain kinds of religious observances and forbade the Hebrews to steal, kill, lie, or commit adultery, thus creating a system of ethical absolutes. From the Ten Commandments a complex system of rules of conduct was created and later written down as Hebrew law.

Like the followers of other religions in the ancient Near East, Jews engaged in rituals through which they showed their devotion. They were also expected to please Yahweh by living up to high moral standards and by worshipping him above all other gods. The first of the Ten Commandments expresses this: "I am the Lord your God . . . you shall have no other gods besides me" (Exodus 20:23). Increasingly this was understood to be a commandment to worship Yahweh alone. The later prophets such as Isaiah created a system of ethical monotheism, in which goodness was understood to come from a single transcendent god, and in which religious obligations included fair and just behavior toward other people as well as rituals.

Like Mesopotamian deities, Yahweh punished people, but the Hebrews also believed he was a loving and forgiving god who would protect and reward all those who obeyed his commandments. The religion of the Hebrews was thus addressed to not only an elite but also the individual. Because kings or other political leaders were not essential to its practice, the rise or fall of a kingdom was not crucial to the religion's continued existence. Religious leaders were important in Judaism, but personally following the instructions of Yahweh was the central task for observant Jews in the ancient world.

Hebrew Family and Society

The Hebrews were originally nomadic, but they adopted settled agriculture in Canaan, and some lived in cities. The shift away from pastoralism affected more than just how people fed themselves. Communal use of land gave way to family or private ownership, and devotion to the traditions of Judaism came to replace tribal identity.

Family relationships reflected evolving circumstances. Marriage and the family were fundamentally important in Jewish life; celibacy was frowned upon and almost all major Jewish thinkers and priests were married. Polygamy was allowed, but the typical marriage was probably monogamous.

As in Mesopotamia and Egypt, marriage was a family matter, too important to be left to the whims of young people. According to biblical rules, sexual relations were a source of impurity that needed to be cleansed with specific rituals, but sex itself was basically good because it was part of Yahweh's creation, and the

| How did the Hebrews create an enduring religious tradition? | What explains the rise and fall of the Assyrians? | How did the Persians consolidate their extensive empire? | ✔ LearningCurve Check what you know. |

41

bearing of children was seen in some ways as a religious function. Sons were especially desired because they maintained the family bloodline, while keeping ancestral property in the family. As in Mesopotamia, land was handed down within families, generally from father to son. A first-born son became the head of the household at his father's death. Mothers oversaw the early education of the children, but as boys grew older, their fathers gave them more of their education. Both men and women were expected to know religious traditions so that they could teach their children and prepare for religious rituals and ceremonies. Women worked in the fields alongside their husbands in rural areas, and in shops in the cities.

The development of urban life among the Jews created new economic opportunities, especially in crafts and trades. People specialized in certain occupations and, as in most ancient societies, these crafts were family trades. Sons worked with their father, daughters with their mother. If the business prospered, the family might be assisted by a few paid workers or slaves. The practitioners of a craft usually lived in a particular section of town. Commerce and trade developed later than crafts. Trade with neighboring countries was handled by foreigners, usually Phoenicians. Jews dealt mainly in local trade, and in most instances craftsmen and farmers sold directly to their customers.

The Torah sets out rules about many aspects of life. Among these was the set of dietary laws known as *kashrut* (from which we derive the English word *kosher*), setting out what plants and animals Jews were forbidden to eat and how foods were to be prepared properly. Later commentators sought to explain these laws as originating in concerns about health or hygiene, but the biblical text simply gives them as rules coming from Yahweh, sometimes expressed in terms of ritual purity or cleanliness.

Beliefs and practices that made Jews distinctive endured, but the Hebrew states did not. Small states like those of the Phoenicians and the Hebrews could exist only in the absence of a major power, and the beginning of the ninth century B.C.E. saw the rise of such a power: the Assyrians of northern Mesopotamia. They conquered the kingdom of Israel, the Phoenician cities, and eventually many other states as well.

> **QUICK REVIEW**

What were the most important differences between Judaism and the other religions of the Near East?

CHAPTER LOCATOR | How did iron technology shape new states after 1200 B.C.E.?

Ashurbanipal and his queen enjoying a banquet

(© The Trustees of the British Museum)

What explains the rise and fall of the Assyrians?

THE ASSYRIAN KINGDOM originated in northern Mesopotamia. The Assyrians built up the military and conquered many of their neighbors, including Babylonia, and took over much of Syria all the way to the Mediterranean. The Assyrians then moved into Anatolia, where the pressure they put on the Hittite Empire was one factor in its collapse. Assyria's success allowed it to become the leading power in the Near East, with an army that at times numbered many tens of thousands.

Assyria's Long Road to Power

The Assyrians had inhabited northern Mesopotamia since the third millennium B.C.E., forming a kingdom that grew and shrank in size and power over the centuries. During the time of Sargon of Akkad, they were part of the Akkadian empire, then independent, then part of the Babylonian empire under Hammurabi, then independent again (see Chapter 1). Warfare with the Babylonians and other Near Eastern states continued off and on, and in the thirteenth century B.C.E., the Assyrians slowly began to create a larger state.

The eleventh century B.C.E.—the time of the Bronze Age Collapse—was a period of instability and retrenchment in the Near East. The Assyrians did not engage in any new wars of conquest but remained fairly secure within their borders. Under the leadership of King Adad-nirari II (r. 911–892 B.C.E.), Assyria began a campaign of expansion and domination, creating what scholars have termed the Neo-Assyrian Empire. The next several turbulent centuries were marked by Assyrian military campaigns, constant efforts by smaller states to maintain or recover their independence, and eventual further Assyrian conquest.

Eighth-century kings continued the expansion of Assyria, which established its capital at Nineveh (NIHN-uh-vuh) on the Tigris River. By means of almost constant warfare, the Assyrians created an empire that stretched from east and north of the Tigris River to central Egypt (**Map 2.1**). Revolt against the Assyrians inevitably promised the rebels bloody battles and cruel sieges followed by surrender, accompanied by systematic torture and slaughter, or by deportations. Like many

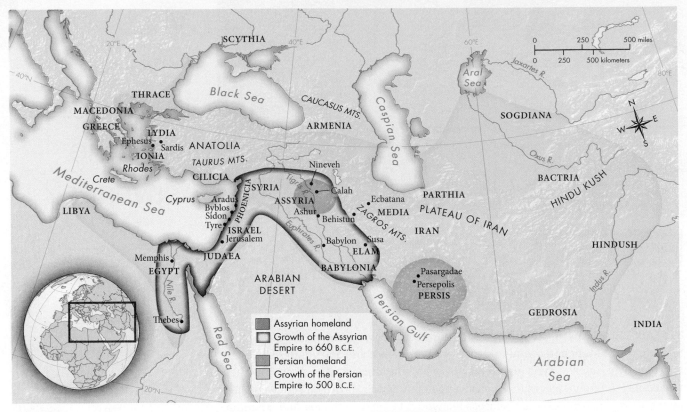

MAP 2.1 ■ The Assyrian and Persian Empires, ca. 1000–500 B.C.E.

At its height around 650 B.C.E., the Assyrian Empire included almost all of the old centers of power in the ancient Near East. By 513 B.C.E., however, the Persian Empire was far larger.

> **MAPPING THE PAST**

ANALYZING THE MAP: How does the Persian Empire compare in size to the Assyrian Empire? What other differences can you identify between the two?

CONNECTIONS: Compare this map to Map 1.1 on page 13. What changes and continuities do you see in the centers of power in the ancient Near East?

conquerors, the Assyrians recognized that relocated peoples were less likely to rebel because they were forced to create new lives for themselves far from their original homelands and that simply relocating leaders might be enough to destroy opposition.

Assyrian methods were certainly harsh, but in practical terms Assyria's success was actually due primarily to the size of its army and the army's sophisticated and effective military organization. By Sargon's time, the Assyrians had invented the mightiest military machine the ancient Near East had ever seen, with perhaps seventy thousand men in the field in an era that typically saw armies of under ten thousand.

Assyrian military genius was remarkable for the development of a wide variety of siege machinery and techniques, including excavation to undermine city walls and battering rams to knock down walls and gates. Never before in the Near East had anyone applied such technical knowledge to warfare. The Assyrians even invented the concept of a corps of engineers, who bridged rivers with pontoons or provided soldiers with inflatable skins for swimming. And the Assyrians knew how to coordinate their efforts, both in open battle and in siege warfare.

CHAPTER LOCATOR | How did iron technology shape new states after 1200 B.C.E.?

CHAPTER 2

44 SMALL KINGDOMS AND MIGHTY EMPIRES IN THE NEAR EAST

Assyrian Rule and Culture

The Assyrians won most of their battles, and they also knew how to use their victories to consolidate their power. The key to success in all empires is to get cooperation from some people in the regions you wish to dominate, and the Assyrians did this well. As early as the reign of Tiglath-pileser III, the Assyrian kings began to organize their conquered territories into an empire. The lands closest to Assyria became provinces governed by Assyrian officials. Kingdoms beyond the provinces were not annexed but became dependent states that followed Assyria's lead and also paid Assyria a hefty tribute. The Assyrian king chose these states' rulers either by regulating the succession of native kings or by supporting native kings who appealed to him. Against more distant states the Assyrian kings waged frequent war in order to conquer them outright or make the dependent states secure. (See "Picturing the Past: Assyrians Besiege a City," page 45.)

In the seventh century B.C.E., Assyrian power seemed firmly established. Yet the downfall of Assyria was swift and complete. Babylon finally won its independence from Assyria in 626 B.C.E. and joined forces with the Medes, an Indo-European-speaking folk from Persia (modern Iran). Together the Babylonians and the Medes destroyed the Assyrian Empire in 612 B.C.E., paving the way for the rise of the Persians. Their cities destroyed and their power shattered, the Assyrians disappeared from history, remembered only as a cruel people of the Old Testament who oppressed the Hebrews. Two hundred years later, when the Greek adventurer and historian Xenophon (ZEH-nuh-fuhn) passed by the ruins of Nineveh, he marveled at the extent of the former city but knew nothing of the Assyrians. The glory of their empire was forgotten.

Modern archaeology has brought the Assyrians out of obscurity. In 1839, the English archaeologist and traveler A. H. Layard began excavations at Nineveh. His findings electrified the world. Layard's workers unearthed masterpieces,

Assyrians Besiege a City

In this Assyrian carving made about 700 B.C.E. from the palace of King Sennacherib at Nineveh, troops attack the Jewish fortified town of Lachish using a variety of siege machinery. At the right, defending soldiers crowd a tower, while men and women carry sacks away from the city.

> PICTURING THE PAST

ANALYZING THE IMAGE: What means of attack do the Assyrians use against the besieged city? How does the artist convey the idea that Assyrian military power was overwhelming?
CONNECTIONS: Based on what you have read in this chapter about the Assyrian kings, why might King Sennacherib have chosen to have this particular scene portrayed in his palace?

How did the Hebrews create an enduring religious tradition?

What explains the rise and fall of the Assyrians?

How did the Persians consolidate their extensive empire?

☑ LearningCurve
Check what you know.

including monumental sculpted figures—huge winged bulls, human-headed lions, and sphinxes—as well as brilliantly sculpted friezes. Among the most renowned of Layard's finds were the Assyrian palace reliefs, whose number has been increased by the discoveries of twentieth-century archaeologists. For the kings' palaces, Assyrian artists carved reliefs that showed scenes of war as a series of episodes that progressed from the time the army marched out until the enemy was conquered.

Equally valuable were the numerous Assyrian cuneiform documents, which ranged from royal accounts of mighty military campaigns to simple letters by common people. The biggest find of these was the library of King Ashurbanipal (r. 668–627 B.C.E.), the last major Assyrian king, in the city of Nineveh. Like many Assyrian kings, Ashurbanipal was described as extremely cruel, but he was also well educated and deeply interested in literary and religious texts, especially those from what was already to him the ancient Mesopotamian past. Included in the tens of thousands of texts in his library were creation accounts from ancient Babylon (some most likely simply confiscated from the city of Babylon, which was part of the Assyrian Empire), the *Epic of Gilgamesh*, and many other mythological and religious texts, as well as word lists, chronicles, and royal documents. Some texts relate to medicine and astronomy, and others to foretelling the future or practicing magic.

The Neo-Babylonian Empire

The decline of Assyria allowed another group of people, the Chaldeans, to create a new dynasty of kings and a somewhat smaller empire centered at Babylon. The Chaldeans were peoples that settled in southern Mesopotamia, where they established their rule, later extending it farther north. They grew strong enough to overthrow Assyrian rule in 626 B.C.E. with the help of another new people, the Medes, who had established themselves in modern western Iran. The Neo- (or new) Babylonian empire they created was marked by an attempt at the restoration of past Babylonian greatness. Their most famous king, Nebuchadnezzar II (neh-buh-kuhd-NEH-zuhr) (r. 604–562 B.C.E.), thrust Babylonian power into Syria and Judah, destroying Jerusalem and forcibly deporting the residents to Babylonia.

The Chaldeans focused on solidifying their power and legitimizing their authority. Kings and priests consciously looked back to the great days of Hammurabi and other earlier kings. They instituted a religious revival that included restoring old temples and sanctuaries, as well as creating new ones in the same tradition. Part of their effort was commercial: they sought to revive the economy in order to resurrect the image of Babylonian greatness. In their hands, the city of Babylon grew and gained a reputation for magnificence and luxury.

The Neo-Babylonians preserved many basic aspects of older Babylonian law, literature, and government, yet they failed to bring peace and prosperity to Mesopotamia. Loss of important trade routes to the north and northeast reduced income, and additional misfortune came in the form of famine and plague. The Neo-Babylonian kingdom was weakened and ultimately conquered in 539 B.C.E. by their former allies, the Medes, who had themselves found new allies, the Persians.

> **QUICK REVIEW**

What strategies did the Assyrians employ to govern their empire and control their subjects?

CHAPTER LOCATOR | How did iron technology shape new states after 1200 B.C.E.?

CHAPTER 2
46   SMALL KINGDOMS AND MIGHTY EMPIRES IN THE NEAR EAST

How did the Persians consolidate their extensive empire?

Gold Plaque from the Persian Empire

In the nineteenth century, a huge collection of silver and gold objects from the fifth and fourth centuries B.C.E., including this gold plaque, was found on the banks of the Oxus River in what is now Tajikistan. The plaque shows a man in the dress of the Medes with a short sword and a bundle of sticks called a *barsom*, which was used in religious ceremonies. (© The Trustees of the British Museum)

THE ASSYRIANS ROSE TO POWER from a base in the Tigris and Euphrates River Valleys of Mesopotamia, which had seen many earlier empires. They were defeated by a coalition that included a Mesopotamian power—Babylon—but also a people with a base of power in a part of the world that had not been the site of earlier urbanized states: Persia (modern-day Iran), a stark land of towering mountains and flaming deserts, with a broad central plateau in the heart of the country (see Map 2.1, page 44). The Persians created an even larger empire than the

How did the Hebrews create an enduring religious tradition?

What explains the rise and fall of the Assyrians?

How did the Persians consolidate their extensive empire?

☑ LearningCurve
Check what you know.

Assyrians did, and one that stretched far to the east. Though as conquerors they willingly used force to accomplish their ends, they also used diplomacy to consolidate their power and generally allowed the peoples that they conquered to practice their existing customs and religions. Thus the Persian Empire was one of political unity and cultural diversity.

Consolidation of the Persian Empire

Iran's geographical position and topography explain its traditional role as the highway between western and eastern Asia. Nomadic peoples migrating south from the broad steppes of Russia and Central Asia have streamed into Iran throughout much of history. Confronting the uncrossable salt deserts, most have turned either westward or eastward, moving on until they reached the advanced and wealthy urban centers of Mesopotamia and India. Cities did emerge along these routes, however, and Iran became the area where nomads met urban dwellers.

Among the nomadic groups were Indo-European-speaking peoples who migrated into this area about 1000 B.C.E. with their flocks and herds. They were also horse breeders, and the horse gave them a decisive military advantage over those who already lived in the area. One of the Indo-European groups was the Medes, who settled in northern Iran. The Medes united under one king and joined the Babylonians in overthrowing the Assyrian Empire. With the rise of the Medes, the balance of power in western Asia shifted for the first time to the area east of Mesopotamia.

In 550 B.C.E., Cyrus the Great (r. 559–530 B.C.E.), king of the Persians and one of the most remarkable statesmen of antiquity, conquered the Medes. (See "Individuals in Society: Cyrus the Great," page 50.) Cyrus's conquest of the Medes resulted not in slavery and slaughter but in the union of the two peoples. Having united Persia and Media, Cyrus set out to achieve two goals. First, he wanted to win control of the shore of the Mediterranean and thus of the terminal ports of the great trade routes that crossed Iran and Anatolia. Second, he strove to secure eastern Iran from the pressure of nomadic invaders.

In a series of major campaigns, Cyrus achieved his goals. He conquered the various kingdoms of the Tigris and Euphrates Valleys, including Babylon in 539 B.C.E. Cyrus then swept into western Anatolia. Cyrus's generals subdued the Greek cities along the coast of Anatolia, thus gaining him important ports on the Mediterranean. From there, Cyrus marched to the far eastern corners of Iran and conquered the regions of Parthia and Bactria in Central Asia, though he ultimately died on the battlefield there.

A text written in cuneiform on a sixth-century-B.C.E. Babylonian clay cylinder presents Cyrus describing the way in which the main Babylonian god Marduk selected him to conquer Babylon and restore proper government and worship. We do not know who actually wrote the text, but whoever did made sure to portray Cyrus as someone who triumphed as the result of divine favor, not simply military conquest, and honored the gods of the regions he conquered.

After his victories, Cyrus made sure that the Persians were portrayed as liberators, and in some cases he was more benevolent than most conquerors were.

CHAPTER LOCATOR | How did iron technology shape new states after 1200 B.C.E.?

According to his own account, he freed all of the captive peoples who were living in forced exile in Babylonia, including the Hebrews. He returned their sacred objects to them and allowed those who wanted to return to Jerusalem to do so, and he paid for the rebuilding of their temple.

Cyrus's successors continued Persian conquests, creating the largest empire the world had yet seen. In 525 B.C.E. Cyrus's son Cambyses (r. 530–522 B.C.E.) subdued the Egyptians and the Nubians. At Cambyses's death (the circumstances of which are disputed), Darius I (r. 521–486 B.C.E.) took over the throne and conquered Scythia in Central Asia, along with much of Thrace and Macedonia, areas north of the Aegean Sea. By 510, the Persians also ruled the western coast of Anatolia and many of the islands of the Aegean. Thus, within forty years, the Persians had transformed themselves from a subject people to the rulers of a vast empire that included all of the oldest kingdoms and peoples of the region, as well as many outlying areas (see Map 2.1, page 44). Unsurprisingly, Darius began to call himself "King of Kings." Invasions of Greece by Darius and his son Xerxes were unsuccessful, but the Persian Empire lasted another two hundred years, until it became part of the empire of Alexander the Great (see Chapter 4).

> ## > Three Generations of Persian Conquerors

- Cyrus the Great (r. 559–530 B.C.E.): Conquered Medes, kingdoms of the Tigris and Euphrates Valleys, western Anatolia, Parthia, and Bactria
- Cambyses (r. 530–522 B.C.E.): Conquered Egyptians and Nubians
- Darius I (r. 521–486 B.C.E.): Conquered Scythia, Thrace, Macedonia, and areas north of the Aegean Sea

The Persians also knew how to preserve the empire they had won on the battlefield. Learning from the Assyrians, they created an efficient administrative system to govern the empire based in their newly built capital city of Persepolis near modern Shiraz, Iran. Under Darius, they divided the empire into districts and appointed either Persian or local nobles as administrators called **satraps** to head each one. The satrap controlled local government, collected taxes, heard legal cases, and maintained order. He was assisted by a council, and also by officials and army leaders sent from Persepolis who made sure that the satrap knew the will of the king and that the king knew what was going on in the provinces. This system lessened opposition to Persian rule by making local elites part of the system of government, although sometimes satraps used their authority to build up independent power.

Communication and trade were eased by a sophisticated system of roads linking the empire from the coast of Asia Minor to the valley of the Indus River. On the roads were way stations where royal messengers could get food and horses, a system that allowed messages to be communicated quickly, much like the famed pony express in the American West. These roads meant that the king was usually in close touch with officials and subjects. The roads also simplified the defense of the empire by making it easier to move Persian armies. In addition the system

satraps
▶ Administrators in the Persian Empire who controlled local government, collected taxes, heard legal cases, and maintained order.

How did the Hebrews create an enduring religious tradition?   What explains the rise and fall of the Assyrians?   **How did the Persians consolidate their extensive empire?**   ✓ LearningCurve Check what you know.

49

INDIVIDUALS IN SOCIETY
Cyrus the Great

Cyrus (r. 559–530 B.C.E.), known to history as "the Great" and the founder of the Persian Empire, began life as a subject of the Medes, an Iranian people very closely related to the Persians. There are few surviving sources describing his early life, and even the date of his birth is uncertain. There are many legends, however, some originating in Persia and others in Greece, as many later Greek leaders and authors admired Cyrus. The Greek historian Herodotus records the legend that Cyrus was the grandson of Astyages, king of the Medes, who ordered him killed to eliminate him as a future threat. Cyrus, like the biblical Moses, escaped the plot and went on to rule both his own Persians and the Medes.

Another story recounted by Herodotus tells how Cyrus's playmates chose him king. He assigned them specific duties, and when one aristocratic boy refused to obey his orders, Cyrus had him "arrested." The boy's father later demanded that Cyrus explain his haughty behavior. Cyrus replied that the other boys had chosen him king, and he did his duty justly, as a king should. He told the man that if he had done anything wrong, he was there to take his punishment. The man and the other boys admired his calm sense of duty and responsibility. Through this anecdote, the historian projected Cyrus's intelligence and good qualities, revealed later in life, back into his boyhood.

Astyages eventually marched against the grown Cyrus and was defeated. Instead of enslaving the Medes, Cyrus incorporated them into the new kingdom of Persia, thus demonstrating his inclusive concept of rule. This relatively mild rule continued with his later conquests. He won the admiration of many Greeks, whom he allowed to continue their religious rituals and intellectual pursuits.

After conquering Babylonia, Cyrus allowed the Jews who had been in forced exile there to return to Jerusalem. Hebrew scripture portrays Cyrus as divinely chosen, as evidenced by this biblical passage, probably written in the late sixth century B.C.E., shortly after the end of the Babylonian Captivity:

> Thus said the Lord to Cyrus, His anointed one—
> Whose right hand He has grasped,
> Treading down nations before him,
> Ungirding the loins of kings,
> Opening doors before him, and letting no gate stay shut:
> I will march before you, and level the hills that loom up;
> I will shatter doors of bronze
> And cut down iron bars.

Statue of Cyrus the Great at the Olympic Park in Sydney, Australia. A replica of a bas-relief in Cyrus's capital city of Pasargadae, this monument was erected in 1994 as a testament to the peaceful coexistence of many different peoples in the Persian Empire. (Courtesy of Siamax)

⯈LaunchPad

ONLINE DOCUMENT PROJECT
What strategies did Persian rulers like Cyrus use to bind together far-flung and diverse peoples under their imperial rule? Keeping the question above in mind, examine sources that illuminate how the Persians saw their empire and how they ruled it, and then complete a writing assignment based on the evidence and details from this chapter. *See inside the front cover to learn more.*

I will give you treasures concealed in the dark
And secret hoards —
So that you may know that it is I the LORD,
The God of Israel, who call you by name. . . .
It was I who roused him [Cyrus] for victory
And who level all roads for him.
He shall rebuild My city
And let My exiled people go
Without price and without payment
   — said the LORD of hosts. (Isaiah 45:1–3, 13)*

Cyrus died in 530 B.C.E. while campaigning in Central Asia. Though much of his life was spent at war, he knew how to govern conquered peoples effectively and acquired a reputation for benevolence and tolerance. Much about his life can never be known, but Cyrus appears to have been a practical man of sound judgment, keenly interested in foreign peoples and their ways of life.

QUESTIONS FOR ANALYSIS

1. How are the Greek stories, as told by Herodotus, and the biblical account similar in their portrayals of Cyrus? How are they different?
2. Herodotus, the Bible, and the inscription on the Cyrus cylinder discussed on page 50 have all been influential in establishing the largely positive historical view of Cyrus. What limitations might there be in using these as historical sources?

*Reprinted from the *Tanakh: The Holy Scriptures* by permission of the University of Nebraska Press. Copyright 1985 The Jewish Publication Society, Philadelphia.

Persian Religion

Iranian religion was originally tied to nature. Ahuramazda (ah-HOOR-uh-MAZ-duh), the chief god, was the creator of all living creatures. Mithra, the sun-god whose cult would later spread throughout the Roman Empire, saw to justice and redemption. Fire was a particularly important god, and fire was often part of religious rituals. A priestly class, the Magi, developed among the Medes to officiate at sacrifices, chant prayers to the gods, and tend the sacred flame.

Around 600 B.C.E., the ideas of Zoroaster, a thinker and preacher (whose dates are uncertain), began to gain prominence. Zoroaster is regarded as the author of key religious texts, later gathered together in a collection of sacred texts called the Avesta. He introduced new spiritual concepts to the Iranian people, stressing devotion to Ahuramazda alone and emphasizing the individual's responsibility to choose between the forces of creation, truth, and order and those of nothingness, chaos, falsehood, and disorder. Zoroaster taught that people possessed the free will to decide between these and that they must rely on their own conscience to guide them through an active life in which they focused on "good thoughts, good words, and good deeds." Their decisions were crucial, he warned, for there would come a time of reckoning. At the end of time, the forces of order would win, and the victorious Ahuramazda, like the Egyptian god Osiris (see Chapter 1, page 22), would preside over a last judgment to determine each person's eternal fate. Those who had lived according to good and truth would enter a divine kingdom. Liars and the wicked, denied this blessed immortality, would be condemned to eternal pain, darkness, and punishment. Thus Zoroaster preached a last judgment that led to a heaven or a hell.

Scholars—and contemporary Zoroastrians—debate whether Zoroaster saw the forces of disorder as a malevolent deity named Angra Mainyu who was co-eternal with and independent from Ahuramazda, or whether he was simply using this

allowed the easy flow of trade, which Persian rulers further encouraged by building canals, including one that linked the Red Sea and the Nile.

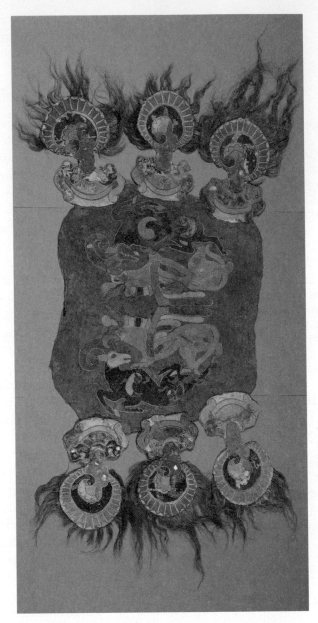

This elaborately painted piece of leather, dating from the fourth or third century B.C.E., shows running goats with huge curved horns. The fact that it survived suggests that it was not actually used but served instead a ceremonial function.
(Hermitage, St. Petersburg, Russia. Photo © Boltin Picture Library/Bridgeman Images)

Zoroastrianism

▶ Religion based on the ideas of Zoroaster that stressed devotion to the god Ahuramazda alone and that emphasized the individual's responsibility to choose between good and evil.

term to mean "evil thoughts" or "a destructive spirit." Later forms of **Zoroastrianism** followed each of these lines of understanding. Most Zoroastrians believed that the good Ahuramazda and the evil Angra Mainyu were locked together in a cosmic battle for the human race, a religious conceptualization that scholars call dualism, which was rejected in Judaism and Christianity. Some had a more monotheistic interpretation, however, and saw Ahuramazda as the only uncreated god.

Whenever he actually lived, Zoroaster's writings were spread by teachers, and King Darius began to use Zoroastrian language and images. Under the protection of the Persian kings, Zoroastrian ideas spread throughout Iran and the rest of the Persian Empire, and then beyond this into central China. It became the official religion of the later Persian Empire ruled by the Sassanid dynasty, and much later Zoroastrians migrated to western India, where they became known as Parsis and

CHAPTER LOCATOR | How did iron technology shape new states after 1200 B.C.E.?

still live today. Zoroastrianism survived the fall of the Persian Empire to influence Christianity, Islam, and Buddhism, largely because of its belief in a just life on earth and a happy afterlife. Good behavior in the world, even though unrecognized at the time, would receive ample reward in the hereafter. Evil, no matter how powerful in life, would be punished after death. In some form or another, Zoroastrian concepts still pervade many modern religions, and Zoroastrianism still exists as a religion.

Persian Art and Culture

The Persians made significant contributions to art and culture. They produced amazing works in gold and silver, often with inlaid jewels and semiprecious stones. They transformed the Assyrian tradition of realistic monumental sculpture from one that celebrated gory details of slaughter to one that showed both the Persians and their subjects as dignified. They noted and carved the physical features of their subjects: their hair, their clothing, their tools and weapons. Because

King Darius Defeats His Enemies King Darius of Persia proclaimed victory over his enemies with a written inscription and sculpture high on a cliff near Mount Behistun so all could see. He attributed his victory to Ahuramazda, the god of Zoroastrianism, whose symbol is carved above the chained prisoners. The proclamation itself was inscribed in three different cuneiform script languages, and it has been a vital tool for scholars as they have deciphered these ancient languages. Robert Harding World Imagery)

How did the Hebrews create an enduring religious tradition? | What explains the rise and fall of the Assyrians? | **How did the Persians consolidate their extensive empire?** | ✓ LearningCurve Check what you know.

53

they depicted both themselves and non-Persians realistically, Persian art serves as an excellent source for learning about the weapons, tools, clothing, and even hairstyles of many peoples of the area.

These carvings adorned temples and other large buildings in cities throughout the empire, and the Persians also built new cities from the ground up. The most spectacular of these was Persepolis, designed as a residence for the kings and an administrative and cultural center. The architecture of Persepolis combined elements found in many parts of the empire. Underneath the city was a system of closed water pipes, drainage canals, and conduits that allowed water from nearby mountains to flow into the city without flooding it, provided water for households and plantings inside the city, and carried away sewage and waste from the city's many residents. The Persians thus further improved the technology for handling water that had been essential in this area since the time of the Sumerians.

The Persians allowed the peoples they conquered to maintain their own customs and beliefs, as long as they paid the proper amount of taxes and did not rebel. Their rule resulted in an empire that brought people together in a new political system, with a culture that blended older and newer religious traditions and ways of seeing the world. Even their opponents, including the Greeks who would stop their expansion and eventually conquer the Persian Empire, admired their art and institutions.

> **QUICK REVIEW**

How did the Persians respond to the challenges created by the cultural diversity of their empire?

CHAPTER LOCATOR | How did iron technology shape new states after 1200 B.C.E.?

CHAPTER 2
54   SMALL KINGDOMS AND MIGHTY EMPIRES IN THE NEAR EAST

LOOKING BACK
LOOKING AHEAD

During the centuries following the Bronze Age Collapse, natives and newcomers brought order to life across the ancient Near East. As Egypt fell, small kingdoms, including those of the Nubians, Phoenicians, and Hebrews, grew and prospered. Regular trade and communication continued, and new products and ideas were transported by sea and land. Beginning about 900 B.C.E., the Assyrians created a large state through military conquest that was often brutal, though they also developed effective structures of rule through which taxes flowed to their leaders. The Persians, an Iranian people whose center of power was east of Mesopotamia, then established an even larger empire, governing through local officials and building beautiful cities.

The lands on the northern shore of the Mediterranean were beyond the borders of the urbanized cultures and centralized empires of the ancient Near East but maintained contact with them through trade and migration. As the Persian Empire continued to expand, it looked further westward toward these lands, including Greece, as possible further conquests. Greek-speaking people living in Anatolia and traveling more widely throughout the area had also absorbed numerous aspects of Persian and other more urbanized cultures they had encountered. They learned of Near Eastern religions and myths, and of the sagas of heroic wars. They also acquired many of the advanced technologies developed by their eastern neighbors, including the use of bronze and later iron, the phonetic alphabet, wine making, and shipbuilding. The Greeks combined these borrowings with their own traditions, ideas, and talents to create a distinct civilization, one that fundamentally shaped the subsequent development of Western society.

LaunchPad

ONLINE DOCUMENT PROJECT
Cyrus the Great

What strategies did Persian rulers like Cyrus use to bind together far-flung and diverse peoples under their imperial rule?

You encountered Cyrus the Great on page 50. Keeping the question above in mind, explore sources that illuminate how Persian rulers saw their empire. *See inside the front cover to learn more.*

How did the Hebrews create an enduring religious tradition?

What explains the rise and fall of the Assyrians?

How did the Persians consolidate their extensive empire?

✓ LearningCurve
Check what you know.

CHAPTER 2 STUDY GUIDE

GET STARTED ONLINE

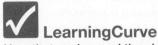
LearningCurve

Now that you've read the chapter, make it stick by completing the LearningCurve activity.

STEP 2

EXPLAIN WHY IT MATTERS

Put your reading into practice. Identify each term below, and then explain why it matters in Western history.

TERM	WHO OR WHAT & WHEN	WHY IT MATTERS
Iron Age (p. 35)		
Kush (p. 36)		
Phoenicians (p. 36)		
Yahweh (p. 38)		
Torah (p. 40)		
Covenant (p. 40)		
satraps (p. 49)		
Zoroastrianism (p. 52)		

STEP 3

MOVE BEYOND THE BASICS

To demonstrate a more advanced understanding, compare and contrast the Assyrian and Persian Empires. Use the chart below to identify key aspects of each empire.

	Assyrian empire	Persian empire
Nature of conquests		
Attitudes and policies toward subjects		
Imperial organization and governmental institutions		

STEP 4 **PUT IT ALL TOGETHER** Now, take a step back and try to explain the big picture. Remember to use specific examples from the chapter in your answers.

KUSH AND PHOENICIA

▶ How did the long history of Egyptian regional domination shape the culture and government of Kush?

▶ What role did the Phoenicians play in the commercial economy of the eastern Mediterranean?

THE HEBREWS

▶ How and why did Hebrew society change between the time the Hebrews arrived in Canaan and the period of Assyrian conquest?

▶ What did the Hebrews expect from Yahweh? What did Yahweh expect in return?

THE ASSYRIAN AND PERSIAN EMPIRES

▶ In your opinion, do the Assyrians deserve their reputation for extraordinary cruelty? Why or why not?

▶ Why was it important to Persian emperors to gain a reputation for being just rulers?

MAKE CONNECTIONS

▶ How did the Assyrian and Persian Empires differ from their Bronze Age counterparts?

▶ What lessons and insights might the Persian Empire have to offer future diverse states and empires? How did the Persians turn potential sources of division into sources of imperial strength?

> IN YOUR OWN WORDS

Imagine that you must give an oral report to the class answering the following question: **How did the Assyrians and the Persians win mighty empires, and how did they rule them once they had been won? What would be the most important points and why?**

3

THE DEVELOPMENT OF GREEK SOCIETY AND CULTURE

CA. 3000–338 B.C.E.

> **What forces shaped the development of Greek society and culture in the Archaic and classical periods?** Chapter 3 examines the development of Greek civilization from the Bronze Age through Greece's classical period. Although geographic conditions made farming difficult and limited the growth of early kingdoms, the people of ancient Greece built on the traditions and ideas of earlier societies to develop a culture that fundamentally shaped the intellectual and cultural traditions of Western civilization. The ancient Greeks were the first to explore many of the questions about the world around them and the place of humans in it, questions that continue to concern thinkers today. They developed ways of understanding and explaining the world around them, which grew into modern philosophy and science. They also created new political forms and new types of literature and art.

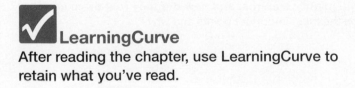

LearningCurve
After reading the chapter, use LearningCurve to
retain what you've read.

> How did the geography of Greece shape its earliest kingdoms?

> What was the role of the polis in Greek society?

> What were the causes and consequences of the major wars of the classical period?

> What were the lasting cultural and intellectual achievements of the classical period?

Religious Life in Hellenic Greece. This painted wooden slab from about 540 B.C.E., found in a cave near Corinth, shows adults and children about to sacrifice a sheep to the deities worshipped in this area. (De Agostini Picture Library/G. Dagli Orti/The Bridgeman Art Library)

> How did the geography of Greece shape its earliest kingdoms?

Mycenaean Dagger Blade
This scene in gold and silver on the blade of an iron dagger depicts hunters armed with spears and protected by shields defending themselves against charging lions. Judging by the number of hunting scenes in surviving Mycenaean art, the Mycenaeans seemed to enjoy the thrill and the danger of hunting. (National Archaeological Museum, Athens/Ancient Art & Architecture Collection/The Bridgeman Art Library)

DURING THE BRONZE AGE, which for Greek history is called the Helladic period, early settlers in Greece began establishing small communities. These communities sometimes joined together to form kingdoms, most prominently the Minoan kingdom on the island of Crete and the Mycenaean kingdom on the mainland. The Minoan and Mycenaean societies flourished for centuries until the Bronze Age Collapse, when Greece entered a period of decline known as the Dark Age (ca. 1100–800 B.C.E.). Epic poems composed by Homer and Hesiod after the Dark Age provide the poets' versions of what life may have been like in these early Greek kingdoms.

Geography and Settlement

Hellas, as the Greeks still call their land, encompassed the Greek peninsula, the islands of the Aegean (ah-GEE-uhn) Sea, and the lands bordering the Aegean, an area known as the Aegean basin (**Map 3.1**). Geography acts as an enormously divisive force in Greek life; mountains divide the land, and although there are good harbors on the sea, there are no navigable rivers. Much of the land is rocky and not very fertile, which meant that food availability was a constant concern.

The major regions of Greece were Thessaly and Macedonia in the north, and Boeotia (bee-OH-shuh) and the large island of Euboea (YOU-boh-ee-ah) in the center, lands marked by fertile plains that helped to sustain a strong population capable of serving as formidable cavalry and infantry. Immediately to the south of Boeotia was Attica, an area of thin soil in which olives and wine grapes flourished. Attica's harbors looked to the Aegean, which invited its inhabitants, the Athenians, to concentrate on maritime commerce. Still farther south, the Peloponnesus (peh-luh-puh-NEE-suhs), a large peninsula connected to the rest of mainland Greece by a very narrow isthmus at Corinth, was a patchwork of high

CHAPTER LOCATOR | How did the geography of Greece shape its earliest kingdoms?

3000 B.C.E.
- Bronze tools and weapons become common in Greece

ca. 1900 B.C.E.
- Minoan culture begins to thrive on Crete

ca. 1650 B.C.E.
- Mycenaean culture develops in Greece

ca. 1300–1100 B.C.E.
- Bronze Age Collapse; migration, destruction

ca. 1100–800 B.C.E.
- Dark Age; population declines; trade decreases; writing disappears

ca. 800–500 B.C.E.
- Archaic age; rise of the polis; Greek colonization of the Mediterranean; Homer and Hesiod compose epics and poetry

ca. 750–500 B.C.E.
- Sparta expands and develops a military state

ca. 600–500 B.C.E.
- Political reforms in Archaic Athens

ca. 600–450 B.C.E.
- Pre-Socratics develop ideas about the nature of the universe

500–338 B.C.E.
- Classical period; development of drama, philosophy, and major building projects in Athens

499–479 B.C.E.
- Persian wars

431–404 B.C.E.
- Peloponnesian War

427–347 B.C.E.
- Life of Plato

384–322 B.C.E.
- Life of Aristotle

371–362 B.C.E.
- Thebes, with an alliance of city-states, rules Greece

338 B.C.E.
- Philip II of Macedonia gains control of Greece

mountains and small plains that divided the area into several regions. Beyond the coast, the islands of the Aegean served as stepping-stones to Anatolia.

The geographical fragmentation of Greece encouraged political fragmentation. Communications were poor, with rocky tracks far more common than roads. Early in Greek history, several kingdoms did emerge, but the rugged terrain prohibited the growth of a great empire like those of Mesopotamia or Egypt. Instead tiny states became the most common form of government.

The Minoans

On the large island of Crete, Bronze Age farmers and fishermen began to trade their surpluses with their neighbors, and cities grew, housing artisans and merchants. Beginning about 2000 B.C.E., Cretan traders voyaged throughout the eastern Mediterranean and the Aegean. Social hierarchies developed, and in many cities certain individuals came to hold power. The Cretans began to use writing about 1900 B.C.E., in a form later scholars called Linear A. This has not been deciphered, but scholars know that the language of Crete was not related to Greek, so they do not consider the Cretans "Greek."

At about the same time that writing began, rulers in several cities of Crete began to build large structures with hundreds of interconnected rooms. The largest of these, at Knossos (NOH-suhs), has over a thousand rooms, with pipes for bringing in drinking water and sewers to get rid of waste. The archaeologists who discovered these huge structures called them "palaces," and they named

What was the role of the polis in Greek society? | What were the causes and consequences of the major wars of the classical period? | What were the lasting cultural and intellectual achievements of the classical period? | ☑ LearningCurve Check what you know.

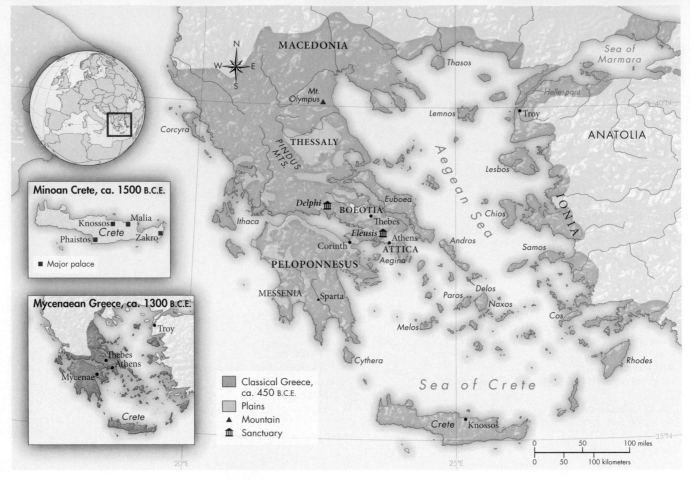

MAP 3.1 ■ Classical Greece, 500–338 B.C.E.

In antiquity, the home of the Greeks included the islands of the Aegean and the western shore of Turkey as well as the Greek peninsula itself. Crete, the home of Minoan civilization, is the large island at the bottom of the map.

Minoan

▶ A wealthy and vibrant culture on Crete from around 1900 B.C.E. to 1450 B.C.E., ruled by a king with a large palace at Knossos.

the flourishing and vibrant culture of this era **Minoan**, after a mythical king of Crete, Minos.

Few specifics are known about Minoan political life except that a king and a group of nobles stood at its head. Minoan life was long thought to have been relatively peaceful, but new excavations are revealing more and more walls around cities, which has called the peaceful nature of Minoan society into question. In terms of their religious life, Minoans appear to have worshipped goddesses far more than gods. Whether this translated into more egalitarian gender roles for real people is unclear, but surviving Minoan art shows women as well as men leading religious activities, watching entertainment, and engaging in athletic competitions.

Beginning about 1700 B.C.E. Minoan society was disrupted by a series of earthquakes and volcanic eruptions on nearby islands, some of which resulted in large tsunamis. The largest of these was a huge volcanic eruption that devastated the island of Thera to the north of Crete. The eruption on Thera was long seen as the most important cause of the collapse of Minoan civilization, but recent scholars have called this theory into question. The eruption seems to have occurred somewhat earlier than 1600 B.C.E., and Minoan society did not collapse until more than two centuries later.

CHAPTER LOCATOR | How did the geography of Greece shape its earliest kingdoms?

The Mycenaeans

As Minoan culture was flourishing on Crete, a different type of society developed on the mainland. This society was founded by groups who had migrated there during the period after 2000 B.C.E. By about 1650 B.C.E., one group of these immigrants had raised palaces and established cities at Thebes, Athens, Mycenae (migh-SEE-nee), and elsewhere. These palace-centers ruled by local kings formed a loose hegemony under the authority of the king of Mycenae, and the archaeologists who first discovered traces of this culture called it **Mycenaean** (migh-see-NEE-an).

As in Crete, the political unit in Mycenaean Greece was the kingdom, and the king and his warrior aristocracy stood at the top of society. The seat and symbol of the king's power was his palace, which was also the economic center of the kingdom. Within the palace's walls, royal artisans fashioned gold jewelry and rich ornaments, made pottery, forged weapons, prepared hides and wool for clothing, and manufactured the other goods needed by the king and his supporters. The Mycenaean economy was marked by an extensive division of labor, and at the bottom of the social scale were male and female slaves.

Palace scribes kept records with a script known as Linear B, which scholars realized was an early form of Greek and have learned to read. Thus, they consider the Mycenaeans the first truly "Greek" culture to emerge in this area. Information on Mycenaean culture comes through inscriptions and other forms of written records as well as buildings and other objects. All of these point to a society in which war was common. Mycenaean cities were all fortified by thick stone walls, and graves contain bronze spears, javelins, swords, helmets, and the first examples of metal armor known in the world. Mycenaean kingdoms appear to have fought regularly with one another.

Contacts between the Minoans and Mycenaeans were originally peaceful, and Minoan culture and trade goods flooded the Greek mainland. But most scholars think that around 1450 B.C.E., the Mycenaeans attacked Crete, destroying many towns and occupying Knossos. For about the next fifty years, the Mycenaeans ruled much of the island. The palaces at Knossos and other cities of the Aegean became grander as wealth gained through trade and tribute flowed into the treasuries of various Mycenaean kings.

Prosperity did not bring peace, however; between 1300 and 1100 B.C.E., various kingdoms in and beyond Greece ravaged one another in a savage series of wars that destroyed both the Minoan and Mycenaean civilizations. Among these wars was perhaps one that later became known as the Trojan War, fought by Greeks in Ionia.

The fall of the Minoans and Mycenaeans was part of what scholars see as a general collapse of Bronze Age civilizations in the eastern Mediterranean (see Chapters 1 and 2). This collapse appears to have had a number of causes: internal economic and social problems; invasions and migrations by outsiders, who destroyed cities and disrupted trade and production; changes in warfare and weaponry, particularly the adoption of iron weapons, which made foot soldiers the most important factor in battles and reduced the power of kings and wealthy nobles fighting from chariots; and natural disasters, which reduced the amount of food and contributed to famines. These factors worked together to usher in a period of poverty and disruption that historians of Greece have traditionally called the Dark Age (ca. 1100–800 B.C.E.).

Mycenaean

▶ A Bronze Age culture that flourished in Greece from about 1650 B.C.E. to 1100 B.C.E., building fortified palaces and cities.

What was the role of the polis in Greek society?

What were the causes and consequences of the major wars of the classical period?

What were the lasting cultural and intellectual achievements of the classical period?

☑ LearningCurve
Check what you know.

63

The Bronze Age Collapse led to the widespread and prolonged movement of Greek peoples, both within Greece itself and beyond. They dispersed beyond mainland Greece farther south to the islands of the Aegean and in greater strength across the Aegean to the shores of Anatolia, arriving at a time when traditional states and empires had collapsed. By the conclusion of the Dark Age, the Greeks had spread their culture throughout the Aegean basin and, like many other cultures around the Mediterranean and the Near East, they had adopted iron.

Homer, Hesiod, and the Epic

Archaeological sources from the Dark Age are less rich than those from the periods that came after, and so they are often used in conjunction with literary sources written in later centuries to give us a more complete picture of the era. Unlike the Hebrews, the Greeks had no sacred book that chronicled their past. Instead they had epics, poetic tales of legendary heroes and of the times when people believed the gods still walked the earth. Of these, the *Iliad* and the *Odyssey* are the most important. Most scholars think they were composed in the eighth or seventh century B.C.E.

The *Iliad* recounts the tale of the Trojan War of the late Bronze Age. As Homer tells it, the Achaeans (uh-KEE-uhnz), the name he gives to the Mycenaeans, sent an expedition to besiege the city of Troy and to retrieve Helen, who was abducted by Paris, the Trojan king's son. The heart of the *Iliad*, however, concerns the quarrel between the Mycenaean king, Agamemnon, and the stormy hero of the poem, Achilles (uh-KIHL-eez), and how this brought suffering to the Achaeans.

Homer's *Odyssey* recounts the adventures of Odysseus (oh-DIH-see-uhs), a wise and fearless hero of the war at Troy, during his ten-year voyage home. He encounters many dangers, storms, and adventures, but he finally reaches his home and unites again with Penelope, the ideal wife, dedicated to her husband and family.

Both of Homer's epics portray engaging but flawed characters who are larger than life yet human. The men and women at the center of the stories display the quality known as *arête* (ah-reh-TAY), that is, excellence and living up to one's fullest potential. Homer was also strikingly successful in depicting the great gods and goddesses, who generally sit on Mount Olympus in the north of Greece and watch the fighting at Troy, although they sometimes participate in the action.

Greeks also learned about the origin and descent of the gods and goddesses of their polytheistic system from another poet, Hesiod (HEH-see-uhd), who most scholars think lived sometime between 750 and 650 B.C.E. Hesiod made the gods the focus of his poem, the *Theogony*. By combining Mesopotamian myths with a variety of Greek oral traditions, Hesiod forged a coherent story of the origin of the gods. In another of Hesiod's poems, *Works and Days*, the gods watch over the earth, looking for justice and injustice, while leaving the great mass of men and women to live lives of hard work and endless toil.

> **QUICK REVIEW**

What factors contributed to the decline of Minoan and Mycenaean society?

CHAPTER LOCATOR | How did the geography of Greece shape its earliest kingdoms?

CHAPTER 3
64   THE DEVELOPMENT OF GREEK SOCIETY AND CULTURE

What was the role of the polis in Greek society?

Spartan Hoplite

This bronze figurine portrays an armed foot soldier about to strike an enemy. His massive helmet with its full crest gives his head nearly complete protection, while a metal corselet covers his chest and back, and greaves (similar to today's shin guards) protect his lower legs. In his right hand he carries a thrusting spear (now broken off), and in his left a large, round shield. (bpk, Berlin/Antikensammlung, Staatliche Museen/Johannes Laurentius/Art Resource, NY)

HOMER AND HESIOD both lived in the era after the Dark Age, which later historians have termed the Archaic age (800–500 B.C.E.). The most important political change in this period was the development of the **polis** (PAH-luhs; plural *poleis*), a word generally translated as "city-state." With the polis, the Greeks established a new type of political structure. During the Archaic period, poleis established colonies throughout much of the Mediterranean, spreading Greek culture. Two particular poleis, each with a distinctive system of government, rose to prominence on the Greek mainland: Sparta and Athens.

polis
▶ Generally translated as "city-state," it was the basic political and institutional unit of Greece in the Hellenic period.

Organization of the Polis

The Greek polis was not the first form of city-state to emerge. The earliest states in Sumer were also city-states, as were many of the small Mycenaean kingdoms. What differentiated the new Greek model from older city-states is the fact that the

What was the role of the polis in Greek society?	What were the causes and consequences of the major wars of the classical period?	What were the lasting cultural and intellectual achievements of the classical period?	 LearningCurve Check what you know.

polis was more than a political institution; it was a community of citizens with their own customs and laws. With one exception, the poleis that emerged after 800 did not have kings but instead were self-governing. The physical, religious, and political forms of the polis varied from place to place, but everywhere the polis was relatively small, reflecting the fragmented geography of Greece. The very smallness of the polis enabled Greeks to see how they fit individually into the overall system—and how the individual parts made up the social whole. This notion of community was fundamental to the polis and was the very badge of Greekness.

Poleis developed from Dark Age towns. When fully developed, each polis normally shared a surprisingly large number of features with other poleis. Physically a polis was a society of people who lived in a city (*asty*) and cultivated the surrounding countryside (*chora*). The countryside was essential to the economy of the polis and provided food to sustain the entire population. By the fifth century B.C.E., the city was generally surrounded by a wall. The city contained a point, usually elevated, called the acropolis, and a public square or marketplace called the agora (ah-guh-RAH). On the acropolis, people built temples, altars, public monuments, and various dedications to the gods of the polis. The agora was the political center of the polis. In the agora were shops, public buildings, and courts.

All poleis, with one exception, did not have standing armies. Instead they relied on their citizens for protection. Wealthy aristocrats often served as cavalry. The backbone of the army, however, was the heavily armed infantry, or **hoplites**, ordinary citizens rather than members of the elite.

hoplites
▶ Heavily armed citizens who served as infantry troops and fought to defend the polis.

Governing Structures

Each Greek polis had one of several different types of government. Monarchy, rule by a king, had been prevalent during the Mycenaean period but declined thereafter. Sporadic periods of violent political and social upheaval often led to the seizure of power by one man, a type of government the Greeks called **tyranny**. Tyrants generally came to power by using their wealth or by negotiating to win a political following that toppled the existing legal government. In contrast to its contemporary meaning, however, tyranny in ancient Greece did not necessarily mean oppressive rule. Some tyrants used their power to benefit average citizens by helping to limit the power of the landowning aristocracy, which made them popular.

Other types of government in the Archaic age were democracy and oligarchy. **Democracy** translates as "the power of the people" but was actually rule by citizens, not the people as a whole. Almost all Greek cities defined a citizen as an adult man with at least one or, at some times and places, two citizen parents. Women were citizens for religious and reproductive purposes, but their citizenship did not give them the right to participate in government. Free men who were not children of a citizen, resident foreigners, and slaves were not citizens and had no political voice.

Oligarchy, which literally means "the rule of the few," was government by citizens who met a minimum property requirement. Many Greeks preferred oligarchy because it provided more political stability than democracy did. Although oligarchy was the government of the prosperous, it left the door open to political and

tyranny
▶ Rule by one man who took over an existing government, generally by using his wealth to gain a political following.

democracy
▶ A type of Greek government in which all citizens administered the workings of government.

oligarchy
▶ A type of Greek government in which citizens who owned a certain amount of property ruled.

social advancement. If members of the polis obtained enough wealth to meet property or money qualifications, they could enter the governing circle.

Overseas Expansion

The development of the polis coincided with the growth of the Greek world in both wealth and numbers, which brought new problems. The increase in population created more demand for food than the land could supply. The resulting social and political tensions drove many people to seek new homes outside Greece.

Greeks from the mainland and Ionia traveled throughout the Mediterranean, sailing in great numbers to Sicily and southern Italy, where there was ample space for expansion (**Map 3.2**). Here they established prosperous cities and often intermarried with local people. Some adventurous Greeks sailed farther west to Sardinia, France, Spain, and perhaps even the Canary Islands. In Sardinia they first established trading stations and then permanent towns. From these new outposts Greek influence extended to southern France.

Colonization changed the entire Greek world, both at home and abroad. In economic terms the expansion of the Greeks created a much larger market for agricultural and manufactured goods. From the east, especially from the northern coast of the Black Sea, came wheat. In return flowed Greek wine and olive

MAP 3.2 ■ Greek Colonization, ca. 750–550 B.C.E.

The Greeks established colonies along the shores of the Mediterranean and the Black Sea, spreading Greek culture and creating a large trading network.

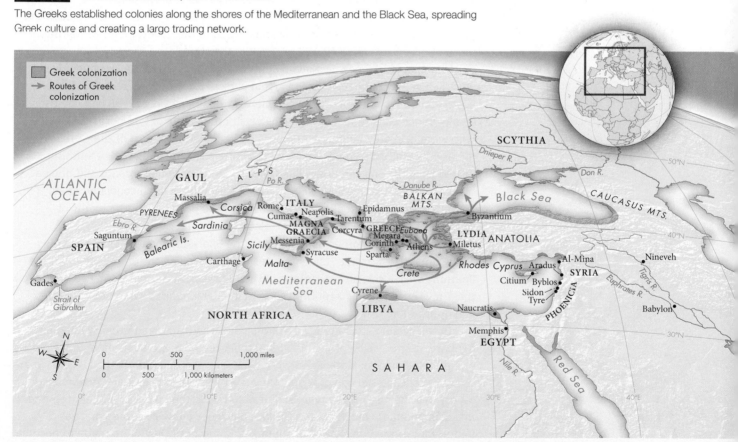

| What was the role of the polis in Greek society? | What were the causes and consequences of the major wars of the classical period? | What were the lasting cultural and intellectual achievements of the classical period? | ✔ LearningCurve Check what you know. |

67

oil, which could not be produced in the harsher climate of the north. Greek-manufactured goods circulated from southern Russia to Spain. During the same period the Greeks adopted the custom of minting coins from metal.

New colonies were planned and initially supplied by the *metropolis,* or "mother city." Once founded, however, they were independent of the metropolis, a pattern that was quite different from most later systems of colonization. Colonization spread the polis and its values far beyond the shores of Greece.

The Growth of Sparta

Many different poleis developed during the Archaic period, but Sparta became the leading military power in Greece. To expand their polis, the Spartans did not establish colonies but set out in about 750 B.C.E. to conquer Messenia (muh-SEE-nee-uh), a rich, fertile region in the southwestern Peloponnesus. This conflict, called the First Messenian War by later Greek historians, lasted for twenty years and ended in a Spartan triumph. The Spartans appropriated Messenian land and turned the Messenians into **helots** (HEH-luhts), unfree residents forced to work state lands.

In about 650 B.C.E., Spartan exploitation and oppression of the Messenian helots, along with Sparta's defeat at the hands of a rival polis, led to a massive helot revolt that became known as the Second Messenian War. After some thirty years of fighting, the Spartans put down the revolt. Nevertheless, the political and social strain it caused led to a transformation of the Spartan polis. After the war, non-nobles who had shared in the fighting as hoplites appear to have demanded rights equal to those of the nobility and a voice in the government. Under intense pressure, the aristocrats agreed to remodel the state into a new system.

The plan for the new system in Sparta was attributed to the lawgiver Lycurgus, who may or may not have been an actual person. According to later Greek sources, political distinctions among Spartan men were eliminated, and all citizens became legally equal. Governance of the polis was in the hands of two hereditary kings who were primarily military leaders. The kings were also part of the *Gerousia* (jeh-roo-SEE-ah), a council of men who had reached the age of sixty and thus retired from the Spartan army. The Gerousia deliberated on foreign and domestic matters and prepared legislation for the assembly, which consisted of all Spartan citizens. The real executive power of the polis was in the hands of five ephors (EH-fuhrs), or overseers, elected from and by all the citizens.

To provide for their economic needs, the Spartans divided the land of Messenia among all citizens. Helots worked the land, raised the crops, provided the Spartans with a certain percentage of their harvest, and occasionally served in the army. The Spartans kept the helots in line by means of systematic brutality and oppression.

In the system attributed to Lycurgus, every citizen owed primary allegiance to Sparta. Suppression of the individual together with emphasis on military prowess led to a barracks state. Family life itself was sacrificed to the polis. Once Spartan boys reached the age of seven, they were enrolled in separate companies with other boys their age. They were required to live in the barracks and eat together in a common mess hall until age thirty. They slept outside on reed mats and underwent rugged physical and military training until they were ready to become

helots
▶ Unfree residents of Sparta forced to work state lands.

Spartan Expansion, ca. 750–500 B.C.E.

■ Spartan homeland
□ Annexed lands
□ Spartan allies

frontline soldiers. For the rest of their lives, Spartan men kept themselves prepared for combat.

Spartans expected women in citizen families to be good wives and strict mothers of future soldiers. They were prohibited from wearing jewelry or ornate clothes. They, too, were supposed to exercise strenuously in the belief that hard physical training promoted the birth of healthy children. Yet Spartan women were freer than many other Greek women. With men in military service much of their lives, women in citizen families owned land and ran the estates and were not physically restricted or secluded.

Along with the emphasis on military values for both sexes, the Spartan system served to instill in society the civic virtues of dedication to the state and a code of moral conduct. These aspects of Spartan society, along with Spartan military successes, were generally admired throughout the Greek world.

The Evolution of Athens

Like Sparta, Athens faced pressing social, economic, and political problems during the Archaic period, but the Athenian response was far different from that of the Spartans. Instead of creating a state devoted to the military, the Athenians created a state that became a democracy.

For Athens, the late seventh century B.C.E. was a time of turmoil, the causes of which are unclear. In 621 B.C.E., Draco (DRAY-koh), an Athenian aristocrat, under pressure from small landholders and with the consent of the nobles, published the first law code of the Athenian polis. His code was harsh, but it embodied the ideal that the law belonged to all citizens. The aristocracy still governed Athens oppressively, however, and the social and economic situation remained dire. Despite Draco's code, noble landholders continued to force small farmers and artisans into economic dependence. Many families were sold into slavery because of debt; others were exiled, and their land was mortgaged to the rich.

One person who recognized these problems clearly was Solon (SOH-luhn), an aristocrat and poet. Reciting his poems in the Athenian agora, where anyone could hear his call for justice and fairness, Solon condemned his fellow aristocrats for their greed and dishonesty. According to later sources, Solon's sincerity and good sense convinced other aristocrats that he was no crazed revolutionary. He also gained the trust of the common people, whose problems provoked them to demand access to political life, much as commoners in Sparta had. Around 594 B.C.E., the nobles elected Solon chief *archon* (AHR-kahn), or magistrate of the Athenian polis, with authority over legal, civic, and military issues.

Solon immediately freed all people enslaved for debt, recalled all exiles, canceled all debts on land, and made enslavement for debt illegal. Solon allowed non-nobles into the old aristocratic assembly, where they could take part in the election of magistrates, including the annual election of the city's nine archons.

Although Solon's reforms solved some immediate problems, they did not satisfy either the aristocrats or the common people completely, and they did not bring peace to Athens. During the sixth century B.C.E., the successful general Pisistratus (pih-SIHS-trah-tuhs) declared himself tyrant. Under his rule, Athens prospered, and his building program began to transform the city into one of the splendors of Greece. He raised the civic consciousness and prestige of the polis by

| What was the role of the polis in Greek society? | What were the causes and consequences of the major wars of the classical period? | What were the lasting cultural and intellectual achievements of the classical period? | ✓ LearningCurve Check what you know. |

69

instituting new cultural festivals that brought people together. Although he had taken over control of the city by force, his reign as tyrant weakened the power of aristocratic families and aroused rudimentary feelings of equality in many Athenian men.

Athens became more democratic under the leadership of Cleisthenes (KLIE-thuh-neez), a wealthy and prominent aristocrat who had won the support of lower-status men and became the leader of Athens in 508 B.C.E. Cleisthenes created the *deme* (deem), a unit of land that kept the roll of citizens, or *demos*, within its jurisdiction. Men enrolled as citizens through their deme instead of through their family group, which brought people of different families together and promoted community and democracy. The demes were grouped into ten tribes, which thus formed the link between the demes and the central government. Each tribe elected a military leader, or *strategos* (plural *strategoi*).

The democracy functioned on the idea that all full citizens were sovereign. In 487 B.C.E., the election of the city's nine archons was replaced by reappointment by lot, which meant that any citizen with a certain amount of property had a chance of becoming an archon. This system gave citizens prestige, although the power of the archons gradually dwindled as the strategoi became the real military leaders of the city. Legislation was in the hands of two bodies, the *boule* (boo-LAY), or council, composed of five hundred members, and the *ecclesia* (ek-lay-SEE-yah), the assembly of all citizens. By supervising the various committees of government and proposing bills to the ecclesia, the boule guided Athenian political life. Nonetheless, the ecclesia had the final word. Open to all male citizens over eighteen years of age, it met at a specific place to vote on matters presented to it.

> **QUICK REVIEW**

Why was the relatively small size of the Greek polis a key to its success as a social and political institution?

CHAPTER LOCATOR | How did the geography of Greece shape its earliest kingdoms?

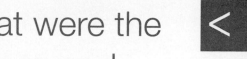

What were the causes and consequences of the major wars of the classical period?

Golden Comb This golden comb, produced about 400 B.C.E. in Scythia (see Map 3.2, page 67), shows a battle among three warriors, perhaps the three brothers who are the legendary founders of Scythia. Their dress shows a combination of Greek and Eastern details; the mounted horseman is clothed with largely Greek armor, while the warriors on foot are wearing Eastern dress. (Hermitage, St. Petersburg, Russia/Bridgeman Images)

FROM THE TIME OF THE MYCENAEANS, violent conflict was common in Greek society, and this did not change in the fifth century B.C.E., the beginning of what scholars later called the classical period of Greek history, which they date from about 500 B.C.E. to the conquest of Greece by Philip of Macedon in 338 B.C.E. First, the Greeks beat back the armies of the Persian Empire. Then, turning their spears against one another, they destroyed their own political system in a century of warfare culminating in the Peloponnesian War. This war and its aftermath proved that the polis had reached the limits of its success as an effective political institution. The Greeks' failure to unify against outsiders led to the rise of a dominant new power: the kingdom of Macedonia.

The Persian Wars

In 499 B.C.E., the Greeks who lived in Ionia rebelled unsuccessfully against the Persian Empire, which had ruled the area for fifty years (see Chapter 2). The Athenians had provided halfhearted help to the Ionians in this failed rebellion, and in 490 B.C.E., the Persians retaliated against Athens, only to be defeated by the Athenian hoplites at the Battle of Marathon.

In 480 B.C.E., the Persian king Xerxes I (r. 485–465 B.C.E.) personally led a massive invasion of Greece. Under the leadership of Sparta, many, though not all, Greek poleis joined together to fight the Persians. The first confrontations between the Persians and the Greeks occurred at the pass of Thermopylae (thuhr-MAWP-uh-lee), where an outnumbered Greek army, including three hundred top Spartan warriors, held off a much larger Persian force for several days. The Greeks at Thermopylae fought heroically, but the Persians won the battle and subsequently occupied and sacked Athens.

The Persian Wars, 499–479 B.C.E.

- Areas of Persian control
- Greek states at war with Persia
- Neutral Greek states

Thermopylae 480 B.C.E.
Artemisium 480 B.C.E.
Plataea 479 B.C.E.
Salamis 480 B.C.E.
Marathon 490 B.C.E.
Crete

What was the role of the polis in Greek society?

What were the causes and consequences of the major wars of the classical period?

What were the lasting cultural and intellectual achievements of the classical period?

✓ LearningCurve
Check what you know.

71

At the same time as the land battle of Thermopylae, Greeks and Persians fought one another in a naval battle at Artemisium off Boetia. The Athenians, led by the general Themistocles, provided the heart of the naval forces with their fleet of triremes, or oar-propelled warships. Storms had wrecked many Persian ships, and neither side won a decisive victory. Only a month or so later, the Greek fleet met the Persian armada at Salamis, an island across from Athens. Though outnumbered, the Greek navy won an overwhelming victory by outmaneuvering the Persians. The remnants of the Persian fleet retired, and in 479 B.C.E., the Greeks overwhelmed the Persian army at Plataea. By defeating the Persians, the Greeks ensured that they would not be ruled by a foreign power.

Growth of the Athenian Empire

The defeat of the Persians created a power vacuum in the Aegean, and the Athenians took advantage of the situation. Led by Themistocles, the Athenians and their allies formed the **Delian League**, a military alliance aimed at protecting the Aegean Islands, liberating Ionia from Persian rule, and keeping the Persians out of Greece. The Delian (DEE-lee-uhn) League was intended to be a free alliance under the leadership of Athens, but as the Athenians drove the Persians out of the Aegean, they also became increasingly imperialistic. Athens began reducing its allies to the status of subjects. Tribute was often collected by force, and the Athenians placed the economic resources of the Delian League under tighter and tighter control. Major allies revolted, and they were put down because the Athenian ideas of freedom and democracy did not extend to the citizens of other cities.

The aggressiveness of Athenian rule also alarmed Sparta and its allies. Relations between Athens and Sparta grew more hostile, particularly when Pericles (PEHR-uh-kleez) (ca. 494–429 B.C.E.), an aristocrat of solid intellectual ability, became the leading statesman in Athens. Like the democracy he led, Pericles was aggressive and imperialistic. In 459 B.C.E., Sparta and Athens went to war over conflicts between Athens and some of Sparta's allies. The war ended in 445 B.C.E with a treaty promising thirty years of peace, and no serious damage to either side. The treaty divided the Greek world between the two great powers, with each agreeing to respect the other and its allies.

Peace lasted thirteen years instead of thirty. Athens continued its severe policies toward its subject allies and came into conflict with Corinth, one of Sparta's leading supporters. In this climate of anger and escalation, Pericles decided to punish the city of Megara, which had switched allegiance from Sparta to Athens and then back again. In 432 B.C.E., Pericles persuaded the Athenians to pass a law that excluded the Megarians from trading with Athens and its empire. In response the Spartans and their allies declared war.

The Peloponnesian War

The Peloponnesian War lasted a generation and brought in its wake disease, famine, civil wars, widespread destruction, and huge loss of life (**Map 3.3**). During the first Spartan invasion of Attica, which began in 431 B.C.E., cramped conditions within the walls of Athens nurtured a dreadful plague that killed huge numbers, eventually claiming Pericles himself. The death of Pericles opened the door to a new breed of politicians, men who were rash, ambitious, and more dedicated to themselves than to Athens. Under the non-aristocratic Cleon, the Athenians coun-

Delian League

▶ A military alliance led by Athens whose aims were to protect the Aegean Islands, liberate Ionia from Persian rule, and keep the Persians out of Greece.

Delian League

Allied with Delian League, 446 B.C.E.

• Athenian military settlement

Thasos

Corcyra

PERSIAN EMPIRE

BEOETIA

Megara Athens

Corinth Delos

Sparta

The Delian League, ca. 478–431 B.C.E.

CHAPTER LOCATOR | How did the geography of Greece shape its earliest kingdoms?

CHAPTER 3

72 THE DEVELOPMENT OF GREEK SOCIETY AND CULTURE

MAP 3.3 ■ The Peloponnesian War, 431–404 B.C.E.

This map shows the alignment of states during the Peloponnesian War.

> MAPPING THE PAST

ANALYZING THE MAP: How would you compare the area controlled by Sparta and its allies to that of Athens and its allies? How would you expect these similarities and/or differences to affect the way that each side chose to conduct its military campaigns?

CONNECTIONS: What does the location of the major battles and sieges suggest about the impact of the war throughout Greece?

terattacked and defeated the Spartans, though Cleon was killed. Recognizing that ten years of war had resulted only in death, destruction, and stalemate, Sparta and Athens concluded the Peace of Nicias (NIH-shee-uhs) in 421 B.C.E.

The Peace of Nicias resulted in a cold war. But even cold war can bring horror and misery. Such was the case when, in 416 B.C.E., the Athenians sent a fleet to the largely neutral island of Melos with an ultimatum: the Melians could surrender or perish. The Melians resisted. The Athenians conquered them, killed the men of military age, and sold the women and children into slavery.

The cold war grew hotter, thanks to the ambitions of Alcibiades (al-suh-BIE-uh-dees) (ca. 450–404 B.C.E.), an aristocrat and a kinsman of Pericles. A shameless opportunist, Alcibiades widened the war to further his own career and increase the power of Athens. He convinced the Athenians to attack Syracuse, the leading polis in Sicily. This action would cut off the grain supply from Sicily to Sparta and its allies, allowing Athens to end the war and become the greatest power in Greece. The undertaking was vast, requiring an enormous fleet and thousands of sailors and soldiers, and it ended in disaster.

The disaster in Sicily ushered in the final phase of the war, which was marked by three major developments: the renewal of war between Athens and Sparta, Persia's intervention in the war, and the revolt of many Athenian subjects. The year 413 B.C.E. saw Sparta's declaration of war against Athens and widespread revolt within the Athenian Empire. The Persians threw their support behind Sparta and built a fleet of ships for them; in exchange they expected Ionia to be returned to them once the Spartans were successful. Now equipped with a fleet, the Spartans challenged the Athenians in the Aegean, and a long series of inconclusive naval battles followed.

| What was the role of the polis in Greek society? | **What were the causes and consequences of the major wars of the classical period?** | What were the lasting cultural and intellectual achievements of the classical period? | ✔️ LearningCurve Check what you know. |

In 405 B.C.E., Spartan forces destroyed the last Athenian fleet at the Battle of Aegospotami, after which the Spartans blockaded Athens until it was starved into submission. In 404 B.C.E., after twenty-seven years of fighting, the Peloponnesian War was over.

The Struggle for Dominance

The decades after the end of the Peloponnesian War were turbulent ones. The chief states—Sparta, Athens, and Thebes—each tried to create a political system in which it would dominate. When Athens surrendered to Sparta in 404 B.C.E., the Spartans used their victory to build an empire. Their decision brought them into conflict with Persia, which now demanded the return of Ionia to its control, as Sparta had promised earlier. From 400 to 386 B.C.E., the Spartans fought the Persians for Ionia, a conflict that eventually engulfed Greece itself. After years of stalemate the Spartans made peace with Persia and their own Greek enemies. The result was a treaty, the King's Peace of 386 B.C.E., in which the Greeks and Persians pledged themselves to live in harmony. This agreement cost Sparta its empire but not its position of dominance in Greece.

The Spartans were not long content with this situation, however, and decided to punish cities that had opposed Sparta during the war. In 378 B.C.E., the Spartans launched an unprovoked attack on Athens. Together the Thebans and the Athenians created what was called the Second Athenian Confederacy, a federation of states to guarantee the terms of the peace treaty. The two fought Sparta until 371 B.C.E., when, due to growing fear of Theban might, Athens made a separate peace with Sparta. Left alone, Thebes defended itself until later that year, when the Thebans routed the Spartan army on the small plain of Leuctra and, in a series of invasions, eliminated Sparta as a major power.

Philip II and Macedonian Supremacy

While the Greek states exhausted themselves in endless conflicts, the new power of Macedonia arose in the north. The kings of Macedonia slowly built up their power over rival states, and in 359 B.C.E., the brilliant and cultured Philip II ascended to the throne. With decades of effort he secured the borders of Macedonia against invaders from the north, and he then launched a series of military operations in the northwestern Aegean. By clever use of his wealth and superb army, he gained control of the area, and in 338 B.C.E., he won a decisive victory over Thebes and Athens that gave him command of Greece. Because the Greeks could not put aside their quarrels, they fell to an invader, and 338 B.C.E. is often seen as marking the end of the classical period.

After his victory, Philip led a combined army of soldiers from Macedonia and from many Greek states in an attempt to liberate the Ionian Greeks from Persian rule. Before he could launch this campaign, however, Philip fell to an assassin's dagger in 336 B.C.E. His young son Alexander vowed to carry on Philip's mission. He would succeed beyond all expectations.

> **QUICK REVIEW**

How did the wars of the classical period shape Greek history?

CHAPTER LOCATOR | How did the geography of Greece shape its earliest kingdoms?

What were the lasting cultural and intellectual achievements of the classical period?

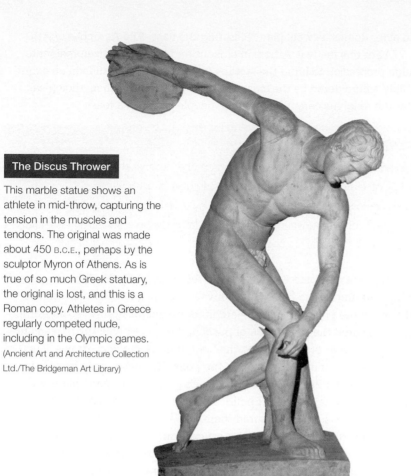

The Discus Thrower

This marble statue shows an athlete in mid-throw, capturing the tension in the muscles and tendons. The original was made about 450 B.C.E., perhaps by the sculptor Myron of Athens. As is true of so much Greek statuary, the original is lost, and this is a Roman copy. Athletes in Greece regularly competed nude, including in the Olympic games. (Ancient Art and Architecture Collection Ltd./The Bridgeman Art Library)

DESPITE THE VIOLENCE THAT DOMINATED GREECE for nearly two centuries beginning in 500 B.C.E., or to some degree because of it, playwrights and thinkers pondered the meaning of the universe and the role of humans in it, and artists and architects created new styles to celebrate Greek achievements. Although warfare was one of the hallmarks of the classical period, intellectual and artistic accomplishments were as well.

Athenian Arts in the Age of Pericles

In the midst of the warfare of the fifth century B.C.E., Pericles turned Athens into the showplace of Greece. He appropriated Delian League funds to pay for a huge building program. Workers erected temples and other buildings as patriotic memorials housing statues and carvings, often painted in bright colors, showing the gods in human form and celebrating the Greek victory over the Persians. Many of the temples were built on the high, rocky Acropolis that stood in the center of the city.

The Athenians normally hiked up the long approach to the Acropolis only for religious festivals, of which the most important and joyous was the Great Panathenaea, held every four years to honor the virgin goddess Athena and perhaps offer

What was the role of the polis in Greek society?　　What were the causes and consequences of the major wars of the classical period?　　**What were the lasting cultural and intellectual achievements of the classical period?**　　✓ LearningCurve Check what you know.

75

sacrifices to older deities as well. (See "Picturing the Past: The Acropolis of Athens," page 77.) For this festival, Athenian citizens and legal noncitizen residents formed a huge procession to bring the statue of Athena in the Parthenon an exquisite robe, richly embroidered by the citizen women of Athens with mythological scenes. After the religious ceremonies, all the people joined in a feast.

> The Great Panathenaea Procession

- Led by an aristocratic young woman carrying an offering basket
- Followed by other richly dressed women carrying gold or silver vessels
- Young men on horseback came next, followed by older men carrying staffs
- Toward the rear came other young men carrying large pitchers or leading sacrificial bulls

The development of drama was tied to the religious festivals of the city, especially those celebrating the god of wine, Dionysus (see page 82). Drama was as rooted in the life of the polis as were the architecture and sculpture of the Acropolis. The polis sponsored the production of plays and required wealthy citizens to pay the expenses of their production. At the beginning of the year, dramatists submitted their plays to the chief archon of the polis. He chose those he considered best and assigned a theatrical troupe to each playwright. Many plays were highly controversial, containing overt political and social commentary, but the archons neither suppressed nor censored them.

Not surprisingly, given the incessant warfare, conflict was a constant element in Athenian drama, and playwrights used their art in attempts to portray, understand, and resolve life's basic conflicts. The Athenian dramatists examined questions about the relationship between humans and the gods, the demands of society on the individual, and the nature of good and evil. Aeschylus (EHS-kuh-lihs) (525–456 B.C.E.), the first of the great Athenian dramatists, was also the first to express the agony of the individual caught in conflict. In his trilogy of plays, *The Oresteia* (ohr-eh-STEE-uh), Aeschylus deals with the themes of betrayal, murder, and reconciliation, urging that reason and justice be applied to reconcile fundamental conflicts.

Sophocles (SOF-uh-klees) (496–406 B.C.E.) also dealt with matters personal and political. Perhaps his most famous plays are *Oedipus* (EHD-uh-puhs) *the King* and its sequel, *Oedipus at Colonus. Oedipus the King* is the tragic story of a man doomed by the gods to kill his father and marry his mother. Try as he might to avoid his fate, his every action brings him closer to its fulfillment. When at last he realizes that he has unwittingly carried out the decree of the gods, Oedipus blinds himself and flees into exile. In *Oedipus at Colonus*, Sophocles dramatizes the last days of the broken king, whose patient suffering and uncomplaining piety win him an exalted position. In the end, the gods honor him for his virtue.

With Euripides (you-RIHP-uh-dees) (ca. 480–406 B.C.E.), drama entered a new and, in many ways, more personal phase. To him the gods were far less important than human beings. The essence of Euripides's tragedy is the flawed character— men and women who bring disaster on themselves and their loved ones because their passions overwhelm reason.

Writers of comedy treated the affairs of the polis and its politicians bawdily and often coarsely. Even so, their plays were also performed at religious festivals.

The Acropolis of Athens

The natural rock formation of the Acropolis probably had a palace on top as early as the Mycenaean period, when it was also surrounded by a defensive wall. Temples were constructed beginning in the sixth century B.C.E., and after the Persian War, Pericles ordered the reconstruction and expansion of many of these, as well as the building of new and more magnificent temples and an extension of the defensive walls. The largest building is the Parthenon, a temple dedicated to the goddess Athena, which originally housed a 40-foot-tall statue of Athena made of ivory and gold sheets attached to a wooden frame. Much of the Parthenon was damaged when it was shelled during a war between Venice and the Ottoman Empire in the seventeenth century C.E., and air pollution continues to eat away at the marble. (Klaas Lingbeek- van Kranen/E+/Getty Images)

> PICTURING THE PAST

ANALYZING THE IMAGE: Imagine yourself as an Athenian walking up the hill toward the Parthenon. What impression would the setting and the building itself convey?
CONNECTIONS: What were the various functions of the Acropolis?

Best known are the comedies of Aristophanes (eh-ruh-STAH-fuh-neez) (ca. 445–386 B.C.E.), an ardent lover of his city and a merciless critic of cranks and quacks. Like Aeschylus, Sophocles, and Euripides, Aristophanes used his art to dramatize his ideas on the right conduct of the citizen and the value of the polis.

Households and Work

In sharp contrast with the rich intellectual and cultural life of Periclean Athens stands the simplicity of its material life. The Athenians, like other Greeks, lived with comparatively few material possessions in houses that were rather simple. Well-to-do Athenians lived in houses consisting of a series of rooms opening onto a central courtyard. Artisans often set aside a room to use as a shop or work area. Larger houses often had a dining room at the front where the men of the family ate and entertained guests at drinking parties called *symposia*, and a **gynaeceum** (also spelled *gynaikeion*), a room or section at the back where the women of the

gynaeceum
▶ Women's quarters at the back of an Athenian house where the women of the family and the female slaves worked, ate, and slept.

What was the role of the polis in Greek society?

What were the causes and consequences of the major wars of the classical period?

What were the lasting cultural and intellectual achievements of the classical period?

☑ LearningCurve
Check what you know.

77

This painting on the side of an amphora from around 500 B.C.E. shows a blacksmith's shop, with the smiths working and other men providing advice. Men often gathered in artisans' shops or on the public square to chat, while women's conversations took place in the home. Although blacksmithing is hot work, a smith would not normally have worked in the nude; showing him naked allowed the painter to demonstrate his ability to depict human musculature. (The Plousios Painter, two-handled jar [amphora]. Greek, Late Archaic Period, about 500–490 B.C.E. Place of Manufacture: Greece, Attica, Athens. Ceramic, Black Figure. Height: 36.1 cm [14³/₁₆ in.]; diameter: 25.9 cm [10 ³/₁₆ in.]. Museum of Fine Arts, Boston. Henry Lillie Pierce Fund, 01.8035. Photograph © 2013 Museum of Fine Arts, Boston.)

family and the female slaves worked, ate, and slept. Other rooms included the kitchen and bathroom. By modern standards there was not much furniture.

Cooking, done over a hearth in the house, provided welcome warmth in the winter. Baking and roasting were done in ovens. Meals consisted primarily of various grains, especially wheat and barley, as well as lentils, olives, figs, grapes, fish, and a little meat. The Greeks used olive oil for cooking, and also as an ointment and as lamp fuel.

In the city a man might support himself as a craftsman—a potter, bronzesmith, sailmaker, or tanner—or he could contract with the polis to work on public buildings. Certain crafts, including spinning and weaving, were generally done by women who produced cloth for their own families and sold it. Men and women without skills worked as paid laborers but competed with slaves for work.

Slavery was commonplace in Greece, as it was throughout the ancient world. Slaves were usually foreigners and often "barbarians," people whose native language was not Greek. Most citizen households in Athens owned at least one slave. Slaves in Athens ranged widely in terms of their type of work and opportunities for escaping slavery. Some male slaves were skilled workers or well-educated teachers and tutors of writing, while others were unskilled laborers in the city, agricultural workers in the countryside, or laborers in mines. Female slaves worked in agriculture or as domestic servants and nurses for children. Slaves received some protection under the law, and those who engaged in skilled labor for which they were paid could buy their freedom. A few ex-slaves even became Athenian citizens.

Gender and Sexuality

The social conditions of Athenian women have been the subject of much debate, in part because the sources are fragmentary. The available sources suggest that women rarely played notable roles in public affairs. However, we do know that

CHAPTER LOCATOR | How did the geography of Greece shape its earliest kingdoms?

the status of a free woman was strictly protected by law and that only the sons of a citizen woman could be citizens. Only she was in charge of the household and the family's possessions, yet the law gave her these rights primarily to protect her husband's interests. Women in Athens and elsewhere in Greece, like those in Mesopotamia, brought dowries to their husbands upon marriage, which went back to their fathers in cases of divorce.

In ancient Athens the main function of women from citizen families was to bear and raise children. Childbirth could be dangerous for both mother and infant, so pregnant women usually made sacrifices or visited temples to ask help from the gods. Women relied on their relatives, on friends, and on midwives to assist in the delivery.

The ideal for Athenian citizen women was apparently a secluded life in which the only men they saw were relatives and tradesmen. The extent to which this ideal was actually a reality is impossible to know, but women in wealthier citizen families probably spent most of their time at home in the gynaeceum, leaving the house only to attend some religious festivals, and perhaps occasionally plays. (See "Individuals in Society: Aspasia," page 80.)

In the gynaeceum, women oversaw domestic slaves and hired labor and, with servants and friends, worked wool into cloth. Women personally cared for slaves who became ill and nursed them back to health and cared for the family's material possessions as well. Women from noncitizen families lived freer lives than citizen women, although they worked harder and had fewer material comforts. They performed manual labor in the fields or sold goods or services in the agora, going about their affairs much as men did.

Among the services that some women and men sold was sex. Women who sold sexual services ranged from poor streetwalkers known as *pornai* to middle-status hired mistresses known as *palakai*, to sophisticated courtesans known as *hetaerae,* who added intellectual accomplishments to physical beauty. Hetaerae accompanied men at dinner parties and in public settings where their wives would not have been welcome, serving men as social as well as sexual partners.

Same-sex relations were generally accepted in all of ancient Greece. In classical Athens part of a male adolescent citizen's training might entail a hierarchical sexual and tutorial relationship with an adult man, who most likely was married and may have had female sexual partners as well. These relationships between young men and

Young Man and Hetaera

In this scene painted on the inside of a drinking cup, a hetaera holds the head of a young man who has clearly had too much to drink. Sexual and comic scenes were common on Greek pottery, particularly on objects that would have been used at a private dinner party hosted by a citizen, known as a symposium. Wives did not attend symposia, but hetaerae and entertainers were often hired to perform for the male guests. (© Martin von Wagner Museum of Universität Wurzburg, Photo: P. Neckermann, respectively E. Oehrlein)

| What was the role of the polis in Greek society? | What were the causes and consequences of the major wars of the classical period? | **What were the lasting cultural and intellectual achievements of the classical period?** | ☑ LearningCurve Check what you know. |

" "If it is necessary for me indeed to speak of female virtues, to those of you who have now become widows, I shall explain the entire situation briefly. It is in your hands whether you will not fall below your nature. The greatest glory to you is to be least talked about by men, either for excellence or blame" (Thucydides 2.46.1). These words were reportedly uttered by Pericles to the widows at a public funeral honoring those killed during the first year of the Peloponnesian War. We have no idea whether Pericles actually said something like this — Thucydides often inserted speeches to make his history more dramatic — but these words express the Athenian ideal of proper behavior for a citizen's wife: she should stay at home and limit her talents to her household. This ideal became the reality for most Athenian women, whose names and actions were not recorded and thus are lost to history.

One exception to this silence is Aspasia (as-PAY-zhuh), who was born in the Greek city of Miletus and came to Athens in about 445 B.C.E. Little is known for certain about her life — Thucydides never mentions her — but she appears to have played a role in Athenian society that was far different from that prescribed in Pericles's speech. Because she was not an Athenian, she could not marry an Athenian citizen. Instead of marrying another non-Athenian, she caught the eye of Pericles. After he had divorced his wife, Aspasia became his mistress and bore him a son, also named Pericles. She may have been a hetaera, one of the high-status courtesans in Athens who provided men with witty conversation at dinner parties as well as sexual services. The first person to mention her status as a hetaera was the comic playwright Aristophanes. Aristophanes was an opponent of Pericles, however, and he may have simply made this up. Other authors, including Plato, do discuss Aspasia, but they focus on her ability with words and her wit (which they see as good) and her influence over Pericles (which they generally see as bad). In one of Plato's dialogues, Socrates even says that Pericles learned his rhetoric from Aspasia and that *she* wrote the famous funeral oration. Most scholars see this not as a statement of fact, but as an attempt by Socrates to ridicule Pericles and criticize his growing power in Athens.

Aspasia herself was accused by various Athenian authors of causing one or another of Athens's wars because of personal vendettas or perverse sexual desires. Pericles's death in 429 B.C.E. in the plague of Athens left Aspasia without a protector, and she disappears from the historical record shortly afterward. Ever more embellished stories about her continued to be told, however. By the time of the Roman

Roman portrait of Aspasia based on a Greek statue. (© Vanni Archive/Art Resource, NY)

biographer Plutarch in the first century C.E., it was said that she held public philosophical discussions, was put on trial for impiety, and became the mistress of another Athenian general after Pericles's death.

It is almost impossible to separate the historical Aspasia from the imaginary one, but what is clear is that her status was dependent on her personal relationships with prominent men. She may well have been a gifted and intelligent speaker, but her actions were severely limited because of her status as a noncitizen in a place where citizenship was essential and even more because of her status as a woman. Thanks largely to her enemies, we do know her name, but Aspasia lacked the honored social position of the anonymous Athenian citizen women that her lover Pericles may have praised.

QUESTIONS FOR ANALYSIS

1. What allowed Aspasia to have a position quite different from that seen as ideal in Pericles's speech?
2. Why might Pericles's enemies have enhanced accounts about her talents and her influence over him? Can you think of more recent parallels?

LaunchPad

ONLINE DOCUMENT PROJECT

What does Aspasia's story reveal about the expectations and ideals surrounding gender in classical Greek society? Keeping the question above in mind, analyze texts and images that testify to Greek attitudes about gender roles during Aspasia's time, and then complete a writing assignment based on the evidence and details from this chapter. *See inside the front cover to learn more.*

older men were often celebrated in literature and art, in part because Athenians regarded perfection as possible only in the male. The perfect body was that of the young male, and perfect love was that between a young man and a slightly older man. The extent to which perfect love was sexual or spiritual was debated among the ancient Greeks. In one of his dialogues, the philosopher Plato (see page 83) argues that the best kind of love is one in which contemplation of the beloved leads to contemplation of the divine, an intellectualized love that came to be known as platonic.

Along with praise of intellectualized love, Greek authors also celebrated physical sex and desire. The soldier-poet Archilochus (d. 652 B.C.E.) preferred "to light upon the flesh of a maid and ram belly to belly and thigh to thigh."[1] The lyric poet Sappho, who lived on the island of Lesbos in the northern Aegean Sea in the sixth century B.C.E., wrote often of powerful desire.

The Hellenic and even more the Hellenistic Greeks regarded Sappho as a great lyric poet, although because some of her poetry is directed toward women, over the last century she has become better known for her sexuality than her writing. Today the English word *lesbian* is derived from Sappho's home island of Lesbos.

Same-sex relations did not mean that people did not marry; Athenians saw the continuation of the family line as essential. Sappho, for example, appears to have been married and had a daughter. Sexual desire and procreation were both important aspects of life, but ancient Greeks did not necessarily link them.

Public and Personal Religion

Like most peoples of the ancient world, the Greeks were polytheists, worshipping a variety of gods and goddesses who were immortal but otherwise acted just like people. Migration, invasion, and colonization brought the Greeks into contact with other peoples and caused their religious beliefs to evolve.

Greek religion was primarily a matter of ritual, with rituals designed to appease the divinities believed to control the forces of the natural world. Processions, festivals, and sacrifices offered to the gods were frequently occasions for people to meet together socially, for times of cheer or even drunken excess.

By the classical era, the primary gods were understood to live metaphorically on Mount Olympus, the highest mountain in Greece. Zeus was the king of the gods and the most powerful of them, and he was married to Hera, who was also his sister. Zeus and Hera had several children, including Ares, the god of war. Zeus was also the father of the god Apollo, who represented the epitome of youth, beauty, and athletic skill, and who served as the patron god of music and poetry. Apollo's half-sister Athena was a warrior-goddess who had been born from the head of Zeus.

The Greeks also honored certain heroes. A hero was born of the union of a god or goddess and a mortal, and was considered an intermediary between the divine and the human. A hero displayed his divine origins by performing deeds beyond the ability of human beings. Herakles (or Hercules, as the Romans called him), the son of Zeus and the mortal woman Alcmene, was the most popular of the Greek heroes. Devotees to Hercules believed that he, like other heroes, protected mortals from supernatural dangers and provided an ideal of vigorous masculinity.

What was the role of the polis in Greek society? | What were the causes and consequences of the major wars of the classical period? | **What were the lasting cultural and intellectual achievements of the classical period?** | ✓ LearningCurve Check what you know.

81

The polis administered cults and festivals, and everyone was expected to participate in these events, comparable to today's patriotic parades or ceremonies. Much religion was local and domestic, and individual families honored various deities privately in their homes. Many people also believed that magic rituals and spells were effective and sought the assistance of individuals reputed to have special knowledge or powers. Even highly educated Greeks sought the assistance of fortune-tellers and soothsayers, from the oracle at Delphi to local figures who examined the flights of birds or the entrails of recently slaughtered chickens for clues about the future.

Along with public and family forms of honoring the gods, some Greeks also participated in what later historians have termed **mystery religions**, in which participants underwent an initiation ritual and gained secret knowledge that they were forbidden to reveal to the uninitiated. The Eleusinian mysteries, held at Eleusis in Attica, are one of the oldest of these. In the sixth century B.C.E., the rulers of nearby Athens made the ritual open to all Greeks, women and slaves included. Many people flocked to the annual ceremonies and learned the mysteries, which by the fourth century B.C.E. appear to have promised life after death to those initiated into them.

Another, somewhat secret religion was that of Dionysus (die-uh-NIE-suhs), the god of wine and powerful emotions. As the god of wine, he also represented freedom from the normal constraints of society, and his worshippers were reported to have danced ecstatically and even to have become a frenzied and uncontrolled mob. Whether or how often this actually happened is impossible to know.

Greeks also shared some public Pan-Hellenic festivals, the chief of which were held at Olympia in honor of Zeus and at Delphi in honor of Apollo. The festivities at Olympia included athletic contests that have inspired the modern Olympic games. Held every four years, these games were for the glory of Zeus. The Pythian (PIH-thee-uhn) games at Delphi were also held every four years and emphasized musical and literary contests as well as athletic prowess. Both the Olympic and the Pythian games were unifying factors in Greek life, bringing Greeks together culturally as well as religiously.

The Flowering of Philosophy

Just as the Greeks developed rituals to honor the gods, they spun myths and epics to explain the origin of the universe. Over time, however, as Greeks encountered other peoples with different beliefs, some of them began to question their old gods and myths, and they sought rational rather than supernatural explanations for natural phenomena. These Greek thinkers, based in Ionia, are called the Pre-Socratics because their rational efforts preceded those of the Athenians. They took individual facts and wove them into general theories that led them to conclude that, despite appearances, the universe is actually simple and subject to natural laws. The Pre-Socratics began an intellectual revolution with their idea that nature was predictable, creating what we now call philosophy and science.

Drawing on their observations, the Pre-Socratics speculated about the basic building blocks of the universe. Thales (THAY-leez) (ca. 600 B.C.E.) thought the basic element of the universe was water, and Heraclitus (hehr-uh-KLIE-tuhs) (ca. 500 B.C.E.) thought it was fire. Democritus (dih-MAH-kruh-tuhs) (ca. 460 B.C.E.)

mystery religions

▶ Belief systems that were characterized by secret doctrines, rituals of initiation, and sometimes the promise of rebirth or an afterlife.

CHAPTER LOCATOR | How did the geography of Greece shape its earliest kingdoms?

CHAPTER 3
82 THE DEVELOPMENT OF GREEK SOCIETY AND CULTURE

broke this down further and created the atomic theory, the idea that the universe is made up of invisible, indestructible particles. The culmination of Pre-Socratic thought was the theory that four simple substances make up the universe: fire, air, earth, and water.

The stream of thought started by the Pre-Socratics branched into several directions. Hippocrates (hih-PAH-kruh-teez) (ca. 470–400 B.C.E.) became the most prominent physician and teacher of medicine of his time. Hippocrates sought natural explanations for diseases and seems to have advocated letting nature take its course and not intervening too much. Illness was caused not by evil spirits, he asserted, but by physical problems in the body, particularly by imbalances in what he saw as four basic bodily fluids: blood, phlegm, black bile, and yellow bile. In a healthy body, these fluids, called humors, were in perfect balance, and the goal of medical treatment of the ill was to help the body bring them back into balance.

The **Sophists** (SOF-ihsts), a group of thinkers in fifth-century-B.C.E. Athens, applied philosophical speculation to politics and language, questioning the beliefs and laws of the polis to understand their origin. They believed that excellence in both politics and language could be taught, and they provided lessons for the young men of Athens who wished to learn how to persuade others. Their later opponents criticized them for charging fees and also accused them of using rhetoric to deceive people instead of presenting the truth.

Socrates (SOK-ruh-teez) (ca. 469–399 B.C.E.), whose ideas are known only through the works of others, also applied philosophy to politics and to people. He seemed, to many Athenians, to be a Sophist because he also questioned Athenian traditions, although he never charged fees. His approach when exploring ethical issues and defining concepts was to start with a general topic or problem and to narrow the matter to its essentials. He did so by continuously questioning participants in a discussion or argument through which they developed critical-thinking skills, a process known as the **Socratic method**.

Socrates was viewed with suspicion by many because he challenged the traditional beliefs and values of Athens. After Athens's disastrous defeat at the hands of Sparta in the Peloponnesian War, Socrates came into serious conflict with the government. Charges were brought against him for corrupting the youth of the city and for impiety, that is, for not believing in the gods honored in the city. Thus, he was essentially charged with being unpatriotic because he criticized the traditions of the city and the decisions of government leaders. He was tried and imprisoned, and though he had several opportunities to escape, in 399 B.C.E., he drank the poison ordered as his method of execution and died.

Most of what we know about Socrates, including the details of his trial and death, comes from his student Plato (427–347 B.C.E.), who wrote dialogues in which Socrates asks questions and who also founded the Academy, a school dedicated to philosophy. Plato developed the theory that there are two worlds: the impermanent, changing world that we know through our senses, and the eternal, unchanging realm of "forms" that constitute the essence of true reality. According to Plato, true knowledge and the possibility of living a virtuous life come from contemplating ideal forms—what later came to be called **Platonic ideals**—not from observing the visible world. Plato believed that the ideal polis could exist only when its citizens were well educated. From education came the possibility of determining all of the virtues of life and combining them into a system that would lead to an intelligent, moral, and ethical life.

Sophists
▶ A group of thinkers in fifth-century-B.C.E. Athens who applied philosophical speculation to politics and language and were accused of deceit.

Socratic method
▶ A method of inquiry used by Socrates based on asking questions, through which participants developed their critical-thinking skills and explored ethical issues.

Platonic ideals
▶ According to Plato, the eternal unchanging ideal forms that are the essence of true reality.

What was the role of the polis in Greek society?

What were the causes and consequences of the major wars of the classical period?

What were the lasting cultural and intellectual achievements of the classical period?

☑ LearningCurve
Check what you know.

This marble head of the philosopher is a later Roman copy of one made in the fourth century B.C.E. by the Greek sculptor Silanion, which had apparently been installed in the Academy of Athens shortly after Plato's death. Idealized portraits in marble of writers, thinkers, rulers, and statesmen became a popular art form in the later classical period and shaped all later depictions of these individuals. (Erin Babnik/Alamy)

Plato's student Aristotle (384–322 B.C.E.) also thought that true knowledge was possible, but he believed that such knowledge came from observation of the world, analysis of natural phenomena, and logical reasoning, not contemplation. Aristotle thought that everything had a purpose so that, to know something, one also had to know its function. Excellence—*arête* in Greek—meant performing one's function to the best of one's ability, whether one was a horse or a person. The range of Aristotle's thought is staggering. His interests embraced logic, ethics, natural science, physics, politics, poetry, and art. He studied the heavens as well as the earth and judged the earth to be the center of the universe, with the stars and planets revolving around it.

Plato's idealism profoundly shaped Western philosophy, but Aristotle came to have an even wider influence; for many centuries in Europe, the authority of Aristotle's ideas was second only to the Bible's. His works—which are actually a combination of his lecture notes and those of his students, copied and recopied many times—were used as the ultimate proof that something was true, even if closer observation of the phenomenon indicated that it was not. Thus, ironically, Aristotle's authority was sometimes invoked in a way that contradicted his own ideas. Despite these limitations, the broader examination of the universe and the place of humans in it that Socrates, Plato, and Aristotle engaged in is widely regarded as Greece's most important intellectual legacy.

> ## QUICK REVIEW

How did Greek philosophers challenge the beliefs and traditions of their contemporaries?

CHAPTER LOCATOR | How did the geography of Greece shape its earliest kingdoms?

LOOKING BACK
LOOKING AHEAD

The ancient Greeks built on the endeavors of earlier societies in the eastern Mediterranean, but they also added new elements, including drama, philosophy, science, and naturalistic art. They created governments that relied on the participation of citizens. These cultural and political achievements developed in a society that, for many centuries, was almost always at war with the Persians and with each other. Those conflicts led many to wonder whether democracy was really a good form of government and to speculate more widely about abstract ideals and the nature of the cosmos. The Greeks carried these ideas with them as they colonized much of the Mediterranean, in migrations that often resulted from the conflicts that were so common in Greece.

The classical Greeks had tremendous influence not only on the parts of the world in which they traveled or settled, but also on all of Western civilization from that point on. As you will see in Chapter 5, Roman art, religion, literature, and many other aspects of culture relied on Greek models. And as you will see in Chapter 12, European thinkers and writers made conscious attempts to return to classical ideals in art, literature, and philosophy during the Renaissance. In the new United States, political leaders from the Revolutionary era on decided that important government buildings should be modeled on the Parthenon or other temples, complete with marble statuary of their own heroes. In some ways, capitol buildings in the United States are perfect symbols of the legacy of Greece—gleaming ideals of harmony, freedom, democracy, and beauty that (as with all ideals) do not always correspond with realities.

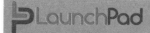

ONLINE DOCUMENT PROJECT
Aspasia

What does Aspasia's story reveal about the expectations and ideals surrounding gender in classical Greek society?

You encountered Aspasia on page 80. Keeping the question above in mind, explore sources that testify to Greek attitudes about gender roles during Aspasia's time. *See inside the front cover to learn more.*

| What was the role of the polis in Greek society? | What were the causes and consequences of the major wars of the classical period? | What were the lasting cultural and intellectual achievements of the classical period? | ✓ **LearningCurve** Check what you know. |

CHAPTER 3 STUDY GUIDE

STEP 1

GET STARTED ONLINE

✓ **LearningCurve**

Now that you've read the chapter, make it stick by completing the LearningCurve activity.

STEP 2

EXPLAIN WHY IT MATTERS

Put your reading into practice. Identify each term below, and then explain why it matters in Western history.

TERM	WHO OR WHAT & WHEN	WHY IT MATTERS
Minoan (p. 62)		
Mycenaean (p. 63)		
polis (p. 65)		
hoplites (p. 66)		
tyranny (p. 66)		
democracy (p. 66)		
oligarchy (p. 66)		
helots (p. 68)		
Delian League (p. 72)		
gynaeceum (p. 77)		
mystery religions (p. 82)		
sophists (p. 83)		
Socratic method (p. 83)		
Platonic ideals (p. 83)		

STEP 3

MOVE BEYOND THE BASICS

To demonstrate a more advanced understanding, compare and contrast Athens and Sparta. Use the chart below to identify key aspects of each city-state.

	Athens	Sparta
Government		
Culture		
Society		
Gender roles		

STEP 4 PUT IT ALL TOGETHER

Now, take a step back and try to explain the big picture. Remember to use specific examples from the chapter in your answers.

THE POLIS

▶ What kinds of governments emerged in Greek city-states after the Dark Age?

▶ How did the early history of Athens and Sparta shape their subsequent development?

CLASSICAL GREECE: WAR AND POLITICS

▶ In your opinion, how much responsibility did Athens bear for the endemic warfare of the classical period?

▶ How did competition between Greek city-states undermine Greek society as a whole?

MAKE CONNECTIONS

▶ How did the Greek polis differ from the Mesopotamian city-state? What might explain the differences you note?

▶ What led to division and conflict within the Greek world? What were the consequences of the inability of the Greeks to develop long-term solutions to their political problems?

CLASSICAL GREECE: LIFE AND CULTURE

▶ What social and cultural values were reflected in Greek religious practices?

▶ Compare and contrast the philosophies of Aristotle and Plato. What were the most important differences?

> IN YOUR OWN WORDS

Imagine that you must give an oral report to the class answering the following question: **What forces shaped the development of Greek society and culture in the Archaic and Classical periods? What would be the most important points and why?**

4

LIFE IN THE HELLENISTIC WORLD

336–30 B.C.E.

> How did the Mediterranean world change in the centuries following Alexander's conquests?

Chapter 4 examines the Hellenistic era, the period following the conquests of Alexander the Great in which Greek culture, the Greek language, and Greek thought spread as far as India, blending with local traditions.

In many ways, life in the Hellenistic world was not much different from life in Hellenic Greece: most people continued to be farmers, raising crops and animals for their own needs and to meet their obligations to their superiors. Those who lived in cities, however, often ate foods and drank wine that came from far away, did business with people who were quite unlike them, and adopted religious practices and ways of thinking unknown to their parents. Hellenistic cities thus offer striking parallels to those of today.

✓ LearningCurve
After reading the chapter, use LearningCurve to retain what you've read.

> How and why did Alexander the Great create an empire?

> How did Greek ideas and traditions spread?

> What new economic connections were created in the Hellenistic period?

> How did religion and philosophy shape everyday life in the Hellenistic world?

> How did science and medicine serve the needs of Hellenistic society?

Hellenistic Married Life. This small terra-cotta figurine from Myrina in what is now Turkey, made in the second century B.C.E., shows a newly married couple sitting on a bridal bed. (Erich Lessing/Art Resource, NY)

How and why did Alexander the Great create an empire?

Alexander at the Battle of Issus

In this first-century-B.C.E. mosaic from the Roman city of Pompeii, Alexander the Great (left), bareheaded and wearing a breastplate, charges King Darius III (right), who is standing in a chariot. Alexander was widely admired by Romans, and this mosaic portrays him in a heroic light, just at the point in the battle when Darius turns to flee from the attack. (C. M. Dixon/Ancient Art & Architecture Collection Ltd.)

Alexander (r. 336–323 B.C.E.) carried out his father Philip's plan to lead the Greeks against the Persians. His campaign swept away the Persian Empire, which had ruled the area for over two hundred years. In its place Alexander established a Macedonian monarchy. Although his rule over these vast territories was never consolidated due to his premature death, he left behind a legacy of political and cultural influence, and a long period of war. Macedonian kings established dynasties and Greek culture spread in this **Hellenistic** era.

Military Campaigns

In 334 B.C.E., Alexander led an army of Macedonians and Greeks into Persian territory in Asia Minor. In the next three years, Alexander moved east into the Persian Empire, winning major battles at the Granicus River and Issus (**Map 4.1**). He moved into Syria and took most of the cities of Phoenicia and the eastern coast of the Mediterranean. He then turned south toward Egypt, which had earlier been conquered by the Persians. The Egyptians saw Alexander as a liberator, and he seized Egypt without a battle. After honoring the priestly class, Alexander was proclaimed pharaoh, the legitimate ruler of the country. He founded a new capital, Alexandria, on the coast of the Mediterranean, which would later grow into an enormous city.

Alexander left Egypt after less than a year and marched into Assyria, where at Gaugamela he defeated the Persian army. After this victory, the principal Per-

Hellenistic

▶ A term that literally means "like the Greek," used to describe the period after the death of Alexander the Great, when Greek culture spread.

CHAPTER LOCATOR | How and why did Alexander the Great create an empire?

90 CHAPTER 4 LIFE IN THE HELLENISTIC WORLD

ca. 342–291 B.C.E.	**323–ca. 300** B.C.E.
– Life of comedy writer Menander	– War of succession leads to the establishment of Antigonid, Ptolemaic, and Seleucid dynasties
340–270 B.C.E.	**ca. 287–212** B.C.E
– Life of Epicurus, on whose ideas Epicureanism was based	– Life of Archimedes
335–262 B.C.E.	**ca. 280** B.C.E.
– Life of Zeno, on whose ideas Stoicism was based	– Founding of the library of Alexandria by the Ptolemies
334–324 B.C.E.	**168** B.C.E.
– Alexander the Great's military campaigns	– Roman overthrow of the Antigonid dynasty
ca. 330–200 B.C.E.	**166–164** B.C.E.
– Establishment of new Hellenistic cities	– Revolt of the Maccabees in Judea
323 B.C.E.	**30** B.C.E.
– Alexander dies at age thirty-two	– Roman conquest of Egypt; end of the Ptolemaic dynasty

sian capital of Persepolis fell to him in a bitterly fought battle. There he performed a symbolic act of retribution by burning the royal buildings of King Xerxes, the invader of Greece during the Persian wars 150 years earlier. In 330 B.C.E., he took Ecbatana, the last Persian capital, and pursued the Persian king Darius III to his death.

The Persian Empire had fallen, but Alexander had no intention of stopping. Many of his troops had been supplied by Greek city-states that had allied with him; he released these troops from their obligations of military service, but then rehired them as mercenaries. Alexander then began his personal odyssey. With his Macedonian soldiers and Greek mercenaries, he set out to conquer more of Asia. He plunged deeper into the East, into lands completely unknown to the Greek world. It took his soldiers four additional years to conquer Bactria (in today's Afghanistan) and the easternmost parts of the now-defunct Persian Empire, but still Alexander was determined to continue his march.

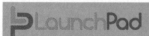

ONLINE DOCUMENT PROJECT

Alexander the Great

What were the motives behind Alexander's conquests, and what were the consequences of Hellenization?

Keeping the question above in mind, explore a variety of ancient perspectives on these questions. *See inside the front cover to learn more.*

| How did Greek ideas and traditions spread? | What new economic connections were created in the Hellenistic period? | How did religion and philosophy shape everyday life in the Hellenistic world? | How did science and medicine serve the needs of Hellenistic society? | ✔️ LearningCurve Check what you know. |

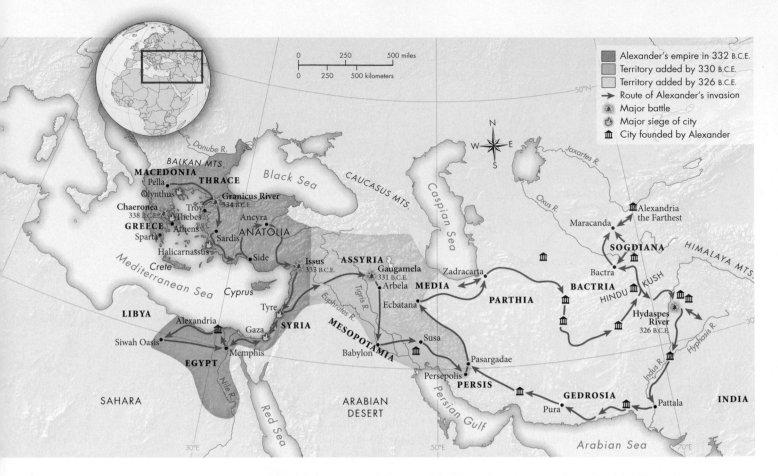

MAP 4.1 ■ Alexander's Conquests, 334–324 B.C.E.

This map shows the course of Alexander's invasion of the Persian Empire. More important than the great success of his military campaigns was the founding of new cities and the expansion of existing ones by Alexander and the Hellenistic rulers who followed him.

In 326 B.C.E., Alexander crossed the Indus River and entered India (in the area that is now Pakistan). There, too, he saw hard fighting, and finally at the Hyphasis (HIH-fuh-sihs) River his troops refused to go farther. Consequently, Alexander turned south to the Arabian Sea, and he waged a bloody and ruthless war against the people of the area. After reaching the Arabian Sea and turning west, he led his army through the Gedrosian Desert (now part of Pakistan and Iran). The army and those who supported the troops with supplies suffered fearfully, and many soldiers died along the way. Nonetheless, in 324 B.C.E., Alexander returned to Susa in the Greek-controlled region of Assyria. His mission was over, but Alexander never returned to his homeland of Macedonia. He died the next year in Babylon from fever, wounds, and excessive drinking.

Alexander's legendary status makes a reasoned interpretation of his goals and character very difficult. His contemporaries from the Greek city-states thought he was a bloody-minded tyrant, but later Greek and Roman writers and political leaders admired him and even regarded him as a philosopher interested in the common good. The most common view today is that Alexander was a brilliant leader who sought personal glory through conquest and who tolerated no opposition.

CHAPTER LOCATOR | How and why did Alexander the Great create an empire?

The Political Legacy

The main question at Alexander's death was whether his vast empire could be held together. Although he fathered a successor, the child was not yet born when Alexander died, and was thus too young to assume the duties of kingship. (Later he and his mother, Roxana, were murdered by one of Alexander's generals, who viewed him as a threat.) This meant that Alexander's empire was a prize for the taking. Several of the chief Macedonian generals aspired to become sole ruler, which led to a civil war lasting for decades. By the end of this conflict, the most successful generals had carved out their own smaller monarchies, although these continued to be threatened by internal splits and external attacks.

Alexander's general Ptolemy (ca. 367–ca. 283 B.C.E.) established the Ptolemaic (TAH-luh-MAY-ihk) kingdom in Egypt. The Ptolemaic dynasty would rule Egypt for nearly three hundred years, until the death of the last Ptolemaic ruler, Cleopatra VII, in 30 B.C.E. (see Chapter 5). Seleucus (ca. 358–281 B.C.E.), another of Alexander's officers, carved out a large kingdom, the Seleucid (SUH-loo-suhd), that stretched from the coast of Asia Minor to India. He was assassinated in 281 B.C.E. on the order of the ruler of the Ptolemaic kingdom; his son succeeded him, however, founding a dynasty that also lasted for centuries, although the kingdom itself shrank as independent states broke off. Antigonus I (382–301 B.C.E.), a third general, became king of Macedonia and established the Antigonid (an-TIH-guh-nuhd) dynasty, which lasted until it was overthrown by the Romans in 168 B.C.E. Rome would go on to conquer the Seleucid and Ptolemaic kingdoms as well (see Chapters 5 and 6).

> Major Hellenistic Dynasties

- **Ptolemaic:** Founded by Ptolemy I (ca. 367–ca. 283 B.C.E.), ruled Egypt
- **Seleucid:** Founded by Seleucus (ca. 358–281 B.C.E.), stretched from the coast of Asia Minor to India
- **Antigonid:** Founded by Antigonus I (382–301 B.C.E.), centered in Macedonia

Hellenistic rulers amassed an enormous amount of wealth from their large kingdoms, and royal patronage provided money for the production of literary works and the research and development that allowed discoveries in science and engineering. To encourage obedience, Hellenistic kings often created ruler cults that linked the king's authority with that of the gods, or they adopted ruler cults that already existed, as Alexander did in Egypt. The kingdoms never won the deep emotional loyalty that Greeks had once felt for the polis, but the ruler cult was an easily understandable symbol of unity within the kingdom.

Hellenistic kingship was hereditary, which gave women who were members of royal families more power than any woman had in democracies such as Athens, where citizenship was limited to men. Wives and mothers of kings had influence over their husbands and sons, and a few women ruled in their own right when there was no male heir.

QUICK REVIEW <

What was the political legacy of Alexander's conquests?

How did Greek ideas and traditions spread?

What new economic connections were created in the Hellenistic period?

How did religion and philosophy shape everyday life in the Hellenistic world?

How did science and medicine serve the needs of Hellenistic society?

LearningCurve
Check what you know.

93

> How did Greek ideas and traditions spread?

The Great Altar of Pergamum A new Hellenistic city needed splendid art and architecture to prove its worth in Greek eyes. In the first half of the second century B.C.E., the king of Pergamum ordered the construction of this huge monumental altar, which is now in a museum in Berlin. The scenes of wildly contorted figures depict the mythical victory of the Greek Olympian gods over the Titans, a race of giants. The altar honors the gods and celebrates Pergamum's military victories, although scholars dispute exactly which victory led to its building. (Bildarchiv Preussischer Kulturbesitz/Art Resource, NY)

Hellenization
▶ The spread of Greek ideas, culture, and traditions to non-Greek groups across a wide area.

Alexander's most important legacy was clearly not political unity. Instead it was the spread of Greek ideas and traditions across a wide area, a process scholars later called **Hellenization**. To maintain contact with the Greek world as he moved farther eastward, he founded new cities and military colonies and expanded existing cities, settling Greek and Macedonian troops and veterans in them. Besides keeping the road back to Greece open, these settlements helped secure the countryside around them. This practice continued after his death, with more than 250 new cities founded in North Africa, West and Central Asia, and southeastern Europe. These cities and colonies became powerful instruments in the spread of Hellenism and in the blending of Greek and other cultures.

Urban Life

In many respects the Hellenistic city resembled a modern city. It was a cultural center, a seat of learning, and a place where people could find amusement. The Hellenistic city was also an economic center that provided a ready market for grain and produce raised in the surrounding countryside. In short, the Hellenistic city offered cultural and economic opportunities for rich and poor alike.

CHAPTER LOCATOR | How and why did Alexander the Great create an empire?

To the Greeks, civilized life was unthinkable outside a city, and Hellenistic kings often gave cities all the external trappings of a polis. Each had an assembly of citizens, a council to prepare legislation, and a board of magistrates to conduct political business. However similar to the Greek polis such a city appeared, it could not engage in diplomatic dealings, make treaties, pursue its own foreign policy, or wage its own wars. The city was required to follow royal orders, and the king often placed his own officials in it to see that his decrees were followed.

A Hellenistic city differed from a Greek polis in other ways as well. The Greek polis had one body of law and one set of customs. In the Hellenistic city, Greeks represented an elite class. Natives and non-Greek foreigners who lived in Hellenistic cities usually possessed lesser rights than Greeks and often had their own laws. In some instances, this disparity spurred natives to assimilate Greek culture in order to rise politically and socially.

The city of Pergamum in northwestern Anatolia is a good example of an older city that underwent changes in the Hellenistic period. Previously an important strategic site, Pergamum was transformed by its new Greek rulers into a magnificent city complete with all the typical buildings of the polis, including gymnasia, baths, and one of the finest libraries in the entire Hellenistic world. The new rulers erected temples to the traditional Greek deities, but they also built imposing temples to other gods. There was a Jewish population in the city, who may have established a synagogue. Especially in the agora, Greeks and indigenous people met to conduct business and exchange goods and ideas. Greeks felt as though they were at home, and the evolving culture mixed Greek and local elements.

The Bactrian city of Ay Khanoum on the Oxus River, on the border of modern Afghanistan, is a good example of a brand-new city where cultures met. Bactria and Parthia had been part of the Seleucid kingdom, but in the third century B.C.E., their governors overthrew the Seleucids and established independent kingdoms in today's Afghanistan and Turkmenistan (**Map 4.2**). Bactria became an outpost of Hellenism, from which the rulers of China and India learned of sophisticated societies other than their own. Along with this very public display of Greek ideals, the city also had temples to local deities and artwork that blended Greek and local styles (for an example, see page 97).

Greeks in Hellenistic Cities

The ruling dynasties of the Hellenistic world were Macedonian, and Macedonians and Greeks filled all the important political, military, and diplomatic positions. Besides building Greek cities, Hellenistic kings offered Greeks land and money as lures to further immigration.

The Hellenistic monarchy, unlike the Greek polis, did not depend solely on its citizens to fulfill its political and military needs, but instead relied on professionals. Talented Greek men had the opportunity to rise quickly in the government bureaucracy. Appointed by the king, these administrators did not have to stand for election each year, unlike many officials of Greek poleis. Greeks also found ready employment in the armies and navies of the Hellenistic monarchies. Hellenistic kings were reluctant to arm the local populations or to allow them to serve in the army, fearing military rebellions among their conquered subjects. The result was the emergence of professional armies and navies consisting primarily of

How did Greek ideas and traditions spread? | What new economic connections were created in the Hellenistic period? | How did religion and philosophy shape everyday life in the Hellenistic world? | How did science and medicine serve the needs of Hellenistic society? | ✓ LearningCurve Check what you know.

95

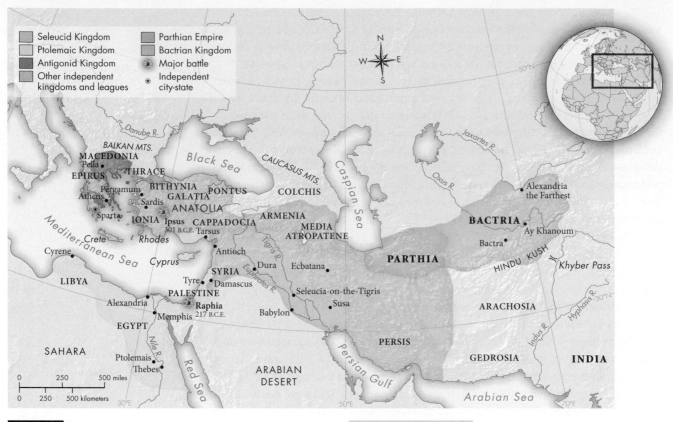

MAP 4.2 ■ The Hellenistic World, ca. 263 B.C.E.

This map depicts the Hellenistic world after Alexander's death.

ANALYZING THE MAP: Compare this map to Map 4.1 on page 92. After Alexander's death, were the Macedonians and Greeks able to retain control of most of the land he had conquered? What areas were lost?

CONNECTIONS: What does this map suggest about the success or failure of Alexander's dreams of conquest?

Greeks, although drawn from many areas of Greece and Macedonia, not simply from one polis. Unlike the citizen hoplites of classical Greece, these men were full-time soldiers. Hellenistic kings paid them well, often giving them land or leasing it to them as an incentive to remain loyal.

Greeks were able to dominate other professions as well. Hellenistic kingdoms and cities recruited Greek writers and artists to create Greek literature, art, and culture. Greek architects, engineers, and skilled craftsmen found themselves in great demand to produce the Greek-style buildings commissioned by the Hellenistic monarchs. Architects and engineers would sometimes design and build whole cities. An enormous wave of construction took place during the Hellenistic period.

Increased physical and social mobility benefited some women as well as men. More women learned to read than before, and they engaged in occupations in which literacy was beneficial, including care of the sick. During the Hellenistic period, women continued to be required to have male guardians to buy, sell, or lease land; to borrow money; and to represent them in other commercial

CHAPTER LOCATOR | How and why did Alexander the Great create an empire?

96 CHAPTER 4
LIFE IN THE HELLENISTIC WORLD

transactions. Yet often such a guardian was present only to fulfill the letter of the law. The woman was the real agent and handled the business being transacted.

Because of the opportunities the Hellenistic monarchies offered, many people moved frequently. Once a Greek man had left home to take service with, for instance, the army or the bureaucracy of the Ptolemies, he had no incentive beyond his pay and the comforts of life in Egypt to keep him there. If the Seleucid king offered him more money or a promotion, he might well accept it and take his talents to Asia Minor. Linguistic changes further facilitated the ease with which people moved. Instead of the different dialects spoken in Greece itself, a new Greek dialect called the *koine* (koy-NAY), which means "common," became the spoken language of traders, the royal court, the bureaucracy, and the army across the Hellenistic world.

As long as Greeks continued to migrate, the kingdoms remained stable and strong. In the process they drew an immense amount of talent from the Greek peninsula. However, the Hellenistic monarchies could not keep recruiting Greeks forever, in spite of their wealth and willingness to spend lavishly. In time, the huge surge of immigration slowed greatly.

Greeks and Non-Greeks

Across the Hellenistic world the prevailing institutions and laws became Greek. Everyone, Greek or non-Greek, who wanted to find an official position or compete in business had to learn Greek. Those who did gained an avenue of social mobility, and as early as the third century B.C.E., local people in some Hellenistic cities began to rise in power and prominence. Once a man knew Greek, he could move more easily to another area for better opportunities, and perhaps even hide his non-Greek origins. He could also join a military unit and perhaps be deployed far from his place of origin. Thus, learning Greek was an avenue of geographic mobility as well.

Cultural influences in the other direction occurred less frequently because they brought fewer advantages. Few Greeks learned a non-Greek language unless they were required to because of their official position. Greeks did begin to worship local deities, but often these were somewhat Hellenized and their qualities blended with those of an existing Greek god or goddess.

Yet the spread of Greek culture was wider than it was deep. Hellenistic kingdoms were never entirely unified in language, customs, and thought. The principal reason for this phenomenon is that Greek culture generally did not extend far beyond the reaches of the cities. Many urban residents adopted the aspects of Hellenism that they found useful, but people in the countryside generally did not embrace it, nor were they encouraged to.

Ptolemaic Egypt provides an excellent example of this situation. The indigenous people were the foundation of the kingdom: they fed it by their labor in the fields and financed its operations with their taxes. Because of this, the Ptolemies tied local people to the land more tightly than they

Metal Plate from Ay Khanoum

This spectacular metal plate, made in the Bactrian city of Ay Khanoum in the second century B.C.E., probably depicts the goddess Cybele being pulled in a chariot by lions with the sun-god above. Worship of Cybele, an earth-mother goddess, spread into Greece from the east and was then spread by her Greek followers as they traveled and migrated. (Courtesy, National Museum of Afganistan, Kabul)

| How did Greek ideas and traditions spread? | What new economic connections were created in the Hellenistic period? | How did religion and philosophy shape everyday life in the Hellenistic world? | How did science and medicine serve the needs of Hellenistic society? | ✓ LearningCurve Check what you know. |

had been before, making it nearly impossible for them to leave their villages. The Ptolemies maintained separate legal systems for Greeks and Egyptians. The bureaucracy of the Ptolemies was relatively efficient, and the indigenous population was viciously and cruelly exploited.

The situation was somewhat different in the booming city of Alexandria, founded by Alexander to be a new seaport, where there had been a small village earlier. Within a century of its founding, it was probably the largest city in the world, with a population numbering in the hundreds of thousands. The ruling elite was primarily Greek, and the Ptolemies tried to keep the Greek and Egyptian populations apart, but this was not always possible. Although the Ptolemies encouraged immigration from Greece, the number of immigrants was relatively low, so intermarriage increased. And the Ptolemies themselves gave privileges to local priests, building temples and sponsoring rituals honoring the local gods. Priestly families became owners of large landed estates and engaged in other sorts of business as well, becoming loyal supporters of the Ptolemaic regime. Even the processions honoring local gods still celebrated Greekness, however, and sometimes became a flash point that sparked protests by Egyptians.

In about 280 B.C.E., the Ptolemies founded a library in Alexandria that both glorified Greek culture and sponsored new scholarship. It eventually contained hundreds of thousands of papyrus scrolls of Greek writings. The library became one of the foremost intellectual centers of the ancient world, pulling in Greek-speaking writers, scholars, scientists, and thinkers from far away and preserving Greek writings.

Greek culture spread more deeply in the Seleucid kingdom than in Egypt, although this was not because the Seleucids had an organized plan for Hellenizing the local population. The primary problem for the Seleucids was holding on to the territory they had inherited. To do this, they established cities and military colonies throughout the region to nurture a vigorous and large Greek-speaking population and to defend the kingdom from their Persian neighbors. Seleucid military colonies were generally founded near existing villages, thus exposing even rural residents to all aspects of Greek life. Many local people found Greek political and cultural forms attractive and imitated them. In Asia Minor and Syria, for instance, numerous villages and towns developed along Greek lines, and some of them grew into Hellenized cities.

> **QUICK REVIEW**

What role did cities play in the spread of Greek culture throughout the Mediterranean world and the Near East?

CHAPTER LOCATOR | How and why did Alexander the Great create an empire?

98   CHAPTER 4
LIFE IN THE HELLENISTIC WORLD

What new economic connections were created in the Hellenistic period?

Harbor and Marketplace at Delos

During the Hellenistic period, the tiny island of Delos in the Aegean became a thriving trading center. From Delos, cargoes were shipped to almost every part of the Mediterranean. (Rolf Richardson/age footstock/superstock)

ALEXANDER'S CONQUESTS brought the Near East and Egypt fully into the sphere of Greek economics. The Hellenistic period did not see widespread improvements, however, in the way people lived and worked. Cities flourished, but many people who lived in rural areas were actually worse off than they had been before because of higher levels of rents and taxes. Alexander and his successors did link East and West in a broad commercial network, however. The spread of Greeks throughout the Near East and Egypt created new markets and stimulated trade.

| How did Greek ideas and traditions spread? | **What new economic connections were created in the Hellenistic period?** | How did religion and philosophy shape everyday life in the Hellenistic world? | How did science and medicine serve the needs of Hellenistic society? | ☑ LearningCurve Check what you know. |

Agriculture and Industry

Much of the revenue for the Hellenistic kingdoms was derived from agricultural products, rents paid by the tenants of royal land, and taxation of land. Trying to improve productivity, the rulers sponsored agricultural experiments and attempted to use their power to dictate agricultural practices and priorities. Such centralized planning was difficult to enforce at the local level, however, especially because the officials appointed to do so switched positions frequently and concentrated most on extracting taxes. Thus, despite royal interest in agriculture and a more studied approach to it in the Hellenistic period, there is no evidence that agricultural productivity increased or that practices changed. Technology was applied to military needs but not to those of food production.

As with agriculture, the production of goods also did not advance from technological developments. Although demand for goods increased during the Hellenistic period, no new techniques of production appear to have developed. Manual labor, not machinery, continued to turn out the raw materials and manufactured goods the Hellenistic world used. Apart from gold and silver, which were used primarily for coins and jewelry, bronze continued to be used for shields. Iron was utilized for weapons and tools.

Pottery remained an important commodity, and most of it was produced locally. The coarse pottery used in the kitchen for plates and cups changed little. Fancier pots and bowls were often decorated with patterns and scenes from mythology, legend, and daily life. Potters often portrayed heroic episodes, such as battles from the *Iliad*, or gods, such as Dionysus at sea. Pots journeyed with Greek merchants, armies, and travelers, so these images spread knowledge of Greek religion and stories west as far as Portugal and east as far as Southeast Asia. Pottery thus served as a means of cultural exchange—of ideas as well as goods—among people scattered across huge portions of the globe.

Commerce

Alexander's conquest of the Persian Empire had immediate effects on trade. In the conquered Persian capitals, Alexander had found vast sums of gold, silver, and other treasure. This wealth financed the creation of new cities, the building of roads, and the development of harbors. It also provided the thousands who participated in his expeditions with booty, with which they could purchase commodities. Whole new fields lay open to Greek merchants, who eagerly took advantage of the new opportunities. Commerce itself was a leading area where Greeks and non-Greeks met on grounds of common interest.

Trade was facilitated by the coining of money. Most of the great monarchies coined their money according to a uniform system, which meant that much of the money used in Hellenistic kingdoms had the same value. Traders were less in need of money changers than in the days when each major power coined money on a different standard.

Overland trade was conducted by caravan, and the backbone of this caravan trade was the camel. Luxury goods that were light, rare, and expensive traveled over the caravan routes to Alexandria or to the harbors of Phoenicia and Syria, from which they were shipped to Greece, Italy, and Spain. In time, these luxury items became more commonplace, in part as the result of an increased volume of

CHAPTER LOCATOR | How and why did Alexander the Great create an empire?

CHAPTER 4
100 LIFE IN THE HELLENISTIC WORLD

trade. Due to the prosperity of the period, more people could afford to buy gold, silver, ivory, precious stones, spices, and a host of other easily transportable goods. Perhaps the most prominent good in terms of volume was silk, and the trade in silk later gave the major East-West route its name: the Great Silk Road. In return, the Greeks and Macedonians sent east manufactured goods, especially metal weapons, cloth, wine, and olive oil. Business customs and languages of trade developed and became standardized so that merchants from different nationalities could communicate in a way understandable to all of them.

The durability and economic importance of the caravan routes are amply demonstrated by the fact that the death of Alexander, the ensuing wars of his successors, and later regional conflicts had little effect on trade. Numerous mercantile cities grew along these routes, and commercial contacts brought people from far-flung regions together, even if sometimes indirectly. The merchants and the caravan cities were links in a chain that reached from the Mediterranean Sea to India and beyond to China, along which ideas as well as goods were passed.

More economically important than the trade in luxury goods were commercial dealings in essential commodities like raw materials and grain and industrial products such as pottery. The Hellenistic monarchies usually raised enough grain for their own needs as well as a surplus for export. This trade in grain was essential for the cities of Greece and the Aegean, many of which could not grow enough on their own (see Map 4.2, page 96).

Olive mill from the Mediterranean. Olives would have been placed in the trough, and the large millstone rolled on top of them, using human or animal power, to extract the oil. (Eric Lessing/ Art Resource, NY)

How did Greek ideas and traditions spread?

What new economic connections were created in the Hellenistic period?

How did religion and philosophy shape everyday life in the Hellenistic world?

How did science and medicine serve the needs of Hellenistic society?

☑ LearningCurve
Check what you know.

Most trade in bulk commodities was seaborne. Maritime trade provided opportunities for workers in other industries and trades; some examples of workers who saw increased opportunity were sailors, shipbuilders, dockworkers, accountants, teamsters, and pirates. Piracy was always a factor in the Hellenistic world, so ships' crews had to be ready to defend their cargoes as well as transport them.

Cities in Greece often paid for their grain by exporting olive oil and wine. When agriculture and oil production developed in Syria, Greek products began to encounter competition from the Seleucid monarchy. Later in the Hellenistic period, Greek oil and wine, shipped in mass-produced pottery jugs called amphoras, found a lucrative market in Italy and throughout the Mediterranean.

Another significant commodity was fish, which for export was salted, pickled, or dried. This trade was especially important because fish provided poor people with protein, an essential element of their diet. Salt, too, was often imported, and there was a very small trade in salted meat, which was a luxury item. Far more important was the trade in honey, dried fruit, nuts, and vegetables. Of raw materials, wood was high in demand, but little trade occurred in manufactured goods.

Slaves were a staple of Hellenistic trade, traveling in all directions on both land and sea routes. War provided prisoners for the slave market; to a lesser extent, so did kidnapping and capture by pirates, although the origins of most slaves is unknown. Both old Greek states and new Hellenistic kingdoms were ready slave markets, and throughout the Mediterranean world, slaves were almost always in demand. Slaves were to be found in the cities and temples of the Hellenistic world; in the shops, fields, armies, and mines; and in the homes of wealthier people.

> **QUICK REVIEW**

How did trade facilitate cultural exchange during the Hellenistic period?

CHAPTER LOCATOR | How and why did Alexander the Great create an empire?

CHAPTER 4
102 LIFE IN THE HELLENISTIC WORLD

How did religion and philosophy shape everyday life in the Hellenistic world?

Isis and Horus

In this small statue from Egypt, the goddess Isis is shown suckling her son Horus. Worship of Isis spread throughout the Hellenistic world; her followers believed that Isis offered them life after death, just as she had brought Horus's father, Osiris, back to life. (Louvre, Paris, France/Peter Willi/The Bridgeman Art Library)

THE MIXING OF PEOPLES in the Hellenistic era influenced religion and philosophy. The Hellenistic kings built temples to the old Olympian gods and promoted rituals and ceremonies like those in earlier Greek cities, but new deities also gained prominence. More people turned to mystery religions, which blended Greek and non-Greek elements. Others turned to practical philosophies that provided advice on how to live a good life.

| How did Greek ideas and traditions spread? | What new economic connections were created in the Hellenistic period? | **How did religion and philosophy shape everyday life in the Hellenistic world?** | How did science and medicine serve the needs of Hellenistic society? | ✓ LearningCurve Check what you know. |

Religion and Magic

When Hellenistic kings founded cities, they also built temples, staffed by priests and supported by taxes, for the Olympian gods of Greece. The transplanted religions, like those in Greece itself, sponsored literary, musical, and athletic contests. These festivities offered bright and lively entertainment, both intellectual and physical. They fostered Greek culture and traditional sports and were attractive to socially aspiring individuals who adopted Greek culture.

Along with the traditional Olympian gods, Greeks and non-Greeks in the Hellenistic world also honored and worshiped deities that had not been important in the Hellenic period or that were a blend of imported Greek and indigenous gods and goddesses. Tyche (TIE-kee), for example, was a new deity, the goddess and personification of luck, fate, chance, and fortune. Temples to her were built in major cities of the eastern Mediterranean, including Antioch and Alexandria, and her image was depicted on coins and bas-reliefs.

Tyche could be blamed for bad things that happened, but Hellenistic people did not simply give in to fate. Instead they honored Tyche with public rituals and more-private ceremonies, and they also turned to professionals who offered spells for various purposes. We generally make a distinction between religion and magic, but for Greeks there was not a clear line. Thus, these professionals would write spells using both ordinary Greek words and special "magical" language known only to the gods, often instructing those who purchased them to carry out specific actions to accompany their words.

Hellenistic kings generally did not suppress indigenous religious practices. Some kings limited the power of existing priesthoods, but they also subsidized them with public money. Priests continued to carry out the rituals that they always had, perhaps now adding the name "Zeus" to that of the local deity or composing their hymns in Greek.

Some Hellenistic kings intentionally sponsored new deities that mixed Egyptian and Greek elements. When Ptolemy I established the Ptolemaic dynasty in Egypt, he thought that a new god was needed who would appeal to both Greeks and Egyptians. Working together, an Egyptian priest and a Greek priest combined elements of the Egyptian god Osiris (god of the afterlife) with aspects of the Greek gods Zeus, Hades (god of the underworld), and Asclepius (god of medicine) to

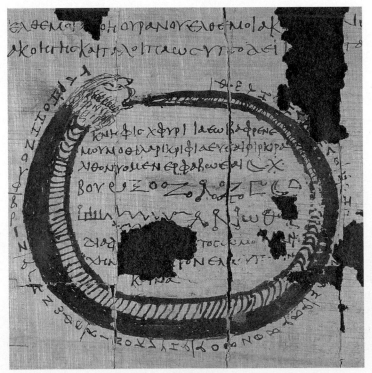

Hellenistic Magical Text

This text, written in Greek and Egyptian on papyrus, presents a magical incantation surrounded by a lion-headed snake. Both Hellenic and Hellenistic Greeks sought to know the future through various means of divination and to control the future through rituals and formulas that called on spirits and gods to intervene. (© British Library Board, PAP.121 fr 3)

CHAPTER LOCATOR | How and why did Alexander the Great create an empire?

create a new god, Serapis. Ptolemy I's successors made Serapis the protector and patron of Alexandria and built a huge temple in the god's honor in the city. His worship spread as intentional government policy, and he was eventually adopted by Romans as well, who blended him with their own chief god, Jupiter.

More and more people were attracted to mystery religions, so called because at the center of each was an inexplicable event that brought union with a god and was not to be divulged to anyone not initiated into the respective religion. Mystery religions incorporated aspects of both Greek and non-Greek religions and claimed to save their adherents from the worst that fate could do. Most taught that by the rites of initiation, in which the secrets of the religion were shared, devotees became united with a deity who had also died and risen from the dead. The sacrifice of the god and his victory over death saved the devotee from eternal death. Similarly, mystery religions demanded a period of preparation in which the converts strove to become pure and holy, that is, to live by the religion's precepts. Once aspirants had prepared themselves, they went through the initiation, usually a ritual of great emotional intensity symbolizing the entry into a new life.

Among the mystery religions, the Egyptian cult of Isis spread widely. In Egyptian mythology Isis brought her husband Osiris back to life (see Chapter 1), and during the Hellenistic era this power came to be understood by her followers as extending to them as well. Isis promised to save any mortal who came to her, and her priests asserted that she had bestowed on humanity the gift of civilization and founded law and literature. Isis was understood to be a devoted mother as well as a devoted wife, and she became the goddess of marriage, conception, and childbirth. She became the most important goddess of the Hellenistic world, where Serapis was often regarded as her consort instead of Osiris. Devotion to Isis, and to many other mystery religions, later spread to the Romans as well as to the Greeks and non-Greeks who lived in Hellenistic cities.

Hellenism and the Jews

Jews in Hellenistic cities were generally treated the same as any other non-Greek group. At first, they were seen as resident aliens. As they grew more numerous, they received permission to form a political corporation, a *politeuma* (pah-lih-TOO-mah), which gave them a great deal of autonomy. The Jewish politeuma, like the rest of the Hellenistic city, was expected to obey the king's commands, but there was almost no royal interference with the Jewish religion.

Antiochus IV Epiphanes (175–ca. 164 B.C.E.) broke with this pattern. He expanded the Seleucid kingdom and nearly conquered Egypt. While he was in Egypt, however, a revolt broke out in Judaea, led by Jews who opposed the Hellenized Jewish leader he had designated for them. Antiochus attacked Jerusalem, killing many, and restored his leader. According to Hebrew scripture, he then banned Jewish practices and worship, ordered copies of the Torah burned, and set up altars to the Greek gods in Jewish temples. These actions sparked a widespread Jewish revolt that began in 166 B.C.E., called the Revolt of the Maccabees, after the name of one of its leaders. Using guerrilla tactics, the Maccabees fought Syrian troops who were fighting under Seleucid commanders, retook Jerusalem, and set up a semi-independent state in 164 B.C.E. This state lasted for about a century, until it was conquered by the Romans.

| How did Greek ideas and traditions spread? | What new economic connections were created in the Hellenistic period? | **How did religion and philosophy shape everyday life in the Hellenistic world?** | How did science and medicine serve the needs of Hellenistic society? | ✓ LearningCurve Check what you know. |

105

Jews living in Hellenistic cities often embraced many aspects of Hellenism. In fact, the Revolt of the Maccabees is seen by some historians as primarily a dispute between Hellenized Jews and those who wanted to retain traditional practices. So many Jews learned Greek, especially in Alexandria, that the Hebrew Bible was translated into Greek and services in the synagogue there were conducted in Greek. Jews often took Greek names, used Greek political forms, adopted Greek practice by forming their own trade associations, and put inscriptions on graves as the Greeks did.

Philosophy and the People

Philosophy during the Hellenic period was the exclusive province of the wealthy and educated; only they had leisure enough to pursue philosophical studies (see Chapter 3, page 82). During the Hellenistic period, however, philosophy came to touch the lives of more men and women than ever before, although it was still directed toward the educated elite. There were several reasons for this development. First, much of Hellenistic life, especially in the new cities of the East, seemed unstable and without venerable traditions. Greeks were far more mobile than they had ever been before, but their very mobility left them feeling uprooted. Second, traditional religions had declined, and there was a growing belief that one could do relatively little to change one's fate. One could honor Tyche, the goddess of fortune, but to protect against the worst that Tyche could do, many Greeks also looked to philosophy. Philosophers themselves became much more numerous, and several new schools of philosophical thought caught the minds and hearts of many contemporary Greeks and some non-Greeks.

One of these new schools of philosophical thought was **Epicureanism** (eh-pih-kyou-REE-uh-nih-zuhm), a practical philosophy of serenity in an often-tumultuous world. Although Epicurus (eh-pih-KYOUR-uhs) (340–270 B.C.E.) did not deny the existence of the gods, he taught that they had no effect on human life. Epicurus used observation and logic to study the world and also to examine the human condition. He decided that the principal goods of human life were contentment and pleasure, which he defined as the absence of pain, fear, and suffering. By encouraging the pursuit of pleasure, he was not advocating drunken revels or sexual excess, which he thought caused pain, but moderation in food, clothing, and shelter.

Epicurus also taught that individuals could attain peace and serenity most easily by ignoring the outside world and looking into their personal feelings and reactions. This ideal was one to which anyone could aspire, no matter what their social standing. Epicurus is reported to have allowed slaves and even women to attend his school, a sharp contrast with the earlier philosopher Plato. Epicureanism taught its followers to ignore politics and other worldly issues because politics led to tumult, which would disturb the soul.

Zeno (335–262 B.C.E.), a philosopher from Cyprus, advanced a different concept of human beings and the universe. Zeno first came to Athens to form his own school, the Stoa, named after the covered walkways where he preferred to teach, and his philosophy, **Stoicism** (STOH-uh-sih-zuhm), in turn, came to be named for his school. Zeno and his followers considered nature an expression of divine will; in their view people could be happy only when living in accordance with nature.

Epicureanism
▶ A system of philosophy based on the teachings of Epicurus, who viewed a life of contentment, free from fear and suffering, as the greatest good.

Stoicism
▶ A philosophy, based on the ideas of Zeno, that people could be happy only when living in accordance with nature and accepting whatever happened.

CHAPTER LOCATOR | How and why did Alexander the Great create an empire?

106 CHAPTER 4 LIFE IN THE HELLENISTIC WORLD

They stressed the unity of humans and the universe, stating that all people were obliged to help one another.

Unlike the Epicureans, the Stoics taught that people should participate in politics and worldly affairs. Yet this idea never led to the belief that individuals should try to change the order of things. The Stoics were indifferent to specific political forms and believed that people should do their duty to the state in which they found themselves. To the Stoics, the important question was not whether they achieved anything, but whether they lived virtuous lives. The patient self-control and fortitude that the Stoics advocated made this a popular philosophy among the Romans later and gave rise to the modern adjective *stoic* to convey these virtues.

The Stoics' most significant practical achievement was the creation of the concept of **natural law**. They concluded that, because all people were kindred, partook of divine reason, and were in harmony with the universe, one law governed them all. This law was part of the natural order of life, not something created by individual states or rulers. Thus, natural law was an abstract matter of ethics and applicable everywhere, not something that applied to everyday political or social life.

Individualistic and individualized themes emerge in Hellenistic art and literature as well as in philosophy. Sculptors looked to the works of the classical period, such as the reliefs and statuary on the Athenian Acropolis, for their models in terms of composition but then created works that show powerful emotions and straining muscles. In contrast to the classical preference for the perfect human form, the artists and the people who bought their works wanted art that showed real people, including those suffering from trauma, disease, and the physical problems that came with aging. Hellenistic art was more naturalistic than Hellenic art—portraying the poor, old, and ugly as well as the young and beautiful.

As had Athens in the classical period, Hellenistic cities offered theater performances to their residents, paid for by the government. People tended to prefer revivals of the tragedies of Aeschylus, Sophocles, and Euripides (see Chapter 3, page 75) over newly written tragic works, but in comedy they wanted new material. This was provided by Menander (ca. 342–291 B.C.E.), whose more than one hundred comedies poked fun at current philosophies and social trends. Menander's comedies tended to be less political than those of Aristophanes, but they still commented on the ruler cults developed by Hellenistic kings, the dangers of the new professionalized mercenary armies to older values, and the conspicuous consumption of the newly rich.

natural law

▶ A Stoic concept that a single law that was part of the natural order of life governed all people.

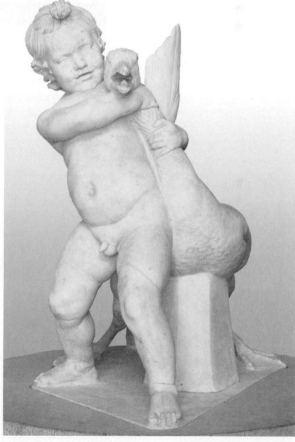

Boy with a Goose

In the Hellenistic culture that developed across a huge area after Alexander the Great's conquests, wealthy urban residents wanted art that showed real people rather than gods. This statue of a little boy wrestling a goose, originally carved about 200 B.C.E., no doubt found an eager buyer. (© Vanni Archive/Art Resource, NY)

QUICK REVIEW <

What larger social, political, and economic trends influenced religion and philosophy in the Hellenistic period?

How did Greek ideas and traditions spread?

What new economic connections were created in the Hellenistic period?

How did religion and philosophy shape everyday life in the Hellenistic world?

How did science and medicine serve the needs of Hellenistic society?

✓ LearningCurve
Check what you know.

> How did science and medicine serve the needs of Hellenistic society?

Physician with Young Patient

This plaster cast from ca. 350 B.C.E. shows a physician examining a child, while Asclepius, the god of healing, observes. Asclepius holds a staff with a snake coiled around it, which remains the symbol of medicine today. This cast was made through a process known as intaglio, in which the picture was carved onto a cylinder-shaped gemstone, then rolled across wet clay to produce the image. (Hulton Archive/Getty Images)

> **PICTURING THE PAST**

ANALYZING THE IMAGE: How is the physician diagnosing the health or illness of the child?
CONNECTIONS: Given what you have read about Hellenistic medicine, why might the artist have included the god Ascelpius in this scene?

IN THE SCHOLARLY REALM, Hellenistic thinkers made advances in mathematics, astronomy, and mechanical design. Physicians used observation and dissection to better understand the way the human body works and to develop treatments for disease. Many of these developments occurred in Alexandria, where the Ptolemies did much to make the city an intellectual, cultural, and scientific center.

Science

The main advances in Hellenistic science came in astronomy, geography, and mechanics. The most notable of the Hellenistic astronomers was Aristarchus (a-ruh-STAHR-kuhs) (ca. 310–230 B.C.E.) of Samos. Aristarchus concluded that the sun is far larger than the earth and that the stars are enormously distant from the earth. He argued against the commonsense observation that the earth was the

CHAPTER LOCATOR | How and why did Alexander the Great create an empire?

center of the universe. Instead, Aristarchus developed the heliocentric theory—that the earth and planets revolve around the sun. His theory was discussed for several centuries but was later forgotten when another astronomer working in Alexandria, Claudius Ptolemy (ca. 90–ca. 168 C.E.) returned the discussion to an earth-centered universe. Aristarchus's heliocentric theory was resurrected in the sixteenth century C.E. by the brilliant Polish astronomer Nicolaus Copernicus.

In geometry, Hellenistic thinkers discovered little that was new, but Euclid (YOU-kluhd) (ca. 300 B.C.E.), a mathematician who lived in Alexandria, compiled a valuable textbook of existing knowledge. His *Elements of Geometry* rapidly became the standard introduction to geometry.

The greatest thinker of the Hellenistic period was Archimedes (ca. 287–212 B.C.E.), a native of Syracuse who was interested in nearly everything. A clever inventor, he devised new artillery for military purposes. In peacetime he perfected the water screw to draw water from a lower to a higher level. He also invented the compound pulley to lift heavy weights. His chief interest, however, lay in pure mathematics. He founded the science of hydrostatics (the study of fluids at rest) and discovered the principle that the volume of a solid floating in a liquid is equal to the volume of the liquid displaced by the solid. (See "Individuals in Society: Archimedes, Scientist and Inventor," page 110.)

Archimedes was willing to share his work with others, among them Eratosthenes (ehr-uh-TAHS-thuh-neez) (285–ca. 204 B.C.E.). Like Archimedes, he was a man of almost universal interests.

Eratosthenes used mathematics to further the geographical studies for which he is most famous. He concluded that the earth was a spherical globe and calculated the circumference of the earth geometrically, estimating it as about 24,675 miles. He was not wrong by much: the earth is actually 24,860 miles in circumference. He drew a map of the earth and discussed the shapes and sizes of land and ocean and the irregularities of the earth's surface. His idea that the earth was divided into large landmasses influenced other geographers and later shaped ordinary people's understanding of the world as well. Eratosthenes declared that to get to India, a ship could sail around Africa or even sail directly westward, an idea that would not be tested until the end of the fifteenth century.

Other Greek geographers also turned their attention southward to Africa. During this period the people of the Mediterranean learned of the climate and customs of Ethiopia and gleaned some information about sub-Saharan Africa from Greek sailors and merchants who had traveled there. Geographers incorporated these travelers' reports into their more theoretical works.

As the new artillery devised by Archimedes indicates, Hellenistic science was used for purposes of war as well as peace. Theories of mechanics were used to build machines that revolutionized warfare. Fully realizing the practical possibilities of the first effective artillery in Western history, Philip of Macedonia had introduced the machines to the broader world in the middle of the fourth century B.C.E. The catapult became the first and most widely used artillery piece, shooting ever-larger projectiles. Generals soon realized that they could also hurl burning bundles over the walls to start fires in a besieged city. As the Assyrians had earlier, engineers built siege towers, large wooden structures that served as artillery platforms, and put them on wheels so that soldiers could roll them up to a city's or town's walls. Once there, archers stationed on top of the siege towers swept the

How did Greek ideas and traditions spread? | What new economic connections were created in the Hellenistic period? | How did religion and philosophy shape everyday life in the Hellenistic world? | **How did science and medicine serve the needs of Hellenistic society?** | ✔ LearningCurve Check what you know.

109

Archimedes (ca. 287–212 B.C.E.) was born in the Greek city of Syracuse in Sicily, an intellectual center where he pursued scientific interests. He was the most original thinker of his time and a practical inventor. In his book *On Plane Equilibriums* he dealt for the first time with the basic principles of mathematics, including the principle of the lever. He once said that if he were given a lever and a suitable place to stand, he could move the world. He also demonstrated how easily his compound pulley could move huge weights with little effort:

> A three-masted merchant ship of the royal fleet had been hauled on land by hard work and many hands. Archimedes put aboard her many men and the usual freight. He sat far away from her; and without haste, but gently working a compound pulley with his hand, he drew her towards him smoothly and without faltering, just as though she were running on the surface.*

He perfected what became known as the Archimedian screw, a pump to bring subterranean water up to irrigate fields, which he had observed in Egypt and which later came into wider use. He worked on issues involving solid geometry, and in his treatise *On Floating Bodies* he founded the science of hydrostatics. He concluded that an object will float if it weighs less than the water it displaces, and that whenever a solid floats in a liquid, the volume of the solid equals the volume of the liquid displaced. The way he made his discovery has become famous:

> When he was devoting his attention to this problem, he happened to go to a public bath. When he climbed down into the bathtub there, he noticed that water in the tub equal to the bulk of his body flowed out. Thus, when he observed this method of solving the problem, he did not wait. Instead, moved with joy, he sprang out of the tub, and rushing home naked he kept indicating in a loud voice that he had indeed discovered what he was seeking. For while running he was shouting repeatedly in Greek, "*Eureka, eureka*" ("I have found it, I have found it").†

War between Rome and Syracuse interrupted Archimedes's scientific life. In 213 B.C.E., during the Second Punic War, the Romans besieged the city. Hiero, its king and Archimedes's friend, asked the scientist for help in repulsing Roman attacks. Archimedes began to design and build remarkable devices that served as artillery. One weapon shot missiles to break up infantry attacks,

Several of Archimedes's treatises were found on a palimpsest, a manuscript that had been scraped and washed so that another text could be written over it, thus reusing the expensive parchment. Reusing parchment was a common practice in the Middle Ages, but the original text can sometimes be reconstructed. Using digital processing with several types of light and X-rays to study this thirteenth-century-C.E. prayer book, scientists were slowly able to decipher the texts by Archimedes that were underneath, including one that had been completely lost. (Image by the Rochester Institute of Technology.)

*Plutarch, *Life of Marcellus*.
†Vitruvius, *On Architecture*, 9 Preface, 10.

and others threw huge masses of stones that fell on the enemy. For use against Roman warships, he is said to have designed a machine with beams from which large claws dropped onto the hulls of warships, hoisted them into the air, and dropped them back into the sea. Later Greek writers reported that he destroyed Roman ships with a series of polished mirrors that focused sunlight and caused the ships to catch fire. Modern experiments re-creating Archimedes's weapons have found that the claw might have been workable, but the mirrors probably were not, as they required a ship to remain stationary for the fire to ignite. It is not certain whether his war machines were actually effective, but later people recounted tales that the Romans became so fearful that whenever they saw a bit of rope or a stick of timber projecting over the wall, they shouted, "There it is—Archimedes is trying some engine on us," and fled. After many months the Roman siege was successful, however, and Archimedes was killed by a Roman soldier.

QUESTIONS FOR ANALYSIS

1. How did Archimedes combine theoretical mathematics and practical issues in his work?
2. What applications do you see in the world around you for the devices Archimedes improved or invented, such as the lever, the pulley, and artillery?

enemy's ramparts with arrows while other soldiers manning catapults added missile fire. As soon as the walls were cleared, soldiers from the siege towers swept over the enemy's ramparts and into the city. To augment the siege towers, generals added battering rams that consisted of long, stout shafts housed in reinforced shells. Inside the shell the crew pushed the ram up to the wall and then heaved the shaft against the wall. Rams proved even more effective than catapults in bringing down large portions of walls.

Over time, Hellenistic generals built larger, more complex, and more effective machines. If these new engines made waging war more efficient, they also added to the misery of the people because war often directly involved the populations of cities. As it had in Periclean Athens (see Chapter 3, page 72), war often contributed to the spread of disease, and battlefields gave surgeons and physicians plenty of opportunities to test their ideas about how the human body would best heal.

Medicine

Doctors as well as scientists combined observation with theory during the Hellenistic period. Herophilus, who lived in the first half of the third century B.C.E., worked at Alexandria and studied the writings attributed to Hippocrates (see Chapter 3, page 82). He approached the study of medicine in a systematic, scientific fashion: he dissected dead bodies and measured what he observed. He was the first to describe the nervous system accurately, and he differentiated between motor and sensory nerves. Herophilus also studied the brain, which he considered the center of intelligence, and discerned the cerebrum and cerebellum. His other work dealt with the liver, lungs, and uterus. His younger contemporary Erasistratus also conducted research on the brain and nervous system and improved on Herophilus's work. Erasistratus, too, followed in the tradition of Hippocrates and believed that the best way for the body to heal itself was through diet and air.

Because Herophilus and Erasistratus followed the teachings of Hippocrates, later writers on medicine labeled them "Dogmatists" or as belonging to the "Dogmatic school," from the Greek word *dogma*, or philosophical idea. Along with their hands-on study of the human body, the Dogmatists also speculated about the nature of disease and argued that there were sometimes hidden causes for illness. Opposing them was an Empiric school begun by a student of Herophilus; doctors in the Empiric school held that observation and experiment were the only ways to advance medical knowledge and viewed the search for hidden causes as useless.

Whether undertaken by Dogmatists or Empiricists, medical study did not lead to effective cures for the infectious diseases that were the leading cause of death for most people, and people used a variety of ways to attempt to combat illness. Medicines prescribed by physicians or prepared at home often included natural products blended with materials thought to work magically. People also invoked Asclepius, the god of medicine, in healing rituals, or focused on other deities who were believed to have power over specific illnesses. (See "Picturing the Past: Physician with Young Patient," page 108.) They paid specialists to devise spells that would cure them or prevent them from becoming ill in the first place (see page 104). Women in childbirth gathered their female friends and relatives around them, and in larger cities they could also hire experienced midwives who knew how to decrease pain and assist in the birthing process if something went wrong. People in the Hellenistic world may have thought that fate determined what would happen, but they also actively sought to make their lives longer and healthier.

> **QUICK REVIEW**

How did science and mathematics alter warfare in the Hellenistic period?

CHAPTER LOCATOR | How and why did Alexander the Great create an empire?

CHAPTER 4
112   LIFE IN THE HELLENISTIC WORLD

LOOKING BACK LOOKING AHEAD

The conquests of Philip and Alexander broadened Greek and Macedonian horizons, but probably not in ways that they had intended. The empire that they created lasted only briefly, but the Hellenistic culture that developed afterward took Greeks even beyond the borders of Alexander's huge empire as conquerors, merchants, artists, and sailors.

The Hellenistic world was largely conquered by the Romans, but in cultural terms the conquest was reversed: The Romans derived their alphabet from the Greek alphabet, though they changed the letters somewhat. Roman statuary was modeled on Greek statuary and was often, in fact, made by Greek sculptors, who found ready customers among wealthy Romans. The major Roman gods and goddesses were largely the same as the Greek ones, though they had different names. The Romans did not seem to have been particularly interested in the speculative philosophy of Socrates and Plato, but they were drawn to the more practical philosophies of the Epicureans and Stoics. And like the Hellenistic Greeks, many Romans turned from traditional religions to mystery religions, which offered secret knowledge and promised eternal life. Among these was Christianity, a new religion that grew in the Roman Empire and whose most important early advocate was Paul of Tarsus, a well-educated Hellenized Jew who wrote in Greek. Significant aspects of Greek culture thus lasted long after the Hellenistic monarchies and even the Roman Empire were gone, shaping all subsequent societies in the Mediterranean and Near East.

> ### ▷LaunchPad
>
> **ONLINE DOCUMENT PROJECT**
> ## Alexander the Great
> What were the motives behind Alexander's conquests, and what were the consequences of Hellenization?
>
> Keeping the question above in mind, explore a variety of ancient perspectives on these questions. *See inside the front cover to learn more.*

| How did Greek ideas and traditions spread? | What new economic connections were created in the Hellenistic period? | How did religion and philosophy shape everyday life in the Hellenistic world? | How did science and medicine serve the needs of Hellenistic society? | ☑ **LearningCurve** Check what you know. |

CHAPTER 4 STUDY GUIDE

 **STEP 1**

GET STARTED ONLINE

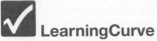 **LearningCurve**

Now that you've read the chapter, make it stick by completing the LearningCurve activity.

 **STEP 2**

EXPLAIN WHY IT MATTERS

Put your reading into practice. Identify each term below, and then explain why it matters in Western history.

TERM	WHO OR WHAT & WHEN	WHY IT MATTERS
Hellenistic (p. 90)		
Hellenization (p. 94)		
epicureanism (p. 106)		
stoicism (p. 106)		
natural law (p. 107)		

STEP 3

MOVE BEYOND THE BASICS

To demonstrate a more advanced understanding of life in a Hellenistic city, use the chart below to help identify its key features. How did the Hellenistic city differ from the Greek polis?

	Hellenistic city	Greek polis
Culture		
Social divisions		
Government		
Economy		
Urban-rural relations		

STEP 4 PUT IT ALL TOGETHER

Now, take a step back and try to explain the big picture. Remember to use specific examples from the chapter in your answers.

HELLENISTIC SOCIETY AND GOVERNMENT

▶ What new opportunities were open to Greek speakers in the Hellenistic period?

▶ What were the most important differences between Hellenic and Hellenistic society?

THE HELLENISTIC ECONOMY

▶ What role did long-distance trade play in the Hellenistic economy?

▶ How did life change, if at all, for the majority of people who lived in the countryside during the Hellenistic era?

HELLENISTIC RELIGION, PHILOSOPHY, AND SCIENCE

▶ What might explain the growing appeal of mystery religions in the Hellenistic period?

▶ Why did philosophy have a wider impact during the Hellenistic period than it had during the Hellenic period?

MAKE CONNECTIONS

▶ What were the most important continuities between the Hellenic and Hellenistic periods? What were the most important discontinuities?

▶ In what ways were Hellenistic cities similar to modern cities? In what ways were they dissimilar?

> IN YOUR OWN WORDS

Imagine that you must give an oral report to the class answering the following question. **How did the Mediterranean world change in the centuries following Alexander's conquests? What** would be the most important points and why?

5

THE RISE OF ROME

CA. 1000–27 B.C.E.

> **How and why did Roman society and government change over the course of the Republican period?** Chapter 5 examines the rise of the Romans from a minor Italian power to the dominant force in the Mediterranean world. At the same time that Alexander the Great's armies were moving from victory to victory, the Romans were gaining control of the Italian peninsula. Beginning in the sixth century B.C.E., the Romans gradually took over more and more territory, first in Italy, then throughout the western Mediterranean basin, and finally in areas in the east that had been part of Alexander's empire. The wars of conquest, however, created serious social, political, and economic problems that, over time, led to the demise of the traditional Roman state and the emergence of a new imperial order.

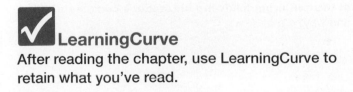

LearningCurve
After reading the chapter, use LearningCurve to retain what you've read.

Life in a Roman City. This intricate mosaic, found in a villa near the city of Pompeii, was buried in the explosion of Mount Vesuvius in 79 C.E. Most of the figures are wearing masks, suggesting they are performing in a theatrical comedy. (Museo Archeologico Nazionale, Naples, Italy/ The Bridgeman Art Library)

> How did the Romans become the dominant power in Italy?

> What were the key institutions of the Roman Republic?

> How did the Romans build a Mediterranean empire?

> How did expansion affect Roman society and culture?

> What led to the fall of the Roman Republic?

> How did the Romans become the dominant power in Italy?

The Temple of Hercules Victory

This round temple, dating from the second century B.C.E., is the oldest surviving marble building in Rome, and was imported from Greece. It once contained a statue of the mythical hero Hercules and was dedicated to him because the temple was the spot where legend told he killed a monster who had stolen some cattle. (Justin Kase z12z/ Alamy)

> PICTURING THE PAST

ANALYZING THE IMAGE: Looking at the pictures of Greek temples and altars in Athens and Pergamum on pages 97 and 77, what stylistic similarities do you see between those buildings and this temple?
CONNECTIONS: How do those similarities, and the fact that this temple was dedicated to Hercules, provide evidence for Roman adoption of Greek religion and culture?

THE COLONIES ESTABLISHED BY GREEK POLEIS (city-states) in the Hellenic era (see Chapter 3) included a number along the coast of southern Italy and Sicily. Although Alexander the Great (see Chapter 4) created an empire that stretched from his homeland of Macedonia to India, his conquests did not reach as far as southern Italy and Sicily. Thus the Greek colonies there remained politically independent. They became part of the Hellenistic cultural world, however, and they transmitted much of that culture to people who lived farther north in the Italian peninsula. These people included the Etruscans, who built the first cities north of the Greek colonies, and then the Romans, who eventually came to dominate the peninsula.

CHAPTER LOCATOR | How did the Romans become the dominant power in Italy?

ca. 1000 B.C.E.
– Earliest settlements in the area that became the city of Rome

264–201; 149–146 B.C.E.
– Punic Wars

753 B.C.E.
– Traditional founding of the city of Rome

133–121 B.C.E.
– Reforms of the Gracchi

509 B.C.E.
– Traditional date of establishment of the Roman Republic

107–31 B.C.E.
– Turmoil in the late republic (see timeline, page 141)

451–449 B.C.E.
– Laws of the Twelve Tables written and issued

44 B.C.E.
– Julius Caesar assassinated

390 B.C.E.
– Gauls sack Rome

31 B.C.E.
– Octavian defeats Antony and Cleopatra at the Battle of Actium

367 B.C.E.
– Licinian-Sextian laws passed

27 B.C.E.
– Senate issues decrees giving Octavian great power

ca. 265 B.C.E.
– Romans control most of Italy

The Geography of Italy

The Italian peninsula occupies the center of the Mediterranean basin and serves as a focal point for the two halves (**Map 5.1**). Italian winters are rainy, but the summer months are dry. Because of the climate, the rivers of Italy usually carry little water during the summer. Most of Italy's other rivers are unsuitable for regular, large-scale shipping and never became major thoroughfares for commerce and communications. Yet the rivers nourished a bountiful agriculture that could produce enough crops for a growing population.

Geography encouraged Italy to look to the Mediterranean. In the north, Italy is protected by the Alps, which form a natural barrier. From the north the Apennine Mountains run southward for the entire length of the Italian boot, cutting off access to the Adriatic Sea for those to their west. This barrier induced Italy to look west to Spain and Carthage rather than east to Greece, but it did not carve up the land in a way that would prevent the development of political unity.

In their southward course, the Apennines leave two broad and fertile plains to their west: Latium and Campania. These plains attracted settlers and invaders from the time that peoples began to move into Italy. Among these peoples were those who would found Rome on the Tiber River in Latium.

This site enjoyed several advantages. The Tiber provided Rome with a constant source of water. Located at an easy crossing point on the Tiber, Rome thus stood astride the main avenue of communications between northern and southern Italy. Positioned amid seven hills, Rome was defensible and safe from the floods of the Tiber. It was also close to the sea through the port of Ostia. Thus, Rome was in an excellent position to develop the resources of Latium and maintain contact with the rest of Italy.

What were the key institutions of the Roman Republic?	How did the Romans build a Mediterranean empire?	How did expansion affect Roman society and culture?	What led to the fall of the Roman Republic?	✔ **LearningCurve** Check what you know.

The Etruscans

The culture that is now called Etruscan developed in north-central Italy about 800 B.C.E. The Etruscans established permanent settlements that evolved into cities resembling the Greek city-states and built a rich cultural life that became the foundation of civilization in much of Italy. The Etruscans spread their influence

MAP 5.1 ■ Roman Italy and the City of Rome, ca. 218 B.C.E.

As Rome expanded, it built roads linking major cities and offered various degrees of citizenship to the territories it conquered or with which it made alliances. The territories outlined in green that are separate from the Italian peninsula were added by 218 B.C.E., largely as a result of the Punic Wars.

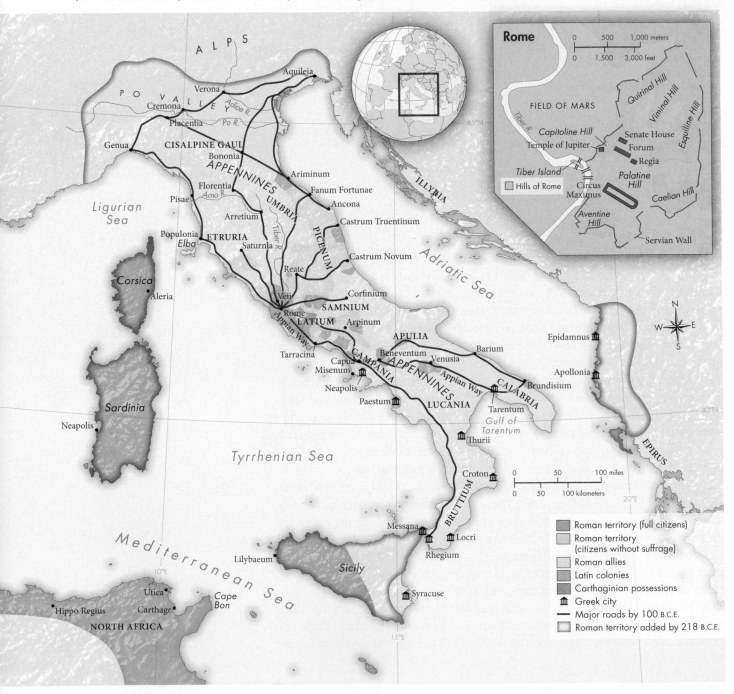

CHAPTER LOCATOR | How did the Romans become the dominant power in Italy?

120 CHAPTER 5
THE RISE OF ROME

over the surrounding countryside. They traded natural products, especially iron, with their Greek neighbors to the south and with other peoples throughout the Mediterranean in exchange for a variety of goods.

Etruscan cities appear to have been organized in leagues and, beginning about 750 B.C.E., the Etruscans expanded southward into central Italy through military actions on land and sea and through the establishment of colony cities. In the process of expansion, they encountered a small collection of villages subsequently called Rome.

The Etruscans, ca. 500 B.C.E.

The Founding of Rome

Archaeological evidence indicates that the ancestors of the Romans began to settle on the hills east of the Tiber during the early Iron Age, around 1000 to 800 B.C.E. Archaeological sources provide the most important information about this earliest period of Roman history, but later Romans told a number of stories about the founding of Rome.

The Romans' foundation myths were told in a number of different versions. In the most common of these, Romulus and Remus founded the city of Rome, an event later Roman authors dated precisely to 753 B.C.E. These twin brothers were the sons of the war god Mars and a human mother. The brothers, who were left to die by a jealous uncle, were raised by a female wolf. When they were grown, they decided to build a city in the hills that became part of Rome, but they quarreled over which hill should be the site of the city. In the end, Romulus killed Remus and named the city after himself. He also established a council of advisers later called the Senate. Romulus and his mostly male followers expanded their power over the neighboring Sabine peoples, in part by abducting and marrying their women. The Sabine women then arranged a peace by throwing themselves between their brothers and their husbands, convincing them that killing kin would make the men cursed. The Romans, favored by the gods, continued their rise to power.

Despite its tales of murder and kidnapping, this founding myth ascribes positive traits to the Romans: they are descended from gods and heroes, can thrive in wild and tough settings, will defend their boundaries at all costs, and mix with other peoples rather than simply conquering them. Also, the story portrays women who were ancestors of Rome as virtuous and brave.

Later Roman historians continued the story by describing a series of kings after Romulus, each elected by the Senate. According to tradition, the last three kings were Etruscan, and another tale about female virtue was told to explain why the Etruscan kings were overthrown. In this story, the son of King Tarquin, the Etruscan king who ruled Rome, raped Lucretia, a virtuous Roman wife, in her own home. Lucretia summoned her husband and father to the house, told them what had happened, and demanded they seek vengeance. She then committed suicide by plunging a knife into her heart.[1] Her father and husband and the other Roman nobles swore on the bloody knife to avenge Lucretia's death by throwing out the Etruscan kings, and they did. Whether any part of this story is true can never be known, but Romans generally accepted it as history and dated the expulsion of the Etruscan kings to 509 B.C.E. They saw this year as marking the end of the monarchical period and the dawn of the republic.

Most historians today view the idea that Etruscan kings ruled the city of Rome as legendary, but they stress the influence of the Etruscans on Rome. The

| What were the key institutions of the Roman Republic? | How did the Romans build a Mediterranean empire? | How did expansion affect Roman society and culture? | What led to the fall of the Roman Republic? | ☑ LearningCurve Check what you know. |

Etruscans transformed Rome from a relatively large town to a real city. The Romans adopted the Etruscan alphabet, which the Etruscans themselves had adopted from the Greeks. Romans adopted the use of a bundle of rods tied together with an ax emerging from the center, which symbolized the Etruscan king's power. This ceremonial object was called the fasces (FAS-eez), and was carried first by Etruscan officials and then by Romans. Even the toga, the white woolen robe worn by citizens, came from the Etruscans, as did gladiatorial combat honoring the dead. In engineering and architecture, the Romans adopted some design elements and the basic plan of their temples, along with paved roads, from the Etruscans.

In this early period, the city of Rome does appear to have been ruled by kings. A hereditary aristocracy also developed; it advised the kings and may have played a role in choosing them. And sometime in the sixth century B.C.E., a group of aristocrats revolted against these kings and established a government in which the main institution of power was in the **Senate**, an assembly of aristocrats, rather than a single monarch. Executive power was in the hands of Senate leaders called **consuls**, but there were always two of them and they were elected for one-year terms only. Rome thereby became a republic, not a monarchy.

Under kings and then the Senate, the villages along the Tiber gradually grew into a single city, whose residents enjoyed contacts with the larger Mediterranean world. Temples and public buildings began to grace Rome, and the Forum, a large plaza between two of Rome's hills, became a public meeting place similar to the Greek agora (see Chapter 3, page 65). The Capitoline Hill became the city's religious center. In addition, trade in metalwork became common, and wealthier Romans began to import fine Greek vases and other luxuries.

The Roman Conquest of Italy

In the years following the establishment of the republic, the Romans fought numerous wars with their neighbors on the Italian peninsula. The Roman army was made up primarily of citizens of Rome organized into legions for military campaigns. War also involved diplomacy, and at an early date, Romans learned the value of alliances, which became a distinguishing feature of Roman expansion in Italy. Alliances with the towns around them in Latium provided a large population that could be tapped for military needs. Some of these townspeople were organized into troops called auxiliaries who fought with the legions.

In 387 B.C.E., the Romans suffered a major setback when the Celts—or Gauls, as the Romans called them—invaded the Italian peninsula from the north, destroyed a Roman army, and sacked the city of Rome. (For more on the Gauls, see Chapter 7, page 194.) More intent on loot than on conquest, the Gauls agreed to abandon Rome in return for a thousand pounds of gold. As the story was later told, when the Gauls provided their own scale, the Romans howled in indignation. The Gallic chieftain Brennus then threw his sword on the scale, exclaiming "*Vae victis*" (woe to the conquered). These words, though legendary, were used by later Romans as an explanation for why they would not surrender, and the city of Rome was not sacked again until 410 C.E.

The Romans rebuilt their city and recouped their losses. They brought Latium and their Latin allies fully under their control and conquered Etruria (see Map 5.1,

Senate
▶ The assembly that was the main institution of power in the Roman Republic, originally composed only of aristocrats.

consuls
▶ Primary executives in the Roman Republic, elected for one-year terms in the Senate who commanded the army in battle, administered state business, and supervised financial affairs.

CHAPTER LOCATOR | How did the Romans become the dominant power in Italy?

122 CHAPTER 5
THE RISE OF ROME

page 120). Starting in 343 B.C.E., they turned south and grappled with the Samnites in a series of bitter wars for the possession of Campania. The Samnites were a formidable enemy and inflicted serious losses on the Romans; in response the Romans reorganized their army to create the mobile legion, a flexible unit of soldiers capable of fighting anywhere. The Romans won in the end and continued their expansion southward. Alarmed by Roman expansion, the Greek city of Tarentum in southern Italy called for help from Pyrrhus (PIHR-uhs), king of Epirus in western Greece, in 280 B.C.E. Pyrrhus won two furious battles but suffered heavy casualties—thus the phrase "Pyrrhic victory" is still used today to describe a victory involving severe losses.

The Romans and the Carthaginians had made a series of treaties to help one another (see page 127), and the Carthaginians attacked Sicily, drawing the armies of Pyrrhus away from Italy for a while and relieving pressure on the Romans. The Romans threw new legions against Pyrrhus's army, which in the end left southern Italy. The Romans made formal alliances with many of the Greek cities in the south then turned north again. Their superior military institutions, organization, and large supply of soldiers allowed the Romans to conquer or take into their sphere of influence most of Italy by about 265 B.C.E.

As they expanded their territory, the Romans spread their religious traditions throughout Italy, blending them with local beliefs and practices. Religion for the Romans was largely a matter of honoring the state and the family. The main goal of religion was to secure the peace of the gods, what was termed *pax deorum,* and to harness divine power for public and private enterprises. Religious rituals were an important way of expressing common values, which for Romans meant those evident in their foundation myths: bravery, morality, seriousness, family, and home. Along with the great gods, the Romans believed in spirits who inhabited fields, forests, crossroads, and even the home itself. These spirits were to be honored with rituals and gifts so that they would be appeased instead of becoming hostile.

Victorious generals made sure to honor the gods of people they had conquered and by doing so transformed them into gods they could also call on for assistance in their future campaigns. Greek deities and mythical heroes were absorbed into the Roman pantheon. (See "Picturing the Past: The Temple of Hercules Victory," page 118.)

Once they had conquered an area, the Romans built roads. These roads provided an easy route for communication between the capital and outlying areas, allowed for the quick movement of armies, and offered an efficient means of trade.

In politics the Romans shared full Roman citizenship with many of their oldest allies, particularly the inhabitants of the cities of Latium. In other instances they granted citizenship without the franchise, that is, without the right to vote or hold Roman office. These allies were subject to Roman taxes and calls for military service but ran their own local affairs. The extension of Roman citizenship strengthened the state and increased its population and wealth, although limitations on this extension would eventually become a source of conflict (see page 138).

QUICK REVIEW <

What role did diplomacy play in the Romans' conquest of Italy?

What were the key institutions of the Roman Republic?

How did the Romans build a Mediterranean empire?

How did expansion affect Roman society and culture?

What led to the fall of the Roman Republic?

☑ LearningCurve
Check what you know.

What were the key institutions of the Roman Republic?

Coin Showing a Voter

This coin from 63 B.C.E. shows a citizen wearing a toga dropping a voting tablet into a voting urn, the Roman equivalent of today's ballot box. The tablet has a *V* on it, meaning a yes vote, and the coin has an inscription giving the name of the moneyer, the official who controlled the production of coins and decided what would be shown on them. Here the moneyer, Lucius Cassius Longinus, depicted a vote held fifty years earlier regarding whether an ancestor of his should be named prosecutor in a trial charging three vestal virgins with unchastity. As was common among moneyers, Longinus chose this image as a means to advance his political career, in this case by suggesting his family's long history of public office. (Snark/Art Resource, NY)

ALONG WITH CITIZENSHIP, the republican government was another important institution of Roman political life. Roman institutions were not static; they changed over time to allow broader access to power and address new problems.

The Roman State

The Romans summed up their political existence in a single phrase: *senatus populusque Romanus*, "the Senate and the Roman people," which they abbreviated SPQR. This sentiment reflects the republican ideal of shared government rather than power concentrated in a monarchy. It stands for the beliefs, customs, and laws of the republic.

In the early republic, social divisions determined the shape of politics. Political power was in the hands of a hereditary aristocracy—the **patricians**, whose privileged legal status was determined by their birth as members of certain families. The common people of Rome, the **plebeians** (plih-BEE-uhns), were free citizens with a voice in politics, but they had few of the patricians' political and social advantages. While some plebeian merchants increased their wealth in the course of Roman expansion and came to rival the patricians economically, most plebeians were poor artisans, small farmers, and landless urban dwellers.

patricians
▸ The Roman hereditary aristocracy; they held most of the political power in the republic.

plebeians
▸ The common people of Rome; they were free but had few of the patricians' advantages.

CHAPTER LOCATOR | How did the Romans become the dominant power in Italy?

The Romans created several assemblies through which men elected high officials and passed legislation. The earliest was the Centuriate Assembly, in which citizens were organized into groups called centuries. Each citizen was assigned to a century depending on his status and amount of wealth, and the patricians possessed the majority of centuries. When an election was ordered, each century met separately and voted as a bloc, which meant that the patricians could easily outvote the plebeians. In 471 B.C.E., plebeian men won the right to meet in an assembly of their own, the *concilium plebis*, and to pass ordinances.

The highest officials of the republic were the two consuls, who were elected for one-year terms by the Centuriate Assembly. The consuls commanded the army in battle, administered state business, presided over the Senate and assemblies, and supervised financial affairs. In effect, they ran the state. The consuls appointed quaestors (KWEH-stuhrs) to assist them in their duties, and in 421 B.C.E. the quaestorship became an elective office open to plebeian men. In 366 B.C.E., the Romans created a new office, that of praetor (PREE-tuhr). When the consuls were away from Rome, the praetors could act in their place; they could also command armies, act as governors in the provinces, interpret law, and administer justice.

The most important institution of the republic was the Senate, a political assembly that most likely originated in the monarchical period as a council of the heads of powerful families who advised the king. During the republic the Senate grew to several hundred members, all of whom had previously been elected to one of the high positions, which automatically conferred Senate membership. Because the Senate sat year after year with the same members, the Senate provided stability and continuity. It passed formal decrees that were technically "advice" to the magistrates, who were not bound to obey them but usually did. The Senate directed the magistrates on the conduct of war and had the power over the expenditure of public money. In times of emergency, it could name a dictator.

Within the city of Rome itself, the Senate's powers were limited by laws and traditions, but as Rome expanded, the Senate had greater authority in the outlying territories. The Romans divided the lands that they conquered into provinces, and the Senate named the governors, most of whom were former consuls or praetors, for each province. Another responsibility of the Senate was to handle relations between Rome and other powers.

A lasting achievement of the Romans was their development of law. Roman civil law, the *ius civile*, consisted of statutes, customs, and forms of procedure that regulated the lives of citizens. As the Romans came into more frequent contact with foreigners, the consuls and praetors applied a broader *ius gentium*, the "law of the peoples," to matters such as peace treaties, the treatment of prisoners of war, and the exchange of diplomats. In the ius gentium, all sides were to be treated the same regardless of their nationality. By the late republic, Roman jurists had widened this principle still further into the concept of *ius naturale*, "natural law," based in part on Stoic beliefs (see Chapter 4, page 106). Natural law, according to these thinkers, is made up of rules that govern human behavior and that come from applying reason rather than customs or traditions, and so apply to all societies.

Social Conflict in Rome

Inequality between plebeians and patricians led to a conflict known as the **Struggle of the Orders**. In this conflict the plebeians sought to increase their power by taking advantage of the fact that Rome's survival depended on its army,

Struggle of the Orders
▶ A conflict in which the plebeians sought political representation and safeguards against patrician domination.

What were the key institutions of the Roman Republic? | How did the Romans build a Mediterranean empire? | How did expansion affect Roman society and culture? | What led to the fall of the Roman Republic? | ☑ LearningCurve Check what you know.

125

tribunes
▶ Plebeian-elected officials; tribunes brought plebeian grievances to the Senate for resolution and protected plebeians from the arbitrary conduct of patrician magistrates.

which needed plebeians to fill the ranks of the infantry. According to tradition, in 494 B.C.E., the plebeians literally walked out of Rome and refused to serve in the army. Their general strike worked, and the patricians grudgingly made important concessions. They allowed the plebeians to elect their own officials, the **tribunes**, who presided over the consilium plebis, brought plebeian grievances to the Senate for resolution, and vetoed the decisions of the consuls if they wished.

The law itself was the plebeians' primary target. Only the patricians knew what the law was, and only they could argue cases in court. All too often they used the law for their own benefit. After much struggle, in 449 B.C.E., the patricians surrendered their legal monopoly and codified and published the Laws of the Twelve Tables, so called because they were inscribed on twelve bronze plaques. The Laws of the Twelve Tables covered many legal issues, including property ownership, guardianship, inheritance, procedure for trials, and punishments for various crimes. The patricians also made legal procedures public so that plebeians could argue cases in court. Later, in 445 B.C.E., the patricians passed a law, the *lex Canuleia*, that for the first time allowed patricians and plebeians to marry one another.

Licinius and Sextius were plebeian tribunes in the fourth century B.C.E. who mounted a sweeping assault on patrician privilege. After a ten-year battle, the Licinian-Sextian laws were passed in 367 B.C.E., giving wealthy plebeians access to all the offices of Rome, including the right to hold one of the two consulships. Once plebeians could hold the consulship, they could also sit in the Senate and advise on policy. Though decisive, this victory did not end the Struggle of the Orders, which happened only in 287 B.C.E. with the passage of the *lex Hortensia*. This law gave the resolutions of the concilium plebis, the plebeian assembly, the force of law for patricians and plebeians alike.

The long Struggle of the Orders had resulted in an expansion of power to wealthy plebeians, but once certain plebeian families could hold the consulship and become members of the Senate, they became as uninterested in the problems of the average plebeian as the patricians had formerly been. In theory, all men could aspire to the highest political offices. In reality, political power had been expanded only slightly and still resided largely in a group of wealthy families, some of whom happened to be plebeian. Access to the highest political offices was still difficult for any plebeian, who often had to get the support of patrician families if he wanted a political career.

patron-client system
▶ An informal system of patronage in which free men promised their votes to a more powerful man in exchange for his help in legal or other matters.

Networks of support were actually important for all Romans involved in public life, not simply aspiring plebeians. Roman politics operated primarily through a **patron-client system** whereby free men promised their votes to a more powerful man in exchange for his help in legal or other matters. The more powerful patron looked after his clients, and his clients' support helped the patron advance his career.

> **QUICK REVIEW**

How did social tensions lead to changes in Roman law and government?

CHAPTER LOCATOR | How did the Romans become the dominant power in Italy?

Roman School In this carved stone relief from the second century c.e., a teacher makes a point to two older students who have scrolls in their hands, while a younger student enters. Roman methods of education developed in the late republic continued in the empire and spread to the provinces. This relief comes from Neumagen, a town in what is now Germany that was founded by the Romans. (Rheinisches Landesmuseum, Trier)

AS THE REPUBLICAN GOVERNMENT WAS DEVELOPING, Roman territory continued to expand. Unlike Alexander the Great, the Romans did not map out grandiose strategies to conquer the world. Rather, they responded to situations as they arose. This meant, however, that they sought to eliminate any state they saw as a military threat.

The Punic Wars

As they pushed southward, incorporating the southern Italian peninsula into their growing territory, the Romans confronted another great power in the western Mediterranean, the Carthaginians. The city of Carthage had been founded by Phoenicians as a trading colony in the eighth century b.c.e. (see Chapter 2). By the

| What were the key institutions of the Roman Republic? | **How did the Romans build a Mediterranean empire?** | How did expansion affect Roman society and culture? | What led to the fall of the Roman Republic? | ✔ LearningCurve Check what you know. |

fourth century B.C.E., the Carthaginians began to expand their holdings. They had one of the largest navies in the Mediterranean and were wealthy enough to hire mercenaries to do much of their fighting. At the end of a long string of wars, the Carthaginians had created and defended a mercantile empire that stretched from western Sicily to the western end of the Mediterranean (see Map 5.1, page 120).

Beginning in the fifth century B.C.E., the Romans and the Carthaginians made a series of treaties with one another that defined their spheres of influence, and they worked together in the 270s B.C.E. to defeat Pyrrhus. But the Greek cities that became Roman allies in southern Italy and Sicily saw Carthage as a competitor in terms of trade. This competition led to the first of the three **Punic Wars** between Rome and Carthage. The First Punic War lasted for twenty-three years (264–241 B.C.E.) and ended with the Romans in possession of Sicily, which became their first real province.

The peace treaty between Rome and Carthage brought no peace because both powers had their sights set on dominating the western half of the Mediterranean. In 238 B.C.E., the Romans took advantage of Carthaginian weakness to seize Sardinia and Corsica. The Carthaginians responded by expanding their holdings in Spain under the leadership of the commander Hamilcar Barca. In the following years, Hamilcar and his son-in-law Hasdrubal (HAHZ-droo-buhl) subjugated much of southern Spain and in the process rebuilt Carthaginian power. Rome first made a treaty with Hasdrubal, setting the boundary between Carthaginian and Roman interests at the Ebro River, and then began to extend its own influence in Spain.

In 221 B.C.E., Hamilcar's son Hannibal became the Carthaginian commander in Spain and laid siege to Saguntum (suh-GUHN-tum), a Roman-allied city that lay within the sphere of Carthaginian interest and was making raids into Carthaginian territories. The Romans declared war, claiming that Carthage had attacked a friendly city. So began the Second Punic War. In 218 B.C.E., Hannibal marched an enormous army from Spain across what is now France and over the Alps into Italy. Once there, he defeated one Roman army after another and, in 216 B.C.E., he won his greatest victory at the Battle of Cannae (KAH-nee). Hannibal then spread devastation throughout the Italian peninsula, and a number of cities in central and southern Italy rebelled against Rome. Yet Hannibal was not able to win areas near Rome in central Italy because Roman allies there, who had been extended citizenship rights, remained loyal. Hannibal's allies did not supply him with enough food and supplies to sustain his troops, and Rome fought back.

In 210 B.C.E., Rome found its answer to the problem of Hannibal in the young commander Scipio Africanus. In the years following 210 B.C.E., Scipio operated in Spain, which in 207 B.C.E. he had wrested from the Carthaginians. That same year, the Romans sealed Hannibal's fate in Italy. At the Battle of Metaurus, the Romans destroyed a major Carthaginian army coming to reinforce Hannibal. Scipio then struck directly at Carthage itself, prompting the Carthaginians to recall Hannibal from Italy to defend their homeland.

In 202 B.C.E., at the town of Zama near Carthage (**Map 5.2**), Scipio defeated Hannibal in a decisive battle. The Carthaginians sued for peace and the Roman Senate agreed.

The Second Punic War contained the seeds of still other wars. Unabated fear of Carthage combined with the encouragement of Cato the Elder (see page 134)

Punic Wars

▶ A series of three wars between Rome and Carthage in which Rome emerged the victor.

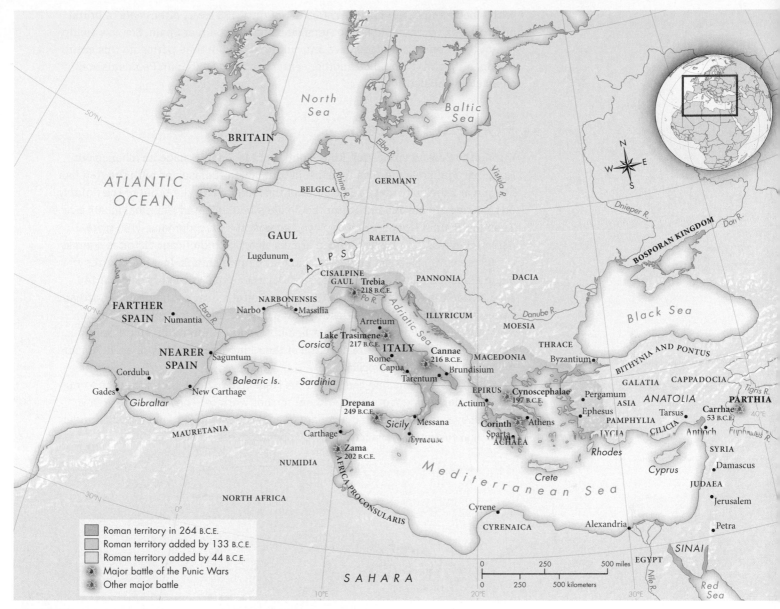

MAP 5.2 ■ Roman Expansion During the Republic, ca. 282–44 B.C.E.

Rome expanded in all directions, first west and then east, eventually controlling every shore of the Mediterranean.

> MAPPING THE PAST

ANALYZING THE MAP: Which years saw the greatest expansion of Roman power during the republic? How might the different geographic features have helped or hindered the expansion into certain areas?

CONNECTIONS: What allowed the Romans to maintain their power across such a wide and diverse area?

led to the Third Punic War, a needless conflict that ended in 146 B.C.E. when Scipio Aemilianus, the grandson by adoption of Scipio Africanus, destroyed the hated rival and burned Carthage to the ground.

During the war with Hannibal, the Romans had invaded the Iberian Peninsula, an area rich in material resources and the home of fierce warriors. They met

| What were the key institutions of the Roman Republic? | **How did the Romans build a Mediterranean empire?** | How did expansion affect Roman society and culture? | What led to the fall of the Roman Republic? | ✓ LearningCurve Check what you know. |

with bloody and determined resistance. Not until 133 B.C.E., after years of brutal and ruthless warfare, did Scipio Aemilianus finally conquer Spain. Scipio's victory meant that Roman language, law, and culture would in time permeate this entire region, although it would be another century before the Iberian Peninsula was completely pacified.

Rome Turns East

During the Second Punic War, King Philip V of Macedonia made an alliance with Hannibal against Rome. The Romans, in turn, allied themselves with the Aetolian League of Greek city-states. The cities of the league bore the brunt of the fighting on the Greek peninsula until after the Romans had defeated Hannibal in 202 B.C.E. Then the Roman legions were deployed against the Macedonians, who were defeated in a series of wars. Roman armies also won significant victories against the forces of the Seleucid emperors, and that empire shrank. In 148 B.C.E., they made Macedonia into a Roman province. Another decisive victory came in 146 B.C.E., when the Romans attacked the city of Corinth. Just as they had at Carthage earlier that year, the Romans destroyed the city, looting it for treasure. In 133 B.C.E., the king of Pergamum bequeathed his kingdom to the Romans. The Ptolemies of Egypt retained formal control of their kingdom, but they obeyed Roman wishes in terms of trade policy.

Once the Romans had conquered the Hellenistic world, they faced the formidable challenge of governing it without further warfare. They began to create political and administrative machinery to hold the Mediterranean together under a political system of provinces ruled by governors sent from Rome.

> **QUICK REVIEW**

How did the Romans take control of the Mediterranean world?

How did expansion affect Roman society and culture?

BY THE SECOND CENTURY B.C.E., the Romans ruled much of the Mediterranean world, and tremendous wealth poured into Rome. Roman institutions, social patterns, and ways of thinking changed to meet the new era. Some looked nostalgically back at what they fondly considered the good old days and idealized the traditional agrarian and family-centered way of life. Others embraced the new urban life and eagerly accepted Greek culture.

Roman Families

The core of traditional Roman society was the family, and the word *family* (*familia*) in ancient Rome actually meant all those under the authority of a male head of household, including nonrelated slaves and servants. In poor families, this group might be very small, but among the wealthy, it could include hundreds of slaves and servants.

The male head of household was called the **paterfamilias**. Just as slave owners held power over their slaves, fathers held great power over their children, which technically lasted for their children's whole lives. Initially this seems to have included power over life and death, but by the second century B.C.E., that had been limited by law and custom. Fathers continued to have the power to decide how family resources should be spent, however, and sons did not inherit until after their fathers had died.

paterfamilias
▶ The oldest dominant male of the family, who held great power over the lives of family members.

| What were the key institutions of the Roman Republic? | How did the Romans build a Mediterranean empire? | **How did expansion affect Roman society and culture?** | What led to the fall of the Roman Republic? | ☑ LearningCurve Check what you know. |

131

In the early republic, legal authority over a woman generally passed from her father to her husband on marriage, but the Laws of the Twelve Tables allowed it to remain with her father even after marriage. That was advantageous to the father, and could also be to the woman, because her father might be willing to take her side in a dispute with her husband, and she could return to her birth family if there was quarreling or abuse. By the late republic, more and more marriages were of this type, and during the time of the empire (27 B.C.E. to 476 C.E.), almost all of them were.

To marry, both spouses had to be free Roman citizens. Marital agreements, especially among the well-to-do, were stipulated with contracts between the families involved. According to Roman law, marriage required a dowry, a payment of money, property, and/or goods that went from the bride's family to the groom. If their owner allowed it, slaves could enter a marriage-like relationship called *contubernium*, which benefited their owner because any children produced from it would be his. People who were not slaves or citizens certainly lived together in marriage-like relationships, but these had no standing before the law and their children could not legally inherit.

Women could inherit and own property under Roman law, though they generally received a smaller portion of any family inheritance than their brothers did. A woman's inheritance usually came as her dowry on marriage. In the earliest Roman marriage laws, men could divorce their wives without any grounds, and women could not divorce their husbands. By the second century B.C.E., however, these laws had changed, and both men and women could initiate divorce. By then, women had also gained greater control over their dowries and other family property, perhaps because Rome's military conquests meant that many husbands were away for long periods of time and women needed some say over family finances.

Although marriages were arranged by families primarily for the handing down of property to legitimate children, the Romans, in something of a contradiction, viewed the model marriage as one in which husbands and wives were loyal to one another and shared interests and activities. The Romans praised women who were virtuous and loyal to their husbands and devoted to their children.

Traditionally minded Romans thought that mothers should nurse their own children and personally see to their welfare. Non-elite Roman women did nurse their own children, although wealthy women increasingly employed slaves as wet nurses and to help them with child rearing. Very young children were under their mother's care, and most children learned the skills they needed from their own parents. For children from wealthier urban families, opportunities for formal education increased in the late republic. Boys and girls might be educated in their homes by tutors, who were often Greek slaves, and boys also might go to a school, paid for by their parents.

Most people in the expanding Roman Republic lived in the countryside. Farmers used oxen and donkeys to plow their fields, collecting the dung of the animals for fertilizer. Along with crops raised for local consumption and to pay their rents and taxes, many farmers raised crops to be sold. These included wheat, flax for making linen cloth, olives, and wine grapes.

Most Romans worked long days, and an influx of slaves from Rome's wars and conquests provided additional labor for the fields, mines, and cities. To the Romans, slavery was a misfortune that befell some people, but it did not entail any racial theories. Slave boys and girls were occasionally formally apprenticed in trades such as leatherworking, weaving, or metalworking. Well-educated slaves

CHAPTER LOCATOR | How did the Romans become the dominant power in Italy?

served as tutors or accountants, ran schools, and designed and made artwork and buildings. For loyal slaves, the Romans always held out the possibility of freedom, and **manumission**, the freeing of individual slaves by their masters, was fairly common, especially for household slaves. Nonetheless, slaves rebelled from time to time, sometimes in large-scale revolts put down by Roman armies (see page 139).

Membership in a family did not end with death; the spirits of the family's ancestors were understood to remain with the family. They and other gods regarded as protectors of the household—collectively these were called the *lares* and *penates*—were represented by small statues that stood in a special cupboard or a niche in the wall. The statues were taken out at meals and given small bits of food, or food was thrown into the household's hearth for them. The lares and penates represented the gods at family celebrations such as weddings, and families took the statues with them when they moved.

manumission

▶ The freeing of individual slaves by their masters.

Greek Influence on Roman Culture

Many aspects of life did not change greatly during the Roman expansion. Most people continued to marry and form families and to live in the countryside, with the rhythm of their days and years determined by the needs of their crops. But with the conquest of the Mediterranean world, Rome became a great city, and many other cities emerged as well. The spoils of war went to build theaters, stadiums, and other places of amusement. Romans and Italian townspeople began to spend more of their time in leisure pursuits. This new urban culture reflected Hellenistic influences. Romans developed a liking for Greek literature, and it became common for an educated Roman to speak both Latin and Greek. The new Hellenism profoundly stimulated the growth and development of Roman art and literature. Roman artists copied many aspects of Greek art, but used art, especially portraiture, to communicate Roman values. Portrait busts in stone were a favored art form. Those who commissioned them wanted to be portrayed as individuals, but also as representing certain admirable qualities, such as wisdom or dignity.

Greek influence was also strong in literature. Roman authors sometimes wrote histories and poetry in Greek, or translated Greek classics into Latin. The poet Ennius (EHN-ee-uhs) (239–169 B.C.E.), the father of Latin poetry, studied Greek philosophy, wrote comedies in Latin, and adapted many of Euripides's tragedies for the Roman stage. Plautus (ca. 254–184 B.C.E.) brought a bawdy humor to his reworkings of Greek plays. The Roman dramatist Terence (ca. 195–159 B.C.E.) wrote comedies of refinement and grace that owed their essential elements to Greek models. All early Roman literature was derived from that of the Greeks, but it flourished because it also spoke to Roman ways of thinking.

The conquest of the Mediterranean world and the wealth it brought gave the Romans leisure, and Hellenism influenced how they spent their free time. Many rich urban dwellers changed their eating habits by consuming elaborate meals of exotic dishes. During the second century B.C.E., the Greek custom of bathing also gained popularity in the Roman world. The Romans built more and more large public buildings containing pools and exercise rooms, and by the period of the early empire, baths had become an essential part of any Roman city.

The baths were socially important places where men and women went to see and be seen. Social climbers tried to talk to the right people and wangle invitations to dinner; politicians took advantage of the occasion to discuss the affairs of the day; marriages were negotiated by wealthy fathers. Baths were also places

| What were the key institutions of the Roman Republic? | How did the Romans build a Mediterranean empire? | **How did expansion affect Roman society and culture?** | What led to the fall of the Roman Republic? | ✔ LearningCurve Check what you know. |

133

Roman Bath This Roman bath in Bath, England (a city to which it gave its name), was built beginning in the first century C.E. around a natural hot spring. The Romans spread the custom of bathing, which they had adopted from the Greeks, to the outer reaches of their empire. In addition to hot water, bathers used oil for massage and metal scrapers (inset) to clean and exfoliate their skin. Many Roman artifacts have been unearthed at Bath, including a number of curse tablets, small tablets made of lead calling on the gods to harm someone, which were common in the Greco-Roman world. Not surprisingly, many of the curse tablets found at Bath relate to the theft of clothing while people were bathing. (bath: Horst Schafer/Peter Arnold Inc.; artifact: Courtesy of the Trustees of the British Museum)

where people could buy sex; the women and men who worked in bathhouses often made extra income through prostitution. Because of this, moralists portrayed them as dens of iniquity, but they were seen by most Romans as a normal part of urban life.

Opposing Views: Cato the Elder and Scipio Aemilianus

Romans differed greatly in their opinions about Hellenism and other new social customs. Two men, Marcus Cato (234–149 B.C.E.) and Scipio Aemilianus (185–129 B.C.E.), both of whom were military commanders and consuls, the highest office in the Roman Republic, can serve as representatives of these opposing views.

CHAPTER LOCATOR | How did the Romans become the dominant power in Italy?

134 CHAPTER 5 THE RISE OF ROME

Marcus Cato was born a plebeian and owned a small rural estate, but his talent and energy caught the eye of high patrician officials and he became their client. He fought in the Second Punic War under Scipio Africanus and then returned to Rome, where he worked his way up through various offices. In 195 B.C.E., he was elected consul. A key issue facing Cato was the heated debate over the repeal of the Oppian Law, which had been passed twenty years earlier, right after Rome's disastrous loss to Carthage at the Battle of Cannae. Rome had needed money to continue the war, and the law decreed that no woman was to own more than a small amount of gold, or wear clothing trimmed in purple, or drive a chariot in the city of Rome itself. These were all proclaimed to be luxuries that wasted money and undermined the war effort. The law was passed in part for financial reasons, but it also had gendered social implications, as there was no corresponding law limiting men's conspicuous consumption. By 195 B.C.E., the war was over and this restriction on women's spending had lost its economic rationale. Roman women publicly protested against it, and Cato led the battle to prevent its repeal. The women's actions were more effective than Cato's speeches, however, and the law was lifted.

Women's spending was not the only problem destroying Roman society, according to Cato. Although he made certain his older son learned Greek as an essential tool in Roman society, he instructed the boy not to take Greek ideas too seriously and viewed the influx of Greek culture in general as dangerous. Cato set himself up as the defender of what he saw as traditional Roman values: discipline, order, morality, frugality, and an agrarian way of life.

Cato held the office of censor, and he attempted to remove from the lists of possible officeholders anyone who did not live up to his standards. Late in life he was a diplomat to Carthage, and after seeing that the city had recovered economically from the war with Rome, he came home declaring, "Carthage must be destroyed." He repeated this often enough that shortly after his death the Romans decided to do just this in the Third Punic War.

Ironically, the mission to Carthage was led by Scipio Aemilianus, the grandson of Scipio Africanus and an avid devotee of Hellenism. Like his grandfather, Scipio believed that broader views had to replace the old Roman narrowness. Rome was no longer a small city; it was the capital of the world, and Romans had to adapt themselves to that fact. Scipio became an innovator in both politics and culture. He developed a more personal style of politics that looked unflinchingly at the broader problems that the success of Rome brought to its people. He embraced Hellenism wholeheartedly and promoted its spread in Roman society. Perhaps more than anyone else of his day, Scipio represented the new Roman— imperial, cultured, and independent. In the end, Scipio's views became more widespread than those of Cato. In general, Rome absorbed and added what it found useful from Hellenism, just as earlier it had absorbed aspects of Etruscan culture.

QUICK REVIEW <

What aspects of Roman life were changed the most by expansion? What aspects were changed the least?

| What were the key institutions of the Roman Republic? | How did the Romans build a Mediterranean empire? | **How did expansion affect Roman society and culture?** | What led to the fall of the Roman Republic? | ☑ LearningCurve Check what you know. |

> What led to the fall of the Roman Republic?

Julius Caesar

In this bust from the first century B.C.E., the sculptor portrays Caesar as a man of power and intensity. Showing individuals as representing certain virtues was common in Roman portraiture. (Museo e Gallerie Nazionali di Capodimonte, Naples, Italy/The Bridgeman Art Library)

THE WARS OF CONQUEST created serious problems for the Romans. The republican constitution had suited the needs of a simple city-state, but it was inadequate to meet the requirements of Rome's new position in international affairs. New armies had to be provided for defense, and systems of administration and tax collection had to be created to support the republic. The people of the Roman Republic came away from the war with differing needs and expectations. Roman generals, who had commanded huge numbers of troops for long periods of time, acquired great power and ambition and were becoming too mighty for the state to control. At the same time, non-Roman inhabitants of Italy who had fought in the wars of expansion began to agitate for full Roman citizenship. Some individuals, including military contractors, profited greatly from the foreign wars, while average soldiers gained little. These complex and explosive problems largely account for the turmoil of the late republic (133–27 B.C.E.).

Reforms for Poor and Landless Citizens

Hannibal's operations and the warfare in Italy had left the countryside a shambles. The prolonged fighting had also drawn untold numbers of Roman and Italian men away from their farms for long periods. Women often ran the farms in their absence, but with so many men away fighting they did not have enough workers

CHAPTER LOCATOR | How did the Romans become the dominant power in Italy?

to keep the land under full cultivation. When the legionaries returned to their farms in Italy, their farms often looked like those they had destroyed in their wars of conquest: land was untilled, buildings were falling down, and animals were wandering.

The wars of conquest had also made some men astoundingly rich, and the newly wealthy invested their money in land. Land won by conquest was generally declared public land, and although officially there was a limit on how much public land one individual could hold, this law was often ignored. Wealthy people created huge estates, which the Romans called **latifundia** (lah-tuh-FUHN-dee-uh). The owners of the latifundia occasionally hired free men as day laborers, but they preferred to use slaves. Using slave labor, and farming on a large scale, owners of latifundia could raise crops at a lower cost than could small farmers.

Confronted by these conditions, veterans and their families took what they could get for their broken and bankrupt farms and tried their luck elsewhere. Sometimes large landowners simply appropriated public land and the small farms of former soldiers. Gradually, Italy was transformed from subsistence farming to an important source of income for the Roman ruling class.

Most veterans migrated to the cities, especially to Rome. Although some found work, most did not. Industry and small manufacturing were generally in the hands of slaves, and even when work was available, slave labor kept the wages of free men low. Instead of a new start, veterans and their families encountered slum-like living conditions and continued dependency on others. If they were Roman citizens, they could vote in citizen's assemblies, however, and tended to back anyone who offered them better prospects.

Growing numbers of landless citizens held ominous consequences for the strength of Rome's armies. The Romans had always believed that only landowners should serve in the army, for only they had something to fight for. The newly landless men may have been veterans of major battles and numerous campaigns, but once they lost their land, they became ineligible for further military service. The landless ex-legionaries wanted to be able to serve in the army again, and they were willing to support any leader who would allow them to.

One man who recognized the plight of Rome's peasant farmers and urban poor was an aristocrat, Tiberius Gracchus (tigh-BEER-ee-uhs GRAK-uhs) (163–133 B.C.E.). After his election as tribune in 133 B.C.E., Tiberius proposed that Rome return to limiting the amount of public land one individual could farm and distribute the rest of the land to the poor in small lots. Although his reform enjoyed the support of some distinguished and popular members of the Senate, it angered those who had usurped large tracts of public land for their own use. This was to be expected, yet Tiberius unquestionably made additional problems for himself. He introduced his land bill in the concilium plebis without officially consulting the Senate. When King Attalus III of Pergamum died and left his wealth and kingdom to the Romans in his will, Tiberius had the money appropriated to finance his reforms—another affront to the Senate, which was responsible for managing the finances of the provinces. As tribune he acted totally within his rights, yet the way in which he proceeded was unprecedented.

Many powerful Romans became suspicious of Tiberius's growing influence with the people. When he sought to be re-elected as tribune, riots erupted among his opponents and supporters, and a group of senators beat Tiberius to death in cold blood. Thus, some of the very people who directed the affairs of state and

| What were the key institutions of the Roman Republic? | How did the Romans build a Mediterranean empire? | How did expansion affect Roman society and culture? | **What led to the fall of the Roman Republic?** | ☑ LearningCurve Check what you know. |

137

administered the law had taken the law into their own hands. The death of Tiberius was the beginning of an era of political violence.

Although Tiberius was dead, his land bill became law, and his brother Gaius (GAY-uhs) Gracchus (153–121 B.C.E.) took up the cause of reform. Gaius was a veteran soldier with an enviable record, and when he became tribune he demanded even more extensive reform than had his brother. To help the urban poor, Gaius pushed legislation to provide them with cheap grain for bread. He defended his brother's land law and proposed that Rome send many of its poor and propertyless people out to form colonies. The prospect of new homes, land, and a fresh start gave the urban poor new hope and made Gaius popular among them.

Like his brother Tiberius, Gaius aroused a great deal of personal and factional opposition. When Gaius failed in 121 B.C.E. to win the tribunate for the third time, he feared for his life. In desperation, he armed his staunchest supporters, whereupon the Senate ordered the consul to restore order. Gaius was killed, and many of his supporters died in the turmoil.

Political Violence

The death of Gaius brought little peace, and trouble came from two sources: the outbreak of new wars in the Mediterranean basin and further political unrest in Rome. In 112 B.C.E., Rome declared war against the rebellious Jugurtha (joo-GUHR-thuh), king of Numidia in North Africa. Numidia had been one of Rome's client kingdoms, a kingdom still ruled by its own king but subject to Rome.

The Roman legions made little headway against Jugurtha until 107 B.C.E., when Gaius Marius (MEHR-ee-uhs), a politician not from the traditional Roman aristocracy, became consul and led troops to Numidia. Marius was unable to defeat Jugurtha directly, but his assistant, Sulla, bribed Jugurtha's father-in-law to betray him, and Jugurtha was captured and later executed in Rome. Marius later claimed this as a victory.

Fighting was also a problem on Rome's northern border, where two German peoples, the Cimbri and Teutones, were moving into Gaul and later into northern Italy. After the Germans had defeated Roman armies sent to repel them, the Senate sent Marius to lead the campaign against them. Before engaging the Germans, Marius encouraged enlistments by promising volunteers land after the war. Poor and landless citizens flocked to him. Marius and his army conquered the Germans, but when Marius proposed a bill to grant land to his troops once they had retired from military service, the Senate refused to act. It was a disastrous mistake. Henceforth the legionaries expected their commanders—not the Senate or the state—to protect their interests.

Rome was dividing into two political factions, both of whom wanted political power. The *populares* attempted to increase their power through the plebeian assembly and the power of the tribunes, while the *optimates* employed the traditional means of patron-client relationships and working primarily through the Senate. Both of these factions were represented in the Senate, and both had their favored general. Marius was the general backed by the populares, while the favored general of the optimates was Sulla.

In 90 B.C.E., many Roman allies in the Italian peninsula rose up against Rome because they were expected to pay taxes and serve in the army, but they had no voice in political decisions because they were not full citizens. This revolt became known as the Social War. Sulla's armies gained a number of victories over the Italian allies, and Sulla gained prestige through his success in fighting them. In the end, however, the Senate agreed to give many allies Roman citizenship in order to end the fighting.

Sulla's military victories led to his election as consul in 88 B.C.E., and he was given command of the Roman army in a campaign against Mithradates, the king of a state that had gained power and territory in what is now northern Turkey and was expanding into Greece. Before he could depart, however, the populares gained the upper hand in the assembly, revoked his consulship, and made Marius the commander of the troops against Mithradates. Riots broke out. Sulla fled the city and returned at the head of an army, an unprecedented move by a Roman general. He quelled the riots, put down his opponents, made some political changes that reduced the power of the assembly, and left again, this time to fight Mithradates.

Sulla's forces were relatively successful against Mithradates, but meanwhile Marius led his own troops into Rome in 86 B.C.E., undid Sulla's changes, and killed many of his supporters. Although Marius died shortly after his return to power, the populares who supported him continued to hold Rome. Sulla returned in 83 B.C.E., and after a brief but intense civil war he entered Rome and ordered a ruthless butchery of his opponents. He then returned all power to the Senate and restored the conservative constitution as it had been before the Gracchian reforms. In 81 B.C.E., he was granted the office of dictator, a position he used to enhance his personal power. Dictators were supposed to step down after six months—and many had done so in Roman history—but Sulla held this position for two years. In 79 B.C.E., Sulla abdicated his dictatorship because he was ill and believed his policies would last. Yet civil war was to be the constant lot of Rome for the next forty-eight years, and Sulla's abuse of political office became the blueprint for later leaders.

Civil War

Sulla's political heirs were Pompey, Crassus, and Julius Caesar, all of them able military leaders and brilliant politicians. Pompey (106–48 B.C.E.) began a meteoric rise to power as a successful commander of troops for Sulla against Marius in Italy, Sicily, and Africa. He then suppressed a rebellion in Spain, led naval forces against pirates in the Mediterranean, and defeated Mithradates and the forces of other rulers as well, transforming their territories into Roman provinces.

Crassus (ca. 115–53 B.C.E.) also began his military career under Sulla and became the wealthiest man in Rome through buying and selling land. In 73 B.C.E., a major slave revolt broke out in Italy, led by Spartacus, a former gladiator. The slave armies defeated several Roman units sent to quash them. Finally Crassus led a large army against them and put down the revolt.

Pompey and Crassus then made an informal agreement with the populares in the Senate. Both were elected consuls in 70 B.C.E. and began to dismantle Sulla's constitution and initiate economic and political reforms. They and the Senate moved too slowly for some people, however, who planned an uprising. This plot was discovered, and the forces of the rebels were put down in 63 B.C.E. by an army sent by Cicero (106–43 B.C.E.), a leader of the optimates who was consul at the time. The rebellion and Cicero's skillful handling of it discredited the populares.

The man who cast the longest shadow over these troubled years was Julius Caesar (100–44 B.C.E.). Military service was an effective stepping-stone to politics,

| What were the key institutions of the Roman Republic? | How did the Romans build a Mediterranean empire? | How did expansion affect Roman society and culture? | **What led to the fall of the Roman Republic?** | ☑ LearningCurve Check what you know. |

139

Tiberius Gracchus (163–133 B.C.E.)	Aristocratic champion of land reform
Gaius Gracchus (153–121 B.C.E.)	Brother of Tiberius Gracchus and champion of land reform
Gaius Marius (157–86 B.C.E.)	General, politician, and rival of Sulla for power
Lucius Cornelius Sulla (138–78 B.C.E.)	General, politician, and Roman dictator
Pompey (106–48 B.C.E.)	Protégé of Sulla, rival and sometime ally of Crassus and Caesar
Crassus (ca. 115–53 B.C.E.)	Wealthiest man in Rome and member of the First Triumvirate
Julius Caesar (100–44 B.C.E.)	General, politician, and victor in power struggle with Pompey
Octavian (63 B.C.E.–14 C.E.)	Nephew of Caesar and eventual victor in civil war
Marc Antony (83–30 B.C.E.)	Lieutenant of Caesar, ally of Octavian in civil war, and final rival of Octavian for power
Cleopatra (69–30 B.C.E.)	Queen of Egypt, lover of Caesar and Antony, partner of Antony in power struggle with Octavian

and Caesar was a military genius who knew how to win battles and turn victories into permanent gains. He was also a shrewd politician of unbridled ambition, who knew how to use the patron-client system to his advantage. He became a protégé of Crassus, who provided cash for Caesar's needs, and at the same time helped the careers of other politicians, who in turn looked after Caesar's interests in Rome when he was away from the city. Caesar launched his military career in Spain, where his courage won the respect and affection of his troops.

In 60 B.C.E., Caesar returned to Rome from Spain, and Pompey returned from military victories in the east. Together with Crassus, the three concluded an informal political alliance later termed the **First Triumvirate** (trigh-UHM-veh-ruht). Crassus's money helped Caesar be elected consul, and Pompey married Caesar's daughter Julia. Crassus was appointed governor of Syria, Pompey of Hispania (present-day Spain), and Caesar of Gaul.

Personal ambitions, however, undermined the First Triumvirate, and it quickly disintegrated. Crassus died in battle while trying to conquer Parthia, and Caesar and Pompey accused each other of treachery. Fearful of Caesar's popularity and growing power, the Senate sided with Pompey and ordered Caesar to disband his army. He refused, and instead in 49 B.C.E. he crossed the Rubicon River in northern Italy—the boundary of his territorial command—with soldiers. Although their forces outnumbered Caesar's, Pompey and the Senate fled Rome, and Caesar entered the city without a fight.

Caesar then led his army against those loyal to Pompey and the Senate in Spain and Greece. In 48 B.C.E., despite being outnumbered, he defeated Pompey and his army at the battle of Pharsalus in central Greece. Pompey fled to Egypt, which was embroiled in a battle for control not between two generals but

First Triumvirate

▶ The name later given to an informal political alliance among Caesar, Crassus, and Pompey in which they agreed to advance one another's interests.

CHAPTER LOCATOR | How did the Romans become the dominant power in Italy?

CHAPTER 5
140 THE RISE OF ROME

between a brother and a sister, Ptolemy XIII and Cleopatra VII (69–30 B.C.E.). Caesar followed Pompey to Egypt, Cleopatra allied herself with Caesar, and Caesar's army defeated Ptolemy's army, ending the power struggle. Pompey was assassinated in Egypt, Cleopatra and Caesar became lovers, and Caesar brought Cleopatra to Rome. (See "Individuals in Society: Queen Cleopatra," page 142.) Caesar put down a revolt against Roman control by the king of Pontus in northern Turkey, then won a major victory over Pompey's army—now commanded by his sons—in Spain.

In the middle of defeating his enemies in battles all around the Mediterranean (see Map 5.2, page 129), Julius Caesar returned to Rome several times and was elected or appointed to various positions, including consul and dictator. He was acclaimed imperator, a title given to victorious military commanders and a term that later gave rise to the word *emperor*. Whatever Caesar's official position, after he crossed the Rubicon he simply made changes on his own authority, though often with the approval of the Senate, which he packed with his supporters. The Senate transformed his temporary positions as consul and dictator into ones he would hold for life.

Caesar began to make a number of legal and economic reforms. He issued laws about debt, the collection of taxes, and the distribution of grain and land. Families who had many children were to receive rewards, and Roman allies in Italy were to have full citizenship. He founded new colonies, which were to be populated by veterans and the poor. He planned even more changes, including transforming elected positions such as consul, tribune, and provincial governor into ones that he appointed.

Caesar was wildly popular with most people in Rome, and even with many senators. Other senators, led by Brutus and Cassius, two patricians who favored the traditional republic, opposed his rise to what was becoming absolute power. In 44 B.C.E., they conspired to kill him and did so on March 15—a date called the "Ides of March" in the Roman calendar—stabbing him multiple times on the steps of the theater of Pompey, where the Senate was meeting that day.

The result of Caesar's assassination was yet another round of civil war. Caesar had named his eighteen-year-old grandnephew and adopted son, Octavian, as his heir. In 43 B.C.E., Octavian joined forces with two of Caesar's lieutenants, Mark Antony and Lepidus (LEH-puh-duhs), in a formal pact known later as the **Second Triumvirate**. Together they hunted down Caesar's killers and defeated the military forces loyal to Pompey's sons and to the conspirators. They agreed to divide the provinces into spheres of influence, with Octavian taking most of the west, Antony the east, and Lepidus the Iberian Peninsula and North Africa. The three came into conflict, and Lepidus was forced into exile by Octavian, leaving the other two to confront one another.

Both Octavian and Antony set their sights on gaining more territory. Cleopatra

TURMOIL IN THE LATE REPUBLIC

107 B.C.E.	Marius, with the aid of Sulla, defeats Jugurtha
104–100 B.C.E.	Marius, backed by populares, is elected consul
90 B.C.E.	Social War
88 B.C.E.	Sulla, backed by optimates, is elected consul
86 B.C.E.	Marius leads his own troops into Rome, kills Sulla's supporters, and seizes consulship
81 B.C.E.	Sulla is elected dictator
79 B.C.E.	Sulla abdicates
73-71 B.C.E.	Spartacus leads major slave revolt
70 B.C.E.	Pompey and Crassus are elected consuls
60 B.C.E.	Pompey, Crassus, and Caesar form the First Triumvirate; Caesar is elected consul
49 B.C.E.	Caesar crosses the Rubicon and takes Rome
48 B.C.E.	Caesar defeats Pompey at the battle of Pharsalus
44 B.C.E.	Caesar is killed by a group of senators

Second Triumvirate

▶ A formal agreement in 43 B.C.E. among Octavian, Mark Antony, and Lepidus to defeat Caesar's murderers.

What were the key institutions of the Roman Republic?   How did the Romans build a Mediterranean empire?   How did expansion affect Roman society and culture?   **What led to the fall of the Roman Republic?**   ☑ LearningCurve Check what you know.

141

INDIVIDUALS IN SOCIETY
Queen Cleopatra

Cleopatra VII (69–30 B.C.E.) was a member of the Ptolemy dynasty, the Hellenistic rulers of Egypt who had established power in the third century B.C.E. Although she was Greek, she was passionately devoted to her Egyptian subjects and was the first in her dynasty who could speak Egyptian in addition to Greek. Just as ancient pharaohs had linked themselves with the gods, she had herself portrayed as the goddess Isis and may have seen herself as a reincarnation of Isis (see Chapter 4).

At the time civil war was raging in the late Roman Republic, Cleopatra and her brother Ptolemy XIII were in a dispute over who would be supreme ruler in Egypt. Julius Caesar captured the Egyptian capital of Alexandria, Cleopatra arranged to meet him, and the two became lovers, although Cleopatra was much younger and Caesar was married. The two apparently had a son, Caesarion, and Caesar's army defeated Ptolemy's army, ending the power struggle. In 46 B.C.E., Cleopatra arrived in Rome, where Caesar put up a statue of her as Isis in one of the city's temples. The Romans hated her because they saw her as a decadent Eastern queen and a threat to what were considered traditional Roman values.

After Caesar's assassination, Cleopatra returned to Alexandria, where she became involved in the continuing Roman civil war that now pitted Octavian, Caesar's grand-nephew and heir, against Mark Antony, who commanded the Roman army in the East. When Antony visited Alexandria in 41 B.C.E., he met Cleopatra and, though he was already married to Octavian's sister, he became her lover. He abandoned (and later divorced) his Roman wife, married Cleopatra in 37 B.C.E., and changed his will to favor his children by Cleopatra. Antony's wedding present to Cleopatra was a huge grant of territory, much of it Roman, that greatly increased her power and that of all her children, including Caesarion. Antony also declared Caesarion to be Julius Caesar's rightful heir.

Octavian used the wedding gift as the reason to declare Antony a traitor. He and other Roman leaders described Antony as a romantic fool captivated by the seductive Cleopatra. Roman troops turned against Antony and joined with Octavian, and at the Battle of Actium in 31 B.C.E., Octavian defeated the army and navy of Antony and Cleopatra. Antony committed suicide, as did Cleopatra shortly afterward. Octavian ordered the teenage Caesarion killed, but the young children of Antony and Cleopatra were allowed to go back to Rome, where they were raised by Antony's ex-wife. Another consequence of Octavian's victory was that Egypt became a Roman province.

Roman sources are openly hostile to Cleopatra, and she became the model of the alluring woman whose sexual attraction led men to their doom. Stories about her beauty, sophistication, lavish spending, desire for power, and ruthlessness abounded and were retold for centuries. The most dramatic story was that she committed suicide through the bite of a poisonous snake, which may have been true

and which has been the subject of countless paintings. Her tumultuous relationships with Caesar and Antony have been portrayed in plays, novels, movies, and television programs.

QUESTIONS FOR ANALYSIS

1. How did Cleopatra benefit from her relationships with Caesar and Antony? How did they benefit from their relationships with her?
2. How did ideas about gender and Roman suspicion of the more sophisticated Greek culture combine to shape Cleopatra's fate and the way she is remembered?
3. In Chapter 1, "Individuals in Society: Hatshepsut and Nefertiti" (see page 27) also focuses on leading female figures in Egypt, but these two women lived more than a thousand years before Cleopatra. How would you compare their situation with hers?

The only portraits of Cleopatra that date from her own lifetime are on the coins that she issued. This one, made at the mint of Alexandria, shows her as quite plain, reinforcing the point made by Cicero that her attractiveness was based more on intelligence and wit than physical beauty. The reverse of the coin shows an eagle, a symbol of rule, and also a mark indicating the coin's value, which was rare in the ancient world. (© Trustees of the British Museum)

LaunchPad

ONLINE DOCUMENT PROJECT

What do Romans' negative depictions of Cleopatra tell us about the attitudes and values of her time? Keeping the question above in mind, explore Roman accounts and representations of Cleopatra to see what light they shed on political, social, and cultural values in the late republic and early empire, and then complete a writing assignment based on your findings. *See inside the front cover to learn more.*

142

had returned to rule Egypt after Caesar's death, and she supported Antony. In 31 B.C.E., Octavian's forces defeated the combined forces of Antony and Cleopatra at the Battle of Actium in Greece, but the two escaped. Octavian pursued them to Egypt, and they committed suicide rather than fall into his hands. Octavian's victory at Actium put an end to an age of civil war. For his success, the Senate in 27 B.C.E. gave Octavian the name Augustus, meaning "revered one." Although the Senate did not mean this to be a decisive break with tradition, that date is generally used to mark the end of the Roman Republic and the start of the Roman Empire.

QUICK REVIEW

Why did political conflicts in the Late Republic so often lead to violence?

LOOKING BACK LOOKING AHEAD As the Greeks were creating urban culture and spreading it around the Mediterranean, other peoples, including the Etruscans and the people who later became the Romans, built their own societies on the Italian peninsula. The Romans spread their way of life throughout Italy by means of conquest and incorporation. After wars in which they defeated the wealthy city of Carthage, they expanded their political dominance throughout the western Mediterranean basin. Then they conquered in the East until they came to view the entire Mediterranean as *mare nostrum*, "our sea." Yet their successes brought war and civil unrest, and they also brought transformations of Roman society and culture as these became Hellenized.

The final days of the republic were filled with war and chaos, and the republican institutions did not survive. Rome became an empire ruled by one man. The laws and administrative practices of the republic shaped those of the empire, however, as well as those of later states in Europe and beyond. When the American constitution was drafted in 1783, its authors—well read in Roman history and law— favored a balance of powers like those they idealized in the Roman Republic, and they chose to call the smaller and more powerful deliberative assembly the Senate. They, too, were divided into those who favored rule by traditional elites and those who favored broader political power, much like the optimates and populares of the Roman Republic. That division is reflected in the fact that the U.S. Congress has two houses, the House of Representatives elected directly by voters, and the Senate, originally elected indirectly by state legislatures.

| What were the key institutions of the Roman Republic? | How did the Romans build a Mediterranean empire? | How did expansion affect Roman society and culture? | **What led to the fall of the Roman Republic?** | ✓ LearningCurve Check what you know. |

143

CHAPTER 5 STUDY GUIDE

 STEP 1 **GET STARTED ONLINE**

 LearningCurve
Now that you've read the chapter, make it stick by completing the LearningCurve activity.

STEP 2 **EXPLAIN WHY IT MATTERS**

Put your reading into practice. Identify each term below, and then explain why it matters in Western history.

TERM	WHO OR WHAT & WHEN	WHY IT MATTERS
Senate (p. 122)		
consuls (p. 122)		
patricians (p. 124)		
plebeians (p. 124)		
Struggle of the Orders (p. 125)		
tribunes (p. 126)		
patron-client system (p. 126)		
Punic Wars (p. 128)		
paterfamilias (p. 131)		
manumission (p. 133)		
latifundia (p. 134)		
First Triumvirate (p. 140)		
Second Triumvirate (p. 141)		

 STEP 3 **MOVE BEYOND THE BASICS**

To demonstrate a more advanced understanding, identify the most important consequences of Roman expansion and conquest. Use the chart below to note the impact of expansion on key aspects of Roman life. Why did Roman military success lead to social and political instability?

Aspect	Consequences of expansion
Republican institutions	
Power of military leaders	
Concentration of wealth	
The Roman economy	
Social and political unity	

144

PUT IT ALL TOGETHER

Now, take a step back and try to explain the big picture. Remember to use specific examples from the chapter in your answers.

EXPANSION AND CONQUEST

▸ How would you explain the Romans' extraordinary military success?

▸ How did the conquest of the Hellenistic world change Roman culture?

POLITICS AND SOCIETY

▸ What were the most important Republican political bodies and institutions? Whose interests did they serve and protect?

▸ How did the Roman family reflect Roman social and moral values?

THE LATE REPUBLIC

▸ Why did political conflicts so frequently lead to political violence during the Late Republic?

▸ What connections can you make between social and economic injustice and political instability during the Late Republic?

MAKE CONNECTIONS

▸ What role did Greek and Etruscan culture play in shaping Roman society and values?

▸ How did the events of the Republican period pave the way for the emergence of Roman autocratic, imperial government?

> IN YOUR OWN WORDS

Imagine that you must give an oral report to the class answering the following question: **How and why did Roman society and government change over the course of the Republican period? What would be the most important points and why?**

6

THE ROMAN EMPIRE

27 B.C.E.–284 C.E.

> **What was life like in the Roman Empire during the period of the pax Romana?** Chapter 6 examines the first three centuries of Roman imperial rule. In 27 B.C.E., the civil wars were largely over and Augustus had emerged the victor. With peace came prosperity, stability, and a new political order that retained the trappings of the republic while concentrating power in the hands of one man. Under Augustus and the rulers that followed him, the boundaries of the Roman Empire expanded in all directions. Gaul, Germany, Britain, and eastern Europe were introduced to Greco-Roman culture. A new religion, Christianity, developed in the eastern Roman province of Judaea, and spread throughout the empire. By the third century C.E., civil wars had returned, however, and it seemed as if Augustus's creation would collapse.

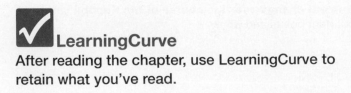

LearningCurve

After reading the chapter, use LearningCurve to retain what you've read.

Life in Imperial Rome. In this terra-cotta relief from the third century C.E., a woman sells fruit. Shops like this one were common in imperial Rome. (De Agostini Picture Library/A. Dagli Orti/The Bridgeman Art Library)

> How did Augustus create a foundation for the Roman Empire?

> How did the Roman state develop after Augustus?

> What was life like in the city of Rome, and what was it like in the provinces?

> How did Christianity grow into a major religious movement?

> What explains the chaos of the third century C.E.?

> How did Augustus create a foundation for the Roman Empire?

AFTER AUGUSTUS (R. 27 B.C.E.–14 C.E.) ENDED THE CIVIL WARS, he faced the monumental problems of reconstruction. He first had to reconstruct the constitution and the organs of government. Next he had to pay his armies for their services and care for the welfare of the provinces. Then he had to address the danger of various groups on Rome's European frontiers.

Augustus was highly successful in meeting these challenges. The result of this work was a system of government in which the emperor held all executive power in both the civil government and the military. The Senate remained as a prestigious advisory body whose members functioned at the desire and request of the emperor.

CHAPTER LOCATOR | How did Augustus create a foundation for the Roman Empire?

The Principate

Augustus claimed that he was restoring the republic, but he actually transformed the government into one in which all real power was held by a single ruler. As he did this, however, he maintained the illusion that the republic still existed.

Augustus fit his own position into the republican constitution not by creating a new office for himself but by gradually taking over many of the offices that traditionally had been held by separate people. The Senate named him often as both consul and tribune. He was also named **imperator**, a title with which the Senate customarily honored a general after a major victory. He held control of the army, which he made a permanent standing organization. Recognizing the importance of religion, he had himself named *pontifex maximus*, or chief priest.

An additional title that Augustus had the Senate bestow on him was *princeps civitatis* (prihn-KEHPS cih-vee-TAH-tees), "first citizen of the state." This title had no official powers attached to it and had been used as an honorific for centuries, so it was inoffensive to Roman ears. The government he created is called the **principate**. One of Augustus's cleverest tactics was to use noninflammatory language for himself and the changes he was making. After what had happened to Julius Caesar, Augustus wisely wielded all his power in the background.

Augustus curtailed the power of the Senate, but it continued to exist as the chief deliberative body of the state, and it continued to act as a court of law. Under Augustus and his successors, it provided officials to administer Rome and its provinces. The Senate's relations with particular emperors were often hostile. In general, however, the Senate adapted itself to the new reality and cooperated in running the empire. Governors sent to the provinces were often members of the Senate, and they took the Roman legal system with them.

Without specifically saying so, Augustus created the office of emperor. The English word *emperor* is derived from the Latin word *imperator*, an origin that reflects the fact that Augustus's command of the army was the main source of his power. Augustus never shared control of the army, and no Roman found it easy to defy him militarily. To solidify his hold on the army and make a more effective fighting force, Augustus professionalized the military even more than it had been in the late republic, and the army became a recognized institution of government.

> CHRONOLOGY

27 B.C.E.–68 C.E.
Julio-Claudian emperors; expansion into northern and western Europe

ca. 50 B.C.E.– 20 C.E.
"Golden age" of Latin literature

ca. 3 B.C.E.–ca. 29 C.E.
Life of Jesus

69–96 C.E.
Flavian emperors; restoration of order

70 C.E.
Rebellion crushed in Judaea

96–180 C.E.
Era of the "five good emperors," with relative peace and prosperity

193–211 C.E.
Emperor Septimius Severus expands Rome's borders in Africa and western Asia

212 C.E.
Edict of Caracalla makes all free males living in Roman Empire citizens

235–284 C.E.
Barracks emperors; civil war; breakdown of the empire; economic decline

imperator
▶ Title given to a Roman general after a major victory; it came to mean "emperor."

principate
▶ Official title of Augustus's form of government, taken from *princeps*, meaning "first citizen."

> The Roman Army

- Largely made up of volunteers
- The Roman legion: units of about 5,000 men, all of whom were Roman citizens
- Auxiliaries: military units made up of noncitizen volunteers or conscripts
- Citizen veterans received land or a cash bonus when they retired
- Auxiliary veterans received Roman citizenship when they retired

| How did the Roman state develop after Augustus? | What was life like in the city of Rome, and what was it like in the provinces? | How did Christianity grow into a major religious movement? | What explains the chaos of the third century C.E.? | ✓ LearningCurve Check what you know. |

Grants of land to veterans had originally been in Italy, but by Augustus's time there was not enough land for this. Instead he gave veterans land in the frontier provinces that had been taken from the people the Romans conquered. These colonies of veterans played an important role in securing the Roman Empire's boundaries and controlling its newly won provinces. Augustus's veterans took abroad with them their Latin language and Roman culture, becoming important agents of Romanization.

Roman Expansion

One of the most significant aspects of Augustus's reign was Roman expansion into northern and western Europe (**Map 6.1**). Augustus began his work in the west and north by completing the conquest of Spain begun by Scipio Africanus in the third century B.C.E. (see Chapter 5, page 127). In Gaul he founded twelve new towns, and the Roman road system linked new settlements with one another and with Italy. In 12 B.C.E., Augustus ordered a major invasion of Germany beyond the Rhine. Roman legions advanced to the Elbe River, and the area north of the Main River and west of the Elbe was on the point of becoming Roman. But in 9 C.E., some twenty thousand Roman troops were annihilated at the Battle of the Teutoburg Forest.

Meanwhile Roman troops penetrated the area of modern Austria, southern Bavaria, and western Hungary. Thereafter the Rhine and the Danube remained the Roman frontier in central Europe. The regions of modern Serbia, Bulgaria, and Romania in the Balkans fell, and the Romans created a land-based link between the eastern and western Mediterranean.

Within the area along the empire's northern border, the legionaries and auxiliaries built fortified camps. Roads linked the camps with one another, and settlements grew around the camps. Traders began to frequent the frontier and to do business with the people who lived there. Thus, Roman culture gradually spread north. As a result, for the first time central and northern Europe came into direct and continuous contact with Mediterranean culture. Many Roman camps grew into cities, transforming the economy of the area around them. Roman cities were the first urban developments in most parts of central and northern Europe.

To fortify the a political and religious bonds between the provinces and Rome, Augustus encouraged the cult of **Roma et Augustus** (Rome and Augustus) as the guardians of the state and the source of all benefits to society. The cult spread rapidly, especially in the eastern Mediterranean, where it built on the ideas of divine kingship developed in the Hellenistic monarchies (see Chapter 4, page 93).

To make his presence felt more keenly, Augustus had himself portrayed on coins standing alongside the goddess Victory, and on celebratory stone arches built to commemorate military victories. In addition, he had temples, stadiums, marketplaces, and public buildings constructed in Rome and other cities. Later emperors expanded this imperial cult, erecting monuments and buildings to honor themselves, their family members, or their predecessors. Many of these were decorated with texts as well as images.

The English historian Edward Gibbon dubbed the stability and relative peace within the empire that Augustus created the **pax Romana**, the "Roman peace," which he saw as lasting about two hundred years, until the end of the reign of Marcus Aurelius in 180 C.E. This peace was enforced by troops who remained on

Roma et Augustus

▶ Patriotic cult encouraged by Augustus and later emperors in which the good of Rome and the good of the emperor were linked.

pax Romana

▶ The "Roman peace," a period during the first and second centuries C.E. of political stability and relative peace.

CHAPTER LOCATOR | How did Augustus create a foundation for the Roman Empire?

Modern place names of Roman cities

Roman name	Modern name
Aquincum	Budapest
Burdigala	Bordeaux
Camulodunum	Colchester
Colonia Claudia Agrippinensis	Cologne
Corduba	Córdoba
Eburacum	York
Emerita Augusta	Merida
Londinium	London
Lugdunum	Lyons
Lutetia Parisiorum	Paris
Massilia	Marseilles
Mediolanum	Milan
Moguntiacum	Mainz
Nemausus	Nimes
Singidunum	Belgrade
Vindobona	Vienna

MAP 6.1 ■ **Roman Expansion Under the Empire, 44 B.C.E.–180 C.E.**

Following Roman expansion during the republic, Augustus added vast tracts of Europe to the Roman Empire, which the emperor Trajan later enlarged by assuming control over parts of central Europe, the Near East, and North Africa.

active duty or as reserves in the provinces and on the frontier, ready to respond to any resistance to Roman dominance. In general, however, Augustus respected local customs and ordered his governors to do the same. Roman governors applied Roman law to Romans living in their territories, but they let local people retain their own laws. As long as they provided taxes and did not rebel, they could continue to run their political and social lives as they had before Roman conquest.

While Romans did not force their culture on local people in Roman territories, local elites with aspirations knew that the best way to rise in stature and power was to adopt aspects of Roman culture. Just as ambitious individuals in the Hellenistic world embraced Greek culture and learned to speak Greek, those determined to get ahead now learned Latin, and sometimes Greek as well if they wished to be truly well educated. As was the case with Hellenization, Romanization and cultural fusion were especially evident in cities.

| How did the Roman state develop after Augustus? | What was life like in the city of Rome, and what was it like in the provinces? | How did Christianity grow into a major religious movement? | What explains the chaos of the third century C.E.? | ✓ LearningCurve Check what you know. |

151

The Flowering of Latin Literature

Many poets and prose writers were active in the late republic and the principate, and the period from about 50 B.C.E. to 20 C.E. is known as the golden age of Latin literature. Roman poets and prose writers produced works that were highly polished, elegant in style, and intellectual in conception. Roman poets referred to the gods often and treated mythological themes, but the core subject matter of their work was human, not divine.

Rome's greatest poet was Virgil (70–19 B.C.E.), who drew on earlier traditions, but gave them new twists. His masterpiece is the *Aeneid* (uh-NEE-ihd), an epic poem that is the Latin equivalent of the Greek *Iliad* and *Odyssey* (see Chapter 3, page 64). Virgil's account of the founding of Rome and the early years of the city gave final form to the legend of Aeneas, the Trojan hero (and ancestor of Romulus and Remus) who escaped to Italy at the fall of Troy. As Virgil told it, Aeneas became the lover of Dido, the widowed queen of Carthage, but left her because his destiny called him to found Rome. In leaving Dido, an "Eastern" queen, Aeneas put duty and the good of the state ahead of marriage or pleasure. The parallels between this story and the very recent real events involving Antony and

Virgil and the *Aeneid*

This third-century mosaic from the prosperous Roman city of Hardrumentum in North Africa shows Virgil holding a copy of his great epic poem and flanked by two Muses. The Muses, nine in all, were minor Greek and Roman goddesses who were thought to inspire artists and writers. The female Muses' role as inspiration, not authors, accurately reflects surviving Latin literature of the Augustan period, all of which, except for a few fragments, is by male authors. (C. M. Dixon/Ancient Art & Architecture Collection)

CHAPTER LOCATOR | How did Augustus create a foundation for the Roman Empire?

CHAPTER 6
152 THE ROMAN EMPIRE

Cleopatra were not lost on Virgil's audience. Making the public aware of these parallels and of Virgil's description of Aeneas as an ancestor of Julius Caesar fit well with Augustus's aims. Therefore, Augustus encouraged Virgil to write the *Aeneid* and made sure it was circulated widely immediately after Virgil died.

The poet Horace (65–8 B.C.E.) rose from humble beginnings to friendship with Augustus. His most important works are a series of odes, short lyric poems often focusing on a single individual or event. One of these commemorated Augustus's victory over Antony and Cleopatra at Actium in 31 B.C.E. Horace depicted Cleopatra as a frenzied queen, drunk with desire to destroy Rome, a view that has influenced opinions about Cleopatra to this day.

Augustus actively encouraged poets and writers, but he could also turn against them. The poet Ovid (AH-vuhd) (43 B.C.E.–17 C.E.) wrote erotic poetry about absent lovers and the joys of seduction, as well as other works about religious festivals and mythology. His best-known work is *The Art of Love*, a satire of the serious instructional poetry that was common in Rome at the time. In 8 B.C.E., Augustus banished Ovid to a city on the Black Sea far from Rome. Why he did so is a mystery. Some scholars argue that Augustus banished Ovid because his poetry celebrated adultery at a time when Augustus was promoting marriage and childbearing, and others say it was because the poet knew about political conspiracies.

Marriage and Morality

Augustus's banishing of Ovid may have simply been an excuse to get rid of him, but concern with morality and with what were perceived as traditional Roman virtues was a matter not just for literature in Augustan Rome but also for law. Augustus promoted marriage and childbearing through legal changes that released free women and freedwomen (female slaves who had been freed) from male guardianship if they had given birth to a certain number of children. Men and women who were unmarried or had no children were restricted in the inheritance of property. Adultery, defined as sex with a married woman or with a woman under male guardianship, was made a crime, not simply the private family matter it had been.

In imperial propaganda, Augustus had his own family depicted as a model of traditional morality. (See "Picturing the Past: Ara Pacis," page 154.) In fact, Augustus's family did not live up to this ideal. Augustus had his daughter Julia arrested and exiled for adultery and treason. Although it is impossible to tell what actually happened, she seems to have had at least one affair after her father forced her to marry a second husband—her stepbrother Tiberius—whom she hated.

Same-sex relationships among men in Rome followed a variety of patterns: some were between social equals and others between men and their slaves. Moralists denounced sexual relationships in which men squandered family money or became subservient to those of lower social status, but no laws were passed against same-sex relationships. We do not know very much about same-sex relationships among women in Rome, though court gossip and criticism of powerful women sometimes included charges of such relationships, along with charges of heterosexual promiscuity and other sexual slander.

How did the Roman state develop after Augustus?

What was life like in the city of Rome, and what was it like in the provinces?

How did Christianity grow into a major religious movement?

What explains the chaos of the third century C.E.?

LearningCurve
Check what you know.

153

Ara Pacis

In the middle years of Augustus's reign, the Roman senate ordered a huge altar, the Ara Pacis, built to honor him and the peace he had brought to the empire. This was decorated with life-size reliefs of Augustus and members of his family, prominent Romans, and other people and deities. One side, shown here, depicts a goddess figure, most likely the goddess Peace herself, with twin babies on her lap, flanked by nymphs representing land and sea, and surrounded by plants and animals. (Scala/Art Resource, NY)

> PICTURING THE PAST

ANALYZING THE IMAGE: What do the elements depicted here most likely symbolize?
CONNECTIONS: The Ara Pacis was among a number of works of public art designed to commemorate the deeds of Augustus. Why might the senate and Augustus have commissioned such works? Can you think of contemporary parallels?

> QUICK REVIEW

Why did Augustus retain the trappings of the republic and take care to avoid creating the appearance of radical change?

CHAPTER LOCATOR | How did Augustus create a foundation for the Roman Empire?

154   CHAPTER 6
THE ROMAN EMPIRE

How did the Roman state develop after Augustus?

AUGUSTUS'S SUCCESS IN CREATING SOLID POLITICAL INSTITUTIONS was tested by the dynasty he created, the Julio-Claudians, whose members schemed against one another trying to win and hold power. The incompetence of one of the Julio-Claudians, Nero, allowed a military commander, Vespasian (veh-SPAY-zhuhn), to claim the throne and establish a new dynasty, the Flavians. The Flavians were followed by the "five good emperors," who were relatively successful militarily and politically.

The Julio-Claudians and the Flavians

Because the principate was not technically an office, Augustus could not legally hand it to a successor. His solution was to adopt his stepson Tiberius (who was also his son-in-law) as his son. Adoption of an heir was a common practice among members of the elite in Rome, who used this method to pass on property to a chosen younger man—often a relative—if they had no sons. Long before his death, Augustus shared his consular and tribunician powers with Tiberius, thus grooming him for the principate. In his will, Augustus left most of his vast fortune to Tiberius, and the Senate formally requested that Tiberius assume the burdens of the principate. Formalities apart, by the time of his death in 14 C.E., Augustus had succeeded in creating a dynasty.

| How did the Roman state develop after Augustus? | What was life like in the city of Rome, and what was it like in the provinces? | How did Christianity grow into a major religious movement? | What explains the chaos of the third century C.E.? | ☑ LearningCurve Check what you know. |

155

■ **The Julio-Claudians**

27 B.C.E.–14 C.E.	Augustus
14 C.E.–37 C.E.	Tiberius
37 C.E.–41 C.E.	Caligula
41 C.E.–54 C.E.	Claudius
54 C.E.–68 C.E.	Nero

■ **The Flavians**

69 C.E.–79 C.E.	Vespasian
79 C.E.–81 C.E.	Titus
81 C.E.–96 C.E.	Domitian

Praetorians
▶ Imperial bodyguard created by Augustus.

For fifty years after Augustus's death, the dynasty that he established provided the emperors of Rome. Two of the Julio-Claudians who followed Augustus, Tiberius and Claudius, were sound rulers and able administrators. The other two, Caligula and Nero, were not.

Augustus's creation of an imperial bodyguard known as the **Praetorians** (pree-TAWR-ee-uhnz) had repercussions for his successors. In 41 C.E., the Praetorians murdered Caligula and forced the Senate to ratify their choice of Claudius as emperor. The events were repeated frequently. During the first three centuries of the empire, the Praetorian Guard often murdered emperors they were supposed to protect and raised to emperor men of their own choosing.

In his early years, Nero ruled fairly well, but he became increasingly paranoid about the power of those around him. In 68 C.E., his erratic actions and his policies led to a revolt by several generals, a revolt that was supported by the Praetorian Guard and members of the Senate. He was declared an enemy of the people and committed suicide. This opened the way to widespread disruption and civil war. In 69 C.E., the "year of the four emperors," four men claimed the position of emperor in quick succession. The man who emerged triumphant was Vespasian, commander of the eastern armies.

To prevent others from claiming the throne, Vespasian designated his sons Titus and Domitian as his successors, thus establishing the Flavian dynasty. Although Roman policy was to rule by peaceful domination whenever possible, he used the army to suppress the rebellions that had begun erupting at the end of Nero's reign. The most famous of these was one that had burst out in Judaea in 66 C.E. Jewish rebels initially defeated the Roman troops stationed in Judaea, but a larger army under the leadership of Vespasian and his son Titus put down the revolt. They destroyed much of the city of Jerusalem, including the Jewish temple, in 70 C.E. and took thousands of Jews as military captives and slaves, dispersing them throughout the empire.

The Flavians carried on Augustus's work in Italy and on the frontiers. During the brief reign of Vespasian's son Titus, Mount Vesuvius in southern Italy erupted, destroying Pompeii and other cities and killing thousands of people. Titus gave money and sent officials to organize the relief effort. His younger brother Domitian, who followed Titus as emperor, won additional territory in Germany, consolidating it into two new provinces. Later in life Domitian became more autocratic, however, and he was killed in 96 C.E. in a plot that involved his own wife, thus ending the Flavian dynasty.

The Age of the "Five Good Emperors"

"five good emperors"
▶ The five Roman emperors (Nerva, Trajan, Hadrian, Antoninus Pius, and Marcus Aurelius) of the second century whose reigns were relatively prosperous and stable.

The Flavians were succeeded by a line of relatively competent emperors known as the **"five good emperors"**—Nerva, Trajan, Hadrian, Antoninus Pius, and Marcus Aurelius. All of these emperors were experienced generals and members of the Senate, and they provided Rome with stable, effective political and military leadership for nearly a century, from 96 C.E. to 180 C.E.

Hadrian is typical of the emperors of the second century. His abilities and intelligence caught the attention of his elder cousin Trajan, the future emperor, who started him on a military career. At age nineteen, Hadrian served on the

CHAPTER LOCATOR │ How did Augustus create a foundation for the Roman Empire?

Danube frontier, where he learned the details of how the Roman army lived and fought and saw for himself the problems of defending the frontiers. When Trajan became emperor in 98 C.E., Hadrian was given important positions in which he learned how to defend and run the empire. Although Trajan did not officially declare Hadrian his successor, at Trajan's death in 117, Hadrian assumed power.

Hadrian established more formal imperial administrative departments and separated civil service from military service. Men with little talent or taste for the army could instead serve the state as administrators. These innovations made running the empire more efficient and increased the authority of the emperor.

Under Trajan the boundaries of the Roman Empire were expanded to their farthest extent, and Hadrian worked to maintain most of these holdings, although he pulled back Roman armies from areas in the East he considered indefensible. No longer a conquering force, the army was expected to defend what had already been won. Forts and watch stations guarded the borders. Outside the forts the Romans built a system of roads that allowed the forts to be supplied and reinforced quickly in times of rebellion or unrest.

Roman soldiers also built walls, of which the most famous was one across northern England built primarily during Hadrian's reign. Hadrian's Wall, as it became known, protected Romans from attacks from the north and also allowed them to regulate immigration and trade through the many gates along the wall. Like all walls around cities or across territory, it served as a symbol and a means of power and control as well as a defensive strategy.

As the empire expanded, the army grew larger, and more and more troops were auxiliary forces of noncitizens. Because army service could lead to citizenship, men from the provinces and even from beyond the borders of the Roman Empire joined the army willingly to gain citizenship, receive a salary, and learn a trade. (See "Individuals in Society: Bithus, a Soldier in the Roman Army," page 158.) The army evolved into a garrison force, with troops guarding specific areas for long periods.

"FIVE GOOD EMPERORS" (THE ANTONINES)

96–98	Nerva
98–117	Trajan
117–138	Hadrian
138–161	Antoninus Pius
161–180	Marcus Aurelius

Roman Britain, ca. 130 C.E.

QUICK REVIEW ‹

In what ways did Hadrian embody the positive qualities of the "five good emperors"?

| **How did the Roman state develop after Augustus?** | What was life like in the city of Rome, and what was it like in the provinces? | How did Christianity grow into a major religious movement? | What explains the chaos of the third century C.E.? | ✔ LearningCurve Check what you know. |

Citizenship and service in the military have long been linked. In classical Athens, the hoplites, who were the backbone of Athenian armies, were all citizens (see Chapter 3). In the United States today, noncitizens serving on active duty in the armed forces may apply for citizenship immediately instead of having to wait the five years that are normally required for civilian noncitizen residents. Citizenship and army service were also connected in the Roman Empire. Only Roman citizens could be members of the Roman legions, but expanding and defending the empire required huge numbers of troops. These were provided by auxiliary units, which were open to all. Some men were drafted into the auxiliaries, but more joined voluntarily, attracted by the offer of pay and by the promise that, at the end of their service and if they survived, they would be awarded Roman citizenship, which would give them legal, social, and economic privileges.

A man's record of army service and his status as a citizen were recorded on what is known as a military diploma, two bronze sheets about the size of a paperback book wired together on which his military career was set out in an inscription. The names of witnesses were also inscribed on the diploma, and their seals attached, which made the document official. One copy of this diploma stayed in Rome, and one was sent to the soldier himself, much as members of the military today receive discharge papers. Most of these diplomas were melted down long ago and their metal was put to other uses, but about a thousand survive. They provide an exact date, which is very rare in ancient sources, so they can be used to trace the movements of units and many other aspects of the military. They also include details about the lives of ordinary soldiers that are unavailable in any other type of source.

One such soldier was the infantryman Bithus, who was born in Thrace in the northeastern region of modern Greece, part of the empire that provided many troops. He joined an auxiliary unit of the Roman army in 63 C.E. and began with basic training, during which he learned to march and to use the standard weapons of a heavily armed infantryman. His training completed, Bithus was sent to Syria, where he spent most of his career. He was one of the thousands of soldiers sent to this area from all parts of the empire because of the revolt in Judaea. There he met others from as far west as Gaul and Spain, from northern Africa, and from other parts of Greece and the Balkans. Unlike many other units that were shifted periodically, his remained in the same area. While in the army, he raised a family, much like soldiers today. The sons of soldiers like Bithus often themselves joined the army, indicating that soldiers' families were a fruitful source for recruitment. After twenty-five years of duty, Bithus received his diploma on November 7, 88. Upon mustering out of the army, he received the grant of Roman citizenship for himself and his family, as his diploma attests. He apparently returned to Thrace because that is where his diploma was found.

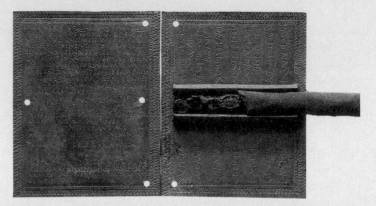

This Roman military diploma, found in present-day Croatia, was issued February 9, 71 C.E., during the reign of Vespasian. This is the outside, with the names of witnesses inscribed on the right-hand side, and their seals attached under the removable cover of the central piece. The left-hand side lists the soldier's tours of duty, described in more detail on the other side, which is the inside when the diploma is closed. (Brodsko Posavlje Museum)

The example of Bithus is important not because he is unusual but because he is typical. The might of the Roman Empire depended on hundreds of thousands of men just like him, who joined the army for the pay and the promise of a better life that it offered.

QUESTIONS FOR ANALYSIS

1. Why would it have been important for a soldier like Bithus to have a permanent record of his military career and status as a citizen?
2. Why did — and does — the promise of citizenship serve as an effective recruiting tool for the armed forces?

Source: *Corpus Inscriptionum Latinarum*, vol. 16, no. 35 (Berlin: G. Reimer, 1882).

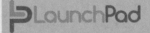

ONLINE DOCUMENT PROJECT

How did the Roman Empire turn countless individuals like Bithus into the most powerful fighting machine the Mediterranean world had ever seen? Keeping the question above in mind, examine documents on the military's role in the expansion of the empire, and then complete a writing assignment based on the evidence and details from this chapter. *See inside the front cover to learn more.*

What was life like in the city of Rome, and what was it like in the provinces?

Gladiator Mosaic Made in the first half of the fourth century, this mosaic from an estate outside Rome includes the name of each gladiator next to the figure. In the back a gladiator stands in a victory pose, while the fallen gladiator in the front is marked with the symbol Ø, indicating that he has died in combat. Many of the gladiators in this mosaic, such as those at the left, appear less fit and fearsome than the gladiators depicted in movies, more closely reflecting the reality that gladiatorial combat was a job undertaken by a variety of people. (Scala/Art Resource, NY)

THE EXPANSION AND STABILIZATION OF THE EMPIRE brought changes to life in the city of Rome and also to life in the provinces in the first two centuries C.E. The city grew to a huge size, bringing the problems that plague any crowded urban area but also opportunities for work and leisure. Roads and secure sea-lanes linked the empire in one vast web, creating a network of commerce and communication. Trade and production flourished in the provinces, and Romans came into indirect contact with China.

Life in Imperial Rome

Rome was truly an extraordinary city, and with a population of over a million it may have been the largest city in the world. Although it boasted stately palaces and beautiful residential areas, most people lived in shoddily constructed houses. They took whatever work was available, producing food, clothing, construction materials, and the many other items needed by the city's residents, or selling these products from small shops or at the city's many marketplaces.

How did the Roman state develop after Augustus?	**What was life like in the city of Rome, and what was it like in the provinces?**	How did Christianity grow into a major religious movement?	What explains the chaos of the third century C.E.?	✓ LearningCurve Check what you know.

Many residents of the city of Rome were slaves, who ranged from highly educated household tutors or government officials and widely sought sculptors to workers who engaged in hard physical tasks. Romans used the possibility of manumission as a means of controlling the behavior of their slaves, and individual Romans did sometimes free their slaves. Often these were house slaves who had become like members of the family and who often stayed with their former owner's family after being freed. Manumission was limited by law, however, in part because freeing slaves made them citizens, allowing them to receive public grain and gifts of money, which some Romans thought debased pure Roman citizenship.

A typical day for the Roman family began with a modest breakfast, which was also true in the days of the republic. Afterward came a trip to the outdoor market for the day's provisions. Seafood was a favorite item because the Romans normally ate meat only at festivals. While poor people ate salt fish, the more prosperous dined on rare fish, oysters, squid, and eels. Wine was the common drink.

As in the republic, children began their education at home, where parents emphasized moral conduct, especially reverence for the gods and the law and respect for elders. Daughters learned how to manage the house, and sons learned the basics of their future calling from their fathers, who also taught them the use of weapons for military service. Wealthy boys gained formal education from tutors or schools, generally favoring rhetoric and law for a political career. Others entered the army, usually as cadets on the staffs of prominent officers.

Approaches to Urban Problems

Fire and crime were serious problems in the city, even after Augustus created urban fire and police forces. Streets were narrow, drainage was inadequate, and sanitation was poor. Private houses generally lacked toilets, so people used chamber pots.

In the second century, urban planning and new construction improved the situation. For example, engineers built an elaborate system that collected sewage from public baths, the ground floors of buildings, and public latrines. They also built hundreds of miles of **aqueducts**, sophisticated systems of canals, channels, and pipes, most of them underground, that brought freshwater into the city from the surrounding hills.

aqueducts
▶ Canals, channels, and pipes that brought freshwater into cities.

Better disposal of sewage was one way that people living in Rome tried to maintain their health, and they also used a range of treatments to stay healthy and cure illness. This included treatments based on the ideas of the Greek physician Hippocrates; folk remedies; prayers and rituals at the temple of the god of medicine, Asclepius; surgery; and combinations of all of these.

The most important medical researcher and physician working in imperial Rome was Galen (ca. 129–ca. 200 C.E.), a Greek born in modern-day Turkey. Building on the work of Hellenistic physicians (see Chapter 4, page 111), Galen wrote a huge number of treatises on anatomy and physiology, and became the personal physician of many prominent Romans, including several emperors. He promoted the idea that imbalances among various bodily fluids caused illness and recommended bloodletting as a cure. His research into the nervous system and the operation of muscles proved to be more accurate than did his ideas about the circulation of fluids. So did his practical advice on the treatment of wounds, much of which grew out of his and others' experiences with soldiers on the battlefield.

CHAPTER LOCATOR | How did Augustus create a foundation for the Roman Empire?

CHAPTER 6
160 THE ROMAN EMPIRE

Pont du Gard The Pont du Gard at Nîmes in France is a bridge over a river carrying an aqueduct that supplied millions of gallons of water per day to the Roman city of Nîmes in Gaul; the water flowed in a channel at the very top. Although this bridge was built largely without mortar or concrete, many Roman aqueducts and bridges relied on concrete and sometimes iron rods for their strength. (Pont du Gard: © Masterfile Royalty Free)

Along with fire and disease, food was an issue in the ever more crowded city. Because of the danger of starvation, the emperor, following republican practice, provided the citizen population with free grain for bread and, later, oil and wine. By feeding the citizenry, the emperor prevented bread riots caused by shortages and high prices. For those who did not enjoy the rights of citizenship, the emperor provided grain at low prices. By maintaining the grain supply, the emperor kept the favor of the people and ensured that Rome's poor did not starve.

Popular Entertainment

In addition to supplying grain, the emperor and other wealthy citizens also entertained the Roman populace, often at vast expense. The most popular forms of public entertainment were gladiatorial contests and chariot racing. Games were advertised on billboards, and spectators were given a program with the names and sometimes the fighting statistics of the pairs so that they could bet more easily.

Men became gladiators through a variety of ways. Many were soldiers captured in war and sent to Rome or other large cities to be gladiators instead of being killed. Some were criminals, especially slaves found guilty of various crimes. By the imperial period, increasing numbers were volunteers, often poor immigrants who saw gladiatorial combat as a way to support themselves. All gladiators were trained in gladiatorial schools and were legally slaves, although they could keep their winnings and a few became quite wealthy. Some gladiatorial matches were to the death, but this was increasingly rare because the owners

| How did the Roman state develop after Augustus? | **What was life like in the city of Rome, and what was it like in the provinces?** | How did Christianity grow into a major religious movement? | What explains the chaos of the third century C.E.? | ✔ LearningCurve Check what you know. |

161

of especially skilled fighters wanted them to continue to compete. Some Romans protested gladiatorial fighting, but the emperors recognized the political value of such spectacles, and most Romans enjoyed them.

The Romans were even more addicted to chariot racing than they were to gladiatorial shows. Under the empire four permanent teams competed against one another. Each had its own color—red, white, green, or blue. Winning charioteers were idolized, just as sports stars are today.

Roman spectacles such as gladiator fights and chariot racing were exciting diversions, but they were not everyday activities for Romans. As is evident on tombstone inscriptions, ordinary Romans were proud of their work and accomplishments and were affectionate toward their families and friends. An impression of them can be gained from their epitaphs.

Prosperity in the Roman Provinces

As the empire grew and stabilized, many Roman provinces grew prosperous. Peace and security opened Britain, Gaul, and the lands of the Danube to settlers from other parts of the Roman Empire (**Map 6.2**). Veterans were given small parcels of land in the provinces, becoming tenant farmers.

The rural population throughout the empire left few records, but the inscriptions that remain point to a melding of cultures. One sphere where this occurred was language. People used Latin for legal and state religious purposes, but gradually Latin blended with the original language of an area and with languages spoken by those who came into the area later. Religion was another site of cultural exchange and mixture. Romans moving into an area learned about and began to venerate local gods, and local people learned about Roman ones. Gradually hybrid deities and rituals developed. The process of cultural exchange was at first more urban than rural, but the importance of cities and towns to the life of the wider countryside ensured that cultural exchanges spread far afield.

The garrison towns that grew around provincial military camps became the centers of organized political life, and some grew into major cities. To supply these administrative centers with food, land around them was cultivated more intensively. Roman merchants became early bankers, loaning money to local people and often controlling them financially. Wealthy Roman officials also sometimes built country estates in rural areas near the city.

During the first and second centuries, Roman Gaul became more prosperous than ever before, and prosperity attracted Roman settlers. Roman veterans mingled with the local population and sometimes married into local families. There was not much difference in many parts of the province between the original Celtic villages and their Roman successors.

In Britain, Roman influence was strongest in the south, where more towns developed. Archaeological evidence indicates healthy trading connections with the north, however, as Roman merchandise moved through the gates of Hadrian's Wall in exchange for food and other local products.

Across eastern Europe, Roman influence was weaker than it was in Gaul or southern Britain, and there appears to have been less intermarriage. In Illyria (ih-LIHR-ee-uh) and Dalmatia, regions of modern Albania, Croatia, and Montenegro, the local population never widely embraced either Roman culture or urban life. To a certain extent, however, Romanization occurred simply because the peoples lived in such close proximity.

CHAPTER LOCATOR | How did Augustus create a foundation for the Roman Empire?

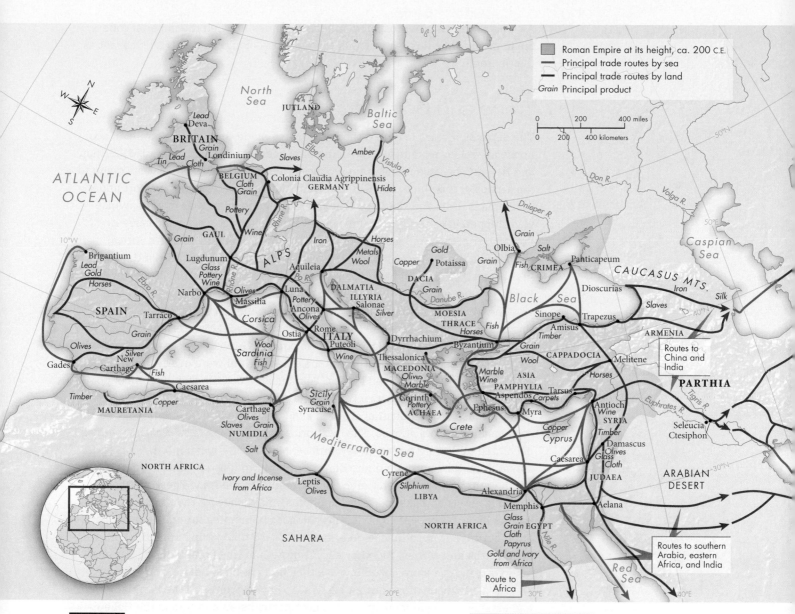

Legend:
- Roman Empire at its height, ca. 200 C.E.
- Principal trade routes by sea
- Principal trade routes by land
- *Grain* Principal product

Map labels (selection): North Sea, JUTLAND, Baltic Sea, ATLANTIC OCEAN, BRITAIN, Lead, Deva, Grain, Londinium, Tin, Lead, Cloth, Slaves, Amber, BELGIUM, Cloth, Grain, Colonia Claudia Agrippinensis, GERMANY, Hides, Pottery, Vistula R., GAUL, Grain, Wine, Rhine R., Elbe R., Iron, Horses, Metals, Wool, Copper, Gold, Potaissa, Olbia, Salt, Grain, Fish, Don R., Volga R., Caspian Sea, Brigantium, Lead, Gold, Horses, Lugdunum, Glass, Pottery, Wine, ALPS, Aquileia, Po R., DACIA, Grain, Danube R., CRIMEA, Panticapeum, CAUCASUS MTS., Iron, Silk, Narbo, Olives, Luna, Pottery, Olives, DALMATIA, ILLYRIA, Salonae, Silver, MOESIA, THRACE, Black Sea, Dioscurias, Slaves, Massilia, Ancona, Horses, Fish, Sinope, Trapezus, ARMENIA, SPAIN, Tarraco, Corsica, Ostia, Rome, ITALY, Puteoli, Dyrrhachium, Byzantium, Amisus, Timber, Grain, CAPPADOCIA, Melitene, Routes to China and India, PARTHIA, Grain, Olives, Silver, New Carthage, Fish, Wool, Sardinia, Fish, Wine, Thessalonica, MACEDONIA, Olives, Marble, Wool, Marble, Wine, ASIA, PAMPHYLIA, Tarsus, Carpets, Horses, Antioch, Wine, SYRIA, Timber, Euphrates R., Tigris R., Seleucia, Ctesiphon, Gades, Caesarea, Fish, Sicily, Grain, Syracuse, Corinth, Pottery, ACHAEA, Ephesus, Myra, Aspendos, Copper, Cyprus, Damascus, Olives, Glass, Cloth, Timber, Copper, MAURETANIA, Carthage, Olives, Slaves, Grain, NUMIDIA, Crete, Caesarea, JUDAEA, ARABIAN DESERT, NORTH AFRICA, Salt, Mediterranean Sea, Cyrene, Silphium, Olives, LIBYA, Alexandria, Aelana, Ivory and Incense from Africa, Leptis, Olives, Memphis, Glass, Grain EGYPT, Cloth, Papyrus, Gold and Ivory from Africa, SAHARA, NORTH AFRICA, Nile R., Route to Africa, Red Sea, Routes to southern Arabia, eastern Africa, and India

MAP 6.2 ■ Production and Trade in the Pax Romana, ca. 27 B.C.E.–180 C.E.

This map gives a good idea of the principal products of various parts of the Roman Empire at its height and the trade routes connecting these regions. Map 10.2 on page 291 is a similar map that shows products and trade in roughly the same area nearly a millennium later. Examine both maps and answer the following questions.

> **MAPPING THE PAST**

ANALYZING THE MAP: What similarities and differences do you see in products during these two periods?
CONNECTIONS: To what extent did Roman trade routes influence later European trade routes?

The Romans were the first to build cities in northern Europe, but in the eastern Mediterranean they ruled cities that had existed before Rome itself was even a village. Here there was much continuity in urban life from the Hellenistic period. There was less construction than in the Roman cities of northern and western Europe because existing buildings could simply be put to new uses.

More than just places to live, cities were centers of intellectual and cultural life. Their residents were in touch with the ideas and events of the day, in a network that spanned the entire Mediterranean and reached as far north as Britain.

| How did the Roman state develop after Augustus? | **What was life like in the city of Rome, and what was it like in the provinces?** | How did Christianity grow into a major religious movement? | What explains the chaos of the third century C.E.? | ✓ LearningCurve Check what you know. |

As long as the empire prospered and the revenues reached the imperial coffers, life in provincial cities — at least for the wealthy — could be nearly as pleasant as that in Rome.

Trade and Commerce

The expansion of trade during the pax Romana made the Roman Empire an economic as well as a political force in the provinces (see Map 6.2, page 163). Britain and Belgium became prime grain producers, with much of their harvests going to the armies of the Rhine, and Britain's wool industry probably got its start under the Romans. Italy and southern Gaul produced huge quantities of wine, which was shipped in large pottery jugs wherever merchant vessels could carry it. Roman colonists introduced the olive to southern Spain and northern Africa, which soon produced most of the oil consumed in the western part of the empire. In the East, the olive oil production of Syrian farmers reached an all-time high, and Egypt produced tons of wheat that fed the Roman populace.

The growth of industry in the provinces was another striking development of this period. Cities in Gaul and Germany eclipsed the old Mediterranean manufacturing centers. Lyons in Gaul and later Cologne in Germany became the new centers of the glassmaking industry, and the cities of Gaul were nearly unrivaled in the manufacture of bronze and brass. The Romans took the manufacture of pottery to an advanced stage by introducing a wider range of vessels and making some of these on an industrial scale, in kilns that were large enough to fire tens of thousands of pots at once. The most prized pottery was *terra sigillata*, reddish decorated tableware with a glossy surface. Methods for making terra sigillata spread from Italy northward into Europe, often introduced by soldiers in the Roman army who had been trained in potterymaking in Italy. These craftsmen set up facilities to make roof tiles, amphoras, and dishes for their units, and local potters began to copy their styles and methods of manufacturing. Terra sigillata often portrayed Greco-Roman gods and heroes, so this pottery spread Mediterranean myths and stories. Aided by all this growth in trade and industry, Europe and western Asia were linked in ways they had not been before.

As the Romans drove farther eastward, they encountered the Parthians, who had established a kingdom in what is now Afghanistan and Iran in the Hellenistic period. In the second century, the Romans tried unsuccessfully to drive out the Parthians, who came to act as a link between Roman and Chinese merchants. Chinese merchants sold their wares to the Parthians, who then carried the goods overland to Mesopotamia or Egypt, from which they were shipped throughout the Roman Empire. Silk was a major commodity traded from the East to the West, along with other luxury goods. In return, the Romans traded glassware, precious gems, and slaves. The pax Romana was also an era of maritime trade, and Roman ships sailed from Egyptian ports to the mouth of the Indus River, where they traded local merchandise and wares imported by the Parthians.

> QUICK REVIEW

How did Roman culture spread and reshape life throughout the empire?

CHAPTER LOCATOR | How did Augustus create a foundation for the Roman Empire?

When Christianity spread in the Roman Empire, many believers purchased household goods with Christian symbols. This pottery lamp for an ordinary home, dating from the fourth century, is marked with a common symbol for Jesus, the letters *XP* (chi rho), the first two letters in Greek for *Christos*, "Christ." (Zev Radovan/www.BibleLandPictures.com)

How did Christianity grow into a major religious movement?

DURING THE REIGN OF THE EMPEROR TIBERIUS (r. 14–37 C.E.), in the Roman province of Judaea, which had been created out of the Jewish kingdom of Judah, a Jewish man named Jesus of Nazareth preached, attracted a following, and was executed on the order of the Roman prefect Pontius Pilate. At the time, all of these events were relatively minor, but Christianity, the religion created by Jesus's followers, came to have an enormous impact, first in the Roman Empire and later throughout the world.

Factors Behind the Rise of Christianity

The civil wars that destroyed the Roman Republic left their mark on Judaea, where Jewish leaders had taken sides in the conflict. The turmoil created a climate of violence throughout the area, and among the Jews, movements in opposition to the Romans spread. Some of these movements, such as the Zealots, encouraged armed rebellion against Roman rule, which would break out several times in the first and second centuries C.E. (see pages 156 and 155). Many Jews came to believe that a final struggle was near and that it would lead to the coming of a savior, or **Messiah**, who would destroy the Roman legions and inaugurate a period of peace, happiness, and prosperity for Jews. This apocalyptic belief was an old one among Jews, but by the first century C.E., it had become more widespread than ever, with many people prophesying the imminent coming of a Messiah and readying themselves for a cataclysmic battle.

Messiah

▶ In Jewish belief, a savior who would bring a period of peace and happiness for Jews.

| How did the Roman state develop after Augustus? | What was life like in the city of Rome, and what was it like in the provinces? | **How did Christianity grow into a major religious movement?** | What explains the chaos of the third century C.E.? | ✓ LearningCurve Check what you know. |

165

pagan

▶ Originally referring to those who lived in the countryside, it came to mean those who practiced religions other than Judaism or Christianity.

The pagan world also played its part in the story of early Christianity. The term **pagan**, derived from a Latin word meaning "rural dweller," came to refer to those who practiced religions other than Judaism or Christianity. This included religions devoted to the traditional Roman gods, syncretistic religions that blended Roman and indigenous deities, the cult of the emperor, and mystery religions that offered the promise of life after death (see Chapter 4, page 104). Many people in the Roman Empire practiced all of these, combining them in whatever way seemed most beneficial or satisfying to them.

The Life and Teachings of Jesus

Into this climate of Messianic hope and Roman religious blending came Jesus of Nazareth (ca. 3 B.C.E.–ca. 29 C.E.). According to Christian scripture, he was born to deeply religious Jewish parents and raised in Galilee, the stronghold of the Zealots and a trading center where Greeks and Romans interacted with Jews. His ministry began when he was about thirty, and he taught by preaching and telling stories.

Like Socrates, Jesus left no writings. Accounts of his sayings and teachings first circulated orally among his followers and were later written down. The principal evidence for his life and deeds are the four Gospels of the Bible (Matthew, Mark, Luke, John), books that are part of what Christians later termed the New Testament. These Gospels—the name means "good news"—are records of Jesus's teachings, written to build a community of faith sometime in the late first century. The Gospels were among the most widely copied and circulated early accounts of Jesus's life, and by the fourth century, officials in the Christian Church decided that they, along with other types of writing such as letters and prophecies, would form Christian scripture.

The Gospels include certain details of Jesus's life, but they were not meant to be biographies. Their authors had probably heard many different people talk about what Jesus said and did, and there are discrepancies among the four accounts. These differences indicate that early followers had a diversity of beliefs about Jesus's nature and purpose.

Earliest Known Depiction of Jesus

This mural, from a Roman camp at Dura-Europos on the Euphrates River, may be the earliest known depiction of Jesus. Dating to 235 C.E., it depicts Jesus healing a paralytic man, an incident described in the New Testament. Early Christians used art to spread their message. (Yale University Art Gallery, Dura-Europos Collection)

CHAPTER LOCATOR | How did Augustus create a foundation for the Roman Empire?

166 CHAPTER 6 THE ROMAN EMPIRE

However, almost all the early sources agree on certain aspects of Jesus's teachings: He preached of a heavenly kingdom of eternal happiness in a life after death and of the importance of devotion to God and love of others. His teachings were based on Hebrew scripture and reflected a conception of God and morality that came from Jewish tradition. The Greek translation of the Hebrew word *Messiah* is *Christos*, the origin of the English word *Christ*. Was Jesus the Messiah, the Christ? A small band of followers thought so, and Jesus claimed that he was. Yet Jesus had his own conception of the Messiah. He would establish a spiritual kingdom, not an earthly one.

The Roman official Pontius Pilate, who had authority over much of Judaea, knew little about Jesus's teachings. Like all Roman officials, he was concerned with maintaining peace and order, which was a difficult task in restive Judaea. According to the New Testament, crowds followed Jesus into Jerusalem at the time of Passover, a highly emotional time in the Jewish year that marked the Jewish people's departure from Egypt under the leadership of Moses (see Chapter 2, page 40). The prospect that these crowds would spark violence no doubt alarmed Pilate. Some Jews believed that Jesus was the long-awaited Messiah. Others hated and feared him because they thought him religiously dangerous. The four Gospels differ somewhat on exactly what actions Jesus took in the city and what Jesus and Pilate said to each other after Jesus was arrested. They agree that Pilate condemned Jesus to death by crucifixion, and his soldiers carried out the sentence. On the third day after Jesus's crucifixion, some of his followers claimed that he had risen from the dead. For his earliest followers and for generations to come, the resurrection of Jesus became a central element of faith.

The Spread of Christianity

The memory of Jesus and his teachings survived and flourished. Believers in his divinity met in small assemblies or congregations to discuss the meaning of Jesus's message and to celebrate a ritual (later called the Eucharist or Lord's Supper) commemorating his last meal with his disciples before his arrest. Because they expected Jesus to return to the world very soon, they regarded earthly life and institutions as unimportant. Only later did these congregations evolve into what came to be called the religion of Christianity, with a formal organization and set of beliefs.

The catalyst in the spread of Jesus's teachings and the formation of the Christian Church was Paul of Tarsus, a well-educated Hellenized Jew who was comfortable in both the Roman and the Jewish worlds. The New Testament reports that at first he persecuted members of the new sect, but when on the road to the city of Damascus in Syria, he was struck blind by a vision of light and heard Jesus's voice. Once converted, Paul traveled all over the Roman Empire and wrote letters of advice to many groups. These letters were copied and widely circulated, transforming Jesus's ideas into more specific moral teachings. He recognized that Christianity would not grow if it remained within Judaism, and so he connected it with the non-Jewish world. As a result of his efforts, Paul became the most important figure in changing Christianity from a Jewish sect into a separate religion, and many of his letters became part of Christian scripture.

The breadth of the Roman Empire was another factor behind the spread of Christianity. If all roads led to Rome, they also led outward to the provinces. This

How did the Roman state develop after Augustus? | What was life like in the city of Rome, and what was it like in the provinces? | **How did Christianity grow into a major religious movement?** | What explains the chaos of the third century c.e.? | ✓ LearningCurve Check what you know.

167

enabled early Christians to spread their faith easily throughout the known world. Though most of the earliest converts seem to have been Jews, or Greeks and Romans who were already interested in Jewish moral teachings, Paul urged that Gentiles, or non-Jews, be accepted on an equal basis. The earliest Christian converts included people from all social classes, and many women were active in spreading Christianity. The growing Christian communities differed about the extent to which women should participate in the workings of the religion; some favored giving women a larger role in church affairs, while others were more restrictive, urging women to be silent on religious matters.

People were attracted to Christian teachings for a variety of reasons. It was, in many ways, a mystery religion, offering its adherents special teachings that would give them immortality. But in contrast to traditional mystery religions, Christianity promised this immortality widely, not only to a select few.

Along with the possibility of life after death, Christianity also offered rewards in this world to adherents. One reward was the possibility of forgiveness; believers accepted that human nature is weak and that even the best Christians could fall into sin. But Jesus loved sinners and forgave those who repented. Christianity was also attractive to many because it gave the Roman world a cause. Instead of passivity, Christians stressed the ideal of striving for a goal. By spreading the word of Christ, Christians played their part in God's plan for the triumph of Christianity on earth. Christianity also gave its devotees a sense of community, which was very welcome in the often highly mobile world of the Roman Empire. Many Christians took Jesus's commandment to love one another as a guide and provided support for widows, orphans, and the poor, just as they did for family members. Such material support became increasingly attractive as Roman social welfare programs broke down in the third century.

The Growing Acceptance and Evolution of Christianity

At first, most Roman officials ignored the followers of Jesus, viewing them simply as one of the many splinter groups within Judaism. Slowly some Roman officials and leaders came to oppose Christian practices and beliefs. They considered Christians to be subversive dissidents because they stopped practicing traditional rituals and they objected—often publicly or in writing—to the cult of the emperor. Some Romans thought that Christianity was one of the worst of the mystery religions, with immoral and indecent rituals. Many in the Roman Empire also feared that the traditional gods would withdraw their favor from the Roman Empire because of the Christian insistence that these gods either did not exist or were evil spirits. The Christian refusal to worship Roman gods, in the opinion of many Romans, endangered Roman lives and society. Others worried that Christians were trying to destroy the Roman family with their insistence on a new type of kinship, and they pointed to Jesus's words in the Gospels saying that salvation was far more important than family relationships. A woman who converted, thought many Romans, might use her new faith to oppose her father's choice of marital partner or even renounce marriage itself, an idea supported by the actions of a few female converts.

CHAPTER LOCATOR | How did Augustus create a foundation for the Roman Empire?

CHAPTER 6
168 THE ROMAN EMPIRE

Persecutions of Christians, including torture and executions, were organized by governors of Roman provinces and sometimes by the emperor, beginning with Nero. Most persecutions were local and sporadic in nature, however, and some of the gory stories about the martyrs are later inventions, designed to strengthen believers with accounts of earlier heroes. Christians differed in their opinions about how to respond to persecution. Some sought out martyrdom, while others thought that doing so went against Christian teachings.

Responses to Christianity on the part of Roman emperors varied. The emperor Trajan forbade his governors to hunt down Christians. Though admitting that he considered Christianity an abomination, he decided it was better policy to leave Christians in peace. Later emperors, including Septimius Severus at the very end of the second century, Decius in the third century, and Diocletian in the fourth century, increased persecutions again, ordering Christians to sacrifice to the emperor and the Roman gods or risk death. Executions followed their edicts, although estimates of how many people were actually martyred in any of these persecutions vary widely.

By the second century C.E., Christianity was also changing. The belief that Jesus was soon coming again gradually waned, and as the number of converts increased, permanent institutions were established instead of simple house churches. These institutions included buildings and a hierarchy of officials often modeled on those of the Roman Empire. **Bishops**, officials with jurisdiction over a certain area, became especially important. They began to assert that they had the right to determine the correct interpretation of Christian teachings and to choose their successors. Councils of bishops determined which writings would be considered canonical, and lines were increasingly drawn between what was considered correct teaching and what was considered incorrect, or **heresy**.

Christianity also began to attract more highly educated individuals who developed complex theological interpretations of issues that were not clear in scripture. Often drawing on Greek philosophy and Roman legal traditions, they worked out understandings of issues such as how Jesus could be both divine and human, and how God could be both a father and a son (and later a spirit as well, a Christian doctrine known as the Trinity). Bishops and theologians often modified teachings that seemed upsetting to Romans, such as Jesus's harsh words about wealth and family ties. Given all these changes, Christianity became more formal in the second century, with power more centralized.

bishops
▶ Christian Church officials with jurisdiction over certain areas and the power to determine the correct interpretation of Christian teachings.

heresy
▶ A religious practice or belief judged unacceptable by church officials.

QUICK REVIEW

What made Christianity so appealing to many Romans? Why did some Romans see the new religion as a threat?

How did the Roman state develop after Augustus?

What was life like in the city of Rome, and what was it like in the provinces?

How did Christianity grow into a major religious movement?

What explains the chaos of the third century C.E.?

✓ LearningCurve
Check what you know.

169

What explains the chaos of the third century C.E.?

The Emperor Marcus Aurelius

This larger-than-life bronze equestrian statue, sculpted to celebrate his military victories shortly after his death in 180 C.E., shows the emperor holding up his hand in the conventional imperial greeting. More than twenty equestrian statues could be seen in late imperial Rome, but this is the only one to survive. In the sixteenth century, Michelangelo built one of the major plazas of Rome around it, although now the original has been moved to a museum for better preservation; a copy stands outdoors. (Tibor Bognar/Alamy)

THE PROSPERITY AND POLITICAL STABILITY of the second century gave way to a period of domestic upheaval and foreign invasion. The third century saw a long series of able but ambitious military commanders who used their legions to make themselves emperors. Law yielded to the sword, and the office of the emperor lost legitimacy. The nature of the army changed, and the economy weakened because of unsound policies.

CHAPTER LOCATOR | How did Augustus create a foundation for the Roman Empire?

Civil Wars and Military Commanders

The reign of Marcus Aurelius (r. 161–180 c.e.), the last of the "five good emperors," was marked by problems. The Tiber River flooded in 162, destroying crops and killing animals, which led to famine. Soldiers returning from wars in the East brought the Antonine plague back to Rome (see page 160) and then carried it northward. Germanic-speaking groups attacked along the Rhine and Danube borders, and the emperor himself took over the campaign against them in 169. He spent most of the rest of his life in military camps along Rome's northern border, where in addition to leading troops he wrote a series of personal reflections in Greek. These *Meditations*, as they later came to be known, are advice to himself about doing one's duty and acting in accordance with nature, ideas that came from Stoic philosophy (see Chapter 4). The *Meditations* are a good key to Marcus Aurelius's character, but they appear not to have circulated very much during the centuries immediately after they were written. Certainly very few later emperors took his advice to heart.

After the death of Marcus Aurelius, misrule by his successors led to a long and intense spasm of fighting. Marcus Aurelius's son Commodus was strangled by a conspiracy that included his wife, and in 193 five men claimed the throne in quick succession. Two of them were also assassinated, and Septimius Severus (r. 193–211) emerged as the victor. He restored order, expanded the borders of the Roman Empire in Africa and western Asia, and invaded Scotland. He increased the size of the army significantly and paid the soldiers better. This made him popular with soldiers, though it also increased the taxes on civilians. Some of his policies regarding the army created additional problems in the long run. Changes in recruiting practices that emphasized local recruiting of non-Romans created a Roman army that became less acculturated to Roman values. This army was no longer the vehicle for Romanization that it had been in earlier centuries. In part to increase the tax base, in 212 Septimius Severus's son Caracalla (r. 198–217) issued an edict making all free male residents of the Roman Empire citizens. This made them eligible to serve in the legions but also made army service less attractive and thus reduced the number of men willing to join.

More than twenty different emperors seized power in the forty-nine years between 235 and 284, a period scholars call the "crisis of the third century." These emperors were generally military commanders from the border provinces, and there were so many that the middle of the third century has become known as the age of the **barracks emperors**. Almost all were either assassinated or died in civil wars, and their concentration on overthrowing the ruling emperor left the borders unguarded. Non-Roman groups on the frontiers took full advantage of the chaos to overrun vast areas. When they reached the Rhine and the Danube, they often found gaping holes in the Roman defenses.

barracks emperors
▶ The emperors of the middle of the third century, so called because they were military commanders.

Turmoil in Economic Life

Chaos on the borders of the empire also disrupted areas far away from these borders. Renegade soldiers and corrupt imperial officials, together with many greedy local agents, preyed on local people. In some places in the countryside, officials

| How did the Roman state develop after Augustus? | What was life like in the city of Rome, and what was it like in the provinces? | How did Christianity grow into a major religious movement? | **What explains the chaos of the third century c.e.?** | ✔ LearningCurve Check what you know. |

171

requisitioned villagers' livestock and compelled them to do forced labor. Farmers appealed to the government for protection so that they could cultivate the land. Although some of those in authority were unsympathetic and even violent toward villagers, many others tried to maintain order. Yet even the best officials also suffered. If they could not meet their tax quotas, which were rising to support the costs of civil war, they had to pay the deficits from their own pockets. Because the local officials were themselves so hard-pressed, they squeezed what they needed from rural families. Many farmers, unable to pay, were driven off their land, and those remaining faced ruin. As a result, agricultural productivity declined.

In response to the economic crisis, the emperors reduced the amount of silver used in coins, replacing it with less valuable metals such as copper, so that they could continue to pay their troops. This tactic led to crippling inflation, however, which wiped out savings and sent prices soaring.

The Romans still controlled the Mediterranean, which nurtured commerce. The road system remained largely intact, though often roads were allowed to fall into disrepair. Trade still flowed, but with reduced efficiency and high costs. By 284 C.E., the empire had reached a crisis that threatened its downfall. The position of emperor was gained no longer by lawful succession but rather by victory in civil war. The empire had failed at the top, and the repercussions of the disaster spread throughout the empire, with dire effects.

> **QUICK REVIEW**

How did political disorder in the third century lead to social and economic disorder?

CHAPTER LOCATOR | How did Augustus create a foundation for the Roman Empire?

CHAPTER 6
172 THE ROMAN EMPIRE

LOOKING BACK
LOOKING AHEAD

The period of the Roman Empire was an era rich in both economic and cultural terms. Roman emperors developed a system of government that ruled over vast areas of diverse people fairly effectively. The resulting stability and peace encouraged agriculture and production. Goods and people moved along roads and sea-lanes, as did ideas, including the new religion of Christianity. As the empire expanded into northern and western Europe, the Romans incorporated indigenous peoples into their way of life. Yet during a long period of internal crisis, civil war, and invasions in the third century, it seemed as if the empire would collapse.

The Roman Empire did not disintegrate in the third century, however. Although emperors came and went in quick and violent succession, the basic institutions and infrastructure of the empire remained intact. Even during the worst of the ordeal, many lower-level officials and ordinary soldiers continued to do their jobs. People like this would be key to passing Roman traditions on to institutions that developed later in Europe, including law courts, city governments, and nations.

LaunchPad

ONLINE DOCUMENT PROJECT

Bithus, a Soldier in the Roman Army

How did the Roman Empire turn countless individuals like Bithus into the most powerful fighting machine the Mediterranean world had ever seen?

You encountered Bithus's story on page 158. Keeping the question above in mind, examine documents on the military's role in the expansion of the empire. *See inside the front cover to learn more.*

How did the Roman state develop after Augustus?

What was life like in the city of Rome, and what was it like in the provinces?

How did Christianity grow into a major religious movement?

What explains the chaos of the third century c.e.?

✔ **LearningCurve**
Check what you know.

CHAPTER 6 STUDY GUIDE

STEP 1 **GET STARTED ONLINE**

 LearningCurve
Now that you've read the chapter, make it stick by completing the LearningCurve activity.

STEP 2 **EXPLAIN WHY IT MATTERS**

Put your reading into practice. Identify each term below, and then explain why it matters in Western history.

TERM	WHO OR WHAT & WHEN	WHY IT MATTERS
imperator (p. 149)		
principate (p. 149)		
Roma et Augustus (p. 150)		
pax Romana (p. 150)		
Praetorians (p. 156)		
"five good emperors" (p. 156)		
aqueducts (p. 160)		
Messiah (p. 165)		
pagan (p. 166)		
bishops (p. 169)		
heresy (p. 169)		
barracks emperors (p. 171)		

STEP 3 **MOVE BEYOND THE BASICS**

To demonstrate a more advanced understanding, use the chart below to trace the imperial succession from Augustus to the barracks emperors.

	Quality of rule	Key developments and policies
Augustus		
Julio-Claudians		
Flavians		
"Five good emperors"		
Barracks emperors		

PUT IT ALL TOGETHER

Now, take a step back and try to explain the big picture. Remember to use specific examples from the chapter in your answers.

IMPERIAL GOVERNMENT

▶ How did the Roman army contribute to the process of Romanization?

▶ In what ways was the power of the Roman army both the empire's greatest strength and one of its most important weaknesses?

ECONOMY AND SOCIETY

▶ What were the most important factors in producing the prosperity of the first and second centuries?

▶ What steps did the Romans take to connect their provinces to Rome and to ensure the loyalty of their provincial subjects?

CHRISTIANITY

▶ What role did Paul play in the transformation of Christianity from a local sect to a major religion?

▶ How did Christianity change in the first two centuries following the death of Jesus?

MAKE CONNECTIONS

▶ Compare and contrast the Roman and the Persian Empires. How did the leaders of each respond to the challenge of ruling diverse subjects?

▶ What were the biggest problems facing Rome at the end of the third century? In your opinion, were they solvable? If so, how? If not, why not?

> IN YOUR OWN WORDS

Imagine that you must give an oral report to the class answering the following question: **What was life like in the Roman Empire during the period of the pax Romana?** What would be the most important points and why?

7
LATE ANTIQUITY
250–600

> In what ways was late antiquity a period marked both by continuity and change?

Chapter 7 examines the period in which the Western Roman Empire slowly disintegrated and ultimately collapsed. The two main agents of continuity in late antiquity were the Christian Church and the Byzantine or Eastern Roman Empire. Missionaries and church officials spread Christianity within and far beyond the borders of the Roman Empire, bringing with them the Latin language and institutions based on Roman models. The Byzantine Empire preserved and transmitted much of ancient Greco-Roman law, philosophy, and institutions. The main agents of change in late antiquity were groups the Romans labeled barbarians migrating into the Roman Empire. The barbarians brought different social, political, and economic structures with them, but as they encountered Roman culture and became Christian, their ways were also transformed.

✓ **LearningCurve**
After reading the chapter, use LearningCurve to retain what you've read.

> How did Diocletian and Constantine try to reform the empire?

> How did the Christian Church become a major force in Europe?

> What were the key characteristics of barbarian society?

> What were some of the causes and consequences of the barbarian migrations?

> How did the church convert barbarian peoples to Christianity?

> How did the Byzantine Empire preserve the legacy of Rome?

Life in Late Antiquity. In this sixth-century ivory carving, a procession of people carry relics of a saint to a Christian church under construction. (akg-images/Newscom.)

> How did Diocletian and Constantine try to reform the empire?

IN THE MIDDLE OF THE THIRD CENTURY, the Roman Empire faced internal turmoil and external attacks. Civil wars tore the empire apart, and barbarian groups migrated and marauded deep within the boundaries of the empire (see Chapter 6). Wars and invasions disrupted normal commerce and agriculture, the primary sources of tax revenues. The barracks emperors of the third century dealt with economic hardship by cutting the silver content of coins until money was virtually worthless. In the early fourth century, the emperor Diocletian (r. 284–305), who was born of low-status parents and had risen through the ranks of the military to become emperor, restored order, and the later emperor Constantine (r. 306–337) continued his work. How Diocletian, Constantine, and their successors responded to the problems facing the empire influenced later developments.

CHAPTER LOCATOR | **How did Diocletian and Constantine try to reform the empire?** | How did the Christian Church become a major force in Europe?

ca. 293
- Diocletian establishes the tetrarchy

313
- Edict of Milan, allowing practice of all religions in the Roman Empire

325
- Council of Nicaea

354–430
- Life of Saint Augustine

378
- Visigoths defeat the Roman army al Adrianople

380
- Theodosius makes Christianity the official religion of the Roman Empire

410
- Visigoths sack Rome

429
- Vandals begin their conquest of North Africa

476
- Odoacer deposes the last Roman emperor in the West

ca. 481–511
- Reign of Clovis

493
- Theoderic establishes an Ostrogothic state in Italy

527–565
- Reign of Justinian

529
- *The Rule of Saint Benedict*

535–572
- Byzantines reconquer and rule Italy

597
- Pope Gregory I sends missionaries to Britain

Political Measures

Diocletian recognized that the empire had become too large for one man to handle and divided it into a western half and an eastern half (**Map 7.1**). Diocletian assumed direct control of the eastern part; he gave the rule of the western part to a colleague, along with the title *augustus*. Around 293 Diocletian further delegated power by appointing two men to assist the augustus and him; each of the four men was given the title *caesar*, and the system was known as the **tetrarchy** (TEH-trahr-kee), meaning "rule of four." He further divided each part of the empire into administrative units called **dioceses**, which were in turn subdivided into small provinces, all governed by an expanded bureaucracy. Although four men ruled the empire, Diocletian was clearly the senior partner and final source of authority.

Diocletian's political reforms were a momentous step. The reorganization made the empire easier to administer and placed each of the four central military commands much closer to borders or other trouble spots so that troops could be sent more quickly when needed. Diocletian hoped that the tetrarchy would supply a clearly defined order of succession and end struggles for power over the emperorship. That did not happen, but much of Diocletian's reorganization remained.

Like Diocletian, Constantine came up through the army and took control after a series of civil wars. He eventually had authority over the entire empire but ruled from the East, where he established a new capital for the empire at Byzantium, an old Greek city on the Bosporus. He named it "New Rome," though it was soon called Constantinople. Constantine built defensive works along the borders of the empire, trying hard to keep it together, and used various means to strengthen the army, as did his successors. The emperors ruling from Constantinople could not

tetrarchy
▶ Diocletian's four-part division of the Roman Empire.

diocese
▶ An administrative unit in the later Roman Empire; adopted by the Christian Church as the territory under the authority of a bishop.

What were the key characteristics of barbarian society?

What were some of the causes and consequences of the barbarian migrations?

How did the church convert barbarian peoples to Christianity?

How did the Byzantine Empire preserve the legacy of Rome?

☑ LearningCurve
Check what you know.

MAP 7.1 ■ The Division of the Roman World, 293

Under Diocletian, the Roman Empire was first divided into a western and an eastern half, a development that foreshadowed the medieval division between the Latin West and the Byzantine East.

provide enough military assistance to repel invaders in the western half of the Roman Empire, however, and Roman authority there slowly disintegrated.

Economic Issues

In response to inflation and declining tax revenues, Diocletian issued an edict that fixed maximum prices and wages throughout the empire. At the same time, taxes became payable in kind, that is, in goods such as grain, sheep, or cloth instead of money, which made them difficult to transport to central authorities. Constantine continued these measures and also made occupations more rigid: all people involved in the growing, preparation, and transportation of food and other essentials were locked into their professions. In this period of severe depression, many individuals and communities could not pay their taxes. In such cases, local tax collectors, who were also bound to their occupations, had to make up the difference from their own funds. This system soon wiped out a whole class of moderately wealthy people and set the stage for the lack of social mobility that was a key characteristic of European society for many centuries to follow.

The emperors' measures did not really address Rome's central economic problems, however. Because of worsening conditions during the third and fourth centuries, many free farmers and their families were killed by invaders or renegade soldiers, fled the land to escape the barbarians, or abandoned farms ravaged in the fighting. Consequently, large tracts of land lay deserted. Landlords with ample resources began at once to reclaim as much of this land as they could; they often hired back the free farmers, who had previously worked the land, as paid labor or tenants. The huge villas that resulted were self-sufficient and became islands of stability in an unsettled world.

Free farmers who remained on the land were exposed to the raids of barbarians or robbers and to the tyranny of imperial officials. In return for the protection and security landlords could offer, small landholders gave over their lands and their freedom. To guarantee a supply of labor, landlords denied them freedom to move elsewhere. Free men and women were becoming tenant farmers bound to the land, what would later be called serfs.

The Acceptance of Christianity

Diocletian stepped up persecution of Christians who would not sacrifice to Rome's traditional deities, portraying them as disloyal to the empire. These persecutions lasted only a few years, however. Increasing numbers of Romans, including mem-

CHAPTER LOCATOR | **How did Diocletian and Constantine try to reform the empire?**

How did the Christian Church become a major force in Europe?

180 CHAPTER 7 LATE ANTIQUITY

bers of prominent families, were converting to Christianity, and many who followed traditional Roman religions no longer saw Christianity as un-Roman (see Chapter 6). Constantine reversed Diocletian's policy and instead ordered toleration of all religions in the Edict of Milan, issued in 313. In addition, he freed the clergy from imperial taxation and endowed the building of Christian churches. In return for his support, Constantine expected the assistance of church officials in maintaining order. Helped in part by its favored position in the empire, Christianity slowly became the leading religion (**Map 7.2**).

Christians disagreed with one another about many issues, which led to schisms (SKIH-zuhms), denunciations, and sometimes violence. In the fourth and fifth centuries, disputes arose over the nature of Christ. For example, **Arianism** (AI-ree-uh-nih-zuhm), developed by Arius (ca. 250–336), a priest of Alexandria,

Arianism

▶ A theological belief that originated with Arius, a priest of Alexandria, denying that Christ was co-eternal with God the Father.

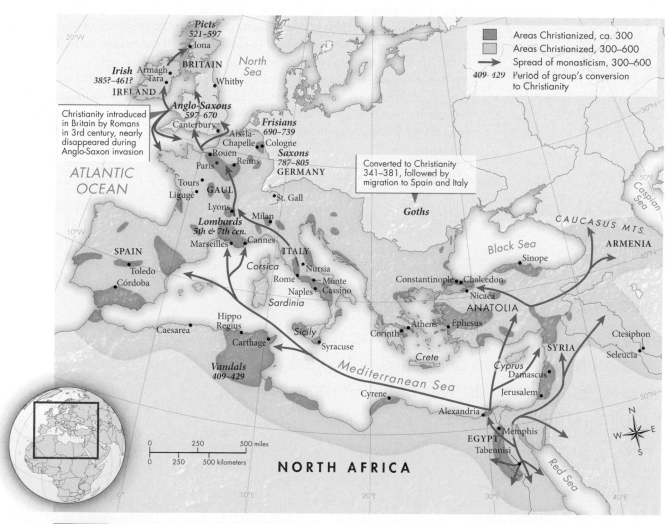

MAP 7.2 ■ The Spread of Christianity to 600

Originating in Judaea, the southern part of modern Israel and Jordan, Christianity first spread throughout the Roman world and then beyond it in all directions.

| What were the key characteristics of barbarian society? | What were some of the causes and consequences of the barbarian migrations? | How did the church convert barbarian peoples to Christianity? | How did the Byzantine Empire preserve the legacy of Rome? | ✓ LearningCurve Check what you know. |

held that Jesus was created by the will of God the Father and thus was not co-eternal with him. This doctrine provoked such controversy that Constantine felt it necessary to intercede. In 325, he summoned church leaders to a council in Nicaea (nigh-SEE-uh) in Asia Minor and presided over it personally. The council produced the Nicene (nigh-SEEN) Creed, which defined the position that Christ is "eternally begotten of the Father" and of the same substance as the Father. Arianism was declared a **heresy**, that is, a belief that contradicted the interpretation the church leaders declared was correct. Interpretations declared correct were termed orthodoxy. These actions did not end Arianism, however. Several later emperors were Arian Christian, and Arian missionaries converted many barbarian tribes.

heresy
▶ The denial of a basic doctrine of faith.

In 380, the emperor Theodosius (thee-uh-DOH-shee-uhs) made Nicene Christianity the official religion of the empire. Theodosius stripped Roman pagan temples of statues, made the practice of the old Roman state religion a treasonable offense, and persecuted Christians who dissented from orthodox doctrine. Most significant, he allowed the church to establish its own courts and to use its own body of law, called canon law. The church courts, not the Roman government, had jurisdiction over the clergy and ecclesiastical disputes. At the death of Theodosius, the Christian Church was considerably independent of the Roman state. The foundation for later growth in church power had been laid.

Later emperors continued the pattern of active involvement in church affairs. They appointed the highest officials of the church hierarchy, the emperors or their representatives presided at ecumenical councils, and the emperors controlled some of the material resources of the church—land, rents, and dependent peasantry.

> ## QUICK REVIEW

Why did the political and economic reforms initiated by Diocletian and Constantine fail to reverse the slow decline of the Roman Empire in the West?

CHAPTER LOCATOR | How did Diocletian and Constantine try to reform the empire? | **How did the Christian Church become a major force in Europe?**

182 CHAPTER 7 LATE ANTIQUITY

How did the Christian Church become a major force in Europe?

AS THE EMPERORS CHANGED THEIR POLICIES about Christianity from persecution to promotion, the church grew, gradually becoming the most important institution in Europe. The able administrators and creative thinkers of the church developed permanent institutions and complex philosophical concepts that drew on the Greco-Roman tradition, which attracted learned Romans.

The Church and Its Leaders

The early Christian Church benefited from the administrative abilities of church leaders. With the empire in decay, educated people joined and worked for the church in the belief that it was the one institution able to provide some stability. Bishop Ambrose of Milan (339–397) is typical of the Roman aristocrats who held high public office, were converted to Christianity, and subsequently became bishops. Like many bishops, Ambrose had a solid education in classical law and rhetoric, which he used to become an eloquent preacher. He had a strong sense of his authority and even stood up to Emperor Theodosius when he ordered Ambrose to

| What were the key characteristics of barbarian society? | What were some of the causes and consequences of the barbarian migrations? | How did the church convert barbarian peoples to Christianity? | How did the Byzantine Empire preserve the legacy of Rome? | ✔ LearningCurve Check what you know. |

hand over his major church—called a basilica—to the emperor. Ambrose argued that the church was supreme in spiritual matters and the state in secular issues, and thus the emperor had no right to the building. In a decision that reflected the growing power of the church, the emperor relented.

Gradually the church adapted the organizational structure of the Roman Empire begun during the reign of Diocletian. The territory under the authority of a bishop was also called a diocese. A bishop's jurisdiction extended throughout the diocese, and he came to control a large amount of land that was given to or purchased by the church. Bishops generally came from prominent families and had both spiritual and political power; as the Roman Empire disintegrated, they became the most important local authority on many types of issues. They claimed to trace their spiritual ancestry back to Jesus's apostles, a doctrine called **apostolic succession**. Because of the special importance of their dioceses, five bishops—those of Antioch, Alexandria, Jerusalem, Constantinople, and Rome—gained the title of patriarch.

After the capital and the emperor moved to Constantinople, the power of the bishop of Rome grew because he was the only patriarch in the Western Roman Empire. The bishops of Rome claimed that Rome had a special place in Christian history. According to tradition, Saint Peter, chief of Jesus's disciples, had lived in Rome and been its first bishop. Thus, as successors of Peter, the bishops of Rome—known as popes, from the Latin word papa, meaning "father"—claimed a privileged position in the church hierarchy, an idea called the **Petrine Doctrine** that built on the notion of apostolic succession. The bishops of Rome stressed their supremacy over other Christian communities and urged other churches to appeal to Rome for the resolution of disputed doctrinal issues. Not surprisingly, the other patriarchs did not agree. They continued to exercise authority in their own regions, and local churches did as well, but the groundwork had been laid for later Roman predominance on religious matters.

Gregory I (pontificate 590–604), later called "the Great," played a particularly important role in cementing the power of the popes. He had been an official for the city of Rome before he became a church official, and his administrative and diplomatic talents helped the church expand. He sent missionaries to the British Isles (see page 199) and wrote letters and guides instructing bishops on practical and spiritual matters. He promoted the ideas of Augustine (see page 187), particularly those that defined church rituals as essential for salvation. The Western Christian Church headed by the pope in Rome would become the most enduring nongovernmental institution in world history.

The Development of Christian Monasticism

Christianity began and spread as a city religion. Since the first century, however, some especially pious Christians had felt that the only alternative to the decadence of urban life was complete separation from the world. This desire to withdraw from ordinary life led to the development of the monastic life. Monasticism began in third-century Egypt, where individuals like Saint Anthony (251?–356) and small groups first withdrew from cities to seek God through prayer in the desert or mountain caves and shelters, giving up all for Christ. Gradually large colonies of monks gathered in the deserts of Upper Egypt, and Christians came to believe that monks, like the early Christian martyrs executed by Roman authorities before

apostolic succession
▶ The doctrine that all bishops can trace their spiritual ancestry back to Jesus's apostles.

Petrine Doctrine
▶ A doctrine stating that the popes (the bishops of Rome) were the successors of Saint Peter and therefore heirs to his highest level of authority as chief of the apostles.

CHAPTER LOCATOR | How did Diocletian and Constantine try to reform the empire? | **How did the Christian Church become a major force in Europe?**

184 CHAPTER 7 LATE ANTIQUITY

them, could speak to God and that their prayers had special influence. These monks were called hermits, from the Greek word eremos, meaning "desert." Many devout women also were attracted to this eremitical (ehr-uh-MIH-tihk-uhl) type of monasticism.

The Egyptian ascetic Pachomius (puh-KOH-mee-uhs) (290–346?) drew thousands of men and women to the monastic life at Tabennisi on the Upper Nile. There were too many for them to live as hermits, so Pachomius organized communities of men and women, creating a new type of monasticism, known as cenobitic (seh-nuh-BIH-tik), that emphasized communal living.

Starting in the fourth century, information about Egyptian monasticism came to the West, and both men and women sought the monastic life. Because of the dangers of living alone in the forests of northern Europe, the eremitical form of monasticism did not take root. Most of the monasticism that developed in Gaul, Italy, Spain, England, and Ireland was cenobitic (**Table 7.1**).

Monastery Life

In 529, Benedict of Nursia (480–543) wrote a brief set of regulations for the monks who had gathered around him at Monte Cassino, between Rome and Naples. Benedict's guide for monastic life, known as *The Rule of Saint Benedict*, came to influence all forms of organized religious life in the Western Christian Church. Men and women in monastic houses all followed sets of rules, first those of Benedict and later those written by other individuals. Because of these rules, men who lived a communal monastic life came to be called **regular clergy**, from the Latin word *regulus* (rule). Priests and bishops who staffed churches in which people worshipped and who were not cut off from the world were called **secular clergy**.

The Rule of Saint Benedict outlined a monastic life of regularity, discipline, and moderation in an atmosphere of silence. Each monk had ample food and adequate sleep. The monk spent part of each day in formal prayer, which consisted of chanting psalms and other prayers from the Bible in the part of the monastery church called the choir. The rest of the day was passed in manual labor, study, and private prayer. The monastic life as conceived by Saint Benedict struck a balance between asceticism (extreme material sacrifice, including fasting and the renunciation of sex) and activity. It thus provided opportunities for men of entirely different abilities and talents—from mechanics to gardeners to literary scholars.

regular clergy
▶ Men and women who lived in monastic houses and followed sets of rules, first those of Benedict and later those written by other individuals.

secular clergy
▶ Priests and bishops who staffed churches where people worshipped and who were not cut off from the world.

TABLE 7.1 ■ Eremitical Monasticism and Cenobitic Monasticism

Eremitical Monasticism	Cenobitic Monasticism
• Began in third-century Egypt	• Developed by the Egyptian ascetic Pachomius (290–346?)
• Centered on individual withdrawal from society	• Centered on organized groups of religious men and women
• Epitomized by Saint Anthony (251?–356)	• Dominant form of monasticism in western Europe
	• Profoundly shaped in the West by Benedict of Nursia (480–543)

What were the key characteristics of barbarian society?

What were some of the causes and consequences of the barbarian migrations?

How did the church convert barbarian peoples to Christianity?

How did the Byzantine Empire preserve the legacy of Rome?

 LearningCurve
Check what you know.

The Benedictine form of religious life also appealed to women because it allowed them to show their devotion and engage in study. Benedict's twin sister Scholastica (480–543) adapted the *Rule* for use by her community of nuns.

Benedictine monasticism also succeeded partly because it was so materially successful. In the seventh and eighth centuries, monasteries pushed back forests and wastelands, drained swamps, and experimented with crop rotation. Benedictine houses thus made a significant contribution to the agricultural development of Europe.

Monasteries also conducted schools for local young people, and monks and nuns copied manuscripts, preserving classical as well as Christian literature. Local and royal governments drew on the services of the literate men and able administrators the monasteries produced.

Christianity and Classical Culture

As Christianity grew from a tiny persecuted group to the official religion of the Roman Empire, its leaders and thinkers gradually incorporated elements of Greek and Roman philosophy and learning into Christian teachings, modifying them to fit with Christian notions. Saint Jerome (340–419), for example, translated the Old and New Testaments from Hebrew and Greek into vernacular Latin. Called the Vulgate, his edition of the Bible served as the official translation until the sixteenth century. Familiar with the writings of classical authors, Saint Jerome maintained that the best ancient literature could and should be interpreted in light of the Christian faith.

Christian Notions of Gender and Sexuality

Early Christians both adopted and adapted the then-contemporary views of women, marriage, and sexuality. In his plan of salvation, Jesus considered women the equal of men. Women were among the earliest converts to Christianity and took an active role in its spread. Because early Christians believed that the Second Coming of Christ was imminent, they devoted their energies to their new spiritual family of co-believers. Women and men joyously accepted the ascetic life, renouncing marriage and procre-

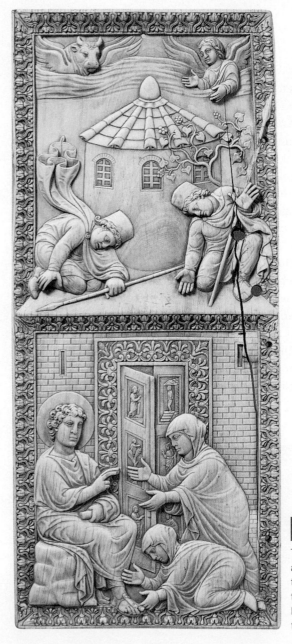

The Marys at Jesus's Tomb

This late-fourth-century ivory panel tells the biblical story of Mary Magdalene and another Mary who went to Jesus's tomb to anoint the body (Matthew 28:1–7). At the top, guards collapse when an angel descends from Heaven; at the bottom, the Marys listen to the angel telling them that Jesus has risen. Here the artist uses Roman artistic styles to convey Christian subject matter, synthesizing classical form and Christian teaching. (Scala/Art Resource, NY)

CHAPTER LOCATOR | How did Diocletian and Constantine try to reform the empire? | **How did the Christian Church become a major force in Europe?**

ation to use their bodies for a higher calling. Some women, either singly or in monastic communities, declared themselves "virgins in the service of Christ." All this initially made Christianity seem dangerous to many Romans, who viewed marriage as the foundation of society and the proper patriarchal order.

Not all Christian teachings about gender were radical, however. In the first century C.E., male church leaders began to place restrictions on female believers. Women were forbidden to preach and were gradually excluded from holding official positions in Christianity other than in women's monasteries. Both Jewish and classical Mediterranean culture viewed women's subordination as natural and proper; thus, in limiting the activities of female believers, the Christian Church was following well-established patterns, just as it did in modeling its official hierarchy after that of the Roman Empire.

Christian teachings about sexuality built on and challenged classical models. The rejection of sexual activity involved an affirmation of the importance of a spiritual life, but it also incorporated the hostility toward the body found in some Hellenistic philosophies and some of the other religions that had spread in the Roman Empire in this era. Christian teachings affirmed that God had created the material world and sanctioned marriage, but most Christian thinkers also taught that celibacy was the better life and that anything that took one's attention from the spiritual world performed an evil function. For most clerical writers (who themselves were male), this temptation came from women, and in some of their writings women themselves are depicted as evil, the "devil's gateway." Thus, the writings of many church fathers contain a strong streak of misogyny (hatred of women), which was passed down to later Christian thinkers.

Saint Augustine on Human Nature, Will, and Sin

The most influential church father in the West was Saint Augustine of Hippo (354–430). Saint Augustine was born into an urban family in what is now Algeria in North Africa. His father, a minor civil servant, was a pagan; his mother, Monica, was a devout Christian. He gained an excellent classical education in philosophy and rhetoric and, as was normal for young Roman men, began relations with a concubine, who later had his son.

Augustine took teaching positions first in Rome and then in Milan, where he had frequent conversations with Bishop Ambrose. Through his discussions with Ambrose and his own reading, Augustine converted to Christianity. He returned to Africa and later became bishop of the seacoast city of Hippo Regius.

Augustine's autobiography, *The Confessions*, is a literary masterpiece and one of the most influential books in the history of Europe. Written in the rhetorical style and language of late Roman antiquity, it marks the synthesis of Greco-Roman forms and Christian thought. *The Confessions* describes Augustine's moral struggle, the conflict between his spiritual and intellectual aspirations and his sensual and material self.

Augustine's ideas on sin, grace, and redemption became the foundation of all subsequent Western Christian theology, Protestant as well as Catholic. He wrote that the basic force in any individual is the will, which he defined as "the power of the soul to hold on to or to obtain an object without constraint." The end or goal

| What were the key characteristics of barbarian society? | What were some of the causes and consequences of the barbarian migrations? | How did the church convert barbarian peoples to Christianity? | How did the Byzantine Empire preserve the legacy of Rome? | ✓ LearningCurve Check what you know. |

187

of the will determines the moral character of the individual. When Adam ate the fruit forbidden by God in the Garden of Eden (Genesis 3:6), he committed the "original sin" and corrupted the will. Adam's sin was not simply his own— it was passed on to all later humans through sexual intercourse; even infants were tainted. Original sin thus became a common social stain, in Augustine's opinion, transmitted by sexual desire. By viewing sexual desire as the result of Adam and Eve's disobedience to divine instructions, Augustine linked sexuality even more clearly with sin than had earlier church fathers. Because Adam disobeyed God and fell, all human beings have an innate tendency to sin: their will is weak. But according to Augustine, God restores the strength of the will through grace, which is transmitted in certain rituals that the church defined as

sacraments

▶ Certain rituals defined by the church in which God bestows benefits on the believer through grace.

sacraments. Grace results from God's decisions, not from any merit on the part of the individual.

When Visigothic forces captured the city of Rome in 410, horrified pagans blamed the disaster on the Christians. In response, Augustine wrote *City of God*. This original work contrasts Christianity with the secular society in which it exists. According to Augustine, history reveals that there are two kinds of people: those who live the life of the flesh, and those who live the life of the spirit in what Augustine called the City of God. The former will endure eternal hellfire; the latter will enjoy eternal bliss.

> **QUICK REVIEW**

How did Greco-Roman traditions shape the development of Church institutions and teachings?

CHAPTER LOCATOR | How did Diocletian and Constantine try to reform the empire? | How did the Christian Church become a major force in Europe?

CHAPTER 7
188 LATE ANTIQUITY

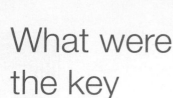

What were the key characteristics of barbarian society?

Visigothic Work and Play

This page comes from one of the very few manuscripts from late antiquity to have survived, a copy of the first five books of the Old Testament — the Pentateuch — made around 600, perhaps in Visigothic Spain or North Africa. The top shows biblical scenes, while the bottom shows people engaged in everyday activities — building a wall, drawing water from a well, and trading punches. (Bibliothèque nationale de France)

AUGUSTINE'S *CITY OF GOD* was written in response to the conquest of Rome by an army of Visigoths, one of the many peoples the Romans—and later historians—labeled "barbarians." Scholars have been hampered in investigating barbarian society because most groups did not write and thus kept no written records before Christian missionaries introduced writing. Greek and Roman authors did describe barbarian society, but they were not always objective observers. Thus, written records must be combined with archaeological evidence to gain a more accurate picture. In addition, historians are increasingly deciphering and using the barbarians' own written records that do exist, especially inscriptions carved in stone, bone, and wood and written in the **runic alphabet**.

runic alphabet
▶ Writing system developed in some barbarian groups that helps to give a more accurate picture of barbarian society.

| What were the key characteristics of barbarian society? | What were some of the causes and consequences of the barbarian migrations? | How did the church convert barbarian peoples to Christianity? | How did the Byzantine Empire preserve the legacy of Rome? | ✓ LearningCurve Check what you know. |

Whalebone Chest This eighth-century chest made of whalebone, depicting warriors, other human figures, and a horse, tells a story in both pictures and words. The runes along the border are one of the varieties from the British Isles. Contact with the Romans led to the increasing use of the Latin alphabet, though runes and Latin letters were used side by side in some parts of northern Europe for centuries. (Erich Lessing/Art Resource, NY)

Barbarians included many different ethnic groups with social and political structures, languages, laws, and beliefs that developed in central and northern Europe over many centuries. Among the largest groups were Celts (whom the Romans called Gauls) and Germans. Celts, Germans, and other barbarians brought their customs and traditions with them when they moved southward, and these gradually combined with classical and Christian patterns to form new types of societies.

Village and Family Life

Barbarian groups usually resided in small villages, and climate and geography determined the basic patterns of how they lived off the land. Many groups lived in small settlements on the edges of clearings where they raised crops. Men and women tilled their fields with simple wooden plows and harvested their grains with small iron sickles. The vast majority of people's caloric intake came from grain in some form; the kernels of grain were eaten as porridge; ground up for flour; or fermented into strong, thick beer.

Within the villages were great differences in wealth and status. Free men and their families constituted the largest class. The number of cattle a man possessed indicated his wealth and determined his social status. Free men also shared in tribal warfare. Slaves acquired through warfare worked as farm laborers, herders, and household servants.

CHAPTER LOCATOR | How did Diocletian and Constantine try to reform the empire? | How did the Christian Church become a major force in Europe?

Ironworking represented the most advanced craft. The typical village had an oven and smiths who produced agricultural tools and instruments of war—one-edged swords, arrowheads, and shields. By the second century C.E., the swords produced by barbarian smiths were superior to the weapons of Roman troops.

In the first two centuries C.E., the quantity and quality of material goods increased dramatically. Goods were used locally and for gift giving, a major social custom. Gift giving conferred status on the giver, whose giving showed his higher (economic) status, cemented friendship, and placed the receiver in his debt. Goods were also traded, though commercial exchange was less important than in the Roman Empire.

Families and kin groups were the basic social units in barbarian society. Families were responsible for the debts and actions of their members and for keeping the peace in general. Barbarian law codes set strict rules of inheritance based on position in the family and often set aside a portion of land that could not be sold or given away by any family member so that the family always retained some land.

Barbarian society was patriarchal: within each household the father had authority over his wife, children, and slaves. Some wealthy and powerful men had more than one wife. Women worked alongside men in the fields and forests. Once women were widowed, they sometimes assumed their husbands' rights over family property and held the guardianship of their children.

Tribes and Hierarchies

The basic social and political unit among barbarian groups was the tribe or confederation, a group whose members believed that they were all descended from a common ancestor. Tribes were led by chieftains. The chief was the member recognized as the strongest and bravest in battle and was elected from among the male members of the most powerful family.

Closely associated with the chief in some tribes was the **comitatus**, or war band. These warriors swore loyalty to the chief, fought with him in battle, and were not supposed to leave the battlefield without him; to do so implied cowardice, disloyalty, and social disgrace. These oaths of loyalty were later more formalized in the development of feudalism (see Chapter 8).

comitatus
▶ A war band of young men in a barbarian tribe who were closely associated with the chief, swore loyalty to him, and fought with him in battle.

Customary and Written Law

Early barbarian tribes had no written laws. Law was custom, but certain individuals were often given special training in remembering and retelling laws from generation to generation. Beginning in the late fifth century, however, some chieftains began to collect, write, and publish lists of their customs and laws.

The law code of the Salian Franks, one of the barbarian tribes, included a feature common to many barbarian codes. Any crime that involved a personal injury, such as assault, rape, and murder, was given a particular monetary value, called the **wergeld** (WUHR-gehld) (literally "man-money" or "money to buy off the spear"), that was to be paid by the perpetrator to the victim or the family. The

wergeld
▶ Compensatory payment for death or injury set in many barbarian law codes.

| **What were the key characteristics of barbarian society?** | What were some of the causes and consequences of the barbarian migrations? | How did the church convert barbarian peoples to Christianity? | How did the Byzantine Empire preserve the legacy of Rome? | ☑ LearningCurve Check what you know. |

wergeld varied according to the severity of the crime and also the social status of the victim.

The wergeld system aimed to prevent or reduce violence. If a person accused of a crime agreed to pay the wergeld and if the victim and his or her family accepted the payment, there was peace. If the accused refused to pay the wergeld or if the victim's family refused to accept it, a blood feud ensued. At first, Romans had been subject to Roman law and barbarians to barbarian custom. As barbarian kings accepted Christianity and as Romans and barbarians increasingly inter-married and assimilated culturally, the distinction between the two sets of law blurred and, in the course of the seventh and eighth centuries, disappeared. The result would be the new feudal law, to which all who lived in certain areas were subject.

Celtic and Germanic Religion

Like Greeks and Romans, barbarians worshipped hundreds of gods and goddesses with specialized functions. They regarded certain mountains, lakes, rivers, or groves of trees as sacred because these were linked to deities. Rituals to honor the gods were held outdoors rather than in temples or churches, often at certain points in the yearly agricultural cycle. Presided over by a priest or priestess, ritu-als sometimes involved animal (and perhaps human) sacrifice. Among the Celts, religious leaders called druids (DROO-ihds) had legal and educational as well as religious functions, orally passing down laws and traditions from generation to generation. Bards singing poems and ballads also passed down myths and stories of heroes and gods, which were written down much later.

> **QUICK REVIEW**

What role did kinship connections play in barbarian society?

CHAPTER LOCATOR | How did Diocletian and Constantine try to reform the empire? | How did the Christian Church become a major force in Europe?

CHAPTER 7
192 LATE ANTIQUITY

What were some of the causes and consequences of the barbarian migrations?

Anglo-Saxon Helmet This ceremonial bronze helmet from seventh-century England was found inside a ship buried at Sutton Hoo. The nearly 100-foot-long ship was dragged overland before being buried completely. It held one body and many grave goods, including swords, gold buckles, and silver bowls made in Byzantium. The unidentified person who was buried here was clearly wealthy and powerful. (© The Trustees of the British Museum)

MIGRATING GROUPS THAT THE ROMANS LABELED BARBARIANS had moved southward and eastward off and on since about 100 B.C.E. (see Chapters 5 and 6). As their movements became more organized in the third and fourth centuries C.E., Roman armies sought to defend the Rhine-Danube border of the Roman Empire. But with troop levels low because Italians were increasingly unwilling to serve in the army, generals were forced to recruit barbarians to fill the ranks. By the fourth century, barbarians made up the majority of those fighting both for and against Rome, and climbed higher and higher in the ranks of the Roman military. Toward the end of the fifth century, this barbarian assumption of authority stretched all the way to the top, and the last person with the title of emperor in the Western Roman Empire was deposed by a Gothic general.

Why did the barbarians migrate? In part they were searching for more regular supplies of food, better farmland, and a warmer climate. In part they were pushed

What were the key characteristics of barbarian society?

What were some of the causes and consequences of the barbarian migrations?

How did the church convert barbarian peoples to Christianity?

How did the Byzantine Empire preserve the legacy of Rome?

✓ LearningCurve
Check what you know.

193

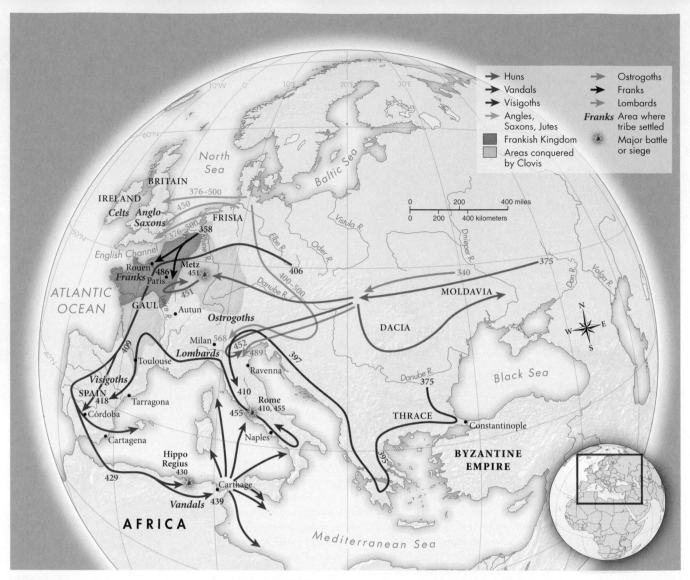

MAP 7.3 ■ The Barbarian Migrations, ca. 340–500

This map shows the migrations of various barbarian groups in late antiquity and can be used to answer the following questions.

> MAPPING THE PAST

ANALYZING THE MAP: The movements of barbarian peoples used to be labeled invasions and are now usually described as migrations. How do the dates on the map support the newer understanding of these movements?

CONNECTIONS: Human migration is caused by a combination of push factors — circumstances that lead people to leave a place — and pull factors — circumstances that attract people to a new location. Based on the information in this and earlier chapters, what push and pull factors might have shaped the migration patterns you see on the map?

by groups living farther eastward, especially by the Huns from Central Asia in the fourth and fifth centuries. Conflicts within and among barbarian groups also led to war and disruption, which motivated groups to move (**Map 7.3**).

Celtic and Germanic People in Gaul and Britain

The Celts present a good example of both assimilation and conflict. Celtic peoples conquered by the Romans often assimilated Roman ways, adapting the Latin language and other aspects of Roman culture. In Roman Gaul and then in Roman

CHAPTER LOCATOR | How did Diocletian and Constantine try to reform the empire? | How did the Christian Church become a major force in Europe?

194 CHAPTER 7 LATE ANTIQUITY

Britain, towns were planned in the Roman fashion, with temples, public baths, theaters, and amphitheaters. In the countryside, large manors controlled the surrounding lands. Roman merchants brought Eastern luxury goods and Eastern religions—including Christianity. The Romans suppressed the Celtic chieftains, and a military aristocracy made up of Romans—some of whom intermarried with Celtic families—governed. In the course of the second and third centuries, many Celts became Roman citizens and joined the Roman army. Celtic culture survived only in areas beyond the borders of the empire.

By the fourth century c.e., Gaul and Britain were under pressure from Germanic groups moving westward, and Rome itself was threatened (see Map 7.3, p. 194). Imperial troops withdrew from Britain in order to defend Rome, and the Picts from Scotland and the Scots from Ireland (both Celtic-speaking peoples) invaded territory held by the Britons. According to the eighth-century historian Bede (BEED), the Briton king Vortigern invited the Saxons from Denmark to help him against his rivals. However, Saxons and other Germanic tribes from the area of modern-day Norway, Sweden, and Denmark turned from assistance to conquest. Their goal was plunder, and at first their invasions led to no permanent settlements. As more Germanic peoples arrived, however, they took over the best lands and eventually conquered most of Britain. Historians have labeled the years 500 to 1066 (the year of the Norman Conquest) the Anglo-Saxon period of English history, after the two largest Germanic groups in England, the Angles and the Saxons.

Anglo-Saxon England was divided along ethnic and political lines. The Germanic kingdoms in the south, east, and center were opposed by the Britons in the west, who wanted to get rid of the invaders. The Anglo-Saxon kingdoms also fought among themselves, causing boundaries to shift constantly. In the ninth century, under pressure from the Viking invasions, King Alfred of Wessex (r. 871–899) created a more unified state with a reorganized army and system of fortresses for defense.

Visigoths and Huns

On the European continent, the Germanic peoples included a number of groups with very different cultural traditions. The largest Germanic group was the Goths, who were further subdivided by scholars into Ostrogoths (eastern Goths) and Visigoths (western Goths) based on their migration patterns. Both of these groups played important roles in the political developments of late antiquity.

Pressured by defeat in battle, starvation, and the movement of other groups, the Visigoths moved westward from their homeland north of the Black Sea, and in 376 they petitioned the Roman emperor Valens to admit them to the empire. They offered to fight for Rome in exchange for the province of Thrace in what is now Greece and Bulgaria. Seeing in the hordes of warriors the solution to his recruitment problem, Valens agreed. However, the deal fell apart when crop failures led to famine and Roman authorities exploited the Visigoths' hunger by forcing them to sell their own people as slaves. The Visigoths revolted, joined with other barbarian enemies of Rome, and defeated the Roman army at the Battle of Adrianople in 378, killing Valens and thousands of Roman soldiers in the process. This left a large barbarian army within the borders of the Roman Empire, and not that far from Constantinople.

What were the key characteristics of barbarian society?

What were some of the causes and consequences of the barbarian migrations?

How did the church convert barbarian peoples to Christianity?

How did the Byzantine Empire preserve the legacy of Rome?

✔ LearningCurve
Check what you know.

195

Valens's successor made peace with the Visigoths, but relations worsened as the Visigoths continued migrating westward (see Map 7.3, p. 194). The Visigothic king Alaric I, who had also been a general in one of the Roman armies in the east, invaded Italy and sacked Rome in 410. The Visigoths burned and looted the city for three days. (See "Picturing the Past: Battle Between Romans and Goths," page 196.) Alaric died a year later, and his successor led his people into southwestern Gaul, where they established the Visigothic kingdom.

One significant factor in the migration of the Visigoths and other Germanic peoples was pressure from nomadic steppe peoples from Central Asia. They included the Alans, Avars, Bulgars, Khazars, and most prominently the Huns, who attacked the Black Sea area and the Byzantine Empire beginning in the fourth century.

Under the leadership of their warrior-king Attila, the Huns attacked the Byzantine Empire in 447 and then turned westward. Several Germanic groups allied with them, as did the sister of the Roman emperor, who hoped to take power from

Battle Between Romans and Goths

Rome's wars with the Germanic-speaking groups along its northern border come to life in this relief from a Roman sarcophagus of the third century C.E., discovered in a tomb in the city of Rome. The Romans are wearing helmets, and the soldier at the right is wearing iron or bronze chain mail, a defensive technology that the Romans adapted from the Celts. (© Vanni Archive/Art Resource, NY)

> PICTURING THE PAST

ANALYZING THE IMAGE: How would you describe this depiction of war? How does the artist show Roman superiority over the barbarians through the placement, dress, and facial features of the soldiers?

CONNECTIONS: How does this funeral sculpture reinforce or challenge what you have learned about Roman expansion and the Romans' treatment of the peoples they conquered?

CHAPTER LOCATOR | How did Diocletian and Constantine try to reform the empire? | How did the Christian Church become a major force in Europe?

CHAPTER 7
196 LATE ANTIQUITY

her brother. Their troops combined with those of the Huns, and a huge army took the city of Metz, now in eastern France. A combined army of Romans and Visigoths stopped the advance of the Huns at Châlons, and they retreated. The following year, they moved into the Western Roman Empire again, crossing the Alps into Italy. Though papal diplomacy was later credited with stopping the advance of the Huns, their dwindling food supplies and a plague that spread among their troops were probably much more important. The Huns retreated from Italy, and within a year Attila was dead. Later leaders were not as effective, and the Huns were never again an important factor in European history. Their conquests had pushed many Germanic groups together, however, transforming smaller bands into larger, more unified peoples who could pick apart the Roman Empire more easily.

Germanic Kingdoms and the End of the Roman Empire

After they conquered an area, barbarians generally established states ruled by kings. The kingdoms did not have definite geographical borders, however, and their locations shifted as tribes moved. In the fifth century, the Burgundians ruled over lands roughly circumscribed by the old Roman army camps in what is now central France and western Switzerland. The Visigoths exercised a weak domination over southern France and much of the Iberian Peninsula. The Vandals, another Germanic tribe whose destructive ways are commemorated in the word vandal, swept across Spain into North Africa in 429 and took over what had been Rome's breadbasket. They established a state that lasted about a century, raided many coastal cities, and even sacked the city of Rome itself in 455.

Barbarian states eventually came to include Italy itself. The Western Roman emperors were generally chosen by the more powerful successors of Constantine in the East, and they increasingly relied on barbarian commanders and their troops to maintain order. In the 470s, a series of these commanders took over authority in name as well as in reality, deposing several Roman emperors. In 476, the barbarian chieftain Odoacer (OH-duh-way-suhr) deposed Romulus Augustus, the last person to have the title of Roman emperor in the West. Emperor Zeno, the Roman emperor in the East ruling from Constantinople, worried about Odoacer's growing power and promised Theoderic (r. 471–526), the leader of the Ostrogoths who had recently settled in the Balkans, the right to rule Italy if he defeated Odoacer. Theoderic's forces were successful, and in 493 Theoderic established an Ostrogothic state in Italy, with his capital at Ravenna.

For centuries, the end of the Roman Empire in the West was seen as a major turning point in history, the fall of the sophisticated and educated classical world to uncouth and illiterate tribes. Over the last several decades, however, many historians have put greater stress on continuities. The Ostrogoths, for example, maintained many Roman ways. Old Roman families continued to run the law courts and the city governments, and well-educated Italians continued to study the Greek classics.

In other barbarian states, aspects of classical culture also continued. Barbarian kings relied on officials trained in Roman law, and Latin remained the language of scholarly communication. Greco-Roman art and architecture still adorned the land,

What were the key characteristics of barbarian society?

What were some of the causes and consequences of the barbarian migrations?

How did the church convert barbarian peoples to Christianity?

How did the Byzantine Empire preserve the legacy of Rome?

LearningCurve
Check what you know.

197

and people continued to use Roman roads, aqueducts, and buildings. The Christian Church in barbarian states modeled its organization on that of Rome, and many bishops were from upper-class families that had governed the empire.

Very recently some historians and archaeologists have returned to an emphasis on change. They note that people may have traveled on Roman roads, but the roads were rarely maintained, and travel itself was much less secure than during the Roman Empire. Merchants no longer traded over long distances, so people's access to goods produced outside their local area plummeted. Knowledge about technological processes such as the making of glass and roof tiles declined or disappeared. There was intermarriage and cultural assimilation among Romans and barbarians, but there was also violence and great physical destruction.

The kingdom established by the Franks is a good example of this combination of peaceful assimilation and violent conflict. The Franks were a confederation of Germanic peoples who originated in the northernmost part of the Roman Empire (see Map 7.3, page 194). In the fourth and fifth centuries, they settled within the empire and allied with the Romans, some attaining high military and civil positions.

The reign of Clovis (KLOH-vis) (ca. 481–511) marks the decisive period in the development of the Franks as a unified people. Through military campaigns, Clovis acquired the central provinces of Roman Gaul and began to conquer southern Gaul and take the spoils from the Burgundians and Visigoths. Clovis's conversion to Roman Christianity brought him the crucial support of the bishops of Gaul in his campaigns against tribes that were still pagan or had accepted the Arian version of Christianity. Along with brutal violence, however, the next two centuries witnessed the steady assimilation of Franks and Romans, as many Franks adopted the Latin language and Roman ways, and Romans copied Frankish customs and Frankish personal names.

From Constantinople, Eastern Roman emperors worked to hold the empire together and to reconquer at least some of the West from barbarian tribes. The emperor Justinian (r. 527–565) waged long and hard-fought wars against the Ostrogoths and temporarily regained Italy and North Africa, but his conquests had disastrous consequences. Justinian's wars exhausted the resources of the state, destroyed Italy's economy, and killed a large part of Italy's population. The wars also paved the way for the easy conquest of Italy by another Germanic tribe, the Lombards, shortly after Justinian's death. In the late sixth century, the territory of the Western Roman Empire came under barbarian sway once again.

> **QUICK REVIEW**

How did Roman leaders respond to the increasing pressure created by barbarian migrations?

CHAPTER LOCATOR | How did Diocletian and Constantine try to reform the empire? | How did the Christian Church become a major force in Europe?

CHAPTER 7
LATE ANTIQUITY
198

How did the church convert barbarian peoples to Christianity?

Staffordshire Hoard Artifact with Biblical Inscription

This strip of gold bears a biblical inscription in somewhat misspelled Latin asking God for help against enemies. Made in the seventh century, it was buried sometime later along with hundreds of garnet-inlaid gold and silver weapon parts, and was discovered in 2009 in Staffordshire, England, as part of the largest hoard of Anglo-Saxon gold ever found. Who made it, who owned it, and who buried it will no doubt be a source of debate for decades as the hoard modifies scholarly opinion about Anglo-Saxon England. (© Birmingham Museums Trust)

THE MEDITERRANEAN SERVED as the highway over which Christianity spread to the cities of the Roman Empire. Christian teachings were initially carried by all types of converts, but they were often spread into the countryside and into areas beyond the borders of the empire by those who had dedicated their lives to the church. Such missionaries were often sent by popes specifically to convert certain groups.

Throughout barbarian Europe, religion was not a private or individual matter; it was a social affair, and the religion of the chieftain or king determined the religion of the people. Thus, missionaries concentrated their initial efforts not on ordinary people but on kings or tribal chieftains and the members of their families, who then ordered their subjects to convert. Germanic kings sometimes accepted Christianity because they came to believe that the Christian God was more powerful than pagan gods and that the Christian God would deliver victory in battle. They also appreciated that Christianity taught obedience to kingly as well as divine authority. Christian missionaries were generally literate, and they taught reading and writing to young men who became priests or officials in the royal household, a service that kings appreciated.

What were the key characteristics of barbarian society?

What were some of the causes and consequences of the barbarian migrations?

How did the church convert barbarian peoples to Christianity?

How did the Byzantine Empire preserve the legacy of Rome?

☑ LearningCurve Check what you know.

199

Missionaries' Actions

During the Roman occupation, small Christian communities were scattered throughout Gaul and Britain. The leaders of some of these, such as Bishop Martin of Tours (ca. 316–397), who founded a monastery and established a rudimentary parish system in his diocese, supported Nicene Christianity (see page 180). Other missionaries were Arian Christians, and they also founded dioceses and converted many barbarian groups.

Tradition identifies the conversion of Ireland with Saint Patrick (ca. 385–461). Born in England to a Christian family of Roman citizenship, Patrick was captured and enslaved by Irish raiders and taken to Ireland, where he worked as a herdsman for six years. He escaped and returned to England, where a vision urged him to Christianize Ireland. In preparation, Patrick studied in Gaul and was consecrated a bishop in 432. He returned to Ireland, where he converted the Irish tribe by tribe, first baptizing the chief of each tribe. By the time of Patrick's death, the majority of the Irish people had received Christian baptism.

In his missionary work, Patrick had the strong support of Bridget of Kildare (ca. 450–528), daughter of a wealthy chieftain. Bridget defied parental pressure to marry and became a nun. She and the other nuns at Kildare instructed relatives and friends in basic Christian doctrine, made religious vestments (clothing) for churches, copied books, taught children, and above all set a religious example by their lives of prayer. In this way, in Ireland and later in continental Europe, women like the nuns at Kildare shared in the process of conversion.

The Christianization of the English began in earnest in 597, when Pope Gregory I sent a delegation of monks under the Roman Augustine to Britain. When Augustine succeeded in converting Ethelbert, king of Kent, the baptism of Ethelbert's people took place as a matter of course. Augustine established his headquarters, or *see*, at Canterbury, the capital of Kent in southern England.

In the course of the seventh century, two Christian forces competed for the conversion of the pagan Anglo-Saxons: Roman-oriented missionaries traveling north from Canterbury, and Celtic monks from Ireland and northwestern Britain. Through the influence of King Oswiu of Northumbria and the dynamic abbess Hilda of Whitby, the Synod (ecclesiastical council) held at Hilda's convent of Whitby in 664 opted to follow Roman practices. The conversion of the English and the close attachment of the English Church to Rome had far-reaching consequences because Britain later served as a base for the Christianization of the European continent (see Map 7.2, page 181), spreading Roman Christian teachings among both pagans and Arians.

The Process of Conversion

When a ruler marched his people to the waters of baptism, the work of Christianization had only begun. Christian kings could order their subjects to be baptized, married, and buried in Christian ceremonies. Churches could be built, and people could be required to attend services and belong to parishes, but the process of conversion was a gradual one.

How did missionaries and priests get masses of pagan and illiterate peoples to understand Christian ideals and teachings? They did so through preaching, assimilation, the ritual of penance, and the veneration of saints. Missionaries

CHAPTER LOCATOR | How did Diocletian and Constantine try to reform the empire? | How did the Christian Church become a major force in Europe?

200 CHAPTER 7 LATE ANTIQUITY

preached the basic teachings of Christianity. In monasteries and cathedrals, men—and a few women—wrote hymns, prayers, and stories about the lives of Christ and the saints. People heard these and slowly became familiar with Christian notions.

Deeply ingrained pagan customs and practices could not be stamped out by words alone, however, or even by royal edicts. Christian missionaries often pursued a policy of assimilation, easing the conversion of pagan men and women by stressing similarities between their customs and beliefs and those of Christianity. In the same way that classically trained scholars such as Jerome and Augustine blended Greco-Roman and Christian ideas, missionaries and converts mixed pagan ideas and practices with Christian ones.

The ritual of penance was also instrumental in teaching people Christian ideas. Christianity taught that certain actions and thoughts were sins, meaning that they were against God's commands. Only by confessing these sins and asking forgiveness could a sinning believer be reconciled with God. Confession was initially a public ritual, but by the fifth century individual confession to a parish priest was more common. The person knelt before the priest, who questioned him or her about sins he or she might have committed. The priest then set a penance such as fasting or saying specific prayers to allow the person to atone for the sin. Penance gave new Christians a sense of expected behavior, encouraged the private examination of conscience, and offered relief from the burden of sinful deeds.

Most religious observances continued to be community matters, as they had been in the ancient world. People joined with family members, friends, and neighbors at their parish church to attend baptisms, weddings, and funerals presided over by a priest. The parish church often housed the **relics** of a saint, that is, bones, articles of clothing, or other objects associated with a person who had lived (or died) in a way that was spiritually heroic or noteworthy. This patron saint was understood to provide protection and assistance for those who came to worship, and the relics served as a link between the material world and the spiritual one.

Christians came to venerate the saints as powerful and holy. They prayed to saints or to the Virgin Mary to intercede with God, or they simply asked the saints to assist and bless them. The entire village participated in processions marking saints' days or points in the agricultural year, often carrying images of saints or their relics around the houses and fields. The decision to become Christian was often made first by an emperor or king, but actual conversion was a local matter, by people who came to feel that the parish priest and the patron saint provided them with benefits in this world and the world to come.

relics
▶ Bones, articles of clothing, or other objects associated with the life of a saint.

QUICK REVIEW <

What distinction must be made between formal conversion and Christianization? Why is the distinction so important?

| What were the key characteristics of barbarian society? | What were some of the causes and consequences of the barbarian migrations? | **How did the church convert barbarian peoples to Christianity?** | How did the Byzantine Empire preserve the legacy of Rome? | ☑ LearningCurve Check what you know. |

How did the Byzantine Empire preserve the legacy of Rome?

Greek Fire In this illustration from a twelfth-century manuscript, sailors shoot Greek fire toward an attacking ship from a pressurized tube that looks strikingly similar to a modern flamethrower. The exact formula for Greek fire has been lost, but it was probably made from a petroleum product because it continued burning on water. Greek fire was particularly important in Byzantine defenses of Constantinople from Muslim forces in the late seventh century. (Prado, Madrid/The Bridgeman Art Library)

BARBARIAN MIGRATIONS AND CHRISTIAN CONVERSIONS occurred throughout all of Europe in late antiquity, but their impact was not the same in the western and eastern halves of the Roman Empire. The Western Roman Empire gradually disintegrated, but the Roman Empire continued in the East. The Byzantine or Eastern Roman Empire (see Map 7.1, page 180) preserved the forms, institutions, and traditions of the old Roman Empire. Byzantine emperors traced their lines back past Constantine to Augustus, and the Senate in Constantinople carried on the traditions of the old Roman Senate. Most important, however, is how Byzantium protected the intellectual heritage of Greco-Roman civilization and then passed it on to the rest of Europe.

Sources of Byzantine Strength

While the western parts of the Roman Empire gradually succumbed to barbarian invaders, the Byzantine Empire survived Germanic, Persian, and Arab attacks **(Map 7.4)**. Why didn't one or a combination of these enemies capture Constantinople as the Ostrogoths had taken Rome? The answer lies in strong military leadership and even more in the city's location and its excellent fortifications. Massive triple walls, built and well maintained by the emperors Constantine and Theodosius II (408–450), protected Constantinople from sea invasion. Within the walls huge cisterns provided water, and vast gardens and grazing areas supplied vegetables and meat, so the defending people could hold out far longer than the besieging army. Attacking Constantinople by land posed greater geographical

CHAPTER LOCATOR | How did Diocletian and Constantine try to reform the empire? | How did the Christian Church become a major force in Europe?

202 CHAPTER 7 LATE ANTIQUITY

and logistical problems than a seventh- or eighth-century government could solve. The site was not absolutely impregnable, but it was almost so. For centuries, the Byzantine Empire served as a bulwark for the West, protecting it against invasions from the East.

The Law Code of Justinian

One of the most splendid achievements of the Byzantine emperors was the preservation of Roman law for the medieval and modern worlds. Roman law had developed from many sources. By the fourth century, it had become a huge, bewildering mass, and its sheer bulk made it almost unusable.

Sweeping and systematic codification took place under the emperor Justinian. He appointed a committee of eminent jurists to sort through and organize the laws. The result was the *Corpus Juris Civilis* (KAWR-puhs JOOR-uhs sih-VIH-luhs) (Body of Civil Law), a multipart collection of laws and legal commentary issued from 529 to 534. The first part of this work, the *Codex*, brought together all the existing imperial laws into a coherent whole, eliminated outmoded laws and contradictions, and clarified the law itself. It began with laws ordering the interpretation of Christian doctrine favored by the emperor, and affirming the power of the emperor in matters of religion. The rest of the *Codex* was structured by topic and

MAP 7.4 ▪ The Byzantine Empire, ca. 600

The strategic position of Constantinople on the waterway between the Black Sea and the Mediterranean was clear to Constantine when he chose the city as the capital of the Eastern Roman Empire. Byzantine territories in Italy were acquired in Emperor Justinian's sixth-century wars and were held for several centuries.

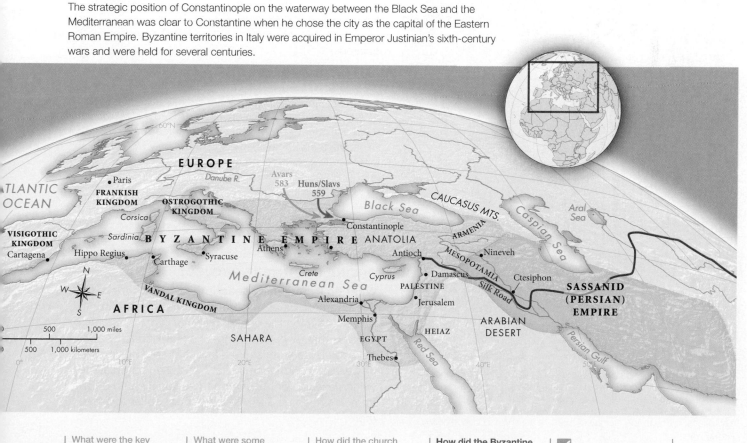

| What were the key characteristics of barbarian society? | What were some of the causes and consequences of the barbarian migrations? | How did the church convert barbarian peoples to Christianity? | **How did the Byzantine Empire preserve the legacy of Rome?** | ✔ LearningCurve Check what you know. |

INDIVIDUALS IN SOCIETY
Theodora of Constantinople

The most powerful woman in Byzantine history was the daughter of a bear trainer for the circus. Theodora (ca. 497–548) grew up in what her contemporaries regarded as an undignified and morally suspect atmosphere, and she worked as a dancer and burlesque actress, both dishonorable occupations in the Roman world. Despite her background, she caught the eye of Justinian, who was then a military leader and whose uncle (and adoptive father) Justin had himself risen from obscurity to become the emperor of the Byzantine Empire. Under Justinian's influence, Justin changed the law to allow an actress who had left her disreputable life to marry whom she liked, and Justinian and Theodora married in 525. When Justinian was proclaimed co-emperor with his uncle Justin on April 1, 527, Theodora received the rare title of *augusta*, or empress. Thereafter, her name was linked with Justinian's in the exercise of imperial power.

Most of our knowledge of Theodora's early life comes from the *Secret History*, a tell-all description of the vices of Justinian and his court written around 550 by Procopius (pruh-KOH-pee-uhs), who was the official court historian and thus spent his days praising those same people. In the *Secret History* he portrays Theodora and Justinian as demonic, greedy, and vicious, killing courtiers to steal their property. In scene after detailed scene, Procopius portrays Theodora as particularly evil, sexually insatiable, depraved, and cruel, a temptress who used sorcery to attract men, including the hapless Justinian.

In one of his official histories, *The History of the Wars of Justinian*, Procopius presents a very different Theodora. Riots between the supporters of two teams in chariot races — who formed associations somewhat like both street gangs and political parties — had turned deadly, and Justinian wavered in his handling of the perpetrators. Both sides turned against the emperor, besieging the palace while Justinian was inside it. Shouting "N-I-K-A" (victory), the rioters swept through the city, burning and looting, and destroyed half of Constantinople. Justinian's counselors urged flight, but, according to Procopius, Theodora rose and declared:

> For one who has reigned, it is intolerable to be an exile. . . . If you wish, O Emperor, to save yourself, there is no difficulty: we have ample funds and there are the ships. Yet reflect whether, when you have once escaped to a place of security, you will not prefer death to safety. I agree with an old saying that the purple [that is, the color worn only by emperors] is a fair winding sheet [to be buried in].

The empress Theodora, shown with a halo, symbolizing piety, and a crown, symbolizing power, in an intricate mosaic of thousands of cubes of colored glass and stone, created in Ravenna, Italy, in the sixth century. Like Justinian, Theodora had power over secular and religious institutions, much to the dismay of many at Justinian's court. (PRISMA ARCHIVO/Alamy)

LaunchPad

ONLINE DOCUMENT PROJECT

What do Procopius's descriptions of Theodora and Justinian tell us about the problems his society faced? Keeping the question above in mind, examine sources that reveal the connections Procopius saw between Byzantium's rulers and the rapid decline he perceived in Byzantine society, and then complete a writing assignment based on the evidence and details from this chapter. *See inside the front cover to learn more.*

Justinian rallied, had the rioters driven into the hippodrome, and ordered between thirty thousand and thirty-five thousand men and women executed. The revolt was crushed and Justinian's authority was restored, an outcome approved by Procopius.

Other sources describe or suggest Theodora's influence on imperial policy. Justinian passed a number of laws that improved the legal status of women, such as allowing women to own property the same way that men could and to be guardians over their own children. Justinian is reputed to have consulted Theodora every day about all aspects of state policy, including religious policy regarding the doctrinal disputes that continued throughout his reign. Theodora's influence over her husband and her power in the Byzantine state continued until she died, perhaps of cancer, twenty years before Justinian. Her influence may have even continued after death, for Justinian continued to pass reforms favoring women and, at the end of his life, accepted her interpretation of Christian doctrine. Institutions that she established, including hospitals, orphanages, houses for the rehabilitation of prostitutes, and churches, continued to be reminders of her charity and piety.

Theodora has been viewed as a symbol of the manipulation of beauty and cleverness to attain position and power, and also as a strong and capable co-ruler who held the empire together during riots, revolts, and deadly epidemics. Just as Procopius expressed both views, the debate has continued to today among writers of science fiction and fantasy as well as biographers and historians.

QUESTIONS FOR ANALYSIS

1. How would you assess the complex legacy of Theodora?
2. Since the official and unofficial views of Procopius are so different regarding the empress, should he be trusted at all as a historical source?

included provisions on every aspect of life, including economic issues, social concerns, and family life.

The second part of Justinian's compilation, the *Digest*, is a collection of the opinions of foremost Roman jurists on complex legal problems, and the third part, the *Institutes*, is a handbook of civil law designed for students and beginning jurists. All three parts were given the force of law and formed the backbone of Byzantine jurisprudence from that point on. The Corpus Juris Civilis was lost in western Europe with the end of the Roman Empire, but it was rediscovered in the eleventh century and came to form the foundation of law for nearly every modern European nation.

Byzantine Intellectual Life

The Byzantines prized education; because of them, many masterpieces of ancient Greek literature have survived to influence the intellectual life of the modern world. The literature of the Byzantine Empire was predominantly Greek, although politicians, scholars, and lawyers also spoke and used Latin. More people could read in Byzantium than anywhere else in Christian Europe at the time, and history was a favorite topic.

The most remarkable Byzantine historian was Procopius (ca. 500–562), who left a rousing account praising Justinian's reconquest of North Africa and Italy but also wrote the *Secret History*, a vicious and uproarious attack on Justinian and his wife, the empress Theodora. (See "Individuals in Society: Theodora of Constantinople," page 204.)

Although the Byzantines discovered little that was new in mathematics and geometry, they made advances in terms of military applications. For example, they invented an explosive liquid that came to be known as "Greek fire." The liquid was heated and propelled by a pump through a bronze tube, and as the jet left the tube, it was ignited—somewhat like a modern flamethrower. In mechanics, Byzantine scientists improved and modified artillery and siege machinery.

The Byzantines devoted a great deal of attention to medicine, and the general level of medical competence was far higher in the Byzantine Empire than in western Europe. Yet their physicians could not cope with the terrible disease, often called the "Justinian plague," that swept through the Byzantine Empire and parts of western Europe between 542 and about 560, claiming the lives of tens of thousands of people.

The epidemic had profound political as well as social consequences: it weakened Justinian's military resources, thus hampering his efforts to restore unity to the Mediterranean world.

By the ninth or tenth century, most major Greek cities had hospitals for the care of the sick. The hospitals might be divided into wards for different illnesses, and hospital staff included surgeons, practitioners, and aids with specialized responsibilities. The imperial Byzantine government bore the costs of these medical facilities.

The Orthodox Church

The continuity of the Roman Empire in the East meant that Christianity developed differently there than it did in the West. The emperors in Constantinople were understood to be Christ's representatives on earth; their palace was considered holy and was filled with relics and religious images, called icons. Emperors convened councils, appointed church officials, and regulated the income of the church. As in Rome, there was a patriarch in Constantinople, but he did not develop the same powers that the pope did in the West because there was never a similar power vacuum into which he needed to step. The **Orthodox Church**, the name generally given to the Eastern Christian Church, was more subject to secular control than the Western Christian Church.

Monasticism in the Orthodox world differed in fundamental ways from the monasticism that evolved in western Europe. While *The Rule of Saint Benedict* gradually became the universal guide for all western European monasteries, each individual house in the Byzantine world developed its own set of rules for organization and behavior. Second, education never became a central feature of Orthodox monasteries. Monks and nuns had to be literate to perform the appropriate rituals, but no Orthodox monastery assumed responsibility for the general training of the local young.

There were also similarities between Western and Eastern monasticism. As in the West, Eastern monasteries became wealthy property owners, with fields, pastures, livestock, and buildings. Since bishops and patriarchs of the Orthodox Church were recruited only from the monasteries, these religious leaders also exercised cultural influence.

Like their counterparts in the West, Byzantine missionaries traveled far beyond the boundaries of the empire in search of converts. In 863, the emperor Michael III sent the brothers Cyril (826–869) and Methodius (815–885) to preach Christianity in Moravia (a region in the modern Czech Republic). Other missionaries succeeded in converting the Russians in the tenth century. Cyril invented a Slavic alphabet using Greek characters, later termed the Cyrillic (suh-RIH-lihk) alphabet in his honor. In the tenth century, other missionaries spread Christianity, the Cyrillic alphabet, and Byzantine art and architecture to Russia. The Byzantines were so successful that the Russians would later claim to be the successors of the Byzantine Empire.

Orthodox Church
▶ Eastern Christian Church in the Byzantine Empire.

> **QUICK REVIEW**

How and why did the Orthodox Church differ from the Roman Christian Church?

CHAPTER LOCATOR | How did Diocletian and Constantine try to reform the empire? | How did the Christian Church become a major force in Europe?

CHAPTER 7
206 LATE ANTIQUITY

LOOKING BACK
LOOKING AHEAD

The Christian Church and the barbarian states absorbed many aspects of Roman culture, and the Roman Empire continued to thrive in the East as the Byzantine Empire, but western Europe in 600 was very different than it had been in 250. The Western Roman Empire had slowly disintegrated under pressure from barbarian groups. Barbarian kings ruled small states from Italy to Norway, while churches and monasteries, rather than emperors and wealthy individuals, took on the role of constructing new buildings and providing education. The city of Rome had shrunk significantly, as had many other cities. As the vast network of Roman urban centers dissolved, economies everywhere became more localized. Commentators such as Augustine advised people to put their faith in the eternal City of God rather than in worldly cities because human history would always bring great change. People who lived with Augustine in Hippo would have certainly understood such counsel: they watched the Vandals besiege their city in 430, move swiftly across North Africa, and bring an end to Roman rule there. Although Justinian's Byzantine forces reclaimed the area a little over a century later, the culture that survived was as much barbarian as Roman, with smaller cities, less trade, and fewer schools.

Two hundred years after the Vandal attack, the residents of Byzantine North Africa confronted another fast-moving army of conquest: Arabian forces carrying a new religion, Islam. This Arabic expansion dramatically shaped the development of Western civilization. Though the end of the Roman Empire in 476 has long been seen as a dramatic break in European history, the expansion of Islam two centuries later may have been even more significant. Many of the patterns set in late antiquity continued, however. Warrior values such as physical prowess, bravery in battle, and loyalty to one's lord remained central and shaped the development of the political system known as feudalism. The Frankish kingdom established by Clovis continued to expand, becoming the most important state in Europe. The economic and political power of the Christian Church expanded as well, with monasteries and convents providing education for their residents. The vast majority of people continued to live in small villages, trying to raise enough grain to feed themselves and their families, and asking the saints for help to overcome life's difficulties.

▷LaunchPad

ONLINE DOCUMENT PROJECT
Theodora of Constantinople

What do Procopius's descriptions of Theodora and Justinian tell us about the problems his society faced?

You encountered Theodora of Constantinople's story on page 204. Keeping the question above in mind, examine sources that reveal the connections Procopius saw between Byzantium's rulers and the rapid decline he perceived in Byzantine society. *See inside the front cover to learn more.*

What were the key characteristics of barbarian society?

What were some of the causes and consequences of the barbarian migrations?

How did the church convert barbarian peoples to Christianity?

How did the Byzantine Empire preserve the legacy of Rome?

☑ LearningCurve
Check what you know.

CHAPTER 7 STUDY GUIDE

STEP 1 GET STARTED ONLINE

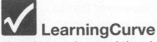 **LearningCurve**

Now that you've read the chapter, make it stick by completing the LearningCurve activity.

STEP 2 EXPLAIN WHY IT MATTERS

Put your reading into practice. Identify each term below, and then explain why it matters in Western history.

TERM	WHO OR WHAT & WHEN	WHY IT MATTERS
tetrarchy (p. 179)		
diocese (p. 179)		
Arianism (p. 181)		
heresy (p. 182)		
apostolic succession (p. 184)		
Petrine Doctrine (p. 184)		
regular clergy (p. 185)		
secular clergy (p. 185)		
sacraments (p. 188)		
runic alphabet (p. 189)		
comitatus (p. 191)		
wergeld (p. 191)		
relics (p. 201)		
Orthodox Church (p. 206)		

STEP 3 MOVE BEYOND THE BASICS

To demonstrate a more advanced understanding of Diocletian's key reforms, their intended purposes, and their actual consequences, complete the chart below.

	Policies	Intended purpose	Actual consequences
Economic policies			
Social policies			
Political policies			

Now, take a step back and try to explain the big picture. Remember to use specific examples from the chapter in your answers.

THE GROWTH AND SPREAD OF CHRISTIANITY

► How did the place of the Christian Church in the Roman Empire change over the course of the third and fourth century?

► Why did Christian missionaries focus initially on the conversion of political and social elites?

BARBARIAN SOCIETY AND MIGRATIONS

► Why were the Romans increasingly unable to resist the penetration of the empire by barbarian peoples?

► In your opinion, did the collapse of the Roman Empire in the west mark a fundamental turning point in Western history? Why or why not?

THE BYZANTINE EMPIRE

► Why did the Roman Empire in the East survive long after the empire in the West fell?

► What role did the Byzantine Empire play in the preservation of the Greco-Roman tradition?

MAKE CONNECTIONS

► In what ways was the collapse of the Roman Empire similar to the collapse of previous empires in the Near East and North Africa? In what ways was it different?

► How did the events of the fourth and fifth centuries lay the foundation for the prominent role the Christian Church would play in European life during the Middle Ages?

> **IN YOUR OWN WORDS**

Imagine that you must give an oral report to the class answering the following question: **In what ways was late antiquity a period marked both by continuity and change?** What would be the most important points and why?

8

EUROPE IN THE EARLY MIDDLE AGES

600–1000

> How did the events and developments of the Early Middle Ages shape European civilization?

Chapter 8 examines the transition from antiquity to the period known as the Middle Ages. The agents in this slow process included not only the barbarian migrations that broke the Roman Empire apart but also the new religion of Islam, Slavic and steppe peoples in eastern Europe, and Christian officials and missionaries. The early Middle Ages, as this period is conventionally known, was a time of disorder and destruction, but it also marked the creation of a new type of society and a cultural revival that influenced later intellectual and literary traditions. While agrarian life continued to dominate Europe, political and economic structures that would influence later European history began to form, and Christianity continued to spread.

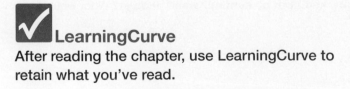

LearningCurve
After reading the chapter, use LearningCurve to retain what you've read.

> What were the origins and early impact of Islam?

> How did the Franks build and govern a European empire?

> What were the significant intellectual and cultural changes in Charlemagne's era?

> What were the consequences of the ninth-century invasions and migrations?

> How did internal conflict and outside threats shape European development?

Life in the Early Middle Ages. In this manuscript illumination from Spain, Muslim fishermen take a rich harvest from the sea. Fish were an important part of the diet of all coastal peoples in medieval Europe. (The Granger Collection, New York)

> What were the origins and early impact of Islam?

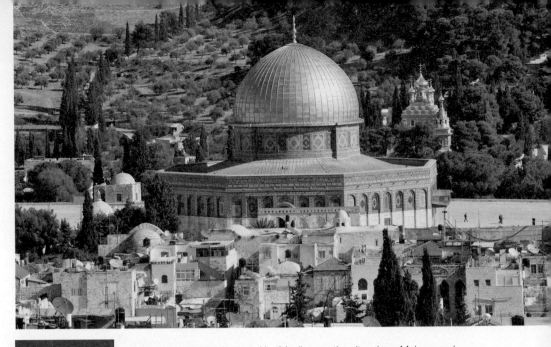

Dome of the Rock, Jerusalem Completed in 691 and revered by Muslims as the site where Muhammad ascended into Heaven, the Dome of the Rock is the oldest surviving Islamic sanctuary and, after Mecca and Medina, the holiest place in Islam. Although influenced by Byzantine and Persian architecture, it also has distinctly Arabic features, such as the 700 feet of carefully selected Qur'anic inscriptions and vegetal motifs that grace the top of the outer walls (imagebroker.net/SuperStock)

IN THE SEVENTH CENTURY C.E., two empires dominated the area today called the Middle East: the Byzantine-Greek-Christian empire and the Sassanid-Persian-Zoroastrian empire. Between the two lay the Arabian peninsula, where a merchant called Muhammad began to have religious visions around 610. By the time he died in 632, all Arabia had accepted his creed of Islam. A century later his followers controlled what is now Syria, Palestine, Egypt, North Africa, Spain, and part of France. This Arabic expansion profoundly affected the development of Western civilization as well as the history of Africa and Asia.

The Arabs

In Muhammad's time, Arabia was inhabited by various tribes, many of them Bedouins (BEH-duh-wuhnz). These nomadic peoples grazed goats and sheep on the sparse patches of grass that dotted the vast semiarid peninsula. Other Arabs lived more settled lives in the southern valleys and coastal towns along the Red Sea, supporting themselves by agriculture and trade.

For all Arabs, the basic social unit was the clan—a group of blood relations connected through the male line. Although the nomadic Bedouins condemned the urbanized lifestyle of the cities as immoral and corrupt, Arabs of all types respected certain aspects of one another's customs and had some religious rules and rituals in common. The city of Mecca was the major religious and economic

CHAPTER LOCATOR | What were the origins and early impact of Islam?

212 CHAPTER 8
EUROPE IN THE EARLY MIDDLE AGES

481–752 – Merovingian dynasty	**800–900** – Free peasants in western Europe increasingly tied to the land as serfs
ca. 571–632 – Life of the Prophet Muhammad	**843** – Treaty of Verdun divides Carolingian kingdom
651 – Official version of the Qur'an published	**850–1000** – Most extensive Viking voyages and conquests
711 – Muslim forces defeat Visigothic kingdom	**ca. 900** – Establishment of Kievan Rus
711–720 – Muslim conquest of Spain	**911** – Vikings establish Normandy
ca. 760–840 – Carolingian Renaissance	**950** – Muslim Córdoba is Europe's largest and most prosperous city
768–814 – Reign of Charlemagne	**1000** – Stephen crowned first king of Hungary
800 – Imperial coronation of Charlemagne	

center of western Arabia. For centuries before the rise of Islam, many Arabs prayed at the Ka'ba (KAH-buh), a temple in Mecca containing a black stone thought to be the dwelling place of a god as well as objects connected to other gods. Economic links also connected Arab peoples, but what eventually molded the diverse Arab tribes into a powerful political and social unity was a new religion based on the teachings of Muhammad.

The Prophet Muhammad

Except for a few vague remarks in the **Qur'an** (kuh-RAHN), the sacred book of Islam, Muhammad (ca. 571–632) left no account of his life. Arab tradition accepts some of the sacred stories that developed about him as historically true, but those accounts were not written down until about a century after his death. Orphaned at the age of six, Muhammad was raised by his grandfather. As a young man he became a merchant in the caravan trade. Later he entered the service of a wealthy widow, and their subsequent marriage brought him financial independence.

The Qur'an reveals Muhammad to be an extremely devout man, ascetic, self-disciplined, and literate, but not formally educated. He prayed regularly, and when he was about forty he began to experience religious visions. Unsure for a time about what he should do, Muhammad discovered his mission after a vision in which the angel Gabriel instructed him to preach.

Muhammad's revelations were written down by his followers during his lifetime and organized into chapters, called *sura*, shortly after his death. In 651, Muhammad's third successor arranged to have an official version of the Qur'an published. At the same time, other sayings and accounts of Muhammad, which

Qur'an
▶ The sacred book of Islam.

How did the Franks build and govern a European empire? | What were the significant intellectual and cultural changes in Charlemagne's era? | What were the consequences of the ninth-century invasions and migrations? | How did internal conflict and outside threats shape European development? | ✓ LearningCurve Check what you know.

gave advice on matters that went beyond the Qur'an, were collected into books termed *hadith* (huh-DEETH). Muslim tradition (*Sunna*) consists of both the Qur'an and the hadith.

Muhammad's visions ordered him to preach a message of a single God and to become God's prophet, which he began to do in his hometown of Mecca. He gathered followers slowly, but also provoked a great deal of resistance because he urged people to give up worship of the gods whose sacred objects were in the Ka'ba and also challenged the power of the local elite. In 622, he migrated with his followers to Medina, an event termed the *hijra* (hih-JIE-ruh). At Medina, Muhammad was much more successful, gaining converts and working out the basic principles of the faith. That same year, through the Charter of Medina, Muhammad formed the first *umma*, a community that united his followers from different tribes and set religious ties above clan loyalty. The charter also extended rights to non-Muslims living in Medina, including Jews and Christians.

In 630, Muhammad returned to Mecca at the head of a large army, and he soon united the nomads of the desert and the merchants of the cities into an even larger umma of Muslims, a word meaning "those who comply with God's will." The religion itself came to be called Islam, which means "submission to God." The Ka'ba was rededicated as a Muslim holy place, and Mecca became the most holy city in Islam.

By the time Muhammad died in 632, the crescent of Islam, the Muslim symbol, prevailed throughout the Arabian peninsula. During the next century, one rich province of the old Roman Empire after another came under Muslim domination—first Syria, then Egypt, and then all of North Africa (**Map 8.1**). Long and bitter wars (572–591, 606–630) between the Byzantine and Persian Empires left both so weak and exhausted that they easily fell to Muslim attack.

The Teachings and Expansion of Islam

Muhammad's religion eventually attracted great numbers of people, partly because of the straightforward nature of its doctrines. The strictly monotheistic theology outlined in the Qur'an has only a few central tenets: Allah, the Arabic word for God, is all-powerful and all-knowing. Muhammad, Allah's prophet, preached his word and carried his message. Muhammad described himself as the successor of both the Jewish patriarch Abraham and Christ, and he claimed that his teachings replaced theirs. He invited and won converts from Judaism and Christianity.

Because Allah is all-powerful, believers must submit themselves to him. All Muslims have the obligation of the *jihad* (literally, "self-exertion") to strive or struggle to lead a virtuous life and to spread God's rule and law. In some cases, striving is an individual struggle against sin; in others, it is social and communal and could involve armed conflict, though this is not an essential part of jihad (jee-HAHD). The Islamic belief of "striving in the path of God" is closely related to the central feature of Muslim doctrine, the coming Day of Judgment. Muslims believe with conviction that the Day of Judgment will come; consequently, all of a Muslim's thoughts and actions should be oriented toward the Last Judgment and the rewards of Heaven.

To merit the rewards of Heaven, a person must follow the strict code of moral behavior that Muhammad prescribed. The Muslim must recite a profession of faith

CHAPTER LOCATOR | What were the origins and early impact of Islam?

214 CHAPTER 8 EUROPE IN THE EARLY MIDDLE AGES

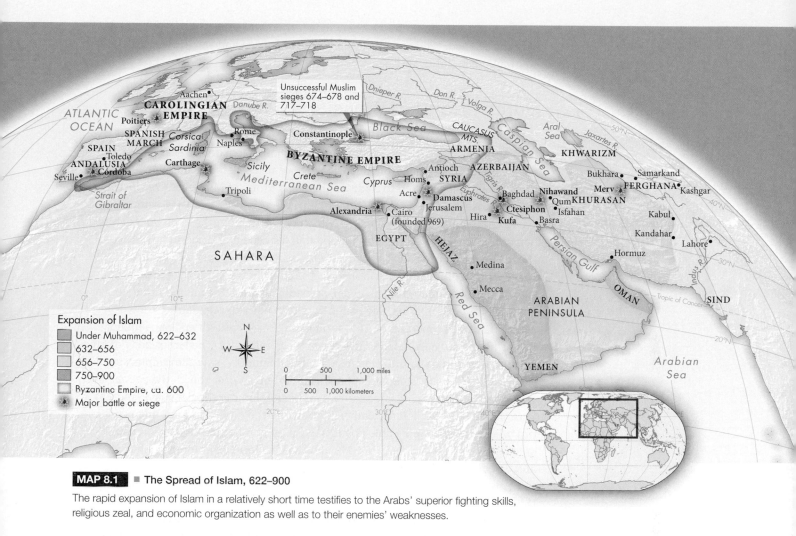

MAP 8.1 ■ The Spread of Islam, 622–900

The rapid expansion of Islam in a relatively short time testifies to the Arabs' superior fighting skills, religious zeal, and economic organization as well as to their enemies' weaknesses.

in God and in Muhammad as God's prophet. The believer must pray five times a day, fast and pray during the sacred month of Ramadan, and contribute alms to the poor and needy. If possible, the believer must make a pilgrimage to Mecca once during his or her lifetime. According to the Muslim *shari'a* (shuh-REE-uh), or sacred law, these five practices constitute the **Five Pillars of Islam**.

The Qur'an forbids alcoholic beverages and gambling, as well as a number of foods, such as pork, a dietary regulation adopted from the Mosaic law of the Hebrews. It condemns business usury—that is, lending money at interest rates or taking advantage of market demand for products by charging high prices for them.

Polygyny, the practice of men having more than one wife, was common in Arab society before Muhammad, though for economic reasons the custom was limited to the well-to-do. The Qur'an limited the number of wives a man could have to four. It also established a strict sexual morality and condemned immoral behavior on the part of men as well as women.

The Qur'an set out rules for inheritance, which privileged sons over daughters. Nonetheless, Muslim women of the early Middle Ages had more rights than Western women. For example, a Muslim woman retained complete jurisdiction

Five Pillars of Islam

▶ The five practices Muslims must fulfill according to the shari'a, or sacred law, including the profession of faith, prayer, fasting, giving alms to the poor, and pilgrimage to Mecca.

How did the Franks build and govern a European empire?

What were the significant intellectual and cultural changes in Charlemagne's era?

What were the consequences of the ninth-century invasions and migrations?

How did internal conflict and outside threats shape European development?

✔ LearningCurve
Check what you know.

over one-third of her property when she married and could dispose of it in any way she wished. Women in most European countries and the United States did not gain these rights until the nineteenth century.

Sunni and Shi'a Divisions

caliph

▶ A successor, as chosen by a group of Muhammad's closest followers.

Despite the clarity and unifying force of Muslim doctrine, divisions developed within the Islamic faith within decades of Muhammad's death. Neither the Qur'an nor the hadith gave clear guidance about how successors to Muhammad were to be chosen but, according to tradition, in 632, a group of Muhammad's closest followers chose Abu Bakr (uh-BOO BAH-kuhr) as **caliph** (KAY-luhf), a word meaning "successor." He was succeeded by two other caliphs, but these provoked opposition, which coalesced around Ali, Muhammad's cousin and son-in-law. Ali was chosen as the fourth caliph in 656 but was assassinated only five years later by backers of the initial line of caliphs. Ali's supporters began to assert that the Prophet had designated Ali as *imam*, or leader, and that he should rightly have been the first caliph; thus, any caliph who was not a descendant of Ali was a usurper. These supporters of Ali—termed Shi'ites—saw Ali and subsequent imams as the divinely inspired leaders of the community. The larger body of Muslims who accepted the first elections—termed Sunnis—saw the caliphs as political leaders. Because Islam did not have an organized priesthood, the caliphs had an additional function of safeguarding and enforcing the religious law (shari'a) with the advice of scholars (*ulama*), particularly the jurists, judges, and scholastics who were knowledgeable about the Qur'an and hadith. Over the centuries, enmity between Sunni and Shi'a Muslims has sometimes erupted into violence, and discord still exists today (**Table 8.1**).

After the assassination of Ali, the caliphate passed to members of the Umayyad (oo-MIE-uhd) clan, who asserted control and brought stability to the growing Muslim empire. They established their capital at Damascus in Syria, and the Muslim faith continued to expand eastward to India and westward across North Africa. That expansion was facilitated everywhere by three main factors: military strength, trade connections, and tolerance toward non-Muslims.

TABLE 8.1 ■ Differences Between Sunni and Shi'a Muslims

Sunni Muslims	Shi'a Muslims
• Believe that Muhammad chose his close friend Abu Bakr as caliph, or successor	• Believe that Muhammad designated his cousin and son-in-law Ali as imam, or leader
• See Abu Bakr and all subsequent caliphs as political leaders	• Believe that any caliph who is not a descendent of Ali is illegitimate
• Constitute the majority of Muslims	• See Ali and all subsequent imams as divinely inspired leaders
	• Remain an important minority within the larger Muslim community

CHAPTER LOCATOR | What were the origins and early impact of Islam?

CHAPTER 8
216 EUROPE IN THE EARLY MIDDLE AGES

Life in Muslim Spain

In Europe, Muslim political and cultural influence was felt most strongly in the Iberian Peninsula. In 711, a Muslim force crossed the Strait of Gibraltar and easily defeated the weak Visigothic kingdom; by 720, the Muslims controlled most of Spain. A member of the Umayyad Dynasty, Abd al-Rahman (AHB-dal-ruh-MAHN) (r. 756–788) established a kingdom in Spain with its capital at Córdoba (KAWR-doh-buh).

Throughout the Islamic world, Muslims used the term **al-Andalus** to describe the part of the Iberian Peninsula under Muslim control. In the eighth century, al-Andalus included the entire peninsula, from Gibraltar in the south to the Cantabrian Mountains in the north (see Map 8.1, page 215).

In the early Middle Ages, the Iberian Peninsula was home to sizable numbers of Jews and Christians as well as Muslims. In business transactions and in much of daily life, all peoples used the Arabic language. With Muslims, Christians, and Jews trading with and learning from one another and occasionally intermarrying, Muslim Spain and Norman Sicily (see Chapter 9) were the only distinctly pluralistic societies in medieval Europe.

Some scholars believe that the eighth and ninth centuries in Andalusia were an era of remarkable interfaith harmony. Jews in Muslim Spain were generally treated well, and Córdoba became a center of Jewish as well as Muslim learning. Many Christians adopted Arabic patterns of speech and dress, gave up eating pork, and developed an appreciation for Arabic music and poetry.

By 950, Córdoba had a population of about a half million, making it Europe's largest and most prosperous city. Many residents lived in large houses and easily purchased the silks and brocades made by the city's thousands of weavers. The streets were well paved and well lit, and there was an abundance of freshwater for drinking and bathing. The largest library contained 400,000 volumes, a vast collection, particularly when compared with the largest library in northern Europe at the Benedictine abbey of St. Gall in Switzerland, which had only 600 books.

In Spain, as elsewhere in the Arab world, the Muslims had an enormous impact on agricultural development. They began the cultivation of rice; sugarcane; citrus fruits; dates; figs; eggplants; carrots; and, after the eleventh century, cotton. These crops, together with new methods of field irrigation, provided the population with food products unknown in the rest of Europe. Muslims also brought technological innovations westward, including new kinds of sails and navigational instruments, as well as paper.

Muslim-Christian Relations

What did early Muslims think of Jesus? Jesus is mentioned many times in the Qur'an. He is described as a righteous prophet chosen by God who performed miracles and continued the work of Abraham and Moses, and he was a sign of the coming Day of Judgment. But Muslims held that Jesus was an apostle only, not God. The Christian doctrine of the Trinity—that there is one God in three persons (Father, Son, and Holy Spirit)—posed a powerful obstacle to Muslim-Christian understanding

al-Andalus

▶ The part of the Iberian Peninsula under Muslim control in the eighth century, encompassing most of modern-day Spain.

Harvesting Dates

This detail from an ivory casket given to a Córdoban prince reflects the importance of fruit cultivation in the Muslim-inspired agricultural expansion in southern Europe in the ninth and tenth centuries. (© RMN-Grand Palais/Art Resource, NY)

| How did the Franks build and govern a European empire? | What were the significant intellectual and cultural changes in Charlemagne's era? | What were the consequences of the ninth-century invasions and migrations? | How did internal conflict and outside threats shape European development? | ☑ LearningCurve Check what you know. |

217

because of Islam's emphasis on the absolute oneness of God. Muslims esteemed the Judeo-Christian Scriptures as part of God's revelation, although they believed that the Qur'an superseded them.

Muslims call Jews and Christians *dhimmis*, or "protected people," because they were "people of the book," that is, the Hebrew Scriptures. Christians and Jews in the areas Muslims conquered were allowed to continue practicing their faith, although they did have to pay a special tax. This toleration was sometimes accompanied by suspicion, however. In Spain, Muslim teachers grew increasingly fearful of close contact with Christians and Jews. Thus, beginning in the late tenth century, Muslim regulations began to prescribe officially what Christians, Jews, and Muslims could do. A Christian or Jew, however much assimilated, remained an **infidel**. An infidel was an unbeliever, and the word carried a pejorative or disparaging connotation.

By about 950, Caliph Abd al-Rahman III (912–961) of the Umayyad Dynasty of Córdoba ruled most of the Iberian Peninsula. Christian Spain consisted of the tiny kingdoms of Castile, León, Catalonia, Aragon, Navarre, and Portugal. Civil wars among al-Rahman's descendants weakened the caliphate, and the small northern Christian kingdoms began to expand southward, sometimes working together. When Christian forces conquered Muslim territory, Christian rulers regarded their Muslim and Jewish subjects as infidels and enacted restrictive measures similar to those imposed on Christians in Muslim lands. Christian bishops worried that even knowledge of Islam would lead to ignorance of essential Christian doctrines, and interfaith contacts declined. Christians' perception of Islam as a menace would help inspire the Crusades of the eleventh through thirteenth centuries (see Chapter 9, page 265).

infidel

▶ A disparaging term used for a person who does not believe in a particular religion.

Cross-Cultural Influences in Science and Medicine

Despite growing suspicions on both sides, the Islamic world profoundly shaped Christian European culture in Spain and elsewhere. Toledo, for example, became an important center of learning through which Arab intellectual achievements entered and influenced western Europe. Arabic knowledge of science, medicine, and mathematics, derived from the Chinese, Greeks, and Hindus, was highly sophisticated, and Middle Eastern Arabs translated and codified the scientific and philosophical learning of Greek and Persian antiquity. In the ninth and tenth centuries, that knowledge was brought to Spain, where between 1150 and 1250 it was translated into Latin. Europeans' knowledge of Aristotle (see Chapter 3, page 82), acquired through Muslim translations, changed the entire direction of European philosophy and theology.

> **QUICK REVIEW**

How did Muslim Spain differ from Christian Europe in the early Middle Ages?

How did the Franks build and govern a European empire?

Saint Radegund and King Clotaire

This eleventh-century manuscript shows the Germanic princess Radegund (ca. 520–586) led before the Merovingian king Clotaire, who became her husband. They had no children, and after Clotaire had Radegund's brother killed, she left him and founded a convent, where she lived the rest of her life. Convents were islands of learning and safety in Merovingian society; from the convent, Radegund corresponded with learned church officials and wrote Latin poems, a few of which have survived. (The Bridgeman Art Library Ltd./Alamy)

OVER TWO CENTURIES BEFORE THE MUSLIM CONQUEST OF SPAIN, the Frankish king Clovis converted to Roman Christianity and established a large kingdom in what had been Roman Gaul. Though at that time the Frankish kingdom was simply one barbarian kingdom among many, it grew to become the most important state in Europe, expanding to become an empire.

The Merovingians

Clovis established the Merovingian dynasty in about 481, and under him the Frankish kingdom included much of what is now France and a large section of southwestern Germany. Following Frankish traditions in which property was divided among male heirs, at Clovis's death the kingdom was divided among his four sons. Historians have long described Merovingian Gaul in the sixth and seventh centuries as wracked by civil wars, chronic violence, and political instability as Clovis's descendants fought among themselves. More recently historians have

| How did the Franks build and govern a European empire? | What were the significant intellectual and cultural changes in Charlemagne's era? | What were the consequences of the ninth-century invasions and migrations? | How did internal conflict and outside threats shape European development? | ✓ LearningCurve Check what you know. |

noted that the Merovingians also created new political institutions, so the era was not uniformly bleak.

Merovingian rulers also developed diverse sources of income, including revenues from the royal estates and the "gifts" of subject peoples. New lands might be conquered and confiscated, and served to replace lands donated as monastic or religious endowments. All free landowners paid a land tax, although some landowners gradually gained immunity from doing so. Fines imposed for criminal offenses and tolls and customs duties also yielded income.

The Franks also based some aspects of their government on Roman principles. For example, the basis of the administrative system in the Frankish kingdom was the **civitas** (SIH-vih-tahs)—Latin for a city and surrounding territory—similar to the political organization of the Roman Empire. A **comites** (KOH-meh-tehs)—a senior official or royal companion, later called a count—presided over the civitas, as had governors in Rome. He collected royal revenue, heard lawsuits, enforced justice, and raised troops. Many comites were not conquerors from outside but came from families that had been administrators in Roman Gaul, were usually native to the regions they administered, and knew their areas well. Frankish royal administration involved another official, the *dux* (dooks) or duke. He was a military leader, commanding troops in the territory of several civitas. Clovis and his descendants also issued capitularies—Roman-style administrative and legislative orders—in an attempt to maintain order in Merovingian society.

Within the royal household, Merovingian politics provided women with opportunities, and some queens not only influenced but occasionally also dominated events. Because the finances of the kingdom were merged with those of the royal family, queens often had control of the royal treasury just as more ordinary women controlled household expenditures. The status of a princess or queen also rested on her diplomatic importance, with her marriage sealing or her divorce breaking an alliance with a foreign kingdom or powerful noble family; on her personal relationship with her husband and her ability to give him sons and heirs; and on her role as the mother and guardian of princes who had not reached legal adulthood.

Merovingian rulers and their successors traveled constantly to check up on local administrators and peoples. Merovingian kings also relied on the comites and bishops to gather and send local information to them. The court or household of Merovingian kings included scribes who kept records, legal officials who advised the king on matters of law, and treasury agents responsible for aspects of royal finance. These officials could all read and write Latin. Over them all presided the mayor of the palace, the most important secular figure after the king, who governed the palace and the kingdom in the king's absence. Mayors were usually from one of the great aristocratic families, which through intermarriage increasingly blended Frankish and Roman elites. These families possessed landed wealth and they often had rich and lavish lifestyles.

The Rise of the Carolingians

From this aristocracy, one family gradually emerged to replace the Merovingian dynasty. The rise of the Carolingians rests on several factors. First, the Carolingian Pippin I (d. 640) acquired the powerful position of mayor of the palace and passed the title to his heirs. Although the mayor of the palace was technically

civitas

▶ The city and surrounding territory that served as a basis of the administrative system in the Frankish kingdoms, based on Roman models.

comites

▶ A senior official or royal companion, later called a count, who presided over the civitas.

employed by the ruling family, the Carolingians would use their influential position to win support for themselves and eventually subvert Merovingian authority. Second, a series of advantageous marriage alliances brought the family estates and influence in different parts of the Frankish world, and provided the Carolingians with landed wealth and treasure with which to reward their allies and followers. Third, military victories over supporters of the Merovingians gave the Carolingians a reputation for strength and ensured their dominance. Pippin I's great-grandson, Charles Martel (r. 714–741), waged war successfully against the Saxons, Frisians, Alamanni, and Bavarians, which further enhanced the family's prestige. In 732, Charles Martel defeated a Muslim force near Poitiers (pwah-tee-AY) in central France. While Muslims saw the battle as nothing more than minor skirmish, Charles Martel and later Carolingians used it to enhance their reputation, portraying themselves as defenders of Christendom against the Muslims.

The Battle of Poitiers helped the Carolingians acquire the support of the church, perhaps their most important asset. Charles Martel and his son Pippin III (r. 751–768) further strengthened their ties to the church by supporting the work of Christian missionaries. As missionaries preached, baptized, and established churches, they included the Christian duty to obey secular authorities as part of their message, thus extending to Frankish rulers the church's support of secular power that had begun with Constantine.

As mayor of the palace, Charles Martel had exercised the power of king of the Franks. His son Pippin III aspired to the title and to the powers it entailed. Pippin's diplomats were able to convince an embattled Pope Zacharias to rule in favor of Pippin against the Merovingians in exchange for military support against the Lombards, who were threatening the papacy. Zacharias invoked his apostolic authority as pope, deposed the Merovingian ruler Chilperic in 752, and declared that Pippin should be king. In 754, when Lombard expansion again threatened the papacy, Pope Stephen II journeyed to the Frankish kingdom seeking help. On this occasion, he personally anointed Pippin with sacred oils and gave him the title "Patrician of the Romans," thus linking him symbolically with the ruling patrician class of ancient Rome. Pippin promised restitution of the papal lands and later made a gift of estates in central Italy. An important alliance had been struck between the papacy and the Frankish monarchs. When Pippin died, his son Charles, generally known as Charlemagne, succeeded him.

The Warrior-Ruler Charlemagne

Charlemagne's adviser and friend Alcuin (ca. 735–804; see page 225) wrote that "a king should be strong against his enemies, humble to Christians, feared by pagans, loved by the poor and judicious in counsel and maintaining justice."[1] Charlemagne worked to realize those ideals in all their aspects. Through brutal military expeditions that brought wealth—lands, booty, slaves, and tribute—and by peaceful travel, personal appearances, and the sheer force of his personality, Charlemagne sought to awe newly conquered peoples and rebellious domestic enemies.

If an ideal king was "strong against his enemies" and "feared by pagans," Charlemagne more than met the standard. His reign was characterized by constant warfare. He subdued all of the north of modern France, but his greatest successes were in today's Germany, where he fought battles he justified as spreading

| How did the Franks build and govern a European empire? | What were the significant intellectual and cultural changes in Charlemagne's era? | What were the consequences of the ninth-century invasions and migrations? | How did internal conflict and outside threats shape European development? | ✔ LearningCurve Check what you know. |

221

Christianity to pagan peoples. In the course of a bloody thirty-year war against the Saxons, he added most of the northwestern German peoples to the Frankish kingdom. He established bishoprics in areas he had conquered, so church officials and church institutions became important means of imposing Frankish rule.

Charlemagne also achieved spectacular results in the south, incorporating Lombardy into the Frankish kingdom. He ended Bavarian independence and defeated the nomadic Avars, opening eastern Germany for later settlement by Franks. He successfully fought the Byzantine Empire for Venetia, Istria, and Dalmatia and temporarily annexed those areas to his kingdom. By around 805, the Frankish kingdom included all of northwestern Europe except Scandinavia and Britain (**Map 8.2**).

Carolingian Government and Society

Charlemagne's empire was not a state as people today understand that term; it was a collection of peoples and clans. For administrative purposes, Charlemagne divided his entire kingdom into counties based closely on the old Merovingian civitas, each governed by a count. Counts were originally sent out from the royal court; later a person native to the region was appointed. As a link between local authorities and the central government, Charlemagne appointed officials called *missi dominici* (mih-see doh-MEH-nee-chee), "agents of the lord king," who checked on the counts and held courts to handle judicial and financial issues.

Considering the size of Charlemagne's empire, the counts and royal agents were few and far between, and the authority of the central government was weak. In the absence of a strong central government, society was held together by alliances among powerful families, along with dependent relationships cemented by oaths promising faith and loyalty.

Family alliances were often cemented by sexual relations, including those of Charlemagne himself. Charlemagne had a total of four legal wives and six concubines. (See "Picturing the Past: Charlemagne and His Wife," page 223.) Charlemagne's personal desires certainly shaped his complicated relationships, but the security and continuation of his dynasty and the need for diplomatic alliances were also important motives.

In terms of social changes, the Carolingian period witnessed moderate population growth. The highest aristocrats and church officials lived well, with fine clothing and at least a few rooms heated by firewood. Male nobles hunted and managed their estates, while female nobles generally oversaw the education of their children and sometimes inherited and controlled land on their own. Craftsmen and craftswomen on manorial estates manufactured textiles, weapons, glass,

MAP 8.2 ■ Charlemagne's Conquests, ca. 768–814

Though Charlemagne's hold on much of his territory was relatively weak, the size of his empire was not equaled again until the nineteenth-century conquests of Napoleon.

Frankish Kingdom, 768
Areas conquered by Charlemagne
Tributary peoples
Byzantine Empire
811 Date of conquest

CHAPTER LOCATOR | What were the origins and early impact of Islam?

222 CHAPTER 8
EUROPE IN THE EARLY MIDDLE AGES

Charlemagne and His Wife

This illumination from a ninth-century manuscript portrays Charlemagne with one of his wives. Marriage was an important tool of diplomacy for Charlemagne, and he had a number of wives and concubines. (Erich Lessing/Art Resource, NY)

> PICTURING THE PAST

ANALYZING THE IMAGE: What does Charlemagne appear to be doing? How would you characterize his wife's reaction?
CONNECTIONS: Does this depiction of a Frankish queen match what you've read about Frankish queens? On what accomplishments did a queen's status rest?

and pottery, primarily for local consumption. Sometimes abbeys and manors served as markets, goods were shipped away to towns and fairs for sale, and a good deal of interregional commerce existed. In the towns, artisans and merchants produced and traded luxury goods for noble and clerical patrons. When compared with earlier Roman cities or with Muslim cities of the time, such as Córdoba and Baghdad, however, Carolingian cities were small and poor.

The modest economic expansion benefited townspeople and nobles, but it did not significantly alter the lives of most people, who continued to live in a vast rural world dotted with isolated estates and small villages. Here life was precarious. Crops could easily be wiped out by bad weather, and transporting food from other areas was impossible. People's diets centered on grain in various forms. To this were added seasonal vegetables such as peas, cabbage, and onions, and tiny amounts of animal protein, mostly cheese. Clothing and household goods were

How did the Franks build and govern a European empire? | What were the significant intellectual and cultural changes in Charlemagne's era? | What were the consequences of the ninth-century invasions and migrations? | How did internal conflict and outside threats shape European development? | ☑ LearningCurve Check what you know.

223

just as simple, and houses were drafty, smoky, and often shared with animals. Work varied by the season, but at all times of the year it was physically demanding and yielded relatively little. What little there was had to be shared with landowners, who demanded their taxes and rents in the form of crops, animals, or labor.

The Imperial Coronation of Charlemagne

In autumn of 800, Charlemagne paid a momentous visit to Rome, during which he was crowned emperor by Pope Leo. For centuries, scholars have debated the reasons for the imperial coronation of Charlemagne. Whose idea was the coronation, Charlemagne's or Leo's? Did Charlemagne plan the ceremony or did he merely accept the title of emperor? What did he have to gain from it? What were Pope Leo's motives?

Though definitive answers will probably never be found, several things seem certain. First, after the coronation, Charlemagne considered himself an emperor ruling a Christian people. Through his motto, *Renovatio romani imperi* (Revival of the Roman Empire), Charlemagne was consciously perpetuating old Roman imperial notions while at the same time identifying with the new Rome of the Christian Church. Second, Leo's ideas about gender and rule undoubtedly influenced his decision to crown Charlemagne. In 800, the ruler of the Byzantine Empire was the empress Irene, the first woman to rule Byzantium in her own name, but Leo did not regard her authority as legitimate because she was female. He thus claimed to be placing Charlemagne on a vacant throne. Third, both parties gained: the Carolingian family received official recognition from the leading spiritual power in Europe, and the papacy gained a military protector.

The coronation of Charlemagne, whether planned by the Carolingian court or by the papacy, was to have a profound effect on the course of German history and on the later history of Europe. In the centuries that followed, German rulers were eager to gain the imperial title and to associate themselves with the legends of Charlemagne and ancient Rome. Ecclesiastical authorities, on the other hand, continually cited the event as proof that the dignity of the imperial crown could be granted only by the pope.

> QUICK REVIEW

What was the relationship between Charlemagne and his elite followers, and how did it shape Carolingian society?

CHAPTER LOCATOR | What were the origins and early impact of Islam?

CHAPTER 8
224 EUROPE IN THE EARLY MIDDLE AGES

What were the significant intellectual and cultural changes in Charlemagne's era?

In the Carolingian period, books played a large role in the spread of Christianity and in the promotion of learning. The development of the clearer script known as Carolingian minuscule shown here made books more legible and copying more efficient because more words could fit on the page. (The Schøyen Collection, MS 76, http://www.schoyencollection.com)

AS HE BUILT AN EMPIRE through conquest and strategic alliances, Charlemagne also set in motion a cultural revival that had long-lasting consequences. The stimulus he gave to scholarship and learning may, in fact, be his most enduring legacy.

The Carolingian Renaissance

In Roman Gaul through the fifth century, the culture of members of the elite rested on an education that stressed grammar, Greco-Roman works of literature and history, and the legal and medical treatises of the Roman world. Beginning in the seventh and eighth centuries, a new cultural tradition common to Gaul, Italy, the British Isles, and to some extent Spain emerged. This culture was based primarily on Christian sources. Scholars have called the new Christian and ecclesiastical culture of the period from about 760 to 840, and the educational foundation on which it was based, the "Carolingian Renaissance" because Charlemagne was its major patron.

Charlemagne directed that every monastery in his kingdom should cultivate learning and educate the monks and secular clergy so that they would have a

How did the Franks build and govern a European empire?

What were the significant intellectual and cultural changes in Charlemagne's era?

What were the consequences of the ninth-century invasions and migrations?

How did internal conflict and outside threats shape European development?

☑ LearningCurve
Check what you know.

225

better understanding of the Christian writings. He also urged the establishment of cathedral and monastic schools where boys might learn to read and to pray properly. Thus the main purpose of this rebirth of learning was to promote an understanding of the Scriptures and of Christian writers and to instruct people to pray and praise God in the correct manner.

Women shared with men the work of evangelization and the new Christian learning. Rulers, noblemen, and noblewomen founded monasteries for nuns, each governed by an abbess. Women's monasteries housed women who were unmarried, and also often widows, children being taught to read and recite prayers and chants, elderly people seeking a safe place to live, and travelers needing hospitality. Some female houses were, in fact, double monasteries in which the abbess governed two adjoining establishments, one for women and one for men. Monks provided protection from attack and did the heavy work on the land in double monasteries, but nuns handled everything else.

In monasteries and cathedral schools, monks, nuns, and scribes copied books and manuscripts and built up libraries. They developed the handwriting known as Carolingian minuscule, from which modern Roman type is derived. In this era before printed books, works could survive only if they were copied. Almost all of the works of Roman authors that we are now able to read, both Christian and secular, were preserved by the efforts of Carolingian scribes. Some scholars went beyond copying to develop their own ideas, and by the middle years of the ninth century there was a great outpouring of more sophisticated original works.

The most important scholar at Charlemagne's court was Alcuin (Al-KYOO-ihn), who came from Northumbria, one of the kingdoms in England. He was the leader of a palace school at Aachen, where Charlemagne assembled learned men from all over Europe. From 781 until his death, Alcuin was the emperor's chief adviser on religious and educational matters.

Through monastic and cathedral schools, basic literacy in Latin was established among some of the clergy and even among some of the nobility. By the tenth century, the patterns of thought and the lifestyles of educated western Europeans were those of Rome and Latin Christianity. Most people, however, continued to live in an oral world. They spoke local languages, which did not have a written form. Christian services continued to be conducted in Latin, but not all village priests were able to attend a school, and many simply learned the service by rote. Some Latin words and phrases gradually penetrated the various vernacular languages, but the Carolingian Renaissance did not trickle down to ordinary people.

Northumbrian Learning and Writing

Charlemagne's court at Aachen was not the only center of learning in early medieval Christian Europe. Another was the Anglo-Saxon kingdom of Northumbria, situated at the northernmost tip of the old Roman world. Northumbrian monasteries produced scores of books: missals (used for the celebration of the Mass); psalters (SAL-tuhrs), which contained the 150 psalms and other prayers used by the monks in their devotions; commentaries on the Scriptures; illuminated manuscripts; law codes; and collections of letters and sermons. (See "Individuals in Society: The Venerable Bede," on page 226.) The finest product of Northumbrian

The Venerable Bede

The finest representative of Northumbrian, and indeed all Anglo-Saxon, scholarship is Bede (ca. 673–735). He was born into a noble family, and when he was seven his parents sent him to Benet Biscop's monastery at Wearmouth as a sign of their religious devotion. Later he was sent to the new monastery at Jarrow five miles away. Surrounded by the hundreds of pagan and Christian books Benet Biscop had brought from Italy, Bede spent the rest of his life there, studying and writing. He wrote textbooks on grammar and writing designed to help students master the intricacies of Latin, commentaries on the Old and New Testaments, historical works relating the lives of abbots and the development of the church, and scientific works on time. His biblical commentaries survive in hundreds of manuscripts, indicating that they were widely studied throughout the Middle Ages. His doctrinal works led him to be honored after his death with the title "*Venerable*," and centuries after his death to be named a "doctor of the church" by the pope.

A manuscript portrait of Bede, set within the first letter of a copy of his *Life of St. Cuthbert*. This is the letter *d*, with the monster's head forming the upward line and Bede's foot the short downward line. There are no contemporary descriptions of Bede, so the later manuscript illuminator was free to imagine what he looked like. (Bodleian Libraries, University of Oxford/The Art Archive at Art Resource/Art Resource, NY)

Bede's religious writings were actually not that innovative, but his historical writings were, particularly his best-known work, the *Ecclesiastical History of the English People*, written about 720. As the title suggests, Bede's main topic is the growth of Christianity in England. The book begins with a short discussion of Christianity in Roman Britain, then skips to Augustine of Canterbury's mission to the Anglo-Saxons. Most of the book tells the story of Christianity's spread from one small kingdom in England to another, with missionaries and the kings who converted as its heroes, and the narrative ends with Bede's own day. Bede searched far and wide for his information, discussed the validity of his evidence, compared various sources, and exercised critical judgment. He includes accounts of miracles, but like the stories of valiant missionaries, these are primarily related to provide moral lessons, which all medieval writers thought was the chief purpose of history.

One of the lessons that Bede sought to impart with his history is that Christianity should be unified, and one feature of the *Ecclesiastical History of the English People* inadvertently provided a powerful model for this. In his history, Bede adopted a way of reckoning time proposed by an earlier monk that would eventually provide a uniform chronology for all Christians. He dated events from the incarnation of Christ, rather than from the foundation of the city of Rome, as the Romans had done, or from the regnal years of kings, as the Germans did. His history was recopied by monks in many parts of Europe, who used this dating method, *anno Domini*, "in the year of the Lord" (later abbreviated A.D.), for their own histories as well. (Though Bede does talk about "before the time of the incarnation of our Lord," the reverse dating system of B.C., "before Christ," does not seem to have been widely used before 1700.) Disputes about whether the year began with the incarnation (that is, the conception) of Christ or his birth, and whether these occurred in 1 B.C. or A.D. 1 (the Christian calendar does not have a year zero), continued after Bede, but his method prevailed.

QUESTIONS FOR ANALYSIS

1. How do the career and accomplishments of Bede fit with the notion of an early medieval "renaissance" of learning?
2. Does Bede's notion that history has a moral purpose still shape the writing of history? Do you agree with him?
3. The Christian calendar dates from a midpoint rather than from a starting point, the way many of the world's calendars do. What advantages does this create in reckoning time? What would you see as the primary reason that the Christian calendar has now been widely adopted worldwide?

LaunchPad

ONLINE DOCUMENT PROJECT

What does Bede's life and work tell us about early medieval intellectual communities? Keeping the question above in mind, find out how knowledge was shared among scholars through excerpts from Bede's writings and those of other Carolingian Renaissance figures. Then complete a writing assignment based on the evidence and details from this chapter. *See inside the front cover to learn more.*

art is probably the Gospel book produced at Lindisfarne monastery around 700. The book was produced by a single scribe working steadily over a period of several years.

As in Charlemagne's empire, women were important participants in Northumbrian Christian culture. Perhaps the most important abbess of the early medieval period anywhere in Europe was Saint Hilda (d. 680). A noblewoman of considerable learning and administrative ability, she ruled the double monastery of Whitby on the Northumbrian coast, advised kings and princes, and encouraged scholars and poets. Hilda played a key role in the adoption of Roman practices by Anglo-Saxon churches (see Chapter 7, page 200).

At about the time the monks at Lindisfarne were producing their Gospel book, another author was probably at work on a nonreligious epic poem, *Beowulf* (BAY-uh-woolf). The poem tells the story of the hero Beowulf's progress from valiant warrior to wise ruler. In contrast to most writings of this era, which were in Latin, *Beowulf* was written in the vernacular Anglo-Saxon. The poem includes descriptions of real historical events that took place in fifth- and sixth-century Denmark and Sweden, which have been confirmed by archaeological excavations. These are mixed in with legends, oral traditions, and material from the Bible. Though it tells a story set in pagan Denmark and Sweden, it was written in Christian England sometime in the eighth to the tenth centuries. *Beowulf* provides evidence of the close relationship between England and the northern European continent in the early Middle Ages. The movements of people and ideas that allowed a work like *Beowulf* to be written only increased in the ninth century, when the North Sea became even more of a highway.

> **QUICK REVIEW**

What were the most important contributions of the Carolingian Renaissance to the emerging European culture?

CHAPTER LOCATOR | What were the origins and early impact of Islam?

CHAPTER 8
228 EUROPE IN THE EARLY MIDDLE AGES

What were the consequences of the ninth-century invasions and migrations?

Animal Headpost from Viking Ship Skilled wood-carvers produced ornamental headposts for ships, sledges, wagons, and bedsteads. The fearsome quality of many carvings suggests that they were intended to ward off evil spirits and to terrify. (Ancient Art and Architecture Collection Ltd./The Bridgeman Art Library)

The Treaty of Verdun, 843

Treaty of Verdun

▶ Treaty, signed in 843 by Charlemagne's grandsons, dividing the Carolingian Empire into three parts and setting the pattern for political boundaries in Europe still in use today.

CHARLEMAGNE LEFT HIS VAST EMPIRE TO HIS SOLE SURVIVING SON, Louis the Pious (r. 814–840), who attempted to keep the empire intact. This proved to be impossible. Members of the nobility engaged in plots and open warfare against the emperor, often allying themselves with one of Louis's three sons, who were in conflict with their father and with one another. In 843, shortly after Louis's death, his sons agreed to the **Treaty of Verdun** (vehr-DUHN), which divided the empire into three parts: Charles the Bald received the western part; Lothair the middle part and the title of emperor; and Louis the eastern part, from which he acquired the title "the German." Though no one knew it at the time, this treaty set the pattern for political boundaries in Europe that has been maintained until today.

After the Treaty of Verdun, continental Europe was fractured politically. All three kingdoms controlled by the sons of Louis the Pious were torn by domestic dissension and disorder. The frontier and coastal defenses erected by Charlemagne and maintained by Louis the Pious were neglected. No European

| How did the Franks build and govern a European empire? | What were the significant intellectual and cultural changes in Charlemagne's era? | **What were the consequences of the ninth-century invasions and migrations?** | How did internal conflict and outside threats shape European development? | ✔ LearningCurve Check what you know. |

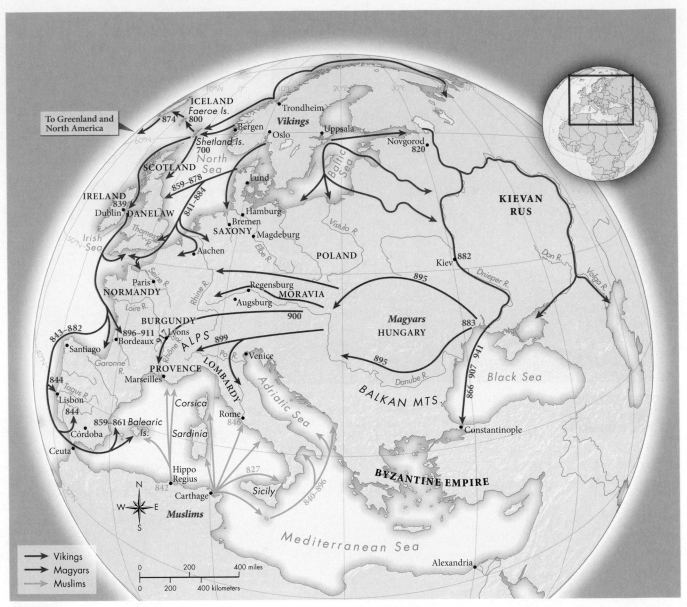

To Greenland and North America

ICELAND
Faeroe Is.
874   800
Shetland Is.
700
SCOTLAND
859–878
IRELAND
839
Dublin   DANELAW
841–884
Irish Sea
Trondheim
Vikings
Bergen   Oslo   Uppsala
North Sea
Lund
Hamburg
Bremen
SAXONY   Magdeburg
Aachen
Novgorod
820
KIEVAN RUS
Baltic Sea
Vistula R.
POLAND
Kiev   882
895
Don R.
Dnieper R.
Volga R.

Thames R.
Paris
NORMANDY
Seine R.
Regensburg
Augsburg
MORAVIA
900
Rhine R.
Loire R.
BURGUNDY
896–911   Lyons
843–882   Bordeaux
Santiago
ALPS
Rhône R.
899
PROVENCE
Marseilles
LOMBARDY
Po R.   Venice
Adriatic Sea
Magyars
HUNGARY
883
866 907 941
Black Sea
895
Danube R.
BALKAN MTS.
Constantinople

844
Tagus R.
Lisbon
844
Córdoba
Ceuta
Garonne R.
859–861   *Balearic Is.*
Corsica
Sardinia
Hippo Regius
842
Carthage
Muslims
827
Rome
846
Sicily
840–896
BYZANTINE EMPIRE

N W E S

Mediterranean Sea

Alexandria

→ Vikings
→ Magyars
→ Muslims

0   200   400 miles
0   200   400 kilometers

MAP 8.3 ■ Invasions and Migrations of the Ninth and Tenth Centuries

This map shows the Viking, Magyar, and Arab invasions and migrations in the ninth and tenth centuries. Compare it with Map 7.3 (page 194) on the barbarian migrations of late antiquity to answer the following questions.

> **MAPPING THE PAST**

ANALYZING THE MAP: What similarities do you see in the patterns of migration in these two periods? What significant differences do you see?
CONNECTIONS: How did the Vikings' expertise in shipbuilding and sailing make their migrations different from those of earlier Germanic tribes? How did this set them apart from the Magyar and Muslim invaders of the ninth century?

political power was strong enough to put up effective resistance to external attacks. Beginning around 850, three main groups began relentless attacks on Europe: Vikings from Scandinavia, representing the final wave of Germanic migrants; Muslims from the Mediterranean; and Magyars from central Europe who were forced westward by other peoples (**Map 8.3**).

CHAPTER LOCATOR | What were the origins and early impact of Islam?

Vikings in Western Europe

Scholars disagree about the reasons for Viking attacks and migrations. A very unstable Danish kingship and disputes over the succession led to civil war and disorder, which may have driven warriors abroad in search of booty and supporters. The population of Scandinavia may have grown too large for the available land to support, and cities on the coasts of northern Europe offered targets for plunder. Goods plundered could then be sold, and looting raids turned into trading ventures. Some scholars assert that the Vikings were looking for trade and new commercial contacts from the beginning.

Whatever the motivations, Viking attacks were savage. Propelled either by oars or by sails, deckless, and about sixty-five feet long, a Viking ship could carry between forty and sixty men—enough to harass an isolated monastery or village. The Vikings burned, looted, and did extensive property damage, although there is little evidence that they caused long-term physical destruction—perhaps because, arriving in small bands, they lacked the manpower to do so. They seized magnates and high churchmen and held them for ransom; they also demanded tribute from kings.

The slave trade represented an important part of Viking plunder and commerce. Slaves, known as *thralls*, were common in Scandinavian society, and Vikings took people from the British Isles and territories along the Baltic Sea as part of their booty. They sold them as slaves in the markets of Magdeburg and Regensburg, at the fairs of Lyons, and in seaports of the Muslim world. Dublin became a center of the Viking slave trade, with hundreds and sometimes thousands of young men and women bought and sold there in any one year.

In the early tenth century, Danish Vikings besieged Paris with fleets of more than a hundred highly maneuverable ships, and the Frankish king Charles the Simple bought them off in 911 by giving them a large part of northern France. There the Vikings established the province of "Northmanland," or Normandy as it was later known, intermarrying with the local population and creating a distinctive Norman culture. From there they sailed around Spain and into the Mediterranean, eventually seizing Sicily from the Muslim Arabs in 1060–1090, while other Normans crossed the English Channel, defeating Anglo-Saxon forces in 1066. Between 850 and 1000, Viking control of northern Europe reached its zenith. Norwegian Vikings moved farther west than any Europeans had before, establishing permanent settlements on Iceland and short-lived settlements in Greenland and Newfoundland in what is now Canada.

The Vikings made positive contributions to the areas they settled. They carried their unrivaled knowledge of shipbuilding and seamanship everywhere. The northeastern and central parts of England where the Vikings settled became known as the *Danelaw* because Danish, not English, laws and customs prevailed there. Scholars believe that some legal institutions, such as the ancestor of the modern grand jury, originated in the Danelaw. Exports from Ireland included iron tools and weapons manufactured there by Viking metal-smiths.

Slavs and Vikings in Eastern Europe

Vikings also brought change in eastern Europe, which was largely populated by Slavs. In antiquity the Slavs lived in central Europe. With the start of the mass migrations of the late Roman Empire, the Slavs moved in different directions and split into what historians later identified as three groups: West, South, and East Slavs.

| How did the Franks build and govern a European empire? | What were the significant intellectual and cultural changes in Charlemagne's era? | **What were the consequences of the ninth-century invasions and migrations?** | How did internal conflict and outside threats shape European development? | ✔ LearningCurve Check what you know. |

231

Kievan Rus, ca. 1050

Kievan Rus

▶ A confederation of Slavic territories, with its capital at Kiev, ruled by descendants of the Vikings.

The group labeled the West Slavs included the Poles, Czechs, Slovaks, and Wends. The South Slavs, comprising peoples who became the Serbs, Croats, Slovenes, Macedonians, and Bosnians, migrated southward into the Balkans. In the seventh century, Slavic peoples of the west and south created the state of Moravia along the banks of the Danube River. By the tenth century, Moravia's residents were Roman Christian, along with most of the other West and South Slavs. In the Balkans, the Serbs accepted Orthodox Christianity, while the Croats became Roman Christian.

Between the fifth and ninth centuries, the eastern Slavs moved into the vast areas of present-day European Russia and Ukraine. This enormous area consisted of an immense virgin forest to the north, where most of the eastern Slavs settled, and an endless prairie grassland to the south.

In the ninth century, the Vikings appeared in the lands of the eastern Slavs. Called Varangians in the old Russian chronicles, the Vikings were interested primarily in gaining wealth through plunder and trade, and the opportunities were good. Moving up and down the rivers, they soon linked Scandinavia and northern Europe to the Black Sea and to the Byzantine Empire's capital at Constantinople. They raided and looted the cities along the Caspian Sea several times in the tenth century, taking booty and slaves, which they then sold elsewhere; thus, raiding turned into trading, and the Scandinavians later established settlements, intermarried, and assimilated with Slavic peoples.

To increase and protect their international commerce and growing wealth, the Vikings declared themselves the rulers of the eastern Slavs. According to tradition, the semi-legendary chieftain Ruirik founded a princely dynasty about 860. In any event, the Varangian ruler Oleg (r. 878–912) established his residence at Kiev in modern-day Ukraine. He and his successors ruled over a loosely united confederation of Slavic territories known as Rus, with its capital at Kiev, until 1054.

Oleg and his clansmen quickly became assimilated into the Slavic population, taking local wives and emerging as the noble class. Missionaries of the Byzantine Empire converted the Vikings and local Slavs to Eastern Orthodox Christianity, accelerating the unification of the two groups. Thus, the rapidly Slavified Vikings left two important legacies for the future: in about 900 they created a loose unification of Slavic territories, **Kievan Rus**, under a single ruling prince and dynasty, and they imposed a basic religious unity by accepting Orthodox Christianity, as opposed to Roman Catholicism, for themselves and the eastern Slavs.

Even at its height under Great Prince Iaroslav (YAHR-uh-slahv) the Wise (r. 1019–1054), the unity of Kievan Rus was extremely tenuous. Trade, not government, was the main concern of the rulers. The Slavified Vikings failed to find a way to transfer power from one generation to the next peacefully. In early Rus, there were apparently no fixed rules, and much strife accompanied each succession. Possibly to avoid such chaos, Great Prince Iaroslav, before his death in 1054, divided Kievan Rus among his five sons, who in turn divided their properties when they died. Between 1054 and 1237, Kievan Rus disintegrated into more and more competing units, each ruled by a prince claiming to be a descendant of Ruirik. The princes divided their land like private property because they thought of it as private property. A prince owned a certain number of farms or landed estates and had them worked directly by his people, mainly slaves, called *kholops* in Russian. Outside these estates, which constituted the princely domain, the prince exercised only limited authority in his principality. Excluding the clergy, two kinds of people lived there: the noble boyars and the commoner peasants.

CHAPTER LOCATOR | What were the origins and early impact of Islam?

The **boyars** were descendants of the original Viking warriors, and they also held their lands as free and clear private property. Although the boyars normally fought in princely armies, the customary law declared that they could serve any prince they wished. The ordinary peasants were also truly free. They could move at will wherever opportunities were greatest. In short, fragmented princely power, private property, and personal freedom all went hand in hand.

boyars
▸ High-ranking nobles in Russia who were descendants of Viking warriors and held their lands as free and clear private property.

Magyars and Muslims

Groups of central European steppe peoples known as Magyars also raided villages in the late ninth century. Moving westward, small bands of Magyars on horseback reached as far as Spain and the Atlantic coast. They subdued northern Italy, compelled Bavaria and Saxony to pay tribute, and even penetrated into the Rhineland and Burgundy (see Map 8.3, page 230).

Magyar forces were defeated by a combined army of Frankish and other Germanic troops at the Battle of Lechfeld near Augsburg in southern Germany in 955, and the Magyars settled in the area that is now Hungary in eastern Europe. The Magyar ruler Géza (GEE-zuh) (r. 970–997), who had been a pagan, became a Roman Christian. This gave him the support of the papacy and offered prospects for alliances with other Roman Christian rulers against the Byzantine Empire, Hungary's southern neighbor. Géza's son Stephen I (r. 997–1038) was officially crowned the king of Hungary by a papal representative on Christmas Day of 1000. Hungary's alliance with the papacy shaped the later history of eastern Europe just as Charlemagne's alliance with the papacy shaped western European history. The Hungarians adopted settled agriculture, wrote law codes, and built towns, and Hungary became an important crossroads of trade for German and Muslim merchants.

The ninth century also saw invasions into Europe from the south. In many ways, these invasions were a continuation of the earlier Muslim conquests in the Iberian Peninsula, but now they focused on Sicily and mainland Italy. In the tenth century, Frankish, papal, and Byzantine forces were able to retake much territory, though the Muslims continued to hold Sicily. Under their rule, agricultural innovations from elsewhere in the Muslim world led to new crops such as cotton and sugar, and fortified cities became centers of Muslim learning. Disputes among the Muslim rulers on the island led one faction to ask the Normans for assistance, and between 1060 and 1090, the Normans gradually conquered all of Sicily.

What was the impact of these invasions? From the perspective of those living in what had been Charlemagne's empire, Viking, Magyar, and Muslim attacks contributed to increasing disorder and violence. People in other parts of Europe might have had a different opinion, however. In Muslim Spain, scholars worked in thriving cities, and new crops such as rice enhanced ordinary people's lives. In eastern Europe, states such as Moravia and Hungary became strong kingdoms. A Viking point of view might be the most positive: by 1100, descendants of the Vikings not only ruled their homelands in Denmark, Norway, and Sweden but also ruled Normandy, England, Sicily, Iceland, and Kievan Rus.

QUICK REVIEW <

How did Viking invaders shape the development of eastern Europe?

How did the Franks build and govern a European empire?

What were the significant intellectual and cultural changes in Charlemagne's era?

What were the consequences of the ninth-century invasions and migrations?

How did internal conflict and outside threats shape European development?

✓ LearningCurve
Check what you know.

How did internal conflict and outside threats shape European development?

THE LARGE-SCALE DIVISION OF CHARLEMAGNE'S EMPIRE into three parts in the ninth century led to a decentralization of power at the local level. Civil wars weakened the power and prestige of kings, who could do little about domestic violence. The great invasions, especially those of the Vikings, also weakened royal authority. The western Frankish kings were unable to halt the invaders, and the local aristocracy had to assume responsibility for defense. Thus, in the ninth and tenth centuries, great aristocratic families increased their authority in the regions of their vested interests, governing virtually independent territories in which distant and weak kings could not interfere. Common people turned for protection to the strongest power, the local counts, whom they considered their rightful rulers, and free peasants sank to the level of serfs.

Decentralization and the Origins of Feudalism

vassal
▶ A warrior who swore loyalty and service to a noble in exchange for land, protection, and support.

fief
▶ A piece of land granted by a feudal lord to a vassal in return for service and loyalty.

feudalism
▶ A term devised by later scholars to describe the political system in which a vassal was generally given a piece of land in return for his loyalty.

The political power of the Carolingian rulers had long rested on the cooperation of the dominant social class, the Frankish aristocracy. Charlemagne and his predecessors relied on the nobles to help wage wars of expansion and suppress rebellions, and in return these families were given a share of the lands and riches confiscated by the rulers. The most powerful nobles were those able to gain the allegiance of warriors, often symbolized in an oath-swearing ceremony in which a warrior (knight) swore his loyalty as a **vassal** to the more powerful individual, who became his lord. In return for the vassal's loyalty, aid, and military assistance, the lord promised him protection and material support, support that most often came in the form of a piece of land called a *feudum* or **fief** (feef). Most legal scholars and historians have seen these personal ties of loyalty cemented by grants of land rather than allegiance to an abstract state as a political and social system they term **feudalism**. They have traced its spread from Frankish areas to other parts of Europe.

CHAPTER LOCATOR | What were the origins and early impact of Islam?

234 CHAPTER 8
EUROPE IN THE EARLY MIDDLE AGES

Vassal-lord relationships provided some degree of cohesiveness in a society that lacked an adequate government bureaucracy or method of taxation. In fact, because vassals owed administrative as well as military service to their lords, vassalage actually functioned as a way to organize political authority. Vassals were expected to serve as advisers to their lord and also to pay him fees for important family events, such as the marriage of the vassal's children.

Along with granting land to knights, lords gave land to the clergy for spiritual services or promises of allegiance. In addition, the church held its own lands, and bishops, archbishops, and abbots and abbesses of monasteries sometimes granted fiefs to their own knightly vassals. Thus the "lord" in a feudal relationship was sometimes an institution. Women other than abbesses were generally not granted fiefs, but in most parts of Europe daughters could inherit them if their fathers had no sons. Occasionally, women did go through ceremonies swearing homage and fealty and swore to send fighters when the lord demanded them. More commonly, women acted as surrogates when their husbands were away, defending the territory from attack and carrying out administrative duties.

Manorialism, Serfdom, and the Slave Trade

In feudal relationships, the "lord" was the individual or institution that had authority over a vassal, but the word *lord* was also used to describe the person or institution that had economic and political authority over peasants who lived in villages and farmed the land. Thus a vassal in one relationship was a slightly different type of lord in another. Most European people in the early Middle Ages were peasants who lived in family groups in villages or small towns and made their living predominantly by raising crops and animals. The village and the land surrounding it were called a manor. Some fiefs might include only one manor, while great lords or kings might have hundreds of manors under their direct control. Residents of manors worked for the lord in exchange for protection, a system that was later referred to as **manorialism**. Free peasants surrendered themselves and their lands to the lord's jurisdiction. The land was given back, but the peasants became tied to it by various kinds of payments and services. Thus, like vassalage, manorialism involved an exchange. Because the economic power of the warring class rested on landed estates worked by peasants, feudalism and manorialism were linked, but they were not the same system.

Local custom determined precisely what services villagers would provide to their lord, but certain practices became common throughout Europe. The peasant was obliged to give the lord a percentage of the annual harvest. The peasant paid a fee to marry someone from outside the lord's estate. To inherit property, the peasant paid a fine. Above all, the peasant became part of the lord's permanent labor force. With vast stretches of uncultivated virgin land and a tiny labor population, manorial lords encouraged population growth and immigration. The most profitable form of capital was not land but laborers.

In entering into a relationship with a manorial lord, free farmers lost status. Their position became servile, and they became **serfs**. That is, they were bound to the land and could not leave it without the lord's permission. Serfdom was not the same as slavery in that lords did not own the person of the serf, but serfs were

manorialism
▶ A system in which peasant residents of manors, or farming villages, provided work and goods for their lord in exchange for protection.

serfs
▶ Peasants bound to the land by a relationship with a manorial lord.

How did the Franks build and govern a European empire?

What were the significant intellectual and cultural changes in Charlemagne's era?

What were the consequences of the ninth-century invasions and migrations?

How did internal conflict and outside threats shape European development?

☑ LearningCurve
Check what you know.

235

subject to the jurisdiction of the lord's court in any dispute over property and in any case of suspected criminal behavior.

The transition from freedom to serfdom was slow. In the late eighth century, there were still many free peasants. And within the legal category of serfdom there were many economic levels, ranging from the highly prosperous to the desperately poor. Nevertheless, a social and legal revolution was taking place. By the year 800, perhaps 60 percent of the population of western Europe—completely free a century before—had been reduced to serfdom. The ninth-century Viking assaults on Europe created extremely unstable conditions and individual insecurity, increasing the need for protection, accelerating the transition to serfdom, and leading to additional loss of personal freedom.

Though serfdom was not slavery, the Carolingian trade in actual slaves was extensive, generally involving persons captured in war or raids. Merchants in early medieval towns used slaves to pay the suppliers of the luxury goods their noble and clerical customers desired, most of which came into Europe from the East. The Muslim conquest of Spain produced thousands of prisoner-slaves, as did Charlemagne's long wars and the Viking raids. When Frankish conquests declined in the tenth century, German and Viking merchants obtained people on the empire's eastern border who spoke Slavic languages, the origin of our word *slave*. Slaves sold across the Mediterranean fetched three or four times the amounts brought within the Carolingian Empire, so most slaves were sold to Muslims. Christian moralists sometimes complained about the sale of Christians to non-Christians, but they did not object to slavery itself.

> ## QUICK REVIEW

How and why did the status of ordinary rural Europeans change over the course of the eighth and ninth centuries?

CHAPTER LOCATOR | What were the origins and early impact of Islam?

CHAPTER 8
236 EUROPE IN THE EARLY MIDDLE AGES

LOOKING BACK
LOOKING AHEAD

The culture that emerged in Europe in the early Middle Ages has justifiably been called the first "European civilization." While it was by no means "civilized" by modern standards, it had definite characteristics that were shared across a wide region. Other than in Muslim Spain and the pagan areas of northern and eastern Europe, almost all people were baptized Christians. Everywhere—including Muslim and pagan areas—most people lived in small villages, supporting themselves and paying their obligations to their superiors by raising crops and animals. These villages were on pieces of land increasingly granted to knights in exchange for loyalty and service to a noble lord. Members of the educated elite were infused with Latin ideas and models for Latin was the common language of educated people in most of Europe.

In the several centuries after 1000, these characteristics—Christianity, village-based agriculture, vassalage, and Latin culture—would not disappear. Historians conventionally term the era from 1000 to about 1300 the "High Middle Ages," but this era built on a foundation that had already been established. Political structures grew from the institutions established in the Carolingian period, and later literary and cultural flowerings followed the model of the Carolingian Renaissance in looking to the classical past. Less positive developments also had their roots in the early Middle Ages, including hostilities between Christians and Muslims that would motivate the Crusades, and the continued expansion of serfdom and other forms of unfree labor.

LaunchPad

ONLINE DOCUMENT PROJECT
The Venerable Bede

What does Bede's life and work tell us about early medieval intellectual communities?

You encountered Bede's story on page 227. Keeping the question above in mind, find out how knowledge was shared among scholars through excerpts from Bede's writings and those of other Carolingian Renaissance figures. *See inside the front cover to learn more.*

| How did the Franks build and govern a European empire? | What were the significant intellectual and cultural changes in Charlemagne's era? | What were the consequences of the ninth-century invasions and migrations? | How did internal conflict and outside threats shape European development? | ✓ LearningCurve Check what you know. |

237

CHAPTER 8 STUDY GUIDE

STEP 1

GET STARTED ONLINE

✓ **LearningCurve**

Now that you've read the chapter, make it stick by completing the LearningCurve activity.

STEP 2

EXPLAIN WHY IT MATTERS

Put your reading into practice. Identify each term below, and then explain why it matters in Western history.

TERM	WHO OR WHAT & WHEN	WHY IT MATTERS
Qur'an (p. 213)		
Five Pillars of Islam (p. 215)		
caliph (p. 216)		
al-Andalus (p. 217)		
infidel (p. 218)		
civitas (p. 220)		
comites (p. 220)		
Treaty of Verdun (p. 229)		
Kievan Rus (p. 232)		
boyars (p. 233)		
vassal (p. 234)		
fief (p. 234)		
feudalism (p. 234)		
manorialism (p. 235)		
serfs (p. 235)		

STEP 3

MOVE BEYOND THE BASICS

To demonstrate a more advanced understanding of ninth- and tenth-century political, economic, and social developments, use the chart below to compare and contrast the key features of feudalism and manorialism. What connections and similarities existed between the two systems? Why is it not correct to include serfs as part of the feudal system?

Feudalism	Manorialism
•	•
•	•
•	•
•	•
•	•

STEP 4 **PUT IT ALL TOGETHER** Now, take a step back and try to explain the big picture. Remember to use specific examples from the chapter in your answers.

THE SPREAD OF ISLAM

▶ What beliefs united all Muslims? What were the sources of division within the Muslim community?

▶ What contributions did Muslim scholars and thinkers make to the development of European civilization?

THE POLITICS AND CULTURE OF THE FRANKISH EMPIRE

▶ What were the most important strengths and weaknesses of Charlemagne's empire?

▶ What motives were behind Charlemagne's patronage of scholarship and education?

INVASIONS, MIGRATIONS, AND POLITICAL FRAGMENTATION

▶ What impact did the Viking invasions have on the areas in which they occurred? How were the Vikings themselves changed by their military success?

▶ What were the most important social and economic consequences of the political fragmentation of the eighth and ninth centuries?

MAKE CONNECTIONS

▶ What Greco-Roman elements were incorporated into the society and culture of the early Middle Ages?

▶ In your opinion, are the early Middle Ages best characterized as a "dark age" or as the dawn of a new era? Why?

> **IN YOUR OWN WORDS**

Imagine that you must give an oral report to the class answering the following question: **How did the events and developments of the Early Middle Ages shape European civilization?** What would be the most important points and why?

239

9

STATE AND CHURCH IN THE HIGH MIDDLE AGES

1000–1300

> **What steps did monarchs take to increase their power and authority during the High Middle Ages?** Chapter 9 examines the development of centralized secular and religious authority in the High Middle Ages. As the invasions and migrations that had contributed to European fragmentation gradually ended, rulers began to develop new institutions of law and government that enabled them to assert their power over lesser lords and the general population. At the same time, energetic popes built their power within the Western Christian Church and tried to assert their superiority over kings and emperors. A papal call to retake Jerusalem led to nearly two centuries of warfare between Christians and Muslims. At the same time, conquest and colonization led to the gradual incorporation of European border regions into a more uniform Christian realm.

✓ **LearningCurve**

After reading the chapter, use LearningCurve to retain what you've read.

> How did monarchs try to centralize political power?

> How did the administration of law evolve in this period?

> What were the political and social roles of nobles?

> How did the papacy reform the church?

> What roles did monks, nuns, and friars play in medieval society?

> What were the causes, course, and consequences of the Crusades?

Life and Death in the High Middle Ages. In this thirteenth-century manuscript, knights of King Henry II stab Archbishop Thomas Becket in Canterbury Cathedral in 1170.

> How did monarchs try to centralize political power?

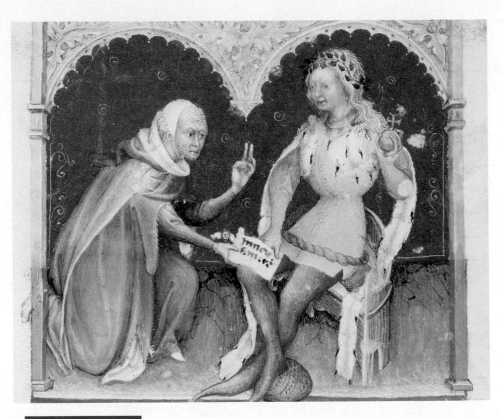

Emperor Frederick II Granting Privileges A young Frederick II signs a grant of privileges for a merchant of the Italian city of Asti in this thirteenth-century manuscript. Frederick wears the flamboyant and fashionable clothing of a high noble, while the merchant seeking his favor is dressed in more sober and less expensive garb. (Scala/Art Resource, NY)

BEGINNING IN THE ELEVENTH CENTURY, rulers in some parts of Europe began to manipulate existing institutions to build up their power, becoming kings over growing and slowly centralizing states. As rulers expanded their territories and extended their authority, they developed larger bureaucracies, armies, judicial systems, and other institutions of state to maintain control and ensure order. Because these institutions cost money, rulers also initiated systems for generating revenue and handling financial matters. Some rulers were more successful than others, and the solutions they found to these problems laid the foundations for modern national states.

CHAPTER LOCATOR | **How did monarchs try to centralize political power?** How did the administration of law evolve in this period?

936–973
- Reign of Otto I in Germany; facilitates spread of Christianity in the Baltics and eastern Europe

1059
- Lateran Council restricts election of the pope to the college of cardinals

1061–1091
- Normans defeat Muslims and Byzantines in Sicily

1066
- Norman conquest of England

1073–1085
- Pontificate of Pope Gregory VII, proponent of Gregorian reforms

1095–1291
- Crusades

1098
- Cistercian order established

1100–1135
- Reign of Henry I of England; establishment of the Exchequer, England's bureau of finance

1100–1200
- Establishment of canon law

1154–1189
- Reign of Henry II of England; revision of legal procedure; beginnings of common law

1170
- Thomas Becket assassinated in England

1180–1223
- Reign of Philip II (Philip Augustus) in France; territory of France greatly expanded

1198–1216
- Innocent III; height of the medieval papacy

1215
- Magna Carta

1216
- Papal recognition of Dominican order

1221
- Papal recognition of Franciscan order

1290
- Jews expelled from England

1298
- Pope Boniface VIII orders all nuns to be cloistered

1302
- Pope Boniface VIII declares all Christians subject to the pope in *Unam Sanctam*

1306
- Jews expelled from France

1397
- Queen Margrete establishes Union of Kalmar

England

Throughout the ninth century, the Vikings had made a concerted effort to conquer and rule all of Anglo-Saxon England. In 878, however, Alfred, king of the West Saxons (or Wessex), defeated the Vikings, inaugurating a period of recovery and stability in England. Alfred and his immediate successors built a system of local defenses and slowly extended royal rule beyond Wessex to other Anglo-Saxon peoples until one law, royal law, took precedence over local custom. England was divided into local units called shires, or counties, each under the jurisdiction of a sheriff appointed by the king. Sheriffs were unpaid officials from well-off families responsible for collecting taxes, catching and trying criminals, and raising infantry when the king required it.

The Viking invasions of England resumed, however, and the island eventually came under Viking rule, with the Viking Canute (r. 1016–1035) making England the

| What were the political and social roles of nobles? | How did the papacy reform the church? | What roles did monks, nuns, and friars play in medieval society? | What were the causes, course, and consequences of the Crusades? | ✓ LearningCurve Check what you know. |

center of his empire. When Canute's heir Edward died childless, there were three claimants to the throne of England—the Anglo-Saxon noble Harold Godwinson (ca. 1022–1066), who had been crowned by English nobles; the Norwegian king Harald III (r. 1045–1066), grandson of Canute; and Duke William of Normandy, who was the illegitimate son of Edward's cousin.

In 1066, the forces of Harold Godwinson crushed Harald's invading army in northern England, then quickly marched south when they heard that William had invaded England with his Norman vassals. Harold was decisively defeated by William at the Battle of Hastings—an event now known as the Norman conquest. In both England and Normandy, William the Conqueror limited the power of the nobles and church officials, and built a unified monarchy. In England, he retained the office of sheriff, but named Normans to the posts. William wanted to determine how much wealth there was in his new kingdom and who held what land. Royal officials were sent to every part of the country, and the resulting record, called the *Domesday Book* (DOOMZ-day), helped William and his descendants tax land appropriately. It also helped William and future English kings regard their country as one unit.

Domesday Book
▶ A general inquiry about the wealth of his lands ordered by William of Normandy.

William's son Henry I (r. 1100–1135) established a bureau of finance called the Exchequer that became the first institution of the government bureaucracy of England. In addition to various taxes and annual gifts, Henry's income came from money paid to the Crown for settling disputes and as penalties for crimes, as well as money due to him in his private position as landowner and lord.

In 1128, Henry's daughter Matilda was married to Geoffrey of Anjou; their son became Henry II of England and inaugurated the Angevin dynasty. Henry II inherited the French provinces of Anjou, Normandy, Maine, and Touraine in northwestern France, and in 1152, he married Eleanor of Aquitaine, who was heir to Aquitaine, Poitou (pwah-TOO), and Gascony in southwestern France. As a result, Henry claimed nearly half of today's France, and the histories of England and France became closely intertwined.

France

French kings overcame the Angevin threat to expand and increasingly unify their realm. Following the death of the last Carolingian ruler in 987, an assembly of nobles selected Hugh Capet (kah-PAY) as his successor. Soon after his own coronation, Hugh crowned his oldest surviving son Robert as king to ensure the succession and prevent disputes after his death. This broke with the earlier practices of elective kingship or dividing a kingdom among one's sons, establishing instead the principle of **primogeniture** (prie-muh-JEH-nuh-tchoor), in which the eldest son inherits all land and titles.

primogeniture
▶ An inheritance system in which the oldest son inherits all land and noble titles.

The Capetian (kuh-PEE-shuhn) kings were weak, but they laid the foundation for later political stability. In the early twelfth century, France still consisted of a number of nearly independent provinces, and the king of France maintained clear jurisdiction over a relatively small area, the Île-de-France. Over time, medieval French kings worked to increase the royal domain and extend their authority over the provinces.

The work of unifying France began under Louis VI's grandson Philip II (r. 1180–1223), also known as Philip Augustus. He took Normandy by force from

CHAPTER LOCATOR | How did monarchs try to centralize political power?   How did the administration of law evolve in this period?

CHAPTER 9
244   STATE AND CHURCH IN THE HIGH MIDDLE AGES

King John of England in 1204 and gained other northern provinces as well. In the thirteenth century, Philip Augustus's descendants acquired important holdings in the south. By the end of the thirteenth century, most of the provinces of modern France had been added to the royal domain through diplomacy, marriage, war, and inheritance (**Map 9.1**).

In addition to expanding the royal territory, Philip Augustus devised a method of governing the provinces and providing for communication between the central government in Paris and local communities. Each province retained its own institutions and laws, but royal agents were sent from Paris into the provinces as the king's official representatives. These agents were never natives of the provinces to which they were assigned, and they could not own land there. This policy reflected the fundamental principle of French administration that officials should gain their power from their connection to the monarchy, not from their own wealth or local alliances.

Central Europe

In central Europe, the German king Otto I (r. 936–973) defeated many other lords to build his power from his original base in Saxony. Otto garnered financial support from church leaders and also asserted the right to control ecclesiastical appointments. This practice, later known as lay investiture, created a grave crisis between the church and the monarchy in the eleventh century (see page 256).

In 955, Otto I inflicted a crushing defeat on the Magyars in the Battle of Lechfeld. In 962, he used this victory to have himself crowned emperor by the pope. Though it was not exactly clear what Otto was the emperor of, by the eleventh century, people were increasingly using the term **Holy Roman Empire** to refer to a loose confederation of principalities, duchies, cities, bishoprics, and other types of regional governments stretching from Denmark to Rome and from Burgundy to Poland (**Map 9.2**).

In this large area of central Europe and northern Italy, the Holy Roman emperors shared power with princes, dukes, archbishops, counts, bishops, abbots, and cities. The office of emperor remained an elected one, though the electors numbered seven—four secular rulers of large territories within the empire and three archbishops.

MAP 9.1 ■ The Growth of the Kingdom of France, 1180–1314

The kings of France expanded their holdings through warfare, diplomacy, and strategic marriages, annexing lands that had belonged to independent nobles and taking over territory from the Angevin kings who also ruled England. The province of Toulouse in the south became part of France as a result of the crusade against the Albigensians (see page 257).

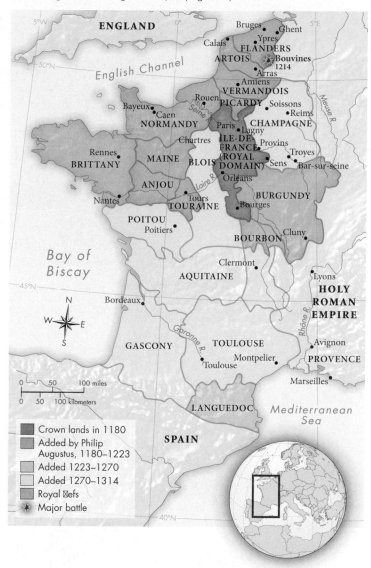

Crown lands in 1180
Added by Philip Augustus, 1180–1223
Added 1223–1270
Added 1270–1314
Royal fiefs
Major battle

Holy Roman Empire

▶ The loose confederation of principalities, duchies, cities, bishoprics, and other types of regional governments stretching from Denmark to Rome and from Burgundy to Poland.

| What were the political and social roles of nobles? | How did the papacy reform the church? | What roles did monks, nuns, and friars play in medieval society? | What were the causes, course, and consequences of the Crusades? | ✔ LearningCurve Check what you know. |

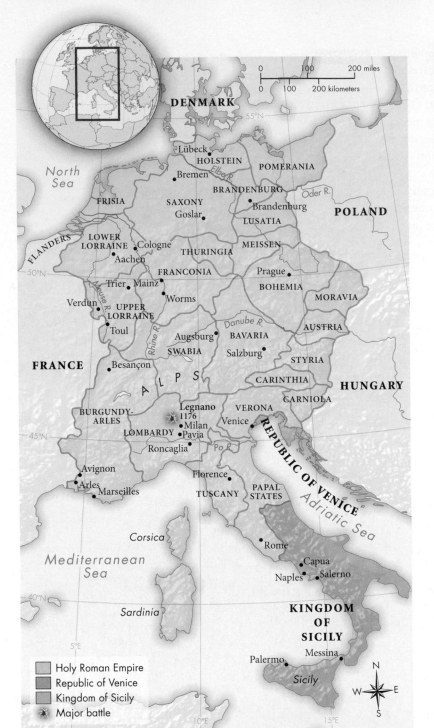

MAP 9.2 ■ The Holy Roman Empire and the Kingdom of Sicily, ca. 1200

Frederick Barbarossa greatly expanded the size of the Holy Roman Empire, but it remained a loose collection of various types of governments. The Christian kingdom of Sicily was created when Norman knights overthrew the Muslim rulers, but it was later ruled by Frederick II, who was also the Holy Roman emperor.

None of Otto's successors were as forceful as he had been, and by the first half of the twelfth century, civil wars wracked the empire. The electors decided the only alternative to continued chaos was the selection of a strong ruler. They chose Frederick Barbarossa of the house of Hohenstaufen (HOH-uhn-shtow-fuhn) (r. 1152–1190). Like William the Conqueror in England and Philip in France, Frederick required vassals to take an oath of allegiance to him as emperor and appointed officials to exercise full imperial authority over local communities.

Between 1154 and 1188, Frederick made six military expeditions into Italy in an effort to assert his imperial rights over the increasingly wealthy towns of northern Italy. While he initially made significant conquests, the Italian cities formed leagues to oppose him and also allied with the papacy. In 1176, Frederick suffered a crushing defeat at Legnano (see Map 9.2). Frederick was forced to recognize the municipal autonomy of the northern Italian cities and the pope's sovereignty in central Italy. His campaigns in Italy took him away from the parts of the empire north of the Alps, and regional rulers there reasserted their authority toward the end of Frederick's reign and in the reigns of his successors. Thus, in contrast to France and England, Germany did not

CHAPTER LOCATOR | How did monarchs try to centralize political power? | How did the administration of law evolve in this period?

246 CHAPTER 9 STATE AND CHURCH IN THE HIGH MIDDLE AGES

become a unified state in the Middle Ages and would not until the nineteenth century.

Italy

The emperor and the pope also came into conflict over Sicily and southern Italy, disputes that eventually involved the kings of France and Spain as well. Between 1061 and 1091, a bold Norman knight, Roger de Hauteville, with papal support and a small band of mercenaries, defeated the Muslims and Byzantines who controlled the island of Sicily. Roger then faced the problem of governing Sicily's heterogeneous population of native Sicilians, Italians, Greeks, Jews, Arabs, and Normans. Roger distributed scattered lands to his followers so no vassal would have a centralized power base. He took an inquest of royal property and forbade his followers to engage in war with one another. To these Norman practices, Roger fused Arabic and Greek institutions, such as the bureau for record keeping and administration that had been established by the previous Muslim rulers.

In 1137, Roger's son and heir, Count Roger II, took the city of Naples and much of the surrounding territory in southern Italy. The entire area came to be known as the kingdom of Sicily (or sometimes the Kingdom of the Two Sicilies).

Roger II's grandson Frederick II (r. 1212–1250) was also the grandson of Frederick Barbarossa of Germany. He was crowned king of the Germans at Aachen and Holy Roman emperor, but he concentrated all his attention on the southern parts of the empire. Frederick had grown up in multicultural Sicily, knew six languages, wrote poetry, and supported scientists, scholars, and artists, whatever their religion or background. In 1224, he founded the University of Naples to train officials for his growing bureaucracy. He tried to administer justice fairly to all his subjects, including Jews and Muslims.

Sicily required constant attention, however, and Frederick's absences on the Crusades and on campaigns in mainland Italy took their toll. Shortly after he died, the unsupervised bureaucracy fell to pieces. The pope, worried about being encircled by imperial power, called in a French prince to rule the kingdom of Sicily. Like Germany, Italy would remain divided until the nineteenth century.

The Iberian Peninsula

From the eleventh to the thirteenth centuries, power in the Iberian Peninsula shifted from Muslim to Christian rulers, with the tide turning decisively in favor of the Christian forces beginning in the early thirteenth century. Alfonso VIII (1158–1214) of Castile, aided by the kings of Aragon, Navarre, and Portugal, won a crushing victory over the Muslims in 1212, accelerating the Christian push southward. Over the next several centuries, successive popes gave Christian warriors in the Iberian Peninsula the same spiritual benefits that they gave those who traveled to Jerusalem, such as granting them forgiveness for their sins. By doing so, the popes transformed this advance into a crusade. Christian troops captured the great Muslim cities of Córdoba in 1236 and Seville in 1248. With this, Christians controlled nearly the entire Iberian Peninsula, save for the small state of

What were the political and social roles of nobles? | How did the papacy reform the church? | What roles did monks, nuns, and friars play in medieval society? | What were the causes, course, and consequences of the Crusades? | ✔ LearningCurve Check what you know.

247

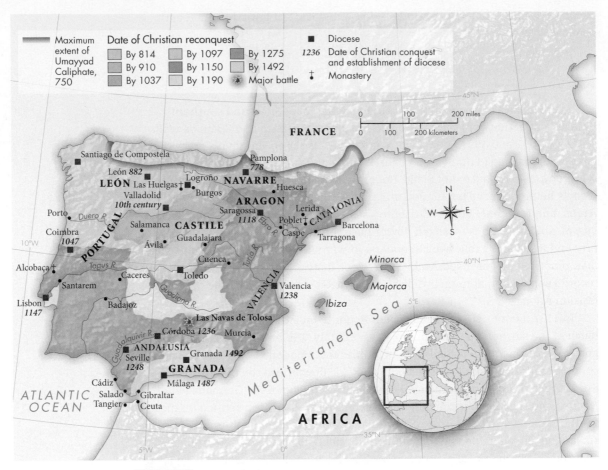

Maximum extent of Umayyad Caliphate, 750

Date of Christian reconquest
By 814
By 910
By 1037
By 1097
By 1150
By 1190
By 1275
By 1492
Major battle

■ Diocese
1236 Date of Christian conquest and establishment of diocese
† Monastery

MAP 9.3 ■ The Reconquista, ca. 750–1492

The Christian conquest of Muslim Spain was followed by ecclesiastical reorganization, with the establishment of dioceses, monasteries, and the Latin liturgy, which gradually tied the peninsula to the heartland of Christian Europe and to the Roman papacy.

reconquista
▶ The Christian term for the conquest of Muslim territories in the Iberian Peninsula by Christian forces.

Granada (**Map 9.3**). The chief mosques in Muslim cities became cathedrals, and Christian rulers recruited immigrants from western and southern Europe. The cities quickly became overwhelmingly Christian, and gradually rural areas did as well. Fourteenth-century clerical writers would call the movement to expel the Muslims the **reconquista** (reconquest), a sacred and patriotic crusade to wrest the country from "alien" Muslim hands.

> **QUICK REVIEW**

What factors contributed to long-term political fragmentation in central Europe and Italy?

CHAPTER LOCATOR | How did monarchs try to centralize political power? | How did the administration of law evolve in this period?

CHAPTER 9
248 STATE AND CHURCH IN THE HIGH MIDDLE AGES

How did the administration of law evolve in this period?

Punishment of Adulterers   A man and a woman found guilty of adultery are led naked through the streets in this thirteenth-century French manuscript, preceded by heralds blowing horns and followed by men carrying sticks. This procession may be driving the couple out of town; banishment was a very common punishment for a number of crimes, including theft and assault. (Bibliothèque municipale, Agen [Lot-et-Garonne]/The Bridgeman Art Library)

THROUGHOUT EUROPE IN 1000, the law was a hodgepodge of local customs and provincial practices. Over the course of the High Middle Ages, national rulers tried to blend these elements into a uniform system of rules acceptable and applicable to all their peoples, though their success at doing so varied.

Local Laws and Royal Courts

In France, this effort to create a royal judicial system was launched by Louis IX (r. 1226–1270). Each French province, even after being made part of the kingdom of France, had retained its unique laws and procedures, but Louis IX published laws for the entire kingdom and sent royal judges to hear complaints of injustice. He established the Parlement of Paris, a kind of supreme court that heard appeals from local administrators and regional courts, and also registered (or announced) royal laws. By the very act of appealing the decisions of local courts to the Parlement of Paris, French people in far-flung provinces were recognizing the superiority of royal justice.

| What were the political and social roles of nobles? | How did the papacy reform the church? | What roles did monks, nuns, and friars play in medieval society? | What were the causes, course, and consequences of the Crusades? |  LearningCurve Check what you know. |

In the Holy Roman Empire, justice was administered at multiple levels. The manorial or seigneurial court, presided over by the local lay or ecclesiastical lord, dealt with matters such as damage to crops and fields, trespass, boundary disputes, and debt. Dukes, counts, bishops, and abbots possessed authority over larger regions, and they dispensed justice in serious criminal cases there. The Holy Roman emperors established a court of appeal similar to that of the French kings, but in their disunited empire it had little power.

England also had a variety of local laws, with procedures and penalties that varied from one part of the country to another. Henry I occasionally sent out circuit judges, royal officials who traveled a given circuit or district, to hear civil and criminal cases. Henry II (r. 1154–1189) made this way of extending royal justice an annual practice. These courts regularized procedures in civil cases, gradually developing the idea of a **common law**, one that applied throughout the whole country. Over the next two or three centuries, common law became a reality as well as a legal theory.

Henry also improved procedure in criminal justice. In 1166, he instructed the sheriffs to summon local juries to conduct inquests and draw up lists of known or suspected criminals. This accusing jury is the ancestor of the modern grand jury. During the course of the thirteenth century, the king's judges gradually adopted the practice of calling on twelve people to consider the question of innocence or guilt; this was the forerunner of the trial jury.

One aspect of Henry II's judicial reforms encountered stiff resistance from an unexpected source. In 1164, Henry insisted that everyone, including clerics, be subject to the royal courts. The archbishop of Canterbury Thomas Becket, who was Henry's friend and former chief adviser, vigorously protested that church law required clerics to be subject to church courts.

The disagreement between king and archbishop dragged on for years. Late in December 1170, in a fit of rage, Henry expressed the wish that Becket be destroyed. Four knights took the king at his word. They rode to Canterbury Cathedral and, as the archbishop was leaving evening services, murdered him. The assassination of an archbishop turned public opinion in England and throughout western Europe against the king, and Henry had to give up his attempts to bring clerics under the authority of the royal courts.

The Magna Carta

In the later years of Henry's reign, his sons fought against their father and one another for power and land. Richard I, known as the Lion-Hearted (r. 1189–1199), won this civil war and acceded to the throne on Henry's death. Soon after, however, he departed on one of the Crusades. Richard was captured on his way back from the Crusades and held by the Holy Roman emperor for a very high ransom, paid primarily through loans and high taxes on the English people.

John (r. 1199–1216) inherited his father's and brother's heavy debts, and his efforts to squeeze money out of his subjects created an atmosphere of resentment. In July 1214, John suffered a severe defeat at the hands of Philip Augustus of France, strengthening the opposition to John back in England. A rebellion begun by northern barons eventually grew to involve many key members of the English nobility. After lengthy negotiations, John met the barons in 1215 at Runnymede and was forced to approve the charter of rights later called **Magna Carta**.

common law
▶ A body of English law established by King Henry II's court that in the next two or three centuries became common to the entire country.

Magna Carta
▶ A peace treaty intended to redress the grievances that particular groups had against King John; it was later viewed as the source of English rights and liberty more generally.

CHAPTER LOCATOR | How did monarchs try to centralize political power? | **How did the administration of law evolve in this period?**

250   CHAPTER 9
STATE AND CHURCH IN THE HIGH MIDDLE AGES

The charter was simply meant to assert traditional rights enjoyed by certain groups and thus state limits on the king's power. In time, however, it came to signify the broader principle that everyone, including the king and the government, must obey the law. The Magna Carta also contains the germ of the idea of "due process of law," meaning that a person has the right to be heard and defended in court and is entitled to the protection of the law.

Law in Everyday Life

Judges determined guilt or innocence in a number of ways. In some cases, particularly those in which there was little clear evidence, they ordered a trial by ordeal. An accused person could be tried by fire or water. In the latter case, the accused was tied hand and foot and dropped in a lake or river. People believed that water was a pure substance and would reject anything foul or unclean. Thus a person who sank was considered innocent; a person who floated was found guilty. Trial by ordeal was a ritual that appealed to the supernatural for judgment.

Trials by ordeal are fascinating to modern audiences, but they were relatively rare, and their use declined over the High Middle Ages as judges and courts increasingly favored more rational procedures. Judges heard testimony, sought witnesses, and read written evidence if it was available. If the accused was found guilty, a punishment was imposed. Murder was a capital crime, as were a number of other violent acts, and executions took place outdoors on a scaffold. Hanging was the most common method of execution, although nobles might be beheaded because hanging was seen as demeaning. Minor crimes were punished by fines, corporal punishments such as whipping, or banishment from the area.

QUICK REVIEW <

What role did monarchs play in the development of law and order in the High Middle Ages?

What were the political and social roles of nobles?

How did the papacy reform the church?

What roles did monks, nuns, and friars play in medieval society?

What were the causes, course, and consequences of the Crusades?

✅ LearningCurve
Check what you know.

> What were the political and social roles of nobles?

Saint Maurice

This sandstone statue from Magdeburg Cathedral, carved around 1250, shows the warrior Saint Maurice. Some of the individuals who were held up to young men as models of ideal chivalry were probably real, but their lives were embellished with many stories. One example was Saint Maurice (d. 287), a soldier apparently executed by the Romans for refusing to renounce his Christian faith. He first emerges in the Carolingian period, and later he was held up as a model knight and declared a patron of the Holy Roman Empire and protector of the imperial army in wars against the pagan Slavs. His image was used on coins, and his cult was promoted by the archbishops of Magdeburg, who moved his relics to their cathedral. Until 1240, he was portrayed as a white man, but after that he was usually represented as a black man, as in this statue. Historians have no idea why this change occurred. (Courtesy, The Menil Foundation, Houston)

THE EXPANSION OF CENTRALIZED ROYAL POWER AND LAW involved limiting the power of the nobility, but rulers also worked through nobles, who retained their privileged status and cultural importance. In fact, the nobility continued to hold real political and social power in Europe into the nineteenth century.

Origins and Status of the Nobility

In the early Middle Ages, noble status was generally limited to a very few families who either were descended from officials at the Carolingian court or were leading families among Germanic tribes. Beginning in the eleventh century, knights in the service of higher nobles or kings began to claim noble status. Although nobles were only a small fraction of the total population, the noble class grew larger and more diverse, ranging from poor knights to dukes and counts.

CHAPTER LOCATOR | How did monarchs try to centralize political power? | How did the administration of law evolve in this period?

Originally, most knights focused solely on military skills, but around 1200 there emerged a different ideal of knighthood, usually termed **chivalry** (SHIH-vuhl-ree). Chivalry was a code of conduct in which fighting to defend the Christian faith and protecting one's countrymen were declared to have a sacred purpose. Other qualities gradually became part of chivalry: bravery, generosity, honor, graciousness, mercy, and eventually gallantry toward women, which came to be called "courtly love."

Training, Marriage, and Inheritance

At about the age of seven, a boy of the noble class who was not intended for the church was placed in the household of one of his father's friends or relatives. There he became a servant to the lord and received formal training in arms. Increasingly, noble youths learned to read and write some Latin. Formal training was concluded around the age of twenty-one, often with the ceremony of knighthood.

The ceremony of knighthood did not necessarily mean attainment of adulthood, power, and responsibility. Sons were completely dependent on their fathers for support. A young man remained a youth until he was in a financial position to marry—that is, until his father died. Increasingly, families adopted primogeniture, with property passing to the oldest son. Younger sons might be forced into the clergy or simply forbidden to marry.

While noble girls were also trained in preparation for their future tasks, that training was quite different. They were often taught to read the local language and perhaps some Latin and to write and do enough arithmetic to keep household accounts. They also learned music, dancing, and embroidery and how to ride and hunt, both common noble pursuits. Much of this training took place in the girl's own home, but, like boys, noble girls were often sent to the homes of relatives or higher nobles to act as servants or ladies in waiting or to learn how to run a household.

Parents often wanted to settle daughters' futures as soon as possible. Men tended to prefer young brides who would have more years to produce children. Therefore, aristocratic girls in the High Middle Ages were married at around the age of sixteen, often to much older men. In the early Middle Ages, the custom was for the groom to present a dowry to the bride and her family, but by the late twelfth century the process was reversed because men were in greater demand.

Power and Responsibility

A male member of the nobility became fully adult when he came into the possession of property. He then acquired authority over lands and people, protecting them from attack, maintaining order, and settling disputes.

Women played a large and important role in the functioning of the estate. They were responsible for the practical management of the household's "inner economy"—cooking, brewing, spinning, weaving, caring for yard animals. When the lord was away for long periods, the women frequently managed the herds, barns, granaries, and outlying fields as well. Often the responsibilities of the estate fell to them permanently as the number of men slain in medieval warfare ran high.

| What were the political and social roles of nobles? | How did the papacy reform the church? | What roles did monks, nuns, and friars play in medieval society? | What were the causes, course, and consequences of the Crusades? | ✓ LearningCurve Check what you know. |

253

The Lady and the Unicorn Tapestry This tapestry, woven in Flanders for a nobleman at the French court, expresses many of the ideals of noble life. A beautiful young woman stands in front of a tent with battle flags. On her right is a lion, symbol of earthly power. On her left is a unicorn, a beast that could be captured only by a virgin. Medieval people viewed the unicorn as an allegory both of Christ (who was "captured" by the Virgin Mary when he was born) and of an earthly lover tamed by his beloved. The enigmatic words on the top of the tent, French for "to my only desire," may refer to either spiritual or romantic love, for both were viewed as appropriate motivations for noble action. (Musée nationale du Moyen Âge et des Thermes de Cluny, Paris/Giraudon/The Bridgeman Art Library)

Throughout the High Middle Ages, fighting remained the dominant feature of the noble lifestyle. The church's preaching and condemnations reduced but did not stop violence, and the military values of the nobles' social class encouraged petty warfare and disorder. The nobility thus represented a constant source of trouble for the monarchy.

> **QUICK REVIEW**

How did the nobility's military function shape its values and lifestyle?

CHAPTER LOCATOR | How did monarchs try to centralize political power? | How did the administration of law evolve in this period?

KINGS AND EMPERORS were not the only rulers consolidating their power in the High Middle Ages. Popes did so as well, through a series of measures that made the church more independent of secular control. The popes' efforts were sometimes challenged by medieval kings and emperors, however, and the wealth of the church came under sharp criticism.

The Gregorian Reforms

During the ninth and tenth centuries, the local church had come under the control of kings and feudal lords, who chose priests and bishops in their territories, granting them land and expecting loyalty and service in return. Church offices were sources of income as well as positions of authority. Officeholders had the right to collect taxes and fees and often to the profits from the land under their control. Church offices were thus sometimes sold outright—a practice called **simony** (SIE-muh-nee). Not surprisingly, clergy at all levels who had bought their positions or had been granted them for political reasons provided little spiritual guidance, and their personal lives were rarely models of high moral standards. Although the Roman Church officially required men to be unmarried in order to be ordained, there were many married priests and others simply living with women. Popes were chosen by wealthy Roman families from among their members, and after gaining the papal office, they paid more attention to their families' political fortunes than to the health of the church.

Serious efforts to change all this began under Pope Leo IX (pontificate 1049–1054). Leo ordered clergy in Rome to dismiss their wives and invalidated the ordination of church officials who had purchased their offices. Pope Leo and several of his successors believed that secular or lay control over the church was largely responsible for its lack of moral leadership, so in a radical shift they proclaimed the church independent of secular rulers. The Lateran Council of 1059 decreed that the authority and power to elect the pope rested solely in the **college of cardinals**, a special group of priests from the major churches in and around Rome.

Leo's successor Pope Gregory VII (pontificate 1073–1085) was even more vigorous in his championing of reform and expansion of papal power. He denounced clerical marriage and simony in harsh language and ordered **excommunication**

simony
▶ The buying and selling of church offices, a policy that was officially prohibited but often practiced.

college of cardinals
▶ A special group of high clergy with the authority and power to elect the pope and the responsibility to govern the church when the office of the pope is vacant.

excommunication
▶ A penalty used by the Christian Church that meant being cut off from the sacraments and all Christian worship.

| What were the political and social roles of nobles? | **How did the papacy reform the church?** | What roles did monks, nuns, and friars play in medieval society? | What were the causes, course, and consequences of the Crusades? |  LearningCurve Check what you know. |

255

(being cut off from the sacraments and all Christian worship) for those who disagreed. He believed that the pope was the vicar of God on earth and that papal orders were thus the orders of God. Gregory was particularly opposed to lay investiture — the selection and appointment of church officials by secular authority. In February 1075, he held a council at Rome that decreed that clerics who accepted investiture from laymen were to be deposed and laymen who invested clerics were to be excommunicated.

In the late eleventh century and throughout the twelfth and thirteenth centuries, the papacy pressed Gregory's campaign for reform of the church. The popes held a series of councils, known as the Lateran Councils, that ratified decisions ending lay investiture, ordered bishops to live less extravagantly, and ordered married priests to give up their wives and children or face dismissal.

Gregory's reforms had a profound effect on nuns and other women in religious orders. The movement built a strict hierarchical church structure with bishops and priests higher in status than nuns, who could not be ordained. The double monasteries of the early Middle Ages were placed under the authority of male abbots. The reformers' emphasis on clerical celibacy and chastity led them to portray women as impure and lustful. Thus, in 1298, in the papal decree *Periculoso*, Pope Boniface VIII ordered all nuns to be strictly cloistered, that is, to remain permanently inside the walls of the convent, and for visits with people from outside the house, including family members, to be limited.

Emperor Versus Pope

Gregory thought that the threat of excommunication would compel rulers to abide by his move against lay investiture. Immediately, however, Henry IV in the Holy Roman Empire, William the Conqueror in England, and Philip I in France protested because the reform would deprive them not only of church income but also of the right to choose which monks and clerics would help them administer their kingdoms. The strongest reaction came from the Holy Roman Empire. Within the empire, religious and secular leaders took sides to pursue their own advantage. In January 1076, many of the German bishops who had been invested by Henry withdrew their allegiance from the pope. Gregory promptly suspended them and excommunicated Henry. The pope told German nobles they no longer owed allegiance to Henry, which obviously delighted them. When powerful nobles invited the pope to come to Germany to settle their dispute with Henry, Gregory traveled to the north. Christmas of 1076 thus witnessed an ironic situation in Germany: the clergy supported the emperor while the great nobility favored the pope.

Henry managed to outwit the pope temporarily. In January 1077, he approached the castle where the pope was staying. According to a letter later sent by Gregory to his German noble allies, Henry stood for three days in the snow, imploring the pope to lift the excommunication. Henry's pleas for forgiveness won him public sympathy, and the pope readmitted the emperor to the Christian community. When the sentence of excommunication was lifted, Henry regained the emperorship and authority over his rebellious subjects; however, he continued his moves against papal power. In 1080, Gregory again excommunicated and deposed the emperor. In return, when Gregory died in 1085, Henry invaded Italy and captured Rome. But Henry won no lasting victory. Gregory's successors encouraged Henry's sons to revolt against their father.

CHAPTER LOCATOR | How did monarchs try to centralize political power? | How did the administration of law evolve in this period?

CHAPTER 9
256   STATE AND CHURCH IN THE HIGH MIDDLE AGES

In 1122, at a conference held at Worms, the issue was settled by compromise. Bishops were to be chosen by the clergy. But since lay rulers were permitted to be present at ecclesiastical elections and to accept or refuse homage from the new prelates, they still possessed an effective veto over ecclesiastical appointments. Papal power was enhanced, but neither side won a clear victory.

The long controversy over lay investiture had tremendous social and political consequences in Germany. The lengthy struggle between papacy and emperor allowed emerging noble dynasties to enhance their position. When the papal-imperial conflict ended in 1122, the nobility held the balance of power in Germany, and later German kings, such as Frederick Barbarossa, would fail in their efforts to strengthen the monarchy. For these reasons, division and local independence characterized the Holy Roman Empire in the High Middle Ages.

Criticism and Heresy

The Gregorian reform movement contributed to dissatisfaction with the church among townspeople as well as monarchs. Papal moves against simony, for example, led to widespread concern about the role of money in the church. Papal efforts to improve the sexual morality of the clergy led some laypersons to assume they could, and indeed should, remove priests for any type of immorality.

Criticism of the church emerged in many places but found its largest audience in the cities, where the contrast between wealth and poverty could be seen more acutely. In northern Italian towns, the monk Arnold of Brescia (BREH-shah) (ca. 1090–1155) denounced clerical wealth. In France, Peter Waldo (ca. 1140–ca. 1218), a rich merchant of the city of Lyons, gave his money to the poor and preached that only prayers, not sacraments, were needed for salvation. The Waldensians (wawl-DEHN-shuhnz)—as Peter's followers were called—bitterly attacked the sacraments and church hierarchy, and they carried these ideas across Europe. In the towns and cities of southern France, the Albigensians (al-buh-JEHN-see-uhns), also known as the Cathars, used the teachings of Jesus about the evils of material goods to call for the church to give up its property. People who rejected worldly things, not wealthy bishops or the papacy, should be the religious leaders.

Critical of the clergy and spiritually unfulfilled, townspeople joined the Waldensians and the Albigensians. The papacy denounced supporters of both movements as heretics and began extensive campaigns to wipe them out. In 1208, Pope Innocent III proclaimed a crusade against the Albigensians, and the French monarchy and northern French knights willingly joined in, eager to gain the lands and wealth of southern French cities. After years of fighting, the leaders agreed to terms of peace, which left the French monarchy the primary beneficiary. Later popes sent inquisitors with the power to seek out and eliminate the remaining heretics.

The Popes and Church Law

Pope Urban II laid the foundations for the papal monarchy by reorganizing the papal *curia* (the central government of the Roman Church) and recognizing the college of cardinals as a definite consultative body. The papal curia had its greatest impact as a court of law. As the highest ecclesiastical tribunal, it formulated

What were the political and social roles of nobles?

How did the papacy reform the church?

What roles did monks, nuns, and friars play in medieval society?

What were the causes, course, and consequences of the Crusades?

☑ LearningCurve
Check what you know.

257

canon law

▶ Church law, which had its own courts and procedures.

church law, termed **canon law**. The church developed a system of courts separate from those of secular rulers that handled disputes over church property and ecclesiastical elections and especially questions of marriage and annulment. Most of the popes in the twelfth and thirteenth centuries were canon lawyers who expanded the authority of church courts.

The most famous of the lawyer-popes was Innocent III (pontificate 1198–1216), who became the most powerful pope in history. During his pontificate, the church in Rome declared itself to be supreme, united, and "catholic" (worldwide), responsible for the earthly well-being as well as the eternal salvation of Christians everywhere.

Innocent called the Fourth Lateran Council in 1215, which affirmed the idea that ordained priests had the power to transform bread and wine during church ceremonies into the body and blood of Christ (a change termed transubstantiation). According to papal doctrine, priests now had the power to mediate for everyone with God, setting the spiritual hierarchy of the church above the secular hierarchies of kings and other rulers.

By the early thirteenth century, papal efforts at reform begun more than a century earlier had attained phenomenal success, and the popes ruled a powerful, centralized institution. At the end of the century, however, the papacy again came into a violent dispute with secular rulers. Pope Boniface VIII (pontificate 1294–1303), arguing from precedent, insisted that King Edward I of England and Philip IV (also known as Philip the Fair) of France obtain his consent for taxes they had imposed on the clergy. Edward immediately denied the clergy the protection of the law, and Philip halted the shipment of all ecclesiastical revenue to Rome. Boniface had to back down.

The battle for power between the papacy and the French monarchy became a bitter war of propaganda, with Philip at one point calling the pope a heretic. In 1302, in a formal written statement known as a papal bull, Boniface insisted that all Christians—including kings—were subject to the pope. In retaliation, French mercenary troops assaulted and arrested the aged pope at Anagni in Italy. Although Boniface was soon freed, he died shortly afterward. The confrontation at Anagni foreshadowed further difficulties in the Christian Church in the fourteenth century.

> **QUICK REVIEW**

What were the primary goals of the Gregorian reform movement? To what extent were those goals achieved?

CHAPTER LOCATOR | How did monarchs try to centralize political power? | How did the administration of law evolve in this period?

258 CHAPTER 9
STATE AND CHURCH IN THE HIGH MIDDLE AGES

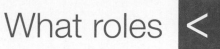

What roles did monks, nuns, and friars play in medieval society?

Saint Francis Gives up His Worldly Possessions
After Francis had given money to a church, his wealthy father ordered Francis to give him back the money. Francis instead took off all his clothes and returned them to his father, signifying his dependence on his father in Heaven rather than his earthly father. The fresco of this event, painted seventy years after Francis's death for the church erected in his honor in Assisi, captures the consternation of Francis's father and the confusion of the local bishop (holding the cloth in front of the naked Francis), who had told the young man to obey his earthly father. By the time the church was built, members of the Franciscan order were in violent disagreement over what Francis would have thought about a huge church built in his honor and other issues of clerical wealth. (San Francesco, Upper Church, Assisi/Giraudon/The Bridgeman Art Library)

MONKS, NUNS, AND FRIARS played significant roles in medieval society, both as individuals and as members of institutions. Medieval people believed that monks and nuns performed an important social service when they prayed for their prayers and chants secured God's blessing for society. The friars worked in the cities, teaching and preaching Christian doctrine but also investigating heretics.

What were the political and social roles of nobles?

How did the papacy reform the church?

What roles did monks, nuns, and friars play in medieval society?

What were the causes, course, and consequences of the Crusades?

✓ **LearningCurve** Check what you know.

Monastic Revival

religious orders

▸ Groups of monastic houses
following a particular rule.

In the early Middle Ages, many religious houses followed the Benedictine *Rule*, while others developed their own patterns (see Chapter 7, page 185). In the High Middle Ages, this diversity became more formalized, and **religious orders**, groups of monastic houses following a particular rule, were established. Historians term the foundation, strengthening, and reform of religious orders in the High Middle Ages the "monastic revival."

In the period of political disorder that followed the disintegration of the Carolingian Empire, many religious houses fell under the control and domination of local lords. Powerful laymen appointed themselves or their relatives as abbots, took the lands and goods of monasteries, and seized monastic revenues. Accordingly, the level of spiritual observance and intellectual activity in monasteries and convents declined. The first sign of reform came in 909, when William the Pious, duke of Aquitaine, established the abbey of Cluny in Burgundy. Duke William declared that the monastery was to be free from any feudal responsibilities to him or any other lord, its members subordinate only to the pope. The monastery at Cluny, which initially held high standards of religious behavior, came to exert vast religious influence. In the eleventh century, Cluny was fortunate to have a series of highly capable abbots who ruled for a long time. In a disorderly world, Cluny gradually came to represent stability. Therefore, laypersons placed lands under its custody and smaller monastic establishments under its jurisdiction. In this way, hundreds of religious houses, primarily in France and Spain, came under Cluny's authority.

Deeply impressed laypeople showered gifts on monasteries with good reputations. But as the monasteries became richer, the lifestyle of the monks grew increasingly luxurious. Monastic observance and spiritual fervor declined. Soon fresh demands for reform were heard, resulting in the founding of new religious orders in the late eleventh and early twelfth centuries.

The Cistercians (sihs-TUHR-shuhnz) best represent the new reforming spirit. In 1098, a group of monks left the rich abbey of Molesmes in Burgundy and founded a new house in the swampy forest of Cîteaux (see-TOH). The early Cistercians determined to keep their services simple and their lives austere, returning to work in the fields and other sorts of manual labor. As with Cluny, their high ideals made them a model, and 525 Cistercian monasteries were founded in the course of the twelfth century all over Europe. The Cistercians' influence on European society was profound because they used new agricultural methods and technology and spread them throughout Europe. Their advanced agricultural approach brought wealth; however, wealth brought power. By the later twelfth century, as with Cluny earlier, economic prosperity and political power had begun to compromise the original Cistercian ideals.

Life in Convents and Monasteries

Medieval monasteries were religious institutions whose organization and structure fulfilled the social needs of the nobility. The monasteries provided noble boys with education and opportunities for ecclesiastical careers. Beginning in the thirteenth century, an increasing number of boys and men from professional and

CHAPTER LOCATOR | How did monarchs try to centralize political power? | How did the administration of law evolve in this period?

merchant families became monks, seeking to take advantage of the opportunities monasteries offered.

Throughout the Middle Ages, social class also defined the kinds of religious life open to women. Kings and nobles usually established convents for their daughters, sisters, aunts, aging mothers, and other women of their class. Like monks, many nuns came into the convent as children.

The office of abbess or prioress was the most powerful position a woman could hold in medieval society. (See "Individuals in Society: Hildegard of Bingen," page 262.) Abbesses were part of the political structure in the same way that bishops and abbots were, with manors under their financial and legal control. Some abbesses in the Holy Roman Empire even had the right to name bishops and send representatives to imperial assemblies. Abbesses also opened and supported hospitals, orphanages, and schools and hired builders, sculptors, and painters to construct and decorate residences and churches.

Monasteries for men were headed by an abbot or prior, who was generally a member of a noble family, often a younger son in a family with several sons. The main body of monks, known as "choir monks" because one of their primary activities was reciting prayers and services while sitting in the part of the church called the choir, were largely of noble or middle-class background and did not till the land themselves. Men from peasant families sometimes became choir monks, but more often they served as lay brothers, doing the manual labor essential to running the monastery. The novice master or novice mistress was responsible for the training of recruits.

The pattern of life within individual monasteries varied widely from one to another and from region to region. One central activity, however, was performed everywhere. Daily life centered on the liturgy or Divine Office, psalms and other prayers offered seven times a day and once during the night. Prayers were offered for peace, rain, good harvests,

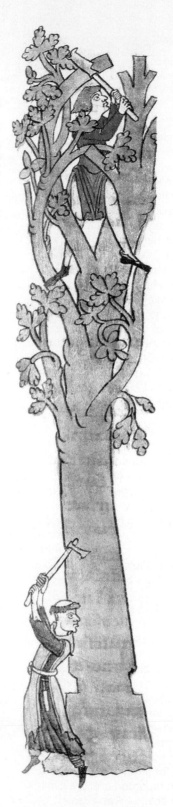

Monastery and Convent Life

Life in monasteries and convents involved physical labor as well as spiritual activities. In this twelfth-century French manuscript, a monk and a lay brother chop down a tree. Such work was a common part of monastic life because monasteries, especially those of the Cistercians, were often built in heavily forested wilderness areas. (Bibliothèque municipale, Dijon, France, Ms 173 f 41/The Bridgeman Art Library)

What were the political and social roles of nobles?

How did the papacy reform the church?

What roles did monks, nuns, and friars play in medieval society?

What were the causes, course, and consequences of the Crusades?

✓ LearningCurve
Check what you know.

The tenth child of a lesser noble family, Hildegard (1098–1179) was given as a child to an abbey in the Rhineland when she was eight years old; there she learned Latin and received a good education. She spent most of her life in various women's religious communities, two of which she founded herself. When she was a child, she began having mystical visions, often of light in the sky, but told few people about them. In middle age, however, her visions became more dramatic: "And it came to pass . . . when I was 42 years and 7 months old, that the heavens were opened and a blinding light of exceptional brilliance flowed through my entire brain. And so it kindled my whole heart and breast like a flame, not burning but warming . . . and suddenly I understood of the meaning of expositions of the books."* She wanted the church to approve of her visions and wrote first to Bernard of Clairvaux, who answered her briefly and dismissively, and then to Pope Eugenius, who encouraged her to write them down. Her first work was *Scivias* (Know the Ways of the Lord), a record of her mystical visions that incorporates vast theological learning.

Possessed of leadership and administrative talents, Hildegard left her abbey in 1147 to found the convent of Rupertsberg near Bingen. There she produced *Physica* (On the Physical Elements) and *Causa et Curae* (Causes and Cures), scientific works on the curative properties of natural elements, as well as poems, a mystery play, and several more works of mysticism. She carried on a huge correspondence with scholars, prelates, and ordinary people. When she was over fifty, she left her community to preach to audiences of clergy and laity, and she was the only woman of her time whose opinions on religious matters were considered authoritative by the church.

Hildegard's visions have been explored by theologians and also by neurologists, who judge that they may have originated in migraine headaches because she reports many of the same phenomena that migraine sufferers do: auras of light around objects, areas of blindness, feelings of intense doubt and intense euphoria. The interpretations that she develops come from her theological insight and learning, however, not illness. That same insight also emerges in her music, for which she is best known today. Eighty of her compositions survive — a huge number for a medieval composer — most of them written to be sung by the nuns in her convent, so they have strong lines for female voices. Many of her songs and chants have been recorded and are available on CD, as downloads, and on several Web sites.

Inspired by heavenly fire, Hildegard begins to dictate her visions to her scribe. The original of this elaborately illustrated twelfth-century copy of *Scivias* disappeared from Hildegard's convent during World War II, but fortunately a facsimile copy had already been made. (Private Collection/The Bridgeman Art Library)

QUESTIONS FOR ANALYSIS

1. Why do you think Hildegard sought church approval for her visions after keeping them secret for so many years?
2. In what ways is Hildegard's life representative of nuns' lives in the High Middle Ages? In what ways were her accomplishments extraordinary?

⫽ LaunchPad

ONLINE DOCUMENT PROJECT

How did Hildegard of Bingen come to be seen as a worthy instrument for the transmission of God's word? Keeping the question above in mind, read excerpts from her correspondence and note the qualities that appealed to so many of her contemporaries. Then complete a writing assignment based on the evidence and details from this chapter. *See inside the front cover to learn more.*

*From *Scivias*, trans. Mother Columba Hart and Jane Bishop, *The Classics of Western Spirituality* (New York/Mahwah: Paulist Press, 1990), p. 65.

the civil authorities, and the monks' families and benefactors. Everything connected with prayer was understood as praise of God, so abbeys spent a large percentage of their income on splendid objects to enhance the service.

In some abbeys, monks and nuns spent much of their time copying books and manuscripts and then illuminating them, decorating them with human and animal figures or elaborate designs. A few monasteries and convents became centers of learning where talented residents wrote their own works as well as copying those of others.

Monks and nuns also performed a variety of social services in an age when there was no state and no conception of social welfare as a public responsibility. Monasteries often ran schools that gave primary education to young boys; convents did the same for girls. Monasteries served as hotels and resting places for travelers, and frequently operated hospitals that provided care and attention to the sick, the aged, and the afflicted.

The Friars

Monks and nuns carried out their spiritual and social services largely within the walls of their institutions, but in the thirteenth century, new types of religious orders were founded whose members lived out in the world. Members of these new groups were **friars**, not monks. Friars stressed apostolic poverty, a life based on the teaching of the Gospels in which they would own no property and depend on Christian people for their material needs. The friars' service to the towns and the poor, their ideal of poverty, and their compassion for the human condition made them popular.

friars
▶ Men belonging to certain religious orders who did not live in monasteries but out in the world.

One order of friars was started by Domingo de Gúzman (1170?–1221), born in Castile. Domingo (later called Dominic), a well-educated priest, accompanied his bishop in 1206 on an unsuccessful mission to win the Albigensians in southern France back to orthodox teaching. Determined to succeed through ardent preaching, he subsequently returned to France with a few followers. In 1216, the Dominicans won papal recognition as a new religious order.

Francesco di Bernardone (1181–1226), son of a wealthy Italian cloth merchant of Assisi, had a religious conversion and decided to live and preach the Gospel in absolute poverty. Francis of Assisi, as he came to be known, did not emphasize withdrawal from the world but joyful devotion. In contrast to the Albigensians, who saw the material world as evil, Francis saw all creation as God-given and good.

The simplicity, humility, and joyful devotion with which Francis carried out his mission soon attracted others. Although he resisted pressure to establish an order, his followers became so numerous that he was obliged to develop some formal structure. In 1221, the papacy approved the Rule of the Little Brothers of Saint Francis, generally called the Franciscans (frahn-SIHS-kuhnz).

Friars worked among the poor but also addressed the spiritual and intellectual needs of the middle classes and the wealthy. The Dominicans preferred that their friars be university graduates in order to better preach to a sophisticated urban society. Dominicans soon held professorial chairs at leading universities, and the Franciscans followed suit.

Beginning in 1231, the papacy also used friars to investigate heretics, sometimes under the auspices of a new ecclesiastical court, the Inquisition.

What were the political and social roles of nobles?

How did the papacy reform the church?

What roles did monks, nuns, and friars play in medieval society?

What were the causes, course, and consequences of the Crusades?

✔ LearningCurve
Check what you know.

Women sought to develop similar orders devoted to active service out in the world. Clare of Assisi (1193–1253) became a follower of Francis, who established a place for her to live in a church in Assisi. She was joined by other women, and they attempted to establish a rule that would follow Francis's ideals of absolute poverty and allow them to serve the poor. This rule was accepted by the papacy only after many decades, and then only because Clare agreed that the order, the Poor Clares, would be cloistered.

In the growing cities of Europe, especially in the Netherlands, groups of laywomen seeking to live religious lives came together in groups that later came to be known as Beguines (bay-GEENS). They lived communally, combining lives of prayer with service to the needy. Beguine spirituality emphasized direct personal communication with God, sometimes through mystical experiences, rather than through the intercession of a saint or official church rituals. Initially some church officials gave guarded approval of the movement, but the church grew increasingly uncomfortable with women who were neither married nor cloistered nuns. By the fourteenth century, beguines were declared heretical, and much of their property was confiscated.

> New Religious Orders

Cistercians	Emphasized austerity and manual labor; helped spread new agricultural methods and technology
Dominicans	Order of friars focused on scholarship, preaching, and combatting heresy
Franciscans	Order of friars that emphasized poverty and work among the poor
Poor Clares	Founded by Clare of Assisi, a follower of Francis; established by papacy after Clare accepted that the new order would be cloistered
Beguines	Groups of laywomen who lived communally and emphasized direct personal communication with God; suppressed in the fourteenth century

> QUICK REVIEW

How and why did monasticism change over the course of the High Middle Ages?

CHAPTER LOCATOR | How did monarchs try to centralize political power? | How did the administration of law evolve in this period?

CHAPTER 9
264 STATE AND CHURCH IN THE HIGH MIDDLE AGES

The Capture of Jerusalem in 1099

In this illustration from a fourteenth-century French version of Archbishop William of Tyre's history of the First Crusade, Crusaders enter the city of Jerusalem on scaling ladders as engines hurl stones to breach the walls. (Bibliothèque nationale de France)

What were the causes, course, and consequences of the Crusades?

> PICTURING THE PAST

ANALYZING THE IMAGE: What do you think the artist's point of view is about the events shown? Would you characterize the painting as a positive or negative depiction of war? What does this suggest about the artist's motives in creating this work?

CONNECTIONS: How might the images shown be different if this had been drawn by a Muslim artist living in Jerusalem?

THE CRUSADES OF THE ELEVENTH AND TWELFTH CENTURIES were the most obvious manifestation of the papal claim to the leadership of Christian society. The **Crusades** were wars sponsored by the papacy for the recovery of the holy city of Jerusalem from the Muslims. The enormous popular response to papal calls for crusading reveals the influence of the reformed papacy and the depth of religious fervor among many different types of people. The Crusades also reflected the church's new understanding of the noble warrior class, for whom war against the church's enemies was understood as a religious duty.

Crusades

▶ Wars sponsored by the papacy for the recovery of Jerusalem and surrounding territories from the Muslims, from the late eleventh to the late thirteenth centuries.

What were the political and social roles of nobles?	How did the papacy reform the church?	What roles did monks, nuns, and friars play in medieval society?	**What were the causes, course, and consequences of the Crusades?**	LearningCurve Check what you know.

Background and Motives of the Crusades

Although conflicts in which Christians fought Christians were troubling to many thinkers, war against non-Christians was another matter. By the ninth century, popes and other church officials encouraged war in defense of Christianity, promising spiritual benefits to those who died fighting. By the eleventh century, these benefits were extended to all those who simply joined a campaign. Around this time, Christian thinkers were developing the concept of purgatory, a place where those on their way to Heaven stayed to do any penance they had not completed while alive. Engaging in holy war could shorten one's time in purgatory, or, as many people understood the promise, allow one to head straight to paradise. Popes signified this by providing **indulgences**, grants with the pope's name on them that lessened earthly penance and postmortem purgatory. Preachers communicated these ideas widely and told stories about warrior-saints who slew hundreds of enemies.

indulgences
▶ Grants by the pope that lessened or eliminated the penance that sinners had to pay on earth and in purgatory before ascending to Heaven.

In the midst of these developments came a change in possession of Jerusalem. The Arabic Muslims who had ruled Jerusalem and the surrounding territory for centuries had allowed Christian pilgrims to travel freely, but in the late eleventh century, the Seljuk (SEHL-jook) Turks took over Palestine, defeating both Arabic and Byzantine armies (**Map 9.4**). The emperor at Constantinople appealed to the West for support, asserting that the Turks would make pilgrimages to holy places more dangerous and that the holy city of Jerusalem should be in Christian hands. The emperor's appeal fit well with papal aims, and in 1095, Pope Urban II called for a great Christian holy war. Urban offered indulgences to those who would fight for and regain the holy city of Jerusalem.

The Course of the Crusades

Thousands of Western Christians of all classes joined the First Crusade, which began in 1096. The First Crusade was successful, mostly because of the dynamic enthusiasm of the participants. The Crusaders had little more than religious zeal. They knew nothing about the geography or climate of the Middle East. Although there were several nobles with military experience among them, the Crusaders could never agree on a leader, and the entire expedition was marked by disputes among the great lords. Lines of supply were never set up, and starvation and disease wracked the army. Nevertheless, the army pressed on, defeating the Turks in several land battles and besieging a few larger towns. In 1099, three years after departing Europe, the Crusaders reached Jerusalem. (See "Picturing the Past: The Capture of Jerusalem in 1099," page 265.) After a month-long siege, they entered the city, where they slaughtered the Muslim defenders.

In the aftermath of the First Crusade, four small Crusader kingdoms—Jerusalem, Edessa, Tripoli, and Antioch—were established (see Map 9.4, page 267). Between 1096 and 1270, the crusading ideal was expressed in eight papally approved expeditions, though none after the First Crusade accomplished very much. Despite this lack of success, members of European noble families from nearly every generation took up the cross for roughly two hundred years.

The Crusades inspired the establishment of new religious orders, particularly military orders dedicated to protecting the Christian kingdoms. The most important was the Knights Templars, founded in 1119. Many people going to the Holy

CHAPTER LOCATOR | How did monarchs try to centralize political power? | How did the administration of law evolve in this period?

CHAPTER 9
266 STATE AND CHURCH IN THE HIGH MIDDLE AGES

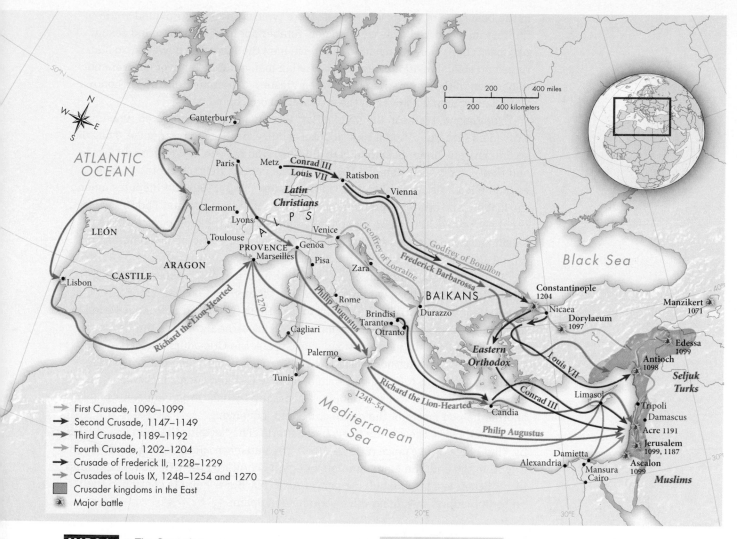

MAP 9.4 ■ The Crusades

This map shows the many different routes that Western Christians took over the centuries to reach Jerusalem.

> **MAPPING THE PAST**

ANALYZING THE MAP: How were the results of the various Crusades shaped by the routes that the Crusaders took?

CONNECTIONS: How did the routes and Crusader kingdoms offer opportunities for profit?

Land put their property in Europe under Templar protection, and by the end of the thirteenth century the order was extremely wealthy. The Templars began serving as moneylenders and bankers, which further increased their wealth. In 1307, King Philip IV of France sought to grab that wealth for himself; he arrested many Templars, accusing them of heresy, blasphemy, and sodomy. They were tortured, a number were burned at the stake. Philip took much of their money, and the Templars were disbanded.

Women from all walks of life participated in the Crusades. When King Louis IX of France was captured on the Seventh Crusade (1248–1254), his wife Queen Marguerite negotiated the surrender of the Egyptian city of Damietta to the Muslims. Some women concealed their sex and fought with the knights. Some joined

| What were the political and social roles of nobles? | How did the papacy reform the church? | What roles did monks, nuns, and friars play in medieval society? | **What were the causes, course, and consequences of the Crusades?** | ✓ LearningCurve Check what you know. |

in the besieging of towns and castles. More typically, women provided water to fighting men, worked as washerwomen, foraged for food, and provided sexual services. There were many more European men than women, however, so marriage and sexual relations between Christian men and Muslim women were not unheard of, although marriages between Western Christian men and Orthodox Christian women who lived in the area were more common.

The Muslim states in the Middle East were politically fragmented when the Crusaders first came, and it took about a century for them to reorganize. They did so dramatically under Saladin (Salah al-Dihn), who first unified Egypt and Syria and then retook Jerusalem in 1187. Christians immediately attempted to take it back in what was later called the Third Crusade (1189–1192), but disputes among the leaders and strategic problems prevented any lasting results. The Crusaders could not retake Jerusalem, though they did keep their hold on port towns, and Saladin allowed pilgrims safe passage to Jerusalem. He also made an agreement with Christian rulers for keeping the peace.

In 1202, Innocent III sent out preachers who called on Christian knights to retake Jerusalem. Those who responded—in what would become the Fourth Crusade—negotiated with the Venetians to take them by boat to Cairo, but Venetian interests combined with a succession struggle over the Byzantine throne led the fleet to go to Constantinople instead. Once there, the Crusaders decided to capture and sack Constantinople. The Byzantines reasserted their control over the empire in 1261, but it was much smaller and weaker and soon consisted of little more than the city of Constantinople. The assault by one Christian people on another helped discredit the entire crusading movement.

Nonetheless, there were a few more efforts. The Seventh Crusade in 1248, led by King Louis IX of France (r. 1223–1270), tried unsuccessfully to come in through Egypt. In the end, the Mamluk rulers of Egypt conquered the Crusader states, and in 1291 their last stronghold, the port of Acre, fell. Some knights continued their crusading efforts by joining the reconquista in Spain.

Consequences of the Crusades

The Crusades gave kings and the pope opportunities to expand their bureaucracies. They also provided kings with the perfect opportunity to get rid of troublemaking knights, particularly restless younger sons. Even some members of the middle class who stayed at home profited from the Crusades. Nobles often had to borrow money from city residents to pay for their expeditions, and they put up part of their land as security. If a noble did not return home or could not pay the interest on the loan, the middle-class creditor took over the land.

The Crusades introduced some Europeans to Eastern luxury goods, but their immediate cultural impact on the West remains debatable. Strong economic and intellectual ties with the East had already been developed by the late eleventh century. The Crusades did greatly benefit Italian merchants, who profited from outfitting military expeditions, the opening of new trade routes, and the establishment of trading communities in the Crusader states. Since commerce with the West benefited both Muslims and Europeans, it continued to flourish even after the Crusader states collapsed.

The Crusades proved to be a disaster for Jewish-Christian relations. In many parts of Europe, Jews lent money, and indebtedness bred resentment. Inspired by

CHAPTER LOCATOR | How did monarchs try to centralize political power? | How did the administration of law evolve in this period?

CHAPTER 9
268 STATE AND CHURCH IN THE HIGH MIDDLE AGES

the ideology of holy war and resentment of Jewish economic activities, Christian armies on their way to Jerusalem during the First Crusade joined with local people to attack Jewish families and sometimes entire Jewish communities. In the German cities along the Rhine River, for example, an army of Crusaders under the leadership of a German noble forced Jews to convert through mass baptisms and killed those who resisted; more than eight hundred Jews were killed in Worms and more than a thousand in Mainz. Later Crusades brought similar violence. As a result of growing hostility, legal restrictions on Jews gradually increased throughout Europe. In 1290, King Edward I of England expelled the Jews from England, and King Philip IV of France followed Edward's example in 1306. The Crusades also left a legacy of deep bitterness between Christians and Muslims. Each side dehumanized the other.

At the same time, the Crusades shaped the identity of the West. They represent the first great colonizing movement beyond the geographical boundaries of Europe. The ideal of a sacred mission to conquer or convert Muslim peoples entered Europeans' consciousness and became a continuing goal. When Christopher Columbus sailed west in 1492, he hoped to reach India in part to establish a Christian base from which a new crusade against Islam could be launched.

The Expansion of Christianity

The Crusades had a profound impact on both Europe and the Middle East, but they were not the only example of Christian expansion in the High Middle Ages. As we saw earlier, Christian kingdoms were established in the Iberian Peninsula through the reconquista. This gradual Christian advance was replicated in northern and eastern Europe in the centuries after 1000. People and ideas moved from western France and western Germany into Ireland, Scandinavia, the Baltic lands, and eastern Europe, with significant consequences for those territories.

Ireland had been Christian since the days of Saint Patrick (see Chapter 7, page 200), but in the twelfth century, Norman knights crossed from England, defeated Irish lords, and established bishoprics with defined territorial dioceses. Latin Christian influences also entered the Scandinavian and Baltic regions primarily through the establishment of dioceses. Otto I established the first Scandinavian dioceses in Denmark. In Norway, Christianity spread in coastal areas beginning in the tenth century, and King Olaf II (r. 1015–1028) brought in clergy and bishops from England and Germany to establish the church more firmly. From Norway, Christianity spread to Iceland; from Denmark, it spread to Sweden and Finland. In all of these areas, royal power advanced institutional Christianity, and traditional Norse religions practiced by the Vikings were outlawed.

In eastern Europe, the German emperor Otto I planted a string of dioceses along his northern and eastern frontiers, hoping to pacify the newly conquered Slavs. German nobles built castles and ruthlessly crushed revolts by Slavic peoples, sometimes using the language of crusade to describe their actions. A military order of German knights founded in Palestine, the Teutonic (too-TAH-nihk) Knights, moved their operations to eastern Europe and waged wars against the pagan Prussians in the Baltic region. After 1230, from a base in Poland, they established a new Christian territory, Prussia, and gradually the entire eastern shore of the Baltic came under their hegemony.

What were the political and social roles of nobles?

How did the papacy reform the church?

What roles did monks, nuns, and friars play in medieval society?

What were the causes, course, and consequences of the Crusades?

✓ LearningCurve
Check what you know.

269

The church also moved into central Europe, first in Bohemia in the tenth century and from there into Poland and Hungary in the eleventh. In the twelfth and thirteenth centuries, thousands of settlers poured into eastern Europe. These immigrants were German in descent, name, language, and law.

Christendom

Christendom

▶ The term used by early medieval writers to refer to the realm of Christianity.

Through the actions of the Roman emperors Constantine and Theodosius (see Chapter 7, page 180), Christianity became in some ways a state as well as a religion. Early medieval writers began to use the word **Christendom** to refer to this Christian realm. When the pope called for holy war against the Muslims, for example, he spoke not only of the retaking of Jerusalem, but also of the defense of Christendom. When missionaries, officials, and soldiers took Christianity into pagan regions, they understood their actions to be aimed at the expansion of Christendom.

From the point of view of popes such as Gregory VII and Innocent III, Christendom was a unified hierarchy with the papacy at the top. They pushed for uniformity of religious worship and campaigned continually for use of the same religious service: the Roman liturgy in Latin, in all countries and places. As we have seen in this chapter, however, not everyone had the same view. Kings and emperors may have accepted the Roman liturgy in their lands, but they had their own ideas of the way power should operate in Christendom, even if this brought them into conflict with the papacy. They remained loyal to Christendom as a concept, but they had a profoundly different idea about how it should be structured and who could best defend it. The battles in the High Middle Ages between popes and kings and between Christians and Muslims were signs of how deeply religion had replaced tribal, political, and ethnic structures as the essence of Western culture.

> **QUICK REVIEW**

How did the Crusades shape the way European Christians saw themselves and their relationship to the larger world?

CHAPTER LOCATOR | How did monarchs try to centralize political power? | How did the administration of law evolve in this period?

CHAPTER 9
270   STATE AND CHURCH IN THE HIGH MIDDLE AGES

LOOKING BACK
LOOKING AHEAD

The High Middle Ages were a time when kings, emperors, and popes expanded their powers and created financial and legal bureaucracies to support those powers. Nobles remained the dominant social group, but as monarchs developed new institutions, their kingdoms began to function more like modern states than disorganized territories. Popes made the church more independent of lay control, established the papal curia and a separate system of canon law, approved new religious orders that provided spiritual and social services, and developed new ways of raising revenue. They supported the expansion of Christianity in southern, northern, and eastern Europe and proclaimed a series of Crusades against Muslims to extend still further the boundaries of a Christendom under their control.

Many of the systems of the High Middle Ages expanded in later centuries and are still in existence today. These systems also contained the seeds of future problems, however, because wealthier nations could sustain longer wars, independent popes could abuse their power more easily, and leaders who espoused crusading ideology could justify the enslavement or extermination of whole peoples.

⊨LaunchPad

ONLINE DOCUMENT PROJECT
Hildegard of Bingen

How did Hildegard of Bingen come to be seen as a worthy instrument for the transmission of God's word?

You encountered Hildegard of Bingen's story on page 262. Keeping the question above in mind, read excerpts from her correspondence and note the qualities that appealed to so many of her contemporaries. *See inside the front cover to learn more.*

| What were the political and social roles of nobles? | How did the papacy reform the church? | What roles did monks, nuns, and friars play in medieval society? | What were the causes, course, and consequences of the Crusades? | ✔ LearningCurve Check what you know. |

CHAPTER 9 STUDY GUIDE

 **STEP 1** GET STARTED ONLINE

 LearningCurve

Now that you've read the chapter, make it stick by completing the LearningCurve activity.

STEP 2 EXPLAIN WHY IT MATTERS

Put your reading into practice. Identify each term below, and then explain why it matters in Western history.

TERM	WHO OR WHAT & WHEN	WHY IT MATTERS
Domesday Book (p. 244)		
primogeniture (p. 244)		
Holy Roman Empire (p. 245)		
reconquista (p. 248)		
common law (p. 250)		
Magna Carta (p. 250)		
chivalry (p. 253)		
simony (p. 255)		
college of cardinals (p. 255)		
excommunication (p. 255)		
canon law (p. 258)		
religious orders (p. 260)		
friars (p. 263)		
Crusades (p. 265)		
indulgences (p. 266)		
Christendom (p. 270)		

 STEP 3 MOVE BEYOND THE BASICS

To demonstrate a more advanced understanding of the politics of the High Middle Ages, complete the chart below to compare and contrast efforts at political centralization in England, France, Central Europe, Italy, and Iberia. Where were centralization efforts most and least successful? Why?

England	France	Central Europe	Italy	Iberia

PUT IT ALL TOGETHER Now, take a step back and try to explain the big picture. Remember to use specific examples from the chapter in your answers.

THE STATE IN THE HIGH MIDDLE AGES

▶ Compare and contrast monarchical efforts at political centralization in England and France. How would you explain the differences you note?

▶ How did medieval monarchs use legal and judicial reforms to enhance their power?

THE CHURCH IN THE HIGH MIDDLE AGES

▶ What steps did reforming popes take to enhance the power and prestige of the church? Who resisted their efforts and why?

▶ What were the guiding principles of the monastic reform movement? How would you explain the movement's success?

THE CRUSADES AND THE EXPANSION OF CHRISTENDOM

▶ What were the most important consequences of the Crusades?

▶ What role did military force play in the expansion of Christendom in the Middle Ages?

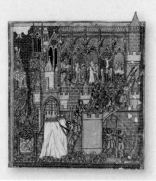

MAKE CONNECTIONS

▶ How did the monarchs of the High Middle Ages build on the accomplishments of their early medieval predecessors?

▶ How did medieval monarchs lay the foundation of modern national states?

> **IN YOUR OWN WORDS**

Imagine that you must give an oral report to the class answering the following question: **What steps did monarchs take to increase their power and authority during the High Middle Ages? What would be the most important points and why?**

10

LIFE IN VILLAGES AND CITIES OF THE HIGH MIDDLE AGES

1000–1300

> **How and why did life change over the course of the High Middle Ages?** Chapter 10 examines the lives of ordinary people during the High Middle Ages. During this period, agricultural improvements led to population growth. Relative security and the increasing food supply allowed for the growth and development of towns and a revival of long-distance trade. Cities developed into intellectual and cultural centers, and the university, a new type of educational institution, came into being. Traditions and values were spread orally and in written form through poems, stories, and songs. Gothic cathedrals were physical manifestations of medieval people's deep faith and pride in their own community.

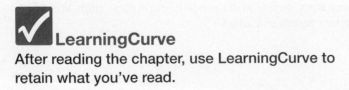

LearningCurve
After reading the chapter, use LearningCurve to retain what you've read.

> What was village life like in medieval Europe?

> How did religion shape everyday life in the High Middle Ages?

> What led to Europe's economic growth and reurbanization?

> What was life like in medieval cities?

> How did universities serve the needs of medieval society?

> How did literature and architecture express medieval values?

Life in the High Middle Ages. In this scene from a German manuscript, the artist shows men and women of different ages sowing seed and harvesting grain. (Rheinisches Landesmuseum, Bonn/ The Bridgeman Art Library)

> What was village life like in medieval Europe?

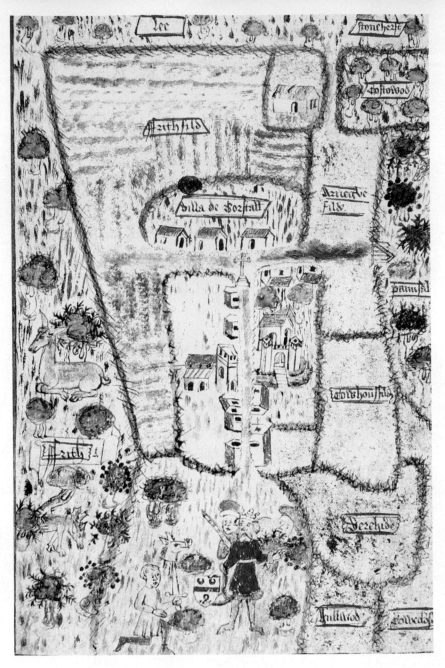

Boarstall Manor, Buckinghamshire

In 1440, Edmund Rede, lord of this estate, had a map made showing his ancestor receiving the title from King Edward I (bottom). Note the manor house, church, and peasants' cottages along the central road. In the common fields, divided by hedges, peasants cultivated on a three-year rotation cycle: winter wheat, spring oats, a year fallow. We don't know whether peasants were allowed to hunt the deer shown in the forest. (Buckinghamshire Record Office, Aylesbury)

THE VAST MAJORITY OF PEOPLE IN MEDIEVAL EUROPE were peasants who lived in small villages and rarely traveled very far, and the aristocratic monks and clerics who wrote the records that serve as historical sources did not spend much time on the peasantry. Today's scholars are far more interested than were their medieval predecessors in the lives of ordinary people, however, and are using archaeological, artistic, and material sources to fill in details that are rarely mentioned in written documents.

CHAPTER LOCATOR | **What was village life like in medieval Europe?** | How did religion shape everyday life in the High Middle Ages?

1050–1300
- Steady rise in population; period of milder climate

ca. 1100
- Merchant guilds become rich and powerful in many cities; artisans begin to found craft guilds

1100–1300
- Height of construction of cathedrals in Europe

1100s
- Hospitals and other homes for the sick begin appearing

1160s
- Silver mines opened in Germany, allowing for more coinage

ca. 1200
- Founding of first universities

1215
- Fourth Lateran Council orders Jews and Muslims to wear distinctive clothing

1225–1274
- Life of Thomas Aquinas; *Summa Theologica*

1241
- Contract between Lübeck and Hamburg, first in the Hanseatic League

ca. 1300
- Bill of exchange becomes most common method of commercial payment in western Europe

1300s
- Clocks in general use throughout Europe

Slavery, Serfdom, and Upward Mobility

There were many levels of peasants, ranging from outright slaves to free but poor peasants, to very rich farmers. The number of slaves who worked the land declined steadily in the High Middle Ages, and most rural people in western Europe during this period were serfs rather than slaves, though the distinction between slave and serf was not always clear. Both lacked freedom and both were subject to the arbitrary will of one person, the manorial lord. Serfs remained bound to the land when their lords died, but unlike slaves they could not be bought and sold outright.

Most serfs worked small plots of land; in addition, all serfs were required to provide a certain number of days of labor a week on a lord's land. Serfs were also often obliged to pay fees on common occurrences, such as marriage or the inheritance of land from one generation to the next. Serfdom was a hereditary condition. As money became more widely available, however, some serfs bought their freedom.

The Manor

Most peasants, free and serf, lived in family groups in small villages. One or more villages and the land surrounding them made up a manor controlled by a noble lord or a church official. Most villages had a church. In some villages, the lord's large residence was right next to the small peasant houses, while in others the lord lived in a castle or manor house separate from the village. Manors varied greatly in size; some contained a number of villages, and some were very small.

The arable land of the manor was divided between the lord and the peasantry, with the lord's portion known as the demesne (dih-MAYN). The manor usually also held pasture or meadowland for grazing livestock and often had some forestland as well. Forests were valuable resources, providing wood, ash, and resin for a variety of purposes.

What led to Europe's economic growth and reurbanization? | What was life like in medieval cities? | How did universities serve the needs of medieval society? | How did literature and architecture express medieval values? | LearningCurve Check what you know.

277

Lords generally appointed officials to oversee the legal and business operations of their manors, collect taxes and fees, and handle disputes. Villages in many parts of Europe also developed institutions of self-government to handle issues such as crop rotation, and villagers themselves chose additional officials. Women had no official voice in running the village, but they did buy, sell, and hold land independently, especially as widows who headed households. In areas of Europe where men left seasonally or more permanently in search of work elsewhere, women played a larger decision-making role, though they generally did not hold official positions.

Manors did not represent the only form of medieval rural economy. In parts of Germany and the Netherlands and in much of southern France, free independent farmers owned land outright, free of rents and service obligations. In Scandinavia, the soil was so poor and the climate so harsh that people tended to live on widely scattered farms rather than in villages.

Work

The peasants' work was typically divided according to gender. Men cleared new land, plowed, and cared for large animals; women cared for small animals, spun yarn, and prepared food. Both sexes planted and harvested.

Once children were able to walk, they helped their parents in the hundreds of chores that had to be done. Small children collected eggs if the family had chickens or gathered twigs and sticks for firewood. As they grew older, children had more responsible tasks, such as weeding the family's vegetable garden, milking the cows, and helping with the planting or harvesting.

open-field system
▶ System in which the arable land of a manor was divided into two or three fields without hedges or fences to mark individual holdings.

In many parts of Europe, medieval farmers employed the **open-field system**, in which the arable land of a manor was divided into two or three fields without hedges or fences to mark the individual holdings of the lord, serfs, and free men. The village as a whole decided what would be planted in each field, rotating the crops according to tradition and need. Some fields would be planted with crops such as wheat, rye, peas, or barley for human consumption, some with oats or other crops for both animals and humans, and some left unworked or fallow to allow the soil to rejuvenate. In most areas with open-field agriculture, the holdings farmed by any one family did not consist of a whole field but consisted instead of strips in many fields. Families worked their own land and the lord's, but also cooperated with other families if they needed help, particularly during harvest time.

Meteorologists think that a slow but steady retreat of polar ice occurred between the ninth and eleventh centuries, and Europe experienced a significant warming trend from 1050 to 1300. The mild winters and dry summers that resulted helped increase agricultural output throughout Europe, particularly in the north.

The tenth and eleventh centuries also witnessed a number of agricultural improvements. Mills driven by wind and water power dramatically reduced the time and labor required to grind grain, crush seeds for oil, and carry out other tasks. Another change, which came in the early twelfth century, was a significant increase in the production of iron. Much of this was used for weapons and armor,

CHAPTER LOCATOR | What was village life like in medieval Europe? | How did religion shape everyday life in the High Middle Ages?

CHAPTER 10
278 LIFE IN VILLAGES AND CITIES OF THE HIGH MIDDLE AGES

Ox Team Plowing From an eleventh-century calendar showing manorial occupations, this illustration for January — the time for sowing winter wheat — shows two pairs of oxen pulling a wheeled plow. Wheeled plows allowed for faster work and deeper tillage but still required large inputs of human labor. Here one man prods the animals, a second directs the plow blade, and a third drops seed in the ground. (© The British Library Board, Cott. Tib. B. V. 3, Min. Pt 1)

but it also filled a growing demand in agriculture. Iron was first used for plowshares (the part of the plow that cuts a deep furrow), and then for pitchforks, spades, and axes.

In central and northern Europe, peasants made increasing use of heavy wheeled iron plows pulled by teams of oxen to break up the rich, clay-filled soil common there, and agricultural productivity increased. Further technological improvements allowed horses to be used for plowing as well as oxen. The development of the padded horse collar that rested on the horse's shoulders and was attached to the load by shafts meant that the animal could put its entire weight into the task of pulling.

By modern standards, medieval agricultural yields were very low, but there was striking improvement between the fifth and the thirteenth centuries. Increased output had a profound impact on society, improving Europeans' health, commerce, industry, and general lifestyle. More food meant that fewer people suffered from hunger and malnourishment and that devastating famines were rarer. Higher yields brought more food for animals as well as people, and the amount of meat that people ate increased slightly. A better diet had an enormous impact on women's lives in particular. More food meant increased body fat, which increased fertility, and more meat—which provided iron—meant that women were less anemic and less subject to disease. Improved opportunities also encouraged people to marry somewhat earlier, which meant larger families and further population growth.

What led to Europe's economic growth and reurbanization?

What was life like in medieval cities?

How did universities serve the needs of medieval society?

How did literature and architecture express medieval values?

☑ LearningCurve
Check what you know.

Home Life

In western and central Europe, villages were generally made up of small houses for individual families. Households consisted of a married couple, their children, and perhaps one or two other relatives. Some homes contained only an unmarried person, a widow, or several unmarried people living together. In southern and eastern Europe, extended families were more likely to live in the same household.

The size and quality of peasants' houses varied according to their relative prosperity, which usually depended on the amount of land held. For most people, however, living space—especially living space close enough to a fire to feel some warmth in cold weather—was cramped, dark, smoky, and smelly, with animals and people both sharing tight quarters, sometimes with each other.

The mainstay of the diet for peasants—and for all other classes—was bread. The main meal was often bread and a thick soup of vegetables and grains eaten around noon. Animals were too valuable to be used for food on a regular basis, but weaker animals were often slaughtered in the fall so that they did not need to be fed through the winter. Their meat was salted for preservation and eaten on great feast days such as Christmas and Easter.

The diet of people with access to a river, lake, or stream would be supplemented with fish, which could be eaten fresh or preserved by salting. People living close to the sea gathered shellfish. Many places had severe laws against hunting and trapping in the forests. Deer, wild boars, and other game were reserved for the king and nobles. These laws were flagrantly violated, however, and rabbits and wild game often found their way to peasants' tables.

Medieval households were not self-sufficient but bought cloth, metal, leather goods, and even some food in village markets. They also bought ale, the universal drink of the common people in northern Europe. Women dominated in the production of ale. Ale not only provided needed calories but also provided some relief from the difficult, monotonous labor that filled people's lives.

The steady rise in population between the mid-eleventh and fourteenth centuries was primarily the result of warmer climate, increased food supply, and a reduction of violence with growing political stability, rather than dramatic changes in health care. Most treatment of illness was handled by home remedies. Treatments were often mixtures of herbal remedies, sayings, specific foods, prayers, amulets, and ritual healing activities. People suffering from wounds, skin diseases, or broken bones sometimes turned to barber-surgeons. For internal ailments, people consulted apothecaries, who suggested and mixed compounds taken internally or applied orally as a salve or ointment.

Beginning in the twelfth century in England, France, and Italy, the clergy, noble men and women, and newly rich merchants also established institutions to care for the sick or for those who could not take care of themselves. Such institutions might be staffed by members of religious orders or by laymen and laywomen who were paid for their work.

Childbirth and Child Abandonment

The most dangerous period of life for any person, peasant or noble, was infancy and early childhood. In normal years perhaps as many as one-third of all children died before age five, and this death rate climbed to more than half in years with

CHAPTER LOCATOR | **What was village life like in medieval Europe?** | How did religion shape everyday life in the High Middle Ages?

CHAPTER 10

280 LIFE IN VILLAGES AND CITIES OF THE HIGH MIDDLE AGES

plagues, droughts, or famines. Once people reached adulthood, however, many lived well into their fifties and sixties.

Childbirth was dangerous for mothers as well as infants. Village women helped one another through childbirth, and women who were more capable acquired midwifery skills. In larger towns and cities, such women gradually developed into professional midwives who were paid for their services and who trained younger women as apprentices. For most women, however, childbirth was handled by female friends and family.

Many infants were abandoned by parents or guardians, who left their children somewhere, sold them, or legally gave authority over them to some other person or institution. Sometimes parents believed that someone of greater means or status might find the child and bring him or her up in better circumstances than they could provide. Christian parents gave their children to monasteries as religious acts, donating them to the service of God in the same way they might donate money.

Donating a child to a monastery was common among the poor until about the year 1000, but less common in the next three hundred years, which saw relative prosperity for peasants. On the other hand, the incidence of noble parents giving their younger sons and daughters to religious houses increased dramatically. This resulted from and also reinforced the system of primogeniture, in which estates were passed intact to the eldest son instead of being divided among heirs (see Chapter 9, page 244). Monasteries provided noble younger sons and daughters with career opportunities, and their being thus disposed of removed them as contenders for family land.

QUICK REVIEW <

What factors contributed to change and growth in rural Europe during the High Middle Ages?

| What led to Europe's economic growth and reurbanization? | What was life like in medieval cities? | How did universities serve the needs of medieval society? | How did literature and architecture express medieval values? | ☑ LearningCurve Check what you know. |

281

How did religion shape everyday life in the High Middle Ages?

Statue of Saint Anne, the Virgin Mary, and the Christ Child

Nearly every church had at least one image of the Virgin Mary, the most important figure of Christian devotion in medieval Europe. In this thirteenth-century wooden sculpture, she is shown holding the infant Jesus, and is herself sitting on the lap of her mother, Anne. Statues such as this reinforced people's sense that the heavenly family was much like theirs, with grandparents who sometimes played important roles. (Scala/Art Resource, NY)

APART FROM THE LAND, the weather, and local legal and social conditions, religion had the greatest impact on the daily lives of ordinary people in the High Middle Ages. Religious practices varied widely from country to country and even from province to province. Most people in medieval Europe were Christian, but there were small Jewish communities scattered in many parts of Europe, and Muslims lived in the Iberian Peninsula, Sicily, and other Mediterranean islands.

Christian Life in Medieval Villages

For Christians, the village church was the center of community life—social, political, and economic, as well as religious—with the parish priest in charge of a host of activities. Although church law placed the priest under the bishop's

CHAPTER LOCATOR | What was village life like in medieval Europe? | How did religion shape everyday life in the High Middle Ages?

CHAPTER 10
282 LIFE IN VILLAGES AND CITIES OF THE HIGH MIDDLE AGES

authority, the manorial lord appointed the priest. Rural priests were peasants and often worked in the fields with the people during the week. On Sundays and holy days, they put on a robe and celebrated mass, or Eucharist, the ceremony in which the priest consecrated bread and wine and distributed it to believers, in a re-enactment of Jesus's Last Supper. At least once a year, villagers were expected to take part in the ceremony and eat the consecrated bread. This usually happened at Easter, after they had confessed their sins to the priest and been assigned a penance.

In everyday life, people engaged in rituals and used language heavy with religious symbolism. Before planting, the village priest customarily went out and sprinkled the fields with water, symbolizing refreshment and life. Everyone participated in village processions to honor the saints and ask their protection. The entire calendar was filled with reference to events in the life of Jesus and his disciples, such as Christmas, Easter, and Pentecost.

Saints and Sacraments

Along with days marking events in the life of Jesus, the Christian calendar was filled with saints' days. People believed that the saints possessed supernatural powers that enabled them to perform miracles, and the saint became the special property of the locality in which his or her relics rested. In return for the saint's healing and support, peasants offered the saint prayers, loyalty, and gifts.

The Virgin Mary, Christ's mother, was the most important saint. In the eleventh century, theologians began to emphasize Mary's spiritual motherhood of all Christians. Special masses commemorated her, churches were built in her honor, and hymns and prayers to her multiplied. Villagers listened intently to sermons telling stories about her life and miracles.

Along with the veneration of saints, sacraments were an important part of religious practice. Twelfth-century theologians expanded on Saint Augustine's understanding of sacraments (see Chapter 7, page 187) and created an entire sacramental system. In 1215, the Fourth Lateran Council formally accepted seven sacraments (baptism, penance, the Eucharist, confirmation, marriage, priestly ordination, anointment of the dying). Medieval Christians believed that these seven sacraments brought God's grace, the divine assistance or help needed to lead a good Christian life and to merit salvation. Most sacraments had to be dispensed by a priest, although spouses officially administered the sacrament of marriage to each other, and laypeople could baptize a dying infant or anoint a dying person if no priest could be found. The sacramental system enhanced the authority of priests over people's lives, but it did not replace strong personal devotion to the saints.

Muslims and Jews

The centrality of Christian ceremonies to daily life for most Europeans meant that those who did not participate were clearly marked as outsiders. Many Muslims left Spain as the Christian "reconquest" proceeded and left Sicily when this became a Christian realm (see Chapter 9, page 268), but others converted. In more isolated villages, people simply continued their Muslim rituals and practices, though they might hide this from the local priest or visiting officials.

| What led to Europe's economic growth and reurbanization? | What was life like in medieval cities? | How did universities serve the needs of medieval society? | How did literature and architecture express medieval values? | ☑ LearningCurve Check what you know. |

283

Islam was geographically limited in medieval Europe, but by the late tenth century, Jews could be found in many areas, often brought in from other areas as clients of rulers to help with finance. Jewish communities could be found in Italian and French cities and in the cities along the Rhine. Jewish dietary laws require meat to be handled in a specific way, so Jews had their own butchers; there were Jewish artisans in many other trades as well. Jews held weekly religious services on Saturday, the Sabbath, and celebrated their own annual cycle of holidays.

Jews could supply other Jews with goods and services, but rulers and city leaders increasingly restricted their trade with Christians to banking and money-lending. This enhanced Christian resentment, as did the ideology of holy war that accompanied the Crusades. Violence against Jews and restrictions on their activities increased further in much of Europe. Jews were expelled from England and later from France. However, Jews continued to live in the independent cities of the Holy Roman Empire and Italy, and some migrated eastward into new towns that were being established in Slavic areas.

Rituals of Marriage and Birth

Increasing suspicion and hostility marked relations between religious groups throughout the Middle Ages, but there were also important similarities in the ways Christians, Jews, and Muslims understood and experienced their religions. In all three traditions, every major life transition was marked by a ceremony that included religious elements.

In Christian weddings, a priest's blessing was often sought, though it was not essential to the marriage. Muslim weddings were also finalized by a contract between the bride and groom and were often overseen by a wedding official. Jewish weddings were guided by statements in Talmudic law that weddings were complete when the bride had entered the *chuppah*, which medieval Jewish authorities interpreted to mean a room in the groom's house. In all three faiths, the wedding ceremony was followed by a wedding party.

Friends and family members had generally been part of the discussions, negotiations, and activities leading up to a marriage; marriage united two families and was far too important to leave up to two people alone. Among serfs, the manorial lord's permission was often required, with a special fee required to obtain it. The involvement of family and friends in choosing one's spouse might lead to conflict, but more often the wishes of the couple and their parents, kin, and community were quite similar: all hoped for marriages that provided economic security, honorable standing, and a good number of healthy children. The best marriages offered companionship, emotional support, and even love, but these were understood to grow out of the marriage, not necessarily precede it. The church forbade divorce, and even among non-Christians marital dissolution by any means other than the death of one spouse was rare.

Most brides hoped to be pregnant soon after the wedding. Christian women hoping for children said special prayers to the Virgin Mary or her mother, Anne. Some wore amulets thought to increase fertility. Others repeated charms and verses, or, in desperate cases, went on pilgrimages to make special supplications. Muslim and Jewish women wore small cases with sacred verses or asked for blessings from religious leaders. Women continued these prayers and rituals throughout pregnancy and childbirth, often combining religious traditions with

CHAPTER LOCATOR | What was village life like in medieval Europe? | **How did religion shape everyday life in the High Middle Ages?**

284 CHAPTER 10 LIFE IN VILLAGES AND CITIES OF THE HIGH MIDDLE AGES

folk beliefs. Judaism, Christianity, and Islam all required women to remain separate from the community for a short time after childbirth and often had special ceremonies welcoming them back once this period was over.

Religious ceremonies also welcomed children into the community. Among Christian families, infants were baptized soon after they were born to ensure that they could enter Heaven. Midwives who delivered children who looked especially weak and sickly often baptized them in an emergency service. In normal baptisms, the women who had assisted the mother in the birth often carried the baby to church, where godparents vowed their support. Godparents were often close friends or relatives, but parents might also choose prominent villagers or even the local lord in the hope that he might later look favorably on the child and provide for him or her in some way.

Within Judaism, a boy was circumcised by a religious official and given his name in a ceremony in his eighth day of life. This *brit milah*, or "covenant of circumcision," was viewed as a reminder of the covenant between God and Abraham described in Hebrew Scripture. Muslims also circumcised boys in a special ritual, though the timing varied from a few days after birth to adolescence.

| What led to Europe's economic growth and reurbanization? | What was life like in medieval cities? | How did universities serve the needs of medieval society? | How did literature and architecture express medieval values? | ✅ LearningCurve Check what you know. |

Death and the Afterlife

Death was similarly marked by religious ceremonies, and among Europeans of all faiths, death did not sever family obligations and connections. Christians called for a priest to perform the sacrament of extreme unction when they thought the hour of death was near.

Once the person had died, the body was washed and dressed in special clothing—or a sack of plain cloth—and buried within a day or two. Family and friends joined in a funeral procession. The wealthy were sometimes buried inside the church—in the walls, under the floor, or under the building itself in a crypt—but most people were buried in the churchyard or a cemetery close by. At the graveside, the priest asked for God's grace for the soul of the deceased and also asked that soul to "rest in peace." This final request was made not only for the benefit of the dead but also for that of the living because the souls of the dead were widely believed to return to earth. Priests were hired to say memorial masses on anniversaries of family deaths, especially one week, one month, and one year afterward.

During the High Middle Ages, learned theologians increasingly emphasized the idea of purgatory, the place where souls on their way to Heaven went after death to make amends for their earthly sins. Memorial masses, prayers, and donations made in the names of the dead could shorten their time in purgatory. So could indulgences (see Chapter 9, page 266), those papal grants that relieved a person from earthly penance. Indulgences were initially granted for performing meritorious acts, such as going on a pilgrimage or crusade, but later they could be obtained by paying a small fee. With this development, their spiritual benefits became transferable, so indulgences could be purchased to shorten the stay in purgatory of one's deceased relatives, as well as to lessen one's own penance or time in purgatory.

The living also had obligations to the dead among Muslims and Jews. In both groups, deceased people were buried quickly, and special prayers were said by mourners and family members. Muslims fasted on behalf of the dead and maintained a brief period of official mourning. The Qur'an promises an eternal paradise with flowing rivers to "those who believe and do good deeds" (Qur'an, 4:57) and a Hell of eternal torment to those who do not.

Jews observed specified periods of mourning during which the normal activities of daily life were curtailed. Every day for eleven months after a death and every year after that on the anniversary of the death, a son of the deceased was to recite Kaddish, a special prayer of praise and glorification of God. Judaism emphasized life on earth more than an afterlife, so beliefs about what happens to the soul after death were more varied; the very righteous might go directly to a place of spiritual reward, but most souls went first to a place of punishment and purification generally referred to as *Gehinnom*. After a period that did not exceed twelve months, the soul ascended to the world to come. Those who were completely wicked during their lifetimes might simply go out of existence or continue in an eternal state of remorse.

> ## QUICK REVIEW

What similarities were there between the religious lives of medieval Christians, Muslims, and Jews?

CHAPTER LOCATOR | What was village life like in medieval Europe? | How did religion shape everyday life in the High Middle Ages?

CHAPTER 10
286 LIFE IN VILLAGES AND CITIES OF THE HIGH MIDDLE AGES

What led to Europe's economic growth and reurbanization?

Lübeck The dominant city in the Hanseatic League, Lübeck is portrayed in this woodcut as densely packed within its walls, with church steeples and the city hall dominating the skyline, and boats carrying goods and people moving swiftly along the river. Even in this stylized scene, the artist captures the key features of the "Queen of the Hansa": crowded, proud, and centered on commerce. (Private Collection/The Stapleton Collection/The Bridgeman Art Library)

LVBECA VRBS IMPERIALIS LIBERA, CIVITATVM WAN' DALICARVM, ET INCLYTÆ HANSEATICÆ SOCIETATIS CAPVT.

MOST PEOPLE CONTINUED TO LIVE IN VILLAGES in the High Middle Ages, but the rise of towns and the growth of a new business and commercial class were central parts of Europe's recovery after the disorders of the tenth century. As towns gained legal and political rights, merchant and craft guilds grew more powerful, and towns became centers of production as well as commerce (**Map 10.1**).

The Rise of Towns

Medieval towns began in many different ways. Some were fortifications erected as a response to ninth-century invasions. Other towns grew around great cathedrals (see page 305) and monasteries. Many other towns grew from the sites of Roman army camps or cities. Still others arose where a trade route crossed a river or a natural harbor allowed ships to moor easily.

Regardless of their origins, medieval towns had a few common characteristics. Each town had a marketplace, and most had a mint for the coining of money. The town also had a court to settle disputes. In addition, medieval towns were

| What led to Europe's economic growth and reurbanization? | What was life like in medieval cities? | How did universities serve the needs of medieval society? | How did literature and architecture express medieval values? |  LearningCurve Check what you know. |

MAP 10.1 ■ European Population Density, ca. 1300

The development of towns and the reinvigoration of trade were directly related in medieval Europe. Using this map, Maps 10.2 and 10.3, and the information in this chapter, answer the following questions.

> **MAPPING THE PAST**

ANALYZING THE MAP: What were the four largest cities in Europe? What part of Europe had the highest density of towns?

CONNECTIONS: What role did textile and other sorts of manufacturing play in the growth of towns? How was the development of towns related to that of universities, monastery schools, and cathedral schools?

---

enclosed by walls. Townspeople supported themselves primarily by exchanging goods and services with one another, becoming artisans, shopkeepers, and merchants. They bought their food from the surrounding countryside and purchased goods from far away brought by traveling merchants.

No matter where people congregated, they settled on someone's land and had to secure permission to live there from the king, count, abbot, or bishop. Aristocratic nobles and churchmen were sometimes hostile to the towns set up on their land, but they soon realized that these could be a source of profits and benefits.

The growing towns of medieval Europe slowly gained legal and political rights, including the rights to hold municipal courts, select the mayor and other

CHAPTER LOCATOR | What was village life like in medieval Europe? | How did religion shape everyday life in the High Middle Ages?

municipal officials, and tax residents and visitors. Lords were often reluctant to grant towns self-government, fearing loss of authority and revenue if they gave the residents full independence. When residents bargained for a town's political independence, however, they offered sizable amounts of ready cash and sometimes promised payments for years to come. Consequently, lords ultimately agreed to self-government.

In addition to working for the independence of the towns, townspeople tried to acquire liberties for themselves. In the Middle Ages, the word *liberties* meant special privileges. The most important privilege a medieval townsperson could gain was personal freedom. It gradually developed that an individual who fled his or her manor and lived in a town for a year and a day was free of servile obligations and status. Thus, the growth of towns contributed to a slow decline of serfdom in western Europe.

> Population of European Cities in 1300	
City	**Approximate Population**
Córdoba	500,000
Constantinople	300,000
Paris	200,000
Venice, Florence, Milan	100,000 each

Merchant and Craft Guilds

The merchants, who were influential in winning towns' independence from feudal lords, also used their power and wealth to control life within the city walls. The merchants of a town joined together to form a **merchant guild** that prohibited nonmembers from trading in the town. Guild members often made up the earliest town government, serving as mayors and members of the city council. By the late eleventh century, especially in the towns of the Low Countries and northern Italy, the leaders of the merchant guilds were rich and politically powerful.

While most towns were initially established as trading centers, they quickly became centers of production as well. Peasants looking for better opportunities

merchant guild
▶ A band of merchants in a town that prohibited nonmembers from trading in that town.

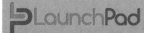

ONLINE DOCUMENT PROJECT
Life in Medieval Towns
How did merchant and craft guilds shape life in medieval towns?

Keeping the question above in mind, examine primary texts and images that illuminate the role of guilds in medieval urban communities. *See inside the front cover to learn more.*

What led to Europe's economic growth and reurbanization?	What was life like in medieval cities?	How did universities serve the needs of medieval society?	How did literature and architecture express medieval values?	 LearningCurve Check what you know.

moved to towns, providing both workers and mouths to feed. Some townspeople began to specialize in certain types of food and clothing production. Over time, some cities specialized in certain items, becoming known for their fine fabrics, their reliable arms and armor, or their elegant gold and silver work.

Like merchants, producers recognized that organizing would bring benefits, and beginning in the twelfth century in many cities, they formed **craft guilds** that regulated most aspects of production. Guilds set quality standards for their particular product and regulated the size of workshops and the conduct of members. In most cities, individual guilds achieved a monopoly in the production of one particular product, forbidding nonmembers to work. The craft guild then chose some of its members to act as inspectors and set up a court to hear disputes between members, though the city court remained the final arbiter.

Each guild set the pattern by which members were trained and the length of the training period. A boy who wanted to become a weaver, for instance, or whose parents wanted him to, spent four to seven years as an apprentice, often bound by a contract. When the apprenticeship was finished, a young artisan spent several years as a journeyman, working in the shop of a master artisan. He then could make his "masterpiece" — in the case of weavers, a long piece of cloth. If the other masters judged the cloth acceptable, and if they thought the market in their town was large enough to support another weaver, the journeyman could then become a master and start a shop. If the guild decided there were already enough masters, he would need to leave that town and try elsewhere.

Many guilds required masters to be married because they recognized the vital role of the master's wife. She assisted in running the shop, often selling the goods her husband had produced. Their children, both male and female, also worked alongside the apprentices and journeymen. The sons were sometimes formally apprenticed, but the daughters were generally not apprenticed because many guilds limited formal membership to males. Most guilds allowed a master's widow to continue operating a shop for a set period of time after her husband's death. In a handful of cities, there were a few all-female guilds, especially in spinning gold thread or weaving silk ribbons for luxury clothing, trades in which girls were formally apprenticed in the same way boys were.

Both craft and merchant guilds were not only economic organizations, but also systems of social support. They took care of elderly masters who could no longer work, and they often supported masters' widows and orphans. They maintained an altar at a city church and provided for the funerals of members and baptisms of their children. Guild members marched together in city parades and reinforced their feelings of solidarity with one another by special ceremonies and distinctive dress.

The Revival of Long-Distance Trade

The growth of towns went hand in hand with a revival of trade as artisans and craftsmen manufactured goods for both local and foreign consumption (**Map 10.2**). Most trade centered in towns and was controlled by professional traders. Long-distance trade was risky and required large investments of capital, Thus, merchants would often pool their resources to finance an expedition to a distant place. When the ship or caravan returned and the cargo was sold, these investors

craft guild

▶ A band of producers in a town that regulated most aspects of production of a good in that town.

CHAPTER LOCATOR | What was village life like in medieval Europe? | How did religion shape everyday life in the High Middle Ages?

290 CHAPTER 10 LIFE IN VILLAGES AND CITIES OF THE HIGH MIDDLE AGES

MAP 10.2 ▪ Trade and Manufacturing in Thirteenth-Century Europe

Note the overland and ocean lines of trade and the sources of silver, iron, copper, lead, paper, wool, carpets and rugs, and slaves.

would share the profits. If disaster struck the caravan, an investor's loss was limited to the amount of that individual's investment.

In the late eleventh century, the Italian cities, especially Venice, led the West in trade in general and completely dominated trade with the East. Venetian ships carried salt from the city's own lagoon, pepper and other spices from India and North Africa, silks and carpets from Central Asia, and slaves from many places. In northern Europe, the towns of Bruges, Ghent, and Ypres (EE-pruh) in Flanders built a vast cloth industry, becoming leaders in both the manufacture and trade of textiles.

What led to Europe's economic growth and reurbanization?	What was life like in medieval cities?	How did universities serve the needs of medieval society?	How did literature and architecture express medieval values?	☑ LearningCurve Check what you know.

From the late eleventh through the thirteenth centuries, Europe enjoyed a steadily expanding volume of international trade. Trade surged markedly with demand for sugar from the Mediterranean islands to replace honey; spices from Asia to season a bland diet; and fine wines from the Rhineland, Burgundy, and Bordeaux to make life more pleasant. Other consumer goods included luxury woolens from Flanders and Tuscany, furs from Ireland and Russia, brocades and tapestries from Flanders, and silks from Constantinople and even China. As the trade volume expanded, the use of cash became more widespread. Beginning in the 1160s, the opening of new silver mines in Germany, Bohemia, northern Italy, northern France, and western England led to the minting and circulation of vast quantities of silver coins.

Business Procedures

The economic surge of the High Middle Ages led merchants to invent new business procedures. Beginning in Italy, merchants formalized their agreements with new types of contracts, including temporary contracts for land and sea trading ventures and permanent partnerships termed *compagnie* (kahm-pah-NYEE). Many of these agreements were initially between brothers or other relatives and in-laws, but they quickly grew to include people who were not family members. In addition, they began to involve individuals—including a few women—who invested only their money, leaving the actual running of the business to the active partners. Commercial correspondence, unnecessary when one businessperson oversaw everything and made direct bargains with buyers and sellers, proliferated. Accounting and record keeping became more sophisticated, and credit facilitated business expansion.

The ventures of the German Hanseatic League illustrate these new business procedures. The **Hanseatic League** was a mercantile association of towns. It originated in agreements between merchants for mutual security and exclusive trading rights, and it gradually developed into agreements among towns themselves. At its height, the league included perhaps two hundred cities from Holland to Poland. From the fourteenth to the sixteenth centuries, the Hanseatic League controlled the trade of northern Europe.

The dramatic increase in trade ran into two serious difficulties in medieval Europe. First, despite investment in mining operations to increase the production of metals, the amount of gold, silver, and copper available for coins was not adequate for the increased flow of commerce. Merchants developed paper bills of exchange, in which coins or goods in one location were exchanged for a sealed letter, which could be used in place of metal coinage elsewhere. This made the long, slow, and very dangerous shipment of coins unnecessary and facilitated the expansion of credit and commerce.

The second problem was a moral and theological one. Church doctrine frowned on lending money at interest, termed *usury* (YOO-zhuh-ree). As money-lending became more important to commercial ventures, the church relaxed its position. It declared that some interest was legitimate as a payment for the risk the investor was taking, and that only interest above a certain level would be considered usury. The church itself then got into the money-lending business, opening pawnshops in cities.

Hanseatic League

▶ A mercantile association of towns begun in northern Europe that provided mutual protection and trading rights.

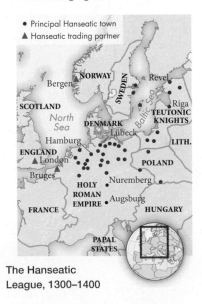

• Principal Hanseatic town
▲ Hanseatic trading partner

The Hanseatic League, 1300–1400

In 1348, when he was a young teenager, Francesco Datini (1335–1410) lost his father, his mother, a brother, and a sister to the Black Death epidemic that swept through Europe (see Chapter 11). Leaving his hometown of Prato in northern Italy, he apprenticed himself to merchants in nearby Florence for several years to learn accounting and other business skills. At fifteen, he moved to Avignon (ah-veen-YOHN) in southern France. The popes were at this point living in Avignon instead of Rome, and the city offered many opportunities for an energetic and enterprising young man. Datini first became involved in the weapons trade, which offered steady profits, and then became a merchant of spices, wool and silk cloth, and jewels. He was very successful, and at thirty-one he married the young daughter of another merchant in an elaborate wedding that was the talk of Avignon.

In 1378, the papacy returned to Italy, and Datini soon followed, setting up trading companies in Prato, Pisa, and Florence. He focused on cloth and leather and sought to control the trade in products used for the preparation of these materials as well, especially the rare dyes that created the brilliant colors favored by wealthy noblemen and townspeople. He eventually had offices all over Europe and became one of the richest men of his day, opening a mercantile bank and a company that produced cloth.

Datini was more successful than most businessmen, but what makes him stand out was his record keeping. He kept careful account books and ledgers, all of them headed by the phrase "in the name of God and profit." He wrote to the managers of each of his offices every week, providing them with careful advice and blunt criticism: "You cannot see a crow in a bowl of milk." Taking on the son of a friend as an employee, he wrote to the young man: "Do your duty well, and you will acquire honor and profit, and you can count on me as if I were your own father. But if you do not, then do not count on me; it will be as if I had never known you."

When Datini was away from home, which was often, he wrote to his wife every day, and she sometimes responded in ways that were less deferential than we might expect of a woman who was many years younger. "I think it is not necessary," she wrote at one point, "to send me a message every Wednesday to say that you will be here on Sunday, for it seems to me that on every Friday you change your mind."

Datini's obsessive record keeping lasted beyond his death, for someone saved all of his records — hundreds of ledgers and contracts, eleven thousand business letters, and over a hundred thousand personal letters — in sacks in his opulent house in Prato, where they were found in the nineteenth century. They provide a detailed picture of medieval business practices and also reveal much about Datini as a person. Ambitious, calculating, luxury loving, and a workaholic, Datini seems similar to a modern CEO.

Statue of Francesco Datini located outside the city hall in Prato. (Peter Horree/Alamy)

Like many of today's self-made billionaires, at the end of his life Datini began to think a bit more about God and less about profit. In his will, he set up a foundation for the poor in Prato and a home for orphans in Florence, both of which are still in operation. In 1967, scholars established an institute for economic history in Prato, naming it in Datini's honor; the institute now manages the collection of Datini's documents and gathers other relevant materials in its archives.

QUESTIONS FOR ANALYSIS

1. How would you evaluate Datini's motto, "In the name of God and profit"? Is it an honest statement of his aims, a hypocritical justification of greed, a blend of both, or something else?
2. Changes in business procedures in the Middle Ages have been described as a "commercial revolution." Do Datini's business ventures support this assessment? How?

Source: Iris Origo, *The Merchant of Prato: Francesco di Marco Datini, 1335–1410* (New York: Alfred A. Knopf, Inc., 1957).

The Commercial Revolution

Changes in business procedures, combined with the growth in trade, led to a transformation of the European economy often called the **commercial revolution** by historians, who see it as the beginning of the modern capitalist economy. In using this label, historians point not only to increases in the sheer volume of trade and in the complexity and sophistication of business procedures, but also to the development of a new capitalist spirit in which making a profit is regarded as a good thing in itself, regardless of the uses to which that profit is put. (See "Individuals in Society: Francesco Datini," page 293.)

The commercial revolution created a great deal of new wealth, which did not escape the attention of kings and other rulers. Wealth could be taxed, and through taxation kings could create strong and centralized states. The commercial revolution also provided the opportunity for thousands of serfs to improve their social position. The slow but steady transformation of European society from almost completely rural and isolated to urban and relatively more sophisticated constituted the greatest effect of the commercial revolution that began in the eleventh century.

Even so, merchants and business people did not run medieval communities other than in central and northern Italy and in the county of Flanders. Kings and nobles maintained ultimate control over most European cities. Most towns remained small, and urban residents never amounted to more than 10 percent of the total European population. The commercial changes of the eleventh through thirteenth centuries did, however, lay the economic foundations for the development of urban life and culture.

> ## QUICK REVIEW

What were the causes and consequences of the medieval commercial revolution?

CHAPTER LOCATOR | What was village life like in medieval Europe? | How did religion shape everyday life In the High Middle Ages?

CHAPTER 10

294 LIFE IN VILLAGES AND CITIES OF THE HIGH MIDDLE AGES

What was life like in medieval cities?

Young Men Playing Stickball With their tunics hitched up in their belts so that they could move around more easily, young men play a game involving hitting a ball with a stick. Games involving bats and balls were popular because the equipment needed was made from simple, inexpensive materials. (The Granger Collection, NYC.)

IN THEIR BACKGROUNDS AND ABILITIES, townspeople represented diversity and change. Their occupations and their preoccupations were different from those of nobles and peasants. Cities were crowded and polluted, though people flocked into them because they offered the possibility of economic advancement, social mobility, and improvement in legal status. Some urban residents grew spectacularly rich, but the numbers of poor swelled as well.

City Life

Walls surrounded almost all medieval towns and cities, and constant repair of these walls was usually the town's greatest expense. Gates pierced the walls, and visitors waited at the gates to gain entrance to the town. Most streets in a medieval town were marketplaces as much as passages for transit. Poor people selling soap, candles, wooden dishes, and similar cheap products stood next to farmers from the surrounding countryside selling eggs, chickens, and vegetables. Because there was no way to preserve food easily, people—usually female family members or servants—had to shop every day, and the market was where they met their neighbors, exchanged information, and talked over recent events.

| What led to Europe's economic growth and reurbanization? | **What was life like in medieval cities?** | How did universities serve the needs of medieval society? | How did literature and architecture express medieval values? | ✓ LearningCurve Check what you know. |

Some selling took place not in the open air but in the craftsman's home. The family lived above the business on the second or third floor. As the business and the family expanded, additional stories were added. Second and third stories jutted out over the ground floor and thus over the street. Because the streets were narrow to begin with, houses lacked fresh air and light. Fire was a constant danger: houses were built close to one another, and fires spread rapidly.

Most medieval cities developed with little planning. As the population increased, space became increasingly limited. Air and water pollution presented serious problems. Horses and oxen, the chief means of transportation and power, dropped tons of dung on the streets every year. It was universal practice in the early towns to dump household waste, both animal and human, into the road in front of one's house.

People of all sorts, from beggars to wealthy merchants, regularly rubbed shoulders in the narrow streets and alleys of crowded medieval cities. This interaction did not mean that people were unaware of social differences, however, because clothing clearly indicated social standing and sometimes occupation. Friars wore black, white, or gray woolen clothing that marked them as members of a particular religious order. Military men and servants who lived in noble households dressed in the nobles' distinctive colors known as livery (LIH-vuh-ree). Wealthier urban residents wore bright colors, imported silk or fine woolen fabrics, and fancy headgear, while poorer ones wore darker clothing made of rough linen or linen and wool blends.

sumptuary laws
▶ Laws that regulated the value and style of clothing and jewelry that various social groups could wear as well as the amount they could spend on celebrations.

In the later Middle Ages, many cities attempted to make clothing distinctions a matter of law as well as of habit. City councils passed **sumptuary laws** that regulated the value of clothing and jewelry that people of different social groups could wear; only members of high social groups could wear velvet, satin, pearls, or fur, for example, or wear clothing embroidered with gold thread or dyed in colors that were especially expensive to produce. Along with enforcing social differences, sumptuary laws also attempted to impose moral standards by prohibiting plunging necklines on women or doublets (fitted buttoned jackets) that were too short on men. Their limits on imported fabrics or other materials also served to protect local industries.

Some of these sumptuary laws called for marking certain individuals as members of groups not fully acceptable in urban society. Many cities ordered prostitutes to wear red or yellow bands on their clothes, and the Fourth Lateran Council required Jews and Muslims to dress in ways that distinguished them from their Christian neighbors. Sumptuary laws were frequently broken and were difficult to enforce, but they provide evidence of the many material goods available to urban dwellers as well as the concern of city leaders about the social mobility and extravagance they saw all around them.

Servants and the Poor

Many urban houses were larger than the tiny village dwellings, so families took in domestic servants. A less wealthy household employed one woman who assisted in all aspects of running the household; a wealthier one employed a large staff of male and female servants with specific duties.

Along with live-in servants, many households hired outside workers to do specific tasks. These workers laundered clothing and household linens, cared for

CHAPTER LOCATOR | What was village life like in medieval Europe? | How did religion shape everyday life in the High Middle Ages?

CHAPTER 10
296 LIFE IN VILLAGES AND CITIES OF THE HIGH MIDDLE AGES

children or invalids, repaired houses and walls, and carried messages or packages around the city or the surrounding countryside. Urban workers had to buy all their food, so they felt any increase in the price of ale or bread immediately. Their wages were generally low, and children from such families sought work at very young ages.

Illegal activities offered another way for people to support themselves. Theft and prostitution were common in medieval cities. Many who engaged in such activities also worked as laundresses, day laborers, porters, peddlers, or street vendors when they could. Cities also drew in orphans, blind people, and the elderly, who resorted to begging for food and money.

Popular Entertainment

Games and sports were common forms of entertainment and relaxation. There were wrestling matches and games in which balls were kicked, hit, and thrown. People played cards, dice, and board games of all types. They trained dogs to fight each other or put them in an enclosure to fight a captured bear. In Spain, Muslim knights confronted and killed bulls from horseback as part of religious feast days, developing a highly ritualized ceremony that would later be further adapted by Spain's Christians. All these sports and games were occasions for wagering and gambling.

Religious and family celebrations also meant dancing. Men and women danced in lines toward a specific object, such as a tree or a maypole, or in circles, groups, or pairs with specific step patterns. They were accompanied by a variety of instruments. Musicians playing string or percussion instruments often sang as well, and people sang without instrumental accompaniment on festive occasions or while working.

QUICK REVIEW <

What was economic life like in Europe's towns and cities during the High Middle Ages?

What led to Europe's economic growth and reurbanization?

What was life like in medieval cities?

How did universities serve the needs of medieval society?

How did literature and architecture express medieval values?

 LearningCurve
Check what you know.

297

How did universities serve the needs of medieval society?

Law Lecture at Bologna This beautifully carved marble sculpture suggests the students' intellectual intensity. The fluid lines of clothing are characteristic of the late Gothic style. (Scala/Art Resource, NY)

JUST AS THE FIRST STRONG SECULAR STATES EMERGED in the thirteenth century, so did the first universities. This was no coincidence. The new bureaucratic states and the church needed educated administrators, and universities were a response to this need.

Origins

In the early Middle Ages, monasteries and cathedral schools had offered most of the available formal instruction. Monastery schools were small, but cathedral schools, run by the bishop and his clergy in bustling cities, gradually grew larger. In the eleventh century, in Italian cities like Bologna (boh-LOH-nyuh), wealthy businessmen established municipal schools. Over the course of the twelfth century, cathedral schools in France and municipal schools in Italy developed into

CHAPTER LOCATOR | What was village life like in medieval Europe? | How did religion shape everyday life in the High Middle Ages?

MAP 10.3 ■ Intellectual Centers of Medieval Europe

Universities provided more sophisticated instruction than did monastery and cathedral schools, but all these institutions served to educate males who had the money to attend.

educational institutions that attracted students from a wide area (**Map 10.3**). These schools were often called *universitas magistrorum et scholarium* (universal society of teachers and students). The first European universities appeared in Italy in Bologna, where the specialty was law, and Salerno, where the specialty was medicine.

| What led to Europe's economic growth and reurbanization? | What was life like in medieval cities? | **How did universities serve the needs of medieval society?** | How did literature and architecture express medieval values? | ✓ LearningCurve Check what you know. |

299

Legal and Medical Training

The growth of the University of Bologna coincided with a revival of interest in Roman law during the investiture controversy. The study of Roman law as embodied in the Justinian *Codex* (see Chapter 7, page 203) had never completely died out in the West, but in the late eleventh century, a complete manuscript of the *Codex* was discovered in a library in Pisa. This discovery led scholars in nearby Bologna to study and teach Roman law intently.

Teachers at Bologna taught law as an organic whole related to the society it regulated, an all-inclusive system based on logical principles that could be applied to difficult practical situations. Thus, as social and economic structures changed, law would change with them. Jurists educated at Bologna—and later at other universities—were hired by rulers and city councils to systematize their law codes and write legal treatises. Canon law was also shaped by the reinvigoration of Roman law, and canon lawyers in ever-greater numbers were hired by church officials or became prominent church officials themselves.

Jewish scholars also produced elaborate commentaries on law and religious tradition. Medieval universities were closed to Jews, but in some cities in the eleventh century special rabbinic academies opened that concentrated on the study of the Talmud, a compilation of legal arguments, proverbs, sayings, and folklore. Men seeking to become rabbis—highly respected figures within the Jewish community, with authority over economic and social as well as religious matters—spent long periods studying the Talmud, which served as the basis for their decisions affecting all areas of life.

Professional medical training began at Salerno. Individuals there began to translate medical works written in Arabic. These translations included writings by the ancient Greek physicians and Muslim medical writers, a blending of knowledge that later occurred on the nearby island of Sicily as well. (See "Picturing the Past: Healthy Living," page 301.) Students of medicine poured into the city.

Medical studies at Salerno were based on classical ideas, particularly those of Hippocrates and Aristotle (see Chapter 3, page 82). Prime among these was the notion of the four bodily humors—blood, phlegm, black bile, and yellow bile—fluids in the body that influenced bodily health. Disease was generally regarded as an imbalance of humors, which could be diagnosed by taking a patient's pulse or examining his or her urine. Treatment was thus an attempt to bring the humors back into balance, which might be accomplished through diet or drugs—mixtures of herbal or mineral substances—or by vomiting, emptying the bowels, or bloodletting.

These ideas spread throughout Europe from Salerno and became the basis of training for physicians at other universities. University training gave physicians high social status and allowed them to charge high fees. They were generally hired directly by patients as needed, though some had more permanent positions as members of the household staffs of especially wealthy nobles or rulers.

Theology and Philosophy

In the Middle Ages, theology was "the queen of sciences" because it involved the study of God, who made all knowledge possible. Paris became the place to study theology. In the first decades of the twelfth century, students from across Europe crowded into the cathedral school of Notre Dame (NOH-truh DAHM) in Paris.

CHAPTER LOCATOR | What was village life like in medieval Europe? | How did religion shape everyday life in the High Middle Ages?

CHAPTER 10

300 LIFE IN VILLAGES AND CITIES OF THE HIGH MIDDLE AGES

Healthy Living

In this illustration from a very popular fourteenth-century Latin handbook on maintaining health and well-being, women with their sleeves rolled up prepare cloth for medical uses; the woman on the left is trimming small threads off with a one-bladed shear, and the woman on the right is boiling the cloth to bleach it. The men in the background eat a meal and drink wine. The text of this handbook was a translation of an Arabic medical treatise, made in the kingdom of Sicily, the site of much cultural borrowing. (Austrian National Library, Vienna/The Bridgeman Art Library)

> PICTURING THE PAST

ANALYZING THE IMAGE: Cleanliness and moderation were recommended as essential to healthy living in this handbook. How does the artist convey these values in this scene?

MAKE CONNECTIONS: Given what you have learned about medieval medical care, why might a handbook like this have been popular with literate urban residents?

| What led to Europe's economic growth and reurbanization? | What was life like in medieval cities? | **How did universities serve the needs of medieval society?** | How did literature and architecture express medieval values? | ☑ LearningCurve Check what you know. |

Scholastics

▶ University professors in the Middle Ages who developed a method of thinking, reasoning, and writing in which questions were raised and authorities cited on both sides of a question.

University professors were known as "schoolmen" or **Scholastics**. They developed a method of thinking, reasoning, and writing in which questions were raised and authorities cited on both sides of a question. The goal of this method was to arrive at definitive answers and to provide rational explanations for what was believed on faith.

The Scholastic approach rested on the recovery of classical philosophical texts. Ancient Greek and Arabic texts entered Europe in the early twelfth century by way of Islamic intellectual centers at Baghdad, Córdoba, and Toledo (see Chapter 8). The major contribution of Arabic culture to the new currents of Western thought rested in the stimulus Arabic philosophers and commentators gave to Europeans' reflections on ancient Greek texts and the ways these texts fit with Christian teachings. One of the young men drawn to Paris was Peter Abelard (1079–1142). Abelard was fascinated by logic, which he believed could be used to solve most problems. He was one of the first Scholastics, and commented, "By doubting we come to questioning, and by questioning we perceive the truth." Abelard was severely censured by a church council, but his cleverness, boldness, and imagination made him a highly popular figure among students.

Abelard's reputation for brilliance drew the attention of one of the cathedral canons, Fulbert, who hired Abelard to tutor his intelligent niece Heloise. The relationship between teacher and pupil passed beyond the intellectual. Heloise became pregnant, and Fulbert pressured the couple to marry. The couple agreed but wanted the marriage kept secret for the sake of Abelard's career. Furious at Abelard, Fulbert hired men to castrate him. Abelard persuaded Heloise to enter a convent, and he became a monk.

In the thirteenth century, Scholastics devoted an enormous amount of time to collecting and organizing knowledge on all topics. Such a collection was published as a *summa* (SOO-muh), or reference book. Saint Thomas Aquinas (1225–1274), a Dominican friar and professor at Paris, produced the most famous of these collections, the *Summa Theologica*, a summation of Christian ideas on a vast number of theological questions, including the nature of God and Christ, moral principles, and the role of the sacraments. In this and many of his other writings, Aquinas used arguments that drew from ancient Greek philosophers, especially Aristotle, as well as earlier Christian writers.

In all of his works, Aquinas stressed the power of human reason to demonstrate many basic Christian principles, including the existence of God. To obtain true Christian understanding, he wrote, one needed both reason and faith. His ideas have been extremely influential in both philosophy and theology: in the former through the philosophical school known as Thomism, and in the latter especially through the Catholic Church, which has affirmed many times that they are foundational to Roman Catholic doctrine.

University Students

The influx of students eager for learning, together with dedicated and imaginative teachers, created the atmosphere in which universities grew. By the end of the fifteenth century there were at least eighty universities in Europe. Some universi-

CHAPTER LOCATOR | What was village life like in medieval Europe? | How did religion shape everyday life in the High Middle Ages?

CHAPTER 10

302 LIFE IN VILLAGES AND CITIES OF THE HIGH MIDDLE AGES

ties also offered younger students training in what were termed the seven liberal arts — grammar, rhetoric, logic, mathematics, geometry, music, and astronomy — that could serve as a foundation for more specialized study in all areas.

University students were generally considered to be lower-level members of the clergy, so any students accused of legal infractions were tried in church, rather than in city, courts. This clerical status, along with widely held ideas about women's lesser intellectual capabilities, meant that university education was restricted to men.

Though university classes were not especially expensive, the many years that a university education required meant that the sons of peasants or artisans could rarely attend unless they could find wealthy patrons who would pay their expenses. Most students were the sons of urban merchants or lower-level nobles. University degrees were initially designed as licenses to teach at the university, but most students staffed the expanding diocesan, royal, and papal administrations as lawyers and officials.

Students did not spend all their time preparing for their degrees. Much information about medieval students concerns what we might call "extracurricular" activities: university regulations forbidding them to throw rocks at professors; sermons about breaking and entering, raping local women, attacking town residents, and disturbing church services; and court records discussing their drunken brawls, riots, and fights and duels.

QUICK REVIEW <

What role did the church play in the growth and development of European educational institutions?

What led to Europe's economic growth and reurbanization?	What was life like in medieval cities?	**How did universities serve the needs of medieval society?**	How did literature and architecture express medieval values?	LearningCurve Check what you know.

303

How did literature and architecture express medieval values?

Notre Dame Cathedral, Paris This view offers a fine example of the twin towers (left), the spire and great rose window over the south portal (center), and the flying buttresses that support the walls and the vaults. Like hundreds of other churches in medieval Europe, it was dedicated to the Virgin Mary. With a spire rising more than 300 feet, Notre Dame was the tallest building in Europe. (David Frazier/Photo Researchers)

THE HIGH MIDDLE AGES saw the creation of new types of literature, architecture, and music. Technological advances in areas such as papermaking and stone masonry made some of these innovations possible, as did the growing wealth and sophistication of patrons. Artists and artisans flourished in the more secure environment of the High Middle Ages, producing works that celebrated the glories of love, war, and God.

Vernacular Literature and Drama

Latin was the language used in university education, scholarly writing, and works of literature. By the High Middle Ages, however, no one spoke Latin as his or her birth tongue. The barbarian invasions, the mixture of peoples, and the usual changes in language that occur over time had resulted in a variety of local dialects that blended words and linguistic forms in various ways. As kings increased the size of their holdings, they often ruled people who spoke many different dialects.

In the High Middle Ages, some authors departed from tradition and began to write in their local dialect, that is, in the everyday language of their region, which linguistic historians call the vernacular. This new **vernacular literature** gradually transformed some local dialects into literary languages, such as French, German, Italian, and English, while other local dialects, such as Breton and Bavarian, remained means of oral communication.

Facilitating this vernacular writing was a technological advance. By the thirteenth century, techniques of making paper from old linen cloth and rags began to spread from Spain, where they had been developed by the Arabs, and provided a much cheaper material on which to write than parchment or vellum (see Chapter 8). People started to write about subjects that were more mundane and less serious in their dialects, using spellings that were often personal and idiosyncratic. These writings included fables, legends, stories, and myths that had circulated orally for generations, adding to the growing body of written vernacular literature.

Stories and songs in the vernacular were composed and performed at the courts of nobles and rulers. In Germany and most of northern Europe, the audiences favored stories and songs recounting the great deeds of warrior heroes. These epics, known as *chansons de geste* (SHAN-suhn duh JEHST; "songs of great deeds"), celebrate violence, slaughter, revenge, and physical power. In southern Europe, especially in Provence in southern France, poets who called themselves **troubadours** (TROO-buh-dorz) wrote and sang lyric verses celebrating love, desire, beauty, and gallantry. Troubadours included a few women, called *trobairitz*, most of whose exact identities are not known.

The songs of the troubadours were widely imitated in Italy, England, and Germany, so they spurred the development of vernacular literature there as well. Most of the troubadours came from and wrote for the aristocratic classes, and their poetry suggests the interests and values of noble culture. Their influence extended to all social groups, however, because people who could not read heard the poems and stories from people who could, so that what had originally come from oral culture was returned to it.

Drama, derived from the church's liturgy, emerged as a distinct art form during the High Middle Ages. Amateurs and later professional actors performed plays based on biblical themes and on the lives of the saints; these dramas were presented in the towns, first in churches and then at the marketplace. By combining comical farce based on ordinary life with serious religious scenes, plays gave ordinary people an opportunity to identify with religious figures and think about their faith.

Churches and Cathedrals

As we have seen, religious devotion was expressed through daily rituals, holiday ceremonies, and the creation of new institutions such as universities and religious orders. People also wanted permanent visible representations of their piety, and both church and city leaders wanted physical symbols of their wealth and power. These aims found their outlet in the building of tens of thousands of churches; chapels; abbeys; and, most spectacularly, **cathedrals** in the twelfth and thirteenth

vernacular literature
▶ Writings in the author's local dialect, that is, in the everyday language of the region.

troubadours
▶ Poets who wrote and sang lyric verses celebrating love, desire, beauty, and gallantry.

cathedral
▶ The church of a bishop and the administrative headquarters of a diocese.

What led to Europe's economic growth and reurbanization?

What was life like in medieval cities?

How did universities serve the needs of medieval society?

How did literature and architecture express medieval values?

✔ LearningCurve
Check what you know.

305

centuries. A cathedral is the church of a bishop and the administrative headquarters of a diocese.

Most of the churches in the early Middle Ages had been built primarily of wood, which meant they were susceptible to fire. They were often small, in a rectangular form with a central aisle, and with a flat roof; this structure, called a basilica, was based on earlier Roman public buildings. With the increasing political stability of the eleventh century, bishops and abbots supported the construction of larger and more fire-resistant churches made almost completely out of stone. As the size of the church grew horizontally, it also grew vertically. Builders adapted Roman-style rounded barrel vaults made of stone for the ceiling; this use of Roman forms led the style to be labeled **Romanesque**.

The next architectural style was **Gothic**. In Gothic churches, the solid stone, barrel-vaulted roof was replaced by a roof made of stone ribs with plaster between them. Because this ceiling was much lighter, side pillars and walls did not need to carry as much weight. Exterior arched stone supports called flying buttresses also carried some of the weight of the roof, so solid walls could be replaced by windows, which let in great amounts of light. Originating in the Île-de-France in the twelfth century, Gothic architecture spread throughout France with the expansion of royal power. From France, the new style spread to England, Germany, Italy, Spain, and eastern Europe.

Extraordinary amounts of money were needed to build these houses of worship. The economic growth of the period meant that merchants, nobles, and the church could afford the costs of this unparalleled building boom. A great number of artisans had to be assembled. Each master craftsman had apprentices, and unskilled laborers had to be recruited for the heavy work. Bishops and abbots sketched out what they wanted and set general guidelines, but they left practical needs and aesthetic considerations to the master mason.

Because cathedrals were symbols of civic pride, towns competed to build the largest and most splendid church. In 1163, the citizens of Paris began Notre Dame Cathedral, planning it to reach the height of 114 feet from the floor to the ceiling at the highest point inside. Many other cathedrals well over 100 feet tall on the inside were built as each bishop and town sought to outdo the neighbors. The construction of a large cathedral was rarely completed in a lifetime; many were never finished at all. Because generation after generation added to the buildings, many of these churches show the architectural influences of two or even three centuries.

Stained glass beautifully reflects the creative energy of the High Middle Ages. It is both an integral part of Gothic architecture and a distinct form of visual art. Windows showed scenes from the Old and New Testaments and the lives of the saints, designed to teach people doctrines of the Christian faith visually. They also showed scenes from the lives of the artisans and merchants who paid for them.

Once at least part of a cathedral had been built, the building began to be used for religious services. Town residents gathered for masses, baptisms, funerals, and saint's day services, and also used it for guild meetings and other secular purposes.

The frenzy to create the most magnificent Gothic cathedrals eventually came to an end. Begun in 1247, the cathedral in Beauvais reached a height of 157 feet in the interior, exceeding all others. Unfortunately, the weight imposed on the vaults was too great, and the building collapsed in 1284. The collapse was viewed as an

Romanesque
▶ An architectural style with rounded arches and small windows.

Gothic
▶ An architectural style typified by pointed arches and large stained-glass windows.

CHAPTER LOCATOR | What was village life like in medieval Europe? | How did religion shape everyday life in the High Middle Ages?

CHAPTER 10
306 LIFE IN VILLAGES AND CITIES OF THE HIGH MIDDLE AGES

aberration, for countless other cathedrals were in various stages of completion at the same time, and none of them fell. In hindsight, however, it can be viewed as a harbinger. Very few cathedrals not yet completed at the time of its collapse were ever finished, and even fewer were started. In the fourteenth century, the church itself splintered, and the cities that had so proudly built cathedrals were decimated by famine and disease.

QUICK REVIEW <

What changes in European culture were marked by the emergence of vernacular literature?

LOOKING BACK
LOOKING AHEAD

The High Middle Ages represent one of the most creative periods in the history of Western society. Institutions that are important parts of the modern world, including universities, jury trials, and investment banks, were all developed in this era. Advances were made in the mechanization of labor, business procedures, architectural design, and education. Through the activities of merchants, Europeans again saw products from Africa and Asia in city marketplaces, as they had in Roman times, and wealthier urban residents bought them. Individuals and groups such as craft guilds provided money for building and decorating magnificent Gothic cathedrals.

Toward the end of the thirteenth century, however, there were increasing signs of impending problems. The ships and caravans bringing exotic goods also brought new pests. The new vernacular literature created a stronger sense of national identity, which increased hostility toward others. The numbers of poor continued to grow, and efforts to aid their suffering were never enough. As the century ended, villagers and city residents alike continued to gather for worship, but they also wondered whether God was punishing them.

LaunchPad

ONLINE DOCUMENT PROJECT
Life in Medieval Towns

How did merchant and craft guilds shape life in medieval towns?

Keeping the question above in mind, examine primary texts and images that illuminate the role of guilds in medieval urban communities. *See inside the front cover to learn more.*

| What led to Europe's economic growth and reurbanization? | What was life like in medieval cities? | How did universities serve the needs of medieval society? | How did literature and architecture express medieval values? | ✓ **LearningCurve** Check what you know. |

CHAPTER 10 STUDY GUIDE

STEP 1 GET STARTED ONLINE

✓ **LearningCurve**

Now that you've read the chapter, make it stick by completing the LearningCurve activity.

STEP 2 EXPLAIN WHY IT MATTERS

Put your reading into practice. Identify each term below, and then explain why it matters in Western history.

TERM	WHO OR WHAT & WHEN	WHY IT MATTERS
open-field system (p. 278)		
merchant guild (p. 289)		
craft guild (p. 290)		
Hanseatic League (p. 292)		
commercial revolution (p. 294)		
sumptuary laws (p. 296)		
Scholastics (p. 302)		
vernacular literature (p. 305)		
troubadours (p. 305)		
cathedral (p. 305)		
Romanesque (p. 306)		
Gothic (p. 306)		

STEP 3 MOVE BEYOND THE BASICS

To demonstrate a more advanced understanding, complete the table below to identify key aspects of medieval religious life. How did religion strengthen the bonds of family and community?

Institutions and officials	
Saints	
Sacraments	
Marriage and birth	
Death and the afterlife	

PUT IT ALL TOGETHER

Now, take a step back and try to explain the big picture. Remember to use specific examples from the chapter in your answers.

RURAL LIFE

► What were the key social and economic characteristics of the typical medieval village?

► How did technological innovations contribute to rural growth?

URBAN LIFE

► How did medieval town life differ from village life?

► What effect did the growth of towns and cities have on European culture?

RELIGION AND CULTURE

► What role did religion play in the daily life of ordinary Europeans?

► What factors contributed to the emergence and growth of universities in the High Middle Ages?

MAKE CONNECTIONS

► In what ways was rural life in the High Middle Ages similar to rural life in previous centuries? In what ways was it different?

► What were the strengths and weaknesses of medieval society? What connections can you make between those weaknesses and the calamities of the fourteenth century?

> IN YOUR OWN WORDS

Imagine that you must give an oral report to the class answering the following question: **How and why did life change over the course of the High Middle Ages?** What would be the most important points and why?

11

THE LATER MIDDLE AGES

1300–1450

> **How did the catastrophes of the Late Middle Ages change European society?** Chapter 11 examines the tumultuous fourteenth century. Between 1300 and 1450, Europeans experienced a frightful series of shocks. The climate turned colder and wetter, leading to poor harvests and famine. In the middle of the fourteenth century, a new disease, probably the bubonic plague, spread throughout Europe, killing millions. War devastated the countryside, leading to widespread discontent and peasant revolts. Workers in cities also revolted, and violent crime and ethnic tensions increased as well. Yet, in spite of all this, important institutions and cultural forms, including representative assemblies and national literatures, emerged. Even institutions that experienced severe crisis, such as the Christian Church, saw new types of vitality.

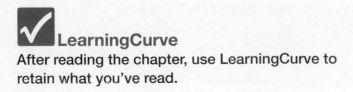

LearningCurve
After reading the chapter, use LearningCurve to
retain what you've read.

> How did climate change shape the late Middle Ages?

> How did the Black Death reshape European society?

> What were the causes, course, and consequences of the Hundred Years' War?

> Why did the church come under increasing criticism?

> What explains the social unrest of the late Middle Ages?

Life and Death in the Late Middle Ages. In this French manuscript illumination from 1465, armored knights kill peasants while they work in the fields or take refuge in a castle. (Musée Condé, Chantilly, France/ The Bridgeman Art Library)

> How did climate change shape the late Middle Ages?

Death from Famine In this fifteenth-century painting, dead bodies lie in the middle of a path, while a funeral procession at the right includes a man with an adult's coffin and a woman with the coffin of an infant under her arm. People did not simply allow the dead to lie in the street in medieval Europe, though during famines and epidemics it was sometimes difficult to maintain normal burial procedures. (Erich Lessing/Art Resource, NY)

TOWARD THE END OF THE THIRTEENTH CENTURY, the expanding European economy began to slow down. In the first half of the fourteenth century, Europe experienced ongoing climate change that led to lower levels of food production, which had dramatic and disastrous ripple effects.

Climate Change and Famine

The period from about 1000 to about 1300 saw a warmer-than-usual climate in Europe, which underlay all the changes and vitality of the High Middle Ages. Around 1300, however, the climate changed for the worse, becoming colder and wetter. Historical geographers refer to the period from 1300 to 1450 as a "little ice age."

Across Europe, an unusual number of storms brought torrential rains, ruining the crops on which people and animals almost everywhere depended. Long-distance transportation of food was expensive and difficult, so most urban areas depended on areas no more than a day's journey away for grain, produce, and meat. Poor harvests led to scarcity and starvation. Almost all of northern Europe suffered a **Great Famine** in the years 1315 to 1322.

Even in non-famine years, the cost of grain, livestock, and dairy products rose sharply, in part because diseases hit cattle and sheep. Increasing prices meant that fewer people could afford to buy food. Reduced caloric intake meant

Great Famine
▶ A terrible famine from 1315 to 1322 that hit much of Europe after a period of climate change.

CHAPTER LOCATOR | How did climate change shape the late Middle Ages?

> CHRONOLOGY

1300–1450 – Little ice age	**1347** – Black Death arrives in Europe
1309–1376 – Babylonian Captivity; papacy in Avignon	**1358** – Jacquerie peasant uprising in France
1310–1320 – Dante writes *Divine Comedy*	**1366** – Statute of Kilkenny
1315–1322 – Great Famine in northern Europe	**1378–1417** – Great Schism
1320s – First large-scale peasant rebellion in Flanders	**1381** – English Peasants' Revolt
1337–1453 – Hundred Years' War	**1387–1400** – Chaucer writes *Canterbury Tales*

increased susceptibility to disease. Workers on reduced diets had less energy, which meant lower productivity, lower output, and higher grain prices.

Social Consequences

The changing climate and resulting agrarian crisis of the fourteenth century had grave social consequences. Poor harvests and famine led to the abandonment of homesteads. In parts of the Low Countries and in the Scottish-English border-lands, entire villages were deserted, and many people became vagabonds, wandering in search of food and work. In Flanders and eastern England, some peasants were forced to mortgage, sublease, or sell their holdings to richer farmers in order to buy food. Throughout the affected areas, young men and women sought work in the towns and delayed marriage.

As the subsistence crisis deepened, starving people focused their anger on the rich, speculators and the Jews. Rumors spread of a plot by Jews and their agents, the lepers, to kill Christians by poisoning wells. Based on "evidence" collected by torture, many lepers and Jews were killed, beaten, or heavily fined.

Meanwhile, the international character of trade and commerce meant that a disaster in one country had serious implications elsewhere. For example, the infection that attacked English sheep in 1318 caused a sharp decline in wool exports in the following years. Without wool, Flemish weavers could not work, and thousands were laid off. Without woolen cloth, the businesses of Flemish, Hanseatic, and Italian merchants suffered. Unemployment encouraged people to turn to crime.

QUICK REVIEW <

What were the social and economic consequences of the food shortages of the early fourteenth century?

How did the Black Death reshape European society?	What were the causes, course, and consequences of the Hundred Years' War?	Why did the church come under increasing criticism?	What explains the social unrest of the late Middle Ages?	 **LearningCurve** Check what you know.

How did the Black Death reshape European society?

Flagellants In this manuscript illumination from 1349, shirtless flagellants scourge themselves with whips as they walk through the streets of the Flemish city of Tournai. The text notes that they are asking for God's grace to return to the city after it had been struck with the "most grave" illness. (Private Collection/The Bridgeman Art Library)

COLDER WEATHER, FAILED HARVESTS, AND RESULTING MALNOURISHMENT left Europe's population susceptible to disease; unfortunately for the continent, a virulent disease appeared in the mid-fourteenth century. Around 1300, improvements in ship design had allowed year-round shipping for the first time. European merchants took advantage of these advances, and ships continually at sea carried all types of cargo. Just as modern air travel has allowed diseases such as AIDS and the H1N1 virus to spread quickly over very long distances, medieval shipping allowed the diseases of the time to do the same. The most frightful of these diseases, carried on Genoese ships, first emerged in western Europe in 1347; the disease was later called the **Black Death**.

Black Death

▶ Plague that first struck Europe in 1347 and killed perhaps one-third of the population.

Pathology

Most historians and microbiologists identify the disease that spread in the fourteenth century as the bubonic plague. The disease normally afflicts rats. Fleas living on the infected rats drink their blood and then pass the bacteria that cause the plague on to the next rat they bite. Usually the disease is limited to rats and

CHAPTER LOCATOR | How did climate change shape the late Middle Ages?

other rodents, but at certain points in history the fleas have jumped from their rodent hosts to humans and other animals.

The classic symptom of the bubonic plague was a growth the size of a nut or an apple in the armpit, in the groin, or on the neck. This was the boil, or *bubo*, that gave the disease its name and caused agonizing pain. If the bubo was lanced and the pus thoroughly drained, the victim had a chance of recovery. If the boil was not lanced, however—and in the fourteenth century, it rarely was—the next stage was the appearance of black spots or blotches caused by bleeding under the skin. After that, the victim began to cough violently and spit blood. This stage signaled the end, and death followed in two or three days. The coughing also released plague pathogens into the air, infecting others when they were breathed in and beginning the deadly cycle again on new victims.

Spread of the Disease

Plague symptoms were first described in 1331 in southwestern China, then part of the Mongol Empire. Plague-infested rats accompanied Mongol armies and merchant caravans carrying silk, spices, and gold across Central Asia in the 1330s. The rats then stowed away on ships, carrying the disease to the ports of the Black Sea by the 1340s.

In October 1347, Genoese ships brought the plague from Kaffa to Messina, from which it spread across Sicily. Venice and Genoa were hit in January 1348, and from the port of Pisa the disease spread south to Rome and east to Florence and all of Tuscany. By late spring, southern Germany was attacked. Frightened French authorities chased a galley bearing plague victims away from the port of Marseilles but not before plague had infected the city, from which it spread to southern France and Spain. In June 1348, two ships entered the Bristol Channel and introduced it into England, and from there it traveled northeast into Scandinavia. The plague seems to have entered Poland through the Baltic seaports and spread eastward from there (**Map 11.1**).

Medieval urban conditions were ideal for the spread of disease. Narrow streets were filled with refuse, human excrement, and dead animals. Houses whose upper stories projected over the lower ones blocked light and air. In addition, people were already weakened by famine, standards of personal hygiene remained frightfully low, and the urban populace was crowded together. Fleas and body lice were universal afflictions: everyone from peasants to archbishops had them. One more bite did not cause much alarm, and the association among rats, fleas, and the plague was unknown. Mortality rates can be only educated guesses because population figures for the period before the arrival of the plague do not exist for most countries and cities. Of a total English population of perhaps 4.2 million, probably 1.4 million died of the Black Death. Densely populated Italian cities endured incredible losses. Florence lost between one-half and two-thirds of its population when the plague visited in 1348. The most widely accepted estimate for western Europe and the Mediterranean is that the plague killed about one-third of the population in the first wave of infection.

Nor did central and eastern Europe escape the ravages of the disease. As the Black Death took its toll on the Holy Roman Empire, waves of emigrants fled to Poland, Bohemia, and Hungary, taking the plague with them. In the Byzantine Empire, the plague ravaged the population.

How did the Black Death reshape European society?	What were the causes, course, and consequences of the Hundred Years' War?	Why did the church come under increasing criticism?	What explains the social unrest of the late Middle Ages?	✓ LearningCurve Check what you know.

315

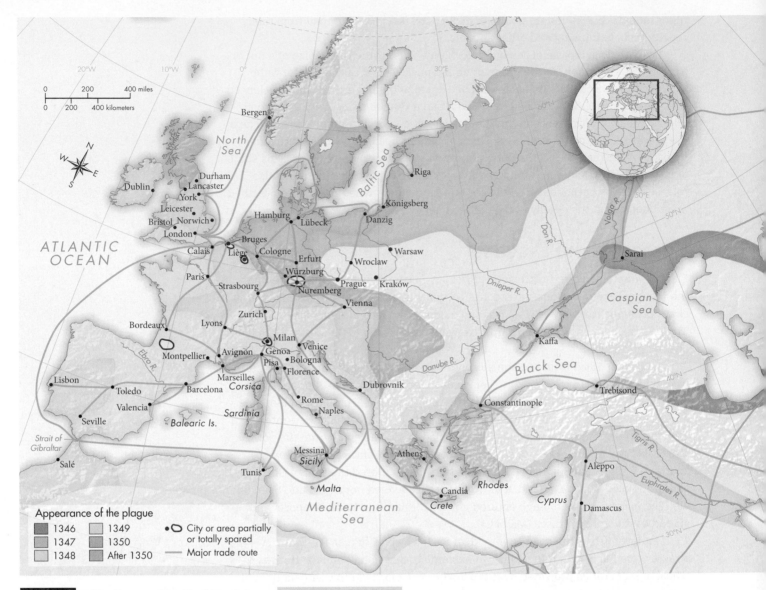

Appearance of the plague

- 1346
- 1347
- 1348
- 1349
- 1350
- After 1350
- • ◯ City or area partially or totally spared
- ── Major trade route

MAP 11.1 ■ **The Course of the Black Death in Fourteenth-Century Europe**

The bubonic plague spread across Europe after beginning in the mid-1340s, with the first cases of disease reported in Black Sea ports.

> MAPPING THE PAST

ANALYZING THE MAP: When did the plague reach Paris? How much time passed before it spread to the rest of northern France and southern Germany? Which cities and regions were spared?

CONNECTIONS: How did the expansion of trade contribute to the spread of the Black Death?

Across Europe, the Black Death recurred intermittently from the 1360s to 1400. It reappeared from time to time over the following centuries as well, though never with the same virulence because by then Europeans now had some resistance. Improved standards of hygiene and strictly enforced quarantine measures also lessened the plague's toll. Only in 1721 did it make its last appearance in Europe, in the French port of Marseilles.

CHAPTER LOCATOR | How did climate change shape the late Middle Ages?

Care of the Sick

Fourteenth-century medical literature indicates that physicians tried many different methods to prevent and treat the plague. People understood that plague and other diseases could be transmitted person to person, and they observed that crowded cities had high death rates, especially when the weather was warm and moist. We now understand that warm, moist conditions make it easier for germs to grow and spread, but fourteenth-century people thought in terms of "poisons" in the air or "corrupted air" coming from swamps, unburied animals, or the positions of the stars. Their treatments thus focused on ridding the air and the body of these poisons and on rebalancing bodily fluids.

It is noteworthy that, in an age of mounting criticism of clerical wealth (see page 327), the behavior of the clergy during the plague was often exemplary. Priests, monks, and nuns cared for the sick and buried the dead. In places like Venice, from which even physicians fled, priests remained to give what ministrations they could. Consequently, their mortality rate was phenomenally high. The German clergy, especially, suffered a severe decline in personnel in the years after 1350.

There were limits to care, however. To avoid contagion, wealthier people often fled the cities for the countryside, though sometimes this simply spread the plague faster. Some cities tried shutting their gates to prevent infected people and animals from coming in, which worked in a few cities. They also walled up houses in which there was plague, trying to isolate those who were sick from those who were still healthy.

Economic, Religious, and Cultural Effects

Economic historians and demographers sharply dispute the impact of the plague on the economy in the late fourteenth century. The traditional view that the plague had a disastrous effect has been greatly modified. By the mid-1300s, the population of Europe had grown somewhat beyond what could easily be supported by available agricultural technology, and the dramatic drop in population allowed less fertile land to be abandoned. People turned to more specialized types of agriculture, such as raising sheep or wine grapes, which in the long run proved to be a better use of the land.

The Black Death did bring on a general European inflation. High mortality produced a fall in production, shortages of goods, and a general rise in prices. This inflation continued to the end of the fourteenth century. But labor shortages resulting from the high mortality caused by the plague meant that workers could demand better wages, and the broad mass of people who survived enjoyed a higher standard of living. The greater demand for labor also meant greater mobility for peasants in rural areas and for artisans in towns and cities.

The plague also affected religious practices. Not surprisingly, some people sought release from the devastating affliction in wild living, but more became more deeply pious. Rather than seeing the plague as a medical issue, they interpreted it as the result of an evil within themselves. God must be punishing them for terrible sins, they thought, so the best remedies were religious ones: asking

| How did the Black Death reshape European society? | What were the causes, course, and consequences of the Hundred Years' War? | Why did the church come under increasing criticism? | What explains the social unrest of the late Middle Ages? | ✓ LearningCurve Check what you know. |

317

for forgiveness, praying, trusting in God, making donations to churches, and trying to live better lives. In Muslim areas, religious leaders urged virtuous living in the face of death: give to the poor, reconcile with your enemies, free your slaves, and say a proper good-bye to your friends and family.

Believing that the Black Death was God's punishment for humanity's wickedness, some Christians turned to the severest forms of asceticism and frenzied religious fervor, joining groups of **flagellants** (FLA-juh-luhnts), who whipped and scourged themselves as penance for their and society's sins. Groups of flagellants traveled from town to town, often growing into unruly mobs. Officials worried that they would provoke violence and riots, and ordered groups to disband or forbade them to enter cities.

flagellants

► People who believed that the plague was God's punishment for sin and sought to do penance by flagellating (whipping) themselves.

Dance of Death

In this fifteenth-century fresco from a tiny church in Croatia, skeletons lead people from all social classes in a procession. (Robert Harding World Imagery/ Alamy)

> PICTURING THE PAST

ANALYZING THE IMAGE: Based on their clothing and the objects they are carrying, who are the people shown in the fresco? What does this suggest was the artist's message about death?

CONNECTIONS: Paintings such as this clearly provide evidence of the preoccupation with death in this era, but does this work highlight other social issues as well? If so, what are they?

CHAPTER LOCATOR | How did climate change shape the late Middle Ages?

CHAPTER 11
318 THE LATER MIDDLE AGES

Along with seeing the plague as a call to reform their own behavior, however, people also searched for scapegoats, and savage cruelty sometimes resulted. As in the decades before the plague, many people believed that the Jews had poisoned the wells of Christian communities and thereby infected the drinking water. Others thought that killing Jews would prevent the plague from spreading to their town, a belief encouraged by flagellant groups. These charges led to the murder of thousands of Jews across Europe, especially in the cities of France and Germany.

The literature and art of the late Middle Ages reveal a people gripped by morbid concern with death. One highly popular literary and artistic motif, the Dance of Death, depicted a dancing skeleton leading away living people, often in order of their rank.

The years of the Black Death witnessed the foundation of new colleges at old universities and of entirely new universities. The foundation charters explain the shortage of priests and the decay of learning as the reasons for their establishment. Whereas older universities such as those at Bologna and Paris had international student bodies, these new institutions established in the wake of the Black Death had more national or local constituencies. Thus, the international character of medieval culture weakened, paving the way for schism (SKIH-zuhm) in the Catholic Church even before the Reformation.

As is often true with devastating events, the plague highlighted central qualities of medieval society: deep religious feeling, suspicion of those who were different, and a view of the world shaped largely by oral tradition, with a bit of classical knowledge mixed in among the educated elite.

QUICK REVIEW <

How did Europeans respond to the devastation produced by the Black Death?

| How did the Black Death reshape European society? | What were the causes, course, and consequences of the Hundred Years' War? | Why did the church come under increasing criticism? | What explains the social unrest of the late Middle Ages? | LearningCurve Check what you know. |

What were the causes, course, and consequences of the Hundred Years' War?

Siege of the Castle of Mortagne Medieval warfare usually consisted of small skirmishes and attacks on castles. This miniature shows the French besieging an English-held castle near Bordeaux in 1377 that held out for six months. Most of the soldiers use longbows, although at the left two men shoot primitive muskets above a pair of cannon. Painted in the late fifteenth century, the scene reflects the military technology available at the time it was painted, not at the time of the actual siege. (© British Library Board, MS Royal 14 e. IV f. 23)

A LONG INTERNATIONAL WAR that began a decade or so before the plague struck and lasted well into the next century added further misery to a disease-ravaged population. England and France had engaged in sporadic military hostilities from the time of the Norman Conquest in 1066, and in the middle of the fourteenth century, these skirmishes became more intense. From 1337 to 1453, the two countries intermittently fought one another in what was the longest war in European history, ultimately dubbed the **Hundred Years' War**, though it actually lasted 116 years.

Hundred Years' War

▶ A war between England and France from 1337 to 1453, with political and economic causes and consequences.

Causes

The Hundred Years' War had a number of causes, including disagreements over rights to land, a dispute over the succession to the French throne, and economic conflicts. Many of these revolved around the duchy of Aquitaine, a province in

CHAPTER LOCATOR | How did climate change shape the late Middle Ages?

southern France that became part of the holdings of the English crown when Eleanor of Aquitaine married King Henry II of England in 1152. French policy in the fourteenth century was strongly expansionist, however, and the French kings resolved to absorb the duchy into the kingdom of France. Aquitaine therefore became a disputed territory.

The immediate political cause of the war was a disagreement over who would inherit the French throne after Charles IV of France, the last surviving son of Philip the Fair, died childless in 1328. Charles IV had a sister—Isabella—but her son was Edward III, king of England. An assembly of French high nobles, meaning to exclude Isabella and Edward from the French throne, proclaimed that, according to French law, "no woman nor her son could succeed to the [French] monarchy." The nobles passed the crown to Philip VI of Valois (r. 1328–1350), a nephew of Philip the Fair.

In 1329, Edward III formally recognized Philip VI's lordship over Aquitaine. Eight years later, Philip, eager to exercise full French jurisdiction there, confiscated the duchy. Edward III interpreted this action as a cause for war. He argued, as the eldest directly surviving male descendant of Philip the Fair, that he deserved the title of king of France. Edward III's dynastic argument upset the feudal order in France: to increase their independent power, many French nobles abandoned Philip VI, using the excuse that they had to transfer their loyalty to a different overlord, Edward III. One reason the war lasted so long was that it became a French civil war, with some French nobles, most important among them the dukes of Burgundy, supporting English monarchs in order to thwart the centralizing goals of the French kings. On the other side, Scotland—resisting English efforts of assimilation—often allied with France.

The governments of both England and France manipulated public opinion to support the war. Kings in both countries instructed the clergy to deliver sermons filled with patriotic sentiment. Royal propaganda on both sides fostered a kind of early nationalism, and both sides developed a deep hatred of the other.

Economic factors involving the wool trade and the control of Flemish towns were linked to these political issues. The wool trade between England and Flanders served as the cornerstone of both countries' economies; they were closely interdependent. Flanders technically belonged to the French crown, and the Flemish aristocracy was highly sympathetic to that monarchy. But the wealth of Flemish merchants and cloth manufacturers depended on English wool, and Flemish burghers strongly supported the claims of Edward III. The disruption of commerce with England threatened their prosperity.

THE HUNDRED YEARS' WAR

1337	Philip VI of France confiscates Aquitaine; war begins
1346	English longbowmen defeat French knights at Crécy
1356	English defeat French at Poitiers
1370s–1380s	French recover some territory
1415	English defeat the French at Agincourt
1429	French victory at Orléans; Charles VII crowned king
1431	Joan of Arc declared a heretic and burned at the stake
1440s	French reconquer Normandy and Aquitaine
1453	War ends
1456	Joan cleared of charges of heresy and declared a martyr

English Successes

The war began with a series of French sea raids on English coastal towns in 1337, but the French fleet was almost completely destroyed when it attempted to land soldiers on English soil, and from that point on the war was fought almost entirely in France and the Low Countries (**Map 11.2**). It consisted mainly of a series

| How did the Black Death reshape European society? | **What were the causes, course, and consequences of the Hundred Years' War?** | Why did the church come under increasing criticism? | What explains the social unrest of the late Middle Ages? | ✓ LearningCurve Check what you know. |

321

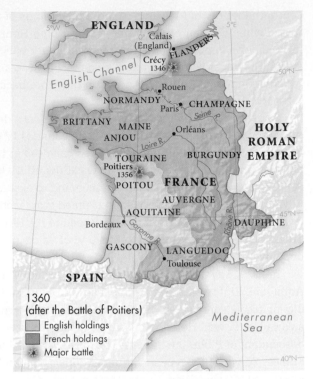

1337
(before the Battle of Crécy)

◻ English holdings
◼ French holdings
▬ Extent of English holdings after Treaty of Paris, 1259

1360
(after the Battle of Poitiers)

◻ English holdings
◼ French holdings
✷ Major battle

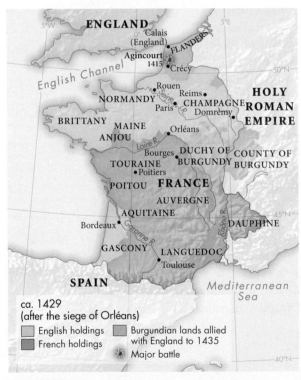

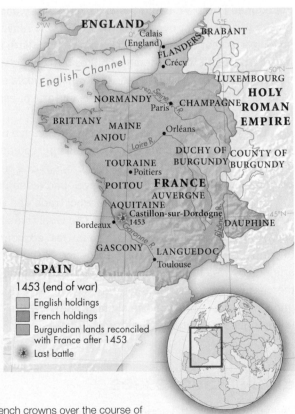

ca. 1429
(after the siege of Orléans)

◻ English holdings
◼ French holdings
◼ Burgundian lands allied with England to 1435
✷ Major battle

1453 (end of war)

◻ English holdings
◼ French holdings
◼ Burgundian lands reconciled with France after 1453
✷ Last battle

MAP 11.2 ■ The Hundred Years' War, 1337–1453

These maps show the change in the land held by the English and French crowns over the course of the Hundred Years' War. Which year marked the greatest extent of English holdings in France?

of random sieges and cavalry raids, fought in fits and starts, with treaties along the way to halt hostilities.

During the war's early stages, England was highly successful. At Crécy in northern France in 1346, English longbowmen scored a great victory over French knights and crossbowmen. Although the aim of longbowmen was not very accurate, the weapon allowed for rapid reloading, and an English archer could send off three arrows to the French crossbowman's one. The roar of English cannon—probably the first use of artillery in the Western world—created further panic. Edward III's son, Edward the Black Prince, used the same tactics ten years later to smash the French at Poitiers, where he captured the French king and held him for ransom. Edward was not able to take all of France, but the English held Aquitaine and other provinces, and allied themselves with many of France's nobles. After a brief peace, the French fought back and recovered some territory during the 1370s and 1380s, and then a treaty again halted hostilities and both sides concentrated on conflicts over power at home.

War began again in 1415 when the able English soldier-king Henry V (r. 1413–1422) invaded France. At Agincourt (AH-jihn-kort), Henry's army defeated a much larger French force, again primarily through the skill of English longbowmen. Henry followed his triumph at Agincourt with the reconquest of Normandy, and by 1419, the English had advanced to the walls of Paris (see Map 11.2, page 322). Henry married the daughter of the French king, and a treaty made Henry and any sons the couple would have heir to the French throne. It appeared as if Henry would indeed rule both England and France, but he died unexpectedly in 1422, leaving an infant son as heir. The English continued their victories, however, and besieged the city of Orléans (or-lay-AHN), the only major city in northern France not under their control. But the French cause was not lost.

Joan of Arc and France's Victory

The ultimate French success rests heavily on the actions of Joan, an obscure French peasant girl whose vision and military leadership revived French fortunes and led to victory. Born in 1412 to well-to-do peasants in the village of Domrémy in Champagne, Joan grew up in a religious household. During adolescence she began to hear voices, which she later said belonged to Saint Michael, Saint Catherine, and Saint Margaret. In 1428, these voices spoke to her with great urgency, telling her that the dauphin (DOH-fuhn), the uncrowned King Charles VII, had to be crowned and the English expelled from France. Joan traveled to the French court wearing male clothing. She had an audience with Charles and was able to secure his support to travel with the French army to Orléans dressed as a knight—with borrowed armor and sword. There she dictated a letter to the English ordering them to surrender.

Such a demand coming from a teenage girl—even one inspired by God—was laughable given the recent course of the conflict, but Joan was amazingly successful. She inspired and led French attacks, forcing the English to retreat from Orléans. The king made Joan co-commander of the entire army, and she led it to a string of victories; other cities simply surrendered without a fight and returned

How did the Black Death reshape European society?

What were the causes, course, and consequences of the Hundred Years' War?

Why did the church come under increasing criticism?

What explains the social unrest of the late Middle Ages?

☑ LearningCurve
Check what you know.

323

their allegiance to France. In July 1429, two months after the end of the siege of Orléans, Charles VII was crowned king at Reims.

Joan and the French army continued their fight against the English and their Burgundian allies. In 1430, the Burgundians captured Joan. Charles refused to ransom her, and she was sold to the English. A church court headed by a pro-English bishop tried her for heresy, and though nothing she had done was heretical by church doctrine, she was found guilty and burned at the stake.

The French army continued its victories without her. Sensing a shift in the balance of power, the Burgundians switched their allegiance to the French, who reconquered Normandy and finally ejected the English from Aquitaine in the 1440s. As the war dragged on, demands for an end increased in England. Parliamentary opposition to additional war grants stiffened, fewer soldiers were sent, and more territory passed into French hands. At the war's end in 1453, only the town of Calais (KA-lay) remained in English hands.

Aftermath

In France, thousands of soldiers and civilians had been slaughtered and hundreds of thousands of acres of rich farmland ruined, leaving the rural economy of many areas in shambles. These losses exacerbated the dreadful losses caused by the plague. The war had disrupted trade and the great trade fairs, resulting in the drastic reduction of French participation in international commerce. Defeat in battle and heavy taxation contributed to widespread dissatisfaction and aggravated peasant grievances.

The war had wreaked havoc in England as well. England spent the huge sum of over £5 million on the war effort, and despite the money raised by some victories, the net result was an enormous financial loss. The government attempted to finance the war by raising taxes on the wool crop, which priced wool out of the export market.

In both England and France, men of all social classes had volunteered to serve in the war in the hope of acquiring booty and becoming rich, and some were successful in the early years of the war. As time went on, however, most fortunes seem to have been squandered as fast as they were made. In addition, the social order was disrupted because the knights who ordinarily served as sheriffs, coroners, jurymen, and justices of the peace were abroad.

The war stimulated technological experimentation, especially with artillery. Cannon revolutionized warfare, making the stone castle no longer impregnable. Because only central governments, not private nobles, could afford cannon, their use strengthened the military power of national states.

The long war also had a profound impact on the political and cultural lives of the two countries. Most notably, it stimulated the development of the English Parliament. Between 1250 and 1450, **representative assemblies** flourished in many European countries. In the English Parliament, German *diets*, and Spanish *cortes*, deliberative practices developed that laid the foundations for the representative institutions of modern democratic nations. While representative assemblies declined in most countries after the fifteenth century, the English Parliament

representative assemblies
▶ Deliberative meetings of lords and wealthy urban residents that flourished in many European countries between 1250 and 1450.

endured. Edward III's constant need for money to pay for the war compelled him to summon not only the great barons and bishops, but knights of the shires and citizens from the towns as well. Parliament met in thirty-seven of the fifty years of Edward's reign.

The frequency of the meetings is significant. Representative assemblies were becoming a habit. Knights and wealthy urban residents—or the "Commons," as they came to be called—recognized their mutual interests and began to meet apart from the great lords. The Commons gradually realized that they held the country's purse strings, and a parliamentary statute of 1341 required parliamentary approval of most new taxes. By signing the law, Edward III acknowledged that the king of England could not tax without Parliament's consent.

In both countries, the war promoted the growth of nationalism—the feeling of unity and identity that binds together a people. After victories, each country experienced a surge of pride in its military strength. Just as English patriotism ran strong after Crécy and Poitiers, so French national confidence rose after Orléans. French national feeling demanded the expulsion of the enemy not merely from Normandy and Aquitaine but from all French soil. Perhaps no one expressed this national consciousness better than Joan when she exulted that the enemy had been "driven out of *France*."

QUICK REVIEW

How did the Hundred Years' War spur the development of nationalism in both England and France?

| How did the Black Death reshape European society? | **What were the causes, course, and consequences of the Hundred Years' War?** | Why did the church come under increasing criticism? | What explains the social unrest of the late Middle Ages? | LearningCurve Check what you know. |

325

Why did the church come under increasing criticism?

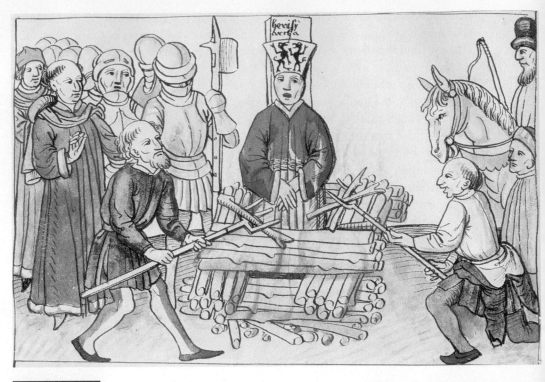

The Execution of Jan Hus This fifteenth-century manuscript illustration shows men placing logs around Hus at the Council of Constance, while soldiers, officials, a priest, and a cardinal look on. Hus became an important symbol of Czech independence, and in 1990, the Czech Republic declared July 6, the date of his execution in 1415, a national holiday. (Gianni Dagli Orti/The Art Archive at Art Resource, NY)

IN TIMES OF CRISIS OR DISASTER, people of all faiths have sought the consolation of religion. In the fourteenth century, however, the official Christian Church offered little solace. Many priests and friars helped the sick and the hungry, but others paid more attention to worldly matters, and the leaders of the church added to the sorrow and misery of the times. In response to this lack of leadership, members of the clergy challenged the power of the pope, and laypeople challenged the authority of the church itself. Women and men increasingly relied on direct approaches to God, often through mystical encounters, rather than on the institutional church.

The Babylonian Captivity and Great Schism

Conflicts between the secular rulers of Europe and the popes were common throughout the High Middle Ages, and in the early fourteenth century the dispute between King Philip the Fair of France and Pope Boniface VIII became particularly bitter (see Chapter 9, page 256). After Boniface's death, Philip pressured the new

CHAPTER LOCATOR | How did climate change shape the late Middle Ages?

pope, Clement V, to settle permanently in Avignon in southeastern France so that he, Philip, could control the church and its policies. The popes lived in Avignon from 1309 to 1376, a period in church history often called the **Babylonian Captivity** (referring to the seventy years the ancient Hebrews were held captive in Mesopotamian Babylon).

The Babylonian Captivity badly damaged papal prestige. The seven popes at Avignon concentrated on bureaucratic and financial matters to the exclusion of spiritual objectives. The general atmosphere was one of luxury and extravagance, which was also the case at many bishops' courts. In 1377, Pope Gregory XI brought the papal court back to Rome, but he died shortly afterward. Roman citizens pressured the cardinals to elect an Italian, and they chose the archbishop of Bari, Bartolomeo Prignano, who took the name Urban VI.

Urban VI (pontificate 1378–1389) had excellent intentions for church reform, but he went about it in a tactless manner. He attacked clerical luxury, denouncing individual cardinals and bishops by name, and even threatened to excommunicate some of them. The cardinals slipped away from Rome and met at Anagni. They declared Urban's election invalid and excommunicated the pope. The cardinals then elected Cardinal Robert of Geneva, the cousin of King Charles V of France, as pope. Cardinal Robert took the name Clement VII. There were thus two popes in 1378—Urban at Rome and Clement VII (pontificate 1378–1394) at Avignon. So began the **Great Schism**, which divided Western Christendom until 1417. The schism weakened the religious faith of many Christians and brought church leadership into serious disrepute.

Critiques, Divisions, and Councils

Criticism of the church during the Avignon papacy and the Great Schism often came from the ranks of highly learned clergy and lay professionals. One of these was William of Occam (1289?–1347?), a Franciscan friar and philosopher who predated the Great Schism but saw the papal court at Avignon during the Babylonian Captivity. Occam argued that governments should have limited powers and be accountable to those they govern and that church and state should be separate.

The Italian lawyer and university official Marsiglio of Padua (ca. 1275–1342) agreed with Occam. In his *Defensor Pacis* (The Defender of the Peace), Marsiglio argued against the medieval idea of a society governed by both church and state, with church supreme. Instead, Marsiglio claimed, the state was the great unifying power in society, and the church should be subordinate to it. Church leadership

Babylonian Captivity

▶ The period from 1309 to 1376 when the popes resided in Avignon rather than in Rome. The phrase refers to the seventy years when the Hebrews were held captive in Babylon.

Great Schism

▶ The division, or split, in church leadership from 1378 to 1417 when there were two, then three, popes.

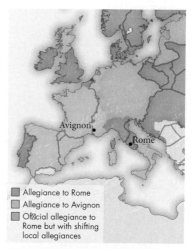

■ Allegiance to Rome
■ Allegiance to Avignon
□ Official allegiance to Rome but with shifting local allegiances

The Great Schism, 1378–1417

TABLE 11.1 ■ The Great Schism

Supporters of Urban VI (Rome)	Supporters of Clement VII (Avignon)
• England • Holy Roman Emperor	• France • Scotland • Aragon • Castile • Portugal • Italian city-states (initially recognized Urban)

How did the Black Death reshape European society?

What were the causes, course, and consequences of the Hundred Years' War?

Why did the church come under increasing criticism?

What explains the social unrest of the late Middle Ages?

✓ LearningCurve
Check what you know.

327

should rest in a general council made up of laymen as well as priests and be superior to the pope. Marsiglio was excommunicated for these radical ideas, and his work was condemned as heresy—as was Occam's—but in the later part of the fourteenth century, many thinkers agreed with these two critics of the papacy. They believed that reform of the church could best be achieved through periodic assemblies, or councils, representing all the Christian people. Those who argued this position were called **conciliarists**.

conciliarists

▶ People who believed that the authority in the Roman Church should rest in a general council composed of clergy, theologians, and laypeople rather than in the pope alone.

The English scholar and theologian John Wyclif (WIH-klihf) (ca. 1330–1384) went further than the conciliarists in his argument against medieval church structure. He wrote that Scripture alone should be the standard of Christian belief and practice and that papal claims of secular power had no foundation in the Scriptures. He urged that the church be stripped of its property. He also wanted Christians to read the Bible for themselves and produced the first complete translation of the Bible into English. Wyclif's followers, dubbed Lollards, spread his ideas and made many copies of his Bible. Lollard teaching allowed women to preach, and women played a significant role in the movement. Lollards were persecuted in the fifteenth century; some were executed, some recanted, and others continued to meet secretly. Bohemian students returning from study at the University of Oxford around 1400 brought Wyclif's ideas with them to Prague. There another university theologian, Jan Hus (ca. 1372–1415), built on them. He also denied papal authority, called for translations of the Bible into the local Czech language, and declared indulgences—papal offers of remission of penance—useless. Hus gained many followers, who linked his theological ideas with their opposition to the church's wealth and power and with a growing sense of Czech nationalism in opposition to the pope's international power. Hus's followers were successful at defeating the combined armies of the pope and the emperor many times. In the 1430s, the emperor finally agreed to recognize the Hussite Church in Bohemia, which survived into the Reformation and then merged with other Protestant churches.

The ongoing schism threatened the church, and in response to continued calls throughout Europe for a council, the cardinals of Rome and Avignon summoned a council at Pisa in 1409. This gathering of prelates and theologians deposed both popes and selected another. Neither the Avignon pope nor the Roman pope would resign, however, and the result was the creation of a threefold schism.

Under pressure from the German emperor Sigismund, a great council met at the imperial city of Constance (1414–1418). The council had three objectives: to wipe out heresy, to end the schism, and to reform the church. The council moved first on the first point: despite being granted a safe-conduct to go to Constance by the emperor, Jan Hus was tried, condemned, and burned at the stake as a heretic in 1415. The council also eventually healed the schism. It deposed both the Roman pope and the successor of the pope chosen at Pisa, and it isolated the Avignon pope. A conclave elected a new leader, the Roman cardinal Colonna, who took the name Martin V (pontificate 1417–1431).

Martin proceeded to dissolve the council. Nothing was done about reform, the third objective of the council. In the later part of the fifteenth century, the papacy concentrated on Italian problems to the exclusion of universal Christian interests. But the schism and the conciliar movement had exposed the need for ecclesiastical reform, thus laying the foundation for the great reform efforts of the sixteenth century.

The Hussite Revolution, 1415–1436

INDIVIDUALS IN SOCIETY
Meister Eckhart

Mysticism — the direct experience of the divine — is an aspect of many world religions and has been part of Christianity throughout its history. During the late Middle Ages, however, the pursuit of mystical union became an important part of the piety of many laypeople, especially in the Rhineland area of Germany. Laypeople were guided by the sermons of the churchman generally known as Meister Eckhart. Born into a German noble family, Eckhart (1260–1329?) joined the Dominican order and studied theology at Paris and Cologne, attaining the academic title of master (*Meister* in German). The leaders of the Dominican order appointed him to a series of administrative and teaching positions, and he wrote learned treatises in Latin that reflected his Scholastic training and deep understanding of classical philosophy.

He also began to preach in German, attracting many listeners through his beautiful language and mystical insights. God, he said, was "an oversoaring being and an overbeing nothingness," whose essence was beyond the ability of humans to express: "if the soul is to know God, it must know Him outside time and place, since God is neither in this or that, but One and above them." Only through "unknowing," emptying oneself, could one come to experience the divine. Yet God was also present in individual human souls, and to a degree in every creature, all of which God had called into being before the beginning of time. Within each human soul there was what Eckhart called a "little spark," an innermost essence that allows the soul — with God's grace and Christ's redemptive action — to come to God. "Our salvation depends upon our knowing and recognizing the Chief Good which is God Himself," preached Eckhart; "the Eye with which I see God is the same Eye with which God sees me." "I have a capacity in my soul for taking in God entirely," he went on, a capacity that was shared by all humans, not only members of the clergy or those with special spiritual gifts. Although Eckhart did not reject church sacraments or the hierarchy, he frequently stressed that union with God was best accomplished through quiet detachment and simple prayer rather than pilgrimages, extensive fasts, or other activities: "If the only prayer you said in your whole life was 'thank you,' that would suffice."*

Eckhart's unusual teachings led to charges of heresy in 1327, which he denied. The pope — who was at this point in Avignon — presided over a trial condemning him, but Eckhart appears to have died during the course of the proceedings or shortly thereafter. His writings were ordered destroyed, but his followers preserved many and spread his teachings.

In the last few decades, Meister Eckhart's ideas have been explored and utilized by philosophers and mystics in Buddhism, Hinduism, and neo-paganism, as well as by Christians. His writings sell widely for their spiritual insights, and quotations from them — including the one above about

A sixteenth-century woodcut of Meister Eckhart teaching. (Visual Connection Archive)

thank-you prayers — can be found on coffee mugs, tote bags, and T-shirts.

QUESTIONS FOR ANALYSIS

1. Why might Meister Eckhart's preaching have been viewed as threatening by the leaders of the church?
2. Given the situation of the church in the late Middle Ages, why might mysticism have been attractive to pious Christians?

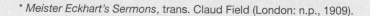 LaunchPad

ONLINE DOCUMENT PROJECT

What does Meister Eckhart's life tell us about the religious climate of the early fourteenth century? Keeping the question above in mind, examine a selection of Eckhart's writings and those of his critics. Then complete a writing assignment based on the evidence and details from this chapter. *See inside the front cover to learn more.*

* *Meister Eckhart's Sermons*, trans. Claud Field (London: n.p., 1909).

Lay Piety and Mysticism

confraternities

▶ Voluntary lay groups organized by occupation, devotional preference, neighborhood, and/or charitable activity.

The failings of the Avignon papacy followed by the scandal of the Great Schism did much to weaken the spiritual mystique of the clergy in the popular mind. Laypeople had already begun to develop their own forms of piety somewhat separate from the authority of priests and bishops, and these forms of piety became more prominent in the fourteenth century.

In the thirteenth century, lay Christian men and women had formed **confraternities**, voluntary lay groups organized by occupation, devotional preference, neighborhood, and/or charitable activity. Like craft guilds, most confraternities were groups of men, but separate women's confraternities were formed in some towns, often to oversee the production of vestments, altar cloths, and other items made of fabric. All confraternities carried out special devotional practices such as prayers or processions, often without the leadership of a priest. Famine, plague, war, and other crises led to an expansion of confraternities in larger cities and many villages.

Beginning in the late fourteenth century in Holland, a group of pious laypeople called the Brethren and Sisters of the Common Life lived in stark simplicity while daily carrying out the Gospel teaching of feeding the hungry, clothing the naked, and visiting the sick. They sought both to ease social problems and to make religion a personal inner experience. In the mid-fifteenth century, the movement founded houses in the Netherlands, in central Germany, and in the Rhineland.

For some individuals, both laypeople and clerics, religious devotion included mystical experiences. (See "Individuals in Society: Meister Eckhart," page 329.) Bridget of Sweden (1303–1373) was a noblewoman who journeyed to Rome after her husband's death. She began to see visions and gave advice based on these visions to both laypeople and church officials.

The confraternities and mystics were generally not considered heretical unless they began to challenge the authority of the papacy the way Wyclif, Hus, and some conciliarists did. However, the movement of lay piety did alter many people's perceptions of their own spiritual power.

> QUICK REVIEW

How and why did laypeople take greater control over their religious lives in the fourteenth and fifteenth centuries?

CHAPTER LOCATOR | How did climate change shape the late Middle Ages?

What explains the social unrest of the late Middle Ages?

City Brothel In this rather fanciful scene of a medieval brothel, two couples share baths and wine, while a third is in bed in the back, and two nobles peer in from a window across the street. Most brothels were not this elaborate, although some did have baths. Many cities also had commercial bathhouses where people paid a small fee to take a hot bath, a luxury otherwise unavailable. Bathhouses did sometimes offer sex, but their main attraction was hot water. (Bibliothèque nationale de France)

AT THE BEGINNING OF THE FOURTEENTH CENTURY, famine and disease profoundly affected the lives of European people. As the century wore on, decades of slaughter and destruction, punctuated by the decimating visits of the Black Death, added further woes. In many parts of France and the Low Countries, fields lay in ruin or untilled for lack of labor. In England, as taxes increased, criticisms of government policy and mismanagement multiplied. Crime and new forms of business organization aggravated economic troubles, and throughout Europe the frustrations of the common people erupted into widespread revolts.

| How did the Black Death reshape European society? | What were the causes, course, and consequences of the Hundred Years' War? | Why did the church come under increasing criticism? | **What explains the social unrest of the late Middle Ages?** | ✓ LearningCurve Check what you know. |

Peasant Revolts

The difficult conditions of the fourteenth and fifteenth centuries spurred a wave of peasant revolts across Europe. Peasants were sometimes joined by those low on the urban social ladder, resulting in a wider revolution of poor against rich.

The first large-scale rebellion was in the Flanders region of present-day Belgium in the 1320s (**Map 11.3**). To satisfy peace agreements, Flemish peasants were forced to pay taxes to the French. Monasteries also pressed peasants for additional money above their customary tithes. In retaliation, peasants burned and pillaged castles and aristocratic country houses. A French army crushed the peasant forces, however, and savage repression and the confiscation of peasant property followed in the 1330s.

MAP 11.3 ■ **Fourteenth-Century Revolts**

In the later Middle Ages, peasant and urban uprisings were endemic, as common as factory strikes in the industrial world. The threat of insurrection served to check unlimited exploitation.

CHAPTER LOCATOR | How did climate change shape the late Middle Ages?

In the following decades, revolts broke out in many other places. In 1358, when French taxation for the Hundred Years' War fell heavily on the poor, the frustrations of the French peasantry exploded in a massive uprising called the **Jacquerie** (zhah-kuh-REE). Peasants blamed the nobility for oppressive taxes, for the criminal banditry of the countryside, for losses on the battlefield, and for the general misery. Artisans and small merchants in cities and parish priests joined the peasants. Rebels committed terrible destruction, and for several weeks the nobles were on the defensive. Then the upper class united to repress the revolt with merciless ferocity. That forcible suppression of social rebellion, without any effort to alleviate its underlying causes, served to drive protest underground.

In England, the Black Death drastically cut the labor supply; as a result, peasants demanded higher wages and fewer manorial obligations. Their lords countered in 1351 with the Statute of Laborers, a law issued by the king that froze wages and bound workers to their manors. This attempt to freeze wages could not be enforced, but a huge gap remained between peasants and their lords. The peasants sought release for their economic frustrations in revolt. Other factors combined with these economic grievances to fuel the rebellion. The south of England, where the revolt broke out, had been subjected to destructive French raids during the Hundred Years' War. The English government did little to protect the region, and villagers grew increasingly frightened and insecure. Decades of aristocratic violence against the weak peasantry had bred hostility and bitterness. Social and religious agitation by the popular preacher John Ball fanned the embers of discontent.

The English revolt was ignited by the reimposition of a tax on all adult males. Despite widespread opposition to the tax in 1380, the royal council ordered the sheriffs to collect it again in 1381. This led to a major uprising known as the **English Peasants' Revolt**, which involved thousands of people. The center of the revolt lay in the highly populated and economically advanced south and east, but sections of the north also witnessed rebellions (see Map 11.3, page 332).

The boy-king Richard II (r. 1377–1399) met the leaders of the revolt, agreed to charters ensuring peasants' freedom, tricked them with false promises, and then crushed the uprising with terrible ferocity. In the aftermath of the revolt, the nobility tried to restore the labor obligations of serfdom, but they were not successful, and the conversion to money rents continued. The English Peasants' Revolt did not bring social equality to England, but rural serfdom continued to decline, disappearing in England by 1550.

Urban Conflicts

In Flanders, France, and England, peasant revolts often blended with conflicts involving workers in cities. Unrest also occurred in Italian, Spanish, and German cities. The urban revolts had their roots in the changing conditions of work. In the thirteenth century, craft guilds had organized the production of most goods, with masters, journeymen, and apprentices working side by side. In the fourteenth century, a new system evolved to make products on a larger scale. Capitalist investors hired many households, with each household performing only one step of the process. Initially these investors were wealthy bankers and merchants, but eventually shop masters themselves embraced the system. In the guilds, this

Jacquerie
▶ A massive uprising by French peasants in 1358 protesting heavy taxation.

English Peasants' Revolt
▶ Revolt by English peasants in 1381 in response to changing economic conditions.

| How did the Black Death reshape European society? | What were the causes, course, and consequences of the Hundred Years' War? | Why did the church come under increasing criticism? | **What explains the social unrest of the late Middle Ages?** | ✔️ LearningCurve Check what you know. |

333

promoted a greater division between wealthier masters and the poorer masters and journeymen they hired.

While capitalism provided opportunities for some artisans to become investors and entrepreneurs, especially in cloth production, for many it led to a decrease in income and status. Guilds sometimes responded to crises by opening up membership, as they did in some places immediately after the Black Death, but they more often responded to competition by limiting membership to existing guild families, which meant that journeymen who were not master's sons or who could not find a master's widow or daughter to marry could never become masters themselves. Remaining journeymen their entire lives, they lost their sense of solidarity with the masters of their craft. Resentment led to rebellion.

Urban uprisings were also sparked by issues involving honor, such as employers who required workers to do tasks they regarded as beneath them. As their actual status and economic prospects declined and their work became basically wage labor, journeymen and poorer masters emphasized skill and honor as qualities that set them apart from less-skilled workers.

Guilds increasingly came to view the honor of their work as tied to an all-male workplace. When urban economies were expanding in the High Middle Ages, the master's wife and daughters worked alongside him. But in the fourteenth century, women's participation in guilds declined despite labor shortages caused by the plague. First, masters' widows were limited in the amount of time they could operate a shop or were prohibited from hiring journeymen; later, female domestic servants were excluded from any productive tasks. Then the number of daughters a master craftsman could employ was limited. When women were allowed to work, it was viewed as a substitute for charity.

Sex in the City

Peasant and urban revolts and riots had clear economic bases, but some historians have suggested that late medieval marital patterns may have also played a role. In northwestern Europe, people believed that couples should be economically independent before they married. Thus, men and women spent long periods as servants or workers in other households, saving money for married life and learning skills, or they waited until their own parents had died and the family property was distributed.

Men of all social groups had long tended to be older than women when they married. In general, men were in their middle or late twenties at first marriage, with wealthier urban merchants often much older. Journeymen and apprentices were often explicitly prohibited from marrying, as were the students at universities.

The prohibitions on marriage for certain groups of men and the late age of marriage for most men meant that cities and villages were filled with large numbers of young adult men with no family responsibilities who often formed the core of riots and unrest. Not surprisingly, this situation also contributed to a steady market for sexual services outside of marriage, services that in later centuries were termed prostitution. In many cities, municipal authorities set up houses or districts for prostitution either outside the city walls or away from respectable neighborhoods.

Young men associated visiting brothels with achieving manhood; for the women themselves, of course, their activities were work. Some women had no

CHAPTER LOCATOR | How did climate change shape the late Middle Ages?

CHAPTER 11
334 THE LATER MIDDLE AGES

choice because they had been traded to the brothel manager by their parents or some other person as payment for debt, or they had quickly become indebted to the manager (most of whom were men) for the clothes and other finery regarded as essential to their occupation. Poor women—and men—also sold sex illegally outside of city brothels, combining this with other sorts of part-time work such as laundering or sewing.

Though selling sex for money was legal in the Middle Ages, the position of women who did so was always marginal. In the late fifteenth century, cities began to limit brothel residents' freedom of movement and choice of clothing, requiring them to wear distinctive head coverings or bands on their clothing. Cities also began to impose harsher penalties on women who did not live in the designated house or section of town. A few women who sold sex did earn enough to donate money to charity or buy property, but most were very poor.

Along with buying sex, young men also took it by force. Unmarried women often found it difficult to avoid sexual contact. Many worked as domestic servants, where their employers or employers' sons or male relatives could easily coerce them, or they worked in proximity to men. Notions of female honor kept upper-class women secluded in their homes, particularly in southern and eastern Europe, but there was little attempt anywhere to protect female servants or day laborers from the risk of seduction or rape. Rape was a capital crime in many parts of Europe, but the actual sentences handed out were more likely to be fines and brief imprisonment, with the severity of the sentence dependent on the social status of the victim and the perpetrator.

Same-sex relations were another feature of medieval life. Same-sex relations were of relatively little concern to church or state authorities in the early Middle

Same-Sex Relations

This illustration, from a thirteenth-century French book of morals, interprets female and male same-sex relations as the work of devils. The illustration was painted at the time that religious and political authorities were increasingly criminalizing same-sex relations. (ONB/Vienna, Picture Archives, Cod. 2554, fol. 2r)

How did the Black Death reshape European society?	What were the causes, course, and consequences of the Hundred Years' War?	Why did the church come under increasing criticism?	**What explains the social unrest of the late Middle Ages?**	✓ LearningCurve Check what you know.

Ages, but this attitude changed beginning in the late twelfth century. By 1300, most areas had defined such actions as "crimes against nature." Same-sex relations, usually termed sodomy, became a capital crime in most of Europe, with adult offenders threatened with execution by fire. The Italian cities of Venice, Florence, and Lucca created special courts to deal with sodomy, which saw thousands of investigations.

How prevalent were same-sex relations? This question is difficult to answer, even in modern society, but the city of Florence provides a provocative case study.[1] Between 1432 and the abolition of the board in 1502, about seventeen thousand men came to its attention, which, even over a seventy-year period, represents a great number in a population of about forty thousand. The men came from all classes of society, but almost all cases involved an adult man and an adolescent boy; they ranged from sex exchanged for money or gifts to long-term affectionate relationships.

Thus, in Florence, and no doubt elsewhere in Europe, sodomy was not a marginal practice, which may account for the fact that, despite harsh laws and special courts, actual executions for sodomy were rare. Same-sex relations often developed within the context of all-male environments, such as the army, the craft shop, and the artistic workshop, and were part of the collective male experience. Homoerotic relationships played important roles in defining stages of life, expressing distinctions of status, and shaping masculine gender identity. Same-sex relations involving women almost never came to the attention of legal authorities, so it is difficult to find out how common they were. However, female-female desire was expressed in songs, plays, and stories, as was male-male desire, offering evidence of the way people understood same-sex relations.

Fur-Collar Crime

The Hundred Years' War had provided employment and opportunity for thousands of idle and fortune-seeking knights. But during periods of truce and after the war finally ended, many nobles once again had little to do. Inflation hurt them. Although many were living on fixed incomes, their chivalric code demanded lavish generosity and an aristocratic lifestyle. Many nobles thus turned to crime as a way of raising money.

This "fur-collar crime" involved both violence and fraud. Groups of noble bandits roamed the English countryside, stealing from both rich and poor. Operating like modern urban racketeers, knightly gangs demanded that peasants pay protection money or else have their hovels burned and their fields destroyed. They seized wealthy travelers and held them for ransom. Corrupt landowners, including some churchmen, pushed peasants to pay higher taxes and extra fees. When accused of wrongdoing, fur-collar criminals intimidated witnesses, threatened jurors, and used their influence to persuade judges to support them—or used cash to bribe them outright.

Ethnic Tensions and Restrictions

Large numbers of people in the twelfth and thirteenth centuries migrated from one part of Europe to another in search of land, food, and work. Everywhere in Europe, towns recruited people from the countryside as well. In frontier regions, townspeople

CHAPTER LOCATOR | How did climate change shape the late Middle Ages?

CHAPTER 11
336   THE LATER MIDDLE AGES

were usually long-distance immigrants, and in eastern Europe, Ireland, and Scotland, they were ethnically different from the surrounding rural population. In eastern Europe, German was the language of the towns; in Irish towns, French, the tongue of Norman or English settlers, predominated. As a result of this colonization and movement to towns, peoples of different ethnic backgrounds lived side by side.

In the early periods of conquest and colonization, and in all regions with extensive migrations, a legal dualism existed: native peoples remained subject to their traditional laws; newcomers brought and were subject to the laws of the countries from which they came. The great exception to this broad pattern of legal pluralism was Ireland. The English distinguished between the free and the unfree, and the entire Irish population, simply by the fact of Irish birth, was unfree. When English legal structures were established beginning in 1210, the Irish were denied access to the common-law courts. In civil (property) disputes, an English defendant did not need to respond to an Irish plaintiff; no Irish person could make a will. In criminal procedures, the murder of an Irishman was not considered a felony.

The later Middle Ages witnessed a movement away from legal pluralism or dualism and toward legal homogeneity and an emphasis on blood descent. The dominant ethnic group in an area tried to bar others from positions of church leadership and guild membership. Marriage laws were instituted that attempted to maintain ethnic purity by prohibiting intermarriage, and some church leaders actively promoted ethnic discrimination.

The most extensive attempt to prevent intermarriage and protect ethnic purity is embodied in the Statute of Kilkenny (1366), a law the ruling English imposed on Ireland, which stated that "there were to be no marriages between those of immigrant and native stock; that the English inhabitants of Ireland must employ the English language and bear English names; that they must ride in the English way [that is, with saddles] and have English apparel; that no Irishmen were to be granted ecclesiastical benefices or admitted to monasteries in the English parts of Ireland."[2]

Statute of Kilkenny
▶ Law issued in 1366 that discriminated against the Irish, forbidding marriage between the English and the Irish, requiring the use of the English language, and denying the Irish access to ecclesiastical offices.

Late medieval chroniclers held that peoples differed according to language, traditions, customs, and laws. None of these were unchangeable, however, and commentators increasingly also described ethnic differences in terms of blood, which made ethnicity heritable. As national consciousness grew with the Hundred Years' War, for example, people began to speak of French blood and English blood. Religious beliefs came to be conceptualized in terms of blood as well, with people regarded as having Jewish blood, Muslim blood, or Christian blood. Blood also came to be used as a way to talk about social differences, especially for nobles. As Europeans increasingly came into contact with people from Africa and Asia, and particularly as they developed colonial empires, these notions about blood also became a way of conceptualizing racial categories.

Literacy and Vernacular Literature

The development of ethnic identities had many negative consequences, but a more positive effect was the increasing use of the vernacular, that is, the local language that people actually spoke, rather than Latin (see Chapter 10, page 304). Two masterpieces of European culture, Dante's *Divine Comedy* (1310–1320) and Chaucer's *Canterbury Tales* (1387–1400), illustrate a sophisticated use of the rhythms and rhymes of the vernacular.

| How did the Black Death reshape European society? | What were the causes, course, and consequences of the Hundred Years' War? | Why did the church come under increasing criticism? | **What explains the social unrest of the late Middle Ages?** | ☑ LearningCurve Check what you know. |

337

The *Divine Comedy* of Dante Alighieri (DAHN-tay ah-luh-GYEHR-ee) (1265–1321) is an epic poem. Each of its three equal parts describes one of the realms of the next world: Hell, Purgatory, and Paradise. The *Divine Comedy* portrays contemporary and historical figures, comments on secular and ecclesiastical affairs, and draws on the Scholastic philosophy of uniting faith and reason. Within the framework of a symbolic pilgrimage, the *Divine Comedy* embodies the psychological tensions of the age. A profoundly Christian poem, it also contains bitter criticism of some church authorities. In its symmetrical structure and use of figures from the ancient world, the poem perpetuates the classical tradition, but as the first major work of literature in the Italian vernacular, it is distinctly modern.

Geoffrey Chaucer (1342–1400) was an official in the administrations of the English kings Edward III and Richard II. His *Canterbury Tales* is a collection of stories in lengthy rhymed narrative. On a pilgrimage to the shrine of Saint Thomas Becket at Canterbury (see Chapter 9, page 249), thirty characters of various social backgrounds tell tales. In depicting the interests and behavior of all types of people, Chaucer presents a rich panorama of English social life in the fourteenth century. Like the *Divine Comedy*, the *Canterbury Tales* reflects the cultural tensions of the times. Ostensibly Christian, many of the pilgrims are also materialistic, sensual, and worldly, suggesting the ambivalence of the broader society's concern for the next world and frank enjoyment of this one.

Beginning in the fourteenth century, a variety of evidence attests to the increasing literacy of laypeople. Wills and inventories reveal that many people, not just nobles, possessed books: mainly devotional texts but also romances, manuals on manners and etiquette, histories, and sometimes legal and philosophical texts. In England, the number of schools in the diocese of York quadrupled between 1350 and 1500. Information from Flemish and German towns is similar: children were sent to schools and were taught the fundamentals of reading, writing, and arithmetic. Laymen increasingly served as managers or stewards of estates and as clerks to guilds and town governments; such positions obviously required the ability to keep administrative and financial records.

The penetration of laymen into the higher positions of governmental administration, long the preserve of clerics, also illustrates rising lay literacy. With growing frequency, the upper classes sent their daughters to convent schools, where, in addi-

Chaucer's Wife of Bath

Chaucer's *Canterbury Tales* were filled with memorable characters, including the often-married Wife of Bath, shown here in a fifteenth-century manuscript. In the prologue that details her life, she denies the value of virginity and criticizes her young and handsome fifth husband for reading a book about "wicked wives." "By God, if women had but written stories, . . ." she comments, "They would have written of men more wickedness / Than all the race of Adam could redress." (Private Collection/The Bridgeman Art Library)

CHAPTER LOCATOR | How did climate change shape the late Middle Ages?

CHAPTER 11
338 THE LATER MIDDLE AGES

tion to instruction in singing, religion, needlework, deportment, and household management, they gained the rudiments of reading and sometimes writing.

The spread of literacy represents a response to the needs of an increasingly complex society. Trade, commerce, and expanding government bureaucracies required an increasing number of literate people. Late medieval culture remained a decidedly oral culture. But by the fifteenth century, the evolution toward a more literate culture was already perceptible, and craftsmen would develop the new technology of the printing press in response to the increased demand for reading materials.

QUICK REVIEW <

How did the Black Death contribute to the rising social and economic tensions of the late Middle Ages?

LOOKING BACK LOOKING AHEAD

The fourteenth and early fifteenth centuries were certainly times of crisis in western Europe. Famine, disease, and war decimated the European population, and traditional institutions, including secular governments and the church, did little or nothing or, in some cases, made things worse. Trading connections that had been reinvigorated in the High Middle Ages spread the most deadly epidemic ever experienced through western Asia, North Africa, and almost all of Europe.

The plague did not destroy the prosperity of the medieval population, however, and it may in fact have indirectly improved the European economy. Wealthy merchants had plenty of money to spend on luxuries and talent. In the century after the plague, Italian artists began to create new styles of painting, writers to pen new literary forms, educators to found new types of schools, and philosophers to develop new ideas about the purpose of human life. These cultural changes eventually spread to the rest of Europe, following the same paths that the plague had traveled.

LaunchPad

ONLINE DOCUMENT PROJECT

Meister Eckhart

What does Meister Eckhart's life tell us about the religious climate of the early fourteenth century?

You encountered Meister Eckart's story on page 329. Keeping the question above in mind, examine Eckhart's writings and those of his critics. Think about why he appealed to lay audiences and what compelled church leaders to condemn his teachings. *See inside the front cover to learn more.*

| How did the Black Death reshape European society? | What were the causes, course, and consequences of the Hundred Years' War? | Why did the church come under increasing criticism? | What explains the social unrest of the late Middle Ages? | ☑ LearningCurve Check what you know. |

CHAPTER 11 STUDY GUIDE

STEP 1 **GET STARTED ONLINE**

✔️ **LearningCurve**

Now that you've read the chapter, make it stick by completing the LearningCurve activity.

STEP 2 **EXPLAIN WHY IT MATTERS**

Put your reading into practice. Identify each term below, and then explain why it matters in Western history.

TERM	WHO OR WHAT & WHEN	WHY IT MATTERS
Great Famine (p. 312)		
Black Death (p. 314)		
flagellants (p. 318)		
Hundred Years' War (p. 320)		
representative assemblies (p. 324)		
Babylonian Captivity (p. 327)		
Great Schism (p. 327)		
conciliarists (p. 328)		
confraternities (p. 330)		
Jacquerie (p. 333)		
English Peasants' Revolt (p. 333)		
Statute of Kilkenny (p. 337)		

STEP 3 **MOVE BEYOND THE BASICS**

To demonstrate a more advanced understanding, complete the chart included below on how the Black Death destabilized existing patterns and institutions and created opportunities for new ones to emerge.

	Economic	Social	Political	Cultural and religious
Consequences of the Black Death				

STEP 4 **PUT IT ALL TOGETHER** Now, take a step back and try to explain the big picture. Remember to use specific examples from the chapter in your answers.

FAMINE, DISEASE, AND WARFARE

▶ How did climate change and disease combine to devastate Europe's population?

▶ Why did the Hundred Years' War drag on as long as it did? What explains the inability of French and English leaders to bring the conflict to a final resolution? Did they even want to?

CHALLENGES TO THE CHURCH

▶ In your opinion, is it fair to describe the fourteenth-century Roman Church as a failed institution? Why or why not?

▶ What does the lay religious activity of the fourteenth century tell us about the values and beliefs of late medieval Europeans? What kind of religious life did fourteenth-century Europeans want? What religious ideals did they hold?

SOCIAL UNREST

▶ Compare and contrast fourteenth-century rebellions and uprisings in England and France. What common causes and conditions linked rebellions in both countries?

▶ Why did perceptions of ethnic difference and ethnic hierarchy sharpen in the fourteenth century? Can you think of any, more recent parallels to this development?

MAKE CONNECTIONS

▶ Why did the growth and vitality of the High Middle Ages prove unsustainable?

▶ In your opinion, are the late Middle Ages best viewed as the end of one of phase of Western development or the beginning of a new one? Why?

> **IN YOUR OWN WORDS**

Imagine that you must give an oral report to the class answering the following question: **How did the catastrophes of the Late Middle Ages change European society?** What would be the most important points and why?

12

EUROPEAN SOCIETY IN THE AGE OF THE RENAISSANCE

1350–1550

> **What new ways of thinking and new forms of cultural expression were developed during the Renaissance?** Chapter 12 examines the emergence of a new culture in southern Europe. The fourteenth century witnessed remarkable changes in Italian intellectual, artistic, and cultural life. Artists and writers thought that they were living in a new golden age, but not until the sixteenth century was this change given the label we use today — the *Renaissance*, derived from the French word for "rebirth." That word was first used by art historian Giorgio Vasari (1511–1574) to describe the art of "rare men of genius." Through their works, Vasari judged, the glory of the classical past had been reborn after centuries of darkness. Over time, the word's meaning was broadened to include many aspects of life during that period. The new attitude had a slow diffusion out of Italy, and thus the Renaissance "happened" at different times in different parts of Europe. The Renaissance was a movement, not a time period.

✓ **LearningCurve**
After reading the chapter, use LearningCurve to retain what you've read.

Life in the Renaissance. In this detail from a fresco, Italian painter Lorenzo Lotto captures the mixing of social groups in a Renaissance Italian city. (Scala/Art Resource, NY)

> How did politics and economics shape the Renaissance?

> What new ideas were associated with the Renaissance?

> How did art reflect new Renaissance ideals?

> What were the key social hierarchies in Renaissance Europe?

> How did nation-states develop in this period?

How did politics and economics shape the Renaissance?

A Florentine Bank Scene

Originally a "bank" was just a counter; money changers who sat behind the counter became "bankers," exchanging different currencies and holding deposits for merchants and business people. In this scene from fifteenth-century Florence, the bank is covered with an imported Ottoman geometric rug, one of many imported luxury items handled by Florentine merchants. (Scala/Art Resource, NY)

Renaissance
▶ A French word meaning "rebirth," used to describe the rebirth of the culture of classical antiquity in Italy during the fourteenth to sixteenth centuries.

patronage
▶ Financial support of writers and artists by cities, groups, and individuals, often to produce specific works or works in specific styles.

THE CULTURE OF THE Renaissance rested on economic and political developments in the city-states of northern Italy. Economic growth laid the material basis for the Italian Renaissance, and ambitious merchants gained political power to match their economic power. They then used their money and power to buy luxuries and hire talent in a system of **patronage**, through which cities, groups, and individuals commissioned writers and artists to produce specific works. Thus, economics, politics, and culture were interconnected.

CHAPTER LOCATOR | How did politics and economics shape the Renaissance?

ca. 1350 – Petrarch develops ideas of humanism	**1478** – Establishment of the Inquisition in Spain
1434–1737 – Medici family in power in Florence	**1492** – Spain conquers Granada, ending reconquista; practicing Jews expelled from Spain
1440s – Invention of movable metal type	**1494** – Invasion of Italy by Charles VIII of France
1447–1535 – Sforza family in power in Milan	**1508–1512** – Michelangelo paints ceiling of Sistine Chapel
1455–1471 – Wars of the Roses in England	**1513** – Machiavelli writes *The Prince*
1469 – Marriage of Isabella of Castile and Ferdinand of Aragon	**1563** – Establishment of first formal academy for artistic training in Florence
1477 – Louis XI conquers Burgundy	

Trade and Prosperity

Northern Italian cities led the way in the great commercial revival of the eleventh century (see Chapter 10, page 287). By the middle of the twelfth century, Venice, supported by a huge merchant marine, had grown enormously rich through overseas trade, as had Genoa and Milan, which had their own sizable fleets. These cities made important strides in shipbuilding that allowed their ships to sail all year-round at accelerated speeds and carrying more and more merchandise.

Another commercial leader, and the city where the Renaissance began, was Florence, situated on fertile soil along the Arno River. Its favorable location on the main road northward from Rome made Florence a commercial hub, and the city grew wealthy buying and selling all types of goods throughout Europe and the Mediterranean.

Florentine merchants also loaned and invested money, and they acquired control of papal banking toward the end of the thirteenth century. Florentine mercantile families began to dominate European banking, setting up offices in major European and North African cities. The banking profits that poured back to Florence were pumped into urban industries such as clothmaking. Profits contributed to the city's economic vitality and allowed banking families to control the city's politics and culture.

By the first quarter of the fourteenth century, the economic foundations of Florence were so strong that even severe crises could not destroy the city. In 1344, King Edward III of England repudiated his huge debts to Florentine bankers, forcing some of them into bankruptcy. Soon after, Florence suffered frightfully from the Black Death, losing at least half its population, and serious labor unrest shook the political establishment. Nevertheless, the basic Florentine economic structure remained stable, and the city grew again. In Florence and other thriving Italian cities, wealth gave many people the free time and resources to appreciate

What new ideas were associated with the Renaissance?	How did art reflect new Renaissance ideals?	What were the key social hierarchies in Renaissance Europe?	How did nation-states develop in this period?	✓ LearningCurve Check what you know.

and patronize the arts. Merchants and bankers commissioned public and private buildings from architects. They hired sculptors and painters to decorate their homes and churches.

Communes and Republics of Northern Italy

communes
▶ Sworn associations of free men in Italian cities led by merchant guilds that sought political and economic independence from local nobles.

The northern Italian cities were **communes**, sworn associations of free men who, like other town residents, began in the twelfth century to seek political and economic independence from local nobles. The local nobles frequently moved into the cities, marrying the daughters of rich commercial families and starting their own businesses. This merger of the northern Italian nobility and the commercial elite created a powerful oligarchy, a small group that ruled the city and surrounding countryside. Yet because of rivalries among competing powerful families within this oligarchy, Italian communes were often politically unstable.

popolo
▶ Disenfranchised common people in Italian cities who resented their exclusion from power.

Unrest from below exacerbated the instability. Merchant elites made citizenship in the communes dependent on a property qualification, years of residence within the city, and social connections. Only a tiny percentage of the male population possessed these qualifications and thus could hold political office. The common people, called the **popolo**, were disenfranchised and heavily taxed, and they bitterly resented their exclusion from power. Throughout most of the thirteenth century, in city after city, the popolo used armed force to take over the city governments. Republican government—in which political power theoretically resides in the people and is exercised by their chosen representatives—was sometimes established in numerous Italian cities. These victories of the popolo proved temporary, however, because they could not establish civil order within their cities. Merchant oligarchies reasserted their power and sometimes brought in powerful military leaders to establish order. These military leaders, called *condottieri* (kahn-duh-TYER-ee; singular *condottiero*), sometimes took over political power once they had supplanted the existing government.

signori
▶ Government by one-man rule in Italian cities such as Milan; also refers to these rulers.

Many cities in Italy became **signori** (seen-YOHR-ee), in which one man ruled and handed down the right to rule to his son. Some signori kept the institutions of communal government in place, but these had no actual power. As a practical matter, there wasn't much difference between oligarchic regimes and signori.

courts
▶ Magnificent households and palaces where signori and other rulers lived, conducted business, and supported the arts.

In the fifteenth and sixteenth centuries, the signori in many cities and the most powerful merchant oligarchs in others transformed their households into **courts**. Courtly culture afforded signori and oligarchs the opportunity to display and assert their wealth and power. They built magnificent palaces in the centers of cities and required all political business to be done there. Ceremonies connected with family births, baptisms, marriages, and funerals offered occasions for magnificent pageantry and elaborate ritual. Cities welcomed rulers who were visiting with magnificent entrance parades. Rulers of nation-states later copied and adapted all these aspects of Italian courts.

City-States and the Balance of Power

Renaissance Italians had a passionate attachment to their individual city-states. Their political loyalty and feeling centered on the city. This intensity of local feeling perpetuated the dozens of small states and hindered the development of one unified Italian state.

CHAPTER LOCATOR | How did politics and economics shape the Renaissance?

CHAPTER 12
346 EUROPEAN SOCIETY IN THE AGE OF THE RENAISSANCE

MAP 12.1 ■ The Italian City-States, ca. 1494

In the fifteenth century, the Italian city-states represented great wealth and cultural sophistication, though the many political divisions throughout the peninsula invited foreign intervention.

HOLY ROMAN EMPIRE

DUCHY OF MILAN

DUCHY OF SAVOY

Brescia

Milan
Pavia

Padua

Turin

Lodi

Venice

Este

SALUZZO

Po R.

MANTUA

Parma

Genoa

FERRARA

Modena

REPUBLIC OF GENOA

Bologna

Ravenna

MODENA

REP. OF FLORENCE

REP. OF LUCCA

Ligurian Sea

Pisa

Florence

Urbino

Arno R.

Arezzo

Siena

Perugia

PAPAL STATES

REP. OF SIENA

Assisi

Elba

Tiber

Corsica (Rep. of Genoa)

Rome

KINGDOM

Bari

Naples

Salerno

OF

NAPLES

Sardinia (Spain)

Tyrrhenian Sea

Mediterranean Sea

Palermo

Sicily (Spain)

AFRICA

Adriatic Sea

REPUBLIC OF VENICE

OTTOMAN EMPIRE

□ Minor city-state
→ Invasion of Charles VIII of France, 1494

0   50   100 miles
0   50   100 kilometers

In the fifteenth century, five powers dominated the Italian peninsula: Venice, Milan, Florence, the Papal States, and the kingdom of Naples (**Map 12.1**). The major Italian powers controlled the smaller city-states and competed furiously among themselves for territory. While the states of northern Europe were moving toward centralization and consolidation, the world of Italian politics resembled a jungle where the powerful dominated the weak.

In one significant respect, however, the Italian city-states anticipated future relations among competing European states after 1500. Whenever one Italian state appeared to gain a predominant position within the peninsula, other states combined against it to establish a balance of power. In the formation of these alliances, Renaissance Italians invented the machinery of modern diplomacy: permanent embassies with resident ambassadors in capitals where political relations and commercial ties needed continual monitoring.

| What new ideas were associated with the Renaissance? | How did art reflect new Renaissance ideals? | What were the key social hierarchies in Renaissance Europe? | How did nation-states develop in this period? | ✓ LearningCurve Check what you know. |

347

At the end of the fifteenth century, Venice, Florence, Milan, and the papacy possessed great wealth and represented high cultural achievement. Wealthy and divided, however, they were also an inviting target for invasion. When Florence and Naples entered into an agreement to acquire Milanese territories, Milan called on France for support, and the French king Charles VIII (r. 1483–1498) invaded Italy in 1494.

Prior to this invasion, the Dominican friar Girolamo Savonarola (1452–1498) had preached in Florence a number of fiery sermons, attended by large crowds, predicting that God would punish Italy for its moral vice and corrupt leadership. Florentines interpreted the French invasion as the fulfillment of this prophecy and expelled the Medici, the powerful banking family that had ruled Florence since 1434. Savonarola became the political and religious leader of a new Florentine republic and promised Florentines even greater glory in the future if they would reform their ways. For a time, Savonarola was wildly popular, but eventually people tired of his moral denunciations. He was excommunicated by the pope, tortured, and burned at the stake, and the Medici returned as the rulers of Florence.

The French invasion inaugurated a new period in Italian and European power politics. Italy became the focus of international ambitions and the battleground of foreign armies, particularly those of the Holy Roman Empire and France in a series of conflicts called the *Habsburg-Valois wars*. The Italian cities suffered severely from continual warfare, especially in the frightful sack of Rome in 1527 by imperial forces under the emperor Charles V. Thus, the failure of the city-states to consolidate, or at least to establish a common foreign policy, led to centuries of subjection by outside invaders. Italy was not to achieve unification until 1870.

> **QUICK REVIEW**

Why and how did Florence emerge as a key center of the Renaissance in the fifteenth century?

CHAPTER LOCATOR | How did politics and economics shape the Renaissance?

CHAPTER 12
348 EUROPEAN SOCIETY IN THE AGE OF THE RENAISSANCE

What new ideas were associated with the Renaissance?

In this reproduction of Gutenberg's printing press, metal type sits in a frame (left) ready to be placed in the bottom part of the press, with a leather-covered ink ball for spreading ink on the type ready nearby. Once the type was in place, paper was placed over the frame and a heavy metal plate (right) was lowered onto the paper with a firm pull of the large wooden handle, a technology adapted from winepresses. (Erich Lessing/Art Resource, NY)

THE RENAISSANCE WAS CHARACTERIZED by self-conscious conviction among educated Italians that they were living in a new era. Through reflecting on the classics of ancient Latin and Greek literature and philosophy, Renaissance thinkers developed new notions of human nature, new plans for education, and new concepts of political rule. The advent of the printing press with movable type would greatly accelerate the spread of these ideas throughout Europe.

Humanism

Francesco Petrarch (1304–1374) spent long hours searching for classical Latin manuscripts in dusty monastery libraries and wandering around the many ruins of the Roman Empire remaining in Italy. He became obsessed with the classical

What new ideas were associated with the Renaissance?	How did art reflect new Renaissance ideals?	What were the key social hierarchies in Renaissance Europe?	How did nation-states develop in this period?	✓ LearningCurve Check what you know.

past and felt that the writers and artists of ancient Rome had reached a level of perfection in their work that had not since been duplicated. Petrarch believed that the recovery of classical texts would bring a new golden age of intellectual achievement, an idea that many others came to share.

Petrarch clearly thought he was witnessing the dawning of a new era in which writers and artists would recapture the glory of the Roman Republic. Around 1350, he proposed a new kind of education in which young men would study the works of ancient Roman authors, using them as models of how to write clearly, argue effectively, and speak persuasively. The study of Latin classics became known as the *studia humanitates* (STOO-dee-uh oo-mahn-ee-TAH-tayz), usually translated as "liberal studies" or the "liberal arts." People who advocated it were known as *humanists* and their program as **humanism**. Humanism was the main intellectual component of the Renaissance. Like all programs of study, humanism contained an implicit philosophy: that human nature and achievements, evident in the classics, were worthy of contemplation.

In the fifteenth century, Florentine humanists became increasingly interested in Greek philosophy as well as Roman literature, especially in the ideas of Plato. Under the patronage of Cosimo de' Medici (1389–1464), the scholar Marsilio Ficino (1433–1499) began to lecture to an informal group of Florence's cultural elite. Ficino regarded Plato as a divinely inspired precursor to Christ. He translated Plato's dialogues into Latin and wrote commentaries attempting to synthesize Christian and Platonic teachings. Plato's emphasis on the spiritual and eternal over the material and transient fit well with Christian teachings about the immortality of the soul. The Platonic idea that the highest form of love was spiritual desire for pure, perfect beauty uncorrupted by bodily desires could easily be interpreted as Christian desire for the perfection of God. For Ficino and his most gifted student, Giovanni Pico della Mirandola (1463–1494), both Christian and classical texts taught that the universe was a hierarchy of beings from God down through spiritual beings to material beings, with humanity, right in the middle, as the crucial link that possessed both material and spiritual natures.

Humanity's divinely bestowed nature meant there were no limits to what people could accomplish. Families, religious brotherhoods, neighborhoods, workers' organizations, and other groups continued to have meaning in peoples' lives, but Renaissance thinkers increasingly viewed these groups as springboards to far greater individual achievement. They were especially interested in individuals who had risen above their background to become brilliant, powerful, or unique. (See "Individuals in Society: Leonardo da Vinci," page 352.) Such individuals had the admirable quality of **virtù** (vihr-TOO), which is not virtue in the sense of moral goodness but instead is their ability to shape the world around them according to their will.

humanism

▶ A program of study designed by Italians that emphasized the critical study of Latin and Greek literature with the goal of understanding human nature.

virtù

▶ The quality of being able to shape the world according to one's own will.

Education

Humanists thought that their recommended course of study in the classics would provide essential skills for future politicians, diplomats, lawyers, military leaders, and businessmen, as well as writers and artists. It would provide a much broader and more practical type of training than that offered at universities, which at the time focused on theology and philosophy or on theoretical training for lawyers and physicians. Humanists poured out treatises on the structure and goals of edu-

CHAPTER LOCATOR | How did politics and economics shape the Renaissance?

cation and the training of rulers and leaders. They taught that a life active in the world should be the aim of all educated individuals and that education was not simply for private or religious purposes but also for the public good.

Humanists put their ideas into practice. Beginning in the early fifteenth century, they opened schools and academies in Italian cities and courts in which pupils began with Latin grammar and rhetoric, went on to study Roman history and political philosophy, and then learned Greek in order to study Greek literature and philosophy. Gradually, humanist education became the basis for intermediate and advanced education for well-to-do urban boys and men.

Humanists disagreed about education for women. Many saw the value of exposing women to classical models of moral behavior and reasoning, but they also wondered whether a program of study that emphasized eloquence and action was proper for women. Women themselves were bolder in their claims about the value of the new learning. Although humanist academies were not open to women, a few women did become educated in the classics. They argued in letters and published writings that reason was not limited to men and that learning was compatible with virtue for women as well as men.

No book on education had broader influence than Baldassare Castiglione's *The Courtier* (1528). This treatise sought to train, discipline, and fashion the young man into the courtly ideal, the gentleman. According to Castiglione (kahsteel-YOH-nay), the educated man should have a broad background in many academic subjects, and should train his spiritual and physical faculties as well as intellect. Castiglione envisioned a man who could compose a sonnet; wrestle; sing a song while accompanying himself on an instrument; ride expertly; solve difficult mathematical problems; and, above all, speak and write eloquently. Castiglione also included discussion of the perfect court lady, who, like the courtier, was to be well educated and able to play a musical instrument, paint, and dance. Physical beauty, delicacy, affability, and modesty were also important qualities for court ladies.

In the sixteenth and seventeenth centuries, *The Courtier* was translated into most European languages and widely read. It influenced the social mores and patterns of conduct of elite groups in Renaissance and early modern Europe; it became a how-to manual for people seeking to improve themselves and rise in the social hierarchy as well. Echoes of its ideal for women have perhaps had an even longer life.

Political Thought

In politics, as with most areas of human activity, humanists looked to the classical past for their models. Some argued that republicanism was the best form of government. Others used the model of Plato's philosopher-king in the *Republic* to argue that rule by an enlightened individual might be best. Both sides agreed that educated men should be active in the political affairs of their city, a position historians have since termed civic humanism.

The most famous (or infamous) civic humanist, and ultimately the best-known political theorist of this era, was Niccolò Machiavelli (1469–1527). After the ouster of the Medici with the French invasion of 1494, Machiavelli was secretary to one of the governing bodies in the city of Florence; he was responsible for diplomatic

| **What new ideas were associated with the Renaissance?** | How did art reflect new Renaissance ideals? | What were the key social hierarchies in Renaissance Europe? | How did nation-states develop in this period? | ✓ LearningCurve Check what you know. |

351

What makes a genius? A deep curiosity about an extensive variety of subjects? A divine spark that emerges in talents that far exceed the norm? Or is it just "one percent inspiration and ninety-nine percent perspiration," as Thomas Edison said? However it is defined, Leonardo da Vinci counts as a genius. In fact, Leonardo was one of the individuals whom the Renaissance label "genius" was designed to describe: a special kind of human being with exceptional creative powers. Leonardo (who, despite the title of a popular novel and film, is always called by his first name) was born in Vinci, near Florence, the illegitimate son of Caterina, a local peasant girl, and Ser Piero da Vinci, a notary public. When Ser Piero's marriage to Donna Albrussia produced no children, he and his wife took in Leonardo, whose mother had married another man. Ser Piero secured Leonardo an apprenticeship with the painter and sculptor Andrea del Verrocchio in Florence. In 1472, when Leonardo was just twenty years old, he was already listed as a master in Florence's Company of Artists.

Leonardo's most famous portrait, *Mona Lisa*, shows a woman with an enigmatic smile that Giorgio Vasari described as "so pleasing that it seemed divine rather than human." The portrait, probably of the young wife of a rich Florentine merchant (her exact identity is hotly debated), may be the best-known painting in the history of art. One of its competitors for that designation would be another work of Leonardo, *The Last Supper*, which has been called "the most revered painting in the world."

Leonardo's reputation as a genius does not rest on his paintings, however, which are actually few in number, but rather on the breadth of his abilities and interests. He is considered by many the first "Renaissance man," a phrase still used for a multitalented individual. Hoping to reproduce what the eye can see, he drew everything he saw around him, including executed criminals hanging on gallows as well as the beauties of nature. Trying to understand how the human body worked, Leonardo studied live and dead bodies, doing autopsies and dissections to investigate muscles and circulation. He carefully analyzed the effects of light, and he experimented with perspective.

Leonardo used his drawings not only as the basis for his paintings but also as a tool of scientific investigation. He drew plans for hundreds of inventions, many of which would become reality centuries later, such as the helicopter, tank, machine gun, and parachute. He was hired by one of the powerful new rulers in Italy, Duke Ludovico Sforza of Milan,

Vitruvian Man, a drawing by Leonardo showing correlations between the ideal human proportions and the geometric shapes of the circle and square, is based on the ideas of the ancient Roman architect Vitruvius, whose works Leonardo read. (Galleria dell' Accademia, Venice, Italy/The Bridgeman Art Library)

to design weapons, fortresses, and water systems, as well as to produce works of art. Leonardo left Milan when Sforza was overthrown, and he spent the last years of his life painting, drawing, and designing for the pope and the French king.

Leonardo experimented with new materials for painting and sculpture, not all of which worked. The experimental method he used to paint *The Last Supper* caused the picture to deteriorate rapidly, and it began to flake off the wall as soon as it was finished. Leonardo regarded it as never quite completed because he could not find a model for the face of Christ who would evoke the spiritual depth he felt the figure deserved. His gigantic equestrian statue in honor of Ludovico's father, Duke Francesco Sforza, was never made, and the clay model collapsed. He planned to write books on many subjects but never finished any of them, leaving only notebooks. Leonardo once said that "a painter is not admirable unless he is universal." The patrons who supported him — and he was supported very well — perhaps wished that his inspirations would have been a bit less universal in scope, or at least accompanied by more perspiration.

Sources: Giorgio Vasari, *Lives of the Artists*, vol. 1, trans. G. Bull (London: Penguin Books, 1965); S. B. Nuland, *Leonardo da Vinci* (New York: Lipper/Viking, 2000).

QUESTIONS FOR ANALYSIS

1. In what ways do the labels "genius" and "Renaissance man" both support and contradict each other? Which better fits Leonardo?
2. Has the idea of artistic genius changed since the Renaissance? How?

ONLINE DOCUMENT PROJECT

How did the needs and desires of Leonardo's patrons influence his work? Keeping the question above in mind, examine letters and visual evidence that sheds light on the dynamic between the artist and his employers, and then complete a writing assignment based on the evidence and details from this chapter. *See inside the front cover to learn more.*

missions and organizing a citizen army. Almost two decades later, the Medici family returned to power, and Machiavelli was arrested, tortured, and imprisoned on suspicion of plotting against them. He was released but had no government position, and he spent the rest of his life writing and making fruitless attempts to regain employment.

Machiavelli's *The Prince* (1513) uses the examples of classical and contemporary rulers to argue that the function of a ruler (or any government) is to preserve order and security. Weakness only leads to disorder, which might end in civil war or conquest by an outsider, situations clearly detrimental to any people's well-being. To preserve the state, a ruler should use whatever means he needs—brutality, lying, manipulation—but should not do anything that would make the populace turn against him; stealing or cruel actions done for a ruler's own pleasure would lead to resentment and destroy the popular support needed for a strong, stable realm.

The Prince is often seen as the first modern guide to politics, though Machiavelli was denounced for writing it, and people later came to use the word *Machiavellian* to mean cunning and ruthless. Medieval political philosophers had debated the proper relation between church and state, but they regarded the standards by which all governments were to be judged as emanating from moral principles established by God. Machiavelli argued that governments should instead be judged by how well they provide security, order, and safety to their populace. A ruler's moral code in maintaining these was not the same as a private individual's because a leader could— indeed, should—use any means necessary. Machiavelli put a new spin on the Renaissance search for perfection, arguing that ideals needed to be measured in the cold light of the real world.

Christian Humanism

In the last quarter of the fifteenth century, students from the Low Countries, France, Germany, and England flocked to Italy, absorbed the so-called new learning, and carried it back to their own countries. Northern humanists shared the ideas of Ficino and Pico about the wisdom of ancient texts, but they went beyond Italian efforts to synthesize the Christian and classical traditions to see humanist learning as a way to bring about reform of the church and

Christian humanists

▶ Northern humanists who interpreted Italian ideas about and attitudes toward classical antiquity and humanism in terms of their own religious traditions.

deep people's spiritual lives. These **Christian humanists**, as they were later called, thought that the best elements of classical and Christian cultures should be combined.

The English humanist Thomas More (1478–1535) began life as a lawyer, studied the classics, and entered government service. Despite his official duties, he had time to write, and he became most famous for his controversial dialogue *Utopia* (1516). *Utopia* describes a community on an island somewhere beyond Europe where all children receive a good education, primarily in the Greco-Roman classics, and adults divide their days between manual labor or business pursuits and intellectual activities. The problems that plagued More's fellow citizens, such as poverty and hunger, have been solved by a beneficent government. There is religious toleration, and order and reason prevail. Because Utopian institutions are perfect, however, dissent and disagreement are not acceptable.

Better known by contemporaries than Thomas More was the Dutch humanist Desiderius Erasmus (dehz-ih-DARE-ee-us ih-RAZ-muhs) (1466?–1536) of Rotterdam. Erasmus's long list of publications includes *The Education of a Christian Prince* (1504), a book combining idealistic and practical suggestions for the formation of a ruler's character through the careful study of the Bible and classical authors; *The Praise of Folly* (1509), a witty satire poking fun at political, social, and especially religious institutions; and, most important, a new Latin translation of the New Testament alongside the first printed edition of the Greek text (1516). In the preface to the New Testament, Erasmus expressed his ideas about Bible translations: "I wish that even the weakest woman should read the Gospel—should read the epistles of Paul. And I wish these were translated into all languages, so that they might be read and understood, not only by Scots and Irishmen, but also by Turks and Saracens."[1]

Two fundamental themes run through all of Erasmus's work. First, education in the Bible and the classics is the means to reform and the key to moral and intellectual improvement. Erasmus called for a renaissance of the ideals of the early church to accompany the renaissance in classical education that was already going on, and he criticized the church of his day for having strayed from these ideals. Second, renewal should be based on what he termed "the philosophy of Christ," an emphasis on inner spirituality and personal morality rather than Scholastic theology or outward observances such as pilgrimages or venerating relics. His ideas, and Christian humanism in general, were important roots of the Protestant Reformation, although Erasmus himself denied this and never became a follower of Luther (see Chapter 13).

The Printed Word

The fourteenth-century humanist Petrarch and the sixteenth-century humanist Erasmus had similar ideas on many topics, but the immediate impact of their ideas was very different because of one thing: the invention of the printing press with movable metal type. The ideas of Petrarch were spread slowly from person to person by hand copying. The ideas of Erasmus were spread quickly through print.

Printing with movable metal type developed in Germany in the 1440s as a combination of existing technologies. Several metal-smiths, most prominently Johann Gutenberg, recognized that the metal stamps used to mark signs on jew-

CHAPTER LOCATOR │ How did politics and economics shape the Renaissance?

354 CHAPTER 12 EUROPEAN SOCIETY IN THE AGE OF THE RENAISSANCE

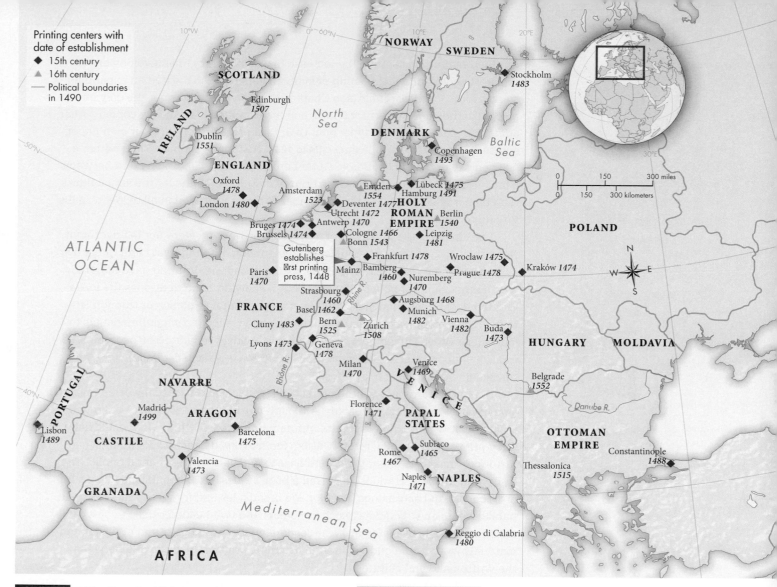

Printing centers with date of establishment
- ◆ 15th century
- ▲ 16th century
- — Political boundaries in 1490

Gutenberg establishes first printing press, 1448

MAP 12.2 ■ The Growth of Printing in Europe, 1448–1552

The speed with which artisans spread printing technology across Europe provides strong evidence for the growing demand for reading material. Presses in the Ottoman Empire were first established by Jewish immigrants who printed works in Hebrew, Greek, and Spanish.

> MAPPING THE PAST

ANALYZING THE MAP: What part of Europe had the greatest number of printing presses by 1550? What explains this?

CONNECTIONS: Printing was developed in response to a market for reading materials. Use Maps 10.2 and 10.3 (pages 291 and 299) to help explain why printing spread the way it did.

---

elry could be covered with ink and used to mark symbols onto a surface in the same way that other craftsmen were using carved wood stamps to print books. (This woodblock printing technique originated in China and Korea centuries earlier.) Gutenberg and his assistants made metal stamps—later called *type*—for every letter of the alphabet and built racks that held the type in rows. This type could be rearranged for every page and so used over and over.

The printing revolution was also made possible by the ready availability of paper, which was produced using techniques that had originated in China. Unlike the printing press, however, papermaking technology had been brought into Europe through Muslim Spain rather than developing independently.

What new ideas were associated with the Renaissance?	How did art reflect new Renaissance ideals?	What were the key social hierarchies in Renaissance Europe?	How did nation-states develop in this period?	✓ LearningCurve Check what you know.

By the fifteenth century, the increase in urban literacy, the development of primary schools, and the opening of more universities had created an expanding market for reading materials (see Chapter 11). Gutenberg was not the only one to recognize the huge market for books, and his invention was quickly copied. Other craftsmen made their own type, built their own presses, bought their own paper, and set themselves up in business (**Map 12.2**). Historians estimate that, within a half century of the publication of Gutenberg's Bible in 1456, somewhere between 8 million and 20 million books were printed in Europe. Whatever the actual figure, the number is far greater than the number of books produced in all of Western history up to that point.

The effects of the invention of movable-type printing were not felt overnight. Nevertheless, movable type radically transformed both the private and the public lives of Europeans by the dawn of the sixteenth century. Printing gave hundreds or even thousands of people identical books, allowing them to discuss the ideas that the books contained more easily with one another in person or through letters. Printed materials reached an invisible public, allowing silent individuals to join causes and allowing groups of individuals widely separated by geography to form a common identity; this new group consciousness could compete with and transcend older, localized loyalties.

Printing also stimulated the literacy of laypeople and eventually came to have a deep effect on their private lives. Although most of the earliest books and pamphlets dealt with religious subjects, printers produced anything that would sell. They printed professional reference sets for lawyers, doctors, and students, and historical romances, biographies, and how-to manuals for the general public. They discovered that illustrations increased a book's sales, so they published books full of woodcuts and engravings. Single-page broadsides and fly sheets allowed great public events and "wonders" such as comets and two-headed calves to be experienced vicariously by a stay-at-home readership. Because books and other printed materials were read aloud to illiterate listeners, print bridged the gap between the written and oral cultures.

> **QUICK REVIEW**

How did liberal arts education reflect humanist values and beliefs?

CHAPTER LOCATOR | How did politics and economics shape the Renaissance?

CHAPTER 12
356 EUROPEAN SOCIETY IN THE AGE OF THE RENAISSANCE

Botticelli, *Primavera* (Spring), ca. 1482 Framed by a grove of orange trees, Venus, goddess of love, is flanked on the right by Flora, goddess of flowers and fertility, and on the left by the Three Graces, goddesses of banquets, dance, and social occasions. Above, Venus's son Cupid, the god of love, shoots darts of desire, while at the far right the wind-god Zephyrus chases the nymph Chloris. The entire scene rests on classical mythology, though some art historians claim that Venus is an allegory for the Virgin Mary. Botticelli captured the ideal for female beauty in the Renaissance: slender, with pale skin, a high forehead, red-blond hair, and sloping shoulders. (Galleria degli Uffizi, Florence, Italy/The Bridgeman Art Library)

NO FEATURE OF THE RENAISSANCE evokes greater admiration than its artistic masterpieces. The 1400s (*quattrocento*) and 1500s (*cinquecento*) bore witness to dazzling creativity in painting, architecture, and sculpture. In all the arts, the city of Florence led the way. But Florence was not the only artistic center; Rome and Venice also became important, and northern Europeans perfected their own styles.

Patronage and Power

In early Renaissance Italy, powerful urban groups often flaunted their wealth by commissioning works of art. These works represented the merchants' dominant influence in the community. In the late fifteenth century, wealthy individuals and rulers, rather than corporate groups, increasingly sponsored works of art. Patrician merchants and bankers, popes, and princes spent vast sums on the arts to glorify themselves and their families.

What new ideas were associated with the Renaissance?	**How did art reflect new Renaissance ideals?**	What were the key social hierarchies in Renaissance Europe?	How did nation-states develop in this period?	✓ LearningCurve Check what you know.

Michelangelo's *David* (1501–1504) and the *Last Judgment* (detail, 1537–1541)

Like all Renaissance artists, Michelangelo worked largely on commissions from patrons. Officials of the city of Florence contracted the young sculptor to produce a statue of the Old Testament hero David (left) to be displayed on the city's main square. Michelangelo portrayed David anticipating his fight against the giant Goliath, and the statue came to symbolize the republic of Florence standing up to its larger and more powerful enemies. More than thirty years later, Michelangelo was commissioned by the pope to paint a scene of the Last Judgment on the altar wall of the Sistine Chapel, where he had earlier spent four years covering the ceiling with magnificent frescoes. The massive work shows a powerful Christ standing in judgment, with souls ascending into Heaven while others are dragged by demons into Hell (above). The *David* captures ideals of human perfection and has come to be an iconic symbol of Renaissance artistic brilliance, while the dramatic and violent *Last Judgment* conveys both terror and divine power. (sculpture: Scala/Ministero per i Beni e le Attività Culturali/Art Resource, NY; painting: Vatican Museums and Galleries, Vatican City/Alinari/The Bridgeman Art Library)

Patrons varied in their level of involvement as a work progressed; some simply ordered a specific subject or scene, while others oversaw the work of the artist or architect very closely, suggesting themes and styles and demanding changes while the work was in progress. For example, Pope Julius II (pontificate 1503–1513), who commissioned Michelangelo to paint the ceiling of the Vatican's Sistine Chapel in 1508, demanded that the artist work as fast as he could and frequently visited him at his work with suggestions and criticisms.

In addition to power, art reveals changing patterns of consumption among the wealthy elite in European society. In the rural world of the Middle Ages, society had been organized for war, and men of wealth spent their money on military gear. As Italian nobles settled in towns (see Chapter 10), they adjusted to an urban culture. Rather than employing knights for warfare, cities hired mercenaries. Accordingly, expenditures on military hardware by nobles declined. For the noble recently arrived from the countryside or the rich merchant of the city, a grand urban palace represented the greatest outlay of cash. Wealthy individuals and families ordered gold dishes, embroidered tablecloths, wall tapestries, paintings on canvas (an innovation), and sculptural decorations to adorn these homes.

After the palace itself, the private chapel within the palace symbolized the largest expenditure for the wealthy of the sixteenth century. Decorated with religious scenes and equipped with ecclesiastical furniture, the chapel served as the center of the household's religious life and its cult of remembrance of the dead.

Changing Artistic Styles

Both the content and style of Renaissance art often differed from those of the Middle Ages. Religious topics remained popular among both patrons and artists, but frequently the patron had himself and his family portrayed in the scene. As the fifteenth century advanced and humanist ideas spread more widely, classical themes and motifs figured increasingly in painting and sculpture, with the facial features of the gods sometimes modeled on living people.

The individual portrait emerged as a distinct artistic genre in this movement. Rather than reflecting a spiritual ideal, as medieval painting and sculpture tended to do, Renaissance portraits showed human ideals, often portrayed in the more realistic style increasingly favored by both artists and patrons. The Florentine painter Giotto (JAH-toh) (1276–1337) led the way in the use of realism; his treatment of the human body and face replaced the formal stiffness and artificiality that had long characterized representation of the human body. Piero della Francesca (frahn-CHAY-skah) (1420–1492) and Andrea Mantegna (mahn-TEHN-yuh) (1430/31–1506) pioneered perspective, the linear representation of distance and space on a flat surface, which enhanced the realism of paintings and differentiated them from the flatter and more stylized images of medieval art. The sculptor Donatello (1386–1466) revived the classical figure, with its balance and self-awareness. In architecture, Filippo Brunelleschi (1377–1446) looked to the classical past for inspiration, creating structures that were carefully thought out to achieve a sense of balance and harmony.

Art produced in northern Europe tended to be more religious in orientation than that produced in Italy. Some Flemish painters, notably Rogier van der Weyden (1399/1400–1464) and Jan van Eyck (1366–1441), were considered the artistic equals of Italian painters and were much admired in Italy. Van Eyck was one of the earliest artists to use oil-based paints successfully, and his religious scenes and portraits all show great realism and remarkable attention to human personality. Albrecht Dürer (1471–1528), from the German city of Nuremberg, studied with artists in Italy and produced woodcuts, engravings, and etchings that rendered the human form and the natural world in amazing detail.

In the early sixteenth century, the center of the new art shifted from Florence to Rome, where wealthy cardinals and popes wanted visual expression of the

| What new ideas were associated with the Renaissance? | **How did art reflect new Renaissance ideals?** | What were the key social hierarchies in Renaissance Europe? | How did nation-states develop in this period? | ☑ LearningCurve Check what you know. |

359

Villa Capra Architecture as well as literature and art aimed to re-create classical styles. The Venetian architect Andrea Palladio modeled this country villa, constructed for a papal official in 1566, on the Pantheon of ancient Rome (see Chapter 6). Surrounded by statues of classical deities, it is completely symmetrical, capturing humanist ideals of perfection and balance. This villa and other buildings that Palladio designed influenced later buildings all over the world, including the U.S. Capitol in Washington, D.C., and countless state capitol buildings. (age fotostock/Superstock)

church's and their own families' power and piety. Renaissance popes expended enormous enthusiasm and huge sums of money to beautify the city. Pope Julius II tore down the old Saint Peter's Basilica and began work on the present structure in 1506. Michelangelo went to Rome from Florence in about 1500 and began the series of statues, paintings, and architectural projects from which he gained an international reputation.

Raphael Sanzio (1483–1520), another Florentine, got the commission for frescoes in the papal apartments, and in his relatively short life he painted hundreds of portraits and devotional images, becoming the most sought-after artist in Europe. Raphael also oversaw a large workshop with many collaborators and apprentices. He wrote treatises on his philosophy of art in which he emphasized the importance of imitating nature and developing an orderly sequence of design and proportion.

Venice became another artistic center in the sixteenth century. Titian (TIH-shuhn) (1490–1576) produced portraits, religious subjects, and mythological scenes. Titian and other sixteenth-century painters developed an artistic style known in English as "mannerism" in which artists sometimes distorted figures, exaggerated musculature, and heightened color to express emotion and drama more intently. (A painting by Titian can be found on page 363; this is also the style in which Michelangelo painted the *Last Judgment* in the Sistine Chapel, shown on page 358.)

CHAPTER LOCATOR | How did politics and economics shape the Renaissance?

The Renaissance Artist

Some patrons rewarded certain artists very well, and some artists gained great public acclaim. This adulation of the artist has led many historians to view the Renaissance as the beginning of the concept of the artist as having a special talent. In the Middle Ages, people believed that only God created, albeit through individuals; the medieval conception recognized no particular value in artistic originality. Renaissance artists and humanists came to think that a work of art was the deliberate creation of a unique personality who transcended traditions, rules, and theories. A genius had a peculiar gift, which ordinary laws should not inhibit. (See "Individuals in Society: Leonardo da Vinci," page 352.)

It is important not to overemphasize the Renaissance notion of genius. As certain artists became popular and well known, they could assert their own artistic styles and pay less attention to the wishes of patrons, but even major artists like Raphael generally worked according to the patron's specific guidelines. Whether in Italy or northern Europe, most Renaissance artists trained in the workshops of older artists. Though they might be men of genius, artists were still expected to be well trained in proper artistic techniques and stylistic conventions. Beginning artists spent years mastering their craft by copying drawings and paintings; learning how to prepare paint and other artistic materials; and, by the sixteenth century, reading books about design and composition. Younger artists gathered together in the evenings for further drawing practice; by the later sixteenth century, some of these informal groups had turned into more formal artistic "academies," the first of which was begun in 1563 in Florence by Vasari under the patronage of the Medici.

The notion of artistic genius that developed in the Renaissance was gendered. All the most famous and most prolific Renaissance artists were male. The types of art in which more women were active, such as textiles, needlework, and painting on porcelain, were not regarded as "major arts," but only as "minor" or "decorative" arts. Like painting, embroidery changed in the Renaissance to become more naturalistic, more visually complex, and more classical in its subject matter. Embroiderers were not trained to view their work as products of individual genius, however, so they rarely included their names on the works, and there is no way to discover their identities.

There are no female architects whose names are known and only one female sculptor, though several women did become well known as painters in their day. Stylistically, their works are different from one another, but their careers show many similarities. The majority of female painters were the daughters of painters or of minor noblemen with ties to artistic circles. Many were eldest daughters or came from families in which there were no sons, so their fathers took unusual interest in their careers. Many women painters began their careers before they were twenty and either produced far fewer paintings after they married or stopped painting entirely. Women were not allowed to study the male nude, a study that was viewed as essential if one wanted to paint large history or biblical paintings with many figures. Women also could not learn the technique of fresco, in which colors are applied directly to wet plaster walls, because such work had to be done in public, which was judged inappropriate for women. Joining a group of male artists for informal practice was also seen as improper, so women had no access to the newly established artistic academies.

| What new ideas were associated with the Renaissance? | **How did art reflect new Renaissance ideals?** | What were the key social hierarchies in Renaissance Europe? | How did nation-states develop in this period? | ☑ LearningCurve Check what you know. |

The Chess Game, 1555 In this oil painting, the Italian artist Sofonisba Anguissola (1532–1625) shows her three younger sisters playing chess, a game that was growing in popularity in the sixteenth century. Each sister looks at the one immediately older than herself, with the girl on the left looking out at her sister, the artist. Anguissola's father, a minor nobleman, recognized his daughter's talent and arranged for her to study with several painters. She became a court painter at the Spanish royal court, where she painted many portraits. Returning to Italy, she continued to be active, painting her last portrait when she was over eighty. (Museum Narodowe, Poznan, Poland/The Bridgeman Art Library)

Women were not alone in being excluded from the institutions of Renaissance culture. Though a few rare men of genius such as Leonardo and Michelangelo emerged from artisanal backgrounds, most scholars and artists came from families with at least some money. The ideas of the highly educated humanists did not influence the lives of most people in cities and did not affect life in the villages at all. For rural people and for less well-off town residents, work and play continued much as they had in the High Middle Ages (see Chapter 10).

> **QUICK REVIEW**

What role did the notion of the artistic "genius" play in Renaissance art?

CHAPTER LOCATOR | How did politics and economics shape the Renaissance?

What were the key social hierarchies in Renaissance Europe?

Laura de Dianti, 1523

The Venetian artist Titian portrays a young Italian woman with a gorgeous blue dress and an elaborate pearl and feather headdress, accompanied by a young black page with a gold earring. Both the African page and the headdress connect the portrait's subject with the exotic, though slaves from Africa and the Ottoman Empire were actually common in wealthy Venetian households. (© Human Bios GmbH, Switzerland. Courtesy, Heinz Kisters Collection.)

THE DIVISION BETWEEN EDUCATED AND UNEDUCATED PEOPLE was only one of many social hierarchies evident in the Renaissance. Social hierarchies in the Renaissance were built on those of the Middle Ages that divided nobles from commoners, but they also developed new concepts that contributed to modern social hierarchies, such as those of race, class, and gender.

Race and Slavery

Renaissance people did not use the word *race* the way we do; they often used *race*, *people*, and *nation* interchangeably for ethnic, national, religious, or other groups. They did make distinctions based on skin color that provide some of the background for later conceptualizations of race, but these distinctions were interwoven with other characteristics when people thought about human differences.

What new ideas were associated with the Renaissance?	How did art reflect new Renaissance ideals?	**What were the key social hierarchies in Renaissance Europe?**	How did nation-states develop in this period?	✓ LearningCurve Check what you know.

363

Since the time of the Roman Republic, a small number of black Africans had lived in western Europe. They had come, along with white slaves, as the spoils of war. Even after the collapse of the Roman Empire, Muslim and Christian merchants continued to import them. The evidence of medieval art attests to the continued presence of Africans in Europe throughout the Middle Ages and to Europeans' awareness of them.

Beginning in the fifteenth century, sizable numbers of black slaves entered Europe. Portuguese sailors brought perhaps a thousand Africans a year to the markets of Seville, Barcelona, Marseilles, and Genoa. In the late fifteenth century, this flow increased, with thousands of people taken from the west coast of Africa. Most of them ended up in Spain and Portugal.

> **People of African Descent in Mid-Sixteenth-Century Portugal**

- 4,000–5,000 African slaves sold to the Portuguese each year
- Blacks, both slave and free, constitute 10 percent of the population of the cities of Lisbon and Évora and 3 percent of the Portuguese population as a whole
- Significant mixed-race populations in Portuguese cities

Although blacks were concentrated in the Iberian Peninsula, some Africans must have lived in northern Europe as well. In the 1580s, for example, Queen Elizabeth I of England complained that there were too many "blackamoores" competing with needy English people for places as domestic servants. Black servants were much sought after; the medieval interest in curiosities, the exotic, and the marvelous continued in the Renaissance. Italian aristocrats had their portraits painted with their black page boys to indicate their wealth (as in the painting of Laura de Dianti on page 363). Blacks were so greatly in demand at the Renaissance courts of northern Italy, in fact, that the Venetians defied papal threats of excommunication to secure them.

Africans were not simply amusements at court. In Portugal, Spain, and Italy, slaves supplemented the labor force in virtually all occupations—as servants, agricultural laborers, craftsmen, and seamen on ships going to Lisbon and Africa. Agriculture in Europe did not involve large plantations, so large-scale agricultural slavery did not develop there as it would in the late fifteenth century in the New World.

Until the voyages down the African coast in the late fifteenth century, Europeans had little concrete knowledge of Africans and their cultures. They perceived Africa as a remote place, the home of strange people isolated by heresy and Islam from superior European civilization. Africans' contact, even as slaves, with Christian Europeans could only "improve" the blacks, they thought. The expanding slave trade reinforced negative preconceptions about the inferiority of black Africans.

Wealth and the Nobility

The word *class* was not used in the Renaissance to describe social divisions, but by the thirteenth century, and even more so by the fifteenth, the idea of a hierarchy based on wealth was emerging. This was particularly true in cities, where

CHAPTER LOCATOR | How did politics and economics shape the Renaissance?

wealthy merchants who oversaw vast trading empires lived in splendor that rivaled the richest nobles. As we saw earlier, the merchants in many cities had gained political power to match their economic might, becoming merchant oligarchs who ruled through city councils. This hierarchy of wealth was more fluid than the older divisions into noble and commoner, which allowed individuals and families to rise—and fall—within one generation.

The development of a hierarchy of wealth did not mean an end to the prominence of nobles, however, and even poorer nobility still had higher status than wealthy commoners. Thus, wealthy Italian merchants enthusiastically bought noble titles and country villas in the fifteenth century, and wealthy English or Spanish merchants eagerly married their daughters and sons into often-impoverished noble families. The nobility maintained its status in most parts of Europe not by maintaining rigid boundaries but by taking in and integrating the new social elite of wealth.

Along with being tied to hierarchies of wealth and family standing, social status was linked to considerations of honor. Among the nobility, for example, certain weapons and battle tactics were favored because they were viewed as more honorable. Among urban dwellers, certain occupations, such as city executioner or manager of the municipal brothel, might be well paid but were understood to be dishonorable and so of low status.

Gender Roles

Renaissance people would not have understood the word *gender* to refer to categories of people, but they would have easily grasped the concept. Toward the end of the fourteenth century, learned men (and a few women) began what was termed the **debate about women** (*querelle des femmes*), a debate about women's character and nature that would last for centuries. Misogynist (muh-SAH-juh-nihst) critiques of women from both clerical and secular authors denounced females as devious, domineering, and demanding. In answer, several authors compiled long lists of famous and praiseworthy women exemplary for their loyalty, bravery, and morality. Christine de Pizan was among the writers who were interested not only in defending women but also in exploring the reasons behind women's secondary status. They were anticipating discussions about the social construction of gender by six hundred years.

Beginning in the sixteenth century, the debate about women also became a debate about female rulers. This debate was sparked primarily by dynastic accidents in many countries, including Spain, England, Scotland, and France, that led to women ruling in their own right or serving as advisers to child kings. The questions were vigorously and at times viciously argued. They directly concerned the social construction of gender: could a woman's being born into a royal family and educated to rule allow her to overcome the limitations of her sex? Should it? Or stated another way: which was (or should be) the stronger determinant of character and social role: gender or rank?

Ideas about women's and men's proper roles determined the actions of ordinary men and women even more forcefully. The dominant notion of the "true" man was that of the married head of household, so men whose social status and age would have normally conferred political power but who remained unmarried

debate about women
▶ Debate among writers and thinkers in the Renaissance about women's qualities and proper role in society.

What new ideas were associated with the Renaissance?

How did art reflect new Renaissance ideals?

What were the key social hierarchies in Renaissance Europe?

How did nation-states develop in this period?

☑ LearningCurve
Check what you know.

365

did not participate in politics to the same level as their married brothers. Unmarried men in Venice, for example, could not be part of the ruling council.

Women were also understood as either "married or to be married." This meant that women's work was not viewed as financially supporting a family — even if it did — and was valued less than men's. If they worked for wages, and many women did, women earned about half to two-thirds of what men did, even for the same work. The maintenance of appropriate power relationships between men and women, with men dominant and women subordinate, served as a symbol of the proper functioning of society as a whole. Disorder in the proper gender hierarchy was linked with social upheaval and was viewed as threatening. Of all the ways in which Renaissance society was hierarchically arranged — social rank, age, level of education, race, occupation — gender was regarded as the most "natural" and therefore the most important to defend.

> ## QUICK REVIEW

How and why did a hierarchy based on wealth emerge in fourteenth- and fifteenth-century Europe?

CHAPTER LOCATOR | How did politics and economics shape the Renaissance?

CHAPTER 12
366 EUROPEAN SOCIETY IN THE AGE OF THE RENAISSANCE

How did nation-states develop in this period?

Tax Collectors

New types of taxes and more effective methods of tax collection were essential to the growth of Renaissance states, but both were often highly unpopular. In this painting from about 1540, the Dutch artist Marinus van Reymerswaele depicts two tax collectors as they count their take and record it in a ledger. Tax collectors were of middling status, but the men shown here wear clothing more appropriate for nobles. (Erich Lessing/Art Resource, NY)

> **PICTURING THE PAST**

ANALYZING THE IMAGE: What elements of the men's clothing suggest wealth? How would you describe the expressions on their faces? What does the painting suggest about the artist's opinion of tax collectors?

CONNECTIONS: In Spain, converso tax collectors were widely resented. What were some of the reasons behind this resentment? How did this hatred shape political developments in Spain?

| What new ideas were associated with the Renaissance? | How did art reflect new Renaissance ideals? | What were the key social hierarchies in Renaissance Europe? | **How did nation-states develop in this period?** | ☑ LearningCurve Check what you know. |

THE HIGH MIDDLE AGES had witnessed the origins of many of the basic institutions of the modern state. The office of sheriffs, inquests, juries, the office of circuit judge, professional bureaucracies, and representative assemblies all trace their origins to the twelfth and thirteenth centuries. The linchpin for the development of states, however, was strong monarchy, and during the period of the Hundred Years' War, no ruler in western Europe was able to provide effective leadership. The resurgent power of feudal nobilities weakened the centralizing work begun earlier.

Beginning in the fifteenth century, however, rulers utilized aggressive methods to rebuild their governments. First in the regional states of Italy, then in the expanding monarchies of France, England, and Spain, rulers began the work of reducing violence, curbing unruly nobles, and establishing domestic order. They attempted to secure their borders and enhanced methods of raising revenue.

France

The Black Death and the Hundred Years' War left France drastically depopulated, commercially ruined, and agriculturally weak. Nonetheless, the ruler whom Joan of Arc had seen crowned at Reims, Charles VII (r. 1422–1461), revived the monarchy and France. Charles reconciled the Burgundians and Armagnacs (ahr-muhn-YAKZ), who had been waging civil war for thirty years. By 1453, French armies had expelled the English from French soil except in Calais. Charles reorganized the royal council, giving increased influence to lawyers and bankers, and strengthened royal finances through taxes on certain products and on land.

By establishing regular companies of cavalry and archers—recruited, paid, and inspected by the state—Charles created the first permanent royal army anywhere in Europe. His son Louis XI (r. 1461–1483) improved on Charles's army and used it to control the nobles' separate militias and to curb urban independence. The army was also employed in 1477 when Louis conquered Burgundy after the death of its ruler Charles the Bold. Three years later, the extinction of the house of Anjou with the death of its last legitimate male heir brought Louis the counties of Anjou, Bar, Maine, and Provence.

The Expansion of France, 1475–1500

Map legend:
- Crown lands, ca. 1475
- Territory added by 1483
- Territory added by 1498
- Independent fiefs
- Boundary of France, ca. 1500

Two further developments strengthened the French monarchy. The marriage of Louis XII (r. 1498–1515) and Anne of Brittany added the large western duchy of Brittany to the state. Then King Francis I and Pope Leo X reached a mutually satisfactory agreement about church and state powers in 1516. The new treaty, the Concordat of Bologna, recognized the French ruler's right to select French bishops and abbots. French kings thereafter effectively controlled the policies of church officials in the kingdom.

England

English society also suffered severely from the disorders of the fifteenth century. The aristocracy dominated the government of Henry IV (r. 1399–1413) and indulged in disruptive violence at the local level (see Chapter 11, page 324). Population continued to decline. Between 1455 and 1471, adherents of the ducal houses of York and Lancaster contended for control of the Crown in a civil war, commonly called the Wars of the Roses. The chronic disorder hurt trade, agriculture, and domestic industry. Under the pious but mentally disturbed Henry VI (r. 1422–1461), the authority of the monarchy sank lower than it had in centuries.

Edward IV (r. 1461–1483), from York, began establishing domestic tranquility. He succeeded in defeating the Lancastrian forces and after 1471 began to reconstruct the monarchy. Edward, his brother Richard III (r. 1483–1485), and Henry VII (r. 1485–1509) of the Welsh house of Tudor worked to restore royal prestige, to crush the power of the nobility, and to establish law and order at the local level.

Edward IV and subsequently the Tudors, except Henry VIII, conducted foreign policy on the basis of diplomacy and avoided expensive wars. Thus, the English monarchy did not have to depend on Parliament for money, and the Crown undercut that source of aristocratic influence.

Henry VII did summon several meetings of Parliament in the early years of his reign, primarily to confirm laws, but the center of royal authority was the royal council, which governed at the national level. Henry VII revealed his distrust of the nobility to the royal council; though not completely excluded, very few great lords were among the king's closest advisers. Instead he chose men from among the smaller landowners and urban residents trained in law. The council dealt with real or potential aristocratic threats through a judicial offshoot, the Court of Star Chamber. The court applied methods that were sometimes terrifying: accused persons were not entitled to see evidence against them, sessions were secret, juries were not called, and torture could be applied to extract confessions. These procedures ran directly counter to English common-law precedents, but they effectively reduced aristocratic troublemaking. When Henry VII died in 1509, he left a country at peace both domestically and internationally, a substantially augmented treasury, an expanding wool trade, and a Crown with its dignity and role much enhanced.

Spain

While England and France laid the foundations of unified nation-states during the Middle Ages, Spain remained a conglomerate of independent kingdoms. By the middle of the fifteenth century, the kingdoms of Castile and Aragon dominated the weaker Navarre, Portugal, and Granada; the Iberian Peninsula, with the exception of Granada, had been won for Christianity (**Map 12.3**). But even the wedding in 1469 of Isabella of Castile and Ferdinand of Aragon did not bring about

| What new ideas were associated with the Renaissance? | How did art reflect new Renaissance ideals? | What were the key social hierarchies in Renaissance Europe? | **How did nation-states develop in this period?** | ✔ LearningCurve Check what you know. |

369

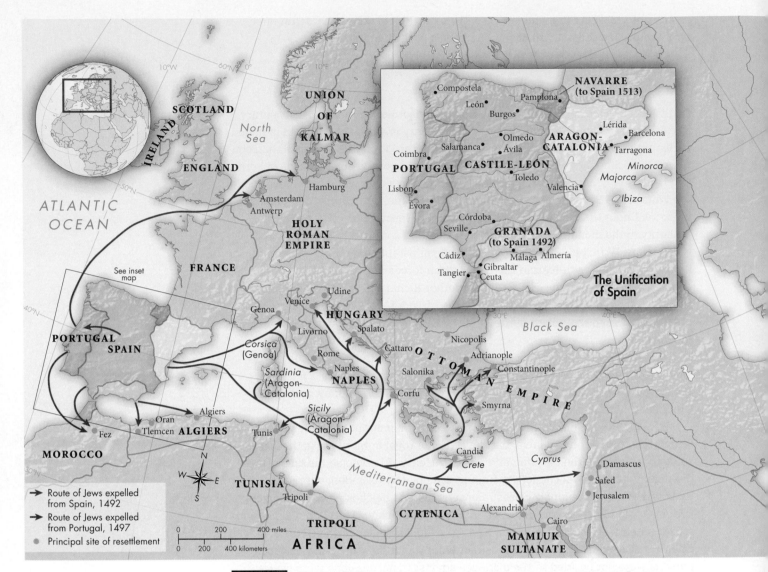

The Unification of Spain

Route of Jews expelled from Spain, 1492

Route of Jews expelled from Portugal, 1497

Principal site of resettlement

MAP 12.3 ■ The Unification of Spain and the Expulsion of the Jews, Fifteenth Century

The marriage of Ferdinand of Aragon and Isabella of Castile in 1469 brought most of the Iberian Peninsula under one monarchy, although different parts of Spain retained distinct cultures, languages, and legal systems. In 1492, Ferdinand and Isabella conquered Granada, where most people were Muslim, and expelled the Jews from all of Spain. Spanish Jews resettled in the cities of Europe and the Mediterranean that allowed them in, including Muslim states such as the Ottoman Empire. Muslims were also expelled from Spain over the course of the sixteenth and early seventeenth centuries.

administrative unity. Their marriage constituted a dynastic union of two royal houses, not the political union of two peoples. Although Ferdinand and Isabella (r. 1474–1516) pursued a common foreign policy, until about 1700, Spain existed as a loose confederation of separate kingdoms, each maintaining its own *cortes* (parliament), laws, courts, and systems of coinage and taxation.

Ferdinand and Isabella were able to exert their authority in ways similar to the rulers of France and England, however. They curbed aristocratic power by

CHAPTER LOCATOR | How did politics and economics shape the Renaissance?

excluding high nobles from the royal council. The council and various government boards recruited men trained in Roman law, which exalted the power of the Crown. They also secured from the Spanish Borgia pope Alexander VI the right to appoint bishops in Spain and in the Hispanic territories in the Americas, enabling them to establish the equivalent of a national church. With the revenues from ecclesiastical estates, they were able to expand their territories to include the remaining land held by Arabs in southern Spain. The victorious entry of Ferdinand and Isabella into Granada on January 6, 1492, signaled the conclusion of the reconquista (see Map 9.3, page 248). Granada was incorporated into the Spanish kingdom, and in 1512, Ferdinand conquered Navarre in the north.

There still remained a sizable and, in the view of the majority of the Spanish people, potentially dangerous minority, the Jews. When the kings of France and England had expelled the Jews from their kingdoms (see Chapter 9, page 268), many had sought refuge in Spain. During the long centuries of the reconquista, Christian kings had recognized Jewish rights and privileges; in fact, Jewish industry, intelligence, and money had supported royal power. While Christians borrowed from Jewish moneylenders and while all who could afford them sought Jewish physicians, a strong undercurrent of resentment of Jewish influence and wealth festered.

In the fourteenth century anti-Semitism in Spain was aggravated by fiery anti-Jewish preaching, by economic dislocation, and by the search for a scapegoat during the Black Death. Anti-Semitic pogroms swept the towns of Spain, and perhaps 40 percent of the Jewish population was killed or forced to convert. Those converted were called *conversos* or **New Christians**. Conversos were often well educated and held prominent positions in government, the church, medicine, law, and business. Numbering perhaps two hundred thousand in a total Spanish population of about 7.5 million, New Christians and Jews in fifteenth-century Spain exercised influence disproportionate to their numbers.

Such successes bred resentment. Aristocratic grandees resented the conversos' financial dependence, the poor hated the converso tax collectors, and churchmen doubted the sincerity of their conversions. (See "Tax Collectors," page 367.) Queen Isabella shared these suspicions, and she and Ferdinand had received permission from Pope Sixtus IV in 1478 to establish their own Inquisition to "search out and punish converts from Judaism who had transgressed against Christianity by secretly adhering to Jewish beliefs and performing rites of the Jews."[2] Investigations and trials began immediately, as officials of the Inquisition looked for conversos who showed any sign of incomplete conversion, such as not eating pork.

Most conversos identified themselves as sincere Christians; many came from families that had received baptism generations before. In response to conversos' statements, officials of the Inquisition developed a new type of anti-Semitism. A person's status as a Jew, they argued, could not be changed by religious conversion, but was in the person's blood and was heritable, so Jews could never be true Christians. In what were known as purity of blood laws, having pure Christian blood became a requirement for noble status. Ideas about Jews developed in Spain were important components in European concepts of race, and discussions of "Jewish blood" later expanded into notions of the "Jewish race."

In 1492, shortly after the conquest of Granada, Isabella and Ferdinand issued an edict expelling all practicing Jews from Spain. Of the community of perhaps

New Christians
▶ A term for Jews and Muslims in the Iberian Peninsula who accepted Christianity; in many cases they included Christians whose families had converted centuries earlier.

| What new ideas were associated with the Renaissance? | How did art reflect new Renaissance ideals? | What were the key social hierarchies in Renaissance Europe? | **How did nation-states develop in this period?** | ✓ LearningCurve Check what you know. |

371

200,000 Jews, 150,000 fled. Many Muslims in Granada were forcibly baptized and became another type of New Christian investigated by the Inquisition. Absolute religious orthodoxy and purity of blood served as the theoretical foundation of the Spanish national state.

The Spanish national state rested on marital politics as well as military victories and religious courts. In 1496, Ferdinand and Isabella married their second daughter, Joanna, heiress to Castile, to the archduke Philip, heir to the Burgundian Netherlands and the Holy Roman Empire. Philip and Joanna's son Charles V (r. 1519–1556) thus succeeded to a vast inheritance. When Charles's son Philip II joined Portugal to the Spanish crown in 1580, the Iberian Peninsula was at last politically united.

> **QUICK REVIEW**

How and why did the rulers of France, England, and Spain seek to undermine the independent power of the aristocracy?

CHAPTER LOCATOR | How did politics and economics shape the Renaissance?

CHAPTER 12
372 EUROPEAN SOCIETY IN THE AGE OF THE RENAISSANCE

LOOKING BACK
LOOKING AHEAD

The art historian Giorgio Vasari, who first called this era the Renaissance, thought that his contemporaries had both revived the classical past and gone beyond it. Vasari's judgment was echoed for centuries as historians sharply contrasted the art, architecture, educational ideas, social structures, and attitude toward life of the Renaissance with those of the Middle Ages: in this view, whereas the Middle Ages were corporate and religious, the Renaissance was individualistic and secular. More recently, historians and other scholars have stressed continuity as well as change. Families, kin networks, guilds, and other corporate groups remained important in the Renaissance, and religious belief remained firm. This re-evaluation changes our view of the relationship between the Middle Ages and the Renaissance. It may also change our view of the relationship between the Renaissance and the dramatic changes in religion that occurred in Europe in the sixteenth century. Those religious changes, the Reformation, used to be viewed as a rejection of the values of the Renaissance and a return to the intense concern with religion of the Middle Ages. This idea of the Reformation as a sort of counter-Renaissance may be true to some degree, but there are powerful continuities as well. Both movements looked back to a time that people regarded as purer and better than their own, and both offered opportunities for strong individuals to shape their world in unexpected ways.

LaunchPad

ONLINE DOCUMENT PROJECT

Leonardo da Vinci

How did the needs and desires of Leonardo's patrons influence his work?

You encountered Leonardo da Vinci's story on page 352. Keeping the question above in mind, examine letters written by Leonardo to his patrons as well as other written and visual evidence that sheds light on the dynamic between the artist and his employers. *See inside the front cover to learn more.*

| What new ideas were associated with the Renaissance? | How did art reflect new Renaissance ideals? | What were the key social hierarchies in Renaissance Europe? | How did nation-states develop in this period? | ✓ **LearningCurve** Check what you know. |

CHAPTER 12 STUDY GUIDE

STEP 1

GET STARTED ONLINE

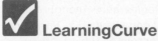 **LearningCurve**

Now that you've read the chapter, make it stick by completing the LearningCurve activity.

STEP 2

EXPLAIN WHY IT MATTERS

Put your reading into practice. Identify each term below, and then explain why it matters in Western history.

TERM	WHO OR WHAT & WHEN	WHY IT MATTERS
Renaissance (p. 344)		
patronage (p. 344)		
communes (p. 346)		
popolo (p. 346)		
signori (p. 346)		
courts (p. 346)		
humanism (p. 350)		
virtù (p. 350)		
Christian humanists (p. 354)		
debate about women (p. 365)		
New Christians (p. 371)		

STEP 3

MOVE BEYOND THE BASICS

To demonstrate a more advanced understanding, fill in the chart included below to identify the historical conditions and trends that made the Renaissance possible.

	Social	Economic	Political	Cultural
The roots of the Renaissance				

STEP 4 **PUT IT ALL TOGETHER** Now, take a step back and try to explain the big picture. Remember to use specific examples from the chapter in your answers.

THE RENAISSANCE

▶ Compare and contrast the city-states of Renaissance Italy and Ancient Greece. What similar patterns and challenges emerged in both contexts?

▶ What might explain the Renaissance interest in artistic "genius"? What does this interest tell you about the values and beliefs of Renaissance thinkers and writers?

SOCIAL HIERARCHIES

▶ What did Renaissance Europeans mean by the term *race*? How does their definition differ from your understanding of the term?

▶ What might explain the increased interest in the differences between men and women during the Renaissance? What connections can you make between the debate about women and larger intellectual trends?

POLITICS AND THE STATE IN WESTERN EUROPE

▶ How did the monarchs of England, France, and Spain use royal councils to augment their own power? What does the use of such councils tell you about the common problems facing the rulers of all three countries?

▶ How were notions of race and religion used in the formation of Spanish national identity? Why might Spanish monarchs have found it advantageous to attack religious and ethnic minorities?

MAKE CONNECTIONS

▶ Suppose you were a scholar or artist of the High Middle Ages. What critique might you offer to the humanists' contention that theirs was an age of rebirth after a millennium of darkness?

▶ In your opinion, is it appropriate to describe the values and attitudes associated with the Renaissance as modern? Why or why not?

> **IN YOUR OWN WORDS**

Imagine that you must give an oral report to the class answering the following question: **What new ways of thinking and new forms of cultural expression were developed during the Renaissance?** What would be the most important points and why?

13

REFORMATIONS AND RELIGIOUS WARS

1500–1600

> ## What were the causes and consequences of religious division in sixteenth-century Europe?

Chapter 13 examines the religious conflicts and divisions of the sixteenth century. Calls for reform of the Christian Church began very early in its history and continued all the way through the fifteenth century. Throughout this long history, a diverse group of reformers, many of whom were members of the clergy, argued that the church had become too worldly, had lost sight of its original mission, or had allowed Christian teachings to be corrupted. What was new in the sixteenth century was the breadth of acceptance and the ultimate impact of the calls for reform. This acceptance was due not only to religious issues and problems within the church, but also to political and social factors. In 1500, there was one Christian Church in western Europe to which all Christians at least nominally belonged. One hundred years later there were many, a situation that continues today.

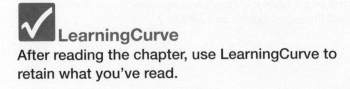

LearningCurve

After reading the chapter, use LearningCurve to retain what you've read.

> What were the
  central ideas of the
  early reformers?

> How did politics in
  Germany shape
  the course of the
  Reformation?

> How did Protestant
  ideas and
  institutions spread
  beyond German-
  speaking lands?

> What reforms did
  the Catholic
  Church make?

> What were the
  causes and
  consequences of
  religious violence?

Religious Violence in Urban Life. This 1590 painting shows Catholic military forces, including friars in their robes, processing through one of the many towns affected by the French religious wars that followed the Reformation. (Musée des Beaux-Arts, Valenciennes, France/Giraudon/The Bridgeman Art Library)

What were the central ideas of the reformers?

Selling Indulgences
A German single-page pamphlet shows a monk offering an indulgence, with the official seals of the pope attached, as people run to put their money in the box in exchange for his promise of heavenly bliss, symbolized by the dove above his head. Indulgences were sold widely in Germany and became the first Catholic practice that Luther criticized openly. This pamphlet also attacks the sale of indulgences, calling this practice devilish and deceitful. Indulgences were often printed fill-in-the-blank forms. (akg-images)

IN EARLY-SIXTEENTH-CENTURY EUROPE, a wide range of people had grievances with the church. Educated laypeople such as Christian humanists and urban residents, villagers and artisans, and church officials themselves called for reform. This widespread dissatisfaction helps explain why the ideas of Martin Luther, an obscure professor, found a ready audience. Within a decade of his first

CHAPTER LOCATOR | What were the central ideas of the reformers?

1517
- Martin Luther writes "Ninety-five Theses on the Power of Indulgences"

1521
- Diet of Worms

1521–1559
- Habsburg-Valois wars

1525
- German Peasants' War

1526
- Turkish victory at Mohács, which allows spread of Protestantism in Hungary

1530s
- Henry VIII ends the authority of the pope in England

1535
- Angela Merici establishes the Ursulines as first women's teaching order

1536
- John Calvin publishes *The Institutes of the Christian Religion*

1540
- Papal approval of Society of Jesus (Jesuits)

1542
- Pope Paul III establishes the Supreme Sacred Congregation of the Roman and Universal Inquisition

1545–1563
- Council of Trent

1553–1558
- Reign of Mary Tudor and temporary restoration of Catholicism in England

1555
- Peace of Augsburg; official recognition of Lutheranism

1558–1603
- Reign of Elizabeth in England

1560–1660
- Height of the European witch-hunt

1568–1578
- Civil war in the Netherlands

1572
- Saint Bartholomew's Day massacre

1588
- England defeats Spanish Armada

1598
- Edict of Nantes

publishing his ideas, much of central Europe and Scandinavia had broken with the Catholic Church, and even more radical concepts of the Christian message were being developed and linked to calls for social change.

The Christian Church in the Early Sixteenth Century

If external religious observances are an indication of conviction, Europeans in the early sixteenth century were deeply pious. Despite—or perhaps because of—the depth of their piety, many people were also highly critical of the Roman Catholic Church and its clergy. The papal conflict with the German emperor Frederick II in the thirteenth century, followed by the Babylonian Captivity and the Great Schism, badly damaged the prestige of church leaders, and the fifteenth-century popes' concentration on artistic patronage and building up family power did not help matters. Papal tax collection methods were attacked orally and in print. Some criticized the papacy itself as an institution. Some groups and individuals argued that certain doctrines taught by the church were incorrect. They suggested measures to reform institutions, improve clerical education and behavior, and alter basic doctrines.

| How did the political situation in Germany shape the course of the Reformation? | How did Protestant ideas and institutions spread beyond German-speaking lands? | What reforms did the Catholic Church make? | What were the causes and consequences of religious violence? | ✔ LearningCurve Check what you know. |

anticlericalism

▶ Opposition to the clergy.

In the early sixteenth century, court records, bishops' visitations of parishes, and popular songs and printed images show widespread **anticlericalism**, or opposition to the clergy. The critics concentrated primarily on three problems: clerical immorality; clerical ignorance; and clerical pluralism (the practice of holding more than one church office at a time), with the related problem of absenteeism. Many priests, monks, and nuns lived pious lives of devotion, learning, and service and had strong support from the laypeople in their areas, but everyone also knew (and repeated) stories about lecherous monks, lustful nuns, and greedy priests.

> **Key Complaints Levied Against the Pre-Reformation Catholic Clergy**

- **Clerical immorality:** Aimed at priests who were drunkards, neglected the rule of celibacy, gambled, or indulged in fancy dress

- **Clerical ignorance:** Motivated by barely literate priests who simply mumbled the Latin words of the Mass by rote without understanding their meaning

- **Absenteeism and pluralism:** Many clerics held several benefices, or offices, simultaneously, but they seldom visited the benefices, let alone performed the spiritual responsibilities those offices entailed

There was also local resentment of clerical privileges and immunities. Priests, monks, and nuns were exempt from civic responsibilities, such as defending the city and paying taxes. Yet religious orders frequently held large amounts of urban property, in some cities as much as one-third. City governments were increasingly determined to integrate the clergy into civic life by reducing their privileges and giving them public responsibilities. Urban leaders wanted some say in who would be appointed to high church offices. This brought city leaders into opposition with bishops and the papacy, which for centuries had stressed the independence of the church from lay control and the distinction between members of the clergy and laypeople.

Martin Luther

By itself, widespread criticism of the church did not lead to the dramatic changes of the sixteenth century. Instead, the personal religious struggle of a German university professor and priest, Martin Luther (1483–1546), propelled the wave of movements we now call the Reformation. Luther's education was intended to prepare him for a legal career. Instead, however, a sense of religious calling led him to join the Augustinian friars, a religious order whose members often preached to, taught, and assisted the poor. Luther was ordained a priest in 1507 and, after additional study, earned a doctorate of theology. From 1512 until his death in 1546, he served as professor of the Scriptures at the new University of Wittenberg.

Martin Luther was a very conscientious friar, but he was plagued with anxieties about sin and his ability to meet God's demands. Through his study of Saint Paul's letters in the New Testament, he gradually arrived at a new understanding of Christian doctrine. His understanding is often summarized as "faith alone, grace alone, Scripture alone." He believed that salvation and justification come through faith. Faith is a free gift of God's grace, not the result of human effort. God's word is revealed only in Scripture, not in the traditions of the church.

CHAPTER LOCATOR | What were the central ideas of the reformers?

At the same time that Luther was engaged in scholarly reflections and professorial lecturing, Pope Leo X authorized the sale of a special Saint Peter's indulgence to finance his building plans in Rome. The archbishop who controlled the area in which Wittenberg was located, Albert of Mainz, was an enthusiastic promoter of this indulgence sale.

What exactly was an **indulgence**? According to Catholic theology, individuals who sin could be reconciled to God by confessing their sins to a priest and by doing an assigned penance. But beginning in the twelfth century, learned theologians increasingly emphasized the idea of purgatory, a place where souls on their way to Heaven went to make further amends for their earthly sins. Both earthly penance and time in purgatory could be shortened by drawing on what was termed the "treasury of merits," which was a collection of all the virtuous acts that Christ, the apostles, and the saints had done during their lives. An indulgence was a document signed by the pope or another church official that substituted a virtuous act from the treasury of merits for penance or time in purgatory.

Archbishop Albert's indulgence sale, run by a Dominican friar named Johann Tetzel, promised that the purchase of indulgences would bring full forgiveness for one's own sins or release from purgatory for a loved one. One of the slogans—"As soon as coin in coffer rings, the soul from purgatory springs"—brought phenomenal success, and people traveled from miles around to buy indulgences.

Luther was severely troubled that many people believed they had no further need for repentance once they had purchased indulgences. In 1517, he wrote a letter to Archbishop Albert on the subject and enclosed in Latin his "Ninety-five Theses on the Power of Indulgences." His argument was that indulgences undermined the seriousness of the sacrament of penance, competed with the preaching of the Gospel, and downplayed the importance of charity in Christian life.

Luther's "Ninety-five Theses" were quickly printed, first in Latin and then in German translation. Luther was ordered to come to Rome; because of the political situation in the empire, however, he was able instead to engage in formal scholarly debate with a representative of the church, Johann Eck, at Leipzig in 1519. He refused to take back his ideas and continued to develop his calls for reform, publicizing them in a series of pamphlets in which he moved further and further away from Catholic theology. Both popes and church councils could err, he wrote, and secular leaders should reform the church if the pope and clerical hierarchy did not. There was no distinction between clergy and laypeople, and requiring clergy to be celibate was a fruitless attempt to control a natural human drive. Luther clearly understood the power of the new medium of print, so he authorized the publication of his works.

The papacy responded with a letter condemning some of Luther's propositions, ordering that his books be burned, and giving him two months to recant or be excommunicated. Luther retaliated by publicly burning the letter. By 1521, when the excommunication was supposed to become final, Luther's theological issues had become interwoven with public controversies about the church's wealth, power, and basic structure. In this highly charged atmosphere, the twenty-one-year-old emperor Charles V held his first diet (assembly of the nobility, clergy, and cities of the Holy Roman Empire) in the German city of Worms and summoned Luther to appear. Luther refused to give in to demands that he take back his ideas. His appearance at the Diet of Worms in 1521 created an even broader audience for reform ideas, and throughout central Europe other individuals began to

How did the political situation in Germany shape the course of the Reformation?

How did Protestant ideas and institutions spread beyond German-speaking lands?

What reforms did the Catholic Church make?

What were the causes and consequences of religious violence?

☑ LearningCurve
Check what you know.

381

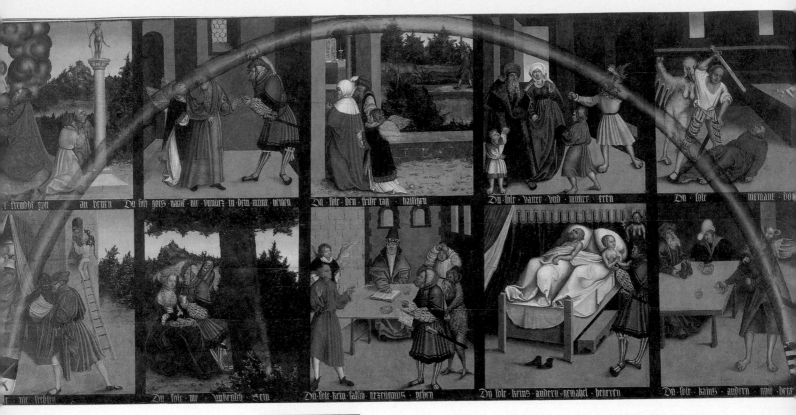

The Ten Commandments Lucas Cranach the Elder, the court painter for the elector of Saxony, painted this giant illustration of the Ten Commandments (more than 5 feet by 11 feet) for the city hall in Wittenberg in 1516, just at the point when Luther was beginning to question Catholic doctrine. Cranach was an early supporter of Luther, and many of his later works depict the reformer and his ideas. Paintings were used by both Protestants and Catholics to teach religious ideas. (Lutherhalle, Wittenberg, Germany/The Bridgeman Art Library)

preach and publish against the existing doctrines and practices of the church, drawing on the long tradition of calls for change as well as on Luther's teachings.

Protestant Thought

The most important early reformer other than Luther was the Swiss humanist, priest, and admirer of Erasmus, Ulrich Zwingli (ZWIHNG-lee) (1484–1531). Zwingli was convinced that Christian life rested on the Scriptures, which were the pure words of God and the sole basis of religious truth. He went on to attack indulgences, the Mass, the institution of monasticism, and clerical celibacy. In his gradual reform of the church in Zurich, he had the strong support of the city authorities, who had long resented the privileges of the clergy.

While they had their differences, Luther, Zwingli, and other early **Protestants** agreed on many things. First, how is a person to be saved? Traditional Catholic teaching held that salvation is achieved by both faith and good works. Protestants held that salvation comes by faith alone, regardless of good works or the sacraments. God, not people, initiates salvation. Second, where does religious authority

Protestants

▶ The name originally given to followers of Luther, which came to mean all non-Catholic Western Christian groups.

CHAPTER LOCATOR | What were the central ideas of the reformers?

reside? Christian doctrine had long maintained that authority rests both in the Bible and in the traditional teaching of the church. For Protestants, authority rested in the Bible alone. For a doctrine or issue to be valid, it had to have a scriptural basis. Because of this scriptural basis, most Protestants rejected Catholic teachings about the sacraments—the rituals that the church had defined as imparting God's benefits on the believer (see Chapter 10, page 283)—holding that only baptism and the Eucharist have scriptural support.

Third, what is the church? Protestants held that the church is a spiritual priesthood of all believers, which differed markedly from the Roman Catholic practice of a hierarchical clerical institution headed by the pope in Rome. Fourth, what is the highest form of Christian life? The medieval church had stressed the superiority of the monastic and religious life over the secular. Protestants disagreed and argued that every person should serve God in his or her individual calling.

The Appeal of Protestant Ideas

Pulpits and printing presses spread the Protestant message all over Germany, and by the middle of the sixteenth century, people of all social classes had rejected Catholic teachings and had become Protestant. What was the immense appeal of Luther's religious ideas and those of other Protestants?

Educated people and many humanists were much attracted by Luther's teachings. He advocated a simpler personal religion based on faith, a return to the spirit of the early church, the centrality of the Scriptures in the liturgy and in Christian life, and the abolition of elaborate ceremonies—precisely the reforms the Christian humanists had been calling for. The Protestant insistence that everyone should read and reflect on the Scriptures attracted literate and thoughtful city residents. In addition, townspeople who envied the church's wealth and resented paying for it were attracted by the notion that the clergy should also pay taxes and should not have special legal privileges.

Scholars in many disciplines have attributed Luther's fame and success to the invention of the printing press, which rapidly reproduced and popularized his ideas. Many printed works included woodcuts and other illustrations, so that even those who could not read could grasp the main ideas. Equally important was Luther's incredible skill with language. Luther's linguistic skill, together with his translation of the New Testament into German in 1523, led to the acceptance of his dialect of German as the standard written version of the German language.

Both Luther and Zwingli recognized that, for reforms to be permanent, political authorities as well as concerned individuals and religious leaders would have to accept them. Zwingli worked closely with the city council of Zurich, and city councils themselves took the lead in other cities and towns of Switzerland and south Germany. They appointed pastors who they knew had accepted Protestant ideas.

Luther lived in a territory ruled by a noble—the elector of Saxony—and he also worked closely with political authorities, viewing them as fully justified in asserting control over the church in their territories. Indeed, he demanded that German rulers reform the papacy and its institutions, and he instructed all Christians to obey their secular rulers, whom he saw as divinely ordained to maintain order.

| How did the political situation in Germany shape the course of the Reformation? | How did Protestant ideas and institutions spread beyond German-speaking lands? | What reforms did the Catholic Church make? | What were the causes and consequences of religious violence? | ✓ LearningCurve Check what you know. |

383

The Radical Reformation and the German Peasants' War

While Luther and Zwingli worked with political authorities, some individuals and groups rejected the idea that church and state needed to be united. Beginning in the 1520s, groups in Switzerland, Germany, and the Netherlands sought instead to create a voluntary community of believers separate from the state, as they understood it to have existed in New Testament times. In terms of theology and spiritual practices, these individuals and groups varied widely, though they are generally termed "radicals" for their insistence on a more extensive break with prevailing ideas. Some adopted the baptism of adult believers, for which they were called by their enemies "Anabaptists," which means "rebaptizers." Some groups attempted communal ownership of property. Some reacted harshly to members who deviated, but others argued for complete religious toleration and individualism.

The radicals' unwillingness to accept a state church marked them as societal outcasts and invited hatred and persecution; both Protestant and Catholic authorities saw a state church as key to maintaining order. Anabaptists and other radicals were banished or cruelly executed by burning, beating, or drowning. (See "Individuals in Society: Anna Jansz of Rotterdam," page 385.) Their community spirit and heroism in the face of martyrdom, however, contributed to the survival of radical ideas.

Radical reformers sometimes called for social as well as religious change, a message that resonated with the increasingly struggling German peasantry. In the early sixteenth century, the economic condition of the peasantry varied from place to place but was generally worse than it had been in the fifteenth century and was deteriorating still further. Crop failures in 1523 and 1524 aggravated an explosive situation. Nobles had aggrieved peasants by seizing village common lands, by imposing new rents and requiring additional services, and by taking the peasants' best livestock whenever a head of household died. The peasants made demands that they believed conformed to the Scriptures, and they cited radical thinkers as well as Luther as proof that their demands did conform.

Initially Luther sided with the peasants, but when rebellion broke out, peasants who expected Luther's support were soon disillusioned. Freedom for Luther meant independence from the authority of the Roman Church; it did not mean opposition to legally established secular powers. Firmly convinced that rebellion would hasten the end of civilized society, Luther wrote the tract *Against the Murderous, Thieving Hordes of the Peasants.* The nobility ferociously crushed the revolt. Historians estimate that more than seventy-five thousand peasants were killed in 1525.

The German Peasants' War of 1525 greatly strengthened the authority of lay rulers. Not surprisingly, the Reformation lost much of its popular appeal after 1525, though peasants and urban rebels sometimes found a place for their social and religious ideas in radical groups. Peasants' economic conditions did moderately improve, however. For example, in many parts of Germany, enclosed fields, meadows, and forests were returned to common use.

Marriage, Sexuality, and the Role of Women

Luther and Zwingli both believed that a priest's or nun's vows of celibacy went against human nature and God's commandments and that marriage brought spiritual advantages, which made it the ideal state for nearly all human beings. Most

CHAPTER LOCATOR | What were the central ideas of the reformers?

INDIVIDUALS IN SOCIETY
Anna Jansz of Rotterdam

Anna Jansz (1509–1539) was born into a well-to-do family in the small city of Briel in the Netherlands. She married, and when she was in her early twenties, she and her husband came to accept Anabaptism after listening to a traveling preacher. They were baptized in 1534 and became part of a group who believed that God would soon come to bring judgment on the wicked and deliver his true followers. Jansz wrote a hymn conveying these apocalyptic beliefs and foretelling vengeance on those who persecuted Anabaptists: "I hear the Trumpet sounding, From far off I hear her blast! . . . O murderous seed, what will you do? Offspring of Cain, you put to death The lambs of the Lord, without just cause — It will be doubly repaid to you! Death now comes riding on horseback, We have seen your fate! The sword is passing over the land, With which you will be killed and slain, And you will not escape from Hell!"

Jansz and her husband traveled to England, where she had a child, but in November 1538, she and her infant son, Isaiah, returned to the Netherlands, along with another woman. As the story was later told, the two women were recognized as Anabaptists by another traveler because of songs they were singing, perhaps her "Trumpet Song" among them. They were arrested and interrogated in the city of Rotterdam, and sentenced to death by drowning. The day she was executed — January 24, 1539 — Anna Jansz wrote a long testament to her son, providing him with spiritual advice: "My son, hear the instruction of your mother, and open your ears to hear the words of my mouth. Watch, today I am travelling the path of the Prophets, Apostles, and Martyrs, and drink from the cup from which they have all tasted. . . . But if you hear of the existence of a poor, lowly, cast-out little company, that has been despised and rejected by the World, go join it. . . . Honor the Lord through the works of your hands. Let the light of Scripture shine in you. Love your Neighbor; with an effusive, passionate heart deal your bread to the hungry."

Anabaptists later compiled accounts of trials and executions, along with letters and other records, into martyrologies designed to inspire deeper faith. One of the most widely read of these describes Jansz on her way to the execution. She offered a certain amount of money to anyone who would care for her son; a poor baker with six children agreed, and she passed the child to him. The martyrology reports that the baker later became quite wealthy, and that her son, Isaiah, became mayor of the city of Rotterdam. As such, he would have easily been able to read the court records of his mother's trial.

An etching of Anna Jansz on the way to her execution, from a 1685 Anabaptist martyrology. (Used by permission of the Mennonite Historical Library, Goshen College, Indiana)

Anna Jansz was one of thousands of people executed for their religious beliefs in sixteenth-century Europe. A few of these were high-profile individuals such as Thomas More, the Catholic former chancellor of England executed by King Henry VIII, but most were quite ordinary people. Many were women. Women's and men's experiences of martyrdom were similar in many ways, but women also confronted additional challenges. Some were pregnant while in prison — execution was delayed until the baby was born — or, like Jansz, had infants with them. They faced procedures of questioning, torture, and execution that brought dishonor as well as pain. Eventually many Anabaptists, as well as others whose religion put them in opposition to their rulers, migrated to parts of Europe that were more tolerant. By the seventeenth century, the Netherlands had become one of the most tolerant places in Europe, and Rotterdam was no longer the site of executions for religious reasons.

QUESTIONS FOR ANALYSIS

1. How did religion, gender, and social class all shape Jansz's experiences and the writings that she left behind?
2. Why might Jansz's hymn and her Anabaptist beliefs have seemed threatening to those who did not share her beliefs?

Source: Quotations are from *Elisabeth's Manly Courage: Testimonials and Songs of Martyred Anabaptist Women in the Low Countries*, ed. and trans. Hermina Joldersma and Louis Peter Grijp (Milwaukee, Wis.: Marquette University Press, 2001).

⬓LaunchPad

ONLINE DOCUMENT PROJECT

What might have led Jansz and thousands like her to die for their religious convictions? Keeping the question above in mind, learn more about Anna Jansz and other Anabaptist martyrs by analyzing images and hymns, and then complete a writing assignment based on the evidence and details from this chapter. *See inside the front cover to learn more.*

Protestant reformers, including Luther and Zwingli, married, and their wives had to create a new and respectable role for themselves—pastor's wife—to overcome being viewed as simply a new type of priest's concubine.

Though they denied that marriage was a sacrament, Protestant reformers stressed that it had been ordained by God when he presented Eve to Adam, served as a "remedy" for the unavoidable sin of lust, provided a site for the pious rearing of the next generation of God-fearing Christians, and offered husbands and wives companionship and consolation. (See "Picturing the Past: Domestic Scene," page 386.) A proper marriage was one that reflected both the spiritual equality of men and women and the proper social hierarchy of husbandly authority and wifely obedience.

Domestic Scene

The Protestant notion that the best form of Christian life was marriage and a family helps explain the appeal of Protestantism to middle-class urban men and women, such as those shown in this domestic scene. The engraving, titled "Concordia" (Harmony), includes the biblical inscription of what Jesus called the greatest commandment — "You shall love the Lord your God with all your heart and all your soul and your neighbor as yourself" (Deuteronomy 6; Matthew 22) — on tablets at the back. The large covered bed at the back was both a standard piece of furniture in urban homes and a symbol of proper marital sexual relations. (Mary Evans Picture Library/The Image Works)

> PICTURING THE PAST

ANALYZING THE IMAGE: What are the different family members doing? What elements of this image suggest that this is a pious Christian family?
CONNECTIONS: How do the various family roles shown here support the Protestant ideal of marriage and family?

CHAPTER LOCATOR | What were the central ideas of the reformers?

CHAPTER 13
386 REFORMATIONS AND RELIGIOUS WARS

Protestants did not break with medieval scholastic theologians in their idea that women were to be subject to men. Men were urged to treat their wives kindly and considerately but also to enforce their authority, through physical coercion if necessary. European marriage manuals used the metaphor of breaking a horse for teaching a wife obedience, though laws did set limits on the husband's power to do so.

Most Protestants came to allow divorce and remarriage. Protestant allowance of divorce differed markedly from Catholic doctrine, which viewed marriage as a sacramental union that, if entered into on valid grounds, could not be dissolved (Catholic canon law allowed only separation with no remarriage). Although permitting divorce was a dramatic legal change, it did not have a dramatic impact on newly Protestant areas. Because marriage was the cornerstone of society socially and economically, divorce was a desperate last resort.

Because Protestants believed that marriage was the only proper remedy for lust, they uniformly condemned prostitution. The licensed brothels that were a common feature of late medieval urban life (see Chapter 11, page 334) were closed in Protestant cities, and harsh punishments were set for prostitution. Many Catholic cities soon closed their brothels as well. Closing brothels did not end the exchange of sex for money, of course, but simply reshaped it. Smaller illegal brothels were established, or women selling sex moved to areas right outside city walls.

The Protestant Reformation clearly had a positive impact on marriage, but its impact on women was more mixed. Many nuns were in convents not out of a strong sense of religious calling but because their parents placed them there. Convents nevertheless provided women of the upper classes with an opportunity to use their literary, artistic, medical, or administrative talents if they could not or would not marry. The Reformation generally brought the closing of monasteries and convents, and marriage became virtually the only occupation for upper-class Protestant women. The Protestant emphasis on marriage made unmarried women (and men) suspect because they did not belong to the type of household regarded as the cornerstone of a proper, godly society.

A few women took Luther's idea about the priesthood of all believers to heart and wrote religious works. No sixteenth-century Protestants allowed women to be members of the clergy, although monarchs such as Elizabeth I of England and female territorial rulers of the states of the Holy Roman Empire did determine religious policies just as male rulers did.

QUICK REVIEW <

Why were the ideas of the Protestant reformers appealing to different social groups?

How did the political situation in Germany shape the course of the Reformation?

How did Protestant ideas and institutions spread beyond German-speaking lands?

What reforms did the Catholic Church make?

What were the causes and consequences of religious violence?

 LearningCurve
Check what you know.

387

> How did the political situation in Germany shape the course of the Reformation?

In this double portrait, artist Giorgio Vasari uses matching hand gestures to indicate agreement between the pope and the emperor, though the pope's red hat and cape make him the dominant figure. Charles V remained loyal to Catholicism, although the political situation and religious wars in Germany eventually required him to compromise with Protestants. (Scala/Art Resource, NY)

ALTHOUGH CRITICISM OF THE CHURCH WAS WIDESPREAD in Europe in the early sixteenth century, reform movements could be squelched more easily by the strong central governments that had evolved in Spain and France. England, too, had a strong monarchy, but the king broke from the Catholic Church for other reasons (see page 393). The Holy Roman Empire, in contrast, included hundreds of largely independent states. Against this background of decentralization and strong local power, Martin Luther had launched a movement to reform the church. Two years after he published the "Ninety-five Theses," the electors of the Holy Roman Empire chose as emperor a nineteen-year-old Habsburg prince who ruled as Charles V (r. 1519–1556). The course of the Reformation was shaped by this election and by the political relationships surrounding it.

CHAPTER LOCATOR | What were the central ideas of the reformers?

The Rise of the Habsburg Dynasty

War and diplomacy were important ways that states increased their power in sixteenth-century Europe, but so was marriage. The benefits of an advantageous marriage stretched across generations, a process that can be seen most dramatically with the Habsburgs. The Holy Roman emperor Frederick III, a Habsburg who was the ruler of most of Austria, acquired only a small amount of territory—but a great deal of money—with his marriage to Princess Eleonore of Portugal in 1452. He arranged for his son Maximilian to marry Europe's most prominent heiress, Mary of Burgundy, in 1477; she inherited the Netherlands, Luxembourg, and the County of Burgundy in what is now eastern France. Through this union with the rich and powerful duchy of Burgundy, the Austrian house of Habsburg, already the strongest ruling family in the empire, became an international power.

Maximilian learned the lesson of marital politics well, marrying his son and daughter to the children of Ferdinand and Isabella, the rulers of Spain, much of southern Italy, and eventually the Spanish New World empire. His grandson Charles V (1500–1558) fell heir to a vast and incredibly diverse collection of states and peoples, each governed in a different manner and held together only by the person of the emperor (**Map 13.1**). Charles, a Catholic, was convinced that it was his duty to maintain the political and religious unity of Western Christendom.

Religious Wars in Switzerland and Germany

In the sixteenth century, the practice of religion remained a public matter. The ruler determined the official form of religious practice in his (or occasionally her) jurisdiction. Almost everyone believed that the presence of a faith different from that of the majority represented a political threat to the security of the state, and few believed in religious liberty.

Luther's ideas appealed to German rulers for a variety of reasons. Though Germany was not a nation, people did have an understanding of being German because of their language and traditions. Luther frequently used the phrase "we Germans" in his attacks on the papacy, and his appeal to national feeling influenced many rulers. Some German rulers were sincerely attracted to Lutheran ideas, but material considerations swayed many others to embrace the new faith. The rejection of Roman Catholicism and adoption of Protestantism would mean the legal confiscation of church property. Thus many political authorities in the empire became Protestant in part to extend their financial and political power and to enhance their independence from the emperor.

Charles V was a vigorous defender of Catholicism, so it is not surprising that the Reformation led to religious wars. The first battleground was Switzerland, a loose confederation of thirteen largely autonomous territories called cantons. Some cantons remained Catholic and some became Protestant; in the late 1520s, the two sides went to war. Zwingli was killed on the battlefield in 1531, and both sides quickly decided that a treaty was preferable to further fighting. The treaty basically allowed each canton to determine its own religion and ordered each side to give up its foreign alliances.

How did the political situation in Germany shape the course of the Reformation?	How did Protestant ideas and institutions spread beyond German-speaking lands?	What reforms did the Catholic Church make?	What were the causes and consequences of religious violence?	✓ LearningCurve Check what you know.

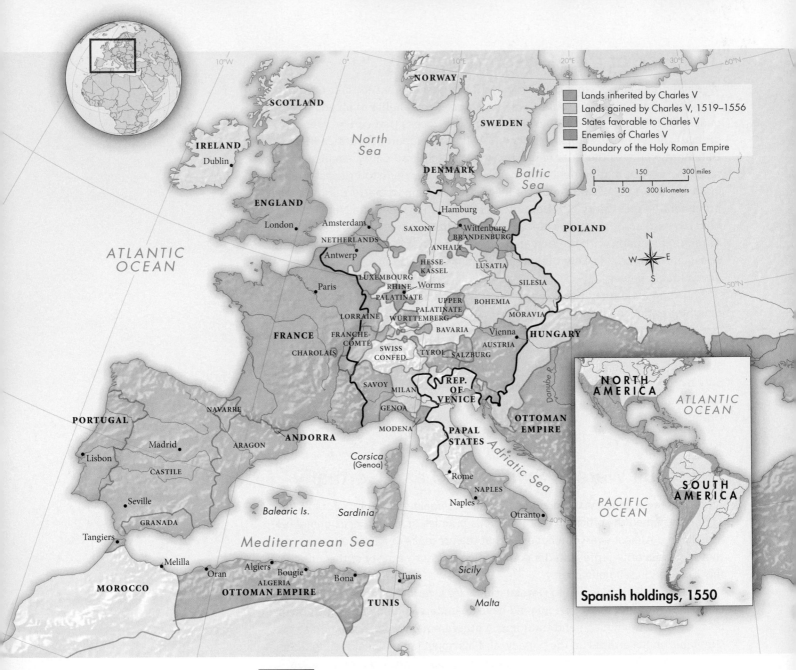

MAP 13.1 ■ The Global Empire of Charles V, ca. 1556

Charles V exercised theoretical jurisdiction over more European territory than anyone since Charlemagne. He also claimed authority over large parts of North and South America (see Map 14.2, page 420), though actual Spanish control was weak in much of the area.

Trying to halt the spread of religious division, Charles V called an Imperial Diet in 1530 to meet at Augsburg. The Lutherans developed a statement of faith, later called the Augsburg Confession, and the Protestant princes presented this to the emperor. Charles refused to accept it; he ordered all Protestants to return to the Catholic Church and give up any confiscated church property. This demand backfired, and Protestant territories in the empire formed a military alliance. The

CHAPTER LOCATOR | What were the central ideas of the reformers?

emperor could not respond militarily because he was in the midst of a series of wars with the French: the Habsburg-Valois wars (1521–1559). The Ottoman Turks had also taken much of Hungary and in 1529 were besieging Vienna.

The 1530s and early 1540s saw complicated political maneuvering among many of the powers of Europe. Various attempts were made to heal the religious split with a church council, but it became increasingly clear that this would not be possible and that war was inevitable. Charles V realized that he was fighting not only for religious unity but also for a more unified state against territorial rulers who wanted to maintain their independence. He was thus defending both church and empire.

Fighting began in 1546, and initially the emperor was very successful. This success alarmed both France and the pope, however, who did not want Charles to become even more powerful. The pope withdrew papal troops, and the Catholic king of France sent money and troops to the Lutheran princes. Finally, in 1555, Charles agreed to the Peace of Augsburg, which officially recognized Lutheranism. The political authority in each territory was permitted to decide whether the territory would be Catholic or Lutheran. Most of northern and central Germany became Lutheran, while the south remained Roman Catholic. There was no freedom of religion within the territories, however. Princes or town councils established state churches to which all subjects of the area had to belong.

The Peace of Augsburg ended religious war in Germany for many decades. His hope of uniting his empire under a single church dashed, Charles V abdicated in 1556 and moved to a monastery, transferring power over his holdings in Spain and the Netherlands to his son Philip and his imperial power to his brother Ferdinand.

QUICK REVIEW <

How did many German princes and city councils use Luther's ideas to further their long-term goal of gaining greater political autonomy?

How did the political situation in Germany shape the course of the Reformation?

How did Protestant ideas and institutions spread beyond German-speaking lands?

What reforms did the Catholic Church make?

What were the causes and consequences of religious violence?

☑ LearningCurve
Check what you know.

How did Protestant ideas and institutions spread beyond German-speaking lands?

Young John Calvin

This oil painting of the reformer as a young man captures his spiritual intensity and determination, qualities that the artist clearly viewed as positive. (De Agostini Picture Library/G. Costa/The Bridgeman Art Library)

STATES WITHIN THE HOLY ROMAN EMPIRE were the earliest territories to accept the Protestant Reformation, but by the later 1520s and 1530s, religious change came to Denmark-Norway, Sweden, England, France, and eastern Europe. In most of these areas, a second generation of reformers built on Lutheran and Zwinglian ideas to develop their own theology and plans for institutional change.

Scandinavia

The first area outside the empire to officially accept the Reformation was the kingdom of Denmark-Norway under King Christian III (r. 1536–1559). In the 1530s, the king officially broke with the Catholic Church, and most clergy followed. The process went smoothly in Denmark, but in northern Norway and Iceland (which Christian also ruled), there were violent reactions, and Lutheranism was only gradually imposed on a largely unwilling populace.

CHAPTER LOCATOR | What were the central ideas of the reformers?

In Sweden, Gustavus Vasa (r. 1523–1560), who came to the throne during a civil war with Denmark, also took over control of church personnel and income. Protestant ideas spread, though the Swedish Church did not officially accept Lutheran theology until later in the century.

Henry VIII and the Reformation in England

As was true on the continent, the Reformation in England had economic and political as well as religious causes. The impetus for England's break with Rome was the desire of King Henry VIII (r. 1509–1547) for a new wife, although his own motives also included political, social, and economic elements.

Henry VIII was married to Catherine of Aragon, the daughter of Ferdinand and Isabella and widow of Henry's older brother, Arthur. Marriage to a brother's widow went against canon law, and Henry had been required to obtain a special papal dispensation to marry Catherine. The marriage had produced only one living heir, a daughter, Mary. By 1527, Henry decided that God was showing his displeasure with the marriage by denying him a son, and he appealed to the pope to have the marriage annulled. He was also in love with a court lady in waiting, Anne Boleyn. Normally an annulment would not have been a problem, but the troops of Emperor Charles V were in Rome at that point, and Pope Clement VII was essentially their prisoner. Charles V was the nephew of Catherine of Aragon and thus was vigorously opposed to an annulment.

With Rome thwarting his matrimonial plans, Henry decided to remove the English Church from papal jurisdiction. In a series of measures during the 1530s, Henry used Parliament to make himself the supreme head of the church in England. Some opposed the king and were beheaded, among them Thomas More, the king's chancellor and author of *Utopia* (see Chapter 12). When Anne Boleyn failed twice to produce a male child, Henry VIII charged her with adulterous incest and in 1536 had her beheaded. His third wife, Jane Seymour, gave Henry the desired son, Edward, but she died in childbirth. Henry went on to three more wives.

Theologically, Henry was conservative, and the English Church retained traditional Catholic practices and doctrines such as confession, clerical celibacy, and transubstantiation. Under the influence of his chief minister, Thomas Cromwell, and the man he had appointed archbishop of Canterbury, Thomas Cranmer, he did agree to place an English Bible in every church. He also decided to dissolve the English monasteries, primarily because he wanted their wealth. Between 1535 and 1539, the king, working through Parliament, ended nine hundred years of English monastic life, dispersing the monks and nuns and confiscating their lands.

The nationalization of the church and the dissolution of the monasteries led to important changes in government administration. Vast tracts of formerly monastic land came temporarily under the Crown's jurisdiction, and new bureaucratic machinery had to be developed to manage those properties. Cromwell reformed and centralized the king's household, the council, the secretariats, and the Exchequer. New departments of state were set up. Surplus funds from all departments went into a liquid fund to be applied to areas where there were deficits. This balancing resulted in greater efficiency and economy, and Henry VIII's reign saw the growth of the modern centralized bureaucratic state.

How did the political situation in Germany shape the course of the Reformation?

How did Protestant ideas and institutions spread beyond German-speaking lands?

What reforms did the Catholic Church make?

What were the causes and consequences of religious violence?

LearningCurve
Check what you know.

Allegory of the Tudor Dynasty The unknown creator of this work intended to glorify the virtues of the Protestant succession; the painting has no historical reality. Henry VIII (seated) hands the sword of justice to his Protestant son Edward VI. The Catholic Queen Mary and her husband Philip of Spain (left) are followed by Mars, god of war, signifying violence and civil disorder. At right, the figures of Peace and Plenty accompany the Protestant Elizabeth I, symbolizing England's happy fate under her rule. (Yale Center for British Art, Paul Mellon Collection/The Bridgeman Art Library)

Did the religious changes under Henry VIII have broad popular support? Historians disagree about this. Some English people had been dissatisfied with the existing Christian Church before Henry's measures, and Protestant literature circulated. Traditional Catholicism exerted an enormously strong and vigorous hold over the imagination and loyalty of the people, however. Recent scholarship points out that people rarely "converted" from Catholicism to Protestantism overnight. People responded to an action of the Crown that was played out in their own neighborhood—the closing of a monastery, the ending of Masses for the dead—with a combination of resistance, acceptance, and collaboration.

Upholding Protestantism in England

In the short reign of Henry's sickly son, Edward VI (r. 1547–1553), Protestant ideas exerted a significant influence on the religious life of the country. Archbishop Thomas Cranmer simplified the liturgy; invited Protestant theologians to

CHAPTER LOCATOR | What were the central ideas of the reformers?

England; and prepared the first *Book of Common Prayer* (1549), which was later approved by Parliament. The *Book of Common Prayer* included the order for all services and prayers of the Church of England.

The equally brief reign of Mary Tudor (r. 1553–1558) witnessed a sharp move back to Catholicism. The devoutly Catholic daughter of Catherine of Aragon, Mary rescinded the Reformation legislation of her father's reign and restored Roman Catholicism. Mary's marriage to her cousin Philip II of Spain (r. 1556–1598), son of the emperor Charles V, proved highly unpopular in England, and her execution of several hundred Protestants further alienated her subjects. Mary's death raised to the throne her half-sister Elizabeth, Henry's daughter with Anne Boleyn, who had been raised a Protestant. Elizabeth's reign from 1558 to 1603 inaugurated the beginnings of religious stability.

At the start of Elizabeth's reign, sharp differences existed in England. On the one hand, Catholics wanted a Roman Catholic ruler. On the other hand, a vocal number of returning exiles wanted all Catholic elements in the Church of England eliminated. The latter, because they wanted to "purify" the church, were called "Puritans."

Shrewdly, Elizabeth chose a middle course between Catholic and Puritan extremes. Working through Parliament, she ordered church and government officials to swear that she was supreme in matters of religion as well as politics, required her subjects to attend services in the Church of England or risk a fine, and called for frequent preaching of Protestant ideas. She did not interfere with people's privately held beliefs, however. The Anglican Church, as the Church of England was called, moved in a moderately Protestant direction.

Toward the end of the sixteenth century, Elizabeth's reign was threatened by European powers attempting to re-establish Catholicism. Philip II of Spain had hoped that his marriage to Mary Tudor would reunite England with Catholic Europe, but Mary's death ended those plans. Another Mary—Mary, Queen of Scots (r. 1560–1567)—provided a new opportunity. Mary was next in line to the English throne, and Elizabeth imprisoned her because she worried—quite rightly—that Mary would become the center of Catholic plots to overthrow her. In 1587, Mary became implicated in a plot to assassinate Elizabeth, a conspiracy that had Philip II's full backing. When the English executed Mary, the Catholic pope urged Philip to retaliate.

Philip prepared a vast fleet to sail from Lisbon to Flanders, where a large army of Spanish troops was stationed because of religious wars in the Netherlands (see page 404). The Spanish ships were to escort barges carrying some of the troops across the English Channel to attack England. On May 9, 1588, the **Spanish Armada** sailed from Lisbon harbor. It met an English fleet in the Channel before it reached Flanders. A combination of storms and squalls; spoiled food and tainted water; inadequate Spanish ammunition; and, to a lesser extent, English fire ships that caused the Spanish to scatter gave England the victory.

The battle in the English Channel has frequently been described as one of the decisive battles in world history. In fact, it had mixed consequences. Spain soon rebuilt its navy and the war between England and Spain dragged on for years. Yet the defeat of the Spanish Armada prevented Philip II from reimposing Catholicism on England by force. In England, the victory contributed to a David and Goliath legend that enhanced English national sentiment.

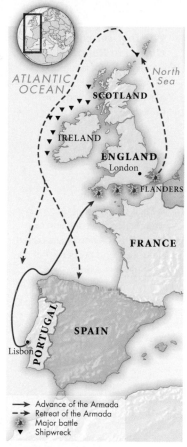

→ Advance of the Armada
⇢ Retreat of the Armada
✳ Major battle
▼ Shipwreck

The Route of the Spanish Armada, 1588

Spanish Armada
▶ The fleet sent by Philip II of Spain in 1588 against England as a religious crusade against Protestantism. Weather and the English fleet defeated it.

How did the political situation in Germany shape the course of the Reformation?

How did Protestant ideas and institutions spread beyond German-speaking lands?

What reforms did the Catholic Church make?

What were the causes and consequences of religious violence?

✓ LearningCurve
Check what you know.

395

Calvinism

John Calvin (1509–1564) was born in Noyon in northwestern France. As a young man he studied law, which had a decisive impact on his mind and later his thought. In 1533, he experienced a religious crisis, and as a result converted to Protestantism.

Calvin believed that God had specifically selected him to reform the church. Accordingly, he accepted an invitation to assist in the reformation of the city of Geneva. There, beginning in 1541, Calvin worked assiduously to establish a well-disciplined Christian society in which church and state acted together.

To understand Calvin's Geneva, it is necessary to understand Calvin's ideas. These he embodied in ***The Institutes of the Christian Religion***, published first in 1536 and in its final form in 1559. The cornerstone of Calvin's theology was his belief in the absolute sovereignty and omnipotence of God and the total weakness of humanity. Before the infinite power of God, he asserted, men and women are as insignificant as grains of sand.

Calvin did not ascribe free will to human beings because that would detract from the sovereignty of God. Men and women cannot actively work to achieve salvation; rather, God in his infinite wisdom decided at the beginning of time who would be saved and who would be damned. This viewpoint constitutes the theological principle called **predestination**. Many people consider the doctrine of predestination, which dates back to Saint Augustine and Saint Paul, to be a pessimistic view of the nature of God. But "this terrible decree," as even Calvin called it, did not lead to pessimism or fatalism. Instead, many Calvinists came to believe that, although one's own actions could do nothing to change one's fate, hard work, thrift, and proper moral conduct could serve as signs that one was among the "elect" chosen for salvation.

Calvin transformed Geneva into a community based on his religious principles. The most powerful organization in the city became the Consistory, a group of laymen and pastors charged with investigating and disciplining deviations from proper doctrine and conduct.

Serious crimes and heresy were handled by the civil authorities, which, with the Consistory's approval, sometimes used torture to extract confessions. Between 1542 and 1546 alone, seventy-six persons were banished from Geneva, and fifty-eight were executed for heresy, adultery, blasphemy, and witchcraft (see page 404).

Geneva became the model of a Christian community for many Protestant reformers. Religious refugees from France, England, Spain, Scotland, and Italy visited Calvin's Geneva. Subsequently, the church of Calvin—often termed "Reformed"—served as the model for the Presbyterian Church in Scotland, the Huguenot Church in France (see page 403), and the Puritan churches in England and New England.

Calvinism became the compelling force in international Protestantism. Calvinists believed that any occupation could be a God-given calling and should be carried out with diligence and dedication. This doctrine encouraged an aggressive, vigorous activism in both work and religious life, and Calvinism became the most dynamic force in sixteenth- and seventeenth-century Protestantism.

The Reformation in Eastern Europe

While political and economic issues determined the course of the Reformation in western and northern Europe, ethnic factors often proved decisive in eastern Europe, where people of diverse backgrounds had settled in the later Middle

The Institutes of the Christian Religion
▶ Calvin's formulation of Christian doctrine, which became a systematic theology for Protestantism.

predestination
▶ The teaching that God has determined the salvation or damnation of individuals based on his will and purpose, not on their merit or works.

CHAPTER LOCATOR | What were the central ideas of the reformers?

Ages. In Bohemia in the fifteenth century, a Czech majority was ruled by Germans. Most Czechs had adopted the ideas of Jan Hus, and the emperor had been forced to recognize a separate Hussite Church (see page 327). Yet Lutheranism appealed to Germans in Bohemia in the 1520s and 1530s, and the nobility embraced Lutheranism in opposition to the Catholic Habsburgs. The forces of the Catholic Reformation (see page 398) promoted a Catholic spiritual revival in Bohemia, and some areas reconverted. This complicated situation would be one of the causes of the Thirty Years' War in the early seventeenth century.

By 1500, Poland and the Grand Duchy of Lithuania were jointly governed by king, senate, and diet (parliament), but the two territories retained separate officials, judicial systems, armies, and forms of citizenship. The population of Poland-Lithuania was also very diverse; Germans, Italians, Tartars, and Jews lived among Poles and Lithuanians. Each group spoke its native language, though all educated people spoke Latin. Luther's ideas took root in Germanized towns but were opposed by King Sigismund I (r. 1506–1548) as well as by ordinary Poles, who held strong anti-German feeling. The Reformed tradition of John Calvin, with its stress on the power of church elders, appealed to the Polish nobility, however. But doctrinal differences among Calvinists, Lutherans, and other groups prevented united opposition to Catholicism, and a Counter-Reformation gained momentum. By 1650, due largely to the efforts of the Jesuits (see page 400), Poland was again staunchly Roman Catholic.

Hungary's experience with the Reformation was even more complex. Lutheranism was spread by Hungarian students who had studied at Wittenberg, and sympathy for it developed at the royal court of King Louis II in Buda. But concern about "the German heresy" by the Catholic hierarchy and among the high nobles found expression in a decree of the Hungarian diet in 1523 that "all Lutherans and those favoring them . . . should have their property confiscated and themselves punished with death as heretics."[1]

Before such measures could be acted on, a military event on August 26, 1526, had profound consequences for both the Hungarian state and the Protestant Reformation there. On the plain of Mohács in southern Hungary, the Ottoman sultan Suleiman the Magnificent inflicted a crushing defeat on the Hungarians, killing King Louis II, many of the nobles, and more than sixteen thousand ordinary soldiers. The Hungarian kingdom was then divided into three parts: the Ottoman Turks absorbed the great plains, including the capital, Buda; the Habsburgs ruled the north and west; and Ottoman-supported Janos Zapolya held eastern Hungary and Transylvania.

The Turks were indifferent to the religious conflicts of Christians, whom they regarded as infidels. Many Magyar (Hungarian) nobles accepted Lutheranism, Lutheran schools and parishes headed by men educated at Wittenberg multiplied, and peasants welcomed the new faith. The majority of Hungarian people were Protestant until the late seventeenth century, when Hungarian nobles recognized Habsburg (Catholic) rule and Ottoman Turkish withdrawal in 1699 led to Catholic restoration.

QUICK REVIEW <

How did Calvinism differ from Lutheranism?

How did the political situation in Germany shape the course of the Reformation?

How did Protestant ideas and institutions spread beyond German-speaking lands?

What reforms did the Catholic Church make?

What were the causes and consequences of religious violence?

☑ LearningCurve
Check what you know.

> What reforms did the Catholic Church make?

Church of the Gesù

Begun in 1568 as the mother church for the Jesuit order, the Church of the Gesù in Rome conveyed a sense of drama, motion, and power through its lavish decorations and shimmering frescoes. Gesù served as a model for Catholic churches elsewhere in Europe and the New World, their triumphant and elaborate style reflecting the dynamic and proselytizing spirit of the Catholic Reformation. (© Alfredo Dagli Orti/The Art Archive/Corbis)

BETWEEN 1517 AND 1547, Protestantism made remarkable advances. Nevertheless, the Roman Catholic Church made a significant comeback. After about 1540, no new large areas of Europe, other than the Netherlands, accepted Protestant beliefs (**Map 13.2**). Many historians see the developments within the Catholic Church after the Protestant Reformation as two interrelated movements: one a drive for internal reform linked to earlier reform efforts, the other a Counter-Reformation that opposed Protestants intellectually, politically, militarily, and institutionally.

Papal Reform and the Council of Trent

Renaissance popes and their advisers were not blind to the need for church reforms, but they resisted calls for a general council representing the entire church and feared that any transformation would mean a loss of power, revenue,

CHAPTER LOCATOR | What were the central ideas of the reformers?

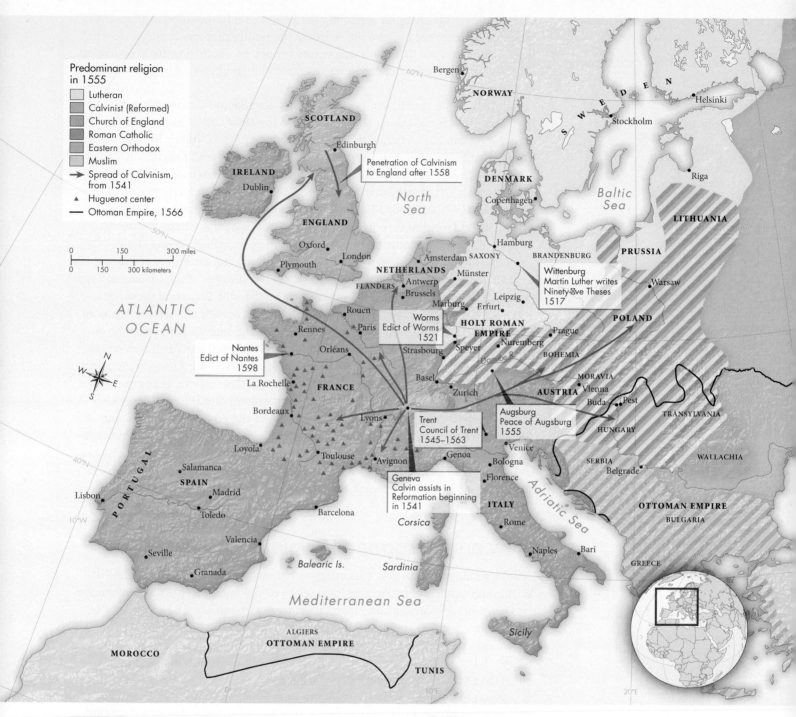

Predominant religion
in 1555

- Lutheran
- Calvinist (Reformed)
- Church of England
- Roman Catholic
- Eastern Orthodox
- Muslim
→ Spread of Calvinism, from 1541
▲ Huguenot center
— Ottoman Empire, 1566

0   150   300 miles
0   150   300 kilometers

Penetration of Calvinism to England after 1558

Wittenburg
Martin Luther writes Ninety-five Theses 1517

Worms
Edict of Worms 1521

Nantes
Edict of Nantes 1598

Trent
Council of Trent 1545–1563

Augsburg
Peace of Augsburg 1555

Geneva
Calvin assists in Reformation beginning in 1541

ATLANTIC OCEAN

North Sea

Baltic Sea

NORWAY   Bergen
SWEDEN   Stockholm   Helsinki
DENMARK   Copenhagen   Riga
LITHUANIA
PRUSSIA
Hamburg   SAXONY   BRANDENBURG
Amsterdam   Münster   Warsaw
SCOTLAND   Edinburgh
IRELAND   Dublin
ENGLAND   Oxford   London
Plymouth
NETHERLANDS   FLANDERS   Antwerp   Brussels
Rouen   Paris   Leipzig   Erfurt   Prague   POLAND
Rennes   Marburg
Orléans   Strasbourg   Speyer   Nuremberg   BOHEMIA
HOLY ROMAN EMPIRE
Basel   Danube R.
La Rochelle   FRANCE   Zurich   AUSTRIA   Vienna   MORAVIA
Bordeaux   Buda   Pest   TRANSYLVANIA
Lyons   HUNGARY
Loyola   Genoa   Venice   WALLACHIA
Salamanca   Toulouse   Avignon   Bologna   SERBIA   Belgrade
SPAIN   Madrid   Florence   ITALY   OTTOMAN EMPIRE
PORTUGAL   Lisbon   Toledo   Corsica   Rome   BULGARIA
Barcelona   Adriatic Sea
Valencia   Naples   Bari
Seville   Balearic Is.   Sardinia   GREECE
Granada
Mediterranean Sea   Sicily
MOROCCO   ALGIERS   OTTOMAN EMPIRE   TUNIS

MAP 13.2 ■ Religious Divisions in Europe, ca. 1555

The Reformations shattered the religious unity of Western Christendom. The situation was even more complicated than a map of this scale can show. Many cities within the Holy Roman Empire, for example, accepted a different faith than the surrounding countryside; Augsburg, Basel, and Strasbourg were all Protestant, though they were surrounded by territory ruled by Catholic nobles.

> MAPPING THE PAST

ANALYZING THE MAP: Which countries were the most religiously diverse in Europe? Which were the least diverse?

CONNECTIONS: Where was the first arena of religious conflict in sixteenth-century Europe, and why did it develop there and not elsewhere? To what degree can nonreligious factors be used as an explanation for the religious divisions in sixteenth-century Europe?

| How did the political situation in Germany shape the course of the Reformation? | How did Protestant ideas and institutions spread beyond German-speaking lands? | **What reforms did the Catholic Church make?** | What were the causes and consequences of religious violence? | ☑ LearningCurve Check what you know. |

and prestige. This changed beginning with Pope Paul III (pontificate 1534–1549), when the papal court became the center of the reform movement rather than its chief opponent. Paul III and his successors supported improvements in education for the clergy, the end of simony (the selling of church offices), and stricter control of clerical life.

In 1542, Pope Paul III established the Supreme Sacred Congregation of the Roman and Universal Inquisition, often called the **Holy Office**, with jurisdiction over the Roman Inquisition, a powerful instrument of the Catholic Reformation. The Roman Inquisition was a committee of six cardinals with judicial authority over all Catholics and the power to arrest, imprison, and execute suspected heretics. The Holy Office published the *Index of Prohibited Books*, a catalogue of forbidden reading that included works by Christian humanists such as Erasmus as well as by Protestants. Within the Papal States, the Inquisition effectively destroyed heresy, but outside the papal territories, its influence was slight.

Pope Paul III also called a general council, which met intermittently from 1545 to 1563 at Trent, an imperial city close to Italy. The decrees of the Council of Trent laid a solid basis for the spiritual renewal of the Catholic Church. It gave equal validity to the Scriptures and to tradition as sources of religious truth and authority. It reaffirmed the seven sacraments and the traditional Catholic teaching on transubstantiation. It tackled the disciplinary matters that had disillusioned the faithful, requiring bishops to reside in their own dioceses, suppressing pluralism and simony, and forbidding the sale of indulgences. Clerics who kept concubines were to give them up, and bishops were given greater authority. The council required every diocese to establish a seminary for the education and training of the clergy. For the first time, great emphasis was laid on preaching and instructing the laity, especially the uneducated. The doctrinal and disciplinary legislation of Trent served as the basis for Roman Catholic faith, organization, and practice through the middle of the twentieth century.

Holy Office

▶ The official Roman Catholic agency founded in 1542 to combat international doctrinal heresy.

New and Reformed Religious Orders

Just as seminaries provided education, so did religious orders, which aimed at raising the moral and intellectual level of the clergy and people. The monasteries and convents of many existing religious orders were reformed so that they followed more rigorous standards. In Spain, for example, the Carmelite nun Teresa of Ávila (1515–1582) founded new convents and reformed her Carmelite order to bring it back to stricter standards of asceticism and poverty, a task she understood God had set for her in mystical visions.

New religious orders were founded, some of which focused on education. The Ursuline order of nuns, for example, founded by Angela Merici (1474–1540), focused on the education of women. Founded in 1535, the Ursulines sought to contribute to the re-Christianizing of society by training future wives and mothers. After receiving papal approval in 1565, the Ursulines rapidly spread to France and the New World.

Jesuits

▶ Members of the Society of Jesus, founded by Ignatius Loyola, whose goal was the spread of the Roman Catholic faith.

The most significant new order was the Society of Jesus, or **Jesuits**. Founded by Ignatius Loyola (1491–1556), the Jesuits played a powerful international role in strengthening Catholicism in Europe and spreading the faith around the world. While recuperating from severe battle wounds in his legs, Loyola studied books

CHAPTER LOCATOR | What were the central ideas of the reformers?

CHAPTER 13
400 REFORMATIONS AND RELIGIOUS WARS

about Christ and the saints and decided to give up his military career and become a soldier of Christ. During a year spent in seclusion, prayer, and asceticism, he gained insights that went into his great classic, *Spiritual Exercises* (1548). This work, intended for study during a four-week period of retreat, set out a training program of structured meditation designed to develop spiritual discipline and allow one to meld one's will with that of God.

After study at universities in Salamanca and Paris, Loyola gathered a group of six companions and in 1540 secured papal approval of the new Society of Jesus. The first Jesuits, recruited primarily from wealthy merchant and professional families, saw their mission as improving people's spiritual condition rather than altering doctrine. Their goal was not to reform the church, but "to help souls."

The Society of Jesus developed into a highly centralized, tightly knit organization. In addition to the traditional vows of poverty, chastity, and obedience, professed members vowed special obedience to the pope. Flexibility and the willingness to respond to the needs of time and circumstance formed the Jesuit tradition, which proved attractive to many young men. The Jesuits achieved phenomenal success for the papacy and the reformed Catholic Church, carrying Christianity to India and Japan before 1550 and to Brazil, North America, and the Congo in the seventeenth century. Within Europe, the Jesuits brought southern Germany and much of eastern Europe back to Catholicism. Jesuit schools adopted the modern humanist curricula and methods, educating the sons of the nobility as well as the poor. As confessors and spiritual directors to kings, Jesuits exerted great political influence.

QUICK REVIEW <

Why is it necessary to speak of both a Catholic Reformation and a Counter-Reformation? What did each accomplish?

How did the political situation in Germany shape the course of the Reformation?

How did Protestant ideas and institutions spread beyond German-speaking lands?

What reforms did the Catholic Church make?

What were the causes and consequences of religious violence?

☑ LearningCurve
Check what you know.

401

What were the causes and consequences of religious violence?

Iconoclasm in the Netherlands Calvinist men and women break stained-glass windows, remove statues, and carry off devotional altarpieces. Iconoclasm, or the destruction of religious images, is often described as a "riot," but here the participants seem very purposeful. Calvinist Protestants regarded pictures and statues as sacrilegious and saw removing them as a way to purify the church. (The Fotomas Index/The Bridgeman Art Library)

IN 1559, **FRANCE AND SPAIN SIGNED** the Treaty of Cateau-Cambrésis (CAH-toh kam-BRAY-sees), which ended the long conflict known as the Habsburg-Valois wars. Spain was the victor. France, exhausted by the struggle, had to acknowledge Spanish dominance in Italy, where much of the fighting had taken place. True peace was elusive, however, and over the next century, religious differences led to riots, civil wars, and international conflicts. Especially in France and the Netherlands, Protestants and Catholics used violent actions as well as preaching and teaching against each other. Catholics and Protestants alike feared people of other faiths, whom they often saw as agents of Satan. Even more, they feared those who were explicitly identified with Satan: witches living in their midst. This era was the time of the most virulent witch persecutions in European history because both Protestants and Catholics tried to make their cities and states more godly.

CHAPTER LOCATOR | What were the central ideas of the reformers?

French Religious Wars

The costs of the Habsburg-Valois wars forced the French to increase taxes and borrow heavily. King Francis I (r. 1515–1547) also tried two new devices to raise revenue: the sale of public offices and a treaty with the papacy. The former proved to be only a temporary source of money: once a man bought an office, he and his heirs were exempt from taxation. But the latter, known as the Concordat of Bologna (see Chapter 12, page 368), gave the French crown the right to appoint all French bishops and abbots, ensuring a rich supplement of money and offices. Because French rulers possessed control over appointments and had a vested financial interest in Catholicism, they had no need to revolt against Rome.

Significant numbers of those ruled, however, were attracted to the Reformed religion of Calvinism. Initially, most French Calvinists, called **Huguenots**, lived in major cities, such as Paris, Lyon, and Rouen. By the time King Henry II (r. 1547–1559) died in 1559, perhaps one-tenth of the population had become Calvinist.

The feebleness of the French monarchy was the seed from which the weeds of civil violence sprang. The three weak sons of Henry II who occupied the throne could not provide the necessary leadership, and they were often dominated by their mother, Catherine de' Medici. The French nobility took advantage of this monarchical weakness. Just as German princes in the Holy Roman Empire had adopted Lutheranism as a way to oppose Emperor Charles V, so French nobles frequently adopted Protestantism as a religious cloak for their independence. Armed clashes between Catholic royalist lords and Calvinist antimonarchical lords occurred in many parts of France.

Calvinist teachings called the power of sacred images into question, and mobs in many cities took down and smashed statues, stained-glass windows, and paintings, viewing this as a way to purify the church. Though it was often inspired by fiery Protestant sermons, this iconoclasm, or destruction of religious images, is an example of ordinary men and women carrying out the Reformation themselves. Catholic mobs responded by defending images, and crowds on both sides killed their opponents, often in gruesome ways.

A savage Catholic attack on Calvinists in Paris on Saint Bartholomew's Day, August 24, 1572, followed the usual pattern. The occasion was the marriage cere-mony of the king's sister Margaret of Valois to the Protestant Henry of Navarre, which was intended to help reconcile Catholics and Huguenots. Instead, Hugue-not wedding guests in Paris were massacred, and other Protestants were slaugh-tered by mobs. Religious violence spread to the provinces, where thousands were killed. This Saint Bartholomew's Day massacre led to a civil war that dragged on for fifteen years.

What ultimately saved France was a small group of moderates of both faiths, called **politiques**, who believed that only the restoration of strong monarchy could reverse the trend toward collapse. The politiques also favored accepting the Huguenots as an officially recognized and organized group. The death of Catherine de' Medici, followed by the assassination of King Henry III, paved the way for the accession of Henry of Navarre, a politique who became Henry IV (r. 1589 1610).

Henry's willingness to sacrifice religious principles to political necessity saved France. He converted to Catholicism but also issued the **Edict of Nantes** in 1598, which granted liberty of conscience and liberty of public worship to

Huguenots
▶ French Calvinists.

politiques
▶ Catholic and Protestant moderates who held that only a strong monarchy could save France from total collapse.

Edict of Nantes
▶ A document issued by Henry IV of France in 1598, granting liberty of conscience and of public worship to Calvinists, which helped restore peace in France.

How did the political situation in Germany shape the course of the Reformation? | How did Protestant ideas and institutions spread beyond German-speaking lands? | What reforms did the Catholic Church make? | **What were the causes and consequences of religious violence?** | ✔ LearningCurve Check what you know.

403

Huguenots in 150 fortified towns. The reign of Henry IV and the Edict of Nantes prepared the way for French absolutism in the seventeenth century by helping restore internal peace in France.

The Netherlands Under Charles V

In the Netherlands, what began as a movement for the reformation of the church developed into a struggle for Dutch independence. Emperor Charles V had inherited the seventeen provinces that compose present-day Belgium and the Netherlands (see page 389). In the Low Countries, as elsewhere, corruption in the Roman Church and the critical spirit of the Renaissance provoked pressure for reform, and Lutheran ideas took root. Charles V had grown up in the Netherlands, however, and he was able to limit the impact of these ideas. But Charles V abdicated in 1556 and transferred power over the Netherlands to his son Philip II, who had grown up in Spain. Protestant ideas spread.

The Netherlands, 1609

- ☐ United Provinces
- ☐ Spanish Netherlands
- — Treaty line, 1609

By the 1560s, Protestants in the Netherlands were primarily Calvinists. Calvinism's intellectual seriousness, moral gravity, and emphasis on any form of labor well done appealed to urban merchants, financiers, and artisans. Whereas Lutherans taught respect for the powers that be, Calvinism tended to encourage opposition to political authorities who were judged to be ungodly. When Spanish authorities attempted to suppress Calvinist worship and raised taxes in the 1560s, rioting ensued. Calvinists sacked thirty Catholic churches in Antwerp, destroying the religious images in them in a wave of iconoclasm. From Antwerp the destruction spread. Philip II sent twenty thousand Spanish troops under the duke of Alva to pacify the Low Countries. Alva interpreted *"pacification"* to mean ruthless extermination of religious and political dissidents. To Calvinists, all this was a clear indication that Spanish rule was ungodly and should be overthrown.

Between 1568 and 1578, civil war raged in the Netherlands between Catholics and Protestants and between the seventeen provinces and Spain. Eventually the ten southern provinces, the Spanish Netherlands (the future Belgium), came under the control of the Spanish Habsburg forces. The seven northern provinces, led by Holland, formed the **Union of Utrecht** and in 1581 declared their independence from Spain. Philip did not accept this declaration, and war continued until 1609, when Spain agreed to a truce that recognized the independence of the United Provinces.

Union of Utrecht

▶ The alliance of seven northern provinces (led by Holland) that declared its independence from Spain and formed the United Provinces of the Netherlands.

The Great European Witch-Hunt

The relationship between the Reformation and the upsurge in trials for witchcraft that occurred at roughly the same time is complex. Increasing persecution for witchcraft actually began before the Reformation in the 1480s, but it became

CHAPTER LOCATOR | What were the central ideas of the reformers?

CHAPTER 13
404 REFORMATIONS AND RELIGIOUS WARS

especially common about 1560, and the mania continued until roughly 1660. Both Protestants and Catholics tried and executed witches, with church officials and secular authorities acting together.

The heightened sense of God's power and divine wrath in the Reformation era was an important factor in the witch-hunts, but so was a change in the idea of what a witch was. In the later Middle Ages, many educated Christian theologians, canon lawyers, and officials added a demonological component to this notion of what a witch was. For them, the essence of witchcraft was making a pact with the Devil. Witches were no longer simply people who used magical power to get what they wanted, but rather people used by the Devil to do what he wanted. Witchcraft was thus spiritualized, and witches became the ultimate heretics, enemies of God.

Scholars estimate that during the sixteenth and seventeenth centuries, between 100,000 and 200,000 people were officially tried for witchcraft and between 40,000 and 60,000 were executed. Though the gender balance varied widely in different parts of Europe, between 75 and 85 percent of those tried and executed were women. Ideas about women and the roles women actually played in society were thus important factors shaping the witch-hunts. Some demonologists expressed virulent misogyny, or hatred of women. Most people viewed women as weaker and so more likely to give in to an offer by the Devil. In both classical and Christian traditions, women were associated with nature, disorder, and the body, all of which were linked with the demonic. Women's actual lack of power in society and gender norms about the use of violence meant that they were more likely to use scolding and cursing to get what they wanted instead of taking people to court or beating them up. Curses were generally expressed (as they often are today) in religious terms; "go to Hell" was calling on the powers of Satan.

Legal changes also played a role in causing, or at least allowing for, massive witch trials. One of these was a change from an accusatorial legal procedure to an inquisitorial procedure. In the former, a suspect knew the accusers and the charges they had brought, and an accuser could in turn be liable for trial if the charges were not proven. In the latter, legal authorities themselves brought the case. This change made people much more willing to accuse others because they never had to take personal responsibility for the accusation or face the accused person's relatives. Inquisitorial procedure involved intense questioning of the suspect, often with torture.

Most witch trials began with a single accusation in a village or town. Individuals accused someone they knew of using magic to spoil food, make children ill, kill animals, raise a hailstorm, or do other types of harm. Tensions within families, households, and neighborhoods often played a role in these accusations. Women number very prominently among accusers and witnesses as well as among those accused of witchcraft because the actions witches were initially charged with, such as harming children or curdling milk, were generally part of women's sphere. A woman also gained economic and social security by conforming to the standard of the good wife and mother and by confronting women who deviated from it.

Once a charge was made, the suspect was brought in for questioning. After the initial suspect had been questioned, and particularly if he or she had been tortured, the people who had been implicated were brought in for questioning. This

How did the political situation in Germany shape the course of the Reformation?

How did Protestant ideas and institutions spread beyond German-speaking lands?

What reforms did the Catholic Church make?

What were the causes and consequences of religious violence?

☑ LearningCurve
Check what you know.

405

might lead to a small hunt, involving from five to ten suspects, and it sometimes grew into a much larger hunt, which historians have called a "witch panic." Panics were most common in the part of Europe that saw the most witch accusations in general: the Holy Roman Empire, Switzerland, and parts of France. Most of this area consisted of very small governmental units that were jealous of each other and, after the Reformation, were divided by religion. The rulers of these small territories often felt more threatened than did the monarchs of western Europe, and they saw persecuting witches as a way to demonstrate their piety and concern for order. Moreover, witch panics often occurred after some type of climatic disaster, such as an unusually cold and wet summer, and they came in waves.

In large-scale panics, a wider variety of suspects were taken in—wealthier people, children, a greater proportion of men. Mass panics tended to end when it became clear to legal authorities, or to the community itself, that the people being questioned or executed were not what they understood witches to be, or that the scope of the accusations was beyond belief.

As the seventeenth century ushered in new ideas about science and reason, many began to question whether witches could make pacts with the Devil or engage in the wild activities attributed to them. Doubts about whether secret denunciations were valid or whether torture would ever yield truthful confessions gradually spread among the same type of religious and legal authorities who had so vigorously persecuted witches. Prosecutions for witchcraft became less common and were gradually outlawed.

> **QUICK REVIEW**

What role did ordinary Europeans play in instigating the religious violence of the sixteenth century? What role did social and political elites play?

CHAPTER LOCATOR | What were the central ideas of the reformers?

LOOKING BACK
LOOKING AHEAD

The Renaissance and the Reformation are often seen as two of the key elements in the creation of the "modern" world. The radical changes brought by the Reformation contained many aspects of continuity, however. Sixteenth-century reformers looked back to the early Christian Church for their inspiration, and many of their reforming ideas had been advocated for centuries. Most Protestant reformers worked with political leaders to make religious changes, just as early church officials had worked with Emperor Constantine and his successors as Christianity became the official religion of the Roman Empire in the fourth century. The spread of Christianity and the spread of Protestantism were accomplished not only by preaching, persuasion, and teaching but also by force and violence. The Catholic Reformation was carried out by activist popes, a church council, and new religious orders, like earlier reforms of the church had been.

Just as they linked with earlier developments, the events of the Reformation were also closely connected with what is often seen as the third element in the modern world: European exploration and colonization. Only a week after Martin Luther stood in front of Charles V at the Diet of Worms declaring his independence in matters of religion, Ferdinand Magellan, a Portuguese sea captain with Spanish ships, was killed in a group of islands off the coast of Southeast Asia. Charles V had provided the backing for Magellan's voyage, the first to circumnavigate the globe. Magellan viewed the spread of Christianity as one of the purposes of his trip, and later in the sixteenth century, institutions created as part of the Catholic Reformation, including the Jesuit order and the Inquisition, would operate in European colonies overseas as well as in Europe itself. The islands where Magellan was killed were later named the Philippines, in honor of Charles's son Philip, who sent the ill-fated Spanish Armada against England. Philip's opponent Queen Elizabeth was similarly honored when English explorers named a huge chunk of territory in North America "Virginia" as a tribute to their "Virgin Queen." The desire for wealth and power was an important motivation in the European voyages and colonial ventures, but so was religious zeal.

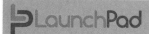 LaunchPad

ONLINE DOCUMENT PROJECT

Anna Jansz of Rotterdam

What might have led Jansz and thousands like her to die for their religious convictions?

You encountered Anna Jansz's story on page 385. Keeping the question above in mind, learn more about Jansz and other Anabaptist martyrs by analyzing images and hymns. *See inside the front cover to learn more.*

How did the political situation in Germany shape the course of the Reformation?

How did Protestant ideas and institutions spread beyond German-speaking lands?

What reforms did the Catholic Church make?

What were the causes and consequences of religious violence?

✔ LearningCurve
Check what you know.

407

CHAPTER 13 STUDY GUIDE

STEP 1

GET STARTED ONLINE

LearningCurve

Now that you've read the chapter, make it stick by completing the LearningCurve activity.

STEP 2

EXPLAIN WHY IT MATTERS

Put your reading into practice. Identify each term below, and then explain why it matters in Western history.

TERM	WHO OR WHAT & WHEN	WHY IT MATTERS
anticlericalism (p. 380)		
indulgence (p. 381)		
Protestants (p. 382)		
Spanish Armada (p. 395)		
The Institutes of the Christian Religion (p. 396)		
predestination (p. 396)		
Holy Office (p. 400)		
Jesuits (p. 400)		
Huguenots (p. 403)		
politiques (p. 403)		
Edict of Nantes (p. 403)		
Union of Utrecht (p. 404)		

STEP 3

MOVE BEYOND THE BASICS

To demonstrate a more advanced understanding, complete the chart below with descriptions of each of the Protestant core beliefs, how each differed from Catholic teachings, and its larger implications for early modern life.

Description of belief	Contrast with Catholicism	Political, social, and cultural implications
Salvation by faith alone		
Sole and absolute authority of the Bible		
Church as a spiritual priesthood of all believers		

PUT IT ALL TOGETHER

Now, take a step back and try to explain the big picture. Remember to use specific examples from the chapter in your answers.

THE REFORMATION

► Why were political elites so important to the spread and entrenchment of Protestant ideas?

► What role did technology play in the spread of Protestant ideas?

THE CATHOLIC REFORMATION AND COUNTER-REFORMATION

► What were the most important outcomes of the Council of Trent?

► How did the Catholic Church actively combat Protestantism and how successful was it?

MAKE CONNECTIONS

► Why and how did Martin Luther's efforts for religious reform produce more dramatic results than those of his predecessors?

   ► Defend or refute the following statement. "More than any other single development, the Reformation marks the end of the Middle Ages and the beginning of a new historical era."

RELIGIOUS VIOLENCE

► Was religion really at the heart of the French religious wars? If not, what was?

► Given the prevalence of belief in witchcraft throughout European history, how would you explain the witchcraft scares of the sixteenth and seventeenth centuries?

> IN YOUR OWN WORDS

Imagine that you must give an oral report to the class answering the following question **What were the causes and consequences of religious division in sixteenth-century Europe?** What would be the most important points and why?

14

EUROPEAN EXPLORATION AND CONQUEST

1450–1650

> **What were the motives behind European overseas expansion, and what were the consequences for Europe, the Americas, and Africa?** Chapter 14 examines European overseas expansion in the early modern era. Before 1450, Europeans were relatively marginal players in a centuries-old trading system that linked Africa, Asia, and Europe. Europeans' search for better access to Asian trade led to a new empire in the Indian Ocean and the accidental discovery of the Western Hemisphere. Within a few decades, European colonies in South and North America would join this worldwide web of commerce. Capitalizing on the goods and riches they found in the Americas, Europeans came to dominate trading networks and built political empires of truly global proportions. The era of globalization had begun, bringing with it new forms of cultural exchange, assimilation, conversion, and resistance.

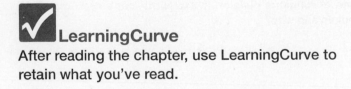

LearningCurve
After reading the chapter, use LearningCurve to retain what you've read.

> What was the Afroeurasian trading world before Columbus?

> How and why did Europeans undertake ambitious voyages of expansion?

> What was the impact of European conquest on the New World?

> How did Europe and the world change after Columbus?

> How did expansion change European attitudes and beliefs?

Life in the Age of Discovery. The arrival of the Portuguese in Japan in 1453 inspired a series of artworks depicting the *namban-jin* or southern barbarians, as they were known. (akg-images/De Agostini Picture Library)

> What was the Afroeurasian trading world before Columbus?

COLUMBUS DID NOT SAIL WEST ON A WHIM. To understand his and other Europeans' explorations, we must first understand late medieval trade networks. Historians now recognize that a type of world economy, known as the Afroeurasian trade world, linked the products and people of Asia, Africa, and Europe in the fifteenth century. The West was not the dominant player before Columbus, and the European voyages derived from a desire to share in and control the wealth coming from the Indian Ocean.

The Trade World of the Indian Ocean

The Indian Ocean was the center of the Afroeurasian trade world. Its location made it a crossroads for exchange among China, India, the Middle East, Africa, and Europe (**Map 14.1**). From the seventh through the fourteenth centuries, the

CHAPTER LOCATOR | What was the Afroeurasian trading world before Columbus?

1271–1295
– Marco Polo travels to China

1443
– Portuguese establish first African trading post at Arguin

1492
– Columbus lands in the Americas

1511
– Portuguese capture Malacca from Muslims

1518
– Spanish king authorizes slave trade to New World colonies

1519–1522
– Magellan's expedition circumnavigates the world

1521
– Cortés conquers the Mexica Empire

1533
– Pizarro conquers the Inca Empire

1602
– Dutch East India Company established

volume of this trade steadily increased, declining only during the years of the Black Death.

Merchants congregated in a series of cosmopolitan port cities strung around the Indian Ocean. The most developed area of this commercial web was in the South China Sea. In the fifteenth century, the port of Malacca became a great commercial entrepôt (AHN-truh-poh), a trading post to which goods were shipped for storage while awaiting redistribution.

The Mongol emperors opened the doors of China to the West, encouraging Europeans, like the Venetian trader and explorer Marco Polo, to do business there. Marco Polo's tales of his travels from 1271 to 1295 and his encounter with the Great Khan fueled Western fantasies about the exotic Orient. After the Mongols fell to the Ming Dynasty in 1368, China entered a period of economic expansion, population growth, and urbanization. By the end of the dynasty in 1644, the Chinese population had tripled to between 150 million and 200 million. Historians agree that China had the most advanced economy in the world until at least the start of the eighteenth century.

China also took the lead in exploration, sending Admiral Zheng He's fleet along the trade web as far west as Egypt. From 1405 to 1433, each of his seven expeditions involved hundreds of ships and tens of thousands of men.[1] Court conflicts and the need to defend against renewed Mongol encroachment led to the abandonment of the maritime expeditions after the deaths of Zheng He and the emperor. China's turning away from external trade opened new opportunities for European states to claim a decisive role in world trade.

Another center of trade in the Indian Ocean was India. The subcontinent had ancient links with its neighbors to the northwest: trade between South Asia and Mesopotamia dates back to the origins of human civilization. Romans had acquired cotton textiles, exotic animals, and other luxury goods from India. Arab merchants who circumnavigated India on their way to trade in the South China Sea established trading posts along the southern coast of India. India was an important contributor of goods to the world trading system; much of the world's pepper was grown there, and Indian cotton textiles were highly prized.

| How and why did Europeans undertake ambitious voyages of expansion? | What was the impact of European conquest on the New World? | How did Europe and the world change after Columbus? | How did expansion change European attitudes and beliefs? | ✔️ LearningCurve Check what you know. |

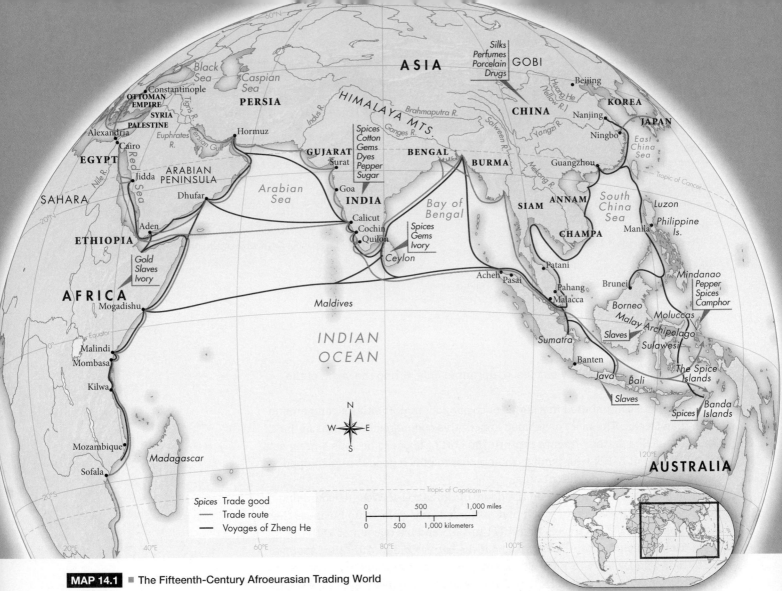

MAP 14.1 ■ The Fifteenth-Century Afroeurasian Trading World

After a period of decline following the Black Death and the Mongol invasions, trade revived in the fifteenth century. Muslim merchants dominated trade, linking ports in East Africa and the Red Sea with those in India and the Malay Archipelago. Chinese admiral Zheng He's voyages (1405–1433) followed the most important Indian Ocean trade routes in the hope of imposing Ming dominance of trade and tribute.

The Trading States of Africa

In the fifteenth century, most of the gold that reached Europe came from the western part of the Sudan region in West Africa and from the Akan (AH-kahn) peoples living near present-day Ghana. Transported across the Sahara by Arab and African traders on camels, the gold was sold in the ports of North Africa. Other trading routes led to the Egyptian cities of Alexandria and Cairo, where the Venetians held commercial privileges.

Nations inland that sat astride the north-south caravan routes grew wealthy from this trade. In the mid-thirteenth century the kingdom of Mali emerged as an important player on the overland trade route, gaining prestige from its ruler Mansa Musa's fabulous pilgrimage to Mecca from 1324–1325. In later centuries,

CHAPTER LOCATOR | What was the Afroeurasian trading world before Columbus?

CHAPTER 14
414 EUROPEAN EXPLORATION AND CONQUEST

the diversion of gold away from the trans-Sahara routes would weaken the inland states of Africa politically and economically.

Gold was one important object of trade; slaves were another. Slavery was practiced in Africa, as it was virtually everywhere else in the world, before the arrival of Europeans. Arabic and African merchants took West African slaves to the Mediterranean to be sold in European, Egyptian, and Middle Eastern markets and also brought eastern Europeans—a major element of European slavery—to West Africa as slaves. In addition, Indian and Arabic merchants traded slaves in the coastal regions of East Africa.

Legends about Africa played an important role in Europeans' imagination of the outside world. They long cherished the belief in a Christian nation in Africa ruled by a mythical king, Prester John, who was believed to be a descendant of one of the three kings who visited Jesus after his birth.

> ## Africa and the Afroeurasian Trading World, ca. 1450

- **North Africa:** Cairo, the capital of the Mamluk Egyptian empire, was a center of Islamic learning and religious authority as well as a hub for Indian Ocean trade goods

- **West Africa:** Connected to Islamic trading networks, West Africa was an important source of slaves, salt, and gold

- **East Africa:** Swahili-speaking city-states engaged in the Indian Ocean trade, exchanging ivory, rhinoceros horn, tortoise shells, and slaves for textiles, spices, cowrie shells, porcelain, and other goods

The Ottoman and Persian Empires

The Middle East served as an intermediary for trade among Asia, Africa, and Europe and was also an important supplier of goods, especially silk and cotton, for foreign exchange. Two great rival empires, the Persian Safavids (sah-FAH-vidz) and the Turkish Ottomans, dominated the region. Persian merchants could be found in trading communities as far away as the Indian Ocean. Persia was also a major producer and exporter of silk.

Under Sultan Mohammed II (r. 1451–1481), the Ottomans captured Europe's largest city, Constantinople, in May 1453. Renamed Istanbul, the city became the capital of the Ottoman Empire. By the mid-sixteenth century, the Ottomans controlled the sea trade in the eastern Mediterranean, Syria, Palestine, Egypt, and the rest of North Africa, and their power extended into Europe as far west as Vienna.

Ottoman expansion frightened Europeans. The Ottoman armies seemed invincible and the empire's desire for expansion limitless. The strength of the Ottomans helps explain some of the missionary fervor Christians brought to new territories. It also raised economic concerns. With trade routes to the East dominated by the Ottomans, Europeans wished to find new trade routes free of Ottoman control.

Genoese and Venetian Middlemen

In the late Middle Ages, the Italian city-states of Venice and Genoa controlled the European luxury trade with the East. In 1304, Venice established formal relations with the sultan of Mamluk Egypt, opening operations in Cairo, the gateway to

| How and why did Europeans undertake ambitious voyages of expansion? | What was the impact of European conquest on the New World? | How did Europe and the world change after Columbus? | How did expansion change European attitudes and beliefs? | ✓ LearningCurve Check what you know. |

415

Asian trade. Venetian merchants specialized in luxury goods which they obtained from middlemen in the eastern Mediterranean and Asia Minor.[2]

Venice's ancient rival was Genoa. In the wake of the Crusades, Genoa dominated the northern route to Asia through the Black Sea. Expansion in the thirteenth and fourteenth centuries took the Genoese as far as Persia and the Far East. In 1291, they sponsored an expedition into the Atlantic in search of India. The ships were lost, and their exact destination and motivations remain unknown. This voyage reveals the long roots of Genoese interest in Atlantic exploration.

In the fifteenth century, with Venice claiming victory in the spice trade, the Genoese shifted focus from trade to finance and from the Black Sea to the western Mediterranean. When Spanish and Portuguese voyages began to explore the western Atlantic (see pages 419–421), Genoese merchants, navigators, and financiers provided their skills to the Iberian monarchs, whose own subjects had much less commercial experience. Genoese merchants would eventually help finance Spanish colonization of the New World.

A major element of Italian trade was slavery. Merchants purchased slaves, many of whom were fellow Christians, in the Balkans. The men were sold to Egypt for the sultan's army or sent to work as agricultural laborers in the Mediterranean. Young girls, who constituted the majority of the trade, were sold in western Mediterranean ports as servants or concubines. After the loss of the Black Sea—and thus the source of slaves—to the Ottomans, the Genoese sought new supplies of slaves in the West, taking the Guanches (indigenous peoples from the Canary Islands), Muslim prisoners and Jewish refugees from Spain, and by the early 1500s both black and Berber Africans. With the growth of Spanish colonies in the New World, Genoese and Venetian merchants would become important players in the Atlantic slave trade.

Italian experience in colonial administration, slaving, and international trade served as a model for the Iberian states as they pushed European expansion to new heights. Mariners, merchants, and financiers from Venice and Genoa—most notably Christopher Columbus—played a crucial role in bringing the fruits of this experience to the Iberian Peninsula and to the New World.

> **QUICK REVIEW**

What role did Europe play in the Afroeurasian trading world prior to 1492?

CHAPTER LOCATOR | What was the
Afroeurasian trading
world before Columbus?

How and why did Europeans undertake ambitious voyages of expansion?

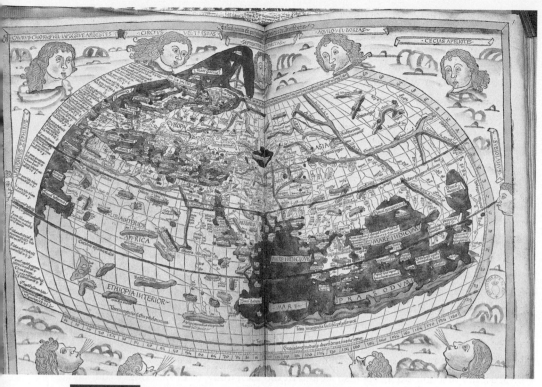

Ptolemy's Geography The recovery of Ptolemy's *Geography* in the early fifteenth century gave Europeans new access to ancient geographical knowledge. This 1486 world map, based on Ptolemy, is a great advance over medieval maps but contains errors with significant consequences for future exploration. It shows a single continent watered by a single ocean, with land covering three-quarters of the world's surface. Africa and Asia are joined with Europe, making the Indian Ocean a landlocked sea and rendering the circumnavigation of Africa impossible. Australia and the Americas are nonexistent, and the continent of Asia is stretched far to the east, greatly shortening the distance from Europe to Asia via the Atlantic. (Bibliothèque nationale de France/Giraudon/The Bridgeman Art Library)

AS WE HAVE SEEN, Europe was by no means isolated before the voyages of exploration and its "discovery" of the New World. But because they did not produce many products desired by Eastern elites, Europeans played only a small role in the Indian Ocean trading world. As Europe recovered after the Black Death, new European players entered the scene with novel technology, eager to spread Christianity and to undo Italian and Ottoman domination of trade with the East. A century after the plague, Iberian explorers began the overseas voyages that helped create the modern world.

Causes of European Expansion

European expansion had multiple causes. By the middle of the fifteenth century, Europe was experiencing a revival of population and economic activity after the lows of the Black Death. This revival created demand for luxuries, especially

How and why did Europeans undertake ambitious voyages of expansion?	What was the impact of European conquest on the New World?	How did Europe and the world change after Columbus?	How did expansion change European attitudes and beliefs?	✓ LearningCurve Check what you know.

417

spices, from the East. The fall of Constantinople and subsequent Ottoman control of trade routes created obstacles to fulfilling these demands. Europeans needed to find new sources of precious metal to trade with the Ottomans or find trade routes that bypassed the Ottomans.

Religious fervor was another important catalyst for expansion. The passion and energy ignited by the Christian reconquista (reconquest) of the Iberian Peninsula encouraged the Portuguese and Spanish to continue the Christian crusade. Overseas exploration was in some ways a transfer of the crusading spirit to new non-Christian territories. Because the remaining Muslim states, such as the mighty Ottoman Empire, were too strong to defeat, Iberians turned their attention elsewhere.

Combined with eagerness to earn profits and to spread Christianity was the desire for glory and the urge to chart new waters. Scholars have frequently described the European discoveries as a manifestation of Renaissance curiosity about the physical universe. The detailed journals many voyagers kept attest to their wonder and fascination with the new peoples and places they visited. Eagerness for exploration was heightened by a lack of opportunity at home. After the reconquista, young men of the Spanish upper classes found their economic and political opportunities greatly limited. The ambitious turned to the sea to seek their fortunes.

Their voyages were made possible by the growth of government power. The Spanish monarchy was stronger than before and in a position to support foreign ventures. In Portugal, explorers also looked to the monarchy, to Prince Henry the Navigator in particular (page 419), for financial support and encouragement. Like voyagers, monarchs shared a mix of motivations, from the desire to please God to the desire to win glory and profit from trade. Competition among European monarchs and between Protestant and Catholic states was an important factor in encouraging the steady stream of expeditions that began in the late fifteenth century.

The people who stayed at home had a powerful impact on the process. Royal ministers and factions at court influenced monarchs to provide or deny support for exploration. The small number of people who could read served as a rapt audience for tales of fantastic places and unknown peoples. Cosmography, natural history, and geography aroused enormous interest among educated people in the fifteenth and sixteenth centuries. One of the most popular books of the time was the fourteenth-century text *The Travels of Sir John Mandeville*, which purported to be a firsthand account of the author's travels in the Holy Land, Egypt, Ethiopia, the Middle East, and India and his service to the Mamluk sultan of Egypt and the Mongol Great Khan of China. Although we now know the stories were fictional, these fantastic tales of cannibals, one-eyed giants, men with the heads of dogs, and other marvels convinced audiences through their vividly and persuasively described details. Christopher Columbus took a copy of Mandeville and the equally popular and more reliable *The Travels of Marco Polo* on his voyage in 1492.

Technology and the Rise of Exploration

Technological developments in shipbuilding, weaponry, and navigation also paved the way for European expansion. Since ancient times, most seagoing vessels had been narrow, open boats called galleys, propelled largely by slaves or convicts manning the oars. Though well suited to the placid waters of the Mediterranean, galleys could not withstand the rough winds and uncharted shoals of

CHAPTER LOCATOR | What was the Afroeurasian trading world before Columbus?

the Atlantic. The need for sturdier craft, as well as population losses caused by the Black Death, forced the development of a new style of ship that would not require much labor to sail. In the course of the fifteenth century, the Portuguese developed the **caravel**, a small, light, three-mast sailing ship. Though somewhat slower than the galley, the caravel held more cargo. Its triangular lateen sails and sternpost rudder also made the caravel a much more maneuverable vessel. When fitted with cannon, it could dominate larger vessels.

Great strides in cartography and navigational aids were also made during this period. Around 1410, Arab scholars reintroduced Europeans to **Ptolemy's *Geography***. Written in the second century C.E., the work synthesized the geographical knowledge of the classical world. Ptolemy's work provided significant improvements over medieval cartography, but it also contained crucial errors. Unaware of the Americas, Ptolemy showed the world as much smaller than it is, so that Asia appeared not very distant from Europe to the west. Based on this work, cartographers fashioned new maps that combined classical knowledge with the latest information from mariners. First the Genoese and Venetians, and then the Portuguese and Spanish, took the lead in these advances.

The magnetic compass enabled sailors to determine their direction and position at sea. The astrolabe, an instrument invented by the ancient Greeks and perfected by Muslim navigators, was used to determine the altitude of the sun and other celestial bodies. It permitted mariners to plot their latitude, that is, their precise position north or south of the equator.

Like the astrolabe, much of the new technology that Europeans used on their voyages was borrowed from the East. Gunpowder, the compass, and the sternpost rudder were Chinese inventions. The lateen sail, which allowed European ships to tack against the wind, was a product of the Indian Ocean trade world. Advances in cartography drew on the rich tradition of Judeo-Arabic mathematical and astronomical learning in Iberia. In exploring new territories, European sailors thus called on techniques and knowledge developed over centuries in China, the Muslim world, and during travels on the Indian Ocean.

The Portuguese Overseas Empire

For centuries, Portugal was a small, poor nation on the margins of European life. The principal activities of its inhabitants were fishing and subsistence farming. Yet Portugal had a long history of seafaring and navigation. Blocked from access to western Europe by Spain, the Portuguese turned to the Atlantic and North Africa, whose waters they knew better than other Europeans. Nature favored the Portuguese: winds blowing along their coast offered passage to Africa, its Atlantic islands, and ultimately Brazil.

In the early phases of Portuguese exploration, Prince Henry (1394–1460), a younger son of the king, played a leading role. A nineteenth-century scholar dubbed Henry "the Navigator" because of his support for the study of geography and navigation and for the annual expeditions he sponsored down the western coast of Africa.

The objectives of Portuguese exploration policy included military glory; the conversion of Muslims; and a quest to find gold, slaves, and an overseas route to the spice markets of India. Portugal's conquest of Ceuta, an Arab city in northern Morocco, in 1415 marked the beginning of European overseas expansion. In the

caravel
▶ A small, maneuverable, three-mast sailing ship developed by the Portuguese in the fifteenth century that gave the Portuguese a distinct advantage in exploration and trade.

Ptolemy's *Geography*
▶ A second-century-C.E. work that synthesized the classical knowledge of geography and introduced the concepts of longitude and latitude. Reintroduced to Europeans about 1410 by Arab scholars, its ideas allowed cartographers to create more accurate maps.

| How and why did Europeans undertake ambitious voyages of expansion? | What was the impact of European conquest on the New World? | How did Europe and the world change after Columbus? | How did expansion change European attitudes and beliefs? | ✓ LearningCurve Check what you know. |

419

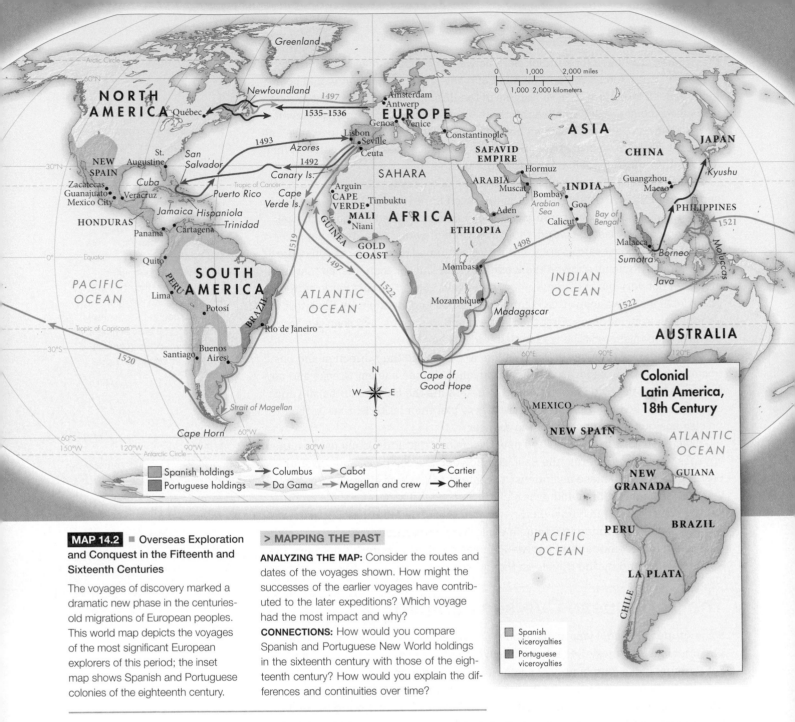

MAP 14.2 ■ Overseas Exploration and Conquest in the Fifteenth and Sixteenth Centuries

The voyages of discovery marked a dramatic new phase in the centuries-old migrations of European peoples. This world map depicts the voyages of the most significant European explorers of this period; the inset map shows Spanish and Portuguese colonies of the eighteenth century.

> MAPPING THE PAST

ANALYZING THE MAP: Consider the routes and dates of the voyages shown. How might the successes of the earlier voyages have contributed to the later expeditions? Which voyage had the most impact and why?

CONNECTIONS: How would you compare Spanish and Portuguese New World holdings in the sixteenth century with those of the eighteenth century? How would you explain the differences and continuities over time?

1420s, under Henry's direction, the Portuguese began to settle the Atlantic islands of Madeira (ca. 1420) and the Azores (1427). In 1443, they founded their first African commercial settlement at Arguin in North Africa. By the time of Henry's death in 1460, his support for exploration was vindicated by thriving sugar plantations on the Atlantic islands, the first arrival of enslaved Africans in Portugal (see page 431), and new access to African gold.

The Portuguese next established trading posts and forts on the gold-rich Guinea coast and penetrated into the African continent all the way to Timbuktu (**Map 14.2**). By 1500, Portugal controlled the flow of African gold to Europe. The golden century of Portuguese prosperity had begun.

CHAPTER LOCATOR | What was the Afroeurasian trading world before Columbus?

CHAPTER 14
420 EUROPEAN EXPLORATION AND CONQUEST

The Portuguese then pushed farther south down the west coast of Africa. In 1487, Bartholomew Diaz rounded the Cape of Good Hope at the southern tip, but storms and a threatened mutiny forced him to turn back. A decade later, Vasco da Gama succeeded in rounding the Cape, and, with the help of an Indian guide, he reached the port of Calicut in India. Overcoming local hostility, he returned to Lisbon loaded with spices and samples of Indian cloth. Thereafter, a Portuguese convoy set out for passage around the Cape every March.

Lisbon became the entrance port for Asian goods into Europe, but this was not accomplished without a fight. Muslim-controlled port city-states had long controlled the rich spice trade of the Indian Ocean, and they did not surrender their dominance willingly. From 1500 to 1511, the Portuguese used a combination of bombardment and diplomatic treaties to establish trading forts at Calicut, Malacca, Hormus, and Goa, thereby laying the foundation for Portuguese imperialism in the sixteenth and seventeenth centuries.

In March 1493, between the voyages of Diaz and da Gama, Spanish ships under a Genoese mariner named Christopher Columbus (1451–1506), in the service of the Spanish crown, entered Lisbon harbor. Spain had also begun the quest for an empire.

The Problem of Christopher Columbus

Christopher Columbus is a controversial figure in history—glorified by some as a courageous explorer, vilified by others as a cruel exploiter of Native Americans. Rather than judging Columbus by debates and standards of our time, it is more important to understand him in the context of his own time. First, what kind of man was Columbus, and what forces or influences shaped him? Second, in sailing westward from Europe, what were his goals? Third, did he achieve his goals, and what did he make of his discoveries?

In his dream of a westward passage to the Indies, Columbus embodied a long-standing Genoese ambition to circumvent Venetian domination of eastward trade, which was now being claimed by the Portuguese. Columbus was very knowledgeable about the sea. He had worked as a mapmaker, and he was familiar with fifteenth-century Portuguese navigational developments and the use of the compass as a nautical instrument. Columbus was also a deeply religious man. Like the Spanish rulers and most Europeans of his age, Columbus understood Christianity as a missionary religion that should be carried to all places of the earth. He viewed himself as a divine agent, fated to spread Christianity beyond Europe.

What was the object of this first voyage? Columbus gave the answer in the very title of the expedition, "The Enterprise of the Indies." He wanted to find a direct ocean trading route to Asia. Rejected for funding by the Portuguese in 1483 and by Ferdinand and Isabella in 1486, the project finally won the backing of the Spanish monarchy in 1492. Inspired by the stories of Mandeville and Marco Polo, Columbus dreamed of reaching the court of the Mongol emperor, the Great Khan (not realizing that the Ming Dynasty had overthrown the Mongols in 1368). Based on Ptolemy's *Geography* and other texts, he expected to pass the islands of Japan and then land on the east coast of China.

How did Columbus interpret what he had found, and in his mind did he achieve what he had set out to do? Columbus's small fleet left Spain on August 3,

How and why did Europeans undertake ambitious voyages of expansion?

What was the impact of European conquest on the New World?

How did Europe and the world change after Columbus?

How did expansion change European attitudes and beliefs?

✓ LearningCurve
Check what you know.

421

1492. He landed in the Bahamas, which he christened San Salvador, on October 12, 1492. Columbus believed he had found some small islands off the east coast of Japan. On encountering natives of the islands, he gave them some beads and "many other trifles of small value," pronouncing them delighted with these gifts and eager to trade. Believing he was in the Indies, he called them "Indians," a name later applied to all inhabitants of the Americas.

Scholars have identified the inhabitants of the islands as the Taino people, speakers of the Arawak language, who inhabited Hispaniola (modern-day Haiti and Dominican Republic) and other islands in the Caribbean. Columbus received reassuring reports from Taino villagers of the presence of gold and of a great king in the vicinity. From San Salvador, Columbus sailed southwest, believing that this course would take him to Japan or the coast of China. He landed instead on Cuba on October 28. Deciding that he must be on the mainland near the coastal city of Quinsay (now Hangzhou), he sent a small embassy inland with letters from Ferdinand and Isabella and instructions to locate the grand city.

The landing party found only small villages. Confronted with this disappointment, Columbus apparently gave up on his aim to meet the Great Khan. Instead, he focused on trying to find gold or other valuables among the peoples he had discovered. The sight of Taino people wearing gold ornaments on Hispaniola seemed to prove that gold was available in the region. In January, confident that its source would soon be found, he headed back to Spain to report on his discovery. News of his voyage spread rapidly across Europe.[3]

Over the next decades, the Spanish would follow a policy of conquest and colonization in the New World rather than one of exchange with equals. On his second voyage, Columbus forcibly subjugated the island of Hispaniola and enslaved its indigenous peoples. On this and subsequent voyages, Columbus brought with him settlers for the new Spanish territories, along with agricultural seed and livestock. Columbus himself, however, had limited skills in governing. Revolt soon broke out against him and his brother on Hispaniola. A royal expedition sent to investigate returned the brothers to Spain in chains. Columbus was cleared of wrongdoing, but the territories remained under royal control.

Columbus was very much a man of his times. To the end of his life in 1506, he believed that he had found small islands off the coast of Asia. He could not know that the scale of his discoveries would revolutionize world power, raising issues of trade, settlement, government bureaucracy, and the rights of native and African peoples.

Columbus's First Voyage to the New World, 1492–1493

Later Explorers

The Florentine navigator Amerigo Vespucci (veh-SPOO-chee) (1454–1512) realized what Columbus had not. Writing about his discoveries on the coast of modern-day Venezuela, Vespucci stated: "Those new regions which we found and explored with the fleet . . . we may rightly call a New World." In recognition of Amerigo's bold claim, the continent was named for him.

To settle competing claims to the Atlantic discoveries, Spain and Portugal turned to Pope Alexander VI. The resulting **Treaty of Tordesillas** (tor-duh-SEE-yuhs) in 1494 gave Spain everything to the west of an imaginary line drawn down the Atlantic and Portugal everything to the east. This arbitrary division worked in

Treaty of Tordesillas

▶ The 1494 agreement giving Spain everything to the west of an imaginary line drawn down the Atlantic and giving Portugal everything to the east.

CHAPTER LOCATOR | What was the Afroeurasian trading world before Columbus?

CHAPTER 14
422 EUROPEAN EXPLORATION AND CONQUEST

Portugal's favor when in 1500 an expedition led by Pedro Alvares Cabral, en route to India, landed on the coast of Brazil, which Cabral claimed as Portuguese territory.

The search for profits determined the direction of Spanish exploration. With insignificant profits from the Caribbean compared to the enormous riches that the Portuguese were reaping in Asia, Spain renewed the search for a western passage to Asia. In 1519, with this goal in mind, Ferdinand Magellan (1480–1521) sailed southwest across the Atlantic to Brazil, and after a long search along the coast, he located the treacherous straits that now bear his name, passing through them into the Pacific (see Map 14.2, page 420). From there, his fleet sailed north up the west coast of South America and then headed west into the immense expanse of the Pacific toward the Malay Archipelago.

Terrible storms, disease, starvation, and violence devastated the expedition. Magellan had set out with a fleet of five ships and around 270 men. Sailors on two of the ships attempted mutiny on the South American coast; one ship was lost, and another ship deserted and returned to Spain before even traversing the straits. The trip across the Pacific took ninety-eight days, and the men survived on rats and sawdust. Magellan himself died in a skirmish in the islands known today as the Philippines. Only one ship, with eighteen men aboard, returned to Spain from the east by way of the Indian Ocean, the Cape of Good Hope, and the Atlantic in 1522. The voyage—the first to circumnavigate the globe—had taken close to three years.

This voyage revolutionized Europeans' understanding of the world by demonstrating the vastness of the Pacific. The earth was clearly much larger than Columbus had believed. Although the voyage made a small profit in spices, it also demonstrated that the westward passage to the Indies was too long and dangerous for commercial purposes. Spain soon abandoned the attempt to oust Portugal from the Eastern spice trade and concentrated on exploiting her New World territories.

Spain's European rivals also set sail across the Atlantic during the early days of exploration in search of a northwest passage to the Indies. In 1497, John Cabot, a Genoese merchant living in London, undertook a voyage to Brazil but discovered Newfoundland instead. The next year he returned and reconnoitered the New England coast. These forays proved futile. Between 1576 and 1578, Martin Frobisher made three voyages in and around the Canadian bay that now bears his name. Frobisher brought a quantity of ore back to England with him, but it proved to be worthless.

Early French exploration of the Atlantic was equally frustrating. Between 1534 and 1541, Frenchman Jacques Cartier made several voyages and explored the St. Lawrence region of Canada, searching for a passage to the wealth of Asia. When this hope proved vain, the French turned to a new source of profit within Canada itself: trade in beavers and other furs. As had the Portuguese in Asia, French traders bartered with local peoples, who maintained control over their trade goods. French fishermen also competed with Spanish and English ships for the teeming schools of cod they found in the Atlantic waters around Newfoundland.

Spanish Conquest in the New World

In 1519, the year Magellan departed on his worldwide expedition, the Spanish sent an exploratory expedition from their post in Cuba to the mainland under the command of the **conquistador** (kahn-KEES-tuh-dor) Hernando Cortés (1485–1547).

conquistador

▶ Spanish for "conqueror"; Spanish soldier-explorers, such as Hernando Cortés and Francisco Pizarro, who sought to conquer the New World for the Spanish crown.

| How and why did Europeans undertake ambitious voyages of expansion? | What was the impact of European conquest on the New World? | How did Europe and the world change after Columbus? | How did expansion change European attitudes and beliefs? | ☑ LearningCurve Check what you know. |

423

Mexica Empire

▶ Also known as the Aztec Empire, a large and complex Native American civilization in modern Mexico and Central America that possessed advanced mathematical, astronomical, and engineering technology.

→ Cortés's original route, 1519
→ Cortés's retreat, 1520
→ Cortés's return route, 1520–1521

Invasion of Tenochtitlán, 1519–1521

Inca Empire

▶ The vast and sophisticated Peruvian empire centered at the capital city of Cuzco that was at its peak from 1438 until 1532.

Cortés was to launch the conquest of the **Mexica Empire**. Its people were later called the Aztecs, but now most scholars prefer to use the term *Mexica* to refer to them and their empire.

The Mexica Empire was ruled by Montezuma II (r. 1502–1520) from his capital at Tenochtitlán (tay-nawch-teet-LAHN), now Mexico City. Larger than any European city of the time, it was the heart of a sophisticated civilization with advanced mathematics, astronomy, and engineering; a complex social system; and oral poetry and historical traditions.

Cortés landed on the coast of the Gulf of Mexico on April 21, 1519. The Spanish camp was soon visited by delegations of unarmed Mexica leaders bearing lavish gifts and news of their great emperor. (See "Picturing the Past: Doña Marina Translating for Hernando Cortés During His Meeting with Montezuma," page 425.) Impressed with the wealth of the local people, Cortés soon began to exploit internal dissension within the empire to his own advantage.

Cortés quickly forged an alliance with the Tlaxcalas (Tlah-scalas) and other subject kingdoms, which chafed under Mexica rule. In October, a combined Spanish-Tlaxcalan force occupied the city of Cholula, the second largest in the empire and its religious capital, and massacred many thousands of inhabitants. Strengthened by this display of power, Cortés made alliances with other native kingdoms. In November 1519, with a few hundred Spanish men and some six thousand indigenous warriors, Cortés marched on Tenochtitlán.

Uncertain of how he should respond, Montezuma refrained from attacking the Spaniards as they advanced toward his capital and welcomed Cortés and his men into Tenochtitlán. His hesitation proved disastrous. When Cortés took Montezuma hostage and tried to rule the Mexica through the emperor's authority, Montezuma's influence over his people crumbled.

In May 1520, Spanish forces massacred Mexica warriors dancing at an indigenous festival. This act provoked an uprising within Tenochtitlán, during which Montezuma was killed. The Spaniards and their allies escaped from the city and began gathering forces against the Mexica. One year later, in May 1521, Cortés laid siege to Tenochtitlán at the head of an army of approximately 1,000 Spanish and 75,000 native warriors.[4] Spanish victory in August 1521 resulted from Spain's superior technology and the effects of the siege and smallpox. After the defeat of Tenochtitlán, Cortés and other conquistadors began the systematic conquest of Mexico.

More surprising than the defeat of the Mexica was the fall of the remote **Inca Empire**. Like the Mexica, the Incas had created a civilization that rivaled that of the Europeans in population and complexity. To unite their vast and well-fortified empire, the Incas built an extensive network of roads, along which traveled a highly efficient postal service. The imperial government, with its capital in the city of Cuzco, taxed, fed, and protected its subjects.

At the time of the Spanish invasion, the Inca Empire had been weakened by an epidemic of disease, possibly smallpox. Even worse, the empire had been embroiled in a civil war over succession. Francisco Pizarro (ca. 1475–1541), a conquistador of modest Spanish origins, landed on the northern coast of Peru on May 13, 1532, the very day Atahualpa (ah-tuh-WAHL-puh) won control of the empire after five years of fighting. As Pizarro advanced across the steep Andes toward Cuzco, Atahualpa was proceeding to the capital for his coronation.

Like Montezuma in Mexico, Atahualpa was aware of the Spaniards' move-

Doña Marina Translating for Hernando Cortés

In April 1519, Doña Marina (or Malintzin as she is known in Nahuatl [NAH-wah-tuhl]) was among twenty women given to the Spanish as slaves. Fluent in Nahuatl and Yucatec Mayan (spoken by a Spanish priest accompanying Cortés), she acted as an interpreter and diplomatic guide for the Spanish. She had a close relationship with Cortés and bore his son, Don Martín Cortés, in 1522. This image, which shows her translating during a meeting between Cortés and Montezuma, was created by Tlaxcalan artists shortly after the conquest of Mexico and represents one indigenous perspective on the events. (The Granger Collection, New York)

> **PICTURING THE PAST**

ANALYZING THE IMAGE: What role does Doña Marina (far right) appear to be playing in this image? Does she appear to be subservient or equal to Cortés (right, seated)? How did the painter indicate her identity as non-Spanish?

CONNECTIONS: How do you think the native rulers negotiating with Cortés might have viewed her? What about a Spanish viewer of this image? What does the absence of other women here suggest about the role of women in these societies?

ments. He sent envoys to invite the Spanish to meet him in the provincial town of Cajamarca. His plan was to lure the Spanish into a trap. With an army of some forty thousand men stationed nearby, Atahualpa felt he had little to fear. Instead, the Spaniards ambushed and captured him, collected an enormous ransom in gold, and then executed him in 1533. The Spanish now marched on the capital of the empire itself, profiting once again from internal conflicts to form alliances with local peoples. When Cuzco fell in 1533, the Spanish plundered immense riches in gold and silver.

| How and why did Europeans undertake ambitious voyages of expansion? | What was the impact of European conquest on the New World? | How did Europe and the world change after Columbus? | How did expansion change European attitudes and beliefs? | ✓ LearningCurve Check what you know. |

425

Early French and English Settlement in the New World

For over a hundred years, the Spanish and the Portuguese dominated settlement in the New World. The first English colony was founded at Roanoke (in what is now North Carolina) in 1585. After a three-year loss of contact with England, the settlers were found to have disappeared; their fate remains a mystery. The colony of Virginia, founded by a private company of investors at Jamestown in 1607, also struggled in its first years and relied on food from the Powhatan Confederacy. Over time, the colony gained a steady hold by producing tobacco for a growing European market.

Settlement on the coast of New England was undertaken for different reasons. There, radical Protestants sought to escape Anglican repression in England and begin new lives. The small and struggling outpost of Plymouth (1620), founded by the Pilgrims who arrived on the *Mayflower*, was followed by Massachusetts (1630), a colony of Puritans that grew into a prosperous settlement.

Whereas the Spanish conquered indigenous empires and established large-scale dominance over Mexico and Peru, English settlements merely hugged the Atlantic coastline. This did not prevent conflict with the indigenous inhabitants over land and resources, however. At Jamestown, for example, English expansion undermined prior cooperation with the Powhatan Confederacy; disease and warfare with the English led to drastic population losses among the Powhatans.

French navigator and explorer Samuel de Champlain founded the first permanent French settlement, at Quebec, in 1608. Ville-Marie, latter-day Montreal, was founded in 1642. Following the waterways of the St. Lawrence, the Great Lakes, and the Mississippi, the French ventured into much of modern-day Canada and at least thirty-five of the fifty states of the United States. French traders forged relations with the Huron Confederacy, a league of four indigenous nations that dominated a large region north of Lake Erie, as a means of gaining access to hunting grounds and trade routes for beaver and other animals. In 1682, French explorer René-Robert Cavelier LaSalle descended the Mississippi to the Gulf of Mexico, opening the way for French occupation of Louisiana.

While establishing their foothold in the north, the French slowly acquired new territories in the West Indies, including Cayenne (1604), St. Christophe (1625), Martinique, Guadeloupe, and Saint-Domingue (1697) on the western side of the island of Hispaniola. These islands became centers of tobacco and then sugar production. French ambitions on the mainland and in the Caribbean sparked a century-long competition with the English.

European involvement in the Americas led to the profound transformation of pre-existing indigenous societies and the rise of a transatlantic slave trade. It also led to an acceleration of global trade and cultural exchange. Over time, the combination of indigenous, European, and African cultures gave birth to new societies in the New World. In turn, the profits of trade and the impact of cultural exchange greatly influenced European society.

> ## QUICK REVIEW

What role did technology play in initiating the European Age of Discovery? What role did ideas and beliefs play?

CHAPTER LOCATOR | What was the Afroeurasian trading world before Columbus?

Mixed Race Procession

Incas used drinking vessels, known as keros, for the ritual consumption of maize beer at feasts. This kero from the early colonial period shows a procession including an Incan leader preceded by a Spanish trumpet player and an African drummer. This is believed to be one of the earliest representations of an African in the Americas. (akg-images/Werner Forman)

THE GROWING EUROPEAN PRESENCE in the New World transformed its land and its peoples forever. Violence and disease wrought devastating losses, while surviving peoples encountered new political, social, and economic organizations imposed by Europeans. The Columbian exchange brought infectious diseases to the Americas, but it also gave new crops to the Old World that altered consumption patterns in Europe and across the globe (see page 430).

Colonial Administration

Spanish conquistadors had claimed the lands they had "discovered" for the Spanish crown. As the wealth of the new territories became apparent, the Spanish government acted to impose its authority and remove that of the original conquerors. The House of Trade, located in Seville, controlled the flow of goods and people to and from the colonies, while the Council of the Indies guided royal policy and served as the highest court for colonial affairs.

The crown divided its New World possessions into two **viceroyalties,** or administrative divisions: New Spain, with the capital at Mexico City, and Peru, with the capital at Lima. Two new viceroyalties added in the eighteenth century were New Granada, with Bogotá as its administrative center, and La Plata, with Buenos Aires as the capital (see Map 14.2, page 420).

The Portuguese adopted similar patterns of rule. India House in Lisbon functioned much like the Spanish House of Trade, and royal representatives oversaw its possessions in West Africa and Asia. To secure the vast expanse of Brazil, the Portuguese implemented the system of captaincies, hereditary grants of land given to nobles and loyal officials who bore the costs of settling and administering their territories. Over time, the Crown secured greater power over the captaincies, appointing royal governors to act as administrators.

viceroyalties
▶ The name for the four administrative units of Spanish possessions in the Americas: New Spain, Peru, New Granada, and La Plata.

| How and why did Europeans undertake ambitious voyages of expansion? | **What was the impact of European conquest on the New World?** | How did Europe and the world change after Columbus? | How did expansion change European attitudes and beliefs? | ✔ LearningCurve Check what you know. |

427

Like their European neighbors, France and England initially entrusted their overseas colonies to individual explorers and monopoly trading companies. By the end of the seventeenth century, the French crown had successfully imposed direct rule over New France and other colonies. The king appointed military governors to rule alongside intendants, royal officials possessed of broad administrative and financial authority within their intendancies.

England's colonies followed a distinctive path. Drawing on English traditions of representative government (see Chapter 15, page 477), English colonists established their own autonomous assemblies to regulate local affairs. Wealthy merchants and landowners dominated the assemblies, although even common men had more say in politics than was the case in England.

Impact of European Settlement on the Lives of Indigenous Peoples

Before Columbus's arrival, the Americas were inhabited by thousands of groups of indigenous peoples, each with distinct cultures and languages. Their patterns of life varied widely, from hunter-gatherer tribes organized into tribal confederations on the North American plains to the large-scale agriculture-based empires of the Mexica and the Inca. Although historians continue to debate the numbers, the best estimate is that in 1492 the peoples of the Americas numbered around 50 million.

Their lives were radically transformed by the arrival of Europeans. In the sixteenth century, perhaps two hundred thousand Spaniards immigrated to the New World. After assisting in the conquest of the Mexica and the Incas, these men carved out vast estates called haciendas in temperate grazing areas and imported Spanish livestock. In coastal tropical areas, the Spanish erected huge plantations to supply sugar to the European market. Around 1550, silver was discovered in present-day Bolivia and Mexico. To work the cattle ranches, sugar plantations, and silver mines, the conquistadors first turned to the indigenous peoples.

encomienda system
▶ A system whereby the Spanish crown granted the conquerors the right to employ groups of Indians forcibly in exchange for providing food, shelter, and Christian teaching.

The Spanish quickly established the **encomienda system**, in which the Crown granted the conquerors the right to employ groups of Native Americans as laborers or to demand tribute from them in exchange for providing food and shelter. Theoretically, the Spanish were supposed to care for the indigenous people under their command and teach them Christianity; in actuality, the system was a brutal form of exploitation only one level removed from slavery.

The new conditions and hardships imposed by conquest and colonization resulted in enormous native population losses. The major cause of death was disease. Having little or no resistance to diseases brought from the Old World, the inhabitants of the New World fell victim to smallpox, typhus, influenza, and other illnesses. Another factor was overwork, from which native workers died in staggering numbers. Forced labor diverted local people from agricultural work, leading to malnutrition, reduced fertility rates, and starvation. Malnutrition and hunger in turn lowered resistance to disease. Many indigenous peoples also died through outright violence in warfare.[5]

The Franciscan Bartolomé de Las Casas (1474–1566) was one of the most outspoken critics of Spanish brutality against indigenous peoples. Las Casas and other missionaries asserted that the Indians had human rights, and through their persistent pressure, the Spanish emperor Charles V abolished the worst abuses of the encomienda system in 1531.

Franciscan, Dominican, and Jesuit missionaries who accompanied the conquistadors and other European settlers played an important role in converting indigenous peoples to Christianity, teaching them European methods of agriculture, and instilling loyalty to their colonial masters. In areas with small Spanish populations, the friars set up missions for a period of ten years, after which established churches and priests would take over and they could move on to new areas. Jesuits in New France also established missions far distant from the centers of French settlement.

Missionaries' success in conversion varied over time and space. In Central and South America, large-scale conversion forged enduring Catholic cultures in Portuguese and Spanish colonies. Galvanized by their opposition to Catholicism and fueled by their own religious fervor, English colonizers also made efforts to convert indigenous peoples. On the whole, however, these attempts were less successful, in part because the English did not establish wholesale dominance over large native populations as did the Spanish.

Rather than a straightforward imposition of Christianity, conversion entailed a complex process of cultural exchange. Catholic friars were among the first Europeans to seek understanding of native cultures and languages as part of their effort to render Christianity comprehensible to indigenous people. In turn, Christian ideas and practices in the New World took on a distinctive character.

The pattern of devastating disease and population loss occurred everywhere Europeans settled. The best estimate of native population loss is a decline from roughly 50 million people in 1492 to around 9 million by 1700. It is important to note, however, that native populations and cultures did survive the conquest period, sometimes by blending with European incomers and sometimes by maintaining cultural autonomy.

For colonial administrators, the main problem posed by the astronomically high death rate was the loss of a subjugated labor force to work the mines and sugar plantations. As early as 1511, King Ferdinand of Spain observed that the Indians seemed to be "very frail" and that "one black could do the work of four Indians."[6] Thus was born an absurd myth, and the new tragedy of the transatlantic slave trade would soon follow (see page 431).

Life in the Colonies

Many factors helped to shape life in European colonies, including geographical location, religion, indigenous cultures and practices, patterns of European settlement, and the cultural attitudes and official policies of the European nations that claimed them as empire. Throughout the New World, colonial settlements were hedged by immense borderlands where European power was weak and Europeans and non-Europeans interacted on a more equal basis.

Women played a crucial role in the creation of new identities and the continuation of old ones. The first explorers formed unions with native women, through coercion or choice, and relied on them as translators and guides and to form alliances with indigenous powers. As settlement developed, the character of each colony was influenced by the presence or absence of European women. Where women and children accompanied men, as in the British colonies and the Spanish mainland colonies, new settlements took on European languages, religion, and ways of life. Where European women did not accompany men, as on the west

How and why did Europeans undertake ambitious voyages of expansion?

What was the impact of European conquest on the New World?

How did Europe and the world change after Columbus?

How did expansion change European attitudes and beliefs?

LearningCurve
Check what you know.

429

coast of Africa and most European outposts in Asia, local populations largely retained their own cultures, to which male Europeans acclimatized themselves.

Most women who crossed the Atlantic were Africans, constituting four-fifths of the female newcomers before 1800.[7] Wherever slavery existed, masters profited from their power to engage in sexual relations with enslaved women. One important difference among European colonies was in the status of children born from such unions. In some colonies, mostly those dominated by the Portuguese, Spanish, or French, substantial populations of free people of color descended from the freed children of such unions. In English colonies, masters were less likely to free children they fathered with female slaves.

The mixing of indigenous peoples with Europeans and Africans created whole new populations and ethnicities and complex self-identities. In Spanish America, the word *mestizo*— *métis* in French—described people of mixed Native American and European descent. The blanket terms "mulatto" and "people of color" were used for those of mixed African and European origin. With its immense slave-based plantation agriculture system, large indigenous population, and relatively low Portuguese immigration, Brazil developed a particularly complex racial and ethnic mosaic.

The Columbian Exchange

Columbian exchange

▶ The exchange of animals, plants, and diseases between the Old and the New Worlds.

The migration of peoples to the New World led to an exchange of animals, plants, and disease, a complex process known as the **Columbian exchange**. Columbus had brought sugar plants on his second voyage; Spaniards also introduced rice and bananas from the Canary Islands, and the Portuguese carried these items to Brazil. Everywhere they settled, the Spanish and Portuguese brought and raised wheat. Grapes and olives brought over from Spain did well in parts of Peru and Chile.

Apart from wild turkeys and game, Native Americans had no animals for food. They did not domesticate animals for travel or use as beasts of burden, except for alpacas and llamas in the Inca Empire. On his second voyage in 1493, Columbus introduced horses, cattle, sheep, dogs, pigs, chickens, and goats. The horse enabled the Spanish conquerors and native populations to travel faster and farther and to transport heavy loads. In turn, Europeans returned home with many food crops that became central elements of their diet.

Disease brought by European people and animals was perhaps the most important form of exchange. The wave of catastrophic epidemic disease that swept the Western Hemisphere after 1492 can be seen as an extension of the swath of devastation wreaked by the Black Death in the 1300s, first in Asia and then in Europe. The world after Columbus was thus unified by disease as well as by trade and colonization.

> ## QUICK REVIEW

What policies and institutions did the Spanish and Portuguese develop to facilitate the exploitation of Indian labor and the natural resources of the Americas?

CHAPTER LOCATOR | What was the Afroeurasian trading world before Columbus?

CHAPTER 14
430 EUROPEAN EXPLORATION AND CONQUEST

How did Europe and the world change after Columbus?

Silver Coin from Potosí After the discovery of the Americas, a wave of new items entered European markets, silver foremost among them. The incredibly rich silver mines at Potosí (in modern-day Bolivia) were the source of this eight-reale coin struck at the mine during the reign of Charles II. Such coins were the original "pieces of eight" prized by pirates and adventurers. (Hoberman Collection/SuperStock)

THE CENTURIES-OLD AFROEURASIAN TRADE WORLD was forever changed by the European voyages of discovery and their aftermath. For the first time, a truly global economy emerged in the sixteenth and seventeenth centuries. The ancient civilizations of Europe, Africa, the Americas, and Asia confronted one another in new and rapidly evolving ways. Those confrontations often led to conquest and exploitation, but they also contributed to cultural exchange and renewal.

Sugar and Slavery

Throughout the Middle Ages, slavery was deeply entrenched in the Mediterranean, but it was not based on race; many slaves were white. How, then, did black African slavery enter the European picture and take root in the Americas? In 1453, the Ottoman capture of Constantinople halted the flow of white slaves from the eastern Mediterranean to western Europe. The successes of the Iberian reconquista also meant that the supply of Muslim captives had drastically diminished. Cut off from its traditional sources of slaves, Mediterranean Europe then turned to sub-Saharan Africa, which had a long history of internal slave trading. (See "Individuals in Society: Juan de Pareja," page 432.) As Portuguese explorers began

| How and why did Europeans undertake ambitious voyages of expansion? | What was the impact of European conquest on the New World? | **How did Europe and the world change after Columbus?** | How did expansion change European attitudes and beliefs? | ☑ LearningCurve Check what you know. |

431

During the long wars of the reconquista, Muslims and Christians captured each other in battle and used the defeated as slaves. As the Muslims were gradually eliminated from Iberia in the fifteenth and sixteenth centuries, the Spanish and Portuguese turned to the west coast of Africa for a new supply of slaves. Most slaves worked as domestic servants rather than in the fields. Some received specialized training as artisans.

Not all people of African descent were slaves, and some experienced both freedom and slavery in a single lifetime. The life and career of Juan de Pareja (pah-REH-huh) illustrates the complexities of the Iberian slave system and the heights of achievement possible for those who gained freedom.

Pareja was born in Antequera, an agricultural region and the old center of Muslim culture near Seville in southern Spain. Of his parents we know nothing. Because a rare surviving document calls him a "mulatto," one of his parents must have been white and the other must have had some African blood. In 1630, Pareja applied to the mayor of Seville

for permission to travel to Madrid to visit his brother and "to perfect his art." The document lists his occupation as "a painter in Seville." Because it mentions no other name, it is reasonable to assume that Pareja arrived in Madrid a free man. Sometime between 1630 and 1648, however, he came into the possession of the artist Diego Velázquez (1599–1660); Pareja became a slave.

How did Velázquez acquire Pareja? By purchase? As a gift? Had Pareja fallen into debt or committed some crime and thereby lost his freedom? We do not know. Velázquez, the greatest Spanish painter of the seventeenth century, had a large studio with many assistants. Pareja was set to grinding powders to make colors and to preparing canvases. He must have demonstrated ability because when Velázquez went to Rome in 1648, he chose Pareja to accompany him.

In 1650, as practice for a portrait of Pope Innocent X, Velázquez painted Pareja. The portrait shows Pareja dressed in fine clothing and gazing self-confidently at the viewer. Displayed in Rome in a public exhibition of Velázquez's work, the painting won acclaim from his contemporaries. That same year, Velázquez signed the document that gave Pareja his freedom, to become effective in 1654. Pareja lived out the rest of his life as an independent painter.

What does the public career of Pareja tell us about the man and his world? Pareja's career suggests that a person of African descent might fall into slavery and yet still acquire professional training and work alongside his master in a position of confidence. If lucky enough to be freed, a former slave could exercise a profession and live his own life in Madrid. Pareja's experience was far from typical for a slave in the seventeenth century, but it reminds us of the myriad forms that slavery took in this period.

Velázquez, *Juan de Pareja*, 1650. (Private Collection/Photo © Christie's Images/ The Bridgeman Art Library)

QUESTIONS FOR ANALYSIS

1. Slavery was an established institution in Spain. Speculate on Velázquez's possible reasons for giving Pareja his freedom.
2. In what ways does Pareja represent Europe's increasing participation in global commerce and exploration?

▷LaunchPad

ONLINE DOCUMENT PROJECT

How could an individual like Pareja experience both slavery and freedom in a single lifetime? Keeping the question above in mind, analyze sources from Pareja's contemporaries that reflect changing ideas about racial identity and slavery, and then complete a writing assignment based on the evidence and details from this chapter. *See inside the front cover to learn more.*

Sources: Jonathan Brown, *Velázquez: Painter and Courtier* (New Haven, Conn.: Yale University Press, 1986); *Grove Dictionary of Art* (New York: Macmillan, 2000); Sister Wendy Beckett, *Sister Wendy's American Collection* (New York: Harper Collins Publishers, 2000), p. 15.

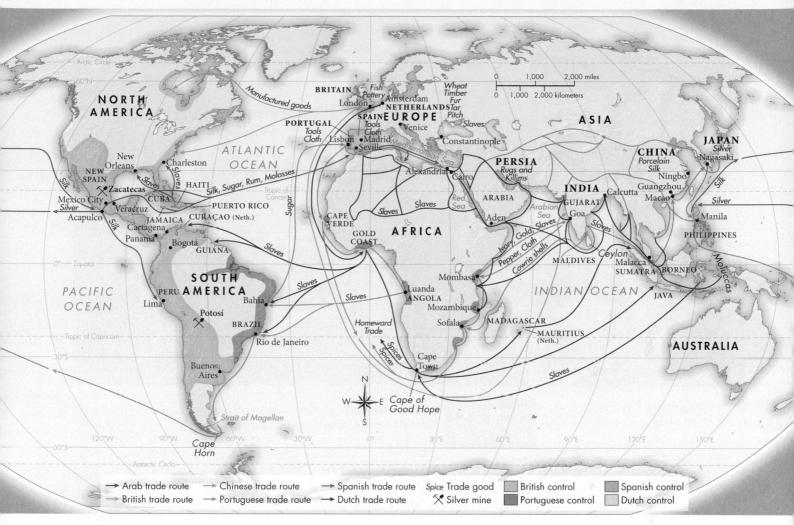

→ Arab trade route	→ Chinese trade route	→ Spanish trade route	*Spice* Trade good	▮ British control	▮ Spanish control
→ British trade route	→ Portuguese trade route	→ Dutch trade route	✗ Silver mine	▮ Portuguese control	▮ Dutch control

MAP 14.3 ■ Seaborne Trading Empires in the Sixteenth and Seventeenth Centuries

By the mid-seventeenth century, trade linked all parts of the world except for Australia. Notice that trade in slaves was not confined to the Atlantic but involved almost all parts of the world.

their voyages along the western coast of Africa, one of the first commodities they sought was slaves. In 1444, the first ship returned to Lisbon with a cargo of enslaved Africans. From 1490 to 1530, Portuguese traders brought hundreds of enslaved Africans to Lisbon each year (**Map 14.3**), where they eventually constituted 10 percent of the city's population.

In this stage of European expansion, the history of slavery became intertwined with the history of sugar. Originally sugar was an expensive luxury that only the very affluent could afford, but population increases and monetary expansion in the fifteenth century led to increasing demand. Native to the South Pacific, sugar was taken in ancient times to India. From there, sugar crops traveled to China and the Mediterranean. When Genoese and other Italians colonized the Canary Islands and the Portuguese settled on the Madeira Islands, sugar plantations came to the Atlantic.

How and why did Europeans undertake ambitious voyages of expansion?	What was the impact of European conquest on the New World?	**How did Europe and the world change after Columbus?**	How did expansion change European attitudes and beliefs?	✔ LearningCurve Check what you know.

A New World Sugar Refinery, Brazil Sugar was the most important and most profitable plantation crop in the New World. This image shows the processing and refinement of sugar on a Brazilian plantation. Sugarcane was grown, harvested, and processed by African slaves, who labored under brutal and ruthless conditions to generate enormous profits for plantation owners. (French School/Getty Images)

Sugar was a particularly difficult and demanding crop to produce for profit. The demands of sugar production only increased with the invention of roller mills to crush the cane more efficiently. Yields could be augmented, but only if a sufficient labor force was found to work the mills. Europeans solved the labor problem by forcing first native islanders and then enslaved Africans to provide the backbreaking work.

Sugar gave New World slavery its distinctive characteristics. Columbus himself brought the first sugar plants to the New World. The transatlantic slave trade began in 1518 when the Spanish emperor Charles V authorized traders to bring enslaved Africans to the Americas. The Portuguese brought slaves to Brazil around 1550; by 1600, four thousand were being imported annually. After its founding in 1621, the Dutch West India Company transported thousands of Africans to Brazil and the Caribbean, mostly to work on sugar plantations. In the midseventeenth century the English got involved.

Conditions for enslaved Africans on the Atlantic passage were often lethal. Before 1700, when slavers decided it was better business to improve conditions, some 20 percent of slaves died on the voyage.[8] To increase profits, slave traders

CHAPTER LOCATOR | What was the Afroeurasian trading world before Columbus?

packed several hundred captives on each ship. On sugar plantations, death rates from the brutal pace of labor were extremely high, leading to a constant stream of new shipments of slaves from Africa.

In total, scholars estimate that European traders shipped over 10 million enslaved Africans across the Atlantic from 1518 to 1800 (of whom roughly 8.5 million disembarked), with the peak of the trade occurring in the eighteenth century.[9] By comparison, only 2 to 2.5 million Europeans migrated to the New World during the same period.

Spanish Silver and Its Economic Effects

The sixteenth century has often been called Spain's golden century, but silver mined in the Americas was the true source of Spain's wealth. In 1545, the Spanish discovered an extraordinary source of silver at Potosí (poh-toh-SEE) (in present-day Bolivia) in territory conquered from the Inca Empire. By 1550, Potosí yielded perhaps 60 percent of all the silver mined in the world. From Potosí and the mines at Zacatecas (za-kuh-TAY-kuhhs) and Guanajuato (gwah-nah-HWAH-toh) in Mexico, huge quantities of precious metals poured forth. Between 1503 and 1650, 35 million pounds of silver and over 600,000 pounds of gold entered Seville's port. Spanish predominance, however, proved temporary.

In the sixteenth century, Spain experienced a steady population increase, creating a sharp rise in the demand for food and goods. Spanish colonies in the Americas also demanded consumer goods, such as cloth and luxury goods. Spain had expelled some of its best farmers and businessmen—the Muslims and Jews—in the fifteenth century; as a result, the Spanish economy was suffering and could not meet the new demands. The excess of demand over supply led to widespread inflation. The result was a rise in production costs and a further decline in Spain's productive capacity.

Did the flood of silver bullion from the Americas cause the inflation? Prices rose most steeply before

Philip II, ca. 1533

This portrait of Philip II as a young man and crown prince of Spain is by the celebrated artist Titian, court painter to Philip's father, Charles V. After taking the throne, Philip became another great patron of the artist. (Palazzo Pitti, Florence, Italy/The Bridgeman Art Library)

| How and why did Europeans undertake ambitious voyages of expansion? | What was the impact of European conquest on the New World? | **How did Europe and the world change after Columbus?** | How did expansion change European attitudes and beliefs? | ✓ LearningCurve Check what you know. |

435

1565, but bullion imports reached their peak between 1580 and 1620. Thus, silver did not cause the initial inflation. It did, however, exacerbate the situation, and, along with the ensuing rise in population, the influx of silver significantly contributed to the upward spiral of prices. Inflation severely strained government budgets. Several times between 1557 and 1647, Spain's King Philip II and his successors wrote off the state debt, thereby undermining confidence in the government and leaving the economy in shambles.

Philip II paid his armies and foreign debts with silver bullion, and Spanish inflation was thus transmitted to the rest of Europe. Between 1560 and 1600, much of Europe experienced large price increases. Spain suffered most severely, but all European countries were affected. Because money bought less, people who lived on fixed incomes, such as nobles, were badly hurt. Those who owed fixed sums of money, such as the middle class, prospered because in a time of rising prices, debts lessened in value each year. Food costs rose most sharply, and the poor fared worst of all.

In many ways, though, it was not Spain but China that controlled the world trade in silver. The Chinese demanded silver for their products and for the payment of imperial taxes. China was thus the main buyer of world silver, absorbing half the world's production. The silver market drove world trade, with New Spain and Japan being mainstays on the supply side and China dominating the demand side. The world trade in silver is one of the best examples of the new global economy that emerged in this period.

The Birth of the Global Economy

With the Europeans' discovery of the Americas and their exploration of the Pacific, the entire world was linked for the first time in history by seaborne trade. The opening of that trade created three successive commercial empires: the Portuguese, the Spanish, and the Dutch.

The Portuguese were the first worldwide traders. In the sixteenth century, they controlled the sea route to India (see Map 14.3, page 433). From their fortified bases at Goa on the Arabian Sea and at Malacca on the Malay Peninsula, ships carried goods to the Portuguese settlement at Macao in the South China Sea. From Macao, Portuguese ships loaded with Chinese silk and porcelain sailed to Japan and the Philippines, where Chinese goods were exchanged for Spanish silver from New Spain. Throughout Asia, the Portuguese traded in slaves. The Portuguese exported horses from Mesopotamia and copper from Arabia to India; from India they exported hawks and peacocks for the Chinese and Japanese markets. They brought back to Portugal Asian spices that had been purchased with textiles produced in India and with gold and ivory from East Africa. They also shipped back sugar from their colony in Brazil, produced by enslaved Africans whom they had transported across the Atlantic.

Coming to empire a few decades later than the Portuguese, the Spanish were determined to claim their place in world trade. The Spanish Empire in the New World was basically a land empire, but across the Pacific the Spaniards built a seaborne empire centered at Manila in the Philippines. The city of Manila served as the transpacific bridge between Spanish America and China. In Manila, Spanish traders used silver from American mines to purchase Chinese silk for Euro-

CHAPTER LOCATOR | What was the Afroeurasian trading world before Columbus?

CHAPTER 14
436 EUROPEAN EXPLORATION AND CONQUEST

pean markets. After 1640, the Spanish silk trade declined in the face of stiff competition from Dutch imports.

The Dutch Empire was initially built on spices. In 1599, a Dutch fleet returned to Amsterdam carrying 600,000 pounds of pepper and 250,000 pounds of cloves and nutmeg. Those who had invested in the expedition received a 100 percent profit. The voyage led to the establishment in 1602 of the Dutch East India Company, founded with the stated intention of capturing the spice trade from the Portuguese.

The Dutch set their sights on gaining direct access to and control of the Indonesian sources of spices. In return for assisting Indonesian princes in local squabbles and disputes with the Portuguese, the Dutch won broad commercial concessions. Through agreements, seizures, and outright military aggression, they gained control of the western access to the Indonesian archipelago in the first half of the seventeenth century. Gradually, they acquired political domination over the archipelago itself. By the 1660s, the Dutch had managed to expel the Portuguese from Ceylon and other East Indian islands, thereby establishing control of the lucrative spice trade.

Not content with challenging the Portuguese in the Indian Ocean, the Dutch also aspired to a role in the Americas. Founded in 1621, when the Dutch were at war with the Spanish, the Dutch West India Company aggressively sought to open trade with North and South America and capture Spanish territories there. The company captured or destroyed hundreds of Spanish ships, seized the Spanish silver fleet in 1628, and captured portions of Brazil and the Caribbean. The Dutch also interceded successfully in the transatlantic slave trade, establishing a large number of trading stations on the west coast of Africa.

QUICK REVIEW <

How was the era of global contact shaped by new commodities, commercial empires, and forced migrations?

| How and why did Europeans undertake ambitious voyages of expansion? | What was the impact of European conquest on the New World? | **How did Europe and the world change after Columbus?** | How did expansion change European attitudes and beliefs? | ✓ LearningCurve Check what you know. |

437

> How did expansion change European attitudes and beliefs?

Titus Andronicus With classical allusions, fifteen murders and executions, a Gothic queen who takes a black lover, and incredible violence, this early Shakespearean tragedy (1594) was a melodramatic thriller that enjoyed enormous popularity with the London audience. The shock value of a dark-skinned character on the English stage is clearly shown in this illustration. (Bibliothèque Nationale, Paris, France/ Giraudon/The Bridgeman Art Library)

THE AGE OF OVERSEAS EXPANSION heightened Europeans' contacts with the rest of the world. These contacts gave birth to new ideas about the inherent superiority or inferiority of different races, in part to justify European participation in the slave trade. Cultural encounters also inspired more positive views. The essays of Michel de Montaigne epitomized a new spirit of skepticism and cultural relativism, while the plays of William Shakespeare reflected the efforts of one great writer to come to terms with the cultural complexity of his day.

CHAPTER LOCATOR | What was the Afroeurasian trading world before Columbus?

New Ideas About Race

At the beginning of the transatlantic slave trade, most Europeans grouped Africans into the despised categories of pagan heathens and Muslim infidels. Africans were certainly not the only peoples subject to such dehumanizing attitudes. Jews were also viewed as alien people who, like Africans, were naturally sinful and depraved. More generally, elite Europeans were accustomed to viewing the peasant masses as a lower form of humanity.[10]

As Europeans turned to Africa for new sources of slaves, they drew on and developed ideas about Africans' primitiveness and barbarity to defend slavery and even argue that enslavement benefited Africans by bringing the light of Christianity to heathen peoples. Over time, the institution of slavery fostered a new level of racial inequality. In contrast to peasants and Jews, Africans gradually became seen as utterly distinct from and wholly inferior to Europeans. Black skin became equated with slavery itself as Europeans at home and in the colonies convinced themselves that blacks were destined by God to serve them as slaves in perpetuity.

After 1700, the emergence of new methods of observing and describing nature led to the use of science to define race. Although the term originally referred to a nation or an ethnic group, henceforth "race" would mean biologically distinct groups of people, whose physical differences produced differences in culture, character, and intelligence.

Michel de Montaigne and Cultural Curiosity

Racism was not the only possible reaction to the new worlds emerging in the sixteenth century. Decades of religious fanaticism, bringing civil anarchy and war, led some Catholics and Protestants to doubt that any one faith contained absolute truth. Added to these doubts was the discovery of peoples in the New World who had radically different ways of life. These shocks helped produce ideas of skepticism and cultural relativism. Skepticism is a school of thought founded on doubt that total certainty or definitive knowledge is ever attainable. Cultural relativism suggests that one culture is not necessarily superior to another, just different. Both notions found expression in the work of Frenchman Michel de Montaigne (mahn-TAYN) (1533–1592).

Montaigne developed a new literary genre, the essay, to express his ideas. Published in 1580, Montaigne's *Essays* consisted of short reflections. Intending his works to be accessible to ordinary people, Montaigne wrote in French rather than Latin and in an engaging conversational style. His essays were quickly translated into other European languages and became some of the most widely read texts of the early modern period.

Montaigne's essay "Of Cannibals" reveals the impact of overseas discoveries on one thoughtful European. In contrast to the prevailing views of his day, he rejected the notion that one culture is superior to another. Speaking of native Brazilians, he wrote, "I find that there is nothing barbarous and savage in this nation [Brazil], . . . except, that everyone gives the title of barbarism to everything that is not according to his usage."[11]

| How and why did Europeans undertake ambitious voyages of expansion? | What was the impact of European conquest on the New World? | How did Europe and the world change after Columbus? | **How did expansion change European attitudes and beliefs?** | ✔ LearningCurve Check what you know. |

439

In his own time, few would have agreed with Montaigne's challenge to ideas of European superiority or his even more radical questioning of the superiority of humans over animals. Nevertheless, his popular essays contributed to a basic shift in attitudes. "Wonder," he said, "is the foundation of all philosophy, research is the means of all learning, and ignorance is the end."[12] Montaigne thus inaugurated an era of doubt.

William Shakespeare and His Influence

In addition to the essay as a literary genre, the period fostered remarkable creativity in other branches of literature. England—especially in the latter part of Queen Elizabeth I's reign and in the first years of her successor, James I (r. 1603–1625)—witnessed remarkable literary expression. The undisputed master of the period was the dramatist William Shakespeare. Born in 1564 to a successful glove manufacturer in Stratford-upon-Avon, Shakespeare grew into a Renaissance man with a deep appreciation of classical culture, individualism, and humanism.

Like Montaigne's essays, Shakespeare's work reveals the impact of the new discoveries and contacts of his day. The title character of *Othello* is described as a "Moor of Venice." In Shakespeare's day, the term "Moor" referred to Muslims of North African origin, including those who had migrated to the Iberian Peninsula. It could also be applied, though, to natives of the Iberian Peninsula who converted to Islam or to non-Muslim Berbers in North Africa. To complicate things even more, references in the play to Othello as "black" in skin color have led many to believe that Shakespeare intended him to be a sub-Saharan African. This confusion in the play aptly reflects the uncertainty in Shakespeare's own time about racial and religious classifications. In contrast to the prevailing view of Moors as inferior, Shakespeare presents Othello as a complex human figure, whose only crime is to have "loved [his wife] not wisely, but too well."

> **QUICK REVIEW**

How did European expansion change the way Europeans saw themselves and their relationships with the other peoples of the world?

CHAPTER LOCATOR | What was the Afroeurasian trading world before Columbus?

CHAPTER 14
440 EUROPEAN EXPLORATION AND CONQUEST

LOOKING BACK
LOOKING AHEAD

In 1517, Martin Luther issued his "Ninety-five Theses," launching the Protestant Reformation; just five years later, Ferdinand Magellan's expedition sailed around the globe, shattering European notions of terrestrial geography. Within a few short years, old medieval certainties about Heaven and earth began to collapse. In the ensuing decades, Europeans struggled to come to terms with religious difference at home and the multitudes of new peoples and places they encountered abroad. While some Europeans were fascinated and inspired by this new diversity, too often the result was violence. Europeans endured decades of civil war between Protestants and Catholics, and indigenous peoples suffered massive population losses as a result of European warfare, disease, and exploitation. Both Catholic and Protestant religious leaders condoned the African slave trade that was to bring suffering and death to millions of Africans.

Even as the voyages of discovery coincided with the fragmentation of European culture, they also belonged to longer-term processes of state centralization and consolidation. The new monarchies of the Renaissance produced stronger and wealthier governments capable of financing the huge expenses of exploration and colonization. Competition to gain overseas colonies became an integral part of European politics. The path from medieval Christendom to the modern nation-state led the world through religious warfare and global encounter.

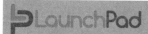

ONLINE DOCUMENT PROJECT
Juan de Pareja

How could an individual like Pareja experience both slavery and freedom in a single lifetime?

You encountered Juan de Pareja's story on page 432. Keeping the question above in mind, examine primary sources from Pareja's time. *See inside the front cover to learn more.*

How and why did Europeans undertake ambitious voyages of expansion?

What was the impact of European conquest on the New World?

How did Europe and the world change after Columbus?

How did expansion change European attitudes and beliefs?

✓ LearningCurve
Check what you know.

441

CHAPTER 14 STUDY GUIDE

STEP 1 GET STARTED ONLINE

✓ LearningCurve

Now that you've read the chapter, make it stick by completing the LearningCurve activity.

STEP 2 EXPLAIN WHY IT MATTERS

Put your reading into practice. Identify each term below, and then explain why it matters in Western history.

TERM	WHO OR WHAT & WHEN	WHY IT MATTERS
caravel (p. 419)		
Ptolemy's *Geography* (p. 419)		
Treaty of Tordesillas (p. 422)		
conquistador (p. 423)		
Mexica Empire (p. 424)		
Inca Empire (p. 424)		
viceroyalties (p. 427)		
encomienda system (p. 428)		
Columbian exchange (p. 430)		

STEP 3 MOVE BEYOND THE BASICS

To demonstrate a more advanced understanding, use the table below to identify the motives behind Spanish expansion across the Atlantic, and describe the motives, actions, and subsequent institutions of the Spanish conquest in the Americas.

Motives	Conquests	Institutions

STEP 4 **PUT IT ALL TOGETHER** Now, take a step back and try to explain the big picture. Remember to use specific examples from the chapter in your answers.

THE EUROPEAN VOYAGES OF DISCOVERY

▶ What role did Europe play in world trade prior to 1492?

▶ What role did governments play in European expansion? What role did technology play?

THE IMPACT OF CONQUEST IN THE AMERICAS

▶ What explains the dramatic decline in native populations after the arrival of Europeans in the New World?

▶ How did the Columbian Exchange transform the Americas?

THE IMPACT OF CONQUEST IN EUROPE AND AROUND THE WORLD

▶ What role did increasing demand for sugar play in shaping the economy and society of the New World?

▶ How did European expansion give rise to new ideas about race?

MAKE CONNECTIONS

▶ How did the developments of the Late Middle Ages create the conditions that made European expansion in the fifteenth and sixteenth centuries possible?

▶ Defend or refute the following statement: "The era of global trade began in the sixteenth century and was initiated by European conquests in the Americas."

> IN YOUR OWN WORDS

Imagine that you must give an oral report to the class answering the following question: **What were the motives behind European overseas expansion, and what were the consequences for Europe, the Americas, and Africa?** What would be the most important points and why?

15

ABSOLUTISM AND CONSTITUTIONALISM

CA. 1589–1725

> **What were the most important political trends in seventeenth-century Europe?** Chapter 15 examines seventeenth-century political developments. The seventeenth century was a period of crisis and transformation in Europe. Agricultural and manufacturing slumps led to food shortages and shrinking population rates. Religious and dynastic conflicts led to almost constant war, visiting violence and destruction on ordinary people and reshaping European states. While absolutism emerged as the solution to these challenges in many European states, a small minority, most notably England and the Dutch Republic, adopted a different path, placing sovereignty in the hands of privileged groups rather than the Crown.

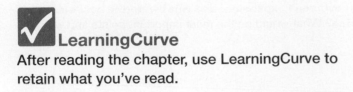

LearningCurve

After reading the chapter, use LearningCurve to retain what you've read.

> What made the seventeenth century an "age of crisis"?

> Why did France rise and Spain fall during this period?

> What explains the rise of absolutism in Prussia and Austria?

> What were the distinctive features of Russian and Ottoman absolutism?

> How and why did the constitutional state triumph in the Dutch Republic and England?

> What was the baroque style in art and music, and where was it popular?

Life at the French Royal Court. King Louis XIV receives foreign ambassadors to celebrate a peace treaty. (Erich Lessing/Art Resource, NY)

> What made the seventeenth century an "age of crisis"?

The Estonians were conquered by German military nobility in the Middle Ages and reduced to serfdom. The German-speaking nobles ruled the Estonian peasants with an iron hand, and Peter the Great reaffirmed their domination when Russia annexed Estonia. (Getty Images)

HISTORIANS OFTEN REFER TO THE SEVENTEENTH CENTURY as an age of crisis. After the economic and demographic growth of the sixteenth century, Europe faltered into stagnation and retrenchment. This was partially due to climate changes beyond anyone's control, but it also resulted from bitter religious divides, increased governmental pressures, and war. In the long run, however, governments proved increasingly able to impose their will on the populace, and the period witnessed spectacular growth in army size as well as new forms of taxation, government bureaucracies, and increased state sovereignty.

The Social Order and Peasant Life

Peasants occupied the lower tiers of a society organized in hierarchical levels. At the top, the monarch was celebrated as a semidivine being, chosen by God to embody the state. In Catholic countries, the clergy occupied the second level. Next came nobles, whose privileged status derived from their ancient bloodlines and military service. Prosperous mercantile families had bought their way into the

CHAPTER LOCATOR | **What made the seventeenth century an "age of crisis"?** | Why did France rise and Spain fall during this period?

CHAPTER 15
446 ABSOLUTISM AND CONSTITUTIONALISM

ca. 1500–1650 – Consolidation of serfdom in eastern Europe	**1665–1683** – Jean-Baptiste Colbert applies mercantilism to France
1533–1584 – Reign of Ivan the Terrible in Russia	**1670** – Charles II agrees to re-Catholicize England in secret agreement with Louis XIV
1589–1610 – Reign of Henry IV in France	**ca. 1680–1750** – Construction of absolutist palaces
1598–1613 – Time of Troubles in Russia	**1682** – Louis XIV moves court to Versailles
1620–1740 – Growth of absolutism in Austria and Prussia	**1682–1725** – Reign of Peter the Great in Russia
1642–1649 – English civil war, which ends with execution of Charles I	**1683–1718** – Habsburgs push the Ottoman Turks from Hungary
1643–1715 – Reign of Louis XIV in France	**1685** – Edict of Nantes revoked in France
1653–1658 – Military rule in England under Oliver Cromwell (the Protectorate)	**1688–1689** – Glorious Revolution in England
1660 – Restoration of English monarchy under Charles II	**1701–1713** – War of the Spanish Succession

nobility through service to the rising monarchies of the fifteenth and sixteenth centuries and constituted a second tier of nobles. Those lower on the social scale, the peasants and artisans who constituted the vast majority of the population, were expected to defer to their betters with humble obedience. This was the so-called Great Chain of Being that linked God to his creation in a series of ranked social groups.

In addition to being rigidly hierarchical, European societies were patriarchal in nature, with men assuming authority over women as a God-given prerogative. The family thus represented a microcosm of this social order. The father ruled his family like a king ruled his domains. Fathers did not possess the power of life and death, but they were entitled to use physical violence, imprisonment, and other forceful measures to impose their authority. These powers were balanced by expectations that a good father would provide and care for his dependents.

In the seventeenth century, most Europeans lived in the countryside. The hub of the rural world was the small peasant village centered on a church and a manor. In western Europe, a small number of peasants in each village owned enough land to feed themselves and had the livestock and plows necessary to work their land. These independent farmers were leaders of the peasant village. They employed the landless poor, rented out livestock and tools, and served as agents for the noble lord. Below them were small landowners and tenant farmers who did not have enough land to be self-sufficient. At the bottom were villagers

| What explains the rise of absolutism in Prussia and Austria? | What were the distinctive features of Russian and Ottoman absolutism? | How and why did the constitutional state triumph in the Dutch Republic and England? | What was the baroque style in art and music, and where was it popular? | ✔ **LearningCurve**
Check what you know. |

who worked as dependent laborers and servants. In eastern Europe, the vast majority of peasants toiled as serfs for noble landowners and did not own land in their own right (see page 462).

Famine and Economic Crisis

European rural society lived on the edge of subsistence. Because of the crude technology and low crop yield, peasants were constantly threatened by scarcity and famine. In the seventeenth century a period of colder and wetter climate throughout Europe, dubbed the "little ice age" by historians, meant a shorter farming season with lower yields. A bad harvest created food shortages; a series of bad harvests could lead to famine. Recurrent famines significantly reduced the population of early modern Europe. Most people did not die of outright starvation but through the spread of diseases like smallpox and typhoid, which were facilitated by malnutrition and exhaustion. Outbreaks of bubonic plague continued in Europe until the 1720s.

Given the harsh conditions of life, industry also suffered. The output of woolen textiles, one of the most important European manufactures, declined sharply in the first half of the seventeenth century. Food prices were high, wages stagnated, and unemployment soared. This economic crisis was not universal: it struck various regions at different times and to different degrees. In the middle decades of the century, for example, Spain, France, Germany, and England all experienced great economic difficulties, but these years were the golden age of the Netherlands.

The urban poor and peasants were the hardest hit. When the price of bread rose beyond their capacity to pay, they frequently expressed their anger by rioting, with women often taking the lead. In towns they invaded bakers' shops to seize bread and resell it at a "just price." In rural areas they attacked convoys taking grain to the cities. Historians have used the term "moral economy" for this vision of a world in which community needs predominate over competition and profit.

The Thirty Years' War

In the first half of the seventeenth century, the fragile balance of life was violently upturned by the ravages of the Thirty Years' War (1618–1648). The Holy Roman Empire was a confederation of hundreds of principalities, independent cities, duchies, and other polities loosely united under an elected emperor. The uneasy truce between Catholics and Protestants created by the Peace of Augsburg in 1555 deteriorated as the faiths of various areas shifted. Lutheran princes felt compelled to form the Protestant Union (1608), and Catholics retaliated with the Catholic League (1609). Each alliance was determined that the other should make no religious or territorial advance. Dynastic interests were also involved; the Spanish Habsburgs strongly supported the goals of their Austrian relatives: the unity of the empire and the preservation of Catholicism within it.

The war began in 1618 with the outbreak of civil war in Bohemia between the Catholic League and the Protestant Union. It would continue for three decades, involve an ever-shifting array of alliances, and draw every major European power into the fighting.

CHAPTER LOCATOR | **What made the seventeenth century an "age of crisis"?** | Why did France rise and Spain fall during this period?

CHAPTER 15
448 ABSOLUTISM AND CONSTITUTIONALISM

- **Bohemian Phase (1618–1625)** Civil war in Bohemia between the Catholic League and the Protestant Union; Catholic forces defeated Protestants at the Battle of the White Mountain (1620)

- **Danish Phase (1625–1629)** So called because of the leadership of the Protestant king Christian IV of Denmark (r. 1588–1648); witnessed additional Catholic victories; the Catholic imperial army swept through Silesia, north to the Baltic, and east into Pomerania

- **Swedish Phase (1630–1635)** Began with the arrival in Germany of the Swedish king Gustavus Adolphus (r. 1594–1632) and his army in support of the empire's Protestants; France subsidized the Swedes, hoping to weaken Habsburg power in Europe; Gustavus Adolphus won two important battles but was fatally wounded in combat

- **French Phase (1635–1648)** Prompted by French fears of Habsburg resurgence; France declared war on Spain and sent military as well as financial assistance; peace was finally achieved in October 1648

The 1648 **Peace of Westphalia** that ended the Thirty Years' War marked a turning point in European history. For the most part, conflicts fought over religious faith receded. The treaties recognized the independent authority of more than three hundred German princes (**Map 15.1**), reconfirming the emperor's severely limited authority. The Augsburg agreement of 1555 became permanent, adding Calvinism to Catholicism and Lutheranism as legally permissible creeds. The north German states remained Protestant, the south German states Catholic.

The Thirty Years' War was the most destructive event for the central European economy and society prior to the world wars of the twentieth century. Perhaps one-third of urban residents and two-fifths of the rural population died, leaving entire areas depopulated. Trade in southern German cities was virtually destroyed. Agricultural areas suffered catastrophically. Many small farmers lost their land, allowing nobles to enlarge their estates and consolidate their control.[1]

Peace of Westphalia

▶ The name of a series of treaties that concluded the Thirty Years' War in 1648 and marked the end of large-scale religious violence in Europe.

Achievements in State-Building

In the context of war and economic depression, seventeenth-century monarchs began to make new demands on their people. Across Europe, states sought to protect and expand their frontiers, raise new taxes, consolidate central control, and compete for new colonies in the New and Old Worlds.

Rulers encountered formidable obstacles in achieving these goals. Some were purely material. Without paved roads, telephones, or other modern technology, it took weeks to convey orders from the central government to the provinces. Rulers also suffered from lack of information about their realms, making it impossible to police and tax the population effectively. Local power structures presented another serious obstacle. Nobles, the church, provincial and national assemblies, town councils, guilds, and other bodies held legal privileges, which could not easily be rescinded. In some kingdoms many people spoke a language different from that of the Crown, further diminishing their willingness to obey its commands.

What explains the rise of absolutism in Prussia and Austria?

What were the distinctive features of Russian and Ottoman absolutism?

How and why did the constitutional state triumph in the Dutch Republic and England?

What was the baroque style in art and music, and where was it popular?

✓ LearningCurve
Check what you know.

449

MAP 15.1 ■ Europe After the Thirty Years' War

This map shows the political division of Europe after the Treaty of Westphalia (1648) ended the war. France emerged as the strongest power in Europe at the end of the Thirty Years' War. Based on this map, what challenges did the French state still face in dominating Europe after 1648? How does the map represent Swedish gains and Spanish losses in the Treaty of Westphalia?

Nonetheless, over the course of the seventeenth century, governments achieved new levels of central control. This increased authority focused on four areas in particular: greater taxation, growth in armed forces, larger and more efficient bureaucracies, and the increased ability to compel obedience from subjects. Over time, centralized power added up to something close to sovereignty. A state may be termed sovereign when it possesses a monopoly over the instruments of

CHAPTER LOCATOR | **What made the seventeenth century an "age of crisis"?** | Why did France rise and Spain fall during this period?

CHAPTER 15
450 ABSOLUTISM AND CONSTITUTIONALISM

justice and the use of force within clearly defined boundaries. In a sovereign state, no system of courts, such as church tribunals, competes with state courts in the dispensation of justice, and private armies, such as those of feudal lords, present no threat to central authority. While seventeenth-century states did not acquire total sovereignty, they made important strides toward that goal.

Warfare and the Growth of Army Size

The driving force of seventeenth-century state-building was warfare. In medieval times, feudal lords had raised armies only for particular wars or campaigns; now monarchs began to recruit their own forces and maintain permanent standing armies. Instead of serving their own interests, army officers were required to be loyal and obedient to those who commanded them. New techniques for training and deploying soldiers meant a rise in the professional standards of the army.

Along with professionalization came an explosive growth in army size. The French took the lead, with the army growing from roughly 125,000 men in the Thirty Years' War to 340,000 at the end of the seventeenth century.[2] Other European powers were quick to follow the French example. The rise of absolutism in central and eastern Europe led to a vast expansion in the size of armies. Great Britain followed a similar, albeit distinctive pattern. Instead of building a land army, the British focused on naval forces and eventually built the largest navy in the world.

Popular Political Action

As governments continuously raised taxes to meet the costs of war, neighborhood riots over the cost of bread turned into armed uprisings. Popular revolts were extremely common in England, France, Spain, Portugal, and Italy during the Thirty Years' War. In 1640, Philip IV of Spain faced revolt in Catalonia, the economic center of his realm. At the same time he struggled to put down uprisings in Portugal and in the northern provinces of the

The Professionalization of the Swedish Army

Swedish king Gustavus Adolphus, surrounded by his generals, gives thanks to God for the safe arrival of his troops in Germany during the Thirty Years' War. (Military Academy of Karlberg)

| What explains the rise of absolutism in Prussia and Austria? | What were the distinctive features of Russian and Ottoman absolutism? | How and why did the constitutional state triumph in the Dutch Republic and England? | What was the baroque style in art and music, and where was it popular? | ✔ LearningCurve Check what you know. |

Netherlands. In 1647, the city of Palermo, in Spanish-occupied Sicily, exploded in protest over food shortages caused by a series of bad harvests. From there, insurgency spread to the rest of the island and eventually to Naples on the mainland. Apart from affordable food, rebels demanded the suppression of extraordinary taxes and participation in municipal government. Some dreamed of a republic that would abolish noble tax exemptions. Despite initial successes, the revolt lacked unity and strong leadership, and it could not withstand the forces of the state.

In France, urban uprisings became a frequent aspect of the social and political landscape. Beginning in 1630 and continuing on and off through the early 1700s, major insurrections occurred at Dijon, Bordeaux (bor-DOH), Montpellier, Lyons, and Amiens. All were characterized by deep popular anger and violence directed at outside officials sent to collect taxes.

Municipal and royal authorities often struggled to overcome popular revolt. They feared that stern repressive measures, such as sending in troops to fire on crowds, would create martyrs and further inflame the situation; full-scale occupation of a city would be very expensive and would detract from military efforts elsewhere. The limitations of royal authority gave some leverage to rebels. To quell riots, royal edicts were sometimes suspended, prisoners released, and discussions initiated.

By the beginning of the eighteenth century, this leverage had largely disappeared. Municipal governments were better integrated into the national structure, and local authorities had prompt military support from the central government. People who publicly opposed royal policies and taxes received swift and severe punishment.

> ## QUICK REVIEW

What were the common crises and achievements of seventeenth-century European states?

Why did France rise and Spain fall in this period?

Spanish Troops The long wars that Spain fought over Dutch independence, in support of Habsburg interests in Germany, and against France left the country militarily exhausted and financially drained by the mid-seventeenth century. In this detail from a painting by Peeter Snayers, Spanish troops — thin, emaciated, and probably unpaid — straggle away from battle. (Prado, Madrid, Spain/Index/The Bridgeman Art Library)

KINGS IN ABSOLUTIST STATES asserted that they were responsible to God alone. They claimed exclusive power to make and enforce laws, denying any other institution or group the authority to check their power. France's Louis XIV is often seen as the epitome of an absolute monarch. In truth, his success relied on collaboration with nobles, and thus his example illustrates both the achievements and the compromises of absolutist rule.

As French power rose in the seventeenth century, the glory of Spain faded. Once the fabulous revenue from American silver declined, Spain's economic stagnation could no longer be disguised, and the country faltered under weak leadership.

The Foundations of Absolutism

Louis XIV's absolutism had long roots. In 1589, his grandfather Henry IV (r. 1589–1610), the founder of the Bourbon dynasty, acquired a devastated country. Civil wars between Protestants and Catholics had wracked France since 1561. Poor harvests had reduced peasants to starvation, and commercial activity had declined drastically. Henri le Grand (Henry the Great), as the king was called, inaugurated a remarkable recovery.

What explains the rise of absolutism in Prussia and Austria?

What were the distinctive features of Russian and Ottoman absolutism?

How and why did the constitutional state triumph in the Dutch Republic and England?

What was the baroque style in art and music, and where was it popular?

LearningCurve
Check what you know.

He did so by keeping France at peace during most of his reign. Although he had converted to Catholicism, he issued the Edict of Nantes, allowing Protestants the right to worship in 150 traditionally Protestant towns throughout France. He sharply lowered taxes and instead charged royal officials an annual fee to guarantee the right to pass their positions down to their heirs. He also improved the infrastructure of the country, building new roads and canals and repairing the ravages of years of civil war. Despite his efforts at peace, Henry was murdered in 1610 by a Catholic zealot, setting off a national crisis.

After the death of Henry IV, his wife, the queen-regent Marie de' Medici, headed the government for the nine-year-old Louis XIII (r. 1610–1643). In 1628 Armand Jean du Plessis—Cardinal Richelieu (1585–1642)—became first minister of the French crown. Richelieu's maneuvers allowed the monarchy to maintain power within Europe and within its own borders despite the turmoil of the Thirty Years' War.

Cardinal Richelieu's political genius is best reflected in the administrative system he established to strengthen royal control. He extended the use of intendants, commissioners for each of France's thirty-two districts who were appointed directly by the monarch, to whom they were solely responsible. As the intendants' power increased under Richelieu, so did the power of the centralized French state.

Under Richelieu, the French monarchy also acted to repress Protestantism. Louis personally supervised the siege of La Rochelle, an important port city and a major commercial center with strong ties to Protestant Holland and England. The fall of La Rochelle in 1628 was one step in the removal of Protestantism as a strong force in French life.

Richelieu did not aim to wipe out Protestantism in the rest of Europe, however. His main foreign policy goal was to destroy the Catholic Habsburgs' grip on territories that surrounded France. Consequently, Richelieu supported Habsburg enemies, including Protestants. For the French cardinal, interests of state outweighed religious considerations.

Richelieu's successor as chief minister for the next child-king, the four-year-old Louis XIV, was Cardinal Jules Mazarin (1602–1661). Along with the regent, Queen Mother Anne of Austria, Mazarin continued Richelieu's centralizing policies. His struggle to increase royal revenues to meet the costs of war led to the uprisings of 1648–1653 known as the **Fronde**. In Paris, magistrates of the Parlement of Paris, the nation's most important court, were outraged by the Crown's autocratic measures. These so-called robe nobles (named for the robes they wore in court) encouraged violent protest by the common people. During the first of several riots, the queen mother fled Paris with Louis XIV. As rebellion spread outside Paris and to the sword nobles (the traditional warrior nobility), civil order broke down completely. In 1651, Anne's regency ended with the declaration of Louis as king in his own right. Much of the rebellion died away, and its leaders came to terms with the government.

The violence of the Fronde had significant results for the future. The twin evils of noble rebellion and popular riots left the French wishing for peace and for a strong monarch to impose order. This was the legacy that Louis XIV inherited in 1661 when he assumed personal rule. Humiliated by his flight from Paris, he was determined to avoid any recurrence of rebellion.

Fronde

▶ A series of violent uprisings during the early reign of Louis XIV triggered by growing royal control and increased taxation.

CHAPTER LOCATOR | What made the seventeenth century an "age of crisis"? | **Why did France rise and Spain fall during this period?**

CHAPTER 15
454 ABSOLUTISM AND CONSTITUTIONALISM

Louis XIV and Absolutism

In the reign of Louis XIV (r. 1643–1715), the longest in European history, the French monarchy reached the peak of absolutist development. In the magnificence of his court and the brilliance of the culture that he presided over, Louis dominated his age. Religion, Anne, and Mazarin all taught Louis the doctrine of the divine right of kings: God had established kings as his rulers on earth, and they were answerable ultimately to him alone. To symbolize his central role in the divine order, when he was fifteen years old Louis danced at a court ballet dressed as the sun, thereby acquiring the title of the Sun King. (See "Picturing the Past: *Louis XIV, King of France and Navarre*, 1701.")

In addition to parading his power before the court, Louis worked very hard at the business of governing. He ruled his realm through several councils of state

Louis XIV, King of France and Navarre, 1701

This was one of Louis XIV's favorite portraits of himself. He liked it so much that he had many copies of the portrait made, in full and half-size format. (Louvre, Paris, France/Giraudon/The Bridgeman Art Library)

> PICTURING THE PAST

ANALYZING THE IMAGE: Why do you think the king liked the portrait so much? What image of the king does it present to the viewer? What details does the painter include, and what impression do they convey?

CONNECTIONS: How does this representation of royal power compare with the images of Peter the Great (page 466) and Charles I (page 473)? Which do you find the most impressive, and why?

| What explains the rise of absolutism in Prussia and Austria? | What were the distinctive features of Russian and Ottoman absolutism? | How and why did the constitutional state triumph in the Dutch Republic and England? | What was the baroque style in art and music, and where was it popular? | ☑ LearningCurve Check what you know. |

455

and insisted on taking a personal role in many of their decisions. He selected councilors from the recently ennobled or the upper middle class because he believed "that the public should know, from the rank of those whom I chose to serve me, that I had no intention of sharing power with them."[3]

Although personally tolerant, Louis hated division within the realm and insisted that religious unity was essential to his royal dignity and to the security of the state. He thus pursued the policy of Protestant repression launched by Richelieu. In 1685, Louis revoked the Edict of Nantes.

Despite his claims to absolute authority, multiple constraints existed on Louis's power. As a representative of divine power, he was obliged to rule in a manner consistent with virtue and benevolence. He had to uphold the laws issued by his royal predecessors. He also relied on the collaboration of nobles. Without their cooperation, it would have been impossible to extend his power throughout France or wage his many foreign wars. Louis's need to elicit noble cooperation led him to revolutionize court life at his spectacular palace at Versailles.

Life at Versailles

Throughout most of the seventeenth century, the French court had no fixed home, following the monarch to his numerous palaces and country residences. In 1682, Louis moved his court and government to the newly renovated palace at Versailles. The palace quickly became the center of political, social, and cultural life. The king required all great nobles to spend at least part of the year in attendance on him there, so he could keep an eye on their activities. Because he controlled the distribution of state power and wealth, nobles had no choice but to obey and compete with each other for his favor at Versailles. The glorious palace, with its sumptuous interiors and extensive formal gardens, was a mirror to the world of French glory, soon copied by would-be absolutist monarchs across Europe.

Louis further revolutionized court life by establishing an elaborate set of etiquette rituals to mark every moment of his day, from waking up and dressing in the morning to removing his clothing and retiring at night. Courtiers vied for the honor of participating in these ceremonies, with the highest in rank claiming the privilege of handing the king his shirt.

These rituals may seem absurd, but they were far from trivial. The king controlled immense resources and privileges; access to him meant favored treatment for government offices, military and religious posts, state pensions, honorary titles, and a host of other benefits. Courtiers sought these rewards for themselves and their family members and followers. A system of patronage—in which a higher-ranked individual protected a lower-ranked one in return for loyalty and services—flowed from the court to the provinces. Through this mechanism, Louis gained cooperation from powerful nobles.

Although they could not hold public offices or posts, women played a central role in the patronage system. At court, the king's wife, mistresses, and other female relatives recommended individuals for honors, advocated policy decisions, and brokered alliances between factions. Noblewomen played a similar role, bringing their family connections to marriage and thus forming powerful social networks.

Louis XIV was also an enthusiastic patron of the arts, commissioning many sculptures and paintings for Versailles as well as performances of dance and music. Louis XIV also loved the stage, and in the plays of Molière and Racine his

CHAPTER LOCATOR | What made the seventeenth century an "age of crisis"? | **Why did France rise and Spain fall during this period?**

456   CHAPTER 15
ABSOLUTISM AND CONSTITUTIONALISM

court witnessed the finest achievements in the history of the French theater. In this period, aristocratic ladies wrote many genres of literature and held salons in their Parisian mansions where they engaged in witty and cultured discussions of poetry, art, theater, and the latest worldly events.

With Versailles as the center of European politics, French culture grew in international prestige. French became the language of polite society and international diplomacy, gradually replacing Latin as the language of scholarship and learning. Royal courts across Europe spoke French, and the great aristocrats of Russia, Sweden, Germany, and elsewhere were often more fluent in French than in the tongues of their homelands. France inspired a cosmopolitan European culture in the late seventeenth century that looked to Versailles as its center.

French Financial Management Under Colbert

France's ability to build armies and fight wars depended on a strong economy. Fortunately for Louis, his controller general, Jean-Baptiste Colbert (1619–1683), proved to be a financial genius. Colbert's central principle was that the wealth and the economy of France should serve the state. To this end, from 1665 to his death in 1683, Colbert rigorously applied mercantilist policies to France.

Mercantilism is a collection of governmental policies for the regulation of economic activities by and for the state. It derives from the idea that a nation's international power is based on its wealth, specifically its supply of gold and silver. To accumulate wealth, a country always had to sell more goods abroad than it bought. To decrease the purchase of goods outside France, Colbert insisted that French industry should produce everything needed by the French people.

To increase exports, Colbert supported old industries and created new ones, focusing especially on textiles, which were the most important sector of the economy. Colbert enacted new production regulations, created guilds to boost quality standards, and encouraged foreign craftsmen to emigrate to France. To encourage the purchase of French goods, he abolished many domestic tariffs and raised tariffs on foreign products. In 1664, Colbert founded the Company of the East Indies with (unfulfilled) hopes of competing with the Dutch for Asian trade. He also hoped to make Canada—rich in untapped minerals and some of the best agricultural land in the world—part of a vast French empire. With this in mind, he sent four thousand colonists to Quebec.

During Colbert's tenure as controller general, Louis was able to pursue his goals without massive tax increases and without creating a stream of new offices. The constant pressure of warfare after Colbert's death, however, undid many of his economic achievements.

mercantilism
▶ A system of economic regulations aimed at increasing the power of the state based on the belief that a nation's international power was based on its wealth, specifically its supply of gold and silver.

Louis XIV's Wars

Louis XIV kept France at war for thirty-three of the fifty-four years of his personal rule. François le Tellier, marquis de Louvois, Louis's secretary of state for war, created a professional army in which the French state, rather than private nobles, employed the soldiers. Uniforms and weapons were standardized, and a rational system of training and promotion was devised. As in so many other matters, his model was followed across Europe.

| What explains the rise of absolutism in Prussia and Austria? | What were the distinctive features of Russian and Ottoman absolutism? | How and why did the constitutional state triumph in the Dutch Republic and England? | What was the baroque style in art and music, and where was it popular? | ✓ LearningCurve Check what you know. |

457

The Acquisitions of Louis XIV, 1668–1713

Territory gained
☐ 1668
■ 1678
▨ 1713

FRANCE
FRANCHE-COMTÉ
•Paris

Peace of Utrecht

▶ A series of treaties, from 1713 to 1715, that ended the War of the Spanish Succession, ended French expansion in Europe, and marked the rise of the British Empire.

Louis's goal was to expand France to what he considered its natural borders. His armies managed to extend French borders to include important commercial centers in the Spanish Netherlands and Flanders as well as the entire province of Franche-Comté between 1667 and 1678. In 1681, Louis seized the city of Strasbourg, and three years later he sent his armies into the province of Lorraine. At that moment the king seemed invincible. In fact, Louis had reached the limit of his expansion. The wars of the 1680s and 1690s brought no additional territories but placed unbearable strains on French resources. Colbert's successors resorted to desperate measures to finance these wars, including devaluation of the currency and new taxes.

Louis's last war was endured by a French people suffering high taxes, crop failure, and widespread malnutrition and death. In 1700, the childless Spanish king Charles II (r. 1665–1700) died, opening a struggle for control of Spain and its colonies. His will bequeathed the Spanish crown and its empire to Philip of Anjou, Louis XIV's grandson (Louis's wife, Maria-Theresa, was Charles's sister). The will violated a prior treaty by which the European powers had agreed to divide the Spanish possessions between the king of France and the Holy Roman emperor, both brothers-in-law of Charles II. Claiming that he was following both Spanish and French interests, Louis broke with the treaty and accepted the will, thereby triggering the War of the Spanish Succession (1701–1713).

In 1701, the English, Dutch, Austrians, and Prussians formed the Grand Alliance against Louis XIV. War dragged on until 1713. The **Peace of Utrecht**, which ended the war, allowed Louis's grandson Philip to remain king of Spain on the understanding that the French and Spanish crowns would never be united. France surrendered Newfoundland, Nova Scotia, and the Hudson Bay territory to England, which also acquired Gibraltar, Minorca, and control of the African slave trade from Spain (**Map 15.2**).

The Peace of Utrecht represented the balance-of-power principle in operation, setting limits on the extent to which any one power—in this case, France—could expand. It also marked the end of French expansion. Thirty-five years of war had given France the rights to all of Alsace and some commercial centers in the north. But at what price? In 1714, an exhausted France hovered on the brink of bankruptcy. It is no wonder that, when Louis XIV died on September 1, 1715, many subjects felt as much relief as they did sorrow.

The Decline of Absolutist Spain in the Seventeenth Century

By the early seventeenth century, the seeds of Spanish disaster were sprouting. Between 1610 and 1650, Spanish trade with the colonies in the New World fell 60 percent due to competition from local industries in the colonies and from Dutch and English traders. At the same time, the native Indian and African slaves who toiled in the South American silver mines suffered frightful epidemics of disease. Ultimately, the mines that filled the empire's treasury started to run dry, and the quantity of metal produced steadily declined after 1620.

In Madrid, however, royal expenditures constantly exceeded income. To meet mountainous state debt, the Crown repeatedly devalued the coinage and declared bankruptcy, which resulted in the collapse of national credit. Meanwhile, manu-

CHAPTER LOCATOR | What made the seventeenth century an "age of crisis"? | Why did France rise and Spain fall during this period?

458 CHAPTER 15 ABSOLUTISM AND CONSTITUTIONALISM

North America, 1714

HUDSON'S BAY COMPANY

Newfoundland

QUEBEC

NEW FRANCE

NOVA SCOTIA

THIRTEEN COLONIES

LOUISIANA

SP. FLORIDA

Claims
British
French
Spanish

0   100   200 miles
0   100   200 kilometers

NORWAY

SCOTLAND
Edinburgh

North Sea

KINGDOM OF DENMARK

Oslo

SWEDEN

Baltic Sea

RUSSIAN EMPIRE

Moscow

Riga

LITHUANIA

Dnieper R.

Smolensk

GREAT BRITAIN
Dublin
IRELAND

Copenhagen

ENGLAND

UNITED NETHERLANDS

London

Utrecht

HANOVER

BRANDENBURG-PRUSSIA

EAST PRUSSIA

POLAND

Berlin

Warsaw

Vistula R.

ATLANTIC OCEAN

Paris

LORRAINE PALATINATE

Strasbourg

ALSACE

FRANCE

Seine R.

Rhine R.

SAXONY

HOLY ROMAN EMPIRE

SILESIA

Oder R.

Kiev

UKRAINE

BOHEMIA

Danube R.

AUSTRIA

BAVARIA

Vienna

Dniester R.

MOLDAVIA

SWITZERLAND

Toulouse

Garonne R.

SAVOY

MILAN

MODENA

GENOA

TUSCANY

REPUBLIC OF VENICE

Buda Pest

HUNGARY

TRANSYLVANIA

CROATIA

SLAVONIA

Belgrade

WALLACHIA

BOSNIA

SERBIA

Danube R.

HERZEGOVINA

Marseilles

PORTUGAL

SPAIN

Duero R.

Ebro R.

Tagus R.

Madrid

Lisbon

CATALONIA

Corsica (Genoa)

PAPAL STATES

Rome

MONTENEGRO

BULGARIA

Constantinople

Balearic Is.

Minorca (Gr. Br.)

Sardinia (Austria)

Naples

KINGDOM OF NAPLES

ALBANIA

OTTOMAN EMPIRE

Adriatic Sea

GIBRALTAR (Gr. Br.)

Mediterranean Sea

Sicily (Savoy)

GREECE

MAP 15.2 ■ Europe After the Peace of Utrecht, 1715

The series of treaties commonly called the Peace of Utrecht ended the War of the Spanish Succession and redrew the map of Europe. A French Bourbon king succeeded to the Spanish throne. France surrendered the Spanish Netherlands (later Belgium), then in French hands, to Austria, and recognized the Hohenzollern rulers of Prussia. Spain ceded Gibraltar to Great Britain, for which it has been a strategic naval station ever since. Spain also granted Britain the *asiento*, the contract for supplying African slaves to the Americas.

> **MAPPING THE PAST**

ANALYZING THE MAP: Identify the areas on the map that changed hands as a result of the Peace of Utrecht. How did these changes affect the balance of power in Europe?

CONNECTIONS: How and why did so many European countries possess scattered or noncontiguous territories? What does this suggest about European politics in this period? Does this map suggest potential for future conflict?

facturing and commerce shrank. In contrast to the other countries of western Europe, Spain had a tiny middle class. To make matters worse, the Crown expelled some three hundred thousand *Moriscos*, or former Muslims, in 1609, significantly reducing the pool of skilled workers and merchants. Those working in the textile industry were forced out of business by steep inflation that pushed their production costs to the point where they could not compete in colonial and international markets.[4]

| What explains the rise of absolutism in Prussia and Austria? | What were the distinctive features of Russian and Ottoman absolutism? | How and why did the constitutional state triumph in the Dutch Republic and England? | What was the baroque style in art and music, and where was it popular? | ✓ LearningCurve Check what you know. |

Spanish aristocrats, attempting to maintain an extravagant lifestyle they could no longer afford, increased the rents on their estates. High rents and heavy taxes in turn drove the peasants from the land, leading to a decline in agricultural productivity. In cities, wages and production stagnated. Spain also ignored new scientific methods that might have improved agricultural and manufacturing techniques because they came from the heretical nations of Holland and England.

The Spanish crown had no solutions to these dire problems. Philip III (r. 1598–1621) handed the running of the government to the duke of Lerma, who used it to advance his personal and familial wealth. Philip IV (r. 1621–1665) left the management of his several kingdoms to Gaspar de Guzmán, Count-Duke of Olivares. Olivares was an able administrator who has often been compared to Richelieu. He succeeded in devising new sources of revenue but clung to the grandiose belief that the solution to Spain's difficulties rested in a return to the imperial tradition of the sixteenth century. Unfortunately, the imperial tradition demanded the revival of war with the Dutch at the expiration of a twelve-year truce in 1622 and a long war with France over Mantua (1628–1659). Spain thus became embroiled in the Thirty Years' War. These conflicts, on top of an empty treasury, brought disaster.

Spain's situation worsened with internal conflicts and fresh military defeats through the remainder of the seventeenth century. In 1640, Spain faced serious revolts in Catalonia and Portugal. In 1643, the French inflicted a crushing defeat on a Spanish army at Rocroi in what is now Belgium. By the Treaty of the Pyrénées of 1659, which ended the French-Spanish conflict, Spain was compelled to surrender extensive territories to France. In 1688, the Spanish crown reluctantly recognized the independence of Portugal, almost a century after the two crowns were joined. The era of Spanish dominance in Europe had ended.

> QUICK REVIEW

What factors led to the rise of the French absolutist state under Louis XIV, and why did absolutist Spain experience decline in the same period?

CHAPTER LOCATOR | What made the seventeenth century an "age of crisis"? | Why did France rise and Spain fall during this period?

CHAPTER 15
460 ABSOLUTISM AND CONSTITUTIONALISM

What explains the rise of absolutism in Prussia and Austria?

A Prussian Giant Grenadier

Frederick William I wanted tall, handsome soldiers. He dressed them in tight, bright uniforms to distinguish them from the peasant population from which most soldiers came. He also ordered several portraits of his favorites, such as this one, from his court painter, J. C. Merk. Grenadiers (greh-nuh-DEERZ) wore the miter cap instead of an ordinary hat so that they could hurl their heavy grenades unimpeded by a broad brim. (Portrait of Grenadier James Kirkland, Irish member of the Potsdamer Riesengarde (giant guards of Potsdam), c.1718, Merk, Johann Christof (fl.1714) / Deutsches Historisches Museum, Berlin, Germany/© DHM/The Bridgeman Art Library)

THE RULERS OF EASTERN EUROPE also labored to build strong absolutist states in the seventeenth century. But they built on social and economic foundations far different from those in western Europe, namely, serfdom and the strong nobility who benefited from it. The most successful states were Austria and Prussia, which witnessed the rise of absolutism between 1620 and 1740.

| What explains the rise of absolutism in Prussia and Austria? | What were the distinctive features of Russian and Ottoman absolutism? | How and why did the constitutional state triumph in the Dutch Republic and England? | What was the baroque style in art and music, and where was it popular? | ✔ LearningCurve Check what you know. |

The Return of Serfdom in the East

While economic and social hardship was common across Europe, important differences existed between east and west. In the west, the demographic losses of the Black Death allowed peasants to escape from serfdom as they acquired enough land to feed themselves. In eastern Europe, seventeenth-century peasants had largely lost their ability to own land independently. Eastern lords dealt with the labor shortages caused by the Black Death by restricting the right of their peasants to move and thus take advantage of better opportunities elsewhere. Lords steadily took more and more of their peasants' land and arbitrarily imposed heavier labor obligations.

The gradual erosion of the peasantry's economic position was bound up with manipulation of the legal system. The local lord was also the local prosecutor, judge, and jailer. There were no independent royal officials to provide justice or uphold the common law. The power of the lord reached far into serfs' everyday lives. Not only was their freedom of movement restricted but they were also required permission to marry or could be forced to marry. Lords could reallocate the lands worked by their serfs at will or sell serfs apart from their families.

Between 1500 and 1650, the consolidation of serfdom in eastern Europe was accompanied by the growth of commercial agriculture, particularly in Poland and eastern Germany. As economic expansion and population growth resumed after 1500, eastern lords increased the production of their estates by squeezing sizable surpluses out of the impoverished peasants. They then sold these surpluses to foreign merchants, who exported them to the growing cities of wealthier western Europe.

It was not only the peasants who suffered in eastern Europe. With the approval of kings, landlords systematically undermined the medieval privileges of the towns and the power of the urban classes. Instead of selling products to local merchants, landlords sold directly to foreigners, bypassing local towns. The population of the towns and the urban middle classes declined greatly. This development both reflected and promoted the supremacy of noble landlords in most of eastern Europe in the sixteenth century.

The Austrian Habsburgs

Like all of central Europe, the Habsburgs emerged from the Thirty Years' War impoverished and exhausted. Their efforts to destroy Protestantism in the German lands and to turn the weak Holy Roman Empire into a real state had failed. Although the Habsburgs remained the hereditary emperors, real power lay in the hands of a bewildering variety of separate political jurisdictions. Defeat in central Europe encouraged the Habsburgs to turn away from a quest for imperial dominance and to focus inward and eastward in an attempt to unify their diverse holdings.

Habsburg victory over Bohemia during the Thirty Years' War was an important step in this direction. Ferdinand II (r. 1619–1637) drastically reduced the power of the Bohemian Estates, the largely Protestant representative assembly. He also confiscated the landholdings of Protestant nobles and gave them to loyal Catholic nobles and to the foreign aristocratic mercenaries who led his armies. After 1650, a large portion of the Bohemian nobility was of recent origin and owed its success to the Habsburgs.

CHAPTER LOCATOR | What made the seventeenth century an "age of crisis"? | Why did France rise and Spain fall during this period?

CHAPTER 15
462 ABSOLUTISM AND CONSTITUTIONALISM

With the support of this new nobility, the Habsburgs established direct rule over Bohemia. Under their rule, the condition of the enserfed peasantry worsened substantially. Protestantism was also stamped out. These changes were important steps in creating absolutist rule in Bohemia.

Ferdinand III (r. 1637–1657) continued to build state power. He centralized the government in the empire's German-speaking provinces, which formed the core Habsburg holdings. For the first time, a permanent standing army was ready to put down any internal opposition. The Habsburg monarchy then turned east toward the plains of Hungary, which had been divided between the Ottomans and the Habsburgs in the early sixteenth century. Between 1683 and 1699, the Habsburgs pushed the Ottomans from most of Hungary and Transylvania. The recovery of all the former kingdom of Hungary was completed in 1718.

The Hungarian nobility, despite its reduced strength, effectively thwarted the full development of Habsburg absolutism. Throughout the seventeenth century, Hungarian nobles rose in revolt against attempts to impose absolute rule. They never triumphed decisively but neither were they crushed the way the nobility in Bohemia had been in 1620. In 1703, with the Habsburgs bogged down in the War of the Spanish Succession, the Hungarians rose in one last patriotic rebellion under Prince Francis Rákóczy. The prince and his forces were eventually defeated, but the Habsburgs agreed to restore many of the traditional privileges of the aristocracy in return for Hungarian acceptance of hereditary Habsburg rule. Thus Hungary, unlike Austria and Bohemia, was never fully integrated into a centralized, absolute Habsburg state.

Despite checks on their ambitions in Hungary, the Habsburgs made significant achievements in state-building elsewhere by forging consensus with the church and the nobility. A sense of common identity and loyalty to the monarchy grew among elites in Habsburg lands, even to a certain extent in Hungary. German became the language of the state, and Catholicism helped fuse a collective identity.

Prussia in the Seventeenth Century

In the fifteenth and sixteenth centuries, the Hohenzollern family had ruled parts of eastern Germany as the imperial electors of Brandenburg and the dukes of Prussia. When he came to power in 1640, twenty-year-old Frederick William, later known as the Great Elector, was determined to unify his three provinces and enlarge his holdings. These provinces were Brandenburg; Prussia, inherited in 1618; and scattered territories along the Rhine inherited in 1614 (**Map 15.3**). Each had its own estates. Although the estates had not met regularly during the chaotic Thirty Years' War, taxes could not be levied without their consent. The estates of Brandenburg and Prussia were dominated by the nobility and the landowning classes, known as the **Junkers**.

Frederick William profited from ongoing European war and the threat of invasion from Russia when he argued for the need for a permanent standing army. In 1660, he persuaded Junkers in the estates to accept taxation without consent in order to fund an army. They agreed to do so in exchange for reconfirmation of their own privileges, including authority over the serfs. Having won over the Junkers, the king crushed potential opposition to his power from the towns. One

Junkers

▶ The nobility of Brandenburg and Prussia, they were reluctant allies of Frederick William in his consolidation of the Prussian state.

| What explains the rise of absolutism in Prussia and Austria? | What were the distinctive features of Russian and Ottoman absolutism? | How and why did the constitutional state triumph in the Dutch Republic and England? | What was the baroque style in art and music, and where was it popular? | ☑ LearningCurve Check what you know. |

463

MAP 15.3 ■ The Growth of Austria and Brandenburg-Prussia to 1748

Austria expanded to the southwest into Hungary and Transylvania at the expense of the Ottoman Empire. It was unable to hold the rich German province of Silesia, however, which was conquered by Brandenburg-Prussia.

by one, Prussian cities were eliminated from the estates and subjected to new taxes on goods and services. Thereafter, the estates' power declined rapidly because the Great Elector had both financial independence and superior force.

During his reign, Frederick William tripled state revenue and expanded the army drastically. In 1688, a population of 1 million supported a peacetime standing army of 30,000. In 1701, the elector's son, Frederick I, received the elevated title of king of Prussia (instead of elector) as a reward for aiding the Holy Roman emperor in the War of the Spanish Succession.

The Consolidation of Prussian Absolutism

Frederick William I, the Soldiers' King (r. 1713–1740), completed his grandfather's work, eliminating the last traces of parliamentary estates and local self-government. He established true Prussian absolutism and transformed Prussia into a military

CHAPTER LOCATOR | What made the seventeenth century an "age of crisis"? | Why did France rise and Spain fall during this period?

state. Frederick William was intensely attached to military life. He always wore an army uniform, and he lived the highly disciplined life of the professional soldier.

Penny-pinching and hard-working, Frederick William achieved results. The king and his ministers built an exceptionally honest and conscientious bureaucracy to administer the country and foster economic development. Twelfth in Europe in population, Prussia had the fourth-largest army by 1740. The Prussian army was the best in Europe, astonishing foreign observers with its precision, skill, and discipline.

Nevertheless, Prussians paid a heavy and lasting price for the obsessions of their royal drillmaster. Army expansion was achieved in part through forced conscription, which was declared lifelong in 1713. Desperate draftees fled the country or injured themselves to avoid service. Finally, in 1733, Frederick William I ordered that all Prussian men would undergo military training and serve as reservists in the army, allowing him to preserve both agricultural production and army size. To appease the Junkers, the king enlisted them to lead his growing army. The proud nobility thus commanded the peasantry in the army as well as on the estates.

With all men harnessed to the war machine, Prussian civil society became rigid and highly disciplined. As a Prussian minister later summed up, "To keep quiet is the first civic duty."[5] Thus the policies of Frederick William I, combined with harsh peasant bondage and Junker tyranny, laid the foundations for a highly militaristic country.

QUICK REVIEW <

What were the social conditions of eastern Europe, and how did the rulers of Austria and Prussia transform their nations into powerful absolutist monarchies?

| What explains the rise of absolutism in Prussia and Austria? | What were the distinctive features of Russian and Ottoman absolutism? | How and why did the constitutional state triumph in the Dutch Republic and England? | What was the baroque style in art and music, and where was it popular? | ✓ LearningCurve Check what you know. |

465

What were the distinctive features of Russian and Ottoman absolutism?

Peter the Great This compelling portrait by Grigory Musikiysky captures the strength and determination of the warrior-tsar in 1723, after more than three decades of personal rule. In his hand Peter holds the scepter, symbol of royal sovereignty, and across his breastplate is draped an ermine fur, a mark of honor. In the background are the battleships of Russia's new Baltic fleet and the famous St. Peter and St. Paul Fortress that Peter built in St. Petersburg. (Hermitage/St. Petersburg, Russia/ Bridgeman Art Library)

A FAVORITE PARLOR GAME of nineteenth-century intellectuals was debating whether Russia was a Western (European) or non-Western (Asian) society. This question was particularly fascinating because it was unanswerable. To this day, Russia differs from the West in some fundamental ways, though its history has paralleled that of the West in other aspects.

There was no question in the minds of Europeans, however, that the Ottomans were outsiders. Even absolutist rulers disdained Ottoman sultans as cruel and tyrannical despots. Despite stereotypes, however, the Ottoman Empire was in many ways more tolerant than its Western counterparts, providing protection and security to other religions while steadfastly maintaining the Muslim faith. Flexibility and openness to other ideas and practices were sources of strength for the empire.

The Mongol Yoke and the Rise of Moscow

The two-hundred-year period of rule by the Mongol khan (king) set the stage for the rise of absolutist Russia. The Mongols, a group of nomadic tribes from present-day Mongolia, established an empire that, at its height, stretched from Korea to

CHAPTER LOCATOR | What made the seventeenth century an "age of crisis"? | Why did France rise and Spain fall during this period?

466 CHAPTER 15 ABSOLUTISM AND CONSTITUTIONALISM

eastern Europe. In the thirteenth century the Mongols conquered the Slavic princes and forced them to pay tribute. The princes of Moscow became particularly adept at serving the Mongols. Ivan III (r. 1462–1505), known as Ivan the Great, successfully expanded the principality of Moscow toward the Baltic Sea.

By 1480, Ivan III was strong enough to defy Mongol control and declare the autonomy of Moscow. To legitimize their new position, the princes of Moscow modeled themselves on the Mongol khans. Like the khans, the Muscovite state forced weaker Slavic principalities to render tribute previously paid to Mongols and borrowed Mongol institutions such as the tax system, postal routes, and census. Loyalty from the highest-ranking nobles, or **boyars**, helped the Muscovite princes consolidate their power.

Another source of legitimacy for Moscow was its claim to the political and religious legacy of the Byzantine Empire. After the fall of Constantinople to the Turks in 1453, the princes of Moscow saw themselves as the heirs of both the caesars (or emperors) and Orthodox Christianity.

boyars

▸ The highest-ranking members of the Russian nobility.

The Tsar and His People

Developments in Russia took a chaotic turn with the reign of Ivan IV (r. 1533–1584), the famous Ivan the Terrible. Ivan's reign was successful in defeating the remnants of Mongol power; adding vast new territories to the realm; and laying the foundations for the huge, multiethnic Russian empire. After the sudden death of his wife, however, Ivan began a campaign of persecution against those he suspected of opposing him. He executed members of leading boyar families, along with their families, friends, servants, and peasants. To replace them, Ivan created a new service nobility, whose loyalty was guaranteed by their dependence on the state for land and titles.

As landlords demanded more from the serfs who survived the persecutions, growing numbers of peasants fled toward wild, recently conquered territories to the east and south. There they joined free groups and warrior bands known as **Cossacks**. Ivan responded by tying peasants more firmly to the land and to noble landholders. Simultaneously, he ordered that urban dwellers be bound to their towns and jobs so that he could tax them more heavily. These restrictions checked the growth of the Russian middle classes and stood in sharp contrast to economic and social developments in western Europe.

After the death of Ivan and his successor, Russia entered a chaotic period known as the Time of Troubles (1598–1613). While Ivan's relatives struggled for power, ordinary people suffered drought, crop failure, and plague. The Cossacks and peasants rebelled against nobles and officials, demanding fair treatment. This social explosion from below brought the nobles, big and small, together. They crushed the Cossack rebellion and brought Ivan's sixteen-year-old grandnephew, Michael Romanov, to the throne (r. 1613–1645).

Although the new tsar successfully reconsolidated central authority, he and his successors did not improve the lot of the common people. In 1649, a law extended serfdom to all peasants in the realm, giving lords unrestricted rights over their serfs and establishing penalties for harboring runaways. Social and religious uprisings among the poor and oppressed continued through the seventeenth century.

Moscow, ca. 1300
Gains by 1505
Gains by 1584
Gains by 1725
Major battle

The Expansion of Russia to 1725

Cossacks

▸ Free groups and outlaw armies originally comprising runaway peasants living on the borders of Russian territory from the fourteenth century onward. By the end of the sixteenth century, they had formed an alliance with the Russian state.

What explains the rise of absolutism in Prussia and Austria?

What were the distinctive features of Russian and Ottoman absolutism?

How and why did the constitutional state triumph in the Dutch Republic and England?

What was the baroque style in art and music, and where was it popular?

✓ LearningCurve
Check what you know.

467

Despite the turbulence of the period, the Romanov tsars, like their Western counterparts, made several important achievements during the second half of the seventeenth century. After a long war, Russia gained land in Ukraine from Poland in 1667 and completed the conquest of Siberia by the end of the century. Territorial expansion was accompanied by growth of the bureaucracy and the army. The tsars employed foreign experts to reform the Russian army, and they enlisted Cossack warriors to fight Siberian campaigns. Russian imperialist expansion to the east paralleled the Western powers' exploration and conquest of the Atlantic world in the same period.

The Reforms of Peter the Great

Heir to Romanov efforts at state-building, Peter the Great (r. 1682–1725) embarked on a tremendous campaign to accelerate and complete these processes. Fascinated by weapons and foreign technology and eager to gain support against the Ottoman Empire, the tsar led a group of 250 Russian officials and young nobles on a tour of western European capitals. Peter met with foreign kings, toured the sites, and learned shipbuilding and other technical skills from local artisans and experts. He was particularly impressed with the growing economic power of the Dutch and the English, and he considered how Russia could profit from their example.

Returning to Russia, Peter entered into a secret alliance with Denmark and Poland to wage a sudden war of aggression against Sweden, with the goal of securing access to the Baltic Sea and opportunities for westward expansion. Eighteen-year-old Charles XII of Sweden (1697–1718), however, surprised Peter. He defeated Denmark quickly in 1700, then turned on Russia. His well-trained professional army attacked and routed unsuspecting Russians besieging the Swedish fortress of Narva on the Baltic coast. It was, for the Russians, a grim beginning to the long and brutal Great Northern War, which lasted from 1700 to 1721.

Peter responded to this defeat with measures designed to increase state power, strengthen his armies, and gain victory. He required all nobles to serve in the army or in the civil administration—for life. A more modern army and government required skilled experts, so Peter created new schools and universities and required every young nobleman to spend five years in education away from home. Peter established an interlocking military-civilian bureaucracy with fourteen ranks, and he decreed that all had to start at the bottom and work toward the top. Drawing on his experience abroad, Peter sought talented foreigners and placed them in his service. These measures gradually combined to make the army and government more powerful and efficient.

Peter also greatly increased the service requirements of commoners. In the wake of the Narva disaster, he established a regular standing army of more than two hundred thousand peasant-soldiers, drafted for life and commanded by noble officers. He added an additional hundred thousand men in special regiments of Cossacks and foreign mercenaries. To fund the army, taxes on peasants increased threefold during Peter's reign. Serfs were also arbitrarily assigned to work in the growing number of factories and mines that supplied the military.

Peter's new war machine was able to crush the small army of Sweden in Ukraine at Poltava in 1709, one of the most significant battles in Russian history.

CHAPTER LOCATOR | What made the seventeenth century an "age of crisis"? | Why did France rise and Spain fall during this period?

CHAPTER 15
468 ABSOLUTISM AND CONSTITUTIONALISM

Saint Basil's Cathedral, Moscow

With its sloping roofs and colorful onion-shaped domes, Saint Basil's is a striking example of powerful Byzantine influences on Russian culture. According to tradition, an enchanted Ivan the Terrible blinded the cathedral's architects to ensure that they would never duplicate their fantastic achievement, which still dazzles the beholder in today's Red Square. (George Holton/Photo Researchers)

Russia's victory against Sweden was conclusive in 1721, and Estonia and present-day Latvia came under Russian rule for the first time. After his victory at Poltava, Peter channeled enormous resources into building St. Petersburg, a new Western-style capital on the Baltic to rival the great cities of Europe.

The government drafted twenty-five thousand to forty thousand men each summer to labor in St. Petersburg. Many of these laborers died from hunger, sickness, and accidents. Nobles were ordered to build costly palaces in St. Petersburg and to live in them most of the year. Merchants and artisans were required to settle and build in the new capital. The building of St. Petersburg was, in truth, an enormous direct tax levied on the wealthy, with the peasantry forced to do the manual labor.

There were other important consequences of Peter's reign. For Peter, modernization meant westernization, and both Westerners and Western ideas flowed into Russia for the first time. He required nobles to shave their heavy beards, wear Western clothing, and attend parties where young men and women would mix

What explains the rise of absolutism in Prussia and Austria?

What were the distinctive features of Russian and Ottoman absolutism?

How and why did the constitutional state triumph in the Dutch Republic and England?

What was the baroque style in art and music, and where was it popular?

☑ LearningCurve
Check what you know.

469

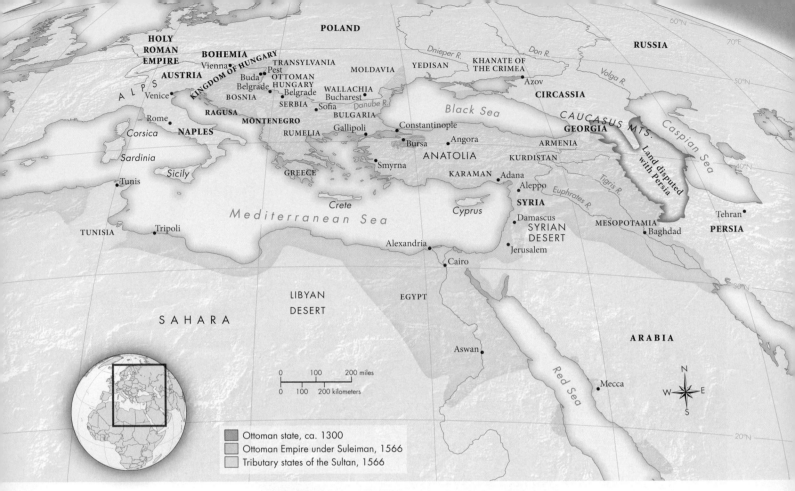

MAP 15.4 ■ The Ottoman Empire at Its Height, 1566

The Ottomans, like their great rivals the Habsburgs, rose to rule a vast dynastic empire encompassing many different peoples and ethnic groups. The army and the bureaucracy served to unite the disparate territories into a single state under an absolutist ruler.

together and freely choose their own spouses. From these efforts, a new elite class of Western-oriented Russians began to emerge.

Peter's reforms were unpopular with many Russians, nobles and serfs alike. Nonetheless, his modernizing and westernizing of Russia paved the way for it to move somewhat closer to the European mainstream in its thought and institutions during the Enlightenment, especially under Catherine the Great.

The Growth of the Ottoman Empire

The Ottomans came out of Central Asia as conquering warriors, settled in Anatolia (present-day Turkey), and, at their peak in the mid-sixteenth century, ruled one of the most powerful empires in the world (see Chapter 14). Their possessions stretched from western Persia across North Africa and into the heart of central Europe (**Map 15.4**).

The Ottoman Empire was built on a unique model of state and society. Agricultural land was the personal hereditary property of the **sultan**, and peasants paid taxes to use the land. Thus, there was an almost complete absence of private landed property and no hereditary nobility.

sultan

▶ The ruler of the Ottoman Empire; he owned all the agricultural land of the empire and was served by an army and bureaucracy composed of highly trained slaves.

CHAPTER LOCATOR | What made the seventeenth century an "age of crisis"? | Why did France rise and Spain fall during this period?

470 CHAPTER 15 ABSOLUTISM AND CONSTITUTIONALISM

The Ottomans also employed a distinctive form of government administration. The top ranks of the bureaucracy were staffed by the sultan's slave corps. Because Muslim law prohibited enslaving other Muslims, the sultan's agents purchased slaves along the borders of the empire. Within the realm, the sultan levied a "tax" of one thousand to three thousand male children on the conquered Christian populations in the Balkans every year. These young slaves were raised in Turkey as Muslims and were trained to fight and to administer. The most talented Ottoman slaves rose to the top of the bureaucracy, where they might acquire wealth and power. The less fortunate formed the core of the sultan's army, the **janissary corps**. These highly organized and efficient troops gave the Ottomans a formidable advantage in war with western Europeans. By 1683, service in the janissary corps had become so prestigious that the sultan ceased recruitment by force, and it became a volunteer army open to Christians and Muslims.

The Ottomans divided their subjects into religious communities, and each *millet*, or "nation," enjoyed autonomous self-government under its religious leaders. The Ottoman Empire recognized Orthodox Christians, Jews, Armenian Christians, and Muslims as distinct millets. The **millet system** created a powerful bond between the Ottoman ruling class and religious leaders, who supported the sultan's rule in return for extensive authority over their own communities.

Istanbul (known outside the empire by its original name, Constantinople) was the capital of the empire. The "old palace" was for the sultan's female family members. The newer Topkapi palace was where officials worked and young slaves trained for future administrative or military careers. Sultans married women of the highest social standing while keeping many concubines of low rank. To prevent the elite families into which they married from acquiring influence over the government, sultans procreated only with their concubines and not with official wives. They also adopted a policy of allowing each concubine to produce only one male heir. At a young age, each son went to govern a province of the empire accompanied by his mother. These practices were intended to stabilize power and prevent a recurrence of the civil wars of the late fourteenth and early fifteenth centuries.

Sultan Suleiman undid these policies when he boldly married his concubine, a former slave of Polish origin named Hürrem, and had several children with her. (See "Individuals in Society: Hürrem," page 472.) Starting with Suleiman, imperial wives began to take on more power. Marriages were arranged between sultans' daughters and high-ranking servants, creating powerful new members of the imperial household. Over time, the sultan's exclusive authority waned in favor of a more bureaucratic administration.

janissary corps
▶ The core of the sultan's army, composed of slave conscripts from non-Muslim parts of the empire; after 1683, it became a volunteer force.

millet system
▶ A system used by the Ottomans whereby subjects were divided into religious communities, with each millet (nation) enjoying autonomous self-government under its religious leaders.

QUICK REVIEW <

What were the commonalities and differences between the development of absolutism in the Russian and Ottoman Empires?

What explains the rise of absolutism in Prussia and Austria?

What were the distinctive features of Russian and Ottoman absolutism?

How and why did the constitutional state triumph in the Dutch Republic and England?

What was the baroque style in art and music, and where was it popular?

 LearningCurve
Check what you know.

I n Muslim culture, *harem* means a sacred place or a sanctuary. The term was applied to the part of the household occupied by women and children and forbidden to men outside the family. The most famous harem member in the history of Ottoman sultans was Hürrem, wife of Suleiman the Magnificent.

Like many of the sultan's concubines, Hürrem (1505?–1558) was of foreign birth. Tradition holds that she was born Aleksandra Lisowska in the kingdom of Poland (present-day Ukraine). Captured during a Tartar raid and enslaved, she entered the imperial harem between 1517 and 1520, when she was about fifteen years old. Reports from Venetian visitors claimed that she was not outstandingly beautiful but was possessed of wonderful grace, charm, and good humor, earning her the Turkish nickname Hürrem, or "joyful one." Soon after her arrival, Hürrem became the imperial favorite.

Suleiman's love for Hürrem led him to set aside all precedents for the role of a concubine, including the rule that concubines must cease having children once they gave birth to a male heir. By 1531, Hürrem had given Suleiman one daughter and five sons. In 1533 or 1534, Suleiman entered formal marriage with his consort — an unprecedented and scandalous honor for a concubine. Suleiman reportedly lavished attention on his wife and defied convention by allowing her to remain in the palace throughout her life instead of accompanying her son to a provincial governorship.

Contemporaries were shocked by Hürrem's influence over the sultan and resentful of the apparent role she played in politics and diplomacy. The Venetian ambassador Bassano wrote that "the Janissaries and the entire court hate her and her children likewise, but because the Sultan loves her, no one dares to speak."* Court rumors circulated that Hürrem used witchcraft to control the sultan and ordered the sultan's execution of his first-born son by another mother.

The correspondence between Suleiman and Hürrem, unavailable until the nineteenth century, along with Suleiman's own diaries, confirms her status as the sultan's most trusted confidant and adviser. During his frequent absences, the pair exchanged passionate love letters. Hürrem included political information and warned of potential uprisings. She also intervened in affairs between the empire and her former home, apparently helping Poland attain its privileged diplomatic status. She brought a feminine touch to diplomatic relations, sending personally embroidered articles to foreign leaders.

Hürrem used her enormous pension to contribute a mosque, two schools, a hospital, a fountain, and two public baths to Istanbul. In Jerusalem, Mecca, and Istanbul, she provided soup kitchens and hospices for pilgrims and the poor. She died in 1558, eight years before her husband. Her son Selim II (r. 1566–1574) inherited the throne.

Relying on Western observers' reports, historians traditionally depicted Hürrem as a manipulative and power-hungry social climber. They portrayed her career as the

Hürrem and her ladies in the harem. (Bibliothèque nationale de France)

beginning of a "sultanate of women" in which strong imperial leadership gave way to court intrigue and debauchery. More recent historians have emphasized the intelligence and courage Hürrem demonstrated in navigating the ruthlessly competitive world of the harem.

Hürrem's journey from Ukrainian maiden to concubine to sultan's wife captured enormous public attention. She is the subject of numerous paintings, plays, and novels, as well as an opera, a ballet, and a symphony by the composer Haydn. Interest in and suspicion of Hürrem continues. In 2003, a Turkish miniseries once more depicted her as a scheming intriguer.

QUESTIONS FOR ANALYSIS

1. What types of power did Hürrem exercise during her lifetime? How did her gender enable her to attain certain kinds of power and also constrain her ability to exercise it?
2. What can an exceptional woman like Hürrem reveal about the broader political and social world in which she lived?

Source: Leslie P. Pierce, *The Imperial Harem: Women and Sovereignty in the Ottoman Empire* (New York: Oxford University Press, 1993).

LaunchPad

ONLINE DOCUMENT PROJECT
What forces shaped Western views of Hürrem? Keeping the question above in mind, examine characterizations of Hürrem as seen through the eyes of a Habsburg diplomat, and then complete a writing assignment based on the evidence and details from this chapter. *See inside the front cover to learn more.*

* Quoted in Galina Yermolenko, "Roxolana: The Greatest Empresse of the East," *The Muslim World* 95 (2005): 235.

How and why did the constitutional state triumph in the Dutch Republic and England?

Van Dyck, *Charles I at the Hunt*, ca. 1635

Anthony Van Dyck was the greatest of Rubens's many students. In 1633, he became court painter to Charles I. This portrait of Charles just dismounted from a horse emphasizes the aristocratic bearing, elegance, and innate authority of the king. Van Dyck had a profound influence on portraiture in England and beyond; some scholars believe that this portrait influenced Rigaud's 1701 portrayal of Louis XIV (see page 455). (Louvre, Paris, France/Giraudon/The Bridgeman Art Library)

WHILE FRANCE, PRUSSIA, RUSSIA, AND AUSTRIA developed absolutist states, England and the Netherlands evolved toward **constitutionalism**, which is the limitation of government by law. Constitutionalism also implies a balance between the authority and power of the government, on the one hand, and the rights and liberties of the subjects, on the other. By definition, all constitutionalist governments have a constitution, be it written or unwritten.

Despite their common commitment to constitutional government, England and the Dutch Republic represented significantly different alternatives to absolute

constitutionalism
► A form of government in which power is limited by law and balanced between the authority and power of the government, on the one hand, and the rights and liberties of the subjects or citizens on the other hand; could include constitutional monarchies or republics.

What explains the rise of absolutism in Prussia and Austria?

What were the distinctive features of Russian and Ottoman absolutism?

How and why did the constitutional state triumph in the Dutch Republic and England?

What was the baroque style in art and music, and where was it popular?

☑ LearningCurve
Check what you know.

republicanism
▶ A form of government in which there is no monarch and power rests in the hands of the people as exercised through elected representatives.

rule. After decades of civil war and an experiment with **republicanism**, the English opted for a constitutional monarchy in 1688. This settlement retained a monarch as the titular head of government but vested sovereignty in an elected parliament. Upon gaining independence from Spain in 1648, the Dutch rejected monarchical rule, adopting a republican form of government in which elected estates held supreme power.

Absolutist Claims in England

In 1603, Queen Elizabeth's Scottish cousin James Stuart succeeded her as James I (r. 1603–1625). James was a firm believer in the divine right of kings. He went so far as to lecture the House of Commons: "There are no privileges and immunities which can stand against a divinely appointed King."[6] Such a view ran directly counter to English traditions that a person's property could not be taken away without due process of law. James I and his son Charles I (r. 1625–1649) considered such constraints intolerable and a threat to their divine-right prerogative. Consequently, bitter squabbles erupted between the Crown and the House of Commons. The expenses of England's intervention in the Thirty Years' War only exacerbated tensions. Charles I's response was to refuse to summon Parliament from 1629 onward.

Religious Divides and the English Civil War

Relations between the king and the House of Commons were also embittered by religious issues. In the early seventeenth century, growing numbers of English people felt dissatisfied with the Church of England established by Henry VIII (r. 1509–1547). Many **Puritans** believed that the Protestant Reformation of the sixteenth century had not gone far enough. They wanted to "purify" the Anglican Church of lingering Roman Catholic elements.

Puritans
▶ Members of a sixteenth- and seventeenth-century reform movement within the Church of England that advocated purifying it of Roman Catholic elements.

James I responded to such ideas by declaring, "No bishop, no king." For James, bishops were among the chief supporters of the throne. His son and successor, Charles I, further antagonized religious sentiments. Not only did he marry a Catholic princess, but he also supported the heavy-handed policies of the archbishop of Canterbury William Laud (1573–1645). In 1637, Laud attempted to impose two new elements on church organization in Scotland: a new prayer book, modeled on the Anglican *Book of Common Prayer*, and bishoprics. The Presbyterian Scots rejected these elements and revolted. To finance an army to put down the Scots, King Charles was compelled to call a meeting of Parliament in November 1640.

Charles had ruled from 1629 to 1640 without Parliament, financing his government through extraordinary stopgap levies considered illegal by most English people. Most members of Parliament were not willing to trust such a despotic king with an army. Many supported the Scots' resistance to Charles's religious innovations. Accordingly, this Parliament, called the "Long Parliament" because it sat from 1640 to 1660, enacted legislation that limited the power of the monarch and made government without Parliament impossible.

In 1641, the Commons passed the Triennial Act, which compelled the king to summon Parliament every three years. The Commons impeached Archbishop

CHAPTER LOCATOR | What made the seventeenth century an "age of crisis"? | Why did France rise and Spain fall during this period?

474 CHAPTER 15 ABSOLUTISM AND CONSTITUTIONALISM

Laud and then threatened to abolish bishops. King Charles, fearful of a Scottish invasion, reluctantly accepted these measures.

The next act in the conflict was precipitated by the outbreak of rebellion in Ireland, where English governors and landlords had long exploited the people. In 1641, the Catholic gentry of Ireland led an uprising in response to a feared invasion by anti-Catholic forces of the British Long Parliament.

Without an army, Charles I could neither come to terms with the Scots nor respond to the Irish rebellion. After a failed attempt to arrest parliamentary leaders, Charles left London for the north of England. There, he recruited an army drawn from the nobility and its cavalry staff, the rural gentry, and mercenaries. In response, Parliament formed its own army, the New Model Army, composed of the militia of the city of London and country squires with business connections.

The English civil war (1642–1649) pitted the king against Parliament. After three years of fighting, Parliament's New Model Army defeated the king's armies at the Battles of Naseby and Langport in the summer of 1645. Charles, though, refused to concede defeat. Both sides jockeyed for position, waiting for a decisive event, which arrived in the form of the army under the leadership of Oliver Cromwell, a member of the House of Commons and a devout Puritan. In 1647, Cromwell's forces captured the king and dismissed anti-Cromwell members of the Parliament. In 1649, the remaining representatives, known as the "Rump Parliament," put Charles on trial for high treason. Charles was found guilty and beheaded on January 30, 1649.

The English Civil War, 1642–1649

Cromwell and Puritanical Absolutism in England

With the execution of Charles, kingship was abolished. In its place, Oliver Cromwell and his supporters enshrined a commonwealth, or republican government, known as the **Protectorate**. Theoretically, legislative power rested in the surviving members of Parliament, and executive power was lodged in a council of state. In fact, the army controlled the government, and Oliver Cromwell controlled the army, ruling what was essentially a military dictatorship.

The fiction of republican government was maintained until 1655 when, after repeated disputes, Cromwell dismissed Parliament. Cromwell continued the standing army and proclaimed quasi-martial law. Reflecting Puritan ideas of morality, Cromwell's state forbade sports, closed the theaters, and rigorously censored the press.

Cromwell had long associated Catholicism in Ireland with sedition and heresy, and led an army there to reconquer the country in August 1649. In the wake of Cromwell's invasion, the English banned Catholicism in Ireland, executed priests, and confiscated land from Catholics for English and Scottish settlers. These brutal acts left a legacy of Irish hatred for England.

Cromwell adopted mercantilist policies similar to those of absolutist France. He enforced a Navigation Act (1651) requiring that English goods be transported on English ships. The act sparked a short but successful war with the commercially threatened Dutch. While mercantilist legislation ultimately benefited English commerce, for ordinary people, the turmoil of foreign war only added to the harsh conditions of life induced by years of civil war.

Protectorate

▶ The English military dictatorship (1653–1658) established by Oliver Cromwell following the execution of Charles I.

What explains the rise of absolutism in Prussia and Austria?

What were the distinctive features of Russian and Ottoman absolutism?

How and why did the constitutional state triumph in the Dutch Republic and England?

What was the baroque style in art and music, and where was it popular?

✔ LearningCurve
Check what you know.

"The Royall Oake of Brittayne"

The chopping down of this tree, as shown in a cartoon from 1649, signifies the end of royal authority, stability, and the rule of law. As pigs graze (representing the unconcerned common people), being fattened for slaughter, Oliver Cromwell, with his feet in Hell, quotes Scripture. This is a royalist view of the collapse of Charles I's government and the rule of Cromwell. (© The British Library Board, E.1052)

The Protectorate collapsed when Cromwell died in 1658 and his ineffectual son succeeded him. Fed up with military rule, the English longed for a return to civilian government and, with it, common law and social stability. By 1660, they were ready to restore the monarchy.

The Restoration of the English Monarchy

The Restoration of 1660 brought to the throne Charles II (r. 1660–1685). Both houses of Parliament were also restored, together with the established Anglican Church. The Restoration failed to resolve two serious problems, however. What was to be the attitude of the state toward Puritans, Catholics, and dissenters from the established church? And what was to be the relationship between the king and Parliament?

CHAPTER LOCATOR | What made the seventeenth century an "age of crisis"? | Why did France rise and Spain fall during this period?

To answer the first question, Parliament enacted the **Test Act** of 1673 against those outside the Church of England, denying them the right to vote, hold public office, preach, teach, attend the universities, or even assemble for meetings. But these restrictions could not be enforced.

In politics, Charles II's initial determination to work well with Parliament did not last long. Finding that Parliament did not grant him an adequate income, Charles entered into a secret agreement with his cousin Louis XIV in 1670. The French king would give Charles £200,000 annually, and in return Charles would relax the laws against Catholics, gradually re-Catholicize England, and convert to Catholicism himself. When the details of this treaty leaked out, a great wave of anti-Catholic sentiment swept England.

When Charles died and his Catholic brother James became king, the worst English anti-Catholic fears were realized. As king, James II (r. 1685–1688) was an active promoter of Catholicism and made no effort to hide his religious agenda. Attempting to broaden his base of support with Protestant dissenters and non-conformists, James granted religious freedom to all.

James's opponents, a powerful coalition of eminent persons in Parliament and the Church of England, offered the English throne to James's heir, his Protestant daughter Mary, and her Dutch husband, Prince William of Orange. In December 1688, James II, his queen, and their infant son fled to France. Early in 1689, William and Mary were crowned king and queen of England.

Constitutional Monarchy and Cabinet Government

The "Glorious Revolution" of 1688–1689 represented the final destruction of the idea of divine-right monarchy. The men who instigated the revolution framed their intentions in the Bill of Rights, which was formulated in direct response to Stuart absolutism. Law was to be made in Parliament; once made, it could not be suspended by the Crown. Parliament had to be called at least once every three years. The independence of the judiciary was established, and there was to be no standing army in peacetime. Significant legal restrictions were imposed on Catholics. William and Mary accepted these principles when they took the throne, and the House of Parliament passed the Bill of Rights in December 1689.

The Glorious Revolution and the concept of representative government found its best defense in political philosopher John Locke's *Second Treatise of Civil Government* (1690). Locke (1632–1704) maintained that a government that oversteps its proper function—protecting the natural rights of life, liberty, and property—becomes a tyranny. Under a tyrannical government, the people have the natural right to rebellion.

During the course of the eighteenth century, the cabinet system of government evolved. In a cabinet system, the leading ministers, who must have seats in and the support of a majority of the House of Commons, formulate common policy and conduct the business of the country. During the administration of one royal minister, Sir Robert Walpole, who led the cabinet from 1721 to 1742, the idea developed that the cabinet was responsible to the House of Commons. In the English cabinet system, both legislative power and executive power are held by the leading ministers, who form the government.

Test Act

► Legislation, passed by the English Parliament in 1673, to secure the position of the Anglican Church by stripping Puritans, Catholics, and other dissenters of the right to vote, preach, assemble, hold public office, and teach at or attend the universities.

What explains the rise of absolutism in Prussia and Austria?

What were the distinctive features of Russian and Ottoman absolutism?

How and why did the constitutional state triumph in the Dutch Republic and England?

What was the baroque style in art and music, and where was it popular?

LearningCurve
Check what you know.

477

The Dutch Republic in the Seventeenth Century

In the late sixteenth century, the seven northern provinces of the Netherlands fought for and won their independence from Spain. The independence of the Republic of the United Provinces of the Netherlands was recognized in 1648 in the treaty that ended the Thirty Years' War. In this period, often called the "golden age of the Netherlands," Dutch ideas and attitudes played a profound role in shaping a new and modern worldview. At the same time, the United Provinces developed its own distinctive model of a constitutional state.

Jan Steen, *The Merry Family*, 1668

In this painting from the Dutch golden age, a happy family enjoys a boisterous song while seated around the dining table. Despite its carefree appearance, the painting was intended to teach a moral lesson. The children are shown drinking wine and smoking, bad habits they have learned from their parents. The inscription hanging over the mantelpiece (upper right) spells out the message clearly: "As the Old Sing, so Pipe the Young." (Album/Art Resource, NY)

CHAPTER LOCATOR | What made the seventeenth century an "age of crisis"? | Why did France rise and Spain fall during this period?

The Dutch established a republic, a state in which power rested in the hands of the people and was exercised through elected representatives. An oligarchy of wealthy businessmen called regents handled domestic affairs in each province's Estates (assemblies). The provincial Estates held almost all the power. A federal assembly, or States General, handled foreign affairs and war, but it did not possess sovereign authority. Holland, the province with the largest navy and the most wealth, usually dominated the republic and the States General.

In each province, the Estates appointed an executive officer, known as the **stadholder**. In theory, the stadholder was freely chosen by the Estates and answerable to them: in practice, however, the strong and influential House of Orange usually held the office of stadholder in several of the seven provinces of the republic. This meant that tensions always lingered between supporters of the House of Orange and those of the staunchly republican Estates, who suspected that the princes of Orange harbored monarchical ambitions.

The political success of the Dutch rested on their phenomenal commercial prosperity. The Dutch came to dominate the shipping business. They boasted the lowest shipping rates and largest merchant marine in Europe, allowing them to undersell foreign competitors (see Chapter 14). Trade and commerce brought the Dutch the highest standard of living in Europe, perhaps in the world. Salaries were high, and all classes of society ate well.

The moral and ethical bases of that commercial wealth were thrift, frugality, and religious toleration. Jews enjoyed a level of acceptance and assimilation in Dutch business and general culture unique in early modern Europe. In the Dutch Republic, toleration paid off: it attracted a great deal of foreign capital and investment.

stadholder
▸ The executive officer in each of the United Provinces of the Netherlands, a position often held by the princes of Orange.

QUICK REVIEW <

What explains the differences between the establishment of constitutionalism in England and the Dutch Republic?

What explains the rise of absolutism in Prussia and Austria?

What were the distinctive features of Russian and Ottoman absolutism?

How and why did the constitutional state triumph in the Dutch Republic and England?

What was the baroque style in art and music, and where was it popular?

 LearningCurve
Check what you know.

479

> What was the baroque style in art and music, and where was it popular?

Rubens, *Garden of Love*, 1633–1634

This painting is an outstanding example of the lavishness and richness of baroque art. Born and raised in northern Europe, Peter Paul Rubens trained as a painter in Italy. Upon his return to the Spanish Netherlands, he became a renowned and amazingly prolific artist, patronized by rulers across Europe. Rubens was a devout Catholic, and his work conveys the emotional fervor of the Catholic Reformation. (Prado, Madrid, Spain/Giraudon/The Bridgeman Art Library)

ROME AND THE REVITALIZED CATHOLIC CHURCH of the late sixteenth century spurred the early development of the baroque style. The papacy and the Jesuits encouraged the growth of an intensely emotional, exuberant art. They wanted artists to appeal to the senses and thereby touch the souls and kindle the faith of ordinary churchgoers while proclaiming the power and confidence of the reformed Catholic Church. In addition to this underlying religious emotionalism, the baroque drew its sense of drama, motion, and ceaseless striving from the Catholic Reformation. The baroque style developed with exceptional vigor in Catholic countries, but it had broad appeal and Protestants accounted for some of the finest examples of baroque style, especially in music.

In painting, the baroque reached maturity early with Peter Paul Rubens (1577–1640), the most outstanding and most representative of baroque painters. Studying in his native Flanders and in Italy, where he was influenced by masters of the High Renaissance such as Michelangelo, Rubens developed his own rich, sensuous, colorful style, which was characterized by animated figures, melodramatic contrasts, and monumental size.

CHAPTER LOCATOR | What made the seventeenth century an "age of crisis"? | Why did France rise and Spain fall during this period?

480 CHAPTER 15 ABSOLUTISM AND CONSTITUTIONALISM

In music, the baroque style reached its culmination almost a century later in the music of Johann Sebastian Bach (1685–1750). Organist and choirmaster of several Lutheran churches across Germany, Bach was equally at home writing secular concertos and sublime religious cantatas. Bach's organ music combined the baroque spirit of invention, tension, and emotion in an unforgettable striving toward the infinite. Unlike Rubens, Bach was not fully appreciated in his lifetime, but since the early nineteenth century his reputation has grown steadily.

QUICK REVIEW <

Why did the Catholic Church promote the baroque style?

LOOKING BACK LOOKING AHEAD
The first half of the seventeenth century was marked by the spread of religious and dynastic warfare across Europe, resulting in the death and dislocation of many millions. This catastrophe was compounded by recurrent episodes of crop failure, famine, and epidemic disease, all of which contributed to a stagnant economy and population loss. In the middle decades of the seventeenth century, the very survival of the European monarchies established in the Renaissance appeared in doubt.

With the re-establishment of order in the second half of the century, maintaining political and social stability was of paramount importance to European rulers and elites. In western and eastern Europe, a host of monarchs proclaimed their God-given and "absolute" authority to rule in the name of peace, unity, and good order. Rulers' ability to impose such claims in reality depended a great deal on compromise with local elites, who acquiesced to state power in exchange for privileges and payoffs. In this way, absolutism and constitutionalism did not always differ as much as they claimed. Both systems relied on political compromises forged from decades of strife.

The eighteenth century was to see this status quo thrown into question by new Enlightenment aspirations for human society, which themselves derived from the inquisitive and self-confident spirit of the Scientific Revolution. By the end of the century, demands for real popular sovereignty would challenge the foundations of the political order so painfully achieved in the seventeenth century.

⊳LaunchPad

ONLINE DOCUMENT PROJECT
Hürrem
What forces shaped Western views of Hürrem?

You encountered Hürrem's story on page 472. Keeping the question above in mind, examine characterizations of Hürrem as seen through the eyes of a Habsburg diplomat. *See inside the front cover to learn more.*

| What explains the rise of absolutism in Prussia and Austria? | What were the distinctive features of Russian and Ottoman absolutism? | How and why did the constitutional state triumph in the Dutch Republic and England? | What was the baroque style in art and music, and where was it popular? | ✔ LearningCurve Check what you know. |

CHAPTER 15 STUDY GUIDE

STEP 1

GET STARTED ONLINE

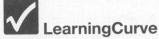 **LearningCurve**

Now that you've read the chapter, make it stick by completing the LearningCurve activity.

STEP 2

EXPLAIN WHY IT MATTERS

Put your reading into practice. Identify each term below, and then explain why it matters in Western history.

TERM	WHO OR WHAT & WHEN	WHY IT MATTERS
Peace of Westphalia (p. 449)		
Fronde (p. 454)		
mercantilism (p. 457)		
Peace of Utrecht (p. 458)		
Junkers (p. 463)		
boyars (p. 467)		
Cossacks (p. 467)		
sultan (p. 470)		
janissary corps (p. 471)		
millet system (p. 471)		
constitutionalism (p. 473)		
republicanism (p. 474)		
Puritans (p. 474)		
Protectorate (p. 475)		
Test Act (p. 477)		
stadholder (p. 479)		

STEP 3

MOVE BEYOND THE BASICS

To demonstrate a more advanced understanding, use the chart to compare and contrast the governments of four European states at the beginning and end of the seventeenth century. How and why did each government change over the course of the century?

Country	1600	1700
France		
England		
Prussia		
Russia		

STEP 4

PUT IT ALL TOGETHER

Now, take a step back and try to explain the big picture. Remember to use specific examples from the chapter in your answers.

ABSOLUTISM

▶ What common challenges were faced by absolutist monarchs? How did the rulers of France, Austria, and Prussia respond to these challenges?

▶ What social and economic trends accompanied the rise of absolutism in eastern Europe?

CONSTITUTIONALISM

▶ Why did the efforts of English monarchs to build an absolutist state fail?

▶ In what ways was the Dutch Republic unique among seventeenth-century states?

RUSSIA AND THE OTTOMAN EMPIRE

▶ How did the Russian tsars gain control over Russia's landowning elite?

▶ How did the Ottoman absolutist state differ from its European counterparts?

MAKE CONNECTIONS

▶ How did the conflicts and tensions unleashed by the Reformation shape seventeenth-century political developments?

▶ What steps were taken during the seventeenth century toward the emergence of the modern nation-state?

▷ IN YOUR OWN WORDS

Imagine that you must give an oral report to the class answering the following question: **What were the most important political trends in seventeenth-century Europe?** What would be the most important points and why?

16

TOWARD A NEW WORLDVIEW

1540–1789

> What new ways of looking at nature, society, and government emerged in the Early Modern period? Chapter 16 examines the Scientific Revolution and the Enlightenment. In the sixteenth and seventeenth centuries, fundamentally new ways of understanding the natural world emerged. The new science entailed the search for precise knowledge of the physical world based on the union of experimental observations with sophisticated mathematics. In the eighteenth century, philosophers extended the use of reason from the study of nature to human society. While the Scientific Revolution ushered in modern science, the Enlightenment created concepts of human rights, equality, progress, universalism, and tolerance that still guide Western societies today. At the same time, some people used their new understanding of nature and reason to proclaim their own superiority, thus rationalizing attitudes such as racism and male chauvinism.

✓**LearningCurve**
After reading the chapter, use LearningCurve to retain what you've read.

> What revolutionary discoveries were made in the sixteenth and seventeenth centuries?

> What intellectual and social changes occurred as a result of the Scientific Revolution?

> What new ideas about society and human relations emerged in the Enlightenment?

> What impact did new ways of thinking have on politics?

Life During the Scientific Revolution. This 1768 painting by Joseph Wright captures the popularization of science and experimentation during the Enlightenment. (National Gallery, London/The Bridgeman Art Library)

> What revolutionary discoveries were made in the sixteenth and seventeenth centuries?

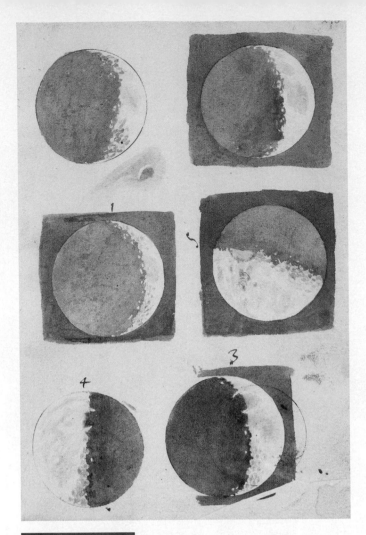

Galileo's Telescopic Observations of the Moon Among the many mechanical devices Galileo invented was a telescope that could magnify objects thirty times (other contemporary telescopes could magnify objects only three times). Using this telescope, he obtained the empirical evidence that proved the Copernican system and sketched many illustrations of his observations, including the six phases of the moon shown here. (akg-images/Rabatti–Domingie)

UNTIL THE MIDDLE OF THE SIXTEENTH CENTURY, Europeans relied on an understanding of motion and matter drawn from the ancient Greek philosopher Aristotle and adapted to Christian theology. The rise of the university, along with the intellectual vitality of the Renaissance and technological advancements, inspired scholars to make closer observations and seek better explanations. From the sun-centered universe proposed by the Polish astronomer Nicolaus Copernicus to the great synthesis of physics and astronomy accomplished by the English scientist Isaac Newton, a revolutionary new understanding of the universe had emerged by the end of the seventeenth century.

CHAPTER LOCATOR | **What revolutionary discoveries were made in the sixteenth and seventeenth centuries?**

ca. 1540–1700 – Scientific Revolution	**ca. 1740–1789** – Salons led by Parisian elites
ca. 1690–1789 – Enlightenment	**1751–1772** – Philosophes publish *Encyclopedia: The Rational Dictionary of the Sciences, the Arts, and the Crafts*
ca. 1700–1800 – Growth of book publishing	**1756–1763** – Seven Years' War
1720–1780 – Rococo style in art and decoration	**1762–1796** – Reign of Catherine the Great of Russia
1740–1748 – War of the Austrian Succession	**1780–1790** – Reign of Joseph II of Austria
1740–1780 – Reign of the empress Maria Theresa of Austria	**1791** – Establishment of the Pale of Settlement
1740–1786 – Reign of Frederick the Great of Prussia	

Scientific Thought in 1500

The term *science* as we use it today came into use only in the nineteenth century. Prior to the Scientific Revolution, many different scholars and practitioners were involved in aspects of what came together to form science. One of the most important disciplines was **natural philosophy**, which focused on fundamental questions about the nature of the universe, its purpose, and how it functioned. In the early 1500s, natural philosophy was still based primarily on the ideas of Aristotle, the great Greek philosopher of the fourth century B.C.E. Medieval theologians brought Aristotelian philosophy into harmony with Christian doctrines. According to the revised Aristotelian view, a motionless earth was fixed at the center of the universe and was encompassed by ten separate concentric crystal spheres that revolved around it. Beyond the tenth sphere was Heaven, with the throne of God and the souls of the saved. Angels kept the spheres moving in perfect circles.

natural philosophy
▶ An early modern term for the study of the nature of the universe, its purpose, and how it functioned; it encompassed what we call science today.

Aristotle's cosmology made intellectual sense, but it could not account for the observed motions of the stars and planets and, in particular, provided no explanation for the apparent backward motion of the planets. The great second-century scholar Ptolemy (see Chapter 14) offered a cunning solution to this dilemma. According to Ptolemy, the planets moved in small circles, called epicycles, each of which moved in turn along a larger circle, or deferent. Ptolemaic astronomy was less elegant than Aristotle's neat nested circles and required complex calculations, but it provided a surprisingly accurate model for predicting planetary motion.

Aristotle's views, revised by medieval philosophers, also dominated thinking about physics and motion on earth. Aristotle had distinguished sharply between the world of the celestial spheres and that of the earth—the sublunar world. The

What intellectual and social changes occurred as a result of the Scientific Revolution?	What new ideas about society and human relations emerged in the Enlightenment?	What impact did new ways of thinking have on politics?	✓ LearningCurve Check what you know.

spheres consisted of a perfect, incorruptible "quintessence." The sublunar world, however, was made up of four imperfect, changeable elements: air, fire, water, and earth. Aristotle and his followers also believed that a uniform force moved an object at a constant speed and that the object would stop as soon as that force was removed.

Origins of the Scientific Revolution

Why did Aristotelian teachings give way to new views about the universe? The Scientific Revolution drew on long-term developments in European culture, as well as borrowings from Arabic scholars. The first important development was the medieval university. By the thirteenth century, permanent universities had been established in western Europe to train the lawyers, doctors, and church leaders society required. By 1300, philosophy had taken its place alongside law, medicine, and theology. Medieval philosophers acquired a limited but real independence from theologians and a sense of free inquiry.

Medieval universities drew on rich traditions of Islamic learning. With the expansion of Islam into lands of the Byzantine Empire in the seventh and eighth centuries, the Muslim world had inherited ancient Greek learning, to which Islamic scholars added their own commentaries and new discoveries. Many Greek texts, which were lost to the West after the fall of the Western Roman Empire in the fifth century, re-entered circulation through translation from Arabic in the twelfth century; these became the basis for the curriculum of the medieval universities. In the fourteenth and fifteenth centuries, leading universities established new professorships of mathematics, astronomy, and optics within their faculties of philosophy. Thus, the stage was set for the union of mathematics with natural philosophy that was to be a hallmark of the Scientific Revolution.

The Renaissance also stimulated scientific progress. Renaissance patrons played a role in funding scientific investigations, as they did for art and literature. Renaissance artists' turn toward realism and their use of geometry to convey three-dimensional perspective encouraged scholars to practice close observation and to use mathematics to describe the natural world. The quest to restore the glories of the ancient past led to the rediscovery of even more classical texts. The fall of Constantinople to the Muslim Ottomans in 1453 resulted in a great influx of little-known Greek works as Christian scholars fled to Italy with their precious texts.

Developments in technology also encouraged the emergence of the Scientific Revolution. The rise of printing in the mid-fifteenth century provided a faster and less expensive way to circulate knowledge across Europe. Fascination with the new discoveries being made in Asia and the Americas greatly increased the demand for printed material. Publishers found an eager audience for the books and images they issued about unknown peoples, plants, animals, and other new findings.

The navigational problems of long sea voyages in the age of overseas expansion, along with the rise of trade and colonization, led to their own series of technological innovations. Navigation and cartography were critical in the development of many new scientific instruments, such as the telescope, barometer, thermometer, pendulum clock, microscope, and air pump. Better instruments, which permitted

CHAPTER LOCATOR | What revolutionary discoveries were made in the sixteenth and seventeenth centuries?

more accurate observations, enabled the rise of experimentation as a crucial method of the Scientific Revolution.

Recent historical research has also focused on the contribution to the Scientific Revolution of practices that no longer belong to the realm of science, such as astrology. Many of the most celebrated astronomers were also astrologers and spent much time devising horoscopes for their patrons. Used as a diagnostic tool in medicine, astrology formed a regular part of the curriculum of medical schools.

Centuries-old practices of magic and alchemy also remained important traditions for natural philosophers. Unlike modern-day conjurers, the practitioners of magic strove to understand and control hidden connections they perceived among different elements of the natural world, such as that between a magnet and iron. The idea that objects possessed invisible or "occult" qualities that allowed them to affect other objects through their innate "sympathy" with each other was a particularly important legacy of the magical tradition.

The Copernican Hypothesis

As a young man, the Polish cleric Nicolaus Copernicus (1473–1543) was drawn to the vitality of the Italian Renaissance. After studies at the University of Kraków, he departed for Italy, where he studied astronomy, medicine, and church law. Copernicus noted that astronomers still depended on the work of Ptolemy for their most accurate calculations, but he felt that Ptolemy's cumbersome and occasionally inaccurate rules detracted from the majesty of a perfect creator. He preferred an alternative ancient Greek idea: that the sun, rather than the earth, was at the center of the universe.

Finishing his university studies and returning to a position in church administration in East Prussia, Copernicus worked on his hypothesis from 1506 to 1530. Without questioning the Aristotelian belief in crystal spheres or the idea that circular motion was divine, Copernicus theorized that the stars and planets, including the earth, revolved around a fixed sun.

The **Copernican hypothesis** had enormous scientific and religious implications, many of which the conservative Copernicus did not anticipate. First, it put the stars at rest, their apparent nightly movement simply a result of the earth's rotation. Thus, his hypothesis destroyed the main reason for believing in crystal spheres capable of moving the stars around the earth. Second, Copernicus's theory suggested a universe of staggering size. If, in the course of a year, the earth moved around the sun and yet the stars appeared to remain in the same place, then the universe was unthinkably large. Third, by using mathematics instead of philosophy to justify his theories, he challenged the traditional hierarchy of the disciplines. And by characterizing the earth as just another planet, Copernicus destroyed the basic idea of Aristotelian physics—that the earthly sphere was quite different from the heavenly one.

Other events were almost as influential as the Copernican hypothesis in creating doubts about traditional astronomy. In 1572, a new star appeared and shone very brightly for almost two years. The new star, which was actually a distant exploding star, made an enormous impression on people. It seemed to contradict the idea that the heavenly spheres were unchanging and therefore perfect. In

Copernican hypothesis
▶ The idea that the sun, not the earth, was the center of the universe.

What intellectual and social changes occurred as a result of the Scientific Revolution?

What new ideas about society and human relations emerged in the Enlightenment?

What impact did new ways of thinking have on politics?

✔ LearningCurve
Check what you know.

489

1577, a new comet suddenly moved through the sky, cutting a straight path across the supposedly impenetrable crystal spheres. It was time, as a sixteenth-century scientific writer put it, for "the radical renovation of astronomy."[1]

Brahe, Kepler, and Galileo: Proving Copernicus Right

Born into a Danish noble family, Tycho Brahe (TEE-koh BRAH-hee) (1546–1601) established himself as Europe's leading astronomer with his detailed observations of the new star of 1572. Aided by generous grants from the king of Denmark, Brahe built the most sophisticated observatory of his day.

Upon the king's death, Brahe acquired a new patron in the Holy Roman emperor Rudolph II and built a new observatory in Prague. For twenty years, Brahe meticulously observed the stars and planets with the naked eye, compiling much more complete and accurate data than ever before. His limited understanding of mathematics and his sudden death in 1601, however, prevented him from making much sense out of his mass of data.

It was left to Brahe's assistant, Johannes Kepler (1571–1630), to rework Brahe's mountain of observations. Kepler's examination of his predecessor's meticulously recorded findings convinced him that Ptolemy's astronomy could not explain them. Abandoning the notion of epicycles and deferents — which even Copernicus had retained in part — Kepler developed three new and revolutionary laws of planetary motion. First, he demonstrated that the orbits of the planets around the sun are elliptical rather than circular. Second, he demonstrated that the planets do not move at a uniform speed in their orbits. When a planet is close to the sun it moves more rapidly, and it slows as it moves farther away from the sun. He also proved that the time a planet takes to make its complete orbit is precisely related to its distance from the sun.

Kepler's contribution was monumental. Whereas Copernicus had used mathematics to

Hevelius and His Wife

Portable sextants were used to chart a ship's position at sea by measuring the altitude of celestial bodies above the horizon. Astronomers used much larger sextants to measure the angular distances between two bodies. Here, Johannes Hevelius uses the great brass sextant at the Danzig observatory, with the help of his wife, Elisabetha. Six feet in radius, this instrument was closely modeled on the one used by Tycho Brahe. (f Typ 620.73.451, Houghton Library, Harvard University)

CHAPTER LOCATOR | **What revolutionary discoveries were made in the sixteenth and seventeenth centuries?**

describe planetary movement, Kepler proved mathematically the precise relations of a sun-centered (solar) system. He thus united for the first time the theoretical cosmology of natural philosophy with mathematics. His work demolished the old system of Aristotle and Ptolemy, and with his third law he came close to formulating the idea of universal gravitation (see page 492).

Beyond his great contribution to astronomy, Kepler pioneered the field of optics. He was the first to explain the role of refraction within the eye in creating vision, and he invented an improved telescope. He was also a great mathematician whose work furnished the basis for integral calculus and advances in geometry.

Kepler was not, however, the consummate modern scientist that these achievements suggest. His duties as court mathematician included casting horoscopes, and he based his own daily life on astrological principles. He also wrote at length on cosmic harmonies and explained, for example, elliptical motion through ideas about the beautiful music created by the combined motion of the planets. His career exemplifies the complex interweaving of ideas and beliefs in the emerging science of his day.

While Kepler was unraveling planetary motion, a young Florentine professor of mathematics named Galileo Galilei (1564–1642) was challenging all the old ideas about motion. His great achievement was the elaboration and consolidation of the **experimental method**. That is, rather than speculate about what might or should happen, Galileo conducted controlled experiments to find out what actually did happen.

In his early experiments, Galileo focused on deficiencies in Aristotle's theories of motion. He measured the movement of a rolling ball across a surface, repeating the action again and again to verify his results. In his famous acceleration experiment, he showed that a uniform force—in this case, gravity—produced a uniform acceleration. Through another experiment, he formulated the **law of inertia**. He found that rest was not the natural state of objects. Rather, an object continues in motion forever unless stopped by some external force. His discoveries proved Aristotelian physics wrong.

Galileo then applied the experimental method to astronomy. On hearing details about the invention of the telescope in Holland, Galileo made one for himself and trained it on the heavens. He quickly discovered the first four moons of Jupiter, which clearly suggested that Jupiter could not possibly be embedded in any impenetrable crystal sphere as Aristotle and Ptolemy maintained. This discovery provided new evidence for the Copernican theory, in which Galileo already believed. Galileo then pointed his telescope at the moon. He wrote in 1610 in *The Sidereal Messenger:* "By the aid of a telescope anyone may behold [the Milky Way] in a manner which so distinctly appeals to the senses that all the disputes which have tormented philosophers through so many ages are exploded by the irrefutable evidence of our eyes, and we are freed from wordy disputes upon the subject."[2]

In 1597, when Johannes Kepler sent Galileo an early publication defending Copernicus, Galileo replied that it was too dangerous to express his support for heliocentrism publicly. The rising fervor of the Catholic Reformation increased the church's hostility to such radical ideas, and in 1616, the Holy Office placed the works of Copernicus and his supporters, including Kepler, on a list of books Catholics were forbidden to read.

Galileo was a devout Catholic who sincerely believed that his theories did not

experimental method
▶ The approach, pioneered by Galileo, that the proper way to explore the workings of the universe was through repeatable experiments rather than speculation.

law of inertia
▶ A law formulated by Galileo that states that motion, not rest, is the natural state of an object, and that an object continues in motion forever unless stopped by some external force.

What intellectual and social changes occurred as a result of the Scientific Revolution?

What new ideas about society and human relations emerged in the Enlightenment?

What impact did new ways of thinking have on politics?

✓ LearningCurve
Check what you know.

491

detract from the perfection of God. Out of caution he silenced his beliefs for several years, until in 1623 he saw new hope with the ascension of Pope Urban VIII, a man sympathetic to developments in the new science. However, Galileo's 1632 *Dialogue on the Two Chief Systems of the World* went too far. Published in Italian and widely read, this work openly lampooned the traditional views of Aristotle and Ptolemy and defended those of Copernicus. The papal Inquisition placed Galileo on trial for heresy. Imprisoned and threatened with torture, the aging Galileo recanted.

Newton's Synthesis

By about 1640, despite the efforts of the church, the work of Brahe, Kepler, and Galileo had been largely accepted by the scientific community. But the new findings failed to explain what forces controlled the movement of the planets and objects on earth. That challenge was taken up by English scientist Isaac Newton (1642–1727).

Newton was born into the lower English gentry in 1642, and he enrolled at Cambridge University in 1661. A genius who spectacularly united the experimental and theoretical-mathematical sides of modern science, Newton was an intensely devout, albeit non-orthodox Christian. Newton was also fascinated by alchemy. He viewed alchemy as one path, alongside mathematics and astronomy, to the truth of God's creation. Like Kepler and other practitioners of the Scientific Revolution, he studied the natural world not for its own sake, but to understand the divine plan.

Newton's towering accomplishment was a single explanatory system that could integrate the astronomy of Copernicus, as corrected by Kepler's laws, with the physics of Galileo and his predecessors. *Philosophicae Naturalis Principia Mathematica* (1687) laid down Newton's three laws of motion, using a set of mathematical laws that explain motion and mechanics. The key feature of the Newtonian synthesis was the **law of universal gravitation**. According to this law, every body in the universe attracts every other body in the universe in a precise mathematical relationship, whereby the force of attraction is proportional to the quantity of matter of the objects and inversely proportional to the square of the distance between them. The whole universe was unified in one coherent system. The German mathematician and philosopher Gottfried von Leibniz, with whom Newton contested the invention of calculus, was outraged by Newton's claim that the "occult" force of gravity could allow bodies to affect one another at great distances. Newton's religious faith, as well as his alchemical belief in the innate powers of certain objects, allowed him to dismiss such criticism.

law of universal gravitation
▶ Newton's law that all objects are attracted to one another and that the force of attraction is proportional to the objects' quantity of matter and inversely proportional to the square of the distance between them.

> ## QUICK REVIEW

In what ways do Newton's breakthroughs represent the culmination of the Scientific Revolution?

CHAPTER LOCATOR | What revolutionary discoveries were made in the sixteenth and seventeenth centuries?

492   CHAPTER 16
TOWARD A NEW WORLDVIEW

What intellectual and social changes occurred as a result of the Scientific Revolution?

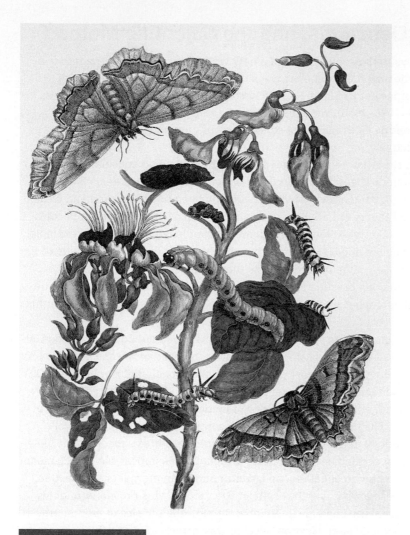

Metamorphoses of the Caterpillar and Moth Maria Sibylla Merian (1647–1717), the stepdaughter of a Dutch painter, became a celebrated scientific illustrator in her own right. Her finely observed pictures of insects in the South American colony of Suriname introduced many new species. For Merian, science was intimately tied with art: she not only painted but also bred caterpillars and performed experiments on them. Her two-year stay in Suriname, accompanied by a teenage daughter, was a daring feat for a seventeenth-century woman. (akg-images)

THE CREATION OF A NEW SCIENCE was not accomplished by a handful of brilliant astronomers working alone. Scholars in many fields—medicine, chemistry, and botany, among others—used new methods to seek answers to long-standing problems, sharing their results in a community that spanned Europe. At the same time, monarchs and entrepreneurs launched explorations to uncover and understand the natural riches of newly conquered empires around the globe.

| What intellectual and social changes occurred as a result of the Scientific Revolution? | What new ideas about society and human relations emerged in the Enlightenment? | What impact did new ways of thinking have on politics? | ✓ LearningCurve Check what you know. |

Bacon, Descartes, and the Scientific Method

One of the keys to the achievement of a new worldview in the seventeenth century was the development of better ways of obtaining knowledge about the world. Two important thinkers, Francis Bacon (1561–1626) and René Descartes (day-KAHRT) (1596–1650), were influential in describing and advocating for improved scientific methods based on experimentation and mathematical reasoning, respectively.

Rejecting the Aristotelian and medieval method of using speculative reasoning to build general theories, the English politician and writer Francis Bacon formalized the empirical method, which had already been used by Brahe and Galileo, into the general theory of inductive reasoning known as **empiricism**. In Bacon's view, the researcher who wants to learn more about leaves or rocks, for example, should not speculate about the subject but should rather collect a multitude of specimens and then compare and analyze them to derive general principles. Bacon's work, and his prestige as lord chancellor under James I, led to the widespread adoption of what was called experimental philosophy in England after his death.

On the continent, more speculative methods retained support. Accepting Galileo's claim that all elements of the universe are composed of the same matter and drawing on ancient Greek atomist philosophies, the French philosopher René Descartes developed the idea that matter was made up of identical "corpuscules" that collided together in an endless series of motions. All occurrences in nature could be analyzed as matter in motion and, according to Descartes, the total "quantity of motion" in the universe was constant. Descartes's mechanistic view of the universe depended on the idea that a vacuum was impossible, which meant that every action had an equal reaction, continuing in an eternal chain reaction.

Although Descartes's hypothesis about the vacuum was proved wrong, his notion of a mechanistic universe intelligible through the physics of motion proved inspirational. Decades later, Newton rejected Descartes's idea of a full universe and several of his other ideas, but retained the notion of a mechanistic universe as a key element of his own system.

Descartes's greatest achievement was to develop his initial vision into a whole philosophy of knowledge and science. The Aristotelian cosmos was appealing in part because it corresponded with the evidence of the human senses. When the senses were proven to be wrong, Descartes decided it was necessary to doubt them and everything that could reasonably be doubted, and then, as in geometry, to use deductive reasoning from self-evident truths, which he called "first principles," to ascertain scientific laws. Descartes's reasoning ultimately reduced all substances to "matter" and "mind"—that is, to the physical and the spiritual. His view of the world as consisting of two fundamental entities is known as **Cartesian dualism**. Descartes's thought was highly influential in France and the Netherlands, but less so in England, where experimental philosophy won the day.

Both Bacon's inductive experimentalism and Descartes's deductive mathematical reasoning had their faults. Bacon's inability to appreciate the importance of mathematics and his obsession with practical results clearly showed the limitations of antitheoretical empiricism. Likewise, some of Descartes's positions demonstrated the inadequacy of rigid, dogmatic rationalism. For example, he believed that it was possible to deduce the whole science of medicine from first principles.

empiricism
▶ A theory of inductive reasoning that calls for acquiring evidence through observation and experimentation rather than deductive reason and speculation.

Cartesian dualism
▶ Descartes's view that all of reality could ultimately be reduced to mind and matter.

CHAPTER LOCATOR | What revolutionary discoveries were made in the sixteenth and seventeenth centuries?

494 CHAPTER 16
TOWARD A NEW WORLDVIEW

Although insufficient on their own, Bacon's and Descartes's extreme approaches are combined in the modern scientific method, which began to crystallize in the late seventeenth century.

Medicine, the Body, and Chemistry

The Scientific Revolution soon inspired renewed study of the microcosm of the human body. For many centuries, the ancient Greek physician Galen's explanation of the body carried the same authority as Aristotle's account of the universe. According to Galen, the body contained four humors. Illness was believed to result from an imbalance of humors, which is why doctors frequently prescribed bloodletting to expel "excess" blood.

Swiss physician and alchemist Paracelsus (1493–1541) was an early proponent of the experimental method in medicine and pioneered the use of chemicals and drugs to address what he saw as chemical, rather than humoral, imbalances. Another experimentalist, Flemish physician Andreas Vesalius (1516–1564), studied anatomy by dissecting human bodies. The experimental approach also led English royal physician William Harvey (1578–1657) to discover the circulation of blood through the veins and arteries in 1628. Harvey was the first to explain that the heart worked like a pump and to explain the function of its muscles and valves.

Some decades later, Irishman Robert Boyle (1627–1691) helped found the modern science of chemistry. Following Paracelsus's lead, he undertook experiments to discover the basic elements of nature, which he believed was composed of infinitely small atoms. Boyle was the first to create a vacuum, thus disproving Descartes's belief that a vacuum could not exist in nature, and he discovered Boyle's law (1662), which states that the pressure of a gas varies inversely with volume.

Empire and Natural History

While the traditional story of the Scientific Revolution focuses exclusively on developments within Europe itself, and in particular on achievements in mathematical astronomy, more recently scholars have emphasized the impact of Europe's overseas empires on the accumulation and transmission of knowledge about the natural world. Building on the rediscovery of classical texts, early modern scholars published new works cataloguing forms of life in northern Europe, Asia, and the Americas that were unknown to the ancients. These encyclopedias of natural history included realistic drawings and descriptions that emphasized the usefulness of animal and plant species for trade, medicine, food, and other practical concerns. Much of the new knowledge contained in such works resulted from scientific expeditions, often sponsored by European governments eager to learn about and profit from their imperial holdings.

MAJOR CONTRIBUTORS TO THE SCIENTIFIC REVOLUTION

■ **Nicolaus Copernicus (1473–1543)**
On the Revolutions of the Heavenly Spheres (1543); theorized that the sun, rather than the earth, was the center of the galaxy

■ **Paracelsus (1493–1541)**
Swiss physician and alchemist who pioneered the use of chemicals and drugs to address illness

■ **Andreas Vesalius (1514–1564)**
On the Structure of the Human Body (1543)

■ **Tycho Brahe (1546–1601)**
Built observatory and compiled data for the *Rudolphine Tables*, a new table of planetary data

■ **Francis Bacon (1561–1626)**
Advocated experimental method, formalizing theory of inductive reasoning known as empiricism

■ **Galileo Galilei (1564–1642)**
Used telescopic observation to provide evidence for Copernican hypothesis; experimented to formulate laws of physics, such as inertia

■ **Johannes Kepler (1571–1630)**
Used Brahe's data to prove the Copernican hypothesis mathematically; his new laws of planetary motion united for the first time natural philosophy and mathematics; completed the *Rudolphine Tables* in 1627

■ **William Harvey (1578–1657)**
Discovery of circulation of blood (1628)

■ **René Descartes (1596–1650)**
Used deductive reasoning to formulate the theory of Cartesian dualism

■ **Robert Boyle (1627–1691)**
Boyle's law (1662) governing the pressure of gases

■ **Isaac Newton (1642–1727)**
Principia Mathematica (1687); set forth the law of universal gravitation, which synthesized previous findings of motion and matter

What intellectual and social changes occurred as a result of the Scientific Revolution?	What new ideas about society and human relations emerged in the Enlightenment?	What impact did new ways of thinking have on politics?	✓ LearningCurve Check what you know.

Science and Society

The rise of modern science had many consequences, some of which are still unfolding. First, it went hand in hand with the rise of a new social group—the international scientific community. Members of this community were linked together by common interests and shared values as well as by journals and the learned scientific societies founded in many countries in the late seventeenth and eighteenth centuries. Second, as governments intervened to support and sometimes direct research, the new scientific community became closely tied to the state and its agendas. At the same time, scientists developed a critical attitude toward established authority that would inspire thinkers to question traditions in other domains as well.

In recent years, historians have emphasized the crossover between the work of artisans and the rise of science, particularly in the development of the experimental method. Many craftsmen developed a strong interest in emerging scientific ideas and, in turn, the practice of science in the seventeenth century often relied on artisans' expertise in making instruments and conducting precise experiments.

Some things did not change in the Scientific Revolution. Scholars have noted that nature was often depicted as a female, whose veil of secrecy needed to be stripped away and penetrated by male experts. New "rational" methods for approaching nature did not question traditional inequalities between the sexes—and may have worsened them in some ways. For example, the rise of universities and other professional institutions for science raised new barriers because most of these organizations did not accept women.

A number of noteworthy exceptions existed, however. In Italy, universities and academies did offer posts to women. Women across Europe worked as makers of wax anatomical models and as botanical and zoological illustrators, like Maria Sibylla Merian. They were also very much involved in informal scientific communities, attending salons (see page 502), participating in scientific experiments, and writing learned treatises. Some female intellectuals became full-fledged members of the philosophical dialogue. In England, Margaret Cavendish, Anne Conway, and Mary Astell all contributed to debates about Descartes's mind-body dualism, among other issues.

By the time Louis XIV died in 1715, many of the scientific ideas that would eventually coalesce into a new worldview had been assembled. Yet Christian Europe was still strongly attached to its established political and social structures and its traditional spiritual beliefs. By 1775, however, a large portion of western Europe's educated elite had embraced the new ideas. This was the work of many men and women across Europe who participated in the Enlightenment, either as publishers, writers, and distributors of texts or as members of the eager public that consumed them.

> **QUICK REVIEW**

How did the ideas of Bacon and Descartes contribute to the development of the scientific method?

CHAPTER LOCATOR | What revolutionary discoveries were made in the sixteenth and seventeenth centuries?

What new ideas about society and human relations emerged in the Enlightenment?

An actor performs the first reading of a new play by Voltaire at the salon of Madame Geoffrin. Voltaire, then in exile, is represented by a bust statue. (Académie des Sciences, Belles-Lettres, Rouen, France/Giraudon/ The Bridgeman Art Library)

> PICTURING THE PAST

ANALYZE THE IMAGE: Which of these people do you think is the hostess, Madame Geoffrin, and why? Using details from the painting to support your answer, how would you describe the status of the people shown?

MAKE CONNECTIONS: What does this image suggest about the reach of Enlightenment ideas to common people? To women? Does the painting of the bookstore on page 503 suggest a broader reach? Why?

THE SCIENTIFIC REVOLUTION was a crucial factor in the creation of the new worldview of the eighteenth-century **Enlightenment**. This worldview grew out of a rich mix of diverse and often conflicting ideas. Nonetheless, three central concepts stand at the core of Enlightenment thinking. The first and foremost idea was that the methods of natural science could and should be used to examine and understand all aspects of life. Nothing was to be accepted on faith; everything was to be submitted to **rationalism**, a secular, critical way of thinking. A second important Enlightenment concept was that the scientific method was capable of discovering the laws of human society as well as those of nature. These tenets led to the third key idea, that of progress. Armed with the proper method of discovering the laws of human existence, Enlightenment thinkers believed, it was at least possible for human beings to create better societies and better people.

Enlightenment
▶ The influential intellectual and cultural movement of the late seventeenth and eighteenth centuries that introduced a new worldview based on the use of reason, the scientific method, and progress.

rationalism
▶ A secular, critical way of thinking in which nothing was to be accepted on faith and everything was to be submitted to reason.

The Emergence of the Enlightenment

The generation that came of age between the publication of Newton's *Principia* in 1687 and the death of Louis XIV in 1715 tied the crucial knot between the Scientific Revolution and a new outlook on life. Whereas medieval and Reformation

What intellectual and social changes occurred as a result of the Scientific Revolution?	**What new ideas about society and human relations emerged in the Enlightenment?**	What impact did new ways of thinking have on politics?	✓ LearningCurve Check what you know.

thinkers had been concerned primarily with abstract concepts of sin and salvation, and Renaissance humanists had drawn their inspiration from the classical past, Enlightenment thinkers believed that their era had gone far beyond antiquity and that intellectual progress was very possible. Talented writers of that generation popularized hard-to-understand scientific achievements and set an agenda of human problems to be addressed through the methods of science.

Like the Scientific Revolution, the Enlightenment was also fueled by Europe's increased contacts with the wider world. In the wake of the great discoveries of the fifteenth and sixteenth centuries, the rapidly growing travel literature taught Europeans that the peoples of China, India, Africa, and the Americas all had their own very different beliefs and customs. Some Europeans began to look at truth and morality in relative, rather than absolute, terms. If anything was possible, who could say what was right or wrong?

The excitement of the Scientific Revolution also generated doubt and uncertainty, contributing to a widespread crisis in late-seventeenth-century European thought. In the wake of the devastation wrought by the Thirty Years' War, some people asked whether ideological conformity in religious matters was really necessary. Others skeptically asked if religious truth could ever be known with absolute certainty and concluded that it could not. The atmosphere of doubt spread from religious to political issues. This was a natural extension, since many rulers viewed religious dissent as a form of political opposition and took harsh measures to stifle unorthodox forms of worship. Thus, questioning religion inevitably led to confrontations with the state.

These concerns combined spectacularly in the career of Pierre Bayle (1647–1706), a French Protestant, or Huguenot, who took refuge from government persecution in the tolerant Dutch Republic. Bayle critically examined the religious beliefs and persecutions of the past in his *Historical and Critical Dictionary* (1697). Demonstrating that human beliefs had been extremely varied and very often mistaken, he concluded that nothing can ever be known beyond all doubt, a view known as skepticism. His very influential *Dictionary* was found in more private libraries of eighteenth-century France than any other book.

Like Bayle, many Huguenots fled France for the Dutch Republic, a center of early Enlightenment thought for people of many faiths. The Dutch Jewish philosopher Baruch Spinoza (1632–1677) borrowed Descartes's emphasis on rationalism and his methods of deductive reasoning, but he rejected the French thinker's mind-body dualism. Instead, Spinoza came to believe that mind and body are united in one substance and that God and nature were merely two names for the same thing. He envisioned a deterministic universe in which good and evil were merely relative values and our actions were shaped by outside circumstances, not free will. Spinoza was excommunicated by the relatively large Jewish community of Amsterdam for his controversial religious ideas, but he was heralded by his Enlightenment successors as a model of personal virtue and courageous intellectual autonomy.

Out of this period of intellectual turmoil came John Locke's *Essay Concerning Human Understanding* (1690). In this work, Locke (1632–1704), a physician and member of the Royal Society, brilliantly set forth a new theory about how human beings learn and form their ideas. Locke insisted that all ideas are derived from experience. The human mind at birth is like a blank tablet, or tabula rasa, on which the environment writes the individual's understanding and beliefs. Human development is therefore determined by education and social institutions. Locke's essay contributed to the theory of sensationalism, the idea that all human ideas and thoughts are produced as a result of sensory impressions. With his emphasis on the role of perception in the acquisition of knowledge, Locke provided a systematic justification of Bacon's emphasis on the importance of observation and experimentation. The *Essay Concerning Human Understanding* passed through many editions and translations and, along with Newton's *Principia*, was one of the dominant intellectual inspirations of the Enlightenment.

The Influence of the Philosophes

The spread of the Enlightenment spirit of inquiry and debate owed a great deal to the work of the **philosophes** (fee-luh-SZOFZ), a group of intellectuals who proudly proclaimed that they, at long last, were bringing the light of reason to their ignorant fellow humans. *Philosophe* is the French word for "philosopher," and in the mid-eighteenth century France became a hub of Enlightenment thought.

philosophes
▶ A group of French intellectuals who proclaimed that they were bringing the light of knowledge to their fellow humans in the Age of Enlightenment.

> Reasons Why France Became a Major Hub of Enlightenment Thought	
French power and prestige	France was the wealthiest and most populous country in Europe; French was the international language of the elite
Political discontent in France	Rising political discontent in France led to calls for reform among educated elite
Ambitions of French philosophes	French philosophes were determined to spread their ideas throughout the international Republic of Letters

One of the greatest philosophes, the baron de Montesquieu (mahn-tuhs-KYOO) (1689–1755), pioneered this approach in *The Persian Letters*, a brilliant and extremely influential social satire published in 1721 and considered the first major work of the French Enlightenment. It consisted of amusing letters supposedly written by two Persian travelers who, as outsiders, saw European customs in unique ways, thereby allowing Montesquieu a vantage point for criticizing existing practices and beliefs.

Having gained fame by using wit as a weapon against cruelty and superstition, Montesquieu set out to apply the critical method to the problem of government in *The Spirit of Laws* (1748). The result was a complex, comparative study of republics, monarchies, and despotisms. Showing that forms of government were shaped by history and geography, Montesquieu focused on the conditions that would promote liberty and prevent tyranny. He argued for a separation of powers, with political power divided and shared by a variety of classes and legal estates.

The most famous and perhaps most representative philosophe was François Marie Arouet, who was known by the pen name Voltaire (vohl-TAIR) (1694–1778). Early in his career, he was arrested on two occasions for insulting noblemen. Voltaire moved to England for three years in order to avoid a longer prison term in France, and in England he came to share Montesquieu's enthusiasm for English liberties and institutions.

Returning to France, Voltaire had the great fortune of meeting Gabrielle-Emilie Le Tonnelier de Breteuil, marquise du Châtelet (SHAH-tuh-lay) (1706–1749),

| What intellectual and social changes occurred as a result of the Scientific Revolution? | **What new ideas about society and human relations emerged in the Enlightenment?** | What impact did new ways of thinking have on politics? | ✔ LearningCurve Check what you know. |

499

a noblewoman with a passion for science. Inviting Voltaire to live in her country house at Cirey in Lorraine and becoming his long-time companion (under the eyes of her tolerant husband), Madame du Châtelet studied physics and mathematics and published scientific articles and translations, including the first—and only—translation of Newton's *Principia* into French.)

While living at Cirey, Voltaire wrote works praising England and popularizing English science. He lauded Newton as history's greatest man because he had used his genius for the benefit of humanity. In the true style of the Enlightenment, Voltaire mixed the glorification of science and reason with an appeal for better individuals and institutions.

Like almost all of the philosophes, however, Voltaire was a reformer, not a revolutionary, in politics. He pessimistically concluded that the best one could hope for in the way of government was a good monarch because human beings "are very rarely worthy to govern themselves." Nor did Voltaire believe in social and economic equality, insisting that the idea of making servants equal to their masters was "absurd and impossible." The only realizable equality, Voltaire thought, was that "by which the citizen only depends on the laws which protect the freedom of the feeble against the ambitions of the strong."[3]

Voltaire's philosophical and religious positions were much more radical than his social and political beliefs. In the tradition of Bayle, his writings challenged the Catholic Church and Christian theology at almost every point. Like many eighteenth-century Enlightenment thinkers, Voltaire was a deist, envisioning God as akin to a clockmaker who set the universe in motion and then ceased to intervene in human affairs. Above all, Voltaire and most of the philosophes hated all forms of religious intolerance, which they believed led to fanaticism.

The ultimate strength of the philosophes lay in their dedication and organization. The philosophes felt keenly that they were engaged in a common undertaking that transcended individuals. Their greatest and most representative intellectual achievement was, quite fittingly, a group effort—the seventeen-volume *Encyclopedia: The Rational Dictionary of the Sciences, the Arts, and the Crafts*, edited by Denis Diderot (DEE-duh-roh) (1713–1784) and Jean le Rond d'Alembert (dah-luhm-BEHR) (1717–1783). Published between 1751 and 1772, it contained seventy-two thousand articles by leading scientists, writers, skilled workers, and progressive priests, and it treated every aspect of life and knowledge. Not every article was daring or original, but the overall effect was little short of revolutionary. Science and the industrial arts were exalted, religion and immortality questioned. Intolerance, legal injustice, and out-of-date social institutions were openly criticized. The encyclopedists were convinced that greater knowledge would result in greater human happiness because knowledge was useful and made possible economic, social, and political progress. Summing up the new worldview of the Enlightenment, the *Encyclopedia* was widely read, especially in less-expensive reprint editions, and it was extremely influential.

Jean-Jacques Rousseau

In the early 1740s, Jean-Jacques Rousseau (1712–1778), the son of a poor Swiss watchmaker, made his way into the Parisian Enlightenment through his brilliant intellect. Like other Enlightenment thinkers, Rousseau was passionately committed to individual freedom. Unlike them, however, he attacked rationalism and civilization as destroying, rather than liberating, the individual. Warm, spontaneous feeling had to complement and correct cold intellect. The basic goodness of the individual and the unspoiled child had to be protected from the cruel refinements of civilization. Rousseau's ideals greatly influenced the early romantic movement, which rebelled against the culture of the Enlightenment in the late eighteenth century.

Rousseau also called for a rigid division of gender roles. According to Rousseau, women and men were radically different beings. Destined by nature to assume a passive role in sexual relations, women should also be subordinate in social life. Women's love for displaying themselves in public, attending social gatherings, and pulling the strings of power was unnatural and had a corrupting effect on both politics and society. Rousseau thus rejected the sophisticated way of life of Parisian elite women. His criticism led to calls for privileged women to renounce their frivolous ways and stay at home to care for their children.

Rousseau's contribution to political theory in *The Social Contract* (1762) was based on two fundamental concepts: the general will and popular sovereignty. According to Rousseau, the general will is sacred and absolute, reflecting the common interests of all the people, who have displaced the monarch as the holder of sovereign power. The general will is not necessarily the will of the majority, however. At times, the general will may be the authentic, long-term needs of the people as correctly interpreted by a farsighted minority. Little noticed in its day, Rousseau's concept of the general will had a great impact on the political aspirations of the American and French Revolutions.

The International Enlightenment

The Enlightenment was a movement of international dimensions, with thinkers traversing borders in a constant exchange of visits, letters, and printed materials. The Republic of Letters was a truly cosmopolitan set of networks stretching from western Europe to its colonies in the Americas, to Russia and eastern Europe, and along the routes of trade and empire to Africa and Asia. Within this broad international conversation, scholars have identified regional and national particularities.

The Scottish Enlightenment, which was centered in Edinburgh, was marked

MAJOR FIGURES OF THE ENLIGHTENMENT

■ **Baruch Spinoza (1632–1677)**
Early Enlightenment thinker excommunicated from the Jewish religion for his concept of a deterministic universe

■ **John Locke (1632–1704)**
Essay Concerning Human Understanding (1690)

■ **Gottfried Wilhelm von Leibniz (1646–1716)**
German philosopher and mathematician known for his optimistic view of the universe

■ **Pierre Bayle (1647–1706)**
Historical and Critical Dictionary (1697)

■ **Montesquieu (1689–1755)**
The Persian Letters (1721); *The Spirit of Laws* (1748)

■ **Voltaire (1694–1778)**
Renowned French philosopher and author of more than seventy works

■ **David Hume (1711–1776)**
Central figure of the Scottish Enlightenment; *Of Natural Characters* (1748)

■ **Jean-Jacques Rousseau (1712–1778)**
The Social Contract (1762)

■ **Denis Diderot (1713–1784) and Jean le Rond d'Alembert (1717–1783)**
Editors of *Encyclopedia: The Rational Dictionary of the Sciences, the Arts, and the Crafts* (1751–1772)

■ **Adam Smith (1723–1790)**
The Theory of Moral Sentiments (1759); *An Inquiry into the Nature and Causes of the Wealth of Nations* (1776)

■ **Immanuel Kant (1724–1804)**
What Is Enlightenment? (1784); *On the Different Races of Man* (1775)

■ **Moses Mendelssohn (1729–1786)**
Major philosopher of the Haskalah, or Jewish Enlightenment

■ **Cesare Beccaria (1738–1794)**
On Crimes and Punishments (1764)

What intellectual and social changes occurred as a result of the Scientific Revolution? | **What new ideas about society and human relations emerged in the Enlightenment?** | What impact did new ways of thinking have on politics? | ✓ LearningCurve Check what you know.

501

by an emphasis on common sense and scientific reasoning. A central figure in Edinburgh was David Hume (1711–1776), whose emphasis on civic morality and religious skepticism had a powerful impact at home and abroad. Building on Locke's teachings on learning, Hume argued that the human mind is really nothing but a bundle of impressions. These impressions originate only in sensory experiences and our habits of joining these experiences together. Because our ideas ultimately reflect only our sensory experiences, our reason cannot tell us anything about questions that cannot be verified by sensory experience (in the form of controlled experiments or mathematics), such as the origin of the universe or the existence of God. Paradoxically, Hume's rationalistic inquiry ended up undermining the Enlightenment's faith in the power of reason.

Another major figure of the Scottish Enlightenment was Adam Smith. In *An Inquiry into the Nature and Causes of the Wealth of Nations* (1776), Smith attacked the laws and regulations that, he argued, prevented commerce from reaching its full capacity (see Chapter 17).

The Enlightenment in British North America was heavily influenced by English and Scottish thinkers, especially John Locke, and by Montesquieu's arguments for checks and balances in government. Leaders of the American Enlightenment, including Benjamin Franklin and Thomas Jefferson, would play a leading role in the American Revolution (see Chapter 19).

After 1760, Enlightenment ideas were hotly debated in the German-speaking states, often in dialogue with Christian theology. Immanuel Kant (1724–1804) was the greatest German philosopher of his day. Kant posed the question of the age when he published a pamphlet in 1784 entitled *What Is Enlightenment?* He answered, "*Sapere Aude* [dare to know]! 'Have the courage to use your own understanding' is therefore the motto of enlightenment." He argued that if intellectuals were granted the freedom to exercise their reason publicly in print, enlightenment would almost surely follow.

Northern Europeans often regarded the Italian states as culturally backward, yet important developments in Enlightenment thought took place in the Italian peninsula. In northern Italy, a central figure was Cesare Beccaria (1738–1794), a nobleman educated at Jesuit schools and the University of Pavia. His *On Crimes and Punishments* (1764) was a passionate plea for reform of the penal system that decried the use of torture, arbitrary imprisonment, and capital punishment, and advocated the prevention of crime over the reliance on punishment.

Urban Culture and Life in the Public Sphere

A series of new institutions and practices encouraged the spread of enlightened ideas in the late seventeenth and eighteenth centuries. First, the European production and consumption of books grew significantly. The types of books people read changed dramatically. The proportion of religious and devotional books published in Paris declined after 1750; history and law held constant; the arts and sciences surged.

Reading more books on many more subjects, the educated public approached reading in a new way. The result was what some scholars have called a **reading revolution**. The old style of reading in Europe had been centered on a core of sacred texts that taught earthly duty and obedience to God. Reading had been patriarchal and communal, with the father slowly reading the text aloud to his

reading revolution

▶ The transition in Europe from a society where literacy consisted of patriarchal and communal reading of religious texts to a society where literacy was commonplace and reading material was broad and diverse.

CHAPTER LOCATOR | What revolutionary discoveries were made in the sixteenth and seventeenth centuries?

CHAPTER 16
502 TOWARD A NEW WORLDVIEW

The French Book Trade Book consumption surged in the eighteenth century and, along with it, new bookstores. This appealing bookshop in France, with its intriguing ads for the latest works, offers to put customers "Under the Protection of Minerva," the Roman goddess of wisdom. Large packets of books sit ready for shipment to foreign countries. (akg-images/De Agostini Picture Library)

assembled family. Now reading involved a broader field of books that constantly changed. Reading became individual and silent, and texts could be questioned. Subtle but profound, the reading revolution ushered in new ways of relating to the written word.

Conversation, discussion, and debate also played a critical role in the Enlightenment. Evolving from the gatherings presided over by the *précieuses* in the late seventeenth century (see Chapter 15), the **salon** was a regular meeting held in the elegant private drawing rooms (or salons) of talented, wealthy men and women. There they encouraged the exchange of witty observations on literature, science, and philosophy among great aristocrats, wealthy middle-class financiers, high-ranking officials, and noteworthy foreigners. Many of the most celebrated salons were hosted by women, known as *salonnières* (sah-lahn-YEHRZ). Invitations to salons were highly coveted; introductions to the rich and powerful could make the career of an ambitious writer, and, in turn, the social elite found amusement and cultural prestige in their ties to up-and-coming artists and men of letters. (See "Picturing the Past: Enlightenment Culture," page 497.)

The salon thus represented an accommodation between the ruling classes and the leaders of Enlightenment thought. Salons were sites in which the philosophes,

salon

▶ Regular social gathering held by talented and rich Parisians in their homes, where philosophes and their followers met to discuss literature, science, and philosophy.

What intellectual and social changes occurred as a result of the Scientific Revolution?

What new ideas about society and human relations emerged in the Enlightenment?

What impact did new ways of thinking have on politics?

✓ LearningCurve
Check what you know.

503

the French nobility, and the prosperous middle classes intermingled and influenced one another while maintaining due deference to social rank. Critical thought about almost any question became fashionable and flourished alongside hopes for human progress through greater knowledge and enlightened public opinion.

Elite women also exercised great influence on artistic taste. Soft pastels, ornate interiors, sentimental portraits, and starry-eyed lovers protected by hovering cupids were all hallmarks of the style they favored. This style, known as **rococo** (ruh-KOH-koh), was popular throughout Europe in the period from 1720 to 1780.

While membership at the salons was restricted to the wellborn, the well connected, and the exceptionally talented, a number of institutions provided the rest of society with access to Enlightenment ideas. Lending libraries served an important function for people who could not afford their own books. The coffeehouses that first appeared in the late seventeenth century became meccas of philosophical discussion. In addition to these institutions, book clubs, debating societies, Masonic lodges (groups of Freemasons, a secret society that accepted craftsmen and shopkeepers as well as middle-class men and nobles), and newspapers all played roles in the creation of a new **public sphere** that celebrated open debate informed by critical reason. The public sphere was an idealized space where members of society came together as individuals to discuss issues relevant to the society, economics, and politics of the day.

What of the common people? Did they participate in the Enlightenment? Enlightenment philosophes did not direct their message to peasants or urban laborers. They believed that the masses had no time or talent for philosophical speculation and that elevating them would be a long and potentially dangerous process. Despite these prejudices, the ideas of the philosophes did find an audience among some members of the common people. At a time of rising literacy, book prices were dropping and many philosophical ideas were popularized in cheap pamphlets and through public reading. Although they were barred from salons and academies, ordinary people were not immune to the new ideas in circulation.

Race and the Enlightenment

If philosophers did not believe the lower classes qualified for enlightenment, how did they regard individuals of different races? In recent years, historians have found in the Scientific Revolution and the Enlightenment a crucial turning point in European ideas about race. A primary catalyst for new ideas about race was the urge to classify nature, an urge unleashed by the Scientific Revolution's insistence on careful empirical observation. As scientists developed taxonomies of plant and animal species, they also began to classify humans into hierarchically ordered "races."

Using the word *race* to designate biologically distinct groups of humans, akin to distinct animal species, was new. Previously, Europeans grouped other peoples into "nations" based on their historical, political, and cultural affiliations, rather than on supposedly innate physical differences. When European thinkers drew up a hierarchical classification of human species, their own "race" was placed, of course, at the top. Europeans had long believed they were culturally superior. Now emerging ideas about racial difference told them they were biologically superior as well. In turn, scientific racism helped legitimate and justify the tremendous growth of slavery that occurred during the eighteenth century.

Racist ideas did not go unchallenged. The abbé Raynal's *History of the Two Indies* (1770) fiercely attacked slavery and the abuses of European colonization.

rococo

► A popular style in Europe in the eighteenth century, known for its soft pastels, ornate interiors, sentimental portraits, and starry-eyed lovers protected by hovering cupids.

public sphere

► An idealized intellectual space that emerged in Europe during the Enlightenment, where the public came together to discuss important issues relating to society, economics, and politics.

Encyclopedia Image of the Cotton Industry

This romanticized image of slavery in the West Indies cotton industry was published in Diderot and d'Alembert's *Encyclopedia*. It shows enslaved men, at right, gathering and picking over cotton bolls, while the woman at left mills the bolls to remove their seeds. The *Encyclopedia* presented mixed views on slavery; one article described it as "indispensable" to economic development, while others argued passionately for the natural right to freedom of all mankind. (Courtesy, Dover Publications. From Denis Diderot, *Pictorial Encyclopedia of Trades and Industry*, edited by Charles C. Gillispie (Dover Publications, 1959).)

Encyclopedia editor Denis Diderot adopted Montesquieu's technique of criticizing European attitudes through the voice of outsiders in his dialogue between Tahitian villagers and their European visitors. Scottish philosopher James Beattie (1735–1803) responded directly to claims of white superiority by pointing out that Europeans had started out as savage as nonwhites supposedly were and that many non-European peoples in the Americas, Asia, and Africa had achieved high levels of civilization. Former slaves, like Olaudah Equiano (see Chapter 17) and Ottobah Cugoana published eloquent memoirs testifying to the horrors of slavery and the innate equality of all humans. These challenges to racism, however, were in the minority. Many other Enlightenment voices supporting racial inequality— Thomas Jefferson among them—may be found.

QUICK REVIEW <

How did Enlightenment thinkers challenge the social, political, and cultural status quo? In what ways did they reinforce it?

What intellectual and social changes occurred as a result of the Scientific Revolution?

What new ideas about society and human relations emerged in the Enlightenment?

What impact did new ways of thinking have on politics?

 LearningCurve
Check what you know.

What impact did new ways of thinking have on politics?

Catherine the Great Strongly influenced by the Enlightenment, Catherine the Great cultivated the French philosophes and instituted moderate reforms, only to reverse them in the aftermath of Pugachev's rebellion. This equestrian portrait now hangs above her throne in the palace throne room in St. Petersburg. (Musée des Beaux-Arts, Chartres/The Bridgeman Art Library)

enlightened absolutism

▶ Term coined by historians to describe the rule of eighteenth-century monarchs who, without renouncing their own absolute authority, adopted Enlightenment ideals of rationalism, progress, and tolerance.

MANY GOVERNMENT OFFICIALS were interested in philosophical ideas. They were among the best-educated members of society, and their daily involvement in complex affairs of state made them naturally attracted to ideas for improving human society. Encouraged and instructed by these officials, some absolutist rulers tried to reform their governments in accordance with Enlightenment ideals— what historians have called the **enlightened absolutism** of the later eighteenth century. The most influential of the new-style monarchs were in Prussia, Russia, and Austria, and their example illustrates both the achievements and the great limitations of enlightened absolutism. France experienced its own brand of enlightened absolutism in the contentious decades prior to the French Revolution (see Chapter 19).

CHAPTER LOCATOR | What revolutionary discoveries were made in the sixteenth and seventeenth centuries?

Frederick the Great of Prussia

Frederick II (r. 1740–1786), commonly known as Frederick the Great, built masterfully on the work of his father, Frederick William I (see Chapter 15). When the young empress Maria Theresa of Austria inherited the Habsburg dominions upon the death of her father Charles VI, Frederick pounced. He invaded her rich province of Silesia (sigh-LEE-zhuh), defying Prussian promises to respect the Pragmatic Sanction, a diplomatic agreement that had guaranteed Maria Theresa's succession. In 1742, as other greedy powers vied for her lands in the European War of the Austrian Succession (1740–1748), Maria Theresa was forced to cede almost all of Silesia to Prussia. In one stroke, Prussia had doubled its population to 6 million people. Now Prussia unquestionably stood as a European Great Power.

Though successful in 1742, Frederick had to fight against great odds to save Prussia from total destruction after the ongoing competition between Britain and France for colonial empire brought another great conflict in 1756. Maria Theresa, seeking to regain Silesia, formed an alliance with the leaders of France and Russia. The aim of the alliance during the resulting Seven Years' War (1756–1763) was to conquer Prussia and divide its territory. Despite invasions from all sides, Frederick fought on with stoic courage. In the end he was miraculously saved: Peter III came to the Russian throne in 1762 and called off the attack against Frederick, whom he greatly admired.

The terrible struggle of the Seven Years' War tempered Frederick's interest in territorial expansion and brought him to consider how more humane policies for his subjects might also strengthen the state. Thus, Frederick went beyond a superficial commitment to Enlightenment culture for himself and his circle. He allowed his subjects to believe as they wished in religious and philosophical matters. He promoted the advancement of knowledge, improving his country's schools and permitting scholars to publish their findings. Frederick tried to improve the lives of his subjects more directly, promoting legal reform and economic growth.

The legal system and the bureaucracy were Frederick's primary tools. Prussia's laws were simplified, torture was abolished, and judges decided cases quickly and impartially. Prussian officials became famous for their hard work and honesty. After the Seven Years' War ended in 1763, Frederick's government energetically promoted the reconstruction of agriculture and industry.

Frederick's dedication to high-minded government went only so far, however. While he condemned serfdom in the abstract, he accepted it in practice and did not free the serfs on his own estates. He accepted and extended the privileges of the nobility, who remained the backbone of the army and the entire Prussian state.

In reforming Prussia's bureaucracy, Frederick drew on the principles of **cameralism**, the German science of public administration that emerged in the decades following the Thirty Years' War. Influential throughout the German lands, cameralism held that monarchy was the best of all forms of government; all elements of society should be placed at the service of the state; and, in turn, the state should make use of its resources and authority to improve society. Predating the Enlightenment, cameralist interest in the public good was usually inspired by the needs of war. Cameralism shared with the Enlightenment an emphasis on rationality, progress, and utilitarianism.

Prussia, 1740
Prussian gains, 1742
Austria, 1740
— Boundary of the Holy Roman Empire

Königsberg

Berlin

POLAND

SILESIA

Prague

Vienna

AUSTRIA

HUNGARY

The War of the Austrian Succession, 1740–1748

cameralism

▶ View that monarchy was the best form of government; all elements of society should serve the monarch; and, in turn, the state should use its resources and authority to increase the public good.

What intellectual and social changes occurred as a result of the Scientific Revolution?

What new ideas about society and human relations emerged in the Enlightenment?

What impact did new ways of thinking have on politics?

☑ LearningCurve
Check what you know.

507

Catherine the Great of Russia

Catherine the Great of Russia (r. 1762–1796) was one of the most remarkable rulers of her age, and the French philosophes adored her. Catherine had drunk deeply at the Enlightenment well. Never questioning that absolute monarchy was the best form of government, she set out to rule in an enlightened manner. She had three main goals. First, she worked hard to continue Peter the Great's effort to bring the culture of western Europe to Russia (see Chapter 15). To do so, she imported Western architects, musicians, and intellectuals. She bought masterpieces of Western art and patronized the philosophes. With these actions, Catherine won good press in the West for herself and for her country. This intellectual ruler, who wrote plays and loved good talk, set the tone for the entire Russian nobility. Peter the Great westernized Russian armies, but it was Catherine who westernized the imagination of the Russian nobility.

Catherine's second goal was domestic reform, and she began her reign with sincere and ambitious projects. In 1767, she appointed a legislative commission to prepare a new law code. This project was never completed, but Catherine did restrict the practice of torture and allowed limited religious toleration. She also tried to improve education and strengthen local government. The philosophes applauded these measures and hoped more would follow.

Such was not the case. In 1773, a Cossack soldier named Emelian Pugachev sparked a gigantic uprising of thousands of serfs. Proclaiming himself the true tsar, Pugachev issued orders abolishing serfdom, taxes, and army service. Pugachev's army proved no match for Catherine's noble-led army, and Pugachev was captured and executed. Pugachev's rebellion put an end to any intentions Catherine had about reforming the system. In 1785, she freed nobles forever from taxes and state service. Under Catherine, the Russian nobility attained its most exalted position, and serfdom entered its most oppressive phase.

Catherine's third goal was territorial expansion, and in this respect she was extremely successful. Her armies subjugated the last descendants of the Mongols and the Crimean Tartars, and began the conquest of the Caucasus (KAW-kuh-suhs). Her greatest coup by far was the partition of Poland (**Map 16.1**). When, between 1768 and 1772, Catherine's armies scored unprecedented victories against the Ottomans and thereby threatened to disturb the balance of power between Russia and Austria in eastern Europe, Frederick of Prussia obligingly came forward with a deal. He proposed that Turkey be let off easily and that Prussia, Austria, and Russia each compensate itself by taking a gigantic slice of the weakly ruled Polish territory. The first partition of Poland took place in 1772. Subsequent partitions in 1793 and 1795 gave away the rest of Polish territory, and the ancient republic of Poland vanished from the map.

The Austrian Habsburgs

Another female monarch, Maria Theresa (r. 1740–1780) of Austria, set out to reform her nation, although traditional power politics was a more important motivation for her than were Enlightenment teachings. Maria Theresa was a remark-

CHAPTER LOCATOR | What revolutionary discoveries were made in the sixteenth and seventeenth centuries?

508 CHAPTER 16 TOWARD A NEW WORLDVIEW

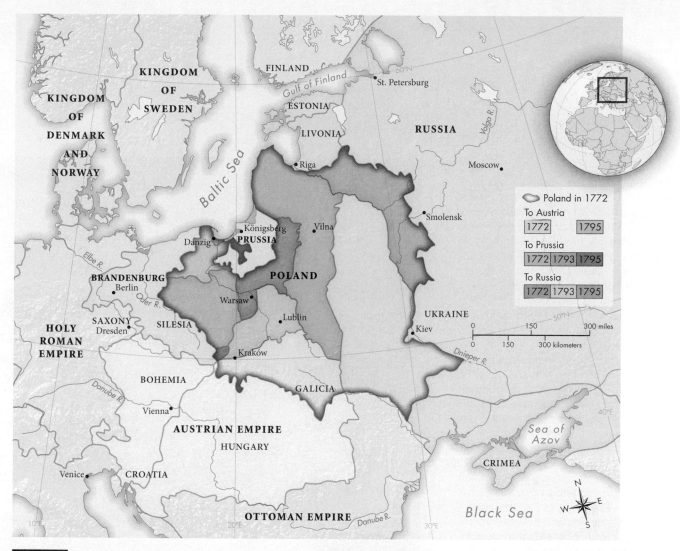

MAP 16.1 ■ The Partition of Poland, 1772–1795

In 1772, war between Russia and Austria threatened over Russian gains from the Ottoman Empire. To satisfy desires for expansion without fighting, Prussia's Frederick the Great proposed that parts of Poland be divided among Austria, Prussia, and Russia. In 1793 and 1795, the three powers partitioned the remainder, and the republic of Poland ceased to exist.

> **MAPPING THE PAST**

ANALYZING THE MAP: Of the three powers that divided the kingdom of Poland, which gained the most territory? How did the partition affect the geographical boundaries of each state, and what was the significance? What border with the former Poland remained unchanged? Why do you think this was the case?

CONNECTIONS: What does it say about European politics at the time that a country could simply cease to exist on the map? Could that happen today?

able but old-fashioned absolutist. Her more radical son, Joseph II (r. 1780–1790), drew on Enlightenment ideals, earning the title of "revolutionary emperor."

Emerging from the long War of the Austrian Succession in 1748 with the serious loss of Silesia, Maria Theresa was determined to introduce reforms that would make the state stronger and more efficient. First, she initiated church reform, with measures aimed at limiting the papacy's influence, eliminating many religious

| What intellectual and social changes occurred as a result of the Scientific Revolution? | What new ideas about society and human relations emerged in the Enlightenment? | **What impact did new ways of thinking have on politics?** | ✓ LearningCurve Check what you know. |

509

INDIVIDUALS IN SOCIETY
Moses Mendelssohn and the Jewish Enlightenment

In 1743, a small, humpbacked Jewish boy with a stammer left his poor parents in Dessau in central Germany and walked eighty miles to Berlin, the capital of Frederick the Great's Prussia. According to one story, when the boy reached the Rosenthaler (ROH-zuhn-taw-lehr) Gate, the only one through which Jews could pass, he told the inquiring watchman that his name was Moses and that he had come to Berlin "to learn." The watchman laughed and waved him through. "Go Moses, the sea has opened before you."*

In Berlin, the young Mendelssohn studied Jewish law and eked out a living copying Hebrew manuscripts in a beautiful hand. But he was soon fascinated by an intellectual world that had been closed to him in the Dessau ghetto, where, like most Jews throughout central Europe, he had spoken Yiddish — a mixture of German, Polish, and Hebrew. Now, working mainly on his own, he mastered German; learned Latin, Greek, French, and English; and studied mathematics and Enlightenment philosophy. Word of his exceptional abilities spread in Berlin's Jewish community (the dwelling of 1,500 of the city's 100,000 inhabitants). He began tutoring the children of a wealthy Jewish silk merchant, and he soon became the merchant's clerk and later his partner. But his great passion remained the life of the mind and the spirit, which he avidly pursued in his off-hours.

Gentle and unassuming in his personal life, Mendelssohn was a bold thinker. Reading eagerly in Western philosophy since antiquity, he was, as a pious Jew, soon convinced that Enlightenment teachings need not be opposed to Jewish thought and religion. He concluded that reason could complement and strengthen religion, although each would retain its integrity as a separate sphere.[†] Developing his idea in his first great work, *On the Immortality of the Soul* (1767), Mendelssohn used the neutral setting of a philosophical dialogue between Socrates and his followers

Lavater (right) attempts to convert Mendelssohn, in a painting by Moritz Oppenheim of an imaginary encounter. (akg-images)

pLaunchPad

ONLINE DOCUMENT PROJECT

How did Moses Mendelssohn fit into the larger Enlightenment debate about religious tolerance?
Examine primary sources written by Mendelssohn and his contemporaries, and then complete a writing assignment based on the evidence and details from this chapter. *See inside the front cover to learn more.*

*H. Kupferberg, *The Mendelssohns: Three Generations of Genius* (New York: Charles Scribner's Sons, 1972), p. 3.
†David Sorkin, *Moses Mendelssohn and the Religious Enlightenment* (Berkeley: University of California Press, 1996), pp. 8ff.

in ancient Greece to argue that the human soul lived forever. In refusing to bring religion and critical thinking into conflict, he was strongly influenced by contemporary German philosophers who argued similarly on behalf of Christianity. He reflected the way the German Enlightenment generally supported established religion, in contrast to the French Enlightenment, which attacked it.

Mendelssohn's treatise on the human soul captivated the educated German public, which marveled that a Jew could have written a philosophical masterpiece. In the excitement, a Christian zealot named Lavater challenged Mendelssohn in a pamphlet to accept Christianity or to demonstrate how the Christian faith was not "reasonable." Replying politely but passionately, the Jewish philosopher affirmed that his studies had only strengthened him in his faith, although he did not seek to convert anyone not born into Judaism. Rather, he urged toleration in religious matters and spoke up courageously against Jewish oppression.

Orthodox Jew and German philosophe, Moses Mendelssohn serenely combined two very different worlds. He built a bridge from the ghetto to the dominant culture over which many Jews would pass, including his novelist daughter Dorothea and his famous grandson, the composer Felix Mendelssohn.

QUESTIONS FOR ANALYSIS

1. How did Mendelssohn seek to influence Jewish religious thought in his time?
2. How do Mendelssohn's ideas compare with those of the French Enlightenment?

holidays, and reducing the number of monasteries. Second, a whole series of administrative renovations strengthened the central bureaucracy, smoothed out some provincial differences, and revamped the tax system, taxing even the lands of nobles, who were previously exempt from taxation. Third, the government sought to improve the lot of the agricultural population, cautiously reducing the power of lords over their hereditary serfs and their partially free peasant tenants.

Coregent with his mother from 1765 onward, Joseph II moved forward rapidly with further reforms when he came to the throne in 1780. Most notably, Joseph abolished serfdom in 1781, and in 1789, he decreed that peasants could pay landlords in cash rather than through labor on their land. This measure was violently rejected not only by the nobility but also by the peasants it was intended to help because they lacked the necessary cash. When a disillusioned Joseph died prematurely at forty-nine, the entire Habsburg empire was in turmoil. His brother Leopold II (r. 1790–1792) canceled Joseph's radical edicts in order to re-establish order.

Despite differences in their policies, Joseph II and the other absolutists of the later eighteenth century combined old-fashioned state-building with the culture and critical thinking of the Enlightenment. In doing so, they succeeded in expanding the role of the state in the life of society. Their failure to implement policies we would recognize as humane and enlightened—such as abolishing serfdom—may reveal inherent limitations in Enlightenment thinking about equality and social justice, rather than deficiencies in their execution of Enlightenment programs.

Jewish Life and the Limits of Enlightened Absolutism

Perhaps the best example of the limitations of enlightened absolutism are the debates surrounding the emancipation of the Jews. Europe's small Jewish populations lived under highly discriminatory laws. For the most part, Jews were confined to tiny, overcrowded ghettos, were excluded by law from most professions, and could be ordered out of a kingdom at a moment's notice.

Haskalah

▶ The Jewish Enlightenment of the second half of the eighteenth century, led by the Prussian philosopher Moses Mendelssohn.

The Pale of Settlement, 1791

In the eighteenth century, an Enlightenment movement known as the Haskalah emerged from within the European Jewish community; it was led by the Prussian philosopher Moses Mendelssohn (1729–1786). (See "Individuals in Society: Moses Mendelssohn and the Jewish Enlightenment," page 510.) Christian and Jewish Enlightenment philosophers, including Mendelssohn, began to advocate for freedom and civil rights for European Jews. In an era of reason and progress, they argued, restrictions on religious grounds could not stand.

Arguments for tolerance won some ground. The British Parliament passed a law allowing naturalization of Jews in 1753 but later repealed the law due to public outrage. The most progressive reforms took place under Austrian emperor Joseph II. Among his liberal edicts of the 1780s were measures intended to integrate Jews more fully into society, including eligibility for military service, admission to higher education and artisanal trades, and removal of requirements for special clothing or emblems.

Many monarchs rejected all ideas of emancipation. Although he permitted freedom of religion to his Christian subjects, Frederick the Great of Prussia firmly opposed any general emancipation for the Jews, as he did for the serfs. Catherine the Great, who acquired most of Poland's large Jewish population when she annexed part of that country in the late eighteenth century, similarly refused. In 1791, she established the Pale of Settlement, a territory including parts of modern-day Poland, Latvia, Lithuania, Ukraine, and Belarus, in which most Jews were required to live. Jewish habitation was restricted to the Pale until the Russian Revolution in 1917.

> ## QUICK REVIEW

What aspects of their states did enlightened monarchs attempt to reform? What aspects did they generally leave untouched?

CHAPTER LOCATOR | What revolutionary discoveries were made in the sixteenth and seventeenth centuries?

LOOKING BACK LOOKING AHEAD

Hailed as the origin of modern thought, the Scientific Revolution must also be seen as a product of its past. Medieval universities gave rise to important new scholarship, and the ambition and wealth of Renaissance patrons nurtured intellectual curiosity. Religious faith also influenced the Scientific Revolution, inspiring thinkers to understand the glory of God's creation while bringing censure and personal tragedy to others. Natural philosophers following Copernicus pioneered new methods of observing and explaining nature while drawing on centuries-old traditions of mysticism, astrology, alchemy, and magic.

The Enlightenment ideas of the eighteenth century were a similar blend of past and present; they could serve as much to bolster absolutist monarchical regimes as to inspire revolutionaries to fight for individual rights and liberties. Although the Enlightenment fostered critical thinking about everything from science to religion, the majority of Europeans, including many prominent thinkers, remained devout Christians.

The achievements of the Scientific Revolution and the Enlightenment are undeniable. Key Western values of rationalism, human rights, and open-mindedness were born from these movements. With their new notions of progress and social improvement, Europeans would embark on important revolutions in industry and politics in the centuries that followed. Nonetheless, others have seen a darker side. For these critics, the mastery over nature permitted by the Scientific Revolution now threatens to overwhelm the earth's fragile equilibrium, and the Enlightenment belief in the universal application of reason can lead to arrogance and intolerance of other people's spiritual, cultural, and political values. Such vivid debates about the legacy of these intellectual and scientific developments testify to their continuing importance in today's world.

LaunchPad

ONLINE DOCUMENT PROJECT
Moses Mendelssohn

How did Moses Mendelssohn fit into the larger Enlightenment debate about religious tolerance?

You encountered Moses Mendelssohn's story on page 510. Keeping the question above in mind, examine primary sources from Mendelssohn's time—including a letter to a contemporary, an excerpt from a play, and a philosophical treatise—to draw your own conclusions. *See inside the front cover to learn more.*

What intellectual and social changes occurred as a result of the Scientific Revolution?

What new ideas about society and human relations emerged in the Enlightenment?

What impact did new ways of thinking have on politics?

✓ **LearningCurve**
Check what you know.

CHAPTER 16 STUDY GUIDE

STEP 1

GET STARTED ONLINE

STEP 2

EXPLAIN WHY IT MATTERS

✓ **LearningCurve**
Now that you've read the chapter, make it stick by completing the LearningCurve activity.

Put your reading into practice. Identify each term below, and then explain why it matters in Western history.

TERM	WHO OR WHAT & WHEN	WHY IT MATTERS
natural philosophy (p. 487)		
Copernican hypothesis (p. 489)		
experimental method (p. 491)		
law of inertia (p. 491)		
law of universal gravitation (p. 492)		
empiricism (p. 494)		
Cartesian dualism (p. 494)		
Enlightenment (p. 497)		
rationalism (p. 497)		
philosophes (p. 499)		
reading revolution (p. 502)		
salon (p. 503)		
rococo (p. 504)		
public sphere (p. 504)		
enlightened absolutism (p. 506)		
cameralism (p. 507)		
Haskalah (p. 512)		

STEP 3

MOVE BEYOND THE BASICS

To demonstrate a more advanced understanding of the Scientific Revolution, fill in the chart included below with descriptions of the major contributions of the figures listed in the chart. Be sure to include both concrete discoveries and contributions to the development of the scientific method.

	Discoveries and contributions
Nicolaus Copernicus	
Tycho Brahe	
Johannes Kepler	
Francis Bacon	
René Descartes	
Galileo Galilei	
Isaac Newton	

STEP 4 PUT IT ALL TOGETHER

Now, take a step back and try to explain the big picture. Remember to use specific examples from the chapter in your answers.

THE SCIENTIFIC REVOLUTION

▶ What was revolutionary about the Scientific Revolution?

▶ What role did religion play in the Scientific Revolution? How did religious belief both stimulate and hinder scientific inquiry?

THE ENLIGHTENMENT

▶ How did the Scientific Revolution contribute to the emergence of the Enlightenment?

▶ How did Enlightenment thinkers deal with issues of gender and race?

ENLIGHTENED ABSOLUTISM

▶ Why did many Enlightenment thinkers see absolute monarchy as a potential force for good?

▶ How did Enlightenment ideas contribute to the expansion of the role of the state in central and eastern European society?

MAKE CONNECTIONS

▶ Compare and contrast medieval and early modern approaches to the study of nature.

▶ Is it accurate to describe the worldview that emerged out of the Scientific Revolution and the Enlightenment as "modern"? Why or why not?

> IN YOUR OWN WORDS

Imagine that you must give an oral report to the class answering the following question: **What new ways of looking at nature, society, and government emerged in the Early Modern period? What would be the most important points and why?**

ENDNOTES

Chapter 3

1. G. Tarditi, *Archilochus Fragmenta* (Rome: Edizioni dell'Ateno, 1968), frag. 112.

Chapter 5

1. Aubrey de Sélincourt, trans., *Livy: The Early History of Rome, Books I-V of the History of Rome from Its Foundation* (Baltimore: Penguin Books, 1960), p. 68.

Chapter 8

1. Quoted in R. McKitterick, *The Frankish Kingdoms Under the Carolingians, 751–987* (New York: Longman, 1983), p. 77.

Chapter 11

1. Michael Rocke, *Forbidden Friendships: Homosexuality and Male Culture in Renaissance Florence* (New York: Oxford University Press, 1996), p. 45.
2. Quoted in R. Bartlett, *The Making of Europe: Conquest, Colonization and Cultural Change, 950–1350* (Princeton, N.J.: Princeton University Press, 1993), p. 239.

Chapter 12

1. Quoted in F. Seebohm, *The Oxford Reformers* (London: J. M. Dent & Sons, 1867), p. 256.
2. Quoted in Benzion Netanyahu, *The Origins of the Inquisition in Fifteenth Century Spain* (New York: Random House, 1995), p. 921.

Chapter 13

1. Quoted in David P. Daniel, "Hungary," in *The Oxford Encyclopedia of the Reformation*, vol. 2, ed. H. J. Hillerbrand (New York: Oxford University Press, 1996), p. 273.

Chapter 14

1. Thomas Benjamin, *The Atlantic World: Europeans, Africans, Indians and Their Shared History, 1400–1900* (Cambridge, U.K.: Cambridge University Press, 2009), p. 56.
2. G. V. Scammell, *The World Encompassed: The First European Maritime Empires, c. 800–1650* (Berkeley: University of California Press, 1981), pp. 101, 104.
3. Peter Hulme, *Colonial Encounters: Europe and the Native Caribbean, 1492–1797* (London: Methuen, 1986), pp. 22–31.
4. Benjamin, *The Atlantic World*, p. 141.
5. Ibid., pp. 35–59.
6. Quoted in L. B. Rout, Jr., *The African Experience in Spanish America* (New York: Cambridge University Press, 1976), p. 23.
7. Cited in Geoffrey Vaughn Scammell, *The First Imperial Age: European Overseas Expansion, c. 1400–1715* (London: Routledge, 2002), p. 432.
8. Herbert S. Klein, "Profits and the Causes of Mortality," in David Northrup, ed., *The Atlantic Slave Trade* (Lexington, Mass.: D. C. Heath and Co., 1994), p. 116.
9. Voyages: The Trans-Atlantic Slave Trade Database, http://www.slavevoyages.org/tast/assessment/estimates.faces.
10. Paul Freedman, *Images of the Medieval Peasant* (Stanford, Calif.: Stanford University Press, 1999).
11. C. Cotton, trans., *The Essays of Michel de Montaigne* (New York: A. L. Burt, 1893), pp. 207, 210.
12. Ibid., p. 523.

Chapter 15

1. H. Kamen, "The Economic and Social Consequences of the Thirty Years' War," *Past and Present* 39 (1968): 44–61.

2. John A. Lynn, "Recalculating French Army Growth," in *The Military Revolution Debate: Readings on the Military Transformation of Early Modern Europe*, ed. Clifford J. Rogers (Boulder, Colo.: Westview Press, 1995), p. 125.
3. Quoted in John A. Lynn, *Giant of the Grand Siècle: The French Army, 1610–1715* (Cambridge, U.K.: Cambridge University Press, 1997), p. 74.
4. J. H. Elliott, *Imperial Spain, 1469–1716* (New York: Mentor Books, 1963), pp. 306–308.
5. H. Rosenberg, *Bureaucracy, Aristocracy, and Autocracy: The Prussian Experience, 1660–1815* (Boston: Beacon Press, 1966), p. 40.
6. For a revisionist interpretation, see J. Wormald, "James VI and I: Two Kings or One?" *History* 62 (1983): 187–209.

Chapter 16
1. Quoted in Herbert Butterfield, *The Origins of Modern Science* (New York: Free Press, 1997), p. 47.
2. Ibid., p. 120.
3. Quoted in G. L. Mosse et al., eds., *Europe in Review* (Chicago: Rand McNally, 1964), p. 156.

INDEX